ULTIMATE Road Trips: USA & CANADA

Hardie Grant

EXPLORE

Introduction

As I write this in February 2022, I'm sitting on a hotel balcony in Biloxi, Mississippi. A ribbon of white-sand beach and, beyond it, the azure Gulf of Mexico stretch out before me as far as the eye can see. Between my balcony and the beach, cars zoom along US 90, a 1633-mile road laid out in 1926 that links the northeast Florida coastal city of Jacksonville with the dusty west Texas town of Van Horn. I can see three dozen cars in the parking lot below, bearing license plates from at least 20 states, from California to Michigan to New Hampshire (that last one's mine). I'm in the middle of an extended road trip, and so are tens of thousands of others.

Travelers have been captivated by automobile touring since the very invention of "horseless carriages" in the mid-1880s. Throughout North America, the popularity of road-tripping has maintained a fairly steady rise over the past 120 years, booming at times (the 1920s, the mid-'40s, and the mid-'60s) to coincide with the construction of new highway systems and an ever-growing selection of services and attractions, from drive-up motels and campgrounds to roadside diners, scenic national park roads, drive-in movie theaters, and kitschy dinosaur statues and neon-lit souvenir shops. It's hardly surprising that this photogenic way of exploring the world has enjoyed a boom in recent years—it lends itself perfectly to our growing love of documenting our adventures on Instagram and other social media.

And then came the pandemic. Following the initial lockdown, when some people gingerly began to take trips again, they mainly did so by car. Driving allowed greater autonomy and easier social distancing. At this moment, road-tripping around the US and Canada has never been more popular. Anyone who's visited a major national park or driven a famous scenic road during the pandemic can attest that this upsurge in car-touring has led to certain challenges, namely overcrowding. But there's a lot of blacktop out there—about 4 million miles of public roads in the US and another 650,000 miles in Canada. If you look a bit beyond the high-profile landmarks, you can still find plenty of incredible places that aren't swarmed by fellow road trippers, even on high-season weekends.

I've been hooked on road-tripping since I was a kid in the '70s. Vacations for our family involved clanking around New England and upstate New York in a wood-sided 1969 Ford Country Squire station wagon. This gas-guzzling tank of a car had only an AM radio and neither air conditioning nor power windows, but I remember loving every minute of those summertime drives through the Adirondacks, coastal Maine, and Cape Cod. Two years out of college in 1993, I quit my job in New York City as a low-level editor with a travel guidebook publisher to embark on a freelance career. I decided I could more easily afford payments on a car than rent on an apartment, so for the next seven years I lived nomadically, crisscrossing the United States and Canada, crashing on sofas, house-sitting, and further solidifying my love of road-tripping. I eventually landed in northern New Mexico for several years and then Portland, Oregon for a decade. And now my partner, Fernando, and I divide our time between a flat in the historic Coyoacán district of Mexico City and a lake house in rural New Hampshire. But exploring by car is still my catnip—my absolute favorite kind of travel experience.

And so here I am in Biloxi, 16 days and 15 states into yet another road trip. The latest Omicron-driven COVID surge is receding and I hope it will be far, far behind us by the time you read these words. I won't try to guess what lies ahead for the pandemic or the state of travel. What I do feel certain about is that people will continue to find ways to explore the world, and that road tripping offers an ideal way to do so. You can go at your own pace and tailor your itinerary to your interests, budget, and level of comfort.

Over the past decade or so, I've driven nearly every mile of roadway I've described in this book, and I've revisited the majority of these itineraries since the start of the pandemic. As a US citizen, I decided against returning to Canada during the pandemic, but I've fact-checked every chapter of this book and only recommended attractions and businesses that I could confirm were open in early 2022. Still, we're living in changing times, and I highly recommend that you call ahead to confirm that places are open, especially if you're driving out of your way to visit them.

I've tried to create itineraries that offer high points for a diverse range of tastes and styles—foodies, families, hikers, retirees, LGBTQ folks, history buffs, art lovers, budget adventurers, and luxury seekers. But above all else, I've designed the drives in this book with the aim of helping you connect North America's must-see road trip experiences—Hwy 1 in California's Big Sur, the Icefields Parkway from Banff to Jasper, the Blue Ridge Parkway in North Carolina and Virginia—with hundreds of less visited gems, from Saguenay Fjord in Quebec to Canyon de Chelly National Monument in Arizona to the blues music towns of the Mississippi Delta.

Enjoy the drive, and if you see a silver 2008 Toyota Highlander with New Hampshire plates that's badly in need of a car wash, be sure to wave hello . . .

ANDREW COLLINS

A road-tripping exhibit at the Henry Ford Museum, Dearborn, MI *Opposite* Badlands National Park, SD

Practical Information

ROAD-TRIPPING IN THE COVID ERA

Traveling by car has become both much more popular since the start of the pandemic and—as with most aspects of our lives—more complicated. As the pandemic and its effects on how we travel continue to change, I've largely refrained from including advisories about COVID-specific policies in this book. The most prudent approach is to call or check websites and social media before visiting attractions, restaurants, and other businesses to confirm hours and other policies.

I undertook a number of short road trips and eight long ones (two weeks or more) during 2020 and 2021, and I encountered relatively few obstacles, but I also planned ahead more than I might have before the pandemic. Some developments during the pandemic have made it easier to travel: many restaurants have added more outdoor space and instituted better reservation and online-ordering systems, busy attractions and parks have helped reduce crowds and traffic bottlenecks by implementing timed-entry policies, and many hotels, museums, and other businesses have vastly upgraded their ventilation and air-filtration systems and improved their overall cleaning practices. But the pandemic, even as it becomes a more manageable part of our everyday lives, continues to present challenges, from staffing shortages to higher costs. My takeaway: patience, both for yourself and for others, is a virtue.

Yosemite National Park, CA

MEASUREMENTS AND CURRENCY CONVERSIONS

The measurements throughout this book are generally given in imperial rather than metric units. The conversion for the units that appear most often are:

1 mile = 1.61 km

1 sq mile = 2.59 sq km

1 foot = 0.305 m

1 acre = 0.405 hectares.

Prices, when they're given, are in USD; Canadian prices appear in some Canada chapters (C$)

HIGHWAY DESIGNATIONS

Numbered roads use the abbreviation *Hwy* (Hwy 17, Hwy 400). However, I generally used Rte instead of Hwy in the US East Coast states to reflect the local vernacular. The two other route abbreviations that appear often are "US," for routes that are part of the United States Numbered Highway System (e.g., US 1 from Maine to Florida, US 90 from Florida to west Texas), and "I," for routes that are part of the newer (and generally faster) US Interstate Highway System (e.g., I-15 from Montana to southern California, I-80 from San Francisco to New Jersey).

TOLL ROADS AND BRIDGES

Quite a few highways (or freeways, as they're more typically known in the western US) as well as bridges and tunnels charge tolls. You sometimes have the option of paying cash and interacting with a human toll collector, but toll agencies are increasingly switching to automated, cashless systems that collect fees through toll transponders that you affix to your windshield. If you don't have a transponder, the toll agency typically charges you by photographing your license plate and mailing you a bill. The pay-by-license-plate option generally works fine, but if you've rented a car, the agency may charge you a hefty fee for tolls they're billed for. When renting a car, I always ask about tolls—many agencies rent transponders or offer other toll-payment options. If you're driving in a region with lots of tolls, consider buying a transponder. E-Z Pass (e-zpassiag.com) covers toll roads and bridges in nearly 20 states, mostly on the East Coast and in the Midwest. If you want to be spared toll-related hassles or expenses, you can also set your GPS to choose routes that avoid tolls.

U.S. States

Alabama (AL)	North Dakota (ND)
Alaska (AK)	Ohio (OH)
Arizona (AZ)	Oklahoma (OK)
Arkansas (AR)	Oregon (OR)
California (CA)	Pennsylvania (PA)
Colorado (CO)	Rhode Island (RI)
Connecticut (CT)	South Carolina (SC)
Delaware (DE)	South Dakota (SD)
District of Columbia (DC)	Tennessee (TN)
Florida (FL)	Texas (TX)
Georgia (GA)	Utah (UT)
Hawai'i (HI)	Vermont (VT)
Idaho (ID)	Virginia (VA)
Illinois (IL)	Washington (WA)
Indiana (IN)	West Virginia (WV)
Iowa (IA)	Wisconsin (WI)
Kansas (KS)	Wyoming (WY)
Kentucky (KY)	
Louisiana (LA)	**Canadian Provinces**
Maine (ME)	**& Territories**
Maryland (MD)	Alberta (AB)
Massachusetts (MA)	British Columbia (BC)
Michigan (MI)	Manitoba (MB)
Minnesota (MN)	New Brunswick (NB)
Mississippi (MS)	Newfoundland & Labrador (NL)
Missouri (MO)	Northwest Territories (NT)
Montana (MT)	Nova Scotia (NS)
Nebraska (NE)	Nunavut (NU)
Nevada (NV)	Ontario (ON)
New Hampshire (NH)	Prince Edward Island (PEI)
New Jersey (NJ)	Quebec (QC)
New Mexico (NM)	Saskatchewan (SK)
New York (NY)	Yukon (YK)
North Carolina (NC)	

CUSTOMS, PASSPORTS, AND BORDER CROSSINGS

Generally speaking, driving back and forth between the US and Canada is a fairly simple process, but even for a quick hop across the border, a passport is a requirement. I recommend carrying your passport if you plan to come anywhere even remotely near a border, as it's nice to have the flexibility to cross on a whim. US and Canadian car insurance policies generally cover you in both countries, and if you rent a car in a state or province on the US-Canada border, your policy typically allows you to drive in both countries, but always check with your rental agency.

Crossing between Canada and the US became significantly more complicated during the pandemic, however, and policies concerning vaccinations, COVID testing, and quarantines continue to change. For the latest rules on COVID restrictions and policies concerning immigration, customs and duties, and real-time border-crossing wait times, check travel.state.gov before visiting the US and travel.gc.ca before heading to Canada. You can typically bring small amounts of alcohol and other goods that you've purchased abroad into the US and Canada duty-free, but you'll be assessed taxes (these can get quite steep for alcohol) for larger quantities. Check online for specific allowances and rates, and never try to sneak booze or other goods across the border. You can face steep fines and other penalties for doing so, and claiming ignorance or that you forgot about those three cases of wine in the trunk will almost surely only make matters worse.

We've included a star or maple leaf symbol in each heading to indicate which countries the road trip includes, to help you plan for border crossings.

★ – **TRAVEL THROUGH USA**

🍁 – **TRAVEL THROUGH CANADA**

TAXES AND TIPPING

In the US, most states and many municipalities charge a sales tax; the five that charge no sales tax are Alaska, Delaware, Montana, New Hampshire, and Oregon. In the other 45 states, sales tax generally ranges from around 4% to 9%. In Canada a 5% GST (goods and services tax) is added to most bills. The federal tax is combined with the provincial rate, which varies in each province and territory so the total added tax rate ranges from 5% to 15%. Additionally, hotels (including Airbnbs and campgrounds) charge occupancy taxes that can add up to 15% to your bill, and taxes on car rentals can run upward of 20% in some states (agencies located at airports often have much higher taxes and fees than off-airport agencies). So be sure to factor in extra taxes and fees into your travel budget.

Tipping is expected in North America, with percentages customarily running a bit higher in the US compared with Canada. Although some restaurants, resorts, and other businesses have instituted no-tip policies (building the cost of tips into their prices instead), most service-industry employees—restaurant servers, housekeeping staff, valet drivers—depend heavily on tips to earn a living wage. In the US the norms are 20% at restaurants, $1 per drink at bars and coffeehouses, $2–$5 per night for housekeeping at hotels, and $2–$5 for valet parking. In Canada a 15% tip is typical in restaurants.

BEST EATS AND SLEEPS

At the end of each itinerary, I've included best accommodation and food suggestions. These represent what I think are the ultimate experiences to be found throughout the trip. As a result, these can often be pricier establishments, but there are also more affordable recommendations scattered throughout the itinerary descriptions, perfect for families and travelers on a budget.

TRAVELING WITH KIDS

Maybe the single most useful approach you can adopt to make road-tripping with kids fun is the same one that will make road-tripping fun for adults: plan each day's route to include lots of stops and breaks, but then let spontaneity be your guide as your day unfolds. Sure, there are the marquee must-see attractions you'll always want to stop for—the touch-friendly aquariums and interactive science centers. But also put together a daily list of possible quick diversions: accessible parks, whimsical shops, ice cream parlors, and offbeat roadside attractions—like the Fremont Troll in Seattle, WA or the world's largest ball of popcorn in Sac City, IA. The goal isn't to stop at all or even most of them, but rather to have plenty of options for taking breaks, playing, and getting the wiggles out each day. As much as possible, let your kids play a central role in deciding where and when to stop—the more they're involved in the planning, or deciding when it's a good time to pull over for a break, the more they'll embrace the role of active adventurer rather than passive passenger.

The same goes for onboard entertainment: choosing the music, podcasts (especially if you've got tweens and teens), audio books, and streaming movies for your journey is more enjoyable as a team activity. Do pack more puzzles, games, and diversions than you might think you'll need, especially if your trip is for a week or longer—after the fourth or fifth day on the road, you'll be glad you have different options on hand. For longer trips, it truly is worth investing in a vehicle that's large enough to give everyone plenty of elbow room. Maybe that means renting an SUV or a minivan when technically your family of four could fit in a sedan, but everyone will be in much better spirits if they have room to spread out and easily access food, games, and gear.

Make sure you have motion-sickness pills (candied ginger really does work, too) and an ample supply of any other medications your family uses, as you can't always count on finding everything on the road that you're used to at home. That leads to the topic of healthy snacks—see Road Trip Hacks, below, for several tips on food strategies on the road. In general, prepare to encounter lots of unhealthy food on the road: ubiquitous fast-food chains and convenience stores are fine in a pinch, but packing as much of your own food as possible results in far healthier eating. By all means, bring along your kids' favorite candies and snacks, too—this is a vacation, after all, and occasionally doling out M&Ms or Cheez-Its can be a nice way to keep the mood upbeat.

Opposite Pets can make great road trip companions

TRAVELING WITH PETS

Road-tripping with your pet has gotten easier in the last decade. More and more hotels and nearly all campgrounds allow pets (though beware that fees can vary wildly), and it's never been easier to find restaurants with pet-friendly patios or decks. There are lots of factors to consider before deciding to bring pets with you, however, especially on a longer adventure. First and foremost, will they truly enjoy traveling with you? Dogs and cats may adore you at home, but if they're unaccustomed to long car rides, unfamiliar spaces, and interacting with strangers, a road trip may cause them more stress than happiness. Before you set out on a long adventure, take your pets with you on an overnight trip within a couple of hours of home and see how they respond. Dogs are better suited to travel than cats, but it's still the case that some enjoy it more than others.

Be sure to consider the weather (traveling during very hot or cold months is less than ideal and can be potentially dangerous) and whether your itinerary really makes sense for pets. Some wilderness areas (especially national parks) prohibit dogs on trails, even leashed, and you may find it challenging to visit museums and other indoor attractions that don't allow pets. You'll also want to make sure your pet's ID tags and vaccinations are current (and medical papers if you're crossing between the US and Canada) and that you pack all of the supplies they need, including toys and bedding, ample food, water, and portable dishes. For the right pets on the right itinerary, a road trip can be a mutually joyful bonding experience—just be sure to plan and prepare correctly.

RVS AND TOWING VEHICLES

If you own an RV or trailer, or you have experience towing a vehicle, you probably already know the ins and outs of traveling with oversized vehicles. Most of the roads I've recommended in this book are fine for RVs and trailers, and the handful of exceptions are noted. National parks or other areas with open terrain aren't always suitable for larger vehicles; dense cities and historic districts with narrow lanes can prove challenging. Some famous national park roads with RV and towing restrictions include Cadillac Summit Road (Acadia), Roaring Fork Motor Nature Trail (Great Smoky Mountains), Going-to-the-Sun Road (Glacier), Rim Drive (Crater Lake), and Howland Hill Road (Redwoods). If you're headed somewhere with remote or rugged scenery, check local websites for details. The free app Togo RV (togorv.com) is useful, too, but I suggest paying the $49 annual fee for the site's more comprehensive parent, Roadpass Pro (roadpass.com/pro), which also gets you access to premium content from the related sites, RV Village and Campendium.

Renting an RV has become an increasingly popular way to tour the US and Canada, with Cruise America being by far the largest RV rental company in North America. Other popular rental companies include Escape Campervans, which offers smaller, colorfully painted, custom-outfitted vans, and RVshare, a peer-to-peer rental marketplace with more than 60,000 owners.

CAMPING

Whether you're driving a luxuriously appointed RV, pitching a tent in the remote backcountry, or opting for a more middle-of-the-road experience—like pulling your vehicle up to a designated site at a commercial campground—camping has never been more popular in North America. There's also glamping, a hybrid approach that typically involves overnighting outdoors but with comfier amenities and shelters—you can book more than 30,000 of these distinctive venues at glampinghub.com.

I've recommended a number of popular campgrounds, both RV and tent-camping venues, at the end of each chapter. But you can also download some outstanding apps, including The Dyrt (a directory of more than 1 million campsites with user reviews, photos, a booking engine, and more) and Hipcamp (an online marketplace on which private landowners rent sites).

BUDGETING YOUR TIME

On the opening page of each chapter, among other quick facts about each road trip, I've recommended how many days it should take you to drive the itinerary. These are minimum guidelines that assume you'll generally drive a few hours each day. In practice, though, these itineraries can vary greatly, depending on how much time you devote to a town or a park along the way, how many rest days you take, and your time and financial resources. I encourage you to add a few days to each itinerary or even double the number of recommended days—you won't run out of things to see and do.

That said, don't be afraid to skip major destinations or so-called must-sees, especially if they're places that you can easily save for a future, perhaps longer, visit. With road trips, the drive itself can sometimes be the main attraction. Maybe that means spending just a couple of hours at the South Rim of the Grand Canyon or doing a quick drive-by of the Gateway Arch on your way through St Louis. Trying to cram in every famous site along a route can be stressful and expensive. I prefer devoting

more time to one or two attractions or experiences each day than rushing through four or five. As you plan out each day on the road, think about what's really going to bring you joy.

Moreover, try to leave parts of your journey unplanned. Although it's often cheaper to book accommodations in advance, and you don't want to show up in a major tourist destination at 10pm during high season without a hotel reservation, leaving some nights open can result in some serendipitous experiences. I've met lifelong friends, eaten incredible meals, and hiked along spectacular trails on portions of road trips that I'd left completely open to chance—to going where fate led me.

Top Petrified Forest National Park, AZ
Opposite top Million Dollar Cowboy Bar in Jackson, WY
Opposite bottom Camping at Jekyll Island, GA

26 Road Trip Tips, Tricks, and Hacks

- **Beware of one-way car-rental fees.** Rental car companies typically impose steep surcharges for returning your car in a different city than where you rented it. This means you may save a bundle by planning a round-trip rather than a one-way road trip.

- **Rent your car from an off-airport agency.** I've sometimes saved $200 to $300 dollars a week by renting at an in-town rather than an airport car-rental location; taxes and fees are often lower, and prices more competitive.

- **Avoid buying insurance from car-rental agencies and decline the prepaid fuel option.** Only buy the insurance if your own policy doesn't cover car rentals (most US and Canadian policies do) or you lack a credit card that provides this coverage (many do). If you do need car-rental insurance, it's usually cheaper to buy it from a third-party provider like Allianz or Rental Cover. And prepaid fuel options are virtually always more expensive than filling the tank yourself and returning it full.

- **Download these apps:** GasBuddy (for finding the cheapest gas stations near you), AllTrails (for details on and peer reviews of more than 200,000 hiking, biking, and recreational trails—I recommend paying for the "pro" version, which unlocks lots of useful features) and Carfax (for tracking your car's maintenance).

- **Make sure you have roadside assistance.** Whether through your insurance company, AAA (or in Canada, CAA) auto clubs, or through your credit card, roadside assistance benefits typically include towing your disabled vehicle, delivering emergency fuel, changing tires, jumping your battery, and unlocking your car. Note that some programs don't cover rental cars, although AAA/CAA always does.

- **Practice changing your tire.** It's really worth brushing up on this skill every couple of years or before you set out on a big trip. At a minimum, whether it's your own car or a rental car, check that your spare is inflated and you have a complete set of tire-changing tools. It's also worth checking that your lug nuts aren't on so tight that you can't manually remove them.

- **Download Google Maps and Waze.** I use Google maps almost exclusively and find it to be extremely reliable, and it's also easy to save maps so you can view them offline, which can be handy in remote areas. Some people prefer Waze, which is owned by Google but also relies on community-based data and constantly updates your routing based on the latest conditions.

- **Keep current with car maintenance.** Change your oil and bring your car in for checkups according to your automaker's maintenance recommendations. If you're planning a trip of more than a few weeks or a few thousand miles, you may want to replace tires, brakes, or other parts that are close to wearing down before you start your adventure.

- **Equip your car for challenging conditions.** If you're driving in remote areas or in extreme weather, keep your gas tank at least half full at all times. It's always a good idea to travel with a first-aid kit (make sure its contents are relatively new and in good working order), a flashlight with fresh batteries, and extra food, water, blankets, gloves, sturdy shoes, and clothing. If driving where snowfall is possible, it's a good idea to travel with chains, an ice scraper, and extra windshield washer fluid.

Enroll in hotel loyalty programs. If you've never felt these programs are worth the bother, you might want to reconsider if you're planning more than a couple of weeks of road-tripping in a given year. The free-night rewards, discounts, and special promotions really do add up, especially when you open an affiliated credit card account that offers a generous sign-up bonus. The brands with the greatest presence of mid-range, road-trip-handy hotels are Hilton, Marriott Bonvoy, IHG, and World of Hyatt, while Best Western and Choice Hotels are good on the budget end.

Buy a national parks pass. A US annual parks pass, good for unlimited admission to more than 2000 federal recreation sites, costs just $80 and is good for all passengers in a vehicle or up to four adults at sites that charge per person. Canada's annual Discovery Pass costs C$145.25 for families and groups (up to seven passengers in a vehicle) and is good for unlimited admission to 80 sites. Given that individual park fees can run as high as $35 in the US and $22 in Canada per vehicle, these annual passes can easily pay for themselves.

Take the ferry. From 10-minute hops across rivers to leisurely cruises across bays and straits that can take a few hours, ferry crossings are a key part of several itineraries in this book. With the exception of some sidetracks to secluded islands, most of these ferry crossings can be bypassed by surface roads. I'm a big fan of taking ferries when possible—they tend to be the more expensive option, and they don't always save a lot of time if you factor in potentially long wait times or limited schedules. (Always check ferry schedules well in advance, and consider booking reservations or buying tickets online when you can.) But I justify the cost by thinking of ferry rides as sightseeing excursions.

- **Consider cities carefully.** Even if you're a diehard urban explorer, you might want to rethink how much time you spend in big cities when road-tripping. In many of North America's largest and densest metropolises, a car is sometimes more of a hindrance than a help— intense traffic, aggressive drivers, and limited, expensive parking can ruin your experience. It may seem crazy to stop only briefly or entirely skip Chicago on a road trip around Lake Michigan, or San Francisco on a drive down Hwy 1, but you might actually enjoy these cities more on some future trip when you're able to spend several days and you don't have a car.

Stick with small luggage. If you're checking into a new hotel nearly every night of your road trip, limit your hassle by limiting how much stuff you carry between your car and your room. I typically keep two or three larger bags in my car filled with all of the clothing, gear, and food I'll need for the duration of my road trip (remember to pack footwear and attire for all of the kinds of weather and conditions you anticipate encountering on our trip). Then I have a couple of smaller bags (a backpack, a carry-on-size roller suitcase) that I take with me from the car to my room each time I check into a new hotel. Every few days I replenish these smaller bags with more supplies and clean clothing from the larger luggage I keep in the car.

Try to secure your valuables, but also try not to stress yourself out worrying. It's a good idea to avoid leaving nice things in your car when you're not in it, but on a long road trip, it can also be impractical to completely empty your car every night. And when you're visiting museums or going on hikes between hotels, you may have to leave most of your belongings in the car. To reduce the risk of someone breaking into your vehicle, stow what you can in the trunk, cover your belongings with cheap-looking blankets, and park in crowded and well-lit areas or secure parking garages. I also keep my important valuables (passport, primary credit cards, cash, backup data drive, and sometimes my laptop) in a lightweight, innocuous-looking tote bag and carry that with me if I'm uneasy about where I've parked my car. And I regularly back up my computer and phone data to the cloud in case I do lose these items. That said, cars and hotel rooms occasionally get broken into (which is a good reason never to bring anything truly irreplaceable with you on your travels). I'm certainly not going to pass up a chance to go on an amazing hike or eat in a cool restaurant because I'm afraid to leave my car unattended with luggage in it.

- **Take the slow road.** Opt for the slower route whenever you can. I've greatly favored local roads versus faster and wider highways, throughout this book, as they tend to offer the most dramatic scenery, and they often pass through colorful towns. When I have recommended an interstate highway, it's because it does offer impressive scenery or the local alternate routes aren't especially appealing.

- **Drive during daylight hours.** The aim of this book is to help you find the most picturesque and engaging roads throughout the US and Canada. You're not going to see what's special about them if you drive them after dark. Moreover, especially when driving through national parks or through rugged terrain, daytime driving is vastly safer—you're less likely to encounter wildlife on the road, and your reaction time to unexpected obstacles is far better. To avoid driving at night, I sometimes plan two-night hotel stays, say near a national park, where I want to spend most of one day exploring. When you are faced with a long nighttime drive, try to favor big highways—they're safer and faster than back roads.

Bend National Park, TX

- **Pay attention to weather conditions.** I typically start my mornings on the road by looking at the 10-day weather forecast, and I frequently adjust my plans accordingly.

- **Invest in a good cooler.** I prefer soft-sided coolers or insulated cooler bags—they're easier to carry and take with you on planes. Each night I transfer the contents to my hotel-room fridge. Coolers work best if you keep them filled to capacity with cold items, so I always pack them with as many cold cans of beer and seltzer as I can fit—this really helps in hot weather.

- **Make sure your hotel room has a small fridge and maybe a microwave.** We rarely use the latter, but it's handy sometimes. The fridge, however, is a must. We also occasionally book rooms with full kitchens, especially if we're staying put for two or three days. Self-catering is a way to save some money and take a break from restaurants, which is especially nice if you're traveling as a family or with a group of friends.

- **Pack some basic tableware.** My partner and I bring along two large bowls (perfect for cereal or yogurt in the morning and soups, instant ramen, store-bought prepared meals, and reheating leftovers), along with a few items of silverware, a paring knife, and a corkscrew–bottle opener combo. That's all we need for picnicking or prepping light meals in hotel rooms. We also bring a small bottle of dish soap and two old pillowcases to protect the bowls. Even basic motels usually supply drinking glasses and mugs (or at least plastic and paper cups), so I never bother with my own glassware, but I do bring an insulated tumbler or thermos.

- **Breakfast is the best meal to supply for yourself.** This may sound counterintuitive because it's the one meal that many hotels offer as a free perk, and for years it never occurred to me to pack breakfast supplies for this reason. Then the pandemic struck, and most hotels temporarily suspended breakfast service. So we started traveling with our own breakfast supplies: granola, bananas, dried fruit, milk, yogurt, cheeses and cold cuts, and good bread. The more we ate our own chosen ingredients, the more we realized how much we preferred them to the bleak breakfasts provided at most hotels—and we also like being able to eat breakfast according to our own schedule, and without having to endure a crowded breakfast room with a TV blaring in the background.

- **Buy groceries at supermarkets.** Convenience stores and little pantries off the lobbies at many hotels may be handy when you need a quick snack on the go, but when we're road-tripping for several days—or weeks—we find it really pays to stock up at a full-service grocery store every three or four days. Prices are lower, and the selection is greater. The beloved US chain Trader Joe's, with its gourmet-on-a-budget ethos, is one of our favorites.

- **Seek out farmers' markets and produce stands.** As much as I rely on grocery stores for staples, they simply can't compete with the peak-season tomatoes, blueberries, apples, and other locally grown goods at farmers' markets, which are also typically great places to enjoy fresh-made breakfast and lunch fare (and people-watching). We also visit local farms and dairies, independently owned bakeries and coffee roasters, and craft breweries and wineries.

- **Bring your own coffee.** I can never quite guess which hotel-room amenity will be more dreadful: the coffeemaker or the coffee itself. Often it's a tie. Some higher-end hotels have upped their coffee game in recent years, but I don't like to take chances—I always bring my own. We've tried traveling with different portable coffee-making devices over the years (AeroPress is our favorite), but ultimately the convenience of cold brew won us over. I stock up on a few bottles of cold brew concentrate before every road trip—Trader Joe's has a decent one, but Chameleon Organic is the best we've found.

- **Pack these indispensable items:** A Bluetooth car adapter in case your rental car doesn't have a stereo with Bluetooth, portable chargers that plug into your car's auxiliary power outlets for your smartphones and laptops (we have a HALO-brand charger that can also jump car batteries), and an extra change of weatherproof outerwear and hiking boots in anticipation of both interesting hiking opportunities and dramatic weather changes.

Map of USA & Canada

AK

YK

MAP LEGEND

NEW YORK ○ Capital/major city

MONTRÉAL ○ Capital/major city/town

Tacoma ○ Town

San Mateo ○ Other population centres/localities

―――― Road trip

―――― Sidetrack route

- - - - Ferry

● **Attractions**

✛ Airport

▲ Mountain

◦ Gorge / Pass

River with waterfall

National park or monument

Other parks or forest

HI

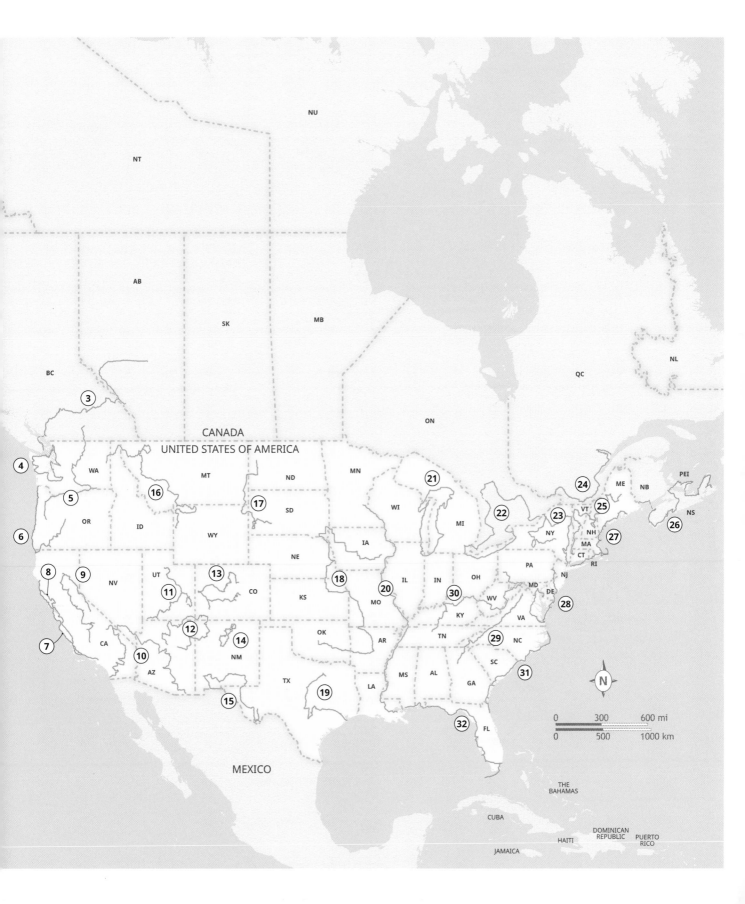

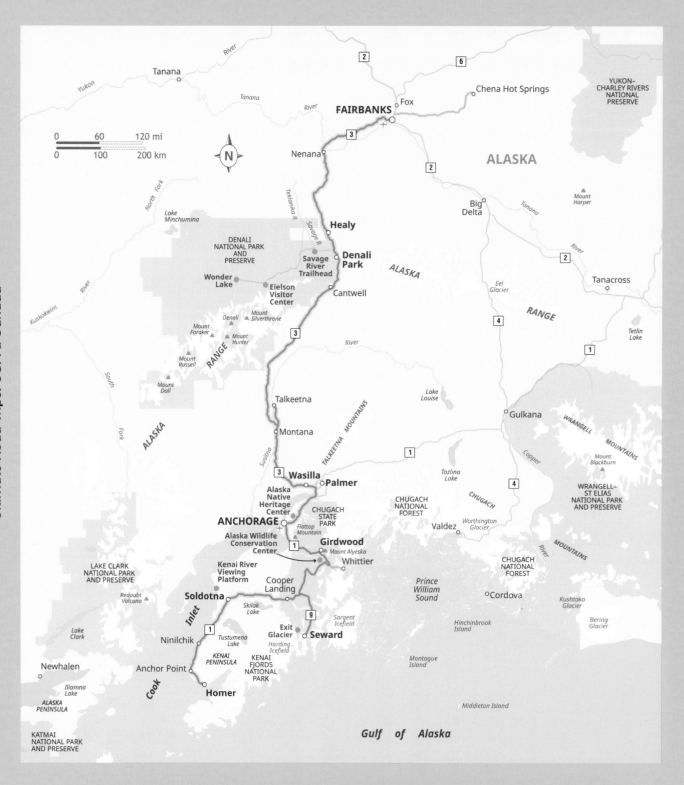

Tanana

Yukon

FAIRBANKS
Fox
Chena Hot Springs

YUKON–
CHARLEY RIVERS
NATIONAL
PRESERVE

Nenana

ALASKA

Tanana

Mount
Harper

Big
Delta

Lake
Minchumina

DENALI
NATIONAL
PARK
AND
PRESERVE

Healy

Denali
Park

ALASKA

Eel
Glacier

Tanacross

Wonder
Lake

Savage
River
Trailhead

Eielson
Visitor
Center

Cantwell

RANGE

Tetlin
Lake

Mount
Foraker

Denali

Mount
Silverthrone

Mount
Hunter

Mount
Russell

Lake
Louise

Gulkana

WRANGELL

MOUNTAINS

Mount
Dall

Talkeetna

Mount
Blackburn

ALASKA

RANGE

Montana

TALKEETNA MOUNTAINS

WRANGELL–
ST ELIAS
NATIONAL
PARK
AND
PRESERVE

Wasilla
Palmer

Tazlina
Lake

CHUGACH

Alaska Native
Heritage
Center

ANCHORAGE

CHUGACH
STATE
PARK

CHUGACH
NATIONAL
FOREST

Valdez

Worthington
Glacier

MOUNTAINS

Flattop
Mountain

Girdwood
Mount Alyeska

Alaska Wildlife
Conservation
Center

Whittier

Prince
William
Sound

CHUGACH
NATIONAL
FOREST

Cordova

Kushtaka
Glacier

LAKE CLARK
NATIONAL PARK
AND PRESERVE

Kenai River
Viewing
Platform

Cooper
Landing

Bering
Glacier

Redoubt
Volcano

Soldotna

Skilak
Lake

Sargent
Icefield

Hinchinbrook
Island

Lake
Clark

Exit
Glacier

Seward

Newhalen

Ninilchik

Tustumena
Lake

KENAI
PENINSULA

KENAI
FJORDS
NATIONAL
PARK

Harding
Icefield

Montague
Island

Middleton Island

Anchor Point

Iliamna
Lake

ALASKA
PENINSULA

Homer

Cook

Inlet

Gulf   of   Alaska

KATMAI
NATIONAL
PARK
AND PRESERVE

The Heart of Alaska ★

See the spectacular glaciers, abundant marine and birdlife, and crystal-clear waters of Alaska's Kenai Peninsula before heading north through vibrant Anchorage to explore Denali National Park and Fairbanks.

HOW LONG?

8 days; add an extra day each to see more of Kenai Fjords and Denali national parks.

WHEN TO GO

Early June to mid-September is ideal, as Denali Park Road and many park services are closed the rest of the year. Summer is peak season and has the best weather but also more crowds and higher rates, so consider the second half of June or first half of September for the best value. It's possible to make this trip in winter and still see a small part of Denali, and this is a great time to see the Northern Lights, but keep in mind that the days are shorter and snowy weather can cause delays.

NEED TO KNOW

This route sticks with paved, well-maintained roads, but it can still be worth renting a four-wheel-drive vehicle to give yourself the freedom of venturing onto rougher roads off the beaten path. Be extremely vigilant driving at night, when wildlife are most apt to cross the road.

Distances
Total distance, one-way: 750 mi (1207 km)
- Homer to Seward: 170 mi (274 km)
- Seward to Anchorage: 130 mi (210 km)
- Anchorage to Talkeetna: (185 km)
- Talkeetna to Denali NP: 145 mi (233 km)
- Denali NP to Fairbanks: 135 mi (217 km)

Daytime Temperatures
January: 0-32°F (-18-0°C)
July: 60-72°F (16-22°C)

More information
- Alaska Tourism, travelalaska.com
- Kenai Peninsula tourism, kenaipeninsula.org
- Kenai Fjords National Park, nps.gov/kefj
- Anchorage tourism, anchorage.net
- Denali National Park, nps.gov/dena
- Fairbanks tourism, explorefairbanks.com

SNAPSHOT

Although most of the largest state in the US is inaccessible by car, a network of smooth, well-trod highways connects many of the dazzling landscapes and distinctive communities for which Alaska is famous. This route begins on the water's edge in the funky fishing town of Homer and ends in the vast interior in the bustling city of Fairbanks. Along the way you'll discover countless natural wonders—including Kenai Fjords and Denali national parks.

HOMER TO SEWARD

If you're traveling here from the southeastern part of the state via the Alaska Marine Highway System, you can take the ferry to Homer to begin your trip. Otherwise, the most practical option is flying into Anchorage, which is served by most major airlines and has plenty of car rental agencies, driving to Homer, and backtracking through Anchorage on your way north. This adds about four or five hours to your trip, but the drive between Anchorage and Homer is so lovely, I never mind making it twice. Also, some rental agencies allow one-way rentals, but there's often a significant surcharge, so it may be worth it to drive the six hours back to Anchorage from Fairbanks at the end of your trip.

Homer is sometimes described as "the end of the road" because of its location at the end of Hwy 1, which is also the terminus of the US highway system—it's 5331 miles, partly through Canada, to get to the farthest-away point in the US (Key West, FL). This friendly fishing town with a year-round population of about 6000 has an artsy, offbeat personality and is popular as a gateway to exploring some of southwestern Alaska's more far-flung communities by boat or plane, including Kodiak Island and Katmai National Park. Narrow and picturesque **Homer Spit** extends 4.5 miles from town into the pristine waters of Kachemak Bay and is lined with casual seafood restaurants, including the excellent La Baleine Cafe, that serve up halibut, salmon, lingcod, and rockfish freshly caught from the town's fleet. You'll also find lots of family-friendly outfitters offering everything from fishing charters to sightseeing cruises.

Downtown has an excellent selection of art galleries and eateries that exceed in both quality and variety what you might expect of such a small, out-of-the-way community. You'll find some interesting attractions, too, including **Pratt Museum and Park**, where you can learn about the natural and human histories of Kachemak Bay, and the outstanding **Alaska Maritime National Wildlife Refuge Visitor Center**, the administrative headquarters for a 7700 sq mile refuge made up of 2400 islands. With engaging exhibits and films on everything from flora and fauna to the Japanese occupation of the Aleutian Islands during World War II, this is a fascinating place that's also surrounded by boardwalk nature trails.

There's just one road out of town, Hwy 1 (aka Sterling Hwy), which curves up through the western side of the Kenai Peninsula, hugging the Cook Inlet for the first 50 miles. A quirky stop along the way is **Anchor Point**, a tiny

unincorporated community that holds the title as the westernmost point on the US highway system. If you've brought food with you, have a picnic at Halibut Campground, whose tables overlook the water—watch for bald eagles, harbor seals, and beluga whales while you dine. About a half hour north, pull over for a quick look around tiny **Ninilchik**, noting the beautiful 1901 Russian Orthodox Church with its ornate green trim and gold-dome spires as well as a small cemetery beside it. The road soon turns inland and passes through one of the peninsula's larger towns, **Soldotna**, where an easy 10-mile side trip leads to the **Kenai River Viewing Platform** and Kenai Beach Dunes. Soldotna is also home to the excellent Kenai River Brewing Co., which produces a refreshing Mexican-style lager called Lime Duck, as well as an excellent steak-and-seafood restaurant, Mykel's. Continue east as Hwy 1 flanks a gorgeous stretch of the Kenai River and passes through **Cooper Landing**, home to several accommodations (Kenai Princess Wilderness Lodge and Drifters Lodge are two great ones) that offer rafting, fishing, and lots of other all-ages activities. About 20 miles later you'll come to the turnoff for Hwy 9, which leads 35 miles south to Seward.

SEWARD TO GIRDWOOD

A spirited port town established in 1903, **Seward** sits at the northern tip of a glacially carved fjord, Resurrection Bay, and is a popular cruise ship stop in part because it lies at the southern terminus of the Alaskan Railroad (which chugs north to Fairbanks, roughly following this driving itinerary). It's also a breathtaking gateway to **Kenai Fjords National**

Park, which in a single day you can explore in two distinct ways: by taking a sightseeing cruise to view humpback whales, Steller sea lions, and glaciers (more than half of the park lies beneath these massive tracts of ice), and then by making the easy 12-mile drive to the foot of gigantic 4 sq mile (though shrinking steadily) **Exit Glacier**. The only part of the park reached by road, it's accurately dubbed a "drive-up" glacier, as an easy, short trail leads from the parking area right to the ice. When I have a few hours, I like making the 8.3-mile round-trip trek through wildflower meadows and cottonwood stands from the parking area to the dramatic Harding Icefield.

Boat trips leave from the busy harbor of Seward's cute and walkable downtown, where a ramble through **Waterfront Park** affords grand views of Mt Alice and the surrounding Kenai Range. Set aside an hour or two to visit the beautifully designed **Alaska SeaLife Center**, a superb aquarium and marine rehabilitation center overlooking the bay that offers up-close opportunities to view tufted puffins, harlequin ducks, spotted seals, and enormous red king crabs. For animal lovers, the fun continues on the drive north; about 40 miles past where Hwy 9 rejoins Hwy 1, stop at the **Alaska Wildlife Conservation Center**, whose mission is to care for wounded or orphaned animals that can't be reintroduced to the wild. You can walk or drive the 1.5-mile loop through this amazing nonprofit sanctuary, stopping to view myriad native species lumbering or scooting about in their spacious enclosures—muskox, brown bears (often swimming in a pond), lynx, and wolves among them. It's another 12 miles north to get to the pretty village of **Girdwood**, whose impressive **Alyeska Resort** contains the state's largest downhill ski area. In summer, ride the aerial tram to the top of Mt Alyeska, go hiking or mountain biking, and enjoy the hotel's extensive and impressive dining and spa facilities.

GIRDWOOD TO ANCHORAGE

It's a quick and scenic one-hour jaunt to sprawling **Anchorage**, which two of every five Alaskans call home. The drive curves dramatically along the shore of Turnagain Arm as it widens before emptying into Cook Inlet. Although water and mountain views greet you here in every direction, Anchorage is less regarded for its beauty than for its lively personality and cultural offerings—much of the city was rebuilt during the decade that followed the catastrophic (magnitude 9.2) Good Friday Earthquake of 1964. Vast as it is (it dwarfs the entire state of Rhode Island), it's easy to navigate and has ample parking. There's an appealing

SIDETRACK

The coolest thing about making a detour to **Whittier**, which is set against soaring mountains at the western end of Prince William Sound's Passage Canal, is the memorable drive. From Hwy 1, head 12 miles on Portage Glacier Road through scenic **Chugach National Forest** and then through the incredibly narrow **Anton Anderson Memorial Tunnel**, which at 2.5 miles is the continent's longest highway tunnel. The mammoth **Portage Glacier** has receded to the degree that you can't see it from the road, but in summer you can score an impressive view by taking a cruise or kayaking excursion on **Portage Lake**, just before you reach the tunnel. Running beneath hulking Maynard Mountain, this one-lane tunnel has the distinction of serving both trains and automobiles; easterly (Whittier-bound) car traffic enters the tunnel on the half-hour, and westerly traffic on the hour, and occasional trains can cause significant delays. It takes about six minutes to drive completely through it, but if you're as claustrophobic as I am, it can feel like an eternity. Whittier is a great spot for kayaking or wildlife cruises, and it's home to the small but excellent **Prince William Sound Museum**. I recommend snagging a seat on the waterfront deck at Oceanfront Cafe and tucking into a bowl of seafood chowder or a kimchi hot dog; it's a good stop for espresso drinks, too.

A bear feasts on salmon at the Alaska Wildlife Conservation Center *Opposite* Mussels at the Little Mermaid in Homer *Previous* Homer and Kachemak Bay

downtown with some interesting historic buildings that survived the quake, plus nice views of Knik Arm (a branch of Cook Inlet) and the mountains beyond. You'll also discover great hiking on the eastern edge of the city, much of it within **Chugach State Park**, including Alaska's most popularly climbed peak, 3510 ft **Flattop Mountain**, which—though a bit steep in places—takes only about two hours to hike round-trip.

Downtown's main thoroughfares of 4th and 5th aves are lined with interesting shops, art galleries, and restaurants, including Red Umbrella Reindeer, my favorite go-to for hearty reindeer sausage hot dogs. Set in a historic Art Deco building, the **Alaska Public Lands Information Center** has enlightening exhibits on the state's flora, fauna, and wilderness and is a great place to pick up maps, hiking tips, and camping advice. Nearby, the **Anchorage Museum** is a must-see for all ages. It occupies a striking, angular contemporary building and contains an amazing collection of Alaska Native art and imaginative exhibits on history and science, plus a terrific restaurant.

ANCHORAGE TO TALKEETNA

About 8 miles out of downtown Anchorage, explore the extensive grounds and fascinating collections at the **Alaska Native Heritage Center**, a vibrant living history museum set on 26 acres and offering visitors the opportunity to view and interact with artists, dancers, and storytellers from the state's many Indigenous cultures. Activities often take place in authentic re-creations of traditional Native buildings. Hwy 1 continues through the **Matanuska-Susitna** (aka **Mat-Su) Valley**, a fertile tract of agricultural land where the Alaska State Fair takes place over two weeks in late August and early September—freakishly prodigious cantaloupes, cabbages, broccoli, and other produce grown here have been recognized as among the largest in the world.

Pick up Hwy 3 and continue through the valley, turning right onto the spur road to the singularly offbeat town of **Talkeetna**, which enjoys an enviable setting on a wide stretch of the Susitna River and is also—despite being 150 miles from the entrance to Denali National Park—one of the best places in the state to see North America's highest peak, 20,320 ft Mt Denali (it's only 55 miles away as the crow flies). For the best photo op on a clear day, walk west a few blocks on to **Talkeetna Riverfront Park**. To get a super close look at the mountain, book a flightseeing excursion (some of these include a short, guided hike on a glacier) from one of the town's tour operators—Talkeetna Air Taxi and K2 Aviation are both highly reputable. Just under 1000 people reside year-round in Talkeetna, which was the inspiration for the endearing '90s TV show *Northern Exposure*. You'll find a smattering of funky shops and cafes, including the colorful West Rib Pub and Grill and adjacent Nagley's general store, which for years was the home of the town's mayor, a sweet orange cat named Stubbs, whom I was fortunate enough to shake paws with on two occasions before he passed away at the ripe old age of 20.

TALKEETNA TO FAIRBANKS

Allow about 2.5 hours to get from Talkeetna to the main visitor center at **Denali National Park**. It's just off Hwy 3 in the small town of **Denali Park**, which with nearby **Healy** acts as a hub of services for park visitors. Slightly larger than the state of New Hampshire and with only one maintained park road, Denali isn't the kind of national park that's geared toward car travel (this is true for all eight of Alaska's remote and rugged national parks). But it's still relatively accessible on this drive.

At a minimum, visit the main **Denali Visitor Center** and walk along several short and easy trails through groves of spruce and open meadows. Then drive your vehicle the first 15 miles of the Park Road to **Savage River** and hike the 2-mile Savage River Loop Trail or steeper 4-mile Savage Alpine Trail. On a clear day, the Alpine Trail may provide you with the chance to see Denali's peak, albeit in the far distance.

If you can, though, I recommend spending the night at one of the properties near the park entrance, then riding a park bus to contemporary **Eielson Visitor Center** at mile marker 66 of the 92-mile Park Road. The ride takes about 3.5 hours each way, and you'll want to spend at least 45 minutes and as long as a few hours exploring the terrain around the visitor center. Both from the visitor center terrace and especially from the lofty Thorofare Ridge Trail, you can take in outstanding views of Mt Denali, which is 33 miles away, and along this spectacularly scenic bus ride, you're likely to see all kinds of wildlife, sometimes within just a few yards of the road: grizzly bears, Dall's sheep, moose, caribou, foxes, and many kinds of birds. Rangers give talks and guided hikes, and although there's no restaurant, it's a great spot to enjoy a picnic lunch.

Plan for a brisk and easy 2 to 2.5-hour drive through gently rolling, relatively open terrain from Denali Park to **Fairbanks**, Alaska's second largest city (pop 30,600). Although less visually dramatic than the Kenai Peninsula or Denali, this laid-back college town—home to the University of Alaska—has some superb museums and, because of its northerly location, is also an ideal place to experience the midnight sun (from late April through late August) and view the northern lights, or aurora borealis (from September to mid-April). Right in the center of downtown, overlooking the Chena River, the striking glass-and-timber **Morris Thompson Cultural and Visitors Center** contains info desks on local attractions and Alaska public lands as well as beautifully rendered dioramas and exhibits that tell the story of the state's people, wildlife, and natural environment. Just west of town, also be sure to check out the exceptional art, cultural, and zoological collections at the extensive and impressively designed **University of Alaska Museum of the North.**

SIDETRACK

Nestled deep in the evergreens about 60 miles east-northeast of Fairbanks, the unincorporated village of **Chena Hot Springs** is set around a unique geothermal hot springs resort. The trip here offers both a lovely woodland drive and the opportunity to soak in an indoor pool or one of several outdoor hot tubs. Come for a few hours, or spend the night in one of the hotel rooms, cabins, or yurts. You can also dine in the inviting restaurant, tour a remarkable ice museum filled with imaginative ice sculptures (it's open year-round, even during the region's often hot summer days), and partake in dog sled (or, in summer, dog cart), horseback, and ATV tours. The lack of light pollution here makes the resort optimal for viewing the northern lights. On your way north from downtown Fairbanks to Chena Hot Springs, you're a quick drive from several other excellent attractions, including the **Fountainhead Antique Auto Museum**, the **Gold Dredge 8** former goldmine, and Silver Gulch Brewing, which serves up tasty brick-oven pizzas and a noteworthy array of craft brews.

A dall sheep taking in the view at Denali National Park

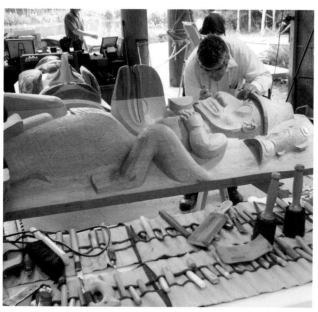

BEST EATS

- **Little Mermaid** The bright and bold contemporary artwork in this downtown Homer bistro matches the colorful, artfully plated seafood, which includes ahi poke, wild-caught prawns with peanut satay sauce, and a hot-stone bowl of local fish and produce. 907-399-9900, littlemermaidhomer.com.

- **The Cookery** A block from Seward's scenic Waterfront Park, this homey spot with imaginatively prepared seafood and a terrific wine list offers both delectable tapas (broiled oysters with house bacon, spot shrimp in garlic-chili oil) and more substantial main plates—the local halibut is always fantastic. 907-422-7459, cookeryseward.com.

- **Double Musky Inn** Apart from the Alyeska Resort, this rambling roadhouse festooned with flags, beer signs, mugs, and colorful Mardi Gras beads might just be the top reason to stop in Girdwood. Since 1962 it's been a beloved go-to for New Orleans-style fare, from crab-stuffed halibut with Creole beurre blanc to shrimp etouffee; there are impressive steaks, too. 907-783-2822, doublemuskyinn.com.

- **Snow City Cafe** Folks line up, especially on weekends, for the chance to feast on snow-crab eggs Benedict and walnut-mandarin orange cream French toast at this cheerful diner-style cafe in downtown Anchorage. Try the salmon BLT at lunch. 907-272-2489, snowcitycafe.com.

- **Pangea** Urbane yet refreshingly unpretentious, this post-industrial-chic space in downtown Anchorage is where you can sample some of the most creative fare in the state. Globally inspired mashups include al pastor-style pork bao buns and banana-cashew-crusted Alaska halibut. 907-222-3949, pangearestaurantandlounge.com.

- **Talkeetna Roadhouse** A rambling log structure built as a freight warehouse in 1917, the roadhouse has long been famous for its mammoth family-style breakfasts, featuring ginormous hotcakes (with daily rotating toppings) from a sourdough starter that dates back to 1902. Fresh-made pies are another specialty, and casual overnight lodgings are offered, too. 907-733-1351, talkeetnaroadhouse.com

Top Downtown Seward *Middle* An artisan at work at the Alaska Native Heritage Center in Anchorage *Bottom* Cabins at Kenai Riverside Lodge

- **229 Parks Restaurant** Named for its mile marker location on the Parks Hwy (Hwy 3), this airy and elegant spot serves some of the tastiest farm-to-table fare in the state from a seasonally changing menu—possibly crisp enoki mushrooms in a smoked-reindeer broth or Alaskan octopus with jalapenos and tangerine oil. Reservations are essential. 907-683-2567, 229parks.com.
- **Pump House** Decorated with Gold Rush-era memorabilia and with extensive deck seating overlooking the picturesque Chena River, this convivial saloon and restaurant 10 miles west of downtown is more about the colorful atmosphere than the food, but the traditional steaks and seafood are still pretty tasty. 907-479-8452, pumphouse.com

---

BEST SLEEPS

- **Homer Inn and Spa** You can't beat the dazzling Kachemak Bay views from the private balconies and decks off every room at this stylish inn with its own waterfront spa (featuring a Finnish sauna, sundeck, hydrotherapy pools, and self-care yurt). The owners also rent out a couple of three-bedroom townhouses in downtown Homer. 907-235-1000, homerinnandspa.com.
- **Bear Creek Inn and Winery** Set on a ridge with commanding bay and mountain views a few miles northeast of downtown Homer, this boutique winery produces semisweet berry and stone-fruit wines and offers three well-appointed accommodations that access a stone hot tub, deck, and waterfall. 907-318-2470, bearcreekwinery.com.
- **Exit Glacier Lodge** This modern 15-room hotel with a Victorian-style facade is less than a 10-minute drive from downtown Seward, on the road to the famed glacier for which it's named. A few good restaurants, including the colorful Le Barn Appetit creperie, as well as a kayak rental and guide service are within walking distance. 907-224-6040, sewardalaskalodging.com.
- **Alyeska Resort** A first-class resort hotel decorated with stunning Native Alaskan artwork and offering its own aerial tram to the top of Mt Alyeska, this chateau-inspired 300-room resort offers plenty of diversions: book a treatment in the hotel's cushy spa, or dine above the clouds—with views of no fewer than seven hanging glaciers—in romantic Seven Glaciers restaurant. 907-754-2111, alyeskaresort.com.

- **Copper Whale Inn** You're steps from downtown Anchorage dining and shopping as well as waterfront Elderberry Park and the Coastal Trail at this cheerful, unpretentious B&B with in-room Roku TVs, tablets, and other thoughtful touches; many rooms have views of Cook Inlet. 907-258-7999, copperwhale.com.
- **Talkeetna Cabins** This small, meticulous compound of fully furnished log cabins along with one larger three-bedroom log house are right in the center of colorful Talkeetna, an easy stroll from Riverfront Park's majestic Mt Denali views as well as Denali Brewpub and Conscious Coffee cafe. 907-733-2227, talkeetnacabins.com.
- **Denali Dome Home B&B** A distinctive alternative to the several utilitarian hotels and lodges near the entrance to Denali National Park, this unusual timber-frame geodesic dome contains eight comfy guestrooms, plenty of indoor and outdoor common spaces, and a peaceful setting on 10 wooded acres. Rates include a generous cooked breakfast. Healy, 907-683-1239, denalidomehome.com.
- **Pike's Waterfront Lodge** Although it's a 10-minute drive west of downtown Fairbanks, the scenic setting on the Chena River is one of this 180-room hotel's prime assets. Other appealing features include a festive restaurant with a riverfront patio, a midnight sun/aurora borealis glass-walled viewing lounge, and a steam room and dry sauna. 907-456-4500, pikeslodge.com.

CAMPING

Alaska in summer is a camping paradise, although you should come fully prepared to spend the night in pristine and sometimes remote wilderness. Encounters with wildlife—including bears—can happen even in Anchorage. There's tent camping near the foot of Exit Glacier in Kenai Fjords National Park and both RV and tent sites at several spots in Denali National Park, with Savage River being one of the most rugged and scenic. In every key community on this itinerary, you'll find at least a few and often many commercial and park campgrounds. Some notable spots include Homer Spit, Williwaw near Portage Lake on the road to Whittier, Eklutna Lake (about 45 minutes northeast of Anchorage, en route to Talkeetna), and K'esugi Ken (between Talkeetna and Denali).

Maui and the Road to Hana ★

The twisting, narrow, and breathtaking Road to Hana is Hawaii's most famous drive, but the rest of Maui—from its sunny west shore beaches to the cool-aired Upcountry—offers plenty of eye-popping scenery, too.

HOW LONG?

2–3 days; add an extra day to spend a night in the Upcountry towns of Kula or Makawao.

WHEN TO GO

April–May and September–October offer perhaps the perfect sweet spot of fewer crowds and lovely weather, but in my experience there's no bad time to visit Maui (or the rest of Hawaii). Keep in mind that although winter is the wet season, and it's especially damp along the main section of the Road to Hana, the frequent rains result in more dramatic waterfalls and rainforests and more frequent rainbows.

NEED TO KNOW

Most car rental companies on Maui void coverage on cars driven around the backside of the Road to Hana—the roughly 10-mile stretch from Kipahulu to Huakini Bay. What this means in practice is that if you have car trouble along here, you're responsible for getting yourself out of this situation (and paying for any towing or repairs). I've taken my chances and driven to central Maui via the Upcountry without incident on several occasions, but in the interest of caution, this itinerary follows the route that doesn't violate car-rental contracts, which means backtracking from Hana to Paia in order to drive into the Upcountry to Kula.

➡ Distances
Total distance, one-way: 175 mi (282 km)
- Kapalua to Kahului: 42 mi (68 km)
- Kahului to Kipahulu: 63 mi (101 km)
- Kipahulu to Kula: 75 mi (121 km)

𝄃 Temperatures
January: 70-82°F (21-28°C)
July: 75-87°F (24-31°C)

ⓘ More information
- Hawaii tourism, gohawaii.com
- Maui tourism, gohawaii.com/islands/maui
- Haleakala National Park, nps.gov/hale

👁 SNAPSHOT

The second largest Hawaiian island, Maui offers an exhilarating mix of postcard-perfect sandy bays, emerald-green rainforests, and arid, rocky volcanic craters and lava fields, along with a great diversity of vacation experiences. Sprawling golf and beach resorts are plentiful, but if you venture a bit off the beaten path, you'll also find more personal and quirky bungalows and historic inns. Several curving scenic roads encircle, and sometimes climb into, the soaring upper elevations of this idyllic island, making it my favorite in Hawaii for car adventures.

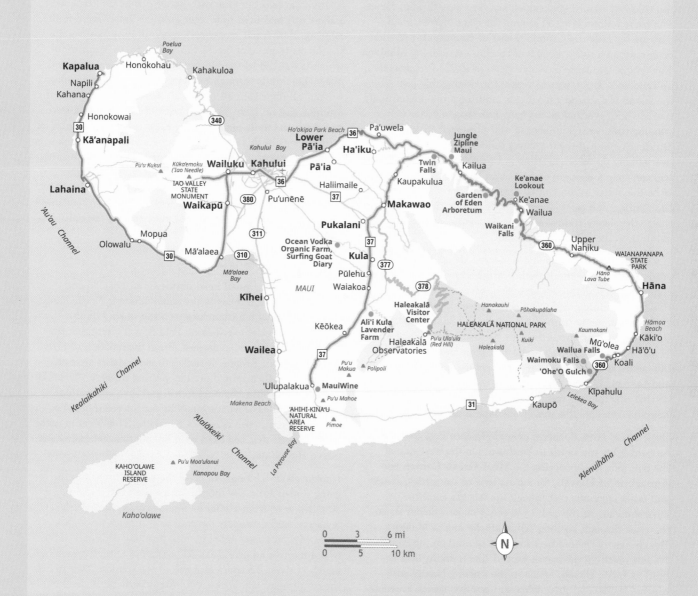

PACIFIC   OCEAN

Hālawa
MOLOKA'I

Kapalua
Napili
Kahana
Honokowai
30
Kā'anapali
Honokohau
Kahakuloa
Poelua Bay
340
Ho'okipa Park Beach
36
Pa'uwela
Lower Pā'ia
Ha'iku
Jungle Zipline Maui
Kailua
Lahaina
Kahului Bay
Kūka'emoku ('Iao Needle)
Pu'u Kukui ▲
Wailuku
Kahului
36
Pā'ia
Haliimaile
37
Kaupakulua
Twin Falls
Garden of Eden Arboretum
Ke'anae Lookout
Ke'anae
Wailua
IAO VALLEY STATE MONUMENT
380
Waikapū
Pu'unēnē
Makawao
Waikani Falls
'Au'au Channel
Mopua
Olowalu
311
Pukalani
360
Upper Nahiku
WAIANAPANAPA STATE PARK
30
Mā'alaea
310
Ocean Vodka Organic Farm, Surfing Goat Diary
37
Kula
377
Hāna Lava Tube
Hāna
Mā'alaea Bay
Pūlehu
MAUI
Waiakoa
Kīhei
Ali'i Kula Lavender Farm
Haleakalā Visitor Center
378
Hanakauhi ▲
Pōhakupālaha
Hāmoa Beach
Kāki'o
Kēōkea
Haleakalā Observatories
Pu'u Ula'ula (Red Hill)
HALEAKALĀ NATIONAL PARK
Kuiki ▲
Kaumakani ▲
Mū'olea
Wailua Falls
Hā'ō'u
Wailea
37
Pu'u Makua ▲
Polipoli
Haleakalā ▲
Waimoku Falls
'Ohe'O Gulch
360
Koali
Kealaikahiki Channel
'Ulupalakua
MauiWine
Pu'u Mahoe ▲
Kīpahulu
Makena Beach
'AHIHI-KINA'U NATURAL AREA RESERVE
Pimoe ▲
31
Kaupō
Lelekea Bay
'Alalākeiki Channel
La Perouse Bay

KAHO'OLAWE ISLAND RESERVE
Pu'u Moa'ulanui ▲
Kanapou Bay

Kaho'olawe

'Alenuihāhā Channel

0   3   6 mi
0   5   10 km

N

KAPALUA TO KAHULUI

Starting a drive around Maui in the rarefied resort community of **Kapalua**, at the northern tip of the island, presents a nice opportunity to soak up plenty of sunshine as well as grand views across Lahaina Roads channel toward the smaller islands of **Molokai** and **Lanai** before you embark on the wild and woolly—and sometimes very wet—Road to Hana. The route follows Hwy 30 around the coast of West Maui, past the big beach and condo resorts of **Kaanapali** and then down around a scenic stretch of beaches overlooking **Maalaea Bay** (you're treated to awesome views of 10,023 ft Haleakala Volcano, too). But my main reason for visiting this part of the island is to spend a few hours strolling around admittedly touristy but nevertheless engaging **Lahaina**, a historic whaling town with a number of well-preserved colonial buildings, many of them holding galleries and boutiques and overlooking the water. Starting in **Courtyard Square**, where you can snap a photo of an enormous banyan tree that's said to be the oldest in the United States, you can venture amid the retailers and cafes along **Front Street**, perhaps popping inside the stately **Baldwin Home Museum**, which has exhibits on the island's rich history.

If you've looked at a map and wondered about the shorter road—Hwy 340, or the **Kahekili Highway**—between Kapalua and Kahului, it's an option, theoretically, but this tight, winding road that's poorly paved in places and somewhat prone to washouts is not for the faint of heart—I find it more treacherous than the backside of the Road to Hana. But if this 22-mile route does offer amazing views of the ocean, so if you're up for an adventure, don't fear heights, and have made sure your car-rental company doesn't prohibit driving this route (some do), go for it—just allow about two hours to complete this mostly one-lane route.

Back where Hwy 30 curves around Maalaea Bay, continuing forward leads you north to **Wailuku**. On the west side of the bay, kids love exploring the **Maui Ocean Center, the Aquarium of Hawaii**, for a close look at sea turtles, sharks, and other creatures that inhabit the island's coral reef environments. At this point you could make a detour down the coast through bustling **Kihei** all the way to **Makena Beach**, one of the prettiest stretches of sand on the island. It's fun watching the sunset here—I like trekking over the bluff to **Little Beach**, which in the evening bustles with hippies, musicians, queer folks, and creative spirits. En route to Makena Beach, you'll pass through the swanky **Wailea Resort**, which is home to some of the most opulent hotels in the state, including the **Four Seasons**, where the biting 2021 HBO series *The White Lotus* was filmed.

When you get to Wailuku, turn left at Honolii Park onto Main Street. If you're interested in learning more about the island's heritage, drop by the **Maui Historical Society Museum**, which occupies an 1833 home that's surrounded by fragrant gardens bursting with native plants. Continue west a short way and then bear right onto Iao Valley Road to the alluring, 1200 ft tall mossy rock monolith, the **Iao Needle**. It's the centerpiece of 6-acre **Iao Valley State Monument**, which is flanked by the soaring West Maui Mountains and offers short trails through one of the wettest and thus most verdant rainforests in all of Hawaii. Return to Wailuku and continue east on Hwy 32 to the heart of Maui's largest town and the home to its main airport, **Kahului**. There aren't a lot of attractions in this prosaic city, but Kahului and neighboring Wailuku do have a number of noteworthy stops for snacking, including friendly Maui Coffee Attic for lattes and light breakfast and lunch fare, and Ululani's for the best shave ice on the island (don't scrimp on the toppings, such as condensed milk, toasted coconut, macadamia nuts, and my favorite, adzuki beans).

KAHULUI TO KIPAHULU

Leaving Kahului, you'll head northeast on Hwy 36 and follow this about 6 miles to the small, amiable North Shore town of **Paia**, which comprises a cluster of surf shops, galleries, and cafes overlooking Paia Bay. It's here that the Road to Hana begins in earnest. From the junction of Hwy 36 and Baldwin Avenue, it snakes around Maui's sparsely populated northeastern shoreline, passing through the small town of Hana after about 44 miles, and then continuing another 11 miles to what's generally considered the end of this scenic route, the village of Kipahulu. This 55-mile route follows a trail that had been used by countless generations of native Hawaiians.

It takes about 2.5 hours to drive the whole thing, and the going is slow for a few mostly fun reasons: the middle 30 miles or so from Haiku to Waianapanapa State Park is narrow and extremely tortuous as it threads through a series of tight curves lined by lush greenery (this part of the island receives an average of 300 inches of rainfall annually, which is about 2.5 times as much as the rainiest town in the continental US, Forks, WA). Many parts of this section, including dozens of bridges and sharp curves, are one-way, so it's critical that you take things slowly. There are lots of turnouts and vista points to pull over and snap a photo, stroll through a fragrant garden or beneath a rushing waterfall, or stop at a farmstand selling local produce, fresh-baked banana bread, or barbecue pork or shrimp. And when you get to the final 15 miles of the route, along the shore of Hana and Kipahulu, you can easily become happily distracted by several beautiful beaches. There's also a less fun reason the drive takes a while: very, very slow traffic. This road has become incredibly famous, and it's sometimes clogged with sightseers. If you can, try driving it Monday through Thursday, and as you make your way, whenever you can safely pull over, let faster traffic pass you—some of these folks are locals just trying to get home from work or running errands.

In terms of where to stop, you'll have the most fun—especially if it's your first time—simply letting your instincts guide you. Whenever a view, a quirky hand-painted sign, or the need to take a pause from driving strikes you, hop out for a gander. Note that quite a few Maui tour operators also offer guided Road to Hana tours, some of which return via the backside road through the Upcountry that rental cars frown upon. These guides (good ones include Hana and Beyond, Mahalo Tours, and—one of the best if you want to see the notorious "backside"—Hoaloha Jeep Adventures) know about the best hikes, waterfalls, and snack stands and are up on the most current weather and road conditions, so consider booking a tour for this stretch of the road, especially if you're keen to sit back and enjoy the scenery.

However you drive the Road to Hana, make time for a few key highlights. As you travel east from Paia, **Twin Falls** is a gorgeous little trek to stunning waterfalls that also has a farmstand selling coconut ice cream, cold brew coffee, and other treats. A family favorite nearby is **Jungle Zipline Maui** aerial adventure park, which has eight lines that traverse a gorgeous green valley. For a stroll through some 30 acres of native trees and plants, stop at **Garden of Eden Arboretum**, and a few miles later, for one of the road's best photo ops, take the little side lane to **Keanae Lookout**, a small promontory of black sand and lava rock that juts out into the sea and offers sweeping views of the surrounding coastal cliffs. The triple cataracts at **Waikani Falls** are another cool sight, and not long after you'll come to **Nahiku Marketplace**, which has a handful of food stalls serving up tacos, Thai food, barbecue chicken, sorbet, and other treats. You're just 6 miles from the town of Hana at this point. Here you can explore one of the true treasures along this journey: 122-acre **Waianapanapa State Park**, with its small crescent-shaped black-sand beach, oft-photographed sea arch, picnic tables, and coastal paths.

Top Sunrise at Haleakala National Park *Bottom* A waterfall on the Road to Hana *Previous* Napili Bay and Kapalua, Maui

With about 1500 years of Native Hawaiian history, **Hana** is one of the best-preserved villages on Maui, thanks in part to its secluded location, which makes commercial development impractical. It supported sugarcane farming from roughly the mid-19th to mid-20th centuries, but these days the town of about 1250 depends mostly on local farming and ecotourism. In addition to Waianapanapa, it's lined with several magical beaches, including the dramatic red-sand beach at **Kaihalulu** and the white sands of **Hamoa Beach**, which is popular for swimming.

From here to **Kipahulu**, the road is a little easier than the stretch before Hana, and it accesses some more memorable sites, including beautiful **Wailua Falls** and the most accessible of three short coastal stretches of **Haleakala National Park**, **Oheo Gulch**. Stop at the **Kipahulu Visitor Center** to learn about the park and pick up trail info, then take the short path to view the pools connected by a rushing stream, or the slightly longer (about 4 miles round-trip) **Pipiwai Trail**, which climbs nearly 1000 ft through a bamboo forest to stunning **Waimoku Falls**. Note that the $30 park entry fee is valid for three days and also gets you into the much larger Upcountry portion of the park that leads into its famous crater. Beyond the park, the paved section of the road continues a few more miles. You can view the grave of notorious former Hana resident Charles Lindbergh along this stretch as well as the neighboring 1857 **Palapala Ho'omau Church**, and you can take a tour and tasting of **Ono Organic Farms**, which grows and sells mouthwatering star apples, durian, rambutans, pink pomelos, and other tasty fruit.

SIDETRACK

By taking the upper of the two main roads through Kula, Hwy 377, you can access Hwy 378, which leads into the heart of 33,000-acre **Haleakala National Park**, whose seminal feature is its massive 10,023 ft namesake volcano, which is dormant at the moment but erupted as recently as 1600. Trails lead into the volcano's 2600 ft deep, 2 mile wide crater, but you can get an impressive view of this otherworldly red-soil expanse by driving to the mountain's summit, where there's an observation platform. Keep in mind that temperatures up here average 45° to 65° F, so bring a jacket (you can pop inside the visitor center to view exhibits about the park and warm up if you're chilly). The favorite time to drive up the steep switchbacking road into the park is early in the morning so you arrive in time to watch one of the most amazing sunrises in the state. Doing this has become so popular that the park now requires reservations if arriving between 3am and 7am; you can book up to 60 days in advance at recreation.gov. The summit is beautiful all day, though, and I find the sunsets (which don't require reservations or waking up at an ungodly hour) to be just as beautiful. As you drive along the park road, keep an eye out for wildlife, especially nene geese—these endangered native creatures are Hawaii's state bird.

Lahaina Town

KIPAHULU TO KULA

Not far west of the Charles Lindbergh grave in Kipahulu, the paved section of the Road to Hana ends. If you're driving a rental car, you'll have to make a decision here about whether to risk continuing west along the narrow, roughly 10-mile unpaved section of Hwy 31 that isn't likely covered in your rental car company's contract or return the way you came. This section of road was historically far more dangerous than it is now—it was little more than a dirt 4WD path with massive potholes, steep drops, and rickety bridges the first time I drove it in the mid-'90s. It has been gradually improved over the years, and the drive is beautiful, but if you do chance it, remember that you're responsible for any repair costs you may incur in the event of a mishap, so drive with extreme care.

Whichever way you proceed, the goal is to get to Maui's mostly rural and agrarian—but also beautiful—Upcountry. If backtracking to get here, turn left up Hwy 365 in Haiku to reach the historic center of **Makawao**, which sits about 1600 ft above sea level on the northwestern slope of East Maui's Mt Haleakala. The town is noteworthy both as a vibrant artists' colony and the state's most celebrated center of paniolo, or Hawaiian cowboy, culture. Each year over July Fourth weekend, the town hosts Hawaii's top paniolo competition, the **Makawao Rodeo**. And year-round, you can get a glimpse of the town's creative spirit by checking out the rotating exhibits at the **Hui No'eau Visual Arts Center** and visiting notable galleries like **Makai Glass Maui** and **Jordanne Gallery**.

From Makawao, Hwy 37 cuts south through **Kula**, gradually ascending to elevations of 2000 to 3000 ft along the western slope of Mt Haleakala. This large Upcountry district of East Maui offers stunning views across the island's western shoreline and out toward Lanai and Molokai and is known for its organic farms and artisanal culinary scene. You could make an afternoon of sampling locally produced delectables: sugarcane spirits at **Ocean Vodka Organic Farm and Distillery**, exceptional soft cheeses and spreads at **Surfing Goat Dairy** (viewing the adorable goats is part of the fun), sipping pineapple wine as well as red and white European varietals at **MauiWine**, sipping herbal tea and perusing bath products at **Alii Kula Lavender Farm**, and stopping at any of several farmstands to snap up fresh produce. All of these properties are set amid lovely gardens or offer dramatic views. MauiWine is about as far south as most drivers go, but if you have some extra time, consider continuing along Hwy 31 through the lava fields that flow down the south slopes of Mt Haleakala until the pavement ends around Huakini Bay.

Remote archipelago though it is, Hawaii is a wonderful state for road-tripping, even if all of its islands can be covered by car in as little as a single day.

The largest of the bunch, **Hawaii Island**—aka the Big Island—can nearly be circumnavigated via a series of coastal roads, but this roughly 250-mile journey takes six hours without stops and easily 10 to 12 hours if you hop out to see the route's top sights: Hawaii Volcanoes National Park, the historic bayfront of Hilo, the Upcountry ranching town of Waimea, the quirky and colorful Hawi town, the upscale resorts along the sunny Kohala Coast, and the coffee plantations of the Kona Coast.

By far the most populous Hawaiian island, **Oahu** has the most developed network of roads, including the state's only true freeways. And although plenty of visitors spend their entire stay in Honolulu and the adjacent Waikiki beachfront (where a car isn't needed and can actually be a drawback given limited or expensive parking), I think making the loop drive around the North Shore is worth renting a car for 24 hours. Start in Honolulu, stop by Pearl Harbor National Memorial, and then head north to check out some of the world's most celebrated surfing beaches in Haleiwa and Pupukea.

Continue around the northeastern tip of the island and down around the secluded coves and beaches on the eastern shore—including Kokololio and Ahupua'a 'O Kahana parks. Cool stops include Kualoa Ranch, where some 80 movies and TV shows (*Lost*, *Godzilla*, *50 First Dates*, *Hawaii Five-O*) have been filmed and a variety of zip line, bike, horseback, and other tours are offered—and Byodo-In Temple.

Aptly nicknamed the Garden Isle, lush **Kauai** is circumnavigated about three-quarters of the way around by absolutely stunning roads. From the airport in Lihue, head southwest along a spectacular road that climbs from the sea up along the 3000 ft elevation rim of 10 mile long Waimea Canyon and on to the waterfalls and temperate rainforest of even higher Kokee State Park. Drive through the majestic scenery of ritzy Princeville Resort and historic Hanalei Bay, which has appeared memorably in such Hollywood blockbusters as *Jurassic World*, *Tropic Thunder*, and *South Pacific*. Dip your toes in the sand at laid-back Ke'e Beach or hike a portion of the legendary Kalalau Trail along the iconic Na Pali Coast.

BEST EATS

- **Star Noodle** Soak up glorious views of Lanai and Molokai and possibly even humpback whales in winter from a patio table of this contemporary pan-Asian restaurant on the Lahaina waterfront. Vietnamese chicken wings, charbroiled miso salmon, and pork ramen are among the specialties. 808-667-5400, starnoodle.com.

- **Mama's Fish House** This legendary—though spendy—Polynesian-style seafood restaurant with bamboo walls and a glorious setting on Paia's scenic Ku'au Cove is a wonderful option for a leisurely lunch at the start of the Road to Hana. Fresh-caught local ono, mahi-mahi, and kanpachi are prepared with artful flourish, and the coconut chiffon cake makes for a memorable dessert. 808-579-8488, mamasfishhouse.com.

- **Island Fresh Cafe** With a lush garden patio and a handy location along Paia's main drag, this cheerful spot offers a wide array of healthy and delicious breakfast and lunch dishes, including pineapple-mango smoothies, acai bowls, avocado toast, and fish tacos. 808-446-0298, islandfreshmaui.com.

- **Hana Farms** On the right side of the road as you enter Hana, a little before you reach Waianapanapa State Park, stop by this lush 7-acre organic farm to pick up fresh papayas and lychees from the farmstand, banana bread and coconut macaroons from the bakery, or kalua pork plates, harvest salads, and wood-fired pizzas from the pitched-roof, high-ceilinged restaurant. 808-248-7371, hanafarms.com.

- **Kula Bistro** In an unassuming vintage storefront across from a 1940s general store, this relaxed restaurant in Upcountry Maui sources local produce and meats for its delicious American and Italian dishes, including hearty penne with vodka-pomodoro sauce, jumbo scallops, and shrimp. 808-871-2960, kulabistro.com.

- **Hali'imaile General Store** Amid scenic pineapple fields a short drive from Makawao, the long-celebrated farm-to-table chef Bev Gannon serves artfully prepared Hawaiian Regional Cuisine in this beautifully restored 1920s building. Expect sterling service, one of the Island's best wine lists, a nice selection of vegetarian and kids' options, and sublime fare like duck steam buns with hoisin sauce and macadamia-nut-crusted catch of the day with a mango-lilikoi butter sauce. 808-572-2666, hgsmaui.com.

BEST SLEEPS

- **Napili Kai Beach Resort** Among the many beach resorts clustered along the Kapalua and Kaanapali coastline, this upscale but reasonably priced 163-room compound overlooking enchanting Napili Bay stands out on several fronts: the tastefully appointed rooms have well-equipped kitchenettes, there are no resort fees, kids eat free and enjoy an array of activities, adults can chill in the excellent little spa, and the service is super-friendly and personal. 808-669-6271, napilikai.com.

- **The Plantation Inn** Just two blocks from Lahaina's historic harborfront, this charmingly intimate boutique hotel has 18 smartly appointed rooms and suites (most with private lanais), a landscaped courtyard with a pool, and rates that include parking as well as a gourmet breakfast prepared by a renowned French chef. 808-667-9225, theplantationinn.com.

- **Paia Inn** This cozy, romantic 1920s inn on a popular surfing beach is right at the start of the Road to Hana and also within walking distance of several appealing shops and eateries, including the property's own hip sushi and cocktail bar, Vana Paia. 808-579-6000, paiainn.com.

- **Hana-Maui Resort** This historic, Hyatt-managed, 66-acre plantation-style resort is the only full-service hotel in tiny Hana, and it's also a bit of a splurge, replete with 74 cushy rooms, suites, and bungalows, one of Maui's most alluring spas, a striking infinity pool with a great little bar, and an acclaimed farm-to-table restaurant (also open to nonguests). It's older and more idiosyncratic than many of the island's luxury properties, but that's the main reason I like it. 808-400-1234, hyatt.com.

- **Guest Houses at Malani** Midway between Hana and Wailua Falls, this pair of warmly appointed bungalows—a one-bedroom and a two-bedroom—is perfect for families or small groups, as each home has a fully stocked kitchen and lots of space to spread out and relax. Gorgeous Hamoa Beach is a 15-minute walk (or quick car ride), and the setting is utterly tranquil. 808-248-8706, hanaguesthouses.com.

- **Banyan Bed & Breakfast Retreat** On the edge of the Upcountry heart of Maui's paniolo country, the town of Makawao, this 2-acre spread dotted with banyan and monkeypod trees has several guest rooms in the main plantation-style house as well as a few simply but cheerfully furnished cottages. The location is near both the start and the end of the Road to Hana. 808-866-6225, bed-breakfast-maui.com.

CAMPING

Tent camping is quite popular in Hawaii, and Maui has some venues for pitching a tent that are more amazing than almost anything you'll experience by staying in a conventional hotel: imagine waking up on a black-sand beach at Hana's Waianapanapa State Park or taking a short stroll from Haleakala National Park's Oheo pools (you can also camp more than 7000 ft above sea level within this park's lunarlike volcanic crater). Other favorite spots include Polipoli Spring in Upcountry Kula, Kipahulu on the south end of the island, and Papalaua Wayside Park, which is one of the only options on the west side of the island. RV and camper camping, though not hugely popular in Hawaii, does have a growing following. You can rent camping vehicles in Maui through several agencies, including Maui Camper Escapes and Campervan Hawaii (the latter company has rentals on Oahu and the Big Island, too).

Top Fresh fruit at Ono Organic Farms *Opposite* Surfing Goat Dairy

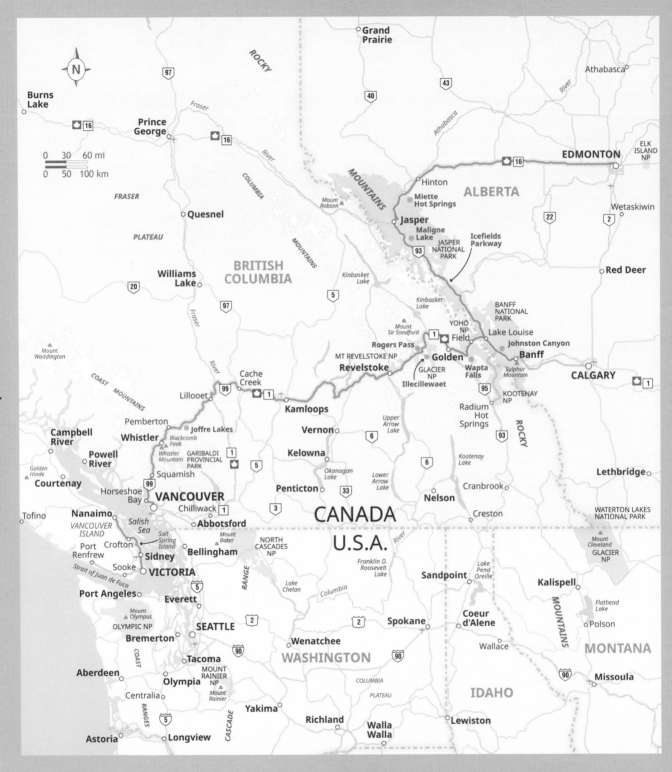

Burns Lake

97

16 Prince George

16

FRASER

Quesnel

PLATEAU

Williams Lake

20

97

BRITISH COLUMBIA

ROCKY

Fraser

COLUMBIA

MOUNTAINS

River

Grand Prairie

43

40

Athabasca

River

Athabasca

MOUNTAINS

Mount Robson

Hinton

Miette Hot Springs

Jasper

Maligne Lake

JASPER NATIONAL PARK

93

ALBERTA

EDMONTON

16

ELK ISLAND NP

Wetaskiwin

2

22

Red Deer

Icefields Parkway

Kinbasket Lake

5

Kinbasket Lake

Mount Sir Sandford

Rogers Pass

MT REVELSTOKE NP

Revelstoke

YOHO NP

1 Field

Golden

GLACIER NP

Illecillewaet

BANFF NATIONAL PARK

Lake Louise

Johnston Canyon

Banff

Wapta Falls

Sulphur Mountain

CALGARY

1

Mount Waddington

COAST MOUNTAINS

River

Lillooet

Cache Creek

99

1

Kamloops

Vernon

Upper Arrow Lake

6

Radium Hot Springs

KOOTENAY NP

95

ROCKY

93

Lethbridge

Campbell River

Powell River

Golden Hinde

Courtenay

Whistler

Joffre Lakes

Blackcomb Peak

Whistler Mountain

GARIBALDI PROVINCIAL PARK

1

Squamish

99

Horseshoe Bay

VANCOUVER

Chilliwack

1

5

Kelowna

Okanagan Lake

Penticton

33

3

Lower Arrow Lake

Kootenay Lake

Nelson

Cranbrook

Creston

CANADA

U.S.A.

WATERTON LAKES NATIONAL PARK

Mount Cleveland

GLACIER NP

Tofino

Nanaimo

VANCOUVER ISLAND

Port Renfrew

Crofton

Sooke

Sidney

VICTORIA

Port Angeles

Salish Sea

Salt Spring Island

Bellingham

Mount Baker

NORTH CASCADES NP

Strait of Juan de Fuca

Everett

Mount Olympus

OLYMPIC NP

SEATTLE

RANGE

Lake Chelan

Franklin D. Roosevelt Lake

Columbia

River

Sandpoint

Lake Pend Oreille

Kalispell

Flathead Lake

Polson

MOUNTAINS

MONTANA

Bremerton

COAST

Tacoma

90

MOUNT RAINIER NP

Mount Rainier

Aberdeen

Olympia

Centralia

RANGES

Yakima

5

CASCADE

Richland

Walla Walla

Wenatchee

2

WASHINGTON

COLUMBIA

PLATEAU

Spokane

2

90

Coeur d'Alene

Wallace

90

Missoula

IDAHO

Lewiston

Astoria

Longview

0 30 60 mi
0 50 100 km

N

Vancouver Island to the Canadian Rockies 🍁

From the temperate rainforests and pristine shores of Vancouver Island to the craggy peaks and glacial lakes of the Canadian Rockies, virtually every mile of this route offers jaw-dropping scenery.

HOW LONG?

12–14 days; add an extra day each to see more of Victoria and Vancouver as well as Banff and Jasper national parks.

WHEN TO GO

This is a great year-round trip, with each season offering rewards. The lush gardens of Vancouver Island and the city of Vancouver burst with color from late spring to early fall, and summer is ideal for hiking and boating in the Rockies. But the entire region is also gorgeous—if wet and rainy near the coast—in winter, which is also perfect for winter recreation at the renowned resorts in Whistler, Revelstoke, Banff, and Jasper.

NEED TO KNOW

Travel with appropriate winter driving gear—chains, first-aid kits, extra warm clothing—in the Rockies from September through May—snowy weather can even happen in summer at the highest elevations. Major winter storms can cause road closures, so watch forecasts closely. Vancouver Island ferries can get crowded on weekends and in summer—make reservations when possible.

➡ Distances
Total distance, one-way: 1150 mi (1851 km)
- Victoria, BC to Whistler, BC: 200 mi (322 km)
- Whistler, BC to Kamloops, BC: 185 mi (298 km)
- Kamloops, BC to Banff, AB: 310 mi (499 km)
- Banff, AB to Jasper, AB: 180 mi (290 km)
- Jasper, AB to Edmonton, AB: 225 mi (362 km)

Daytime Temperatures
January: 20-50°F (-6-10°C)
July: 60-85°F (16-29°C)

More information
- Victoria tourism, tourismvictoria.com
- Vancouver tourism, destinationvancouver.com
- Whistler tourism, whistler.com
- Revelstoke tourism, seerevelstoke.com
- Banff tourism, banfflakelouise.com
- Jasper tourism, jasper.travel
- Edmonton tourism, exploreedmonton.com

👁 SNAPSHOT

The vertiginous drive from coastal British Columbia to the peaks of western Alberta packs as many awe-inspiring sights as any auto adventure in Canada. Just offshore from dignified, old-world Victoria, you might see orcas and humpback whales breaching in the open sea. On the mainland, views from the undulating highways that climb through Whistler and the Canadian Rockies can include hulking glaciers, turquoise alpine lakes, bears cavorting in wildflower meadows, and roaring rivers and waterfalls. All along the route—even in small towns—it's easy to find rustic-chic lodges and grand hotels and restaurants specializing in locally sourced ingredients.

SIDETRACK

For a splendid coastal drive, make the two-hour trek to **Sooke**, with its farm-to-table restaurants and posh country inns, and Port Renfrew, which lies literally at the end of the road. From Victoria, take gently rolling and lushly forested Hwy 14 to Sooke Basin bay and then onward through town along Vancouver Island's southwestern shore. The views of Washington's Olympic Mountains are spectacular, and a number of parks and beaches line the route, among them **French Beach**, **Jordan River Regional Park** (where you might stop inside the funky Cold Shoulder Cafe for an Earl Grey latte or a bowl of chanterelle mushroom soup), and—via a short drive and then hike from the main route— **Sombrío Beach**. At the end of Hwy 14 lies **Port Renfrew**, a small hamlet where the San Juan and Gordon rivers empty into the sea. Wonderful spots for a stroll include the tidepools and dramatic rock formations of **Botanical Beach Provincial Park** and **Avatar Grove**, with its massive, gnarled old-growth cedars. You can return to Victoria the way you came, or you can make a half hour longer scenic loop through dense conifer forests to **Lake Cowichan** and then along the west side of Saanich Inlet.

VICTORIA, BC TO WHISTLER, BC

Although it's possible to start this trip on the mainland, I prefer ferrying 20 miles across the Georgia Strait and beginning on **Vancouver Island**, a huge—it's more than twice the size of Prince Edward Island—tract of sculpted inlets, mammoth mountains, and temperate rainforest that offers scenery completely different from, but every bit as spectacular as, the Rockies. Start in the island's largest city and BC's capital, **Victoria**, strolling around downtown's picturesque **Inner Harbour**, which is anchored by the ornately neo-Baroque provincial parliament buildings, the engrossing **Royal BC Museum**, and the **Fairmont Empress** hotel.

High tea in this elegant hotel is a treasured rite, which perhaps isn't surprising given Victoria's traditional—some might say stodgy—British reputation; but this city of around 85,000 has become younger and more diverse in recent years, and locals are now more likely to spend the afternoon at a lively brewpub, a third-wave coffeehouse, or one of the laid-back seafood shacks lining the harbor—maybe Red Fish Blue Fish beside the seaplane terminal or the Fish Store at colorful **Fisherman's Wharf**. It's a short walk from the waterfront to the city's most famous patch of greenery, **Beacon Hill Park**, which is laced with evergreen-shaded trails that lead south to **Spiral Beach** and **Finlayson Point**, where you're treated to views across the Strait of San Juan de Fuca of Washington's snowcapped Olympic Mountains. My favorite part of the park is **Beacon Hill Children's Farm**, where you can see and sometimes pet potbellied pigs, miniature donkeys, goats, and other cute critters. I always time my visit to watch absurdly adorable daily goat stampedes at around 10 and 4.

Drive along scenic **Dallas Road** and **Beach Road**, following the curving shoreline and admiring genteel **Oak Bay**, and then take Hwy 17 north to the cute port town of **Sidney** (where ferries depart for Washington's San Juan Islands), which is home to the terrific **Shaw Centre for the Salish Sea** aquarium. On the way to Sidney, I suggest detouring a few miles west on Keating Cross Road to famous **Butchart Gardens**, a 55-acre former limestone quarry on Brentwood Bay that in 1921 was transformed into a series of dramatic gardens.

Drive to **Swartz Bay** to make the short ferry ride to **Salt Spring Island**, the largest of the **Gulf Islands** and a scenic archipelago just off the southeastern coast of Vancouver Island. Plenty of artists, makers, and other creative spirits are among the 10,500 year-round residents of this hilly, agrarian island anchored by the animated harborfront village of

City View
Vancouver

Framed by mountains and water, Vancouver is blessed with an incredible natural setting—you can be paddling a kayak in **English Bay** in the morning and skiing on **Grouse Mountain** by mid-afternoon. From just about anywhere in the **City Center** and the adjacent **West End**, you can walk or bike to museums, beaches, and strips of lively bars and restaurants, from chic **Yaletown** to LGBTQ-popular **Davie Village**. With so much to see and do, there's good reason to spend a couple of days here.

Car-friendly rating: Poor. Vancouver is the only city in North America without any freeways, which means it can be a little slow-going getting around. Street parking is limited, and City Center lots and garages can be pricey, so it's best to ditch the car and move about on foot or via the excellent public transit network of Sky Train light rail, buses, and even ferries and water taxis. I often park in an outlying neighborhood and take public transit into town.

What to see in a day: Start with a walk around the cobblestone streets of historic **Gastown**, with its trendy shops and eateries, such as Salt Tasting Room and the Alibi Pub. Head to the snazzy **Yaletown** area for more great shopping and gallery-hopping, and then catch a water taxi to **Granville Island**, a former shipping and processing center for the city's logging industry that's been transformed into a dazzling public market with galleries and artists' studios, too. Just steps from the West End you'll discover beautiful, rugged **Stanley Park**, which occupies a peninsula of more than 1000 unspoiled acres of lush greenery, forests of cedar and Douglas fir, sandy beaches, and panoramic maritime vistas. From here it's a short drive to the kid-approved attractions of **North Vancouver**, home to great hiking at **Grouse Mountain** and the nearby 450 ft long **Capilano Suspension Bridge**, which oscillates gently some 230 ft above the river below.

Where to stay: The best hotels tend to be in the City Center, which is also where parking rates are highest, but both **The Burrard** and the **Granville Island Hotel** have a great location and fairly affordable parking. You'll also find nice options in North Vancouver, including the **Lonsdale Quay Hotel** and **Pinnacle Hotel at the Pier**, which are within walking distance of the ferry to the City Center, and the **SureStay Hotel by Best Western North Shore**, which has free parking but is a short drive from the ferry.

Top Granville Market *Bottom* Siwash Rock, Stanley Park
Opposite A totem pole by Doug LaFortune of the Tsawout First Nation at Butchart Gardens, near Victoria
Previous Downtown Banff

Ganges. For a great view of the harbor, grab a seat on the waterfront deck at Moby's Pub, which serves up tasty burgers and great beer. Scenic roads lace the island and access the coastal trails of **Ruckle Provincial Park**, an excellent place for viewing whales and sea lions in Captain Passage, and **Mt Maxwell Provincial Park**, where you can drive a gravel road or hike well-maintained trails to 1175 ft high Baynes Peak for panoramic island vistas. Depart by ferry from **Vesuvius** and then drive from **Crofton** to **Nanaimo**, a laid-back coastal city of about 91,000 with a pretty harborfront walking path and a good selection of international restaurants, among them Nanda Chicken, Nori Japanese, and Kim's Korean BBQ House. I like to treat myself to a Nanaimo bar—the famous local chocolate-layered confection—at Mon Petit Choux bakery.

Take the ferry from Nanaimo to **Horseshoe Bay,** and continue to Vancouver, from which there are three main options for driving to Kamloops, the gateway to the Canadian Rockies. The quickest (four hours) is via the Trans-Canada Hwy (Hwy 1) and Hwy 5 (aka the Coquihalla Hwy), a route that climbs up and over a dramatic section of the Cascade Range. Or you could follow the Trans-Canada Hwy (Hwy 1) the entire way (five hours), as it twists and turns through the steep-sided Fraser Canyon at Hells Gate and then follows the Thompson River to Kamloops via Cache Creek. Both of these drives offer plenty of amazing scenery, but I recommend the even more breathtaking and varied third option, Hwy 99 (the aptly named Sea to Sky Hwy) via Whistler, which takes about 5.5 hours without stops—although you really should stop (and ideally overnight) in Whistler. Hwy 99 is prone to snowstorms, so check conditions in winter.

It takes a little under two hours to get from Vancouver to **Whistler** via Howe Sound and small but fast-growing **Squamish**, which has become popular with outdoorsy types priced out of Vancouver and Whistler. The road ascends some 2000 ft over the next 35 miles en route to luxurious Whistler, whose leviathan **Whistler Blackcomb** ski resort was the center of the action during the 2010 Vancouver Olympics. It's no less of an outdoor recreation wonderland in summer, with zip-lining, hiking, spa-going, and mountain-biking galore. Be sure to ride between the resort's two main summits on the **Peak 2 Peak Gondola,** one of the world's highest (at 1430 ft above the valley) aerial trams, and then have lunch with a view at one of the slopeside restaurants. I like to end the day by hopping among the soothingly hot and bracingly cold outdoor pools at **Scandinave Spa,** which has an idyllic evergreen setting.

SIDETRACK

It's a three-hour drive from Nanaimo, via Hwys 19 and 4, through prolific logging towns and across the **Pacific Coast Mountains** to secluded **Tofino,** a nature lover's utopia that fringes **Pacific Rim National Park Reserve** and enjoys a magical, windswept setting where Clayoquot Sound meets the ocean. Surfers, hikers, and wildlife viewers flock here year-round, even during the winter months, when storms off the Pacific pack some incredible visual drama best viewed from a cozy room with a fireplace at one of the town's beach hotels, such as the posh **Wickaninnish Inn** and eco-chic **Duffin Cove Oceanfront Lodging**. Numerous outfitters offer sea kayaking expeditions, whale-watching and deep-sea fishing cruises, and surfing lessons, or you could just venture out on your own for a hike through the surrounding temperate rainforests. For a town of fewer than 2000 residents, Tofino has a fantastic culinary scene, too.

WHISTLER, BC TO KAMLOOPS, BC

From Whistler it's a roughly four-hour drive to Kamloops via the inviting little town of **Pemberton.** Fans of artisanal spirits should stop by **Pemberton Distillery** to sample the fine gins and unique organic hemp vodka, and the friendly Mile One Eating House is an inviting spot for lunch. Afterward, go for a short hike to **Nairn Falls** before enjoying the spectacular scenery of both **Joffre Lake** and **Duffey Lake** provincial parks on your drive northeast. The highest point (4183 ft above sea level) on Hwy 99, **Cayoosh Pass,** is just past **Lower Joffre Lake.** Hop out for a hike along the **Joffre Lakes Trail** (about 2.5 miles, much of it uphill, to Upper Joffre Lake, but the scenery is quite stunning even if you hike just the first half hour or so). **Lillooet,** one of the oldest continuously inhabited communities in North America, is a center of the St'at'imc Nation. Here you'll drive alongside a stretch of BC's longest river (at 855 miles), the Fraser, on your way to **Cache Creek** and the Trans-Canada Hwy.

About an hour later, you'll reach **Kamloops,** a sunny, semi-arid city where the two main branches of the Thompson River meet. The name Kamloops is derived from the Secwepemc word Tk'emlups, which means "where the rivers meet". Kamloops is somewhat sprawly, but there are some nice spots downtown for stretching your legs, including **Riverside** and **Pioneer** parks and the historic **Kamloops Heritage Railway,** which offers scenic steam train rides from a historic station. Mostly, though, Kamloops is a good place to break up the long drive.

KAMLOOPS, BC TO BANFF, AB

Staying on Hwy 1, the drive continues along the Thompson River and passes through Kamloops's small but up-and-coming wine region—**Harper's Trail Estate, Sagewood,** and **Monte Creek** all have excellent tasting rooms. The highway continues northeast, curving around **Shuswap Lake** and passing by **Enchanted Forest,** a fanciful roadside attraction with nature walks through fairy-tale–inspired tree houses, paddle boat rides, and an adventure park through the treetops of evergreens.

The celebrated ski town of **Revelstoke** is on a broad and beautiful stretch of the Columbia River, the very waterway that snakes down through Washington and eventually empties into the Pacific Ocean. It's home to **Mt Revelstoke National Park,** the highlight of which is driving **Meadows in the Sky Parkway,** a 16-mile scenic park road that zigzags 4500 ft from town to alpine **Balsam Lake.** You can ride a shuttle bus a bit farther to the summit, which is crowned by a historic fire tower and accesses several trails. Back in town there's a good mix of shops and restaurants along the riverfront, and the **Revelstoke Railway Museum** features impressive old locomotives and railroad memorabilia.

Hwy 1 continues through two more national parks en route to Banff. The first is **Glacier National Park of Canada,** which—as the name suggests—stands out for its myriad glaciers, more than 130 in all, and also boasts an extensive network of caves. Much of the park is geared to backcountry exploration, but right off the highway **Hemlock Grove Boardwalk** and the **Rockgarden Trail** offer easy but stunning strolls. Another interesting feature is **Rogers Pass National Historic Site,** which is where in 1885 the Canadian Pacific Railway successfully laid tracks through the formidable Selkirk Mountains; the **Rogers Pass Discovery Centre** has cool exhibits on how engineers have managed to control, or at least limit damage from, the massive avalanches common to this part of the Rockies. From the highway, you can also clearly view one of the most impressive of the park's glaciers, **Illecillewaet.**

Top Whistler Peak Suspension Bridge *Bottom* By the ferry terminal at Fulford Harbour, Salt Spring Island

Hwy 1 continues through **Golden**, a logging and railroad town that has become popular as a less spendy and crowded alternative to Banff, and then enters **Yoho National Park**. At 507 square miles, it's about one-fifth the size of Banff, and several of its most impressive features are easy to reach from Hwy 1, including thundering **Wapta Falls**, which you can hike to on a fairly easy 3-mile round-trip trail. The park's main village, **Field**, offers several picturesque lodging and dining options. From here it's a 15-minute drive to **Emerald Lake**, a stunning glacial lake with a lodge and restaurant that's perfect for a scenic lunch. If you have time, make the 25-minute drive along Yoho Valley Road to the base of 833 ft **Takakkaw Falls**, a glacier-fed cataract. On your way east from Field, keep an eye out for the **Lower Spiral Tunnel** observation area, from which you can see the ingeniously engineered spiral tunnels constructed in 1909 as a way to reduce the speed of trains chugging down the west slope of the Rockies.

On the east side of the park, Hwy 1 crosses **Kicking Horse Pass** at the British Columbia–Alberta border and is one of the main routes into **Banff National Park**. Designated in 1885 as the country's first national park, Banff adjoins not just Yoho but also Kootenay and even bigger Jasper; together these four national parks cover an area of nearly 8000 sq miles. With incredible scenery, grand hotels, and a beautiful little town at its core, Banff easily lives up to its acclaimed reputation, but it also teems with tourists in summer. Try visiting on a weekday or during the shoulder seasons (May to mid-June and mid-September to October) if you can.

Hwy 1 meets with Hwy 93, the famed Icefields Parkway, where you should exit and drive 10 minutes west to behold one of the most iconic views in Canada: turquoise

SIDETRACK

From the park's southern border, it's just over an hour's drive to Alberta's largest city, **Calgary**, a lively metropolis on the Bow River offering plenty of diversions as well as a first-rate food scene, with places like Proof Cocktail Bar, Ten Foot Henry, Bridgette Bar, Foreign Concept, and Charcut Roast House earning serious kudos among foodies. The world-famous **Calgary Stampede**—a rollicking rodeo with concerts, competitions, and all kinds of entertaining all-ages events—takes place over 10 days each July. Several other prominent attractions are an easy drive from the city core and include the **Calgary Zoo**, hilly **Prince's Island Park** in the Bow River, and **Heritage Park Historical Village**, the nation's largest living history museum.

SIDETRACK

About 20 miles north of the town of Banff, a left turn onto Hwy 93 leads 7 miles west to **Vermilion Pass**, the border between Alberta and BC, and between Banff and Kootenay national parks. Created in 1920 and laid out with road trippers in mind, **Kootenay National Park** spans about five miles on either side of Hwy 93 (aka the Banff-Windermere Highway) as it zigzags for about 60 miles south to the small town of **Radium Hot Springs**, where you'll find several accommodations and restaurants. The park's unusual linear shape means that all of its key attractions—the steep walls of **Sinclair Canyon and Redwall Fault**, the hot mineral pools at **Radium Hot Springs**, and the dramatic **Marble Canyon Gorge**—can be easily accessed by car.

Lake Louise framed against the snowcapped peaks of Mts Temple, Whyte, and Niblock. Past the imposing (I think a bit severe) **Fairmont Chateau Lake House** hotel, walk along the **Lake Louise Lakeshore Trail** to fully soak up the panorama, or rent a kayak or canoe to paddle across it. I recommend continuing your drive south through the park by skipping faster Hwy 1 in favor of the more relaxing and even more breathtaking 32-mile **Bow Valley Parkway** (Hwy 1A), which parallels both the Bow River and the Canadian Pacific railroad tracks. For a somewhat strenuous but stunning three-hour ramble, hike the 4.5-mile round-trip trail to **Castle Mountain Lookout**. Another highlight is **Johnston Canyon**, a spectacular limestone gorge.

With a year-round population of about 8000 and more than 3500 hotel rooms, picture-perfect **Banff** lies entirely within the national park. Settled in 1883, it contains dozens of historic buildings, including the chateauesque **Fairmont Banff Springs Hotel**—try to have a meal in this storied building even if you don't spend the night. While in this part of the park, ride the **Banff Gondola** to the top of **Sulphur Mountain** for a knockout view of town and the mountains (and perhaps to have lunch or dinner at Sky Bistro) and take a scenic cruise on **Lake Minnewanka**, the second longest lake in the Rockies.

BANFF, AB TO EDMONTON, AB

Allow four to five hours, depending on how often you stop to get from the town of Banff to the town of Jasper, which anchors Jasper National Park. The drive along **Icefields Parkway** (Hwy 93) offers eye-popping scenery of not just the mountains, but of bears, elk, and other wildlife.

Jasper National Park is more than one and a half times the size of Banff, but in part because it's farther north, it receives about 1.5 million fewer annual visitors. Like Banff, the park offers a slew of recreational activities, from whitewater rafting on the **Athabasca River** to skiing and snowboarding at **Marmot Basin** to miles of fantastic hiking and mountain-biking trails. The main town of **Jasper** was settled in 1813 as a fur-trade outpost but became a hub for park visitors in the early 1900s. On a short visit, set aside about three hours to make the scenic drive to **Maligne Lake**, with its glacial-fed turquoise waters and backdrop of rugged mountain peaks. It's one of the best hiking destinations in the park, with options for every ability level, and you can take a breathtakingly beautiful cruise along this narrow fjord-like lake to oft-Instagrammed **Spirit Island**.

From Jasper it's just under an hour's drive via Hwy 16 (the Yellowhead Hwy) to the park's eastern entrance, but on your way you'll want to stop to see **Jasper Lake** and the extensive system of sand dunes along its eastern shore—on a hot day, it's fun to stroll across the sand and wade into this quite shallow lake. Shortly before exiting the park, note the right-hand turn for **Miette Hot Springs**, reached via a 10-mile drive through the verdant Fiddle Valley. Here you can soak your bones in a pool fed by the hottest natural springs in the Rockies (104 degrees F) and even stay the night in a simple, comfy 1930s bungalow.

Just outside the park, **Hinton** is a good place to fuel up before making the fairly straight, flat three-hour drive through the Canadian prairies to **Edmonton**. Alberta's capital is home to the largest shopping center in North America, **West Edmonton Mall**, which actually is worth a visit even if you're not much of a shopper, especially if you're traveling with kids, as it features a giant waterpark, an underground aquarium with sharks and sea lions, and an NHL-size ice hockey rink. But there's more to this friendly city known for its long, sunny days in summer (and great views of the northern lights in winter). The four glass pyramids that dominate the skyline comprise **Muttart Conservatory**, a lush botanical garden with a first-rate restaurant. When the weather is warm, explore some of the more than 20 patches of greenery that collectively make up Canada's largest urban park, the **River Valley**—these include **Henrietta Muir Edwards Park**, adjacent to Muttart, and **Louise McKinney Riverfront Park**, which is just across the North Saskatchewan River. A few blocks away, check out the superb **Art Gallery of Alberta**, which occupies a fanciful contemporary building. A 10-minute drive south, stroll along **Whyte Avenue** (aka 82 Avenue), a lively thoroughfare of vintage buildings that cuts through the decidedly bohemian and hip **Old Strathcona District**. This is one of Edmonton's hubs of foodie culture—standouts include Block 1912, MEAT, Pho Boy, and El Cortez Mexican Kitchen.

Opposite Icefields Parkway, from Banff to Jasper

BEST EATS

- **Little Jumbo** The discreet entrance, dim lighting, and cozy confines of this trendy spot near Victoria's Inner Harbour create a fun speakeasy vibe, and indeed, the expertly mixed cocktails are superb. 778-433-5535, littlejumbo.ca.

- **Finn's Seafood Chops Cocktails** Giant windows and a large patio afford wonderful views of the Inner Harbour at this festive 1880s warehouse space that offers everything from casual fish and chips and pizzas to prime steaks with Alaskan king crab legs. 250-360-1808, finnsvictoria.com.

- **Rock Salt Restaurant** Couples, families, boaters, and hikers mix and mingle over breakfast, lunch, and dinner at this cheerful waterfront eatery by the ferry dock in Salt Spring Island's Fulford Harbour. 250-653-4833, rocksaltrestaurant.com.

- **Araxi** Steps from the gondola in Whistler Village, this sophisticated purveyor of contemporary Canadian fare has an enchanting heated patio with mountain views, an impressive wine list, and some of the best fresh seafood and chops in town. 604-932-4540, araxi.com.

- **Kitchen at Fort Berens** Enjoy the dramatic Coast Mountains scenery during your drive from Whistler to Kamloops with lunch on the patio at the sleekly designed kitchen and tasting room of this acclaimed BC winery. Pickled veggie and charcuterie platters pair perfectly with Fort Berens's well-crafted Pinot Noirs, Rosés, and Grüner Veltliners. 250-256-7788, fortberens.ca.

- **Noble Pig** Located conveniently beside downtown Kamloops's Thompson Hotel and offering seats in a fireplace-warmed dining room and on a trellised garden patio, this casual brewpub serves reliably tasty ales and comfort food. 778-471-5999, thenoblepig.ca.

- **Old School Eatery** This lively, family-friendly eatery set in a handsomely converted brick school building in Revelstoke serves modern comfort food and offers plenty of outdoor seating. 250-814-4144, oldschooleatery.ca.

- **Eleven22** Creative, internationally inflected fare draws diners to this intimate, art-filled restaurant in Golden, between Glacier and Yoho national parks. 250-344-2443, eleven22restaurant.com

- **Truffle Pigs Bistro** Inside a contemporary guest lodge surrounded by the lofty peaks of Yoho National Park, this cheerful eatery serves eclectic, seasonally inspired fare. Field, 250-343-6303, trufflepigs.com.

- **Whitehorn Bistro** Ride the gondola to the top of the Lake Louise ski area and have a seat on the spacious deck, soaking up stunning views while you sample deftly prepared contemporary Canadian cuisine. 403-522-1310, skilouise.com.

- **Farm and Fire Bistro** Serving wood-grilled pizzas, rotisserie-chicken sandwiches, and beef tartare with black-garlic aioli, this airy bistro in downtown Banff is a perfect spot to relax and reinvigorate. 403-760-3298, banffjaspercollection.com.

- **Raven Bistro** With stylish, intimate digs in downtown Jasper, this upbeat and upmarket purveyor of pan-Mediterranean food is perfect for anything from a casual pre-hike brunch to a special-occasion dinner. 780-852-5151, theravenbistro.com.

- **Hanjan** In addition to serving flavorful, authentic Korean standbys like bibimbap and grilled kalbi short ribs, this casual spot with three locations, including one by Old Strathcona's colorful Whyte Street, specializes in elaborate shave-ice desserts. Edmonton, 587-454-3333, hanjan.ca.

BEST SLEEPS

- **Inn at Laurel Point** Enjoy views of the ferries, yachts, and seaplanes that ply Victoria's Inner Harbour from the balcony of your room at this fashionably sleek low-rise with a Japanese garden, pool, and excellent Pacific Rim-inspired restaurant. 250-386-8721, laurelpoint.com.

- **Abigail's** An old-world Tudor Revival inn built in the 1930s, Abigail's stands out for its attentive service and gourmet breakfasts. It's close to Beacon Park and historic downtown. 250-388-5363, abigailshotel.com.

- **Sidney Pier Hotel** With a full-service spa and a superb location steps from Glass Beach and the Shaw Centre for the Salish Sea aquarium, this contemporary mid-rise is also just a short drive from the ferries to the San Juan and Gulf islands. Sidney, 250-655-9445, sidneypier.com

- **Salt Spring Inn** This reasonably priced inn with warmly appointed rooms and a convivial restaurant is right in the heart of Ganges Village, steps from the harbor and within an easy drive of Salt Spring Island's parks and beaches. 250-537-9339, saltspringinn.com.

- **Nita Lake Lodge** Within walking distance of Creekside Village, which is a bit mellower than Whistler Village, this upscale lakeside property has roomy suites with fireplaces. There's a full spa and a fantastic restaurant. 604-966-5700, nitalakelodge.com.

- **South Thompson Inn** You'll find plenty of perfectly suitable chain hotels in downtown Kamloops but none with as picturesque a setting as this 55-acre boutique resort in a river valley dotted with wineries. 250-573-3777, souththompsonhotelkamloops.com.

- **Explorers Society Hotel** The nine spacious rooms in this stately 1911 redbrick building in downtown Revelstoke have tall windows, locally crafted furnishings, and a hip, clean aesthetic. Relax in the spacious indoor-outdoor rooftop lounge, and there's a terrific restaurant, Quartermaster Eatery. 250-814-2565, explorers-society.com.

- **Heather Mountain Lodge** Just off the Trans-Canada Hwy beyond the East Gate of Glacier National Park of Canada, this upscale contemporary lodge enjoys a spectacular alpine setting, with mountain views from most rooms and cabins. Although 40 minutes from Golden's dining scene, the lodge has its own exceptional restaurant. 250-344-7490, heathermountainlodge.com.

- **Cathedral Mountain Lodge** Close to the famous Spiral railroad tunnels of Yoho National Park, this swanky modern chalet with 31 handsome rooms and cabins sits along the pristine Yoho River. The knowledgeable staff can help you arrange park activities. 250-343-6442, cathedralmountainlodge.com.

- **Fairmont Banff Springs** The crown jewel of Canada's national park lodges, this castle-like structure rises 11 stories above the Bow and Spray rivers. With more than 750 rooms and a slew of amenities and dining options, it can feel a bit like its own miniature kingdom. 403-762-2211, fairmont.com/banff-springs.

- **Storm Mountain Lodge** Away from the hubbub of Banff village and Lake Louise, this 1920s compound of rustic-chic bungalows, many with wood-burning fireplaces and deep soaker tubs, boasts a wonderfully cozy and romantic restaurant that's worth a visit even if you don't stay here. It's inside Banff National Park but very close to Kootenay National Park. 403-762-4155, stormmountainlodge.com.

- **Fairmont Park Jasper Lodge** This single-story lodge and its surrounding log cabins are designed to fit in with the rugged landscape, although all 442 accommodations are still utterly plush. The 700-acre resort curves around the shore of Beauvert Lake, offers a full slate of services in its spa, and adjoins what's arguably the country's most celebrated golf course. 780-852-3301, fairmont.com/jasper.

- **Pyramid Lake Resort** A 10-minute drive up a scenic road from downtown Jasper, this smartly designed 62-room lodge offers a lakefront setting and rents canoes, kayaks, mountain bikes, and other equipment to enjoy in this peaceful section of Jasper National Park. 780-852-4900, banffjaspercollection.com.

- **Metterra Hotel on Whyte** This mid-priced property has affordable parking, elegant yet modern rooms, and a prime location in Edmonton's hip Old Strathcona neighborhood. 780-465-8150, metterra.com

---

CAMPING

From maritime landscapes near the coast to the national parks of the Canadian Rockies, it's easy to find glorious campsites all along this scenic route. On Vancouver Island, Goldstream Campground has a peaceful, wooded setting just outside Victoria, and both Mowhinna Creek and Ruckle Provincial Park are terrific options on Salt Spring Island. As you make your way up through Whistler, consider Mamquam River Campground just north of Squamish. The four contiguous national parks of the Rockies—Kootenay, Yoho, Banff, and Jasper—offer an array of designated campgrounds, all of them managed by Parks Canada, through which you can make reservations, which are essential, especially in summer and on weekends. With 14 campgrounds, Banff has the most options, with Johnston Canyon and the two large areas at Lake Louise among the most popular. Jasper also has quite a few venues—Whistlers and Wabasso are favorites. You'll find fewer choices in smaller Yoho and Kootenay, and these can fill up fast (especially Lake O'Hara and Takakkaw Falls).

Fairmont Banff Springs

Washington: the Mountains and the Sea ★

On this journey through western Washington, you're always within view of snowcapped peaks, cool-blue bays, and conifer-carpeted islands.

HOW LONG?

7 days; add an extra day or two each to see more of Seattle, Tacoma, and Olympic and Mt Rainier national parks.

WHEN TO GO

Sunny and dry summer offers the best views, comfort, and scenery, but hotel rates skyrocket and the national parks can get extremely crowded. You might encounter drippy days (although not always) during the May to mid-June and mid-September to October shoulder seasons, but hotels are cheaper then, too. In winter, snow and limited facilities at Mt Rainier and other mountain locales present a challenge, as does rain everywhere else, but this can also be a beautiful time to book a room with a cozy fireplace to watch the dramatic storms on the coast.

NEED TO KNOW

The main ferry routes on this itinerary don't require reservations, but if taking a car on the sidetrack to the San Juan Islands, it's wise to book in advance (by several days on summer weekends). The mountains receive lots of snow in winter, and road closures are common—check conditions before you go and always stick to well-established routes.

➡ Distances

Total distance, one-way: 800 mi (1287 km)
- Seattle to Bellingham: 140 mi (225 km)
- Bellingham to Port Angeles: 120 mi (193 km)
- Port Angeles to Olympia: 240 mi (386 km)
- Olympia to Mt Rainier National Park: 140 mi (225 km)
- Mt Rainier National Park to Bainbridge Island: 135 mi (217 km)

⦚ Daytime Temperatures

January: 25-48°F (-4-9°C)
July: 60-78°F (16-26°C)

ⓘ More information

- Seattle tourism, visitseattle.org
- Bellingham tourism, bellingham.org
- Olympic Peninsula tourism, olympicpeninsula.org
- Olympic National Park, nps.gov/olym
- Mt Rainier National Park, nps.gov/mora
- Tacoma tourism, traveltacoma.com

⊙ SNAPSHOT

Western Washington is home to some of the nation's most alluring natural scenery, all of it within a three-hour drive of exciting and inviting Seattle. Part of what makes driving around this region so memorable are its extremes—even on sunny summer days, you can usually spy snowy mountain peaks out the car window. And nowhere on this trip are you more than 50 miles from the jagged shores of the Salish Sea, a stunning international waterway comprising Puget Sound and the Strait of Juan de Fuca (along with Canada's adjacent Georgia Strait).

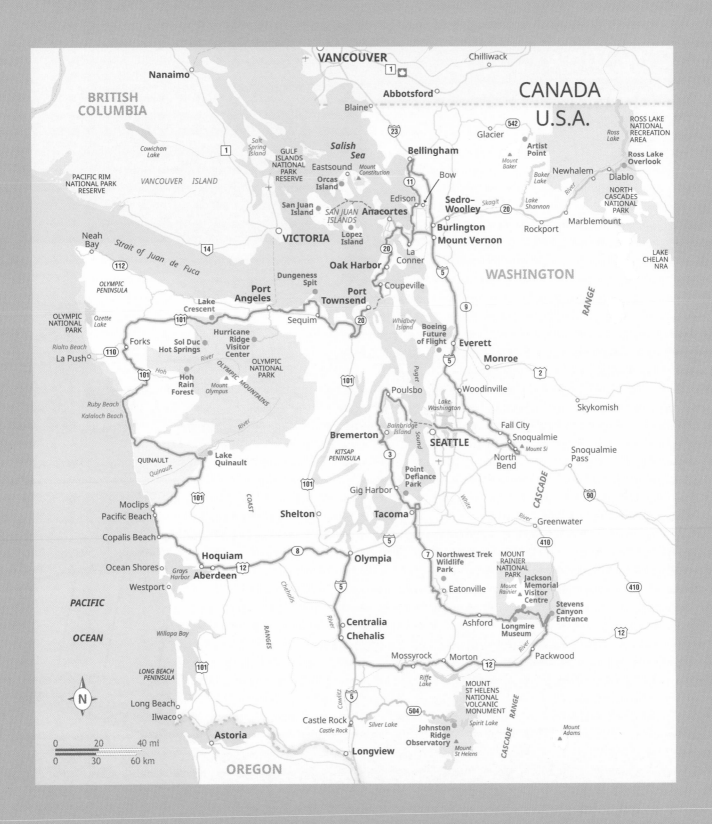

City View

Seattle

A fast-growing tech hub with a storied setting, this dynamic city of 760,000 is a delightful place to spend at least a day before exploring the scenic waterways and snowcapped mountains that frame it. Seattle has a diverse arts scene that you can get to know through its eclectic museums, outdoor art installations, grand performance venues, and maker-driven shops. And if you love to eat and drink your way across a city, well, loosen your belt—the Emerald City offers an astonishing assortment of innovative restaurants, coffeehouses, and lounges.

Car-friendly rating: Fair. With its steep streets, high density, noxious rush hour traffic, and expensive hotel parking, it's best to leave the car behind in Downtown Seattle and get around on foot or via the fairly efficient public transit system. As you venture into outlying neighborhoods, however, it becomes easier to find metered or free street parking and less expensive lots, and a car can actually be an asset.

What to see in a day: It may be relentlessly touristy, but I never tire of visiting the colorful food stalls of Downtown's oft-photographed **Pike Place Market**. If it's a nice day, I like to gather up my food purchases (which usually include a grilled aged-cheddar sandwich from Beecher's Handmade Cheese), walk through the Crafts Market, and snag a picnic table on the Sundeck at MarketFront Plaza, with its views of the bustling piers down below on Elliott Bay. Sunny days also warrant a visit a few blocks north to the waterfront **Olympic Sculpture Park** and then over to the **Seattle Center** for an incredible view of the city from the 520 ft tall observation deck atop the retro-futuristic **Space Needle**. Be sure to set aside time to check out the cool exhibits next door in the Frank Gehry-designed **Museum of Pop Culture**, and if you're in the mood for lunch, head nearby to inviting Toulouse Petit to sample its hearty Cajun and Creole seafood. In the afternoon, explore the one-of-a-kind indie shops and eateries of **Capitol Hill**'s LGBTQ-popular **Pine and Pike** corridor—Ooink ramen, Plum vegan bistro, and Mamnoon Middle Eastern are all splendid food options. Turn north for a stroll through leafy **Volunteer Park** to visit the excellent **Seattle Asian Art Museum** and walk the gorgeous trails nearby at the **Washington Park Arboretum**. Then cross the Lake Washington Ship Canal to investigate the fab food and retail scenes of **Fremont** and **Ballard**, where you can also visit the excellent **National Nordic Museum** and enjoy a sunset stroll over **Ballard Locks**.

Where to stay: This is a great city for fans of design-driven lodgings. In the Downtown area, consider the sleek and supremely opulent **Thompson Seattle** and the arty **Lotte Hotel**, with its Philippe Starck interiors, as well as the beautifully restored **Kimpton Palladian**. You'll find some appealing options in more car-friendly outlying areas, too, such as the dapper **Silver Cloud** in Capitol Hill, the **Graduate Seattle** near the University of Washington campus (don't miss the rooftop bar), and the stylish **Hotel Ballard**, set along one of the city's trendiest restaurant rows.

SEATTLE TO BELLINGHAM

Although this adventure ultimately continues due north to Bellingham, I like starting with a foray east of Seattle to **North Bend** and **Snoqualmie** for a brief taste of the Cascades—there's great hiking here, including the 7.5-mile round-trip climb to the 4167 ft summit of **Mt Si**. Auteur filmmaker David Lynch shot his early '90s TV series *Twin Peaks* in these picturesque towns—old-fashioned Twede's Cafe in downtown North Bend served as the Double R Diner on the show, and you'll surely recognize 268 ft **Snoqualmie Falls** from the opening credits. Staying atop these soaring cascades at the **Salish Lodge** is an absolute treat—at the very least, have breakfast or lunch as near as possible to a window in the excellent restaurant.

Head northwest through the eastern Seattle suburbs to **Woodinville**, a once modest farming town that over the past several decades has exploded into a renowned wine destination. You'll find more than 130 wineries and tasting rooms, most of them concentrated in compact walkable areas, yet virtually no vineyards—wine produced and sold here is sourced from grapes grown elsewhere in the state. My favorite neighborhood for winery-hopping is the **Hollywood District**—you can't go wrong with **DeLittle**, **àMaurice**, or **Brian Carter Cellars** among the more than 30 options. Head north up I-5, stopping in the small waterfront city of **Everett**. Here, surrounding Paine Field Airport, you can take a fascinating 90-minute factory tour at **Boeing Future of Flight**, where the company's 767, 777, and 787 Dreamliners are manufactured, and also visit the **Flying Heritage and Combat Armor Museum**, which comprises a pair of hangars packed not only with impressive old planes but also tanks and military equipment amassed by the late tech magnate Paul Allen. From Everett, it's a straight one-hour shot up the interstate to Bellingham.

BELLINGHAM TO PORT ANGELES

Situated on beautiful Bellingham Bay, with views of the Cascades to the east and the San Juan Islands to the west, lively **Bellingham** (pop 96,000) is an enjoyable destination with a wealth of boutiques, bars, and cafes—many of them filled with students from Western Washington University. Stroll through both downtown and the quaint **Old Fairhaven District**, with its late-Victorian buildings. Stop for an espresso or cocoa at Evolve Chocolate + Cafe on the top floor of Village Books, and peruse the fine art in the village's superb galleries. If you're here for an extra day, make the 60-mile drive east through a soaring canyon and into a

SIDETRACK

In **Burlington**, exit I-5 onto Hwy 20 east for a one-hour drive to **North Cascades National Park**, a magnificent if slightly overlooked 1070 sq mile tract of massive peaks, pristine lakes, and more than 300 glaciers. One reason North Cascades is far less visited than Washington's other two national parks (Olympic and Mt Rainier) is that you have to venture deep into the backcountry to access many of its most spectacular features. However, Hwy 20 passes through a stunning cross-section of the park. I recommend driving at least as far as Ross Lake. Stop by the main **North Cascades Visitor Center** in **Newhalem** to view displays on the park's ecosystems, and then go for a walk around the imposing 1920s **Gorge Powerhouse** and adjacent **Ladder Creek Falls** along the roaring Skagit River. Continuing east over the next 15 miles to **Ross Lake Overlook**, you'll come to a series of short hikes and dramatic overlooks (turquoise **Diablo Lake** is a must photo op). Note that from late fall through early spring, Hwy 20 closes east of Ross Lake.

pristine section of the Cascade Range to **Artist Point**, where you can hike through wildflower meadows for a panoramic view of 10,778 ft **Mt Baker**.

Depart Bellingham via **Chuckanut Drive** (Hwy 11), a famously scenic 23-mile road constructed in 1916 that meanders through dense stands of Douglas fir and cedar trees. To stretch your legs, make the 5.5-mile loop hike to **Fragrance Lake** at **Larrabee State Park**, and if you're hungry, take heart: the drive passes several esteemed oyster restaurants—I'm partial to the Samish Oyster Bar and Shellfish Market at Taylor Farms, where you can sip wine and sup on fresh-shucked oysters and clams on a deck overlooking the bay. At the twin villages of **Bow** and **Edison**, which are also renowned for their U-pick farms, more artisan-driven eating awaits: pick up black-olive ciabatta or coconut shortbread cookies at Breadfarm and chive-flecked unripened Ladysmith cheese at Samish Bay dairy before cutting west from Hwy 11 and driving down along the water, stopping for a quick walk along the 2.3-mile **Shore Trail** at **Padilla Bay National Estuarine Reserve's Breazeale Interpretive Center**. In **Mount Vernon**, stop to smell the flowers at **RozenGaarde**, one of the country's largest flower growers and the host of April's famous Skagit Valley Tulip Festival. Then explore charming **La Conner's** colorful shops and eateries, the wooden boardwalk along the banks of Swinomish Channel, and its handful of small but excellent regional art and history museums.

Follow Hwy 20 west to the seaside town of **Anacortes**, where ferries depart for the **San Juan Islands**, a ruggedly sublime archipelago of about 175 islands in the Salish Sea. Although entirely in Washington, they're just off the southeast coast of Canada's Vancouver Island. In fact, continuing by ferry to Victoria, BC, for a night or two and then taking a second ferry across the Strait of Juan de Fuca makes a highly enjoyable alternate route to the Olympic Peninsula. If you have a day to explore the San Juans, take an early morning ferry out to one of the three main inhabited islands. The most populous, **San Juan Island** has a gallery and restaurant-filled downtown and is also known for its fantastic orca whale-watching along the western shore (Lime Kiln Point State Park is a favorite place to watch for them in summer). Smaller and relatively flat **Lopez Island** is a top destination for biking. My favorite is **Orcas Island** because I like to hike its dramatically hilly trails—either climbing up to the summit of 2409 ft Mt Constitution at **Moran State Park** or to Turtlehead Point at **Turtleback Mountain Reserve**, which offers wonderful views of Canada's Gulf Islands. But you need a car to get around this large and fairly rural island—even just to get from the ferry terminal to the lovely main village, **Eastsound**, where you can dine on exceptional pizza at Hogstone's Wood Oven and craft cocktails and bar snacks at The Barnacle. The entire archipelago is utterly relaxing and captivating in its natural beauty. If you can spare the time, I highly recommend taking your car on the ferry and spending two or three days exploring.

Top Salish Lodge, atop Snoqualmie Falls *Bottom* Orcas Island

After taking Hwy 20 over the majestic 180 ft tall bridge through **Deception Pass State Park**, continue south through **Whidbey Island**, a narrow 37 mile long landmass with an irregular shoreline that curves through the heart of Puget Sound. Once you pass the more developed US Navy town of **Oak Harbor**, the island feels quainter and more agrarian. Stop for a ramble around **Coupeville**, with its colorfully painted ice cream stands, art galleries, and gift shops. Walk out to the end of the wharf for a clear view of **Penn Cove**, which is famous for its sweet and fleshy mussels—they appear on menus all over the country. Excellent places in town to sample them include divy Toby's Tavern and the stylish Oystercatcher. It's a short drive south, beyond the picturesque beaches of Fort Ebey and Fort Casey state parks, to board a ferry for the relaxing 30-minute ride to **Port Townsend**.

Established in 1851, this steep-sloping town on the tip of the Quimper Peninsula, which itself lies at the northeastern tip of the Olympic Peninsula, exudes charm. The stately redbrick Victorian buildings hint at the hopes that its founders had for Port Townsend becoming the western terminus of the Northern Pacific Railroad. That honor ultimately went to Seattle and Tacoma, and this easygoing seaport of around 10,000 has instead developed into an arts colony and weekend getaway. Be sure to visit the **Northwest Maritime Center**, where you'll often see craftspersons at work building boats; this airy contemporary building with a terrific nautical shop and coffeehouse hosts the popular Wooden Boat Festival in September. Just up the hill, walk around the stately **Fort Worden State Park**. Its 432-acre campus of regal military buildings appeared in the 1982 hit film *An Officer and a Gentleman*. Some buildings are now available as overnight accommodations, and attractions include the engaging

Townsend Marine Science Center as well as a network of hiking trails—a particularly scenic 2.7-mile loop leads out to the 1913 lighthouse at the tip of Point Wilson.

US 101 continues across the northern Olympic Peninsula through the pretty farming town of **Sequim**, which is famous for its lavender farms. For a lovely coastal adventure, pick up a to-go lunch at Pacific Pantry market or Salty Girls Seafood and then head north to **Cline Spit County Park** for a picnic with views across the bay of narrow **Dungeness Spit**, which curves 5.5 miles out around the coast. The shoreline is a bonanza of migratory birdwatching during the spring and fall months, and its rugged cliffs offer views of mountainous Vancouver Island, 15 miles across the Strait of Juan de Fuca. Continue into the peninsula's largest municipality, **Port Angeles**, a busy lumber and fishing town that's also the gateway to **Olympic National Park**. Go for a walk on the **City Pier**, stopping by the small **Feiro Marine Life Center** to visit the kid-friendly touch tanks, then drive a few miles inland to the **Olympic National Park Visitor Center** to pick up maps and information about this majestic 1442-sq-mile wilderness of snowy mountain peaks, mossy temperate rainforests, and driftwood-strewn beaches.

PORT ANGELES TO OLYMPIA

Your first mission in Olympic National Park is making the 50-minute drive a mile in elevation up the park road to **Hurricane Ridge**, stopping by the modern visitor center and hiking 1.6 miles and back to **Hurricane Hill** for a 360-degree view of the peninsula and surrounding waters (in winter it's a popular ski area). Returning to Port Angeles, follow US 101 counterclockwise around the peninsula, stopping by rustic **Lake Crescent Lodge**, a 1916 structure with a pine-walled restaurant overlooking the tranquil lake for which it's named, then rent a kayak or paddleboard for a spin along the shore. Detouring south through a lush river valley to **Sol Duc Hot Springs** for a hike and a soak in one of the three roughly 100-degree sulfuric springs is a satisfying way to soothe sore muscles, but this adds a couple of hours to your trip—skip it if time is short. Continue to the old lumber town of **Forks**, whose dewy green meadows and fern-fringed valleys are the setting of Stephenie Meyer's feverishly adored *Twilight* novels—an entire cottage industry has grown up around them. Averaging more than 110 inches of rain and seven inches of snow per year, Forks is considered the wettest town in the lower 48 states. From here, make a side trip on Hwy 110 out to the Quileute tribal community of **La Push** for lunch overlooking the ocean at River's Edge Restaurant

(try the salmon burger), and then go beachcombing across the Quillayute River on **Rialto Beach**, with its massive piles of driftwood and towering sea stacks.

Return to US 101 and continue to the 19-mile turnoff for the **Hoh Rain Forest**, which is sometimes described as the quietest place on the continent. I believe it. I've heard nothing but an occasional bird chirp on my short hikes along the **Hall of Mosses Trail**, where the massive limbs of old-growth maples hang heavy with velvety moss. Continue on US 101 along a spectacular stretch of coast, which you can access directly via short trails from several parking areas—**Ruby Beach** and **Kalaloch Beach** are a couple of the gems. At the latter, I recommend soaking up the ocean view while savoring a hearty lunch or a dish of blackberry cobbler at the **Kalaloch Lodge**'s Creekside Restaurant. US 101 then meanders inland and upland through the mountains and to one last magical park setting, **Lake Quinault**, where you can make a short stroll to see what's billed as the "World's Largest Sitka Spruce" and stop either for a meal, overnight stay, or just a walk among the gardens and lawns at the historic **Lake Quinault Lodge**.

From here to Washington's small state capital Olympia, it's less than a two-hour drive via the most direct route, but I prefer detouring southwest through the Indigenous **Quinault Reservation** and rejoining the coast in **Moclips** and then making the leisurely drive down Hwy 109 through **Pacific Beach** and **Copalis Beach**. From there, head inland along the north shore of **Grays Harbor**, a broad estuary at the mouth of the Chehalis River. You'll go through the historic port towns of **Hoquiam** and **Aberdeen**, a rather gruff port city and hometown of grunge icon Kurt Cobain (you can visit a small memorial and murals devoted to him under the Young Street Bridge), before continuing east to Olympia.

OLYMPIA TO MT RAINIER NATIONAL PARK

With a skyline dominated by the 287 ft tall dome of the **Washington State Capitol**, Olympia lies at the southern tip of Puget Sound and makes a good overnight base, with a pleasant mix of hotels and eateries. Follow I-5 south through **Centralia** and **Chehalis**, where you can pick up US 12 east into the Cascades.

From roughly late May through mid-October (depending on snowfall), you can follow US 12 through the bucolic villages of **Mossyrock**, **Morton**, and **Packwood** (which has a handful of pleasant, mid-priced lodging options) and then up and around to the southeastern **Stevens Canyon Entrance** of **Mt Rainier National Park** (if it's winter, you can access

From Chehalis it's a half-hour drive south on I-5 to **Castle Rock** to make the 52-mile scenic drive east on Hwy 504, known as **Spirit Lake Hwy**. The road leads through the site of one of the most famous volcanic events of the past century: the May 1980 eruption of **Mt St Helens**, which laid to waste an area of 229 sq miles, resulting in 57 deaths. Just a few miles into your drive on Spirit Lake Hwy, you can learn about the eruption and the mountain's geological history at **Mt St Helens Visitor Center**. As you venture into the blast zone, you'll encounter more evidence, although the forest has healed significantly. From mid-May until early November, you can drive the final few miles from **Castle Lake Viewpoint** to **Johnston Ridge Observatory**, which presents an enthralling, if rather chilling, movie about the eruption and displays instruments that monitor the still highly active volcano. From the observation terrace, you can look 6 miles across the valley to the gaping scar across the northern slopes of this peak, which the blast reduced in elevation from 9677 to 8365 ft.

the park via **Ashford** and then through the southwestern **Nisqually Entrance**). The centerpiece of this 369 sq mile park is its formidable 14,410 ft namesake peak. Each year, around 5000 (very experienced) climbers summit this active volcano, which is the most glaciated peak in the contiguous US. There's lots to do on the lower slopes, however. Start by viewing the exhibits inside the **Henry M. Jackson Memorial Visitor Center**. From here you can set out on the aptly named **Skyline Trail**, a 5-mile loop through brilliant wildflower meadows and thick conifer groves to 6800 ft **Panorama Point** for an unparalleled view of the Cascades. Lower on the mountain, other great treks include the 3.5-mile round-trip expedition from serene **Reflection Lake** to roaring **Narada Falls** and—near the Stevens Canyon Entrance—the easy 1.1-mile trail through the centuries-old Western red cedars, silver and Douglas firs, and hemlocks that thrive in the magnificent **Grove of the Patriarchs**. Exiting the park to the west, stop at the 1916 **Longmire Museum** to admire its wonderful old park photos and natural history exhibits. Then follow Hwy 706 into densely wooded **Ashford**, stopping for a slice of blackberry pie at the captivatingly creaky old **Copper Creek Restaurant**.

Lime Kiln Point State Park, San Juan Island

MT RAINIER NATIONAL PARK TO BAINBRIDGE ISLAND

From Ashford it's a pleasant 60-mile drive northwest to Tacoma through the foothills of the Cascades. Stop in **Eatonville** to drive through the impressive **Northwest Trek Wildlife Park**, a 720-acre preserve that's home to more than 40 animals native to the Pacific Northwest, including Canadian lynx, grizzly bears, and gray wolves. I consider **Tacoma** to be one of the West Coast's most overlooked cities. It has several truly world-class museums, including the **Washington State History Museum**, the **Tacoma Art Museum**, and the **Museum of Glass**, which are all within walking distance of one another and connected by a 500 ft long pedestrian overpass lined with art-glass installations by native son Dale Chihuly. The sleek **LeMay–America's Car Museum** is also a must for fans of automotive history. But this hilly and attractive city on Puget Sound also boasts stately residential neighborhoods and flourishing greenways, including 760-acre **Point Defiance Park**, with its excellent **Point Defiance Zoo and Aquarium** and 22-acre rhododendron garden.

Take Hwy 16 across the monumental **Tacoma Narrows Bridge** to the snug maritime community of **Gig Harbor**, with its walkable downtown waterfront. Have lunch overlooking the water at Tides Tavern or Devoted Kiss Cafe, and check out the extensive exhibits at the **Harbor History Museum**. This is also a great little town for renting kayaks or SUPs, or even booking a romantic ride in a Venetian gondola around the harbor. Continue up Hwy 16 through the colorful **Kitsap Peninsula**, passing through the industrious Navy town of **Bremerton**—with its engaging museum aboard the **USS *Turner Joy*** naval destroyer ship. Then curve up around Liberty Bay and into the quaint Scandinavian village of **Poulsbo**, where you can investigate the touch-friendly exhibits at the family-oriented **SEA Discovery Center** aquarium and marine science museum, afterward stopping for delicious donuts and apple fritters at Sluys, a traditional Norwegian bakery that opened more than a century ago. Take Hwy 305 southeast to end your adventure on scenic **Bainbridge Island**. Strolling through the tranquil Asian-inspired gardens of **Bloedel Reserve** is a must, but also set aside time to walk around the island's lively downtown, which is home to several winery tasting rooms and top-notch seafood restaurants. From here it's a lovely 35-minute hop by commuter car ferry across Elliott Bay back to Seattle.

BEST EATS

- **Herbfarm** This hallowed locavore restaurant at Woodinville's posh Willows Lodge resort is the ultimate destination for a sublime nine-course dinner after spending an afternoon exploring the town's world-class wineries. 425-485-5300, theherbfarm.com.

- **Bantam 46** This bi-level downtown Bellingham tavern serves up fantastic Southern fare and is especially beloved for its buttermilk and Nashville-style spicy fried chicken—best enjoyed with a side of fluffy biscuits and honey. Note the impressive craft cocktail lists. 360-788-4507, bantambellingham.com.

- **Oyster and Thistle** Plan for a leisurely lunch or dinner of artfully prepared Pacific Northwest-influenced country French cuisine—panfried Samish Bay oysters with lemon-caper aioli, crispy duck confit with roasted mission figs—at this warmly lighted bistro in downtown La Conner. 360-766-6179, theoysterandthistle.com.

- **Finistère** A few blocks up the hill from Port Townsend's historic downtown, this minimalist-chic Uptown eatery presents seasonal, locally sourced regional American cuisine and a thoughtfully curated list of Washington-focused wine and beer. The house-made pastas are fantastic. 360-344-8127, restaurantfinistere.com.

- **Chelsea Farms Oyster Bar** Snag a table in this handsome, high-ceilinged seafood bistro in downtown Olympia's hip 222 Market hall. Several varieties of local oyster are served on the half shell, along with a lengthy array of regional specialties from the sea: geoduck ceviche, steelhead tartare, and whole-fried trout among them. 360-915-7784, chelseafarms.net.

- **Wooden City** This rustic-chic space on a hilly street in Tacoma's eclectic Theater District serves stellar wood-fired pizzas, savory-tangy beet ravioli with goat cheese and pistachio butter, and hefty burgers with Swiss, mushrooms, and onion jam. The well-curated wine list leans toward French, Italian, and Pacific Northwestern. 714 Pacific Ave, 253-503-0762.

- **NetShed 9** Set in one of Gig Harbor's historic waterfront fishing-net sheds, this charming bistro serves tantalizing breakfast and lunch fare, as well as dinners on weekends. Start the day with a cast-iron-skillet-fried cinnamon roll and a sausage breakfast burger, or tuck into the chile-rubbed pork shoulder burrito at lunch. 253-858-7175, netshed9.com.

- **Ba Sa** Talented young chefs and siblings Trinh and Thai Nguyen serve sensational modern Vietnamese food—including wild-mushroom pho, butter beef with garlic rice, and spicy truffle wontons with grilled shrimp and pork—in this homey modern restaurant in the village of Winslow on Bainbridge Island. 206-565-3287, basabainbridgeisland.com.

BEST SLEEPS

- **Salish Lodge** Perched atop the dramatic waterfall that is the star attraction of Snoqualmie, this luxurious but unpretentious 86-room hotel stands out not only for its magical setting but also for its cushy spa and soaking pools and the area's best restaurants. 425-888-2556, salishlodge.com.
- **Hotel Leo** Set in a beautifully retrofitted 1883 apartment tower in downtown Bellingham, this hostelry with high-tech rooms and comfy bedding is within a few blocks of first-rate restaurants as well as great museums. The owners run the more affordable mid-century modern motel, the Heliotrope. 360-739-0250, thehotelleo.com.
- **Old Consulate Inn** All six rooms in this brick-red Queen Anne mansion overlooking Port Townsend Bay are individually—and gorgeously—appointed, and rates include a decadent gourmet breakfast as well as homemade cookies and espresso, tea, or cocoa in the afternoon. 360-385-6753, oldconsulate.com.
- **Olympic National Park lodgings** Each of the five properties inside this sprawling park has its own distinct personality and setting, and the three best for road-tripping—as they're all on or near US 101—are also arguably the three prettiest. The 1916 Lake Crescent Lodge is closest to Port Angeles and has some of the park's most economical rooms (these have shared baths). With its glorious alpine waterfront setting, Lake Quinault Lodge connects directly with trails into an old-growth forest and has an inviting lobby warmed by a huge fireplace. And perched on a bluff on a stunning beach, Kalaloch Lodge was built in the '50s and is less architecturally distinctive—but wow, the setting. nps.gov/olym.

- **Mt Rainier National Park lodgings** Both hotels inside the park date to the early 20th century, with the lofty Paradise Inn—set a mile above sea level and offering knockout views of the mountain—as the showstopper, with a classic steep-roof design and warmly furnished common areas. However, it has a few cons: it books far in advance, its least pricey rooms share a bath, and it's only open late spring to early autumn. You'll find simpler accommodations at the 25-room National Park Inn, which has a lower elevation in historic Longmire and is open year-round.
- **Hotel Murano** This 26-room contemporary hotel in Tacoma's Theater District taps into the region's reputation for contemporary glassblowing; installations by renowned glass artists fill the public areas, and the city's famous Museum of Glass is a 10-minute stroll down the hill. 253-238-8000, hotelmuranotacoma.com.
- **Waterfront Inn** This cozy 1918 inn with a commanding location at the end of Gig Harbor has five spacious, well-appointed rooms with private entrances that allow easy access to the deck and 150 ft pier. Guests can borrow a kayak to paddle around the harbor, and there are several good restaurants nearby. 253-857-0770, waterfront-inn.com.

CAMPING

RV and tent venues abound throughout this part of the state. Olympic National Park is a veritable campers' paradise, with magnificent settings along the coast (Kalaloch and Ozette) and in the rainforest steps from hot springs (Hoh and Sol Duc). At Mt Rainier, favorite locales for pitching a tent include Cougar Rock, which is close to the trails and amenities of the park's Paradise village, and Ohanapecosh at the southeastern edge of the park, near the Grove of the Patriarchs. Other beautiful campgrounds include Larrabee State Park near Bellingham, Fort Ebey State Park on Whidbey Island, Fort Worden State Park in Port Townsend, and Fay Bainbridge Park on Bainbridge Island.

Top Paradise Inn, Mt Rainier National Park

Pacific Northwest
Wine Country ★ 🍁

On this journey through the temperate, emerald valleys and sunny high-desert ridges of Oregon, Washington, and British Columbia, you'll pass within a few miles of no fewer than 1300 wineries.

HOW LONG?

7 days; add an extra day each to see more of Portland, Walla Walla, and Kelowna.

WHEN TO GO

April to mid-June and mid-September to October are ideal, as many wineries hold barrel tastings in spring and harvest events in the fall, and the weather is typically mild (if potentially a bit rainy). Summer means sunshine but also hot (though dry) weather throughout the region, plus high-season hotel rates. Personally, I don't mind the damp chill of Pacific Northwest winters and find this to be a nice time to go, as hotels cost less and tasting rooms are less crowded—just keep in mind that many wineries have reduced hours.

NEED TO KNOW

If carrying wine or other alcohol across the border, the best strategy is to declare it and present receipts at customs. Duty taxes can be hefty, and it's a rather byzantine system that varies between US and Canada and also—potentially—from one customs officer to the next. I've sometimes been waved on, and sometimes been assessed taxes, but being upfront about my purchases has made the process fairly quick and pleasant. Many tasting rooms strongly encourage, or even require, reservations—at the very least, check winery websites or social media before visiting.

👁 SNAPSHOT

Wine production and its ancillary elements—posh country inns, artfully designed tasting rooms, sophisticated locavore cuisine—have escalated so rapidly in parts of the Pacific Northwest that you may not even recognize the bustling and urbane downtowns of places like McMinnville, Walla Walla, and Kelowna if you haven't been in a decade or two. The wine countries of Oregon, Washington, and British Columbia now earn effusive praise from top wine critics, and the entire region abounds with bewitching natural scenery, including the snowcapped peaks of the Cascade Range, the rocky palisades of the Columbia River, and the pristine shorelines of Chelan and Okanagan lakes.

→ Distances

Total distance, one-way: 850 mi (1368 km)
- Eugene, OR to Hood River, OR: 190 mi (306 km)
- Hood River, OR to Walla Walla, WA: 180 mi (290 km)
- Walla Walla, WA to Yakima, WA: 130 mi (209 km)
- Yakima, WA to Chelan, WA: 150 mi (241 km)
- Chelan, WA to Kelowna, BC: 185 mi (298 km)

Daytime Temperatures

January: 35-48°F (2-9°C)
July: 80-90°F (27-32°C)

① More information

- Oregon Wine tourism, oregonwine.org
- Willamette Valley tourism, willamettevalley.org
- Portland tourism, travelportland.com
- Columbia Gorge tourism, hood-gorge.com
- Washington Wine tourism, washingtonwine.org
- Walla Walla tourism, wallawalla.org
- Yakima Valley tourism, visityakima.com
- Chelan and Leavenworth tourism, visitchelancounty.com
- British Columbia Wine tourism, winebc.com
- Okanagan Valley tourism, okanagan.com

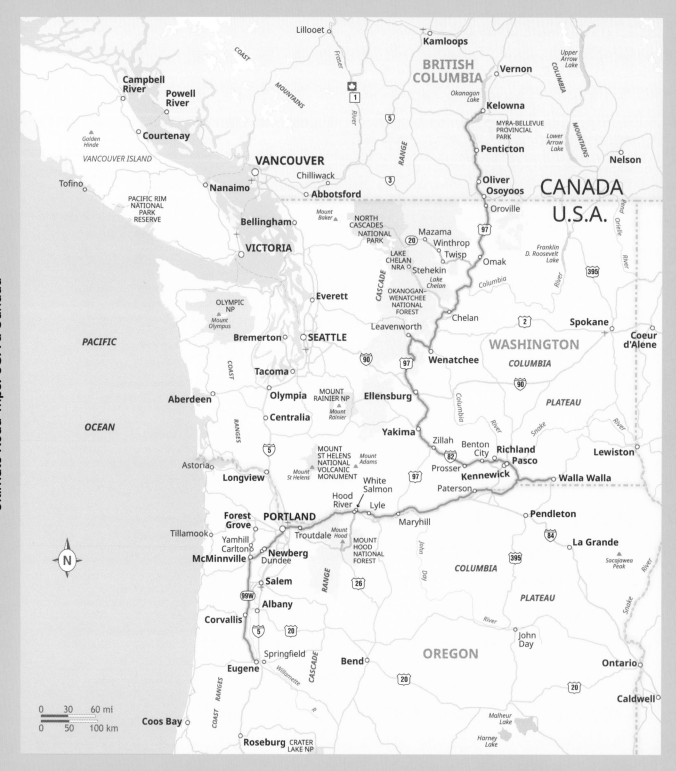

Lillooet

Kamloops

BRITISH COLUMBIA

Vernon

Upper Arrow Lake

Campbell River

Powell River

COAST

MOUNTAINS

Okanagan Lake

Kelowna

COLUMBIA

Courtenay

Golden Hinde

5

Penticton

MYRA-BELLEVUE PROVINCIAL PARK

Lower Arrow Lake

MOUNTAINS

Nelson

VANCOUVER ISLAND

River

RANGE

3

VANCOUVER

Chilliwack

Oliver

CANADA

Tofino

Nanaimo

Abbotsford

Osoyoos

U.S.A.

PACIFIC RIM NATIONAL PARK RESERVE

Oroville

Pend Orielle

River

Bellingham

Mount Baker

NORTH CASCADES NATIONAL PARK

20

Mazama

Winthrop

97

Franklin D. Roosevelt Lake

395

VICTORIA

LAKE CHELAN NRA

Twisp

Omak

Stehekin

Columbia

Lake Chelan

River

OLYMPIC NP

Everett

CASCADE

OKANOGAN–WENATCHEE NATIONAL FOREST

Chelan

2

Spokane

Mount Olympus

Leavenworth

WASHINGTON

Coeur d'Alene

PACIFIC

Bremerton

SEATTLE

97

Wenatchee

COLUMBIA

90

Tacoma

90

Columbia

PLATEAU

COAST

Olympia

MOUNT RAINIER NP

Ellensburg

River

OCEAN

Aberdeen

Centralia

Mount Rainier

River

Snake

Lewiston

RANGES

Yakima

Zillah

Benton City

Richland

5

MOUNT ST HELENS NATIONAL VOLCANIC MONUMENT

Mount Adams

82

Prosser

Kennewick

Pasco

Lewiston

Astoria

Mount St Helens

97

Paterson

Walla Walla

Longview

White Salmon

Hood River

Lyle

84

Pendleton

PORTLAND

Maryhill

La Grande

Tillamook

Forest Grove

Troutdale

Mount Hood

395

Sacajawea Peak

Yamhill Carlton

Newberg

MOUNT HOOD NATIONAL FOREST

COLUMBIA

McMinnville

Dundee

John Day

River

Salem

RANGE

26

PLATEAU

99W

Albany

John Day

Corvallis

5

20

River

Springfield

Bend

OREGON

Ontario

Eugene

CASCADE

20

Coos Bay

COAST RANGES

Willamette

R

20

Caldwell

Malheur Lake

Roseburg

CRATER LAKE NP

Harney Lake

N

0   30   60 mi
0   50   100 km

EUGENE, OR TO HOOD RIVER, OR

Oregon's second largest city, **Eugene** lies at the southern end of the **Willamette Valley** (it's pronounced Wuh-LAM-ett), a 150-mile stretch of undulating, nutrient-rich, volcanic terrain punctuated by unpretentious agricultural communities, some of which—especially up north closer to Portland—now pop with buzzy farm-to-table eateries and fancy inns. The region's first vineyards were begun by California transplants in the late '60s, and the valley now rivals France's Burgundy for its sublime Pinot Noir. Nearly all of the region's 700 wineries specialize in Pinot Noir along with a slate of cool-weather-conducive whites, such as Pinot Gris, Chardonnay, and Riesling. I enjoy a lean, earthy Pinot Noir as much as the next person, but tasting this same varietal over and over can have diminishing returns, so I've tried to include some wineries on this itinerary that offer more diverse types of wines (sometimes sourcing additional grapes from warmer parts of the state).

Home to the University of Oregon and its excellent museums, which include the superb **Jordan Schnitzer Museum of Art,** Eugene is a progressive, bike-friendly, food-forward city of around 175,000 with lots of parks and some notable culinary neighborhoods, in particular the **Market District,** which is centered around lively **5th Street Public Market** and skirts the forested slopes and trails of **Skinner Butte Park,** extending west to hip and arty **Whiteaker.** The neighborhood has some excellent urban wineries, including **Oregon Wine LAB** and **Capitello Wines,** which has roots in both Oregon and New Zealand (and pours exceptional Pinot Noir from both regions). There's also a rich variety of eateries, bars, and markets and a superb cidery, **WildCraft.** Start the day with coffee, avocado toast, or an almond brioche at Tailored Coffee Roasters, then snack on pork steam buns at Legend of Szechuan or a soft-shell-crab taco at Tacovore later in the day. Before heading north, consider a quick detour to the very southern edge of the Willamette Valley, which is home to such vaunted wineries as **Sweet Cheeks** and **King Estate,** with its stunning hilltop setting and superb restaurant.

From Eugene, follow Hwy 99W north. Framed by the Oregon Coast Range to the west and the much higher and more dramatic Cascades to the east, it's a pleasant, relaxing 85-mile drive past pockets of vineyards and through the college town of **Corvallis** (Oregon State University) to **McMinnville,** a dapper farming and logging town that's morphed into a hotbed of foodie culture. The tree-shaded downtown is filled with tasting rooms, including **Troon** and **R. Stuart and Co.** On the outskirts, you'll pass a field with

SIDETRACK

North of McMinnville lies a constellation of wineries that includes some of Oregon's brightest stars. Follow Hwy 47 to the cute, walkable town of **Carlton,** which has a cluster of notable tasting rooms, such as **Ken Wright Cellars** and **Flâneur Wines.** I like relaxing with a game of bocce at **Cana's Feast,** which offers an expansive selection of Italian and Bordeaux reds, and checking out the up-and-coming makers at the nearby **Carlton Winemakers Studio,** a cooperative that's home to 16 different small-lot outfits. Continue north through **Yamhill,** where you can foray into the eastern hills to visit such world-renowned Pinot producers as **Lemelson** and **Penner-Ash,** and then up to pretty **Forest Grove,** which is home to some lovely tasting rooms set in the breezy foothills of the Coast Range, such as **David Hill Vineyards** and **Montinore Estate.**

two giant airplane hangars—this is the **Evergreen Aviation and Space Museum,** and touring the nearly 200 aircraft, which include Howard Hughes's huge all-wooden *Spruce Goose,* is a blast, especially if you have kids with you. The complex includes **Wings and Waves Waterpark,** in which you can plunge down a waterslide that starts in the Boeing 747 on the roof of the building.

The 15-mile Hwy 99W corridor from McMinnville to Newberg contains some of the region's most exciting wineries. The two musts for me are **Sokol Blosser** because of its stunning, linear architecture and **Stoller Family Estate,** where you can hang out in Adirondack chairs on an expansive lawn while sipping a glass of crisp Chardonnay. There are also notable tasting rooms along the main drag in **Dundee,** such as **Argyle** and **Alit Wines,** and you can stop for lunch or picnic supplies at Red Hills Market (the wood-fired roast beef sandwich with blue cheese and caramelized onions has attained near cult status). **Newberg** has a similarly buzz-worthy downtown tasting scene, with venues like **Artisanal Wine Cellars** and **Wolves and People Farmhouse Brewery** well worth visiting.

Roll down the windows and make sure your phone has ample data storage: the drive to Hood River through the **Columbia Gorge** is one of the true stunners of the West. Head from Portland to **Troutdale,** stopping for brunch or to sample spirits or wine at **McMenamins Edgefield,** an eccentric hotel fashioned out of a 1911 former home for the

City View
Portland

Set at the confluence of the Columbia and Willamette rivers, verdant and outdoorsy Portland (pop 645,000) is a key stop on any serious Northwestern wine vacation. The city's culinary cred has soared off the charts in recent decades, and there are enough nationally acclaimed restaurants, bakeries, food trucks, breweries, coffeehouses, distilleries, and urban wineries to keep you busy for days, if not weeks. On a short visit, it's best to focus on two or three food-focused neighborhoods.

Car-friendly rating: Fair-Good. In a city that faithfully promotes its bike-friendly infrastructure and excellent public transportation (which includes the user-friendly MAX light rail, sleek streetcars, and efficient buses), it feels almost blasphemous to point out that it's also a pretty easy place to get around by car. The denser Downtown core is better suited to walking and public transit (street parking is more limited here, and garages can get spendy), but there's plenty of free street parking in even the trendy neighborhoods on the East Side.

What to see in a day: The true "attractions" in Portland are its lively outer neighborhoods, although the **Portland Art Museum** on Downtown's leafy Park Blocks is a bona fide gem. Also set aside at least two hours to visit **Washington Park**, where you can saunter amid the 10,000 bushes in the **International Rose Test Garden** and walk by koi ponds, ornamental trees, and striking buildings in the **Portland Japanese Garden**, which offers exceptional views toward Mt Hood. Enchanting foot trails lead deeper into Washington Park and amid the hemlocks and Douglas firs of adjacent 5157-acre **Forest Park**. Down the hill in the **Pearl District**, you can browse the aisles at legendary **Powell's City of Books** and taste wine at some exceptional tasting rooms, including **Battle Creek Cellars** and **Erath**. The city's edgiest and most intriguing food neighborhoods are across the Willamette River. A good plan is to arrive with an empty stomach and eat and drink to your heart's content on **Northeast Alberta Street**, **North Mississippi Avenue**, **Southeast Division Street**, and—my personal favorite—the **Central East Side**, a roughly 50-block quadrant of converted warehouses and striking newer buildings that houses some of the city's most exciting culinary destinations.

Where to stay: Portland has experienced a major hip-hotel boom since the mid-2010s. Most of the city's top lodgings are Downtown (note that overnight parking can run $50 or higher) and include the **Nines** and the **Woodlark**, as well as **Kimpton RiverPlace**, with its quieter and wonderfully picturesque marina setting on the river. But some stylish options have opened closer to the East Side's corridors of coolness. I like the snug but comfy rooms at the Scandinavian-chic **KEX Portland**, which also has my favorite lobby-restaurant for both eating and lounging. Other good bets on the East Side include the **Hotel Grand Stark** and the **McMenamins Kennedy School**.

Top Downtown food trucks *Bottom* Portland sign

From Portland to the vineyards of the Columbia Gorge, the craggy, snowcapped summit of Oregon's tallest peak, 11,240 ft **Mt Hood** is ever present. It's a breathtaking 40-mile drive south from Hood River to get a closer look at this striking mountain that the region's Indigenous people call Wy'East. As the road curves around Mt Hood's southern slope, pull off for an easy, refreshing 3.4-mile round-trip hike to shimmering **Tamanawas Falls**. Continue south, bearing right onto US 26 and then take Timberline Highway on its climb 5.5 miles to iconic **Timberline Lodge**, which was designed by Gilbert Stanley Underwood (famous for Yosemite's Ahwahnee Hotel) and constructed by the WPA in the 1930s—its exterior served as that of the haunted Overlook Hotel in Stanley Kubrick's *The Shining*. You can spend the night in one of the simple, cozy rooms. I like visiting the small museum on the ground floor and then enjoying drinks and fondue in the circular **Ram's Head Bar** with its towering ceilings and massive central fireplace.

Portland Japanese Garden

indigent that abounds with terraces, gardens, tasting rooms, and eateries. Or save your appetite for Sugarpine Drive-In, a classic roadside eatery that serves farm-to-table sandwiches and salads and house-made soft-serve ice cream with creative toppings (I'm crazy about the Larch Mountain sundae, a decadent concoction of vanilla-chocolate-swirl ice cream topped with a Blondie brownie, pine nut–honeycomb crunch, and blueberry-lavender sauce). Crossing the bridge over the Sandy River, turn right onto the **Historic Columbia River Highway** and follow this narrow, curving road constructed in 1922 to attract tourists to the awesome Columbia Gorge, a 74-mile-long span of the Columbia River that cuts through the Cascade Range. Steep cliffs and mountains rise 4500 ft on both sides of the Gorge, and there are several must-see stops (which can get wildly crowded, so go on a weekday if possible). Definitely pull over at **Vista House at Crown Point**, a historic octagonal building that offers panoramic views up and down the river, and **Multnomah Falls**, where you can stand at the base of a 620 ft cascade and, if you're up for a short workout, climb a 1.25-mile paved trail to the top. Gorgeous hikes line this drive—**Angel's Rest** and **Wahkeena Falls** are good ones you can complete in less than three hours.

East of Multnomah Falls, take I-84 to **Cascade Locks**, and for a break, have beer overlooking the river at Thunder Island Brewing. Cross the **Bridge of the Gods** (which you may recognize from the movie *Wild*) into Washington, and continue through the Gorge on Hwy 14, stopping 20 miles later to visit a couple of the superb wineries that cling to the hills in **Underwood**. Tastings at **AniChe Cellars** take place on a patio with eye-popping Gorge views, and **Savage Grace** pours some of the area's most interesting wines— including a distinctive orange Gewürztraminer. Cross back into Oregon to explore **Hood River**, a cheerful river town that has about three dozen excellent wineries, most of them along a meandering 35-mile scenic route known as the **Fruit Loop** and named for its many pear, cherry, peach, and other fruit orchards. **Marchesi**, with its refined Nebbiolos and Sangioveses, and **Stave and Stone** are excellent stops for vino, as is the **Gorge White House**, where you can sample hard ciders and wines, dine on burgers and flatbreads in the lush garden, and scoop up fruit and flowers in the U-pick gardens and orchards. You'll find excellent restaurants in Hood River's historic downtown and also by the modern **Waterfront Park** on the river—savor delicious pizza at Solstice Wood Fire and outstanding beer and tasty gastropub fare at Pfriem Family Brewers.

Downtown Leavenworth *Opposite* AniChe Cellars

HOOD RIVER, OR TO WALLA WALLA, WA

Cross back into Washington, stopping in cute **White Salmon** to pick up cheese and charcuterie or gourmet sandwiches at Feast Market and Delicatessen or White Salmon Baking Company, and continue east through Bingen, home of the chic, Scandinavian-inspired **Society Hotel**. Hwy 14 continues through the beautiful, more desert-like eastern half of the Gorge. The town of **Lyle** is home to several stellar wineries that specialize in Rhone varietals, including **Syncline** (my favorite winery in either state) and **COR Cellars**. As you make your way east over soaring ridges and beneath rocky basalt cliffs, stop for a tasting at renowned **Maryhill Winery** and to admire the sculpture gardens and eclectic holdings (about 80 sculptures and molds by Rodin and an impressive set of antique chess sets) at the stately **Maryhill Museum of Art**. A few miles farther east, walk around a full-size concrete replica of **Stonehenge** built by Maryhill Museum's founder as a memorial to soldiers lost in World War II.

It's a picturesque 2.5-hour drive east to **Walla Walla**, a former hub of wheat, onion, and legume farming nestled in the sun-kissed golden hills of southeastern Washington's sparsely settled **Palouse** region. Since a handful of pioneering vintners swapped acres of grains for grapes in the 1970s, this easygoing town has vaulted into winery stardom, earning comparisons with Napa and Sonoma for the incredibly high quality (yet comparatively lower costs) of its vibrant Cabernet Sauvignons, Syrahs, Merlots, Malbecs, and other big and bold reds. You can walk among about 40 tasting rooms downtown, which are interspersed among stylish boutiques and buzzy eateries. Or head east a few miles to another compact cluster of tasting rooms in the **Airport Wineries District**. But for the best mix of scenery and vino, drive down through the **South Walla Walla Valley**, enjoying the sweeping mountain views and stopping for tastes at some of the area's architecturally stunning tasting rooms, such as **Amavi Cellars**, **Revelry Vintners**, and **Valdemar Estates**. Note that a handful of Walla Walla's wineries offer inviting overnight accommodations—the farmhouse-chic digs at 38-acre **Abeja Winery** are my favorite.

WALLA WALLA, WA TO CHELAN, WA

Backtrack from Walla Walla on US 12, stopping to sample the exceptional wines at **Waterbrook Winery** and **L'Ecole No 41**, to **Tri-Cities**, a metroplex of three contiguous small cities—**Richland**, **Pasco**, and **Kennewick**—at the confluence of the Snake and Columbia rivers. Soak up the scenery with a walk or bike ride along the **Sacagawea Heritage Trail** or through verdant **Columbia Park**, near which you can stop by **Bartholomew** and **Monarcha** wineries for tastings. For the next 85 miles to Yakima, you're in Washington's most prolific wine country, with more than 140 tasting rooms. I suggest narrowing down your adventures to two relatively compact areas. The most picturesque is **Red Mountain**, near tiny **Benton City**, which has several outstanding tasting rooms— the grounds and architecture at **Col Solare** and **Hedges** are breathtaking, but I like the wines at **Fidélitas** and **Frichette** every bit as much.

Follow I-82 west to my other favorite Yakima Valley wine town, **Prosser**, which is considered the birthplace of Washington's wine industry and has more than 30 tasting rooms. Many are within walking distance of one another at **Vintners Village**: family-operated **Martinez & Martinez** produces a heady Carménère, and **Milbrandt Cellars** scores high marks for its silky Syrahs and Cabernet Sauvignons. Stop for lunch on the patio at **Wine o'Clock Wine Bar and Bistro** before driving over to **Prosser Wine and Food Park**, an unassuming semi-industrial area that's home to such outstanding wineries as **Kestrel** and **Alexandria Nicole**. Continue northwest through this arid valley, stopping in the region's largest city, **Yakima** (pop 98,000) and visiting two more terrific vintners—the sparkling wine specialist **Treveri Cellars** and the Bordeaux-blend exemplar **Owen Roe**.

There's great craft-brewing around here, too. Nearly 50% of the world's hops is grown in this valley, and **Bale Breaker Brewing** is an excellent place to taste bright and hoppy IPAs produced with hops grown on the property.

From Yakima exit the interstate and drive up slower but far more beautiful Hwy 821, which snakes through dramatic **Yakima Canyon**. Along the route, **Canyon River Grill**— helmed by James Beard–recognized chef Kevin Davis—is a memorable stop for lunch. Continue north to the friendly college town (home to Central Washington University) of **Ellensburg**, which famously hosts the **Ellensburg Rodeo** each Labor Day and is also home to the renowned **Gallery One Visual Arts Center** and **Clymer Museum of Art** as well as several acclaimed tasting rooms and restaurants. Leave the high desert and follow US 97 on a captivatingly crooked path through the coniferous-shaded slopes of **Okanogan-Wenatchee National Forest**, breathing in the cool air of the eastern Cascade Range.

You may feel as though you've been airlifted into the Bavarian Alps when you pull into **Leavenworth**, with its colorful buildings—many of them housing romantic inns— festooned with ornate gingerbread trim, hanging baskets of petunias and geraniums, and folky signs with Old German typeface. I found the kitsch factor a bit excessive the first time I visited, but this once-prosaic town's efforts to rebrand in the 1960s as an Alpine-inspired weekend destination have grown on me, especially when I'm here in winter and actual icicles hang from the town's chalet-style eaves and balconies. It also helps that Leavenworth's food scene has improved dramatically. You can still find traditional German restaurants with beamed ceilings and servers in dirndls and lederhosen (**Andreas Keller** is a fine choice for that), but they're joined by eclectic and adventuresome options like hip **Yodelin Broth Company** and contemporary **Watershed Cafe**, plus more than 15 tasting rooms representing some of the state's top wineries. There's also lots of beautiful hiking— just outside town and abundant with wildflowers in spring and colorful foliage in the fall, the 5.5-mile **Icicle Ridge Trail** offers an enjoyable way to burn some calories.

Not more than 15 miles east you'll emerge from the cloistered woods of the Cascades back out into the sunny Columbia River Valley. Stop in **Wenatchee** to walk among the ferns and rippling rock pools of historic **Ohme Gardens** or for a bite to eat downtown at **Pybus Public Market**, a grand modern marketplace with stalls proffering all sorts of local goodies. Then follow US 97 along the west shore of the Columbia, turning left onto Hwy 971 and continuing a few miles to the southern shore of **Lake Chelan**, a pristine 50.5-mile, 1453 ft deep fjord. Excellent wineries with sunny patios set on ridges with expansive water views line the lake's southern shore. **Karma Vineyards** and **Tsillan Cellars** (which has a superb Italian restaurant) are great places to sample the Riesling, Gewürztraminer, and Pinot Noir that this relatively cool Washington AVA specializes in. Drive east through the attractive town of **Chelan** and pick up Hwy 150 to explore the area's estimable North Shore wineries. Several of these—including **C.R. Sandidge** and **CheVal**—are along the main drag of **Manson**, while others are up in the hills and offer yet more glorious views of the mountains and lake. For its setting, it's hard to beat **Benson Vineyards**, but I also like **Hard Road to Hoe**, an acclaimed woman-owned vineyard with a cheeky bordello theme, a peaceful garden tasting area, and seriously accomplished wines.

CHELAN, WA TO KELOWNA, BC

From Chelan it's about a two-hour drive on US 97, through a series of small towns along the Okanogan River, to **Osoyoos**, British Columbia. Almost immediately after crossing the border into Canada, vineyards—acres and acres of them—dominate your view. There's actually a great little family-run boutique winery, **Lariana Cellars**, that's just 50 ft from the US border. As you continue north around Osoyoos Lake and through this town that's popular with retirees (it's considered the warmest place in Canada), you'll enter the **Oliver-Osoyoos Wine Country** at the southern end of the **Okanagan Valley**. Here, more than 80% of British Columbia's wines are produced—only southern Ontario rivals this area in volume and quality of Canadian wine. The Oliver-Osoyoos region's relatively warm weather and glacial soil are ideal for growing a wide range of grapes, especially Cabernet Sauvignon, Syrah, and Merlot. On your way north, notable stops for tasting include Indigenous-owned **Nk'Mip Cellars**, Golden Mile Bench–situated **Road 13 Vineyards**, and

SIDETRACK

You can only drive the first 15 miles of Lake Chelan's shore, but you can traverse this majestic fjord via a scenic boat ride through **Lake Chelan Boat Co.**, disembarking at the quaint and remote village of **Stehekin**. Unless you're planning to spend the night in one of the 15 comfy cabins at **Stehekin Valley Ranch**, give yourself about six hours in town, perhaps having lunch at Stehekin Pastry Company or making a hike either along the shore or across **Purple Creek** and up to about the 3-mile mark, where you'll be treated to wondrous views. Stehekin is in the **Lake Chelan National Recreation Area** portion of North Cascades National Park and is accessible only by boat or hiking trails. You can pick up maps and info at the **Golden West Visitor Center**.

SIDETRACK

About 20 miles north of Chelan, follow US 97 along a serpentine stretch of the Columbia River, turn left onto Hwy 153, and follow the eastern edge of the Cascades through the curving **Methow Valley** (it's pronounced Meh-tow). For a bite to eat, stop in quaint downtown **Twisp**—the Cinnamon Twisp Bakery is beloved for its decadent cinnamon roll-esque pastries, and in the evening Tappi serves up fantastic pizzas and offers an excellent wine list. Turn onto Hwy 20 and 10 miles northwest you'll enter **Winthrop**, which like Leavenworth solved its faltering economic fortunes in the 1970s by reinventing itself, in this case as a Wild West theme town. Buildings have colorful wood-frame facades and contain gift shops, galleries, and cafes, and many have decks or patios overlooking the Chewuch and Methow rivers. Continue west on Hwy 20 through the outdoor recreation village of **Mazama**, with its colorful Mazama Store stocked with everything from cast-iron baking pans to local honey, and then into the east side of **North Cascades National Park** (*see* Washington: the Mountains and the Sea chapter p. 26). From late spring until around mid-September, depending on snowfall, you can drive Hwy 20 completely through the park. From Twisp, to continue north to BC, follow Hwy 20 about 35 miles east to rejoin US 97 in Omak.

Burrowing Owl Estate, which offers elegant accommodations and refined dining. Also worth a stop is **District Wine Village**, a collection of 16 artisanal producers of wine, spirits, and beer that opened in 2021 in **Oliver** near the cottonwood groves and birdwatching of **Inkaneep Provincial Park**.

As Hwy 97 reaches the cliff-fringed shores of narrow **Vaseux Lake**, you'll enter the most visually alluring stretch of the Okanagan Valley. The scenery really pops for the next 20 miles as you continue past noted Pinot Noir and Pinot Gris producers around **Okanagan Falls**, such as **Noble Ridge** and **Blue Mountain Vineyard**, and then up along the western shore of deep-blue **Skaha Lake**, which leads to the valley's third largest city, **Penticton** (pop 34,000). Here at the southern tip of 85 mile long **Kelowna Lake**, make a 10-mile detour along the eastern shore to one of BC's most respected wine regions, the sunny **Naramata Bench**. About 30 wineries thrive among the moderating lake breezes and ample sunshine, which are a boon to growing both light- and full-bodied wines, from Chardonnay and Sauvignon Blanc to Merlot and Malbec. Notable tasting rooms include **La Frenz** and **Terravista Vineyards**, a small producer of superb Spanish-style whites, including a knockout Albariño. Return through **Penticton** to Hwy 97, and stop for a sip or two at some of the gorgeous tasting rooms in pastoral **Summerland**, where you can also book a 90-minute journey aboard a restored locomotive on the **Kettle Valley Steam Railway**. **Silkscarf Estate** and **Dirty Laundry Vineyard** (don't miss the delicious pizzas) are top wineries in this cooler area that specializes in Gewürztraminer, Pinot Noir, and Riesling.

Hwy 97 continues north through **West Kelowna**, which is home to some of the Okanogan Valley's largest and most prestigious winemaking operations, including **Mission Hill** and **Quails' Gate**, as well the excellent **Indigenous World Winery**. Established in 2016, it's the province's only 100% Indigenous-owned wine company, and it offers tastings in a sleek, glass-walled space with a patio and grand lake views. Crossing a modern pontoon bridge leads you right into the center of fast-growing **Kelowna**, which with a population of 142,000 is the region's primary service center. The paved and boardwalked **Waterfront Promenade** curves for 1.5 miles along the picturesque downtown lakeshore, connecting two verdant parks with the attractions of the **Cultural District**: the beautifully landscaped **Kasugai Japanese Garden**, the intimate **Kelowna Art Gallery**, and the informative **Okanagan Wine and Orchard Museum**, next to which you can stroll through adjacent **Laurel Square Park**, where interpretive signs tell the story of the area's rich

agricultural and winegrowing heritage. The nearby **North End** is becoming a trendy hub of craft-beverage production; sample the goods at **Kettle River Brewing**, **BC Tree Fruits Cider Company**, **Sandhill Wines**, and **Jackknife Brewing**, which is well regarded for its creative pizzas.

A wonderland of outdoor recreation, Kelowna is surrounded by rugged natural scenery. On the north edge of downtown, **Knox Mountain Park** has 580 acres of both easy and more rigorous hiking trails to lofty promontories with dazzling lake and city views. Just southeast of Kelowna, **Myra-Bellevue Provincial Park** offers hiking and biking along a breathtaking 8-mile section of the regional **Kettle Valley Rail Trail**—it cuts through narrow rock passes and tunnels and over a series of dramatic wooden trestles with impressive lake vistas. Nearby, family-friendly **Myra Canyon Adventure Park** offers zip-lining and tree-top canopy tours. More wine-touring awaits on the eastern side of the lake, where you can visit architecturally striking **Summerhill Pyramid Winery** and its acclaimed organic bistro or continue north up Hwy 97 to renowned **50th Parallel Estate**, about 15 miles from the region's northernmost city, **Vernon**. Here you could extend your stay at a snazzy resort—such as **Sparkling Hill** or **Predator Ridge**—or continue farther via Hwy 1, the Trans-Canada Highway, into the Canadian Rockies.

Vineyards in Kelowna

BEST EATS

- **Izakaya Meiji** In this dimly lit modern Japanese restaurant in Eugene's trendy Whiteaker neighborhood, sup on eminently snackable and shareable small plates—fried chicken teriyaki burgers, mushroom curry udon, shredded salmon-belly rice balls—and sip from a well-curated list of sakes, wines, and beers. 541-505-8804, izakayameiji.com.

- **La Rambla** Boldly flavored, beautifully composed Spanish fare, from traditional Valencia-style seafood paella to lamb skewers with harissa and crab cakes with Calabrian aioli, is the draw at this elegant restaurant set in an 1880s building in downtown McMinnville. 503-435-2126, laramblaonthird.com.

- **Newbergundian Bistro** A luminary among several destination-worthy restaurants in Newberg, this playfully named French eatery celebrates the food and wine of both Oregon and Burgundy. House-made charcuterie and classic coq au vin with locally foraged mushrooms are among the standout dishes. 971-832-8687, newbergundian.com.

- **Pixán Taqueria and Cantina** I was happily surprised to taste some of the most flavorful Mexican cuisine I've eaten on the West Coast in the tiny Columbia Gorge town of White Salmon. Opened in 2020, this handsome spot serves both simple (roasted potato, carne asada) and more elaborate (cochinita pibil, charred cauliflower with hazelnuts and yuca mash) tacos, along with well-crafted mezcal and tequila cocktails. 509-310-3855, pixantacos.com.

- **Hattaway's** Wrap up an afternoon of tasting room-hopping in downtown Walla Walla at this intimate brick-walled bistro, which presents an always interesting mashup of Southeast and Northwest dishes. Think sautéed mussels and collard greens with house-cured pork belly and cold-smoked duck breast with dirty rice and kimchi. 509-525-4433, hattawaysonalder.com.

- **Brasserie Four** Seating at this beloved Walla Walla eatery includes a casually smart dining room with pressed-tin ceilings and a sunny tree-lined sidewalk. The old-school country French cuisine—escargot in parsley-garlic butter, hearty Provençal bouillabaisse—pairs wonderfully with the extensive selection of local wines. 509-529-2011, brasseriefour.com.

- **Mana** Set aside about 2.5 hours and prepare to be dazzled by the artful, locally sourced eight-course meals served in this bright cottage in downtown Leavenworth. The chefs happily accommodate vegetarian and other dietary requests, and well-considered wine or nonalcoholic-drink pairings are offered. 509-548-1662, manamountain.com.

- **Vin du Lac Bistro** With an airy terrace offering splendid views of Lake Chelan and the surrounding peaks, this inviting farmstead is both a first-rate winery open for tastings and a gracious restaurant serving creative takes on hearty American fare, from elk meatloaf to smoked gouda mac-and-cheese. 509-682-2882, vindulac.com.

- **Miradoro** Situated at beautiful Tinhorn Creek Vineyards in BC's prolific Oliver-Osoyoos Wine Country, this airy and modern restaurant serves superb Mediterranean fare, from mussels steamed in a saffron broth with chorizo to pappardelle pasta with foraged wild mushrooms. 250-498-3742, tinhorn.com.

- **Elma** Have a seat in the airy and colorful dining room of this contemporary Turkish bistro in Penticton, savoring grand views of Okanagan Lake's southern shoreline and feasting on pureed eggplant with pomegranate molasses and lamb kebabs with garlic yogurt. 236-422-3562, eatatelma.com.

- **Home Block** Tables at this chic restaurant at Kelowna's acclaimed CedarCreek Estate Winery enjoy dramatic views through a wall of floor-to-ceiling windows. Three-course, wine-paired dinners feature artfully crafted, locally sourced cuisine. 250-980-4663, cedarcreek.bc.ca.

BEST SLEEPS

- **Gordon Hotel** You're steps from the cool urban wineries and eateries of Eugene's bustling Market District at this dapper contemporary mid-rise that offers plenty of pleasing amenities, from loaner bikes to local snacks, wine, and beer. 541-762-0555.

- **Atticus Hotel** The 36 rooms and suites in this glamorous four-story boutique hotel in downtown McMinnville have soaring 13 ft ceilings, are filled with well-chosen local art, and are outfitted with wine refrigerators, premium sound systems, French press coffeemakers, and beautiful handcrafted furnishings. Red Hills Kitchen features exceptional regional Pacific Northwestern fare and local wines. 503-472-1975, atticushotel.com.

- **Allison Inn and Spa** The ultimate opulent wine country retreat, this contemporary resort nestled among Newberg's vineyards has a superb farm-to-table restaurant, an expansive spa with a dozen treatment rooms and an indoor pool, and 85 rooms kitted out with gas fireplaces, wet bars, and deep soaking tubs. 503-554-2525, theallison.com.

- **Hood River Hotel** Staying in this mid-priced historic property in the heart of downtown Hood River puts you within easy reach of more than 50 Columbia Gorge wineries, not to mention the hiking and skiing at Mt Hood. Just off the lobby, hip Broder Øst serves Scandinavian brunch fare, including delectable lefse potato crepes stuffed with chevre and topped with baked eggs. 541-386-1900, hoodriverhotel.com.

- **The Finch** Fashioned out of a gloriously updated mid-1960s motel in downtown Walla Walla, this striking 80-room vision of mid-century modernism is decked out in thoughtfully curated local artwork and offers a slew of pleasing creature comforts, from premium coffee in the morning to an inviting common outdoor space with a wood-burning fireplace. 509-956-4994, finchwallawalla.com.

- **Inn at Desert Wind Winery** Designed with an elegant Southwestern flair that befits the sunny high-desert climate of the Yakima Valley, this luxurious four-room retreat in Prosser is part of the esteemed Desert Wind winery, where you can book tastings and fascinating behind-the-scenes tours. 509-786-7277, desertwindwinery.com.

- **Abendblume** Overlooking wildflower meadows a short drive from the bustle of downtown Leavenworth, this handsome old-world chalet with ornate balconies has over-the-top rooms outfitted with fireplaces, heated marble bathroom floors, double whirlpool tubs, handmade sleigh beds, and other cushy features. Wake up in the morning to a feast of aebleskivers with apple syrup. 509-548-4059, abendblume.com.

- **Warm Springs Inn and Winery** Set amid nearly 10 acres of gardens and vineyards along a lovely stretch of the Wenatchee River, this peaceful early-20th-century B&B has six plush antiques-filled rooms and includes lavish breakfasts with its rates. On-site Brender Canyon Vineyard produces first-rate wines. 509-662-5863, warmspringsinn.com.

- **Spirit Ridge Resort** Set on a bluff near the US border overlooking the beautiful lakefront in Osoyoos, this elegant retreat overlooks acres of vineyards and a superb golf course. Enjoy a massage in the soothing spa or a tasting at on-site Nk'Mip Cellars. 250-495-5445, Hyatt.com.

- **Summerland Waterfront Resort** The spacious suites in this family-friendly retreat on the southwestern shore of Okanagan Lake have balconies and well-equipped kitchens, and a full slate of activities awaits, including kayaks, SUPs, bikes, pools, a kids' playground, and an adult spa. 250-494-8180, summerlandresorthotel.com.

- **Hotel Eldorado** Set on a picturesque marina just south of downtown Kelowna, this 1920s boutique hotel with an upscale newer wing has beautifully appointed rooms with balconies and mountain views. Tender steaks and an impressive BC wine list are among the draws in the romantic lakefront restaurant. 250-763-7500, hoteleldoradokelowna.com.

CAMPING

A handful of wineries in the Pacific Northwest offer camping and glamping experiences, among them Oregon's Eola Hills Wine Cellars and Washington's Cultura and Cave B, which also has a fine restaurant and elegant bungalows on a cliff in the central Columbia Valley. You can book many of these, and find lots of others, through the RVing-winery stay website HarvestHosts.com. You can also rent a stylishly outfitted antique Airstream at Vintages Trailer Resort, a Willamette Valley compound that's between McMinnville and Dundee and is adjacent to Willamette Wine Country RV Park. Other great campgrounds include Silver Falls State Park in the Willamette Valley, Memaloose State Park in the Columbia Gorge, Blue Valley RV Park in Walla Walla, Alpine View RV Park in Leavenworth, and Lake Chelan State Park. Across the border in the Okanagan Valley, try Nk'mip Campground on Osoyoos Lake, Summerland Beach RV and Campground on the west shore of Okanagan Lake, and Canyon Farms RV Park near Myra Canyon in Kelowna.

Opposite The skyline of Kelowna and the William R. Bennett Bridge

Oregon Coast and The Cascades ★

Drive along Oregon's spectacular coastline before exploring northern California's skyscraping redwood trees then turning inland through the sunny Rogue Valley and around gorgeous Crater Lake.

HOW LONG?

7 days; add an extra day each to see more of Redwood National and State Parks, Ashland, Crater Lake, and Bend.

WHEN TO GO

Late May through June is perfect, as dry weather is likely, summer crowds haven't yet materialized, all of Crater Lake's roads should have reopened for the season, and wildfires aren't yet a threat. September to mid-October is my second choice, but wildfires and smoke, mainly in the interior, can be a problem. Summer is lovely, too, but for the increased crowds and hotel rates. I actually love winter's dramatically stormy coastal weather and powdery snow in the mountains (resulting in the closure of much of Crater Lake, but you can still access the South Rim).

NEED TO KNOW

In summer, book hotel rooms far in advance at Crater Lake and along the coast. Always stick with well-established routes when traveling over the mountains in Oregon; GPS sometimes recommends rough logging roads that aren't maintained and can become impassable from October through May.

→ Distances

Total distance, one-way: 770 mi (1239 km)
- Astoria, OR to Florence, OR: 185 mi (298 km)
- Florence, OR to Crescent City, CA: 200 mi (322 km)
- Crescent City, CA to Ashland, OR: 130 mi (209 km)
- Ashland, OR to Bend, OR: 200 mi (322 km)

Daytime Temperatures

January: 40-55°F (4-13°C)
July: 65-82°F (18-28°C)

More information
- Oregon Coast tourism, visittheoregoncoast.com
- Crescent City tourism, visitdelnortecounty.com
- Redwood National and State Parks, nps.gov/redw
- Southern Oregon tourism, southernoregon.org
- Crater Lake National Park, nps.gov/crla
- Bend tourism, visitbend.com

◉ SNAPSHOT

Relatively remote, the Oregon Coast is less visited than many US coastal regions, yet its rugged beauty is almost unmatched. US 101 twists and turns for 365 miles from the gaping mouth of the Columbia River through low-key fishing towns, over breathtaking headlands, and past towering sand dunes, before accessing California's redwoods. This route then jogs inland through Oregon's increasingly acclaimed Rogue Valley wine country, through the theater town of Ashland, and up around the mesmerizing blue waters of Crater Lake, before ending in the sunny recreation mecca of Bend.

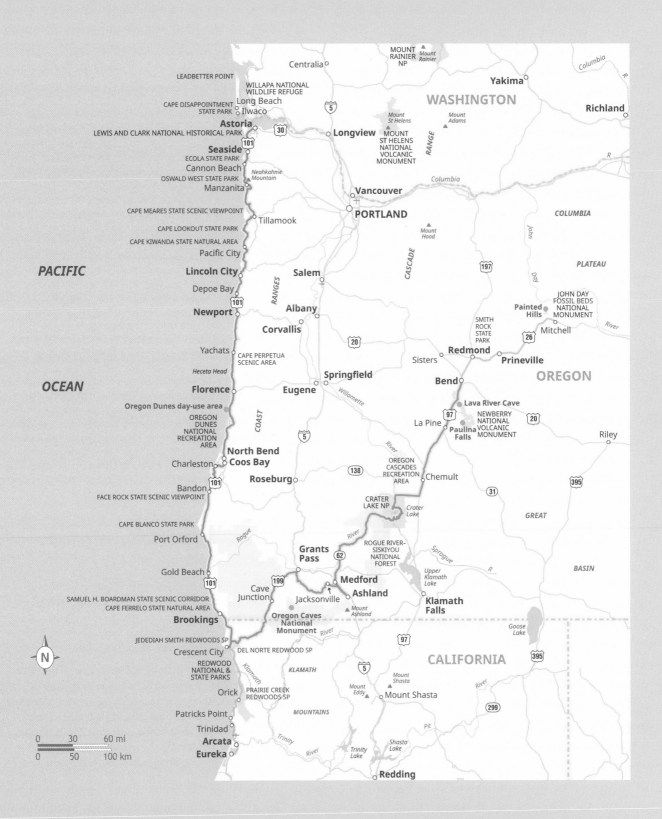

ASTORIA, OR TO FLORENCE, OR

With its handsome 19th-century industrial buildings, buzzy maker-and-foodie scene, and a rough-and-tumble seaport history, **Astoria** feels a bit like Portland's little sister by the sea. This hilly burgh predates Portland by about 40 years and lies at the mouth of the mighty Columbia River. Once known for its thriving fish canneries, Astoria today is dependent more on tourism and offers a great mix of standard chains and historic indie hotels (some cool economical options include the **Commodore** and the **Norblad**). Two hours west of Portland, it's an appealing starting point for an Oregon coast adventure. For an incredible view of the sea and mountains, drive up the hill to the **Astoria Column** and climb the 164 steps to the observation deck atop this 125 ft tall muraled obelisk. Then explore the riverfront, poking around the antique equipment and photos at the former Bumble Bee Seafood cannery on **Pier 39** and visiting the exceptional **Columbia River Maritime Museum**, where fascinating exhibits relate the dangers ship captains have always faced navigating the perilous waters of the Columbia Bar (where the river meets the ocean). Kids love to walk out on the dock and below deck of the lightship *Columbia*, a decommissioned 128 ft US Coast Guard vessel.

For a snack, drop by funky Blue Scorcher Bakery for heavenly pastries and sandwiches in a sunny hilltop dining room or Astoria Coffeehouse for craft coffees and delicious made-from-scratch breakfast, lunch, and dinner fare (the rockfish tacos are delish). As you leave town, peek inside the **Oregon Film Museum**, which fans of the cult kids classic *The Goonies* may recognize from that movie's jail scenes. Exhibits and memorabilia touch on dozens of other Hollywood features shot around the state, from *One Flew Over the Cuckoo's Nest* to *Animal House*. US 101 begins its snaky path down the Oregon Coast just west of **Fort Clatsop**, where you can visit a replica of the crude timber garrison in which members of the Lewis and Clark expedition encamped during the winter of 1805–06. It's part of **Lewis and Clark National Historic Park**, which also lies across the river at Washington's Cape Disappointment State Park.

Drive south on US 101, stopping briefly in **Seaside**, a honky-tonk beach town whose bustling main drag feels like one giant vintage candy shop/video arcade—very popular with kids or kids-at-heart. About 5 miles farther, you enter a dramatic coastal stretch, starting with dapper **Cannon Beach**, with its breezy art galleries and tasteful hotels. Massive 235 ft tall **Haystack Rock** dominates the beachfront beside a broad

SIDETRACK

From Astoria it's a short jog over the graceful Astoria-Megler Bridge to Washington's beautiful **Long Beach Peninsula**. Follow US 101 along the north bank of the Columbia River into **Ilwaco**, stopping for a bowl of steamer clams or Dungeness crab mac-and-cheese on the riverfront deck of the Salt Pub. Continue into **Cape Disappointment State Park**, which encompasses a lush 2000-acre headland with beautiful hiking trails that traverse 200 ft sea cliffs as well as the **Lewis and Clark Interpretive Center** and the West Coast's oldest operating lighthouse—it dates to 1856. Detour briefly before exiting the park to stroll around a second lighthouse, stately **North Head** (the historic Lighthouse Keepers' Residence now serves as a vacation rental) and continue up Hwy 103 to explore this 28 mile long peninsula known for its wide beaches, peaceful nature preserves, and oyster farms and cranberry bogs. At the top of the peninsula **Leadbetter Point State Park** and neighboring **Willapa National Wildlife Refuge** offer contemplative hiking through rolling dunes and some of the Pacific Northwest's best coastal migratory bird-watching. The peninsula's southern half abounds with family-oriented diversions, especially around the towns of **Seaview** and **Long Beach**. Visit the **World Kite Museum** and have lunch or dinner at Pickled Fish, which has grand ocean views from its third-floor perch atop the inviting **Adrift Hotel**. Then follow **Long Beach Boardwalk** for a look at the massive skeleton of a gray whale.

swath of hard-packed sand—there's great tide-pooling at low tide. The area's true star, however, is **Ecola State Park**, which is reached down a narrow lane through a temperate rainforest. The views of massive sea stacks and cliffs are impressive. I suggest hiking down to the beach (which is typically far less crowded than Cannon Beach) and making the 3.5-mile loop hike for a cliff-top view across an expanse of ocean to lonely **Tillamook Rock Lighthouse**.

US 101 continues south through a narrow tunnel and into **Oswald West State Park**, which is my favorite slice of wilderness on the Oregon Coast. I like to amble out to watch the surfers at **Short Sand Beach**, and then when time allows hike up to the 1680 ft summit of **Mt Neahkahnie**. This challenging climb takes a few hours, but the 40-mile vistas down the spectacular shoreline are incredible (and

every bit as majestic as California's Hwy 1, but with fewer crowds). Stop for a stroll in impossibly cute **Manzanita**, then drive about 25 miles until you see the big, new, and shiny **Tillamook Cheese Factory**. On a self-guided tour you can see how this famed dairy's beloved cheddar is produced, but the real fun is gobbling up free samples and then stopping in the stylish food hall for a snack (I recommend the marionberry pie ice cream).

For the best coastal scenery, break off of US 101 for a bit and explore the majestic 42-mile **Three Capes Loop**, stopping first at **Cape Meares State Scenic Viewpoint** to tour the lighthouse and kerosene-powered Fresnel lens, pose for a picture beside a famously massive, multi-trunked Sitka spruce, and view a rookery of cormorants, common murres, and pigeon guillemots from a cliff overlook. Continue along the sweeping beach at **Cape Lookout State Park** and down to **Cape Kiwanda State Natural Area** in the small fishing hamlet of Pacific City. Offshore lies another monolith called Haystack Rock (it's 92 ft higher than the more famous one in Cannon Beach), and you can scamper up a 200 ft sand dune, which is more of a butt-kicking adventure than it looks. Reward yourself with a smooth Pre-Prohibition Cream Ale and a bowl of clam chowder at beachfront Pelican Brewing before crossing the Nestucca River and rejoining US 101.

The route passes through the string of touristy but family-popular vacation villages known collectively as **Lincoln City** (the **Lincoln City Glass Center** is worth a stop to watch artisans hand-blow brightly colored paperweights, floats, and

votives) and then through **Depoe Bay**, the whale-watching capital of Oregon. At the mouth of what's been deemed the "world's smallest navigable harbor," stop inside the **OPRD Whale Watching Center** to learn about the roughly 20,000 gray whales that migrate down the coast from Alaska to Baja Mexico from mid-December to mid-January, and then return from late March to early June. You'll also find out about the many excellent coastal spots for viewing the gray whales who reside in Oregon's waters year-round, as well as orcas, humpbacks, dolphins, and porpoises. You can book whale-watching cruises through several reliable companies, **Whale Research EcoExcursions** among them. About 15 miles south at the **Oregon Coast Aquarium**, walk through tunnels beneath a huge tank with enormous bat rays, schools of mackerel, and five kinds of sharks; watch sea otters at play in a lagoon; and view horned puffins, black oystercatchers, and dozens of other birds in an aviary. Across **Yaquina Bay**, commercial (walk right past Ripley's Believe It Or Not) but colorful **Newport** has some engaging shops—you'll almost always hear and often see barking sea lions cavorting in the marina. Overlooking the ocean, Newport's quieter **Nye Beach** neighborhood has a cluster of cute eateries—I like ordering a mocha latte and a snickerdoodle at bric-a-brac-filled Blue Pig Bakery and then walking off my sugar high on the lovely beach.

Top Crater Lake *Previous* Sand dunes on the Oregon Coast

NEWPORT, OR TO CRESCENT CITY, CA

The southern half of the Oregon Coast is every bit as visually spectacular as the northern half, but with fewer and generally smaller towns and formal attractions. Assume a leisurely pace, and make time for a few beach or cliff hikes. Without stops, it's five hours from Newport to Crescent City, CA. I like breaking things up with a night in Bandon or Gold Beach, which have ample hotel options.

The 50-mile stretch of coast from Newport to Florence rivals any in Oregon for sheer natural beauty, especially **Yachats**, a lively but laid-back beach town that's counterintuitively pronounced YAH-hots. This is a great place for dining—maybe a wild mushroom frittata at cozy Beach Street Kitchen or a platter of local king salmon, albacore, and halibut at Luna Sea Fish House. Cross the Yachats River and round a few dramatic bends en route to **Cape Perpetua Scenic Area**, where you should start at the informative visitor center. You can drive to **Cape Perpetua Overlook** for dazzling vistas up and down the coast, but I prefer the short (2.5-mile round-trip) but steep (700 ft gain) hike through a spruce forest to the summit. Then saunter along the dramatic rocky shore and gaze into the seemingly endless depths of the **Thor's Well**

sinkhole. The road continues to **Heceta Head**, where you can pull off and drive beneath the striking Cape Creek Bridge, park by the beautiful beach, and walk out to a red-roofed 19th-century lighthouse. For the best photo op, stop at the viewing atop a massive headland just south on US 101. Then continue to **Florence**'s enchanting Old Town along the Siuslaw River. It's a great spot to stretch your legs, browse for art and gifts, or get caffeinated at River Roasters—sip your espresso from the observation deck in the small adjacent park. Gazing beneath the **Siuslaw River Bridge**, which is one of many ornate bridges built by the WPA in the 1930s along US 101, you'll see the natural feature that defines the coast for the next 40 miles or so: massive sand dunes.

Crossing the Siuslaw River, US 101 enters one of the world's largest coastal dune habitats, 45 sq mile **Oregon Dunes National Recreation Area**. There are several well-signed day-use areas along the route, including **Honeyman Memorial State Park**, where you can rent sandboards to cavort among these mounds of sand, which reach heights of 500 ft, and boats to paddle around Cleawox Lake. My favorite spot for quick gambol in a particularly striking area is the **Oregon Dunes Day-Use Overlook** off US 101, which is just north of Crown Zellerbach Campground.

South of the Oregon Dunes, the highway crosses another impressive historic bridge into **North Bend** and **Coos Bay**, neighboring timber and transportation hubs a few miles inland. Stop by the excellent **Coos History Museum and Maritime Collection**, which occupies a striking building with an exhaustive collection of photos and artifacts and a beautiful bay setting. Detour west on Hwy 540 through the fishing village of **Charleston** and down a rugged stretch of coast with three state parks—the two most interesting being **Cape Arago**, whose rocky trails are well suited to bird- and whale-watching, and **Shore Acres**, where peaceful pathways lead through rose and Japanese gardens that surround the former estate of a local lumber tycoon.

Oregon's final 120 miles of US 101 traverse an even quieter and often sunnier section of coastline. Stop in **Bandon**, home to the Scottish links–style golf resort **Bandon Dunes Golf Resort**, which ranks among the world's most exacting and exclusive places to play the game. With patio tables overlooking the Coquille River on an inviting boardwalk, no-frills Tony's Crab Shack is one of my favorite spots for whole Dungeness crab dinners (I'm partial to the the full meal with a half-pound of steamer clams and three jumbo prawns in a garlic–butter–white wine broth). Drive up over the headlands to view the awesome sea stacks just offshore at **Kronenburg County Park** and **Face Rock State Scenic Viewpoint**. Farther south, depending on how much time you have, stop at a few more enthralling parks. Best bets include **Cape Blanco State Park**, which has a striking lighthouse, and the **Samuel H. Boardman State Scenic Corridor**, a 12-mile stretch of vistas accessed by mostly short, dramatic hikes. My favorite areas are the arched formations and blowholes at **Natural Bridges** overlook and the easy mile-long trek to **Cape Ferrelo** (it's stunning at sunset). You'll find some quirky attractions, too, such as **Port Orford**'s Crazy Norwegian, which doles out perfectly battered fish and chips and fresh-baked pies, and the **Prehistoric Gardens**, an old-fashioned park with trails through a temperate rainforest dotted with 23 life-size dinosaur sculptures—this place looks as you'd imagine it depicted on a 1956 postcard. **Brookings** is a good-size town near the California border that has some acclaimed eateries, including Oxenfrē for creative comfort fare and Chetco Brewing to sample first-rate sour beers and the satisfying Imperial Coconut Porter.

Opposite Oregon Dunes National Recreation Area

CRESCENT CITY, CA TO ASHLAND, OR

About 20 miles south of the California border, **Crescent City** serves as the northern gateway to **Redwood National and State Parks**. First stroll around **Battery Point Lighthouse** and savor a lunch of creative wood-fired pizzas and well-crafted ales at the excellent SeaQuake Brewing. Much of the park extends south down US 101, but just outside town you can get an up-close look at hundreds of immense redwoods at **Jedediah Smith Redwoods State Park**. See a short film about the park's ecology at the **Hiouchi Information Center** and then view the excellent exhibits and inquire about ranger-led walks at the nearby **Jedediah Smith Visitor Center**. In **Stout Grove**, drive along unpaved Howland Hill Rd, which snakes for 10 miles through a vast old-growth stand of these monumental ancient trees that can grow as tall as a 35-story building.

From Crescent City, US 199 twists and turns alongside the swift-moving Smith River into the remote southwestern corner of Oregon's **Rogue River–Siskiyou National Forest**. At **Cave Junction** spelunkers should take note: a right turn onto Hwy 46 leads 20 miles to **Oregon Caves National Monument**, where from spring through fall you can tour an impressive network of marble caverns. Continue to **Grants Pass**, a laid-back, picturesque gateway for whitewater rafting and jet-boat excursions through the spectacular **Hellgate Canyon** corridor of the Rogue River—**Orange Torpedo** is a reliable, family-friendly outfitter. Head southeast onto Hwy 238 into the **Applegate Valley**, an increasingly celebrated winemaking region with two dozen tasting rooms, many with garden patios overlooking rolling vineyards. A couple of gems include **Wooldridge Creek Winery**, where you can visit the friendly goats who produce this farm's delicious cheeses, and **Red Lily**, which pours Spanish-style wines in a striking contemporary building by the Applegate River. Then saunter through the quaint center of **Jacksonville**, whose 19th-century brick and wood-frame buildings look right out of a Hollywood Western—many of them housing galleries and gift shops. In a pastoral amphitheater the Britt Music and Arts Festival offers first-rate performances over several weekends from late July until Labor Day. Just east lies fast-growing **Medford** (pop 82,000), which has an attractive downtown with an especially impressive selection of craft breweries and distilleries, with Common Block Brewing and Jefferson Spirits leading the way. South along Hwy 99 toward Ashland, stop at the flagship store of **Harry & David**, famous for its massive gourmet baskets, to stock up on fruits, nuts, and candies.

If your relatively brief mingle with the giant trees around Crescent City has piqued your interest, continue down US 101 for a fuller exploration of **Redwood National and State Parks**. Ideally spend a night or two; there are a couple of alluring lodgings in the park, **Elk Meadow Cabins** and the **Historic Requa Inn**, and many more just south in the sea-cliff-perched village of Trinidad (the romantic **Lost Whale Inn** is a stunner) as well as in historic Eureka. Park highlights include **Fern Canyon**, a verdant 80 ft deep gully of hanging gardens that you may recognize from *Jurassic Park 2*. The park fringes a gorgeous 50-mile span of the Pacific Ocean, parts of it flanked by US 101, but I also recommend exploring 9-mile **Coastal Drive**, a well-maintained but partly unpaved scenic loop with dramatic seaside panoramas (keep an eye open for gray whales). South of Klamath, hop onto the 10-mile **Newton B. Drury Scenic Parkway**, which directly bisects an amazing redwood forest. The historic visitor center at **Prairie Creek Redwoods State Park** accesses several short and kid-friendly trails through pristine groves and areas for viewing the park's impressive herd of Roosevelt elk. To the south, just beyond the beachfront **Thomas H. Kuchel Visitor Center** near **Orick**, stop at **Humboldt Lagoons State Park** and rent kayaks for a scenic paddle. US 101 continues south to **Trinidad** with its homey restaurants—such as Trinidad Bay Eatery and the Larrupin Cafe—and the emerald forests and vibrant tidepools at **Patrick's Point State Park**. It then passes through the nonconformist college town of **Arcata** and around big, blue Arcata Bay into **Eureka**, with its Victorian buildings—many with colorful murals—in the adjoining **Old Town** and **Waterfront** districts. A popular family attraction, the excellent **Sequoia Park Zoo** contains a network of elevated walkways through a canopy of redwoods. You'll find terrific seafood restaurants south of the park, such as the stylish, upmarket Salt Fish House in Arcata and the convivial oyster and wine bar Humboldt Bay Provisions in Eureka.

ASHLAND, OR TO BEND, OR

In the shadows of 7533 ft **Mt Ashland** ski area, anchored by the tree-shaded campus of **Southern Oregon University** and famous for the **Oregon Shakespeare Festival**, friendly **Ashland** appeals to outdoorsy types, academics, and artists. The Shakespeare Festival presents 11 plays—some by the Bard and others by Shaw, Ibsen, and contemporary playwrights—from mid-February through mid-November in three beautiful venues in Ashland's attractive downtown, which abounds with sophisticated eateries, wine bars, and B&Bs. The largest theater overlooks 93-acre **Lithia Park**, an enchanting swatch of greenery, paths, gardens, and duck ponds that's named for the mineral springs that gurgle beneath it; you can have a sip from several historic water fountains.

From Medford, follow Hwy 62 about 70 miles through the pine-shaded southern end of the Cascade Mountains to the **Annie Springs Entrance** of Crater Lake National Park. I always pull over about 15 miles before the park for a slice of huckleberry pie at **Beckie's Cafe**, a sweetly intimate roadhouse that's been doling out down-home American fare since the 1920s. **Crater Lake National Park** was designated in 1902 to preserve its central feature—the country's deepest lake (at 1943 ft). It was created by the violent explosion nearly 8000 years ago of Mt Mazama, whose caldera of cliffs now forms the lake's steep shoreline. You can drive scenic 33-mile **Rim Drive** around the lake in two to four hours, depending on how often you stop for photos or hikes. Check out the historic stone-and-timber **Rim Visitor Center** and adjacent **Sinnott Memorial Overlook** for a sweeping view of the lake's surface, nearly 1000 ft below. Then take a narrated cruise around the lake; some of these trips, which all depart from Cleetwood Cove on the north shore, stop at **Wizard Island**, a striking cinder cone that's great for a picnic or a hike to the 755 ft summit.

Keeping in mind that Crater Lake's **North Entrance** closes due to snow from mid-autumn to late spring (at which time you can detour around the park's west side on Hwy 230), it's a relaxing and picturesque 2- to 2.5-hour drive north through to fast-growing **Bend**, which has more than quintupled in population, to more than 111,000, since 1990. Locals and visitors appreciate the sunny, semi-arid climate—famously rainy Oregon is actually quite dry east of the Cascades—and the proximity to myriad forms of recreation, from powdery skiing and snowboarding to mountain-biking, hiking, fishing, rafting, and rock climbing. There are plenty of hotels for every budget, and downtown has great restaurants and—of cities its size—maybe the nation's best craft-brewing scene. Bend's top two attractions are a little south of town: the **High Desert Museum** is set on a pine-dotted 135-acre spread with indoor exhibits and outdoor enclosures that allow an up-close look at the region's wildlife and an understanding of its rich human history. A short drive south is 86 sq mile **Newberry National Volcanic Monument.** Start at the informative **Lava Lands Visitor Center,** driving or hiking to the top of a jet-black cinder cone. Continue south to scramble through 1-mile **Lava River Cave** and for a drive through the heart **Newberry Caldera,** an active shield volcano with miles of trails—the most rewarding one is a quick half-mile jaunt to 80 ft **Paulina Falls.**

SIDETRACK

From Bend you can find spectacular scenery and thrilling opportunities for outdoor fun in every direction. Drive east 85 miles on US 26 to explore the colorful striated badlands of **John Day Fossil Beds National Monument**, which has three units, the closest being the **Painted Hills**. Head north 25 miles on US 97 to see the peaks and canyons of **Smith Rock State Park**, which is bisected by a gorgeous stretch of the Crooked River and is renowned for rock climbing—there are plenty of easy and moderately challenging hiking trails. Finally, drive west 20 miles to the lively ski and mountain town of **Sisters** on the eastern edge of the Cascades. Consider tacking on an extra night or two at the rustic-chic **FivePine Lodge** or a bit farther west at the stylish **Suttle Lodge & Boathouse**, which overlooks a pristine alpine lake and boasts a stellar restaurant. Sisters is also a good overnight stop en route back to Portland, about three hours northwest.

Top Ecola State Park, Cannon Beach *Middle* Jedediah Smith Redwoods State Park, Crescent City *Bottom* Ashland

BEST EATS

- **Buoy Beer Company** The wharfside brewery gastropub in a century-old Astoria warehouse serves seriously delicious ales (I like the fresh Czech Pils) and terrific food—try the beer tempura-battered fish and chips and the grilled bratwurst, and be sure to look through the plexiglass panel floor to admire the sea lions beneath the building. 503-325-4540, buoybeer.com.

- **Castaways** Channel your inner beach bum at this convivial Cannon Beach tiki bar and restaurant that turns out hearty platters of Cajun-seasoned grilled prawns with etouffee sauce, jerk-spiced baby-back ribs with mango-habanero sauce, and other Caribbean- and Creole-inspired fare. Note the potent pineapple-chili margaritas. 503-436-4444, facebook.com/cbcastaways.com.

- **Restaurant Beck** James Beard semifinalist Justin Wills produces tantalizing, gorgeously plated farm- and surf-to-table fare at this understatedly elegant, airy space inside Depoe Bay's chichi Whale Cove Inn. The wine list is superb. 541-765-3220, restaurantbeck.com

- **Local Ocean Seafoods** This contemporary bistro and shellfish market overlooking the boating, fishing, and barking sea lions in Newport's Yaquina Bay is my go-to for razor-clam chowder with a crisp glass of Oregon Pinot Gris, but you'll find always-delicious bigger plates, too: wild king salmon with tomato-saffron sauce and Brazilian-style shellfish stew among them. 541-574-7959, localocean.net.

- **Yachats Brewing** Set in a cool mid-century-modern building remodeled with salvaged timber and wine barrels, this light-filled restaurant leans heavily on the fermentation process not just with its exceptional beers, but also with house-brewed kombucha and kefir sodas and much of its flavorful food—from kimchi rice bowls to pulled pork sandwiches with "probiotic" slaw. 541-547-3884, yachatsbrewing.com.

- **Waterfront Depot** An old wood-frame train station was hauled down the Siuslaw River and converted into this warmly lighted tavern in Old Town Florence. Eclectic Pacific Northwestern fare stars on the menu and might include Caesar salad topped with local Dungeness crab cakes or seared, five-spice-rubbed duck. 541-902-9100, thewaterfrontdepot.com.

- **Redfish** The soaring floor-to-ceiling windows drew me into this modern bistro in tiny Port Orford a few years ago. I marveled at a magnificent sunset, and soon learned that Redfish deserves just as much praise for its well-crafted coastal Oregon fare, from grilled rockfish with hazelnut brown butter to locally sourced lamb burgers with jalapeno jam. 541-366-2200, redfishportorford.com.

- **Pacific Sushi & Grill** One of only a few Asian restaurants along the southern Oregon coast, this inviting Japanese eatery in Brookings is justly known for its fresh and creative sushi rolls and nigiri, but don't overlook the perfectly grilled hanger steak with a bourbon demi-glace and wasabi-mashed potatoes. 541-251-7707, pacificsushi.com.

- **Twisted Cork Wine Bar** An excellent place to get acquainted with the exceptional wines of the Rogue and Umpqua valleys (try a flight for the fullest immersion), this bustling Grants Pass storefront space with a mix of tables and armchairs also serves an extensive roster of shareable tapas, salads, and flatbreads. Save room for a slice of dark-chocolate blackberry Zinfandel cake. 541-295-3094, thetwistedcorkgrantspass.com.

- **Hearsay** Have a seat in the lush garden or the lively piano bar in this convivial restaurant set inside a 1910s church that also contains Ashland's esteemed Oregon Cabaret Theatre. There's an extensive cocktail and wine program, and the kitchen serves creative takes on American classics, from St Louis-style pork ribs to pan-seared Columbia River steelhead. 541-625-0505, hearsayashland.com.

- **Wild Rose Thai** The authentic northern Thai cuisine at this inviting family-run bistro in downtown Bend compares favorably with anything I've eaten in the Pacific Northwest. Specialties include the spicy larb kua, in which rich pork blood is added to the ground pork and belly, and whole game hen steamed with a fragrant yellow curry broth. 541-382-0441, wildrosethai.com.

BEST SLEEPS

- **Cannery Pier Hotel** Set on a wharf that juts out into the Columbia River, this stylish property has waterfront balconies in every one of its 54 spacious rooms. An Aveda spa offers a range of relaxing treatments, and at the base of the pier, Bridgewater Bistro serves stellar contemporary coastal Oregon cuisine. 503-325-4996, cannerypierhotel.com.

- **Inn at Cannon Beach** You're just a block from the sand in Cannon Beach's quieter Tolovana section at this casually upscale retreat comprising cheerful, bungalow-style buildings set around a garden courtyard. Rooms have fireplaces, and homemade cookies in the afternoon and an expansive continental breakfast buffet in the morning are included. 503-436-9085, innatcannonbeach.com.

- **Headlands Coastal Lodge** In the shadows of Cape Kiwanda's towering dunes, this luxurious boutique beach resort is perfect for a night of oceanfront pampering. Just off the inviting lobby, Meridian Restaurant & Bar serves

exceptional farm-to-table cuisine with splendid sunset views. 503-483-3000, headlandslodge.com.

- **Sylvia Beach Hotel** The 20 rooms in this offbeat, literary-themed hotel overlooking the ocean in Newport's Nye Beach are named for noted writers, including Herman Melville, Gertrude Stein, and Oregon's own Beat Generation novelist, Ken Kesey. In the cozy common areas, you can visit the feline innkeeping staff and gaze out at the sea. 541-265-5428, sylviabeachhotel.com.

- **Heceta Head Lighthouse B&B** Although it's a bit of a drive from the nearest town, this secluded six-room inn that occupies the former lightkeeper's residence at Heceta Head Lightstation is utterly romantic and perfect for storm-watching, star-gazing, and getting away from it all. Your stay includes a decadent seven-course breakfast. 541-547-3696, hecetalighthouse.com.

- **Tu' Tun Lodge** A 15-minute drive inland from Gold Beach, this posh 20-room retreat is set on a patch of lawns and gardens that roll down to a beautiful bend in the Rogue River—fly-fishing, jet-boating, kayaking, and stand-up paddle-boarding are among the guest activities. You can also book a riverside massage and sup on rarefied Pacific Northwestern cuisine on the restaurant's tranquil terrace. 541-247-6664, tututun.com.

- **Curly Redwood Lodge** Fashioned out of one single, massive redwood tree, this mid-century-modern motor court in Crescent City is a handy and affordable base for exploring the northern reaches of Redwood National and State Parks. 707-464-2137, curlyredwoodlodge.com.

- **Weasku Inn** This rambling 1920s compound of finely appointed cabins and suites has an ideal location for touring Southern Oregon's wineries or fishing or rafting along the federally designated "Wild and Scenic" Rogue River. Grants Pass, 541-471-8000, weaskuinn.com.

- **Ashland Hills Hotel and Suites** Although it's just off the interstate a bit east of charming downtown Ashland, this rambling 173-room compound has plenty going for it: spacious and reasonably priced rooms with colorful retro-chic furnishings, two tennis courts and a big outdoor pool, and a well-curated market and cafe. The owners operate several other inviting lodgings in the area. 541-482-8310, ashlandhillshotel.com.

- **Crater Lake National Park lodgings** Perched on the rim of the caldera with stunning views, the Crater Lake Lodge was built in 1915 in the classic National Park style. I stayed in one of these cozy, simple rooms that lack air-conditioning one hot summer night, and I still wouldn't have traded the experience for comfier digs elsewhere—there's just nothing like awakening to a perfect view of Crater Lake. It does also book up months in advance, but at least check out the charming public spaces and lobby museum, and try to snag a reservation in the restaurant. Several miles south of the lake but in a pretty wooded glade, the Cabins at Mazama Village are basic but inexpensive. 541-594-2255, craterlakelodges.com.

- **McMenamins Old St Francis School** This funky 60-room hotel fashioned out of a 1930s school building is a short walk from downtown Bend's impressive restaurant scene and the scenic Deschutes River. Intriguing amenities include five eateries and bars, a movie theater, and a soaking pool, and many rooms and suites have kitchenettes and private patios. 541-382-5174, www.mcmenamins.com.

CAMPING

You'll find beautiful, breezy campsites up and down the Oregon coast. Venues with especially spectacular settings include Astoria/Warrenton/Seaside KOA Resort, Short Sand Beach in Oswald West State Park, and Cape Kiwanda State Natural Area on the upper half of the coast. On the lower half, consider Heceta Beach RV Park, Honeyman Memorial State Park, Sunset Bay State Park, Cape Blanco State Park, and Harris Beach State Recreation Area. In Crescent City, Jedediah Smith Campground offers tent and RV sites surrounded by majestic old-growth redwoods. Cantrall Buckley County Park has peaceful camping just outside Jacksonville, and Emigrant Lake County Park has a beautiful setting near Ashland. Crater Lake has a pair of developed campgrounds—neither has lake views, but both enjoy scenic wooded settings. Mazama is the largest and most developed (it has a restaurant and market within walking distance), while smaller Lost Creek Campground is for tents only and has 16 primitive but peaceful sites. Good bets near Bend include Tumalo State Park and Crown Villa RV Resort.

Top Heceta Head Lighthouse B&B

California Highway 1 ★

One of the world's most celebrated scenic roads, Hwy 1 traverses California's long, curving coastline, connecting wild and spectacular stretches of undeveloped sea cliffs and beaches with the storied cities of San Francisco and Los Angeles.

HOW LONG?

7 days; add an extra day each to see more of San Francisco, Monterey Bay, and Los Angeles.

WHEN TO GO

Try to avoid summer or holiday periods, as traffic can slow along the most popular sections, especially Big Sur, and hotel rates are highest. Mid-March to May and September to mid-November offer the best balance of sunny weather and fewer crowds. Winter is prone to intense spells of rain and wind, but the coast can still be entrancing with stormy skies, and hotels are cheaper, especially along the northern half of the route.

NEED TO KNOW

Portions of Hwy 1 in Big Sur and from San Francisco north to Mendocino County are windy, narrow, and slow going; give yourself plenty of time, take frequent breaks, and avoid driving after dark or in heavy rain. On weekends, especially in summer, reserve hotels at least a few days in advance.

→ Distances

Total distance, one-way: 700 mi (1127 km)
- Leggett to Point Reyes Station: 185 mi (298 km)
- Point Reyes Station to Carmel-by-the-Sea: 160 mi (257 km)
- Carmel-by-the-Sea to San Luis Obispo: 135 mi (217 km)
- San Luis Obispo to Los Angeles: 200 mi (322 km)

ⓘ Daytime Temperatures

January: 55-70°F (13-21°C)
July: 67-85°F (19-29°C)

ⓘ More information

- Mendocino tourism, visitmendocino.com
- Marin County tourism, visitmarin.org
- San Francisco tourism, sftravel.com
- Santa Cruz tourism, santacruz.org
- Monterey tourism, seemonterey.com
- San Luis Obispo tourism, slocal.com
- Santa Barbara tourism, santabarbaraca.com
- Los Angeles tourism, discoverlosangeles.com

◉ SNAPSHOT

With its forever coastal vistas, precipitous sea cliffs, boisterous sea lion colonies, and heady mix of laid-back surfer towns and sophisticated culinary hubs, California's Hwy 1 is the most celebrated scenic road in North America and perhaps the apogee of early-20th-century road and bridge engineering. Even when it's flooded with dawdling drivers, it's still possible—with a little effort—to find tranquil trails and wooded roadside overlooks where you can commune with nature. Coastal California also abounds with amazing purveyors of food, wine, craft beer, and artisan coffee, so you can expect to dine well on this magical journey.

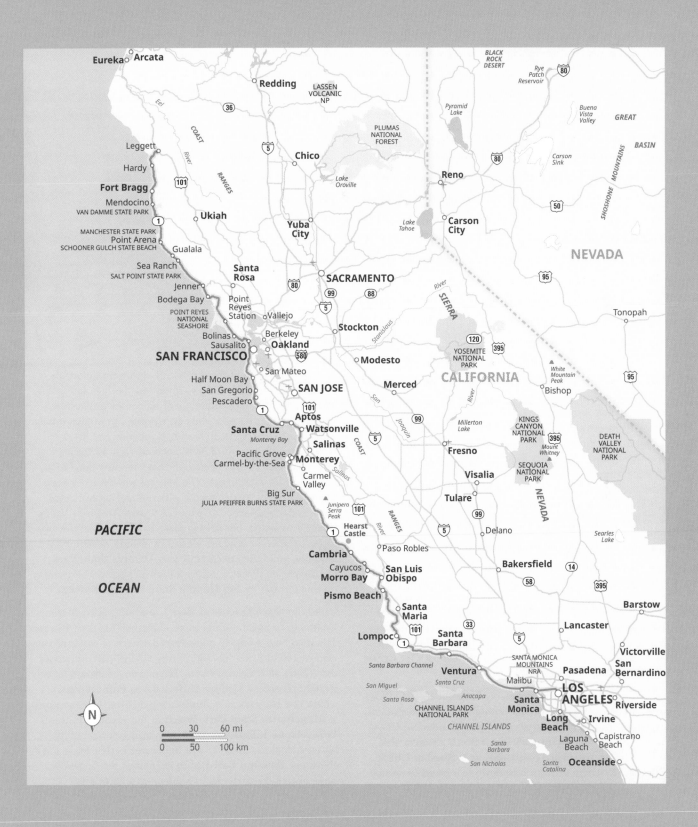

LEGGETT TO POINT REYES STATION

The famous twists and turns of Hwy 1 are nowhere more dramatic than in remote Mendocino County, from its start beneath the redwoods at the junction with US 101 in tiny **Leggett** to its first glimpse of ocean near **Hardy Rock** and continuing down into **Fort Bragg**. In Leggett, stop for a classic California photo op by driving through the hole that's been carved into the base of **Chandelier Tree**, an ancient 276 ft tall redwood. A narrow ribbon of blacktop lined with lush greenery and skirting atop dramatic headlands, Hwy 1 climbs, banks, and zigzags for 45 miles to Fort Bragg, which has a wealth of hotels and services. Explore the downtown of this former lumber and transportation center, visiting the cool little **Sea Glass Museum**. Fort Bragg has one of the highest concentrations of sea glass in the world, largely because in the early 20th century the town's **Glass Beach** served as a landfill (you can visit the beach, just off Noyo Point Road, but removing sea glass is prohibited). You'll also find some great little spots for snacking, including Cowlick's Ice Cream and Headlands Coffeehouse.

As you head south to the impossibly beautiful coastal village of **Mendocino**, stop for a walk through stands of magnolias, camellias, and rhododendrons at 47-acre **Mendocino Coast Botanic Gardens**. **Point Cabrillo** is worth a stop to visit its handsome, red-roofed lighthouse, as is **Russian Gulch State Park**, where you can hike down to a gorgeous swatch

of sand with views of the ocean and up toward gracefully arcing Russian Gulch Bridge, which was built in late 1930s and is one of the most dramatic of numerous bridges that you'll drive over on your journey. Upscale but unpretentious Mendocino sits atop steep seaside headlands and has a picturesque downtown of New England–style Victorian buildings. It's convincing enough that the town stood in as Crabapple Cove, Maine, in the beloved whodunit TV series *Murder She Wrote*. With inviting galleries and sophisticated eateries that showcase the wines of nearby Anderson Valley, this is a romantic, bewitching place to spend a night or two. Opportunities for outdoor adventure abound, whether it's kayaking amid the sea caves of **Van Damme State Park** or scampering through pygmy forests and down a series of marine terraces at **Jug Handle State Natural Reserve**.

I find the next 130 miles of Hwy 1 south to coastal Marin County to be just as—if not more—breathtaking than Big Sur. The road hugs a largely undeveloped stretch of coastline that's interrupted by just a handful of tiny villages. After crossing the Albion and Navarro rivers, Hwy 1 runs along a relatively straight section of high sea cliffs down to **Point Arena**, where you can walk in solitude along driftwood-strewn sands at **Manchester State Park Beach** or out around 115 ft tall **Point Arena Lighthouse** and its dramatic coastal bluffs. A bit farther, at the north end of **Schooner Gulch State Park**, check out **Bowling Ball Beach**, so named for its strange array of round sedimentary boulders, or concretions.

At the Sonoma County line, the road soon enters **Gualala** (pop 2100), where at Trinks you can stop for an espresso, a slice of berry cobbler, or a sandwich to enjoy on the patio. Set in a striking wood-and-glass building, the **Gualala Arts Center** has beautiful gardens and presents engaging exhibits; it's also home to the superb Dolphin Gallery & Gift Shop. A few miles south in the planned resort community of **Sea Ranch**, stop for a contemplative stroll around and inside **Sea Ranch Chapel**, a remarkable nondenominational structure built from copper and redwood in 1984 to resemble a seashell. Hwy 1 soon passes **Kruse Rhododendron State Natural Reserve**, where you can stretch your legs on a serene 2.3-mile loop trail that's especially dramatic during the mid-April to mid-June blooming season but is lovely year-round, with its stands of Douglas fir, redwoods, and tanbark oak trees.

For the next 20 miles, Hwy 1 is a bit of a rollercoaster, and a wonderfully scenic one at that, as it plunges down around beautiful coves and climbs over emerald meadows where extremely happy-looking dairy cows graze. **Gerstle Cove** at **Salt Point State Park** is a favorite stop for tidepooling, and at **Fort Ross State Historic Park** you can view a reconstructed wood-frame chapel and other distinctive buildings that relate to the Russian fur-trading settlement that stood here in the early 19th century. You'll soon come to the cute coastal village of **Jenner** at the mouth of the Russian River, where you can watch sea lions rolling about beneath **Jenner Point Lookout**. Savor a light breakfast or lunch from one of the waterfront Adirondack chairs at Cafe Aquatica, or rent sea kayaks for a paddle around the river. The road continues along sweeping headlands that could easily pass for northern Scotland before passing through **Bodega Bay**, whose sweet, innocuous demeanor contrasted perfectly with the terror that Alfred Hitchcock unleashed upon it in his horror masterpiece *The Birds*. Overlooking the bay, casual Spud Point Crab Company is a must for rich clam chowder and Dungeness crab sandwiches.

Crossing into Marin County, Hwy 1 fringes the picturesque eastern shore of **Tomales Bay**—famous for its oyster farms and restaurants, among them Hog Island Oyster Company and the Marshall Store—on its way into the amiable village of **Point Reyes Station**, the gateway to breathtaking **Point Reyes National Seashore**, which spreads out over a 71,028-acre peninsula that's geographically demarcated from the mainland by a pronounced span of the famously jittery San

Andreas Fault. Pick up picnic supplies at the venerable Cowgirl Creamery Barn Shop & Cantina or trendy Side Street Kitchen and give yourself at least a couple of hours to drive all the way to the end of the Point Reyes Seashore's stunning Sir Francis Drake Boulevard, where you can make the short trek out along the 150 ft cliffs of **Chimney Rock**, a fantastic perch for observing whales offshore (most commonly during the January to mid-April migratory season) and viewing barking elephant seals on the beach below. You can get a nice little workout by descending the 313 steps to the visitor center and observation deck at famed 1870 **Point Reyes Lighthouse**. Other highlights of this rugged cape dotted with stands of Bishop pine and Douglas fir include **Tomales Point**, a great place for viewing tule elk, and **Abbotts Lagoon**, an idyllic spot for birdwatching.

POINT REYES STATION TO CARMEL-BY-THE-SEA

The route continues through mesmerizing coastal scenery of the insular arts community of **Bolinas**, surfing and kite-flying at offbeat **Stinson Beach**, and the sweeping slopes of **Mt Tamalpais State Park**. Hwy 1 then climbs inland; here you'll pass **Muir Woods National Monument**, which though famous for its redwoods, is prone to crowding and requires reservations. I recommend skipping it and continuing through the tony town of **Sausalito** to the **Marin Headlands** for a drive along Conzelman Rd, where you can stop at several overlooks for awe-inspiring views of Golden Gate Bridge and the San Francisco skyline. If time allows, follow the road through this section of **Golden Gate National Recreation Area** to visit beautiful **Black Sands** and **Rodeo** beaches, the Project Space exhibits at **Headlands Center for the Arts**, the **Point Bonita Lighthouse**, and the miles of trails around historic **Fort Barry** and **Fort Baker**. Then continue south across the **Golden Gate Bridge** into one of the world's most alluring cities.

Hwy 1 meanders south from San Francisco through the **Pedro Point Headlands** and Tom Lantos Tunnels, and then alongside steep sea cliffs en route to **Half Moon Bay**, an oceanfront community of about 13,000 that's close enough to both San Francisco and Silicon Valley to be a commuter suburb but so picturesque and laid-back that it feels miles away from the city. Both **Francis** and **Poplar** beaches are lovely places to curl your toes in the sand. Hwy 1 curves south and then east around the lower end of the San Francisco Peninsula. You'll find myriad magical beaches along this largely undeveloped 50-mile stretch, from **San Gregorio** at the north end to **Año Nuevo State Park** in the

Opposite Hearst Castle *Previous* Bixby Creek Bridge, Big Sur

City View
San Francisco

Hwy 1 passes directly through this peninsular city famed for its colorfully painted Victorian homes, mind-bogglingly steep streets, deliciously diverse food, and notoriously fickle weather. Even if you're just zipping through on your way down the coast, there's both gorgeous natural scenery and captivating cultural attractions within a stone's throw of Hwy 1. If you're able to spend a night or two, you can really immerse yourself in the city, seeing iconic sights like Alcatraz Island, Coit Tower, and The Exploratorium, with its engaging interactive kid-friendly exhibits.

Car-friendly rating: Fair. If you stick to the Hwy 1 corridor or even the western two-thirds of the city—keeping roughly west of Van Ness Ave—San Francisco is relatively easy to navigate by car. This side of the city has a fair amount of street and lot parking, and the few lodgings often have reasonably priced or even free parking. East of Van Ness—which includes Union Square, the Financial District, and SoMa—is another story entirely: street parking is hard to come by, garage and hotel parking is costly, and traffic can be maddening. Fortunately, the city's extensive BART subway and MUNI bus, light rail, streetcar, and cable car networks are highly efficient for exploring this part of the city.

What to see in a day: From the Golden Gate Bridge, exit into the northern end of the Presidio, the nearly 1500-acre hub of **San Francisco National Park at Golden Gate** that served as a military base from 1776 until it was decommissioned and transferred to the National Park Service in 1994. The engaging diversions here are many: lazing on the beach at **Crissy Field**, enjoying the videos and movie memorabilia at **Walt Disney Family Museum**, viewing the dozens of stately old military buildings, and wandering through the lushly landscaped 23-acre campus of George Lucas's **Letterman Digital Arts Center**. Continue south to Geary Blvd, and turn right to reach **Lands End** for a walk along its cypress-dotted **Coastal Trail**, which offers a different vantage point for photographing the Golden Gate Bridge, the fascinating ruins of **Sutro Baths**, and a nifty contemporary visitor center. Then drive south along the long beachfront to the western edge of **Golden Gate Park**, a long, rectangular patch of greenery that includes the **San Francisco Botanical Garden** and **Conservatory of Flowers**, which are musts for nature lovers. The park's first-rate cultural institutions include the LEED-Platinum-certified **California Academy of Sciences**, which contains four different attractions, an aquarium, natural history museum, rainforest, and planetarium; and the distinctive, copper-shrouded **de Young Museum**, whose collections specialize in African and Oceanic art. Take the elevator to the museum's ninth-floor observatory for a great view of the park. The surrounding **Richmond** and **Sunset** districts are home to some of the city's best international restaurants: try buzzy Burma Superstar for fragrant curries and stir-fries, Fiorella for mouthwatering wood-fired pizzas and pastas, and no-frills San Tung Chinese for spicy dry-fried chicken wings (I've decided the brusque service is actually part of the charm). Save room for a scoop of black sesame or miso caramel ice cream at Polly Ann.

Where to stay: Although most of the city's hotels are downtown, there are several good options in the western half of the city, closer to Hwy 1, including the historic and upscale **Lodge at Presidio** and **Inn at Presidio** within San Francisco National Park at Golden Gate. The **Laurel Inn** is a stylish boutique hotel set in lovely Pacific Heights; many of its casually chic rooms have kitchenettes. In the heart of the LGBTQ-popular Castro District, **Beck's Motor Lodge** is a smartly renovated, budget-friendly, midcentury-modern motel with free parking.

The Castro

middle to **Scott Creek** and **Bonny Dune** down near Santa Cruz. The secluded ranching village of **Pescadero** is worth a quick visit, especially if you're hungry; since 1894, old-school Duarte's Tavern has been serving hearty Portuguese-American food—creamy artichoke soup is a specialty.

The easygoing surfing and college town of **Santa Cruz** sits at the northern end of Monterey Bay and offers an engaging mix of attractions for every age. There's the retro-fun **Santa Cruz Beach Boardwalk**, where you can ride such iconic amusements as an 1890s Looff Carousel with an original 342-pipe organ and the Giant Dipper, a massive wooden roller coaster built in 1924. Nearby you can walk out to the end of 2745 ft **Santa Cruz Wharf** (the West Coast's longest pier) to peruse the colorful souvenir shops and seafood shacks and admire the sea lions barking down below. Then drive or walk along Cliff Dr to visit the great little **Santa Cruz Surfing Museum**, which documents the area's 140-year love affair with this now-ubiquitous sport—appropriately, it overlooks world-famous Steamer Lane, where you'll see talented surfers testing their mettle against a roaring surf. Bustling downtown Santa Cruz abounds with one-of-a-kind shops and eateries as well as the excellent **Santa Cruz Museum of Art and History**, and on the west side of town, a cool little food-and-drink sector is growing up along **Swift St** and includes excellent Santa Cruz Mountain Brewing and Venus Spirits Tasting Room. For the best scenery, continue south on the local coastal roads through charming **Capitola** and **Aptos** rather than Hwy 1, which is a modern freeway from Santa Cruz to **Watsonville**.

At the southern end of the bay, the Spanish Colonial city of **Monterey**—a former fishing and shipping hub—shares a dramatic, rocky peninsula with the exclusive resort community of Pacific Grove. If you have even a modest interest in marine life, set aside a couple of hours for **Monterey Bay Aquarium**, which is one of the world's foremost and contains more than 200 exhibits plus interactive touch tanks that are a hit with young children. However, the aquarium is expensive, a bit crowded and surrounded by touristy **Cannery Row**, so if you're not moved to visit (or you've already been), don't feel bad about breezing through and following the local streets to **Pacific Grove**. Here you can motor along legendary **17-mile Drive**, noting the $10.50 fee (it's free to bicyclists). The road is a stunner, as it curves around **Cypress Point** and beside the fairways of the world-famous golf courses of **Pebble Beach**, but I often skip this, too, given that plenty of breathtaking (and free) coastal scenery lies ahead.

Drive south into one of the most enchanting little villages on the West Coast, **Carmel-by-the-Sea**. Walk along **Ocean Avenue**, which is lined with swanky boutiques, rarefied winery tasting rooms, and elegant eateries set inside cozy Tudor-style cottages with lush courtyards. Relax on the sugary white sands of beautiful **Carmel Beach**, and then drive or walk south along **Scenic Road**, which curls around the peninsula past the Frank Lloyd Wright–designed Clinton Walker House and beside uncrowded **Carmel River Beach**, and then inland to stately 1797 **Carmel Mission Basilica**, which has gardens and a fine museum. Note the turnoff east on Hwy G16 into **Carmel Valley**—this sunny and swanky community is worth a brief inland detour if you're a fan of Monterey County's exceptional wines. There are some 40 tasting rooms, among them **Holman Ranch** and **Folktale**, not to mention several acclaimed restaurants and ultra-posh inns, favorites being **Bernardus Lodge and Spa** and **Carmel Valley Ranch**.

CARMEL-BY-THE-SEA TO SAN LUIS OBISPO

Just south of Carmel and **Point Lobos State Natural Reserve**, where you can hike through stands of colorful cypress trees to a sheltered teal-hued cove, Hwy 1 enters iconic **Big Sur**, which is the name of both an 80-mile stretch of virtually unspoiled coastline and a miniscule unincorporated village in the heart of it. It took engineers and laborers about 20 years—ending in 1937—to build the two-lane stretch of Hwy 1 through this corridor of 1000-plus-ft sea cliffs and untrammeled beaches. The road itself is Big Sur's key attraction, and the joy of experiencing it lies in stopping at designated pullouts to take in the million-dollar views and embarking on short or quite extensive hikes in the many parks along the route. There are dozens of memorable waysides—some favorites include **Garrapata State Park**, where you can hike a 1.8-mile, wildflower-strewn loop to Soberanes Point; and 715 ft long **Bixby Creek Bridge**, a graceful, much-photographed 1932 structure that rises some 300 ft above an emerald canyon. At **Pfeiffer Beach**, you can hike the nearly 2-mile Valley View Trail and amble along the sheltered sands for a clear view of Keyhole Arch, a curious rock formation through which the sun sometimes peeks dramatically before sunset. And in **Julia Pfeiffer Burns State Park**, be sure to make the easy half-mile jaunt to view McWay Falls, which flows over an 80 ft cliff down to the pristine beach below. Note that along the northern stretch of Big Sur, you'll pass a handful of celebrated spots for cliff-top lunch or a sunset dinner, such as Nepenthe, once owned by Orson Welles and Rita Hayworth and now known for its incredible ocean views and delicious Ambrosia Burgers, and the glass-walled restaurant at the super posh Post Ranch Inn.

At the south end of Big Sur, a few miles before you reach pint-sized **San Simeon**, stop at **Elephant Seal Vista Point** at Piedras Blancas, so named for the throngs of 5000-pound elephant seals that frolic, grunt, laze, and swim along a roughly half-mile stretch of sand. At San Simeon, look north into the surrounding hills to behold the soaring twin turrets of one of the largest and most renowned residential buildings in the country, **Hearst Castle**, which publishing magnate William Randolph Hearst commissioned architect Julia Morgan to construct over about three decades, ending in 1947. An array of guided tours offer an up-close glimpse of this amazing 115-room mansion and its extensive grounds, all of which are now operated by California's division of state parks; the Grand Rooms tour is my favorite for getting a full sense of the estate.

Hwy 1 then passes through **Cambria**, with its many appealing beach hotels, fun tidepooling on Moonstone Beach at **Leffingwell Landing Park**, and an inviting pine-shaded downtown with several good restaurants, including Linn's, where you'll want to pause for a slice of olallieberry-apple pie. If you're not too sugared out when you get to the genial village of **Cayucos**, with its striking 1872 pier, pop inside

the Brown Butter Cookie Company to pick up a bag of what I consider to be the world's most sublimely delicious sugar cookies. In Morro Bay, snap a photo of 576 ft tall **Morro Rock**, perhaps while feasting on fresh seafood at one of the bay-front eateries—Tognazzini's Dockside, known for delicious fish and chips, is a standout. Hwy 1 then cuts inland 15 miles to **San Luis Obispo** (*see* California Wine Country chapter p. 67), where it joins with US 101 and enters **Pismo Beach**. Here you can book a horseback ride at **Pismo Preserve** or drive out around **Avila Beach** to **Point San Luis Lighthouse**.

SAN LUIS OBISPO, CA TO LOS ANGELES, CA

At Pismo Beach, Hwy 1 separates from US 101 and passes through a series of small towns—the most prominent being **Lompoc**, a small winemaking hub and gateway to Vandenberg Air Force Base—before again rejoining US 101 and fringing the south-central California Coast into the historic and monied enclave of **Santa Barbara** (*see* California Wine Country chapter p. 67). At a minimum, enjoy a meal at one of the breezy waterfront restaurants, such as the Boathouse at Hendry's Beach or Brophy Bros, and go for a walk along **East Beach** or out to the end of **Stearns Wharf**. Visible less than

25 miles offshore lies one of the West Coast's most underrated treasures, **Channel Islands National Park**, which comprises five unspoiled islands. Although the only part of this park you can drive to is the **Robert J. Lagomarsino Visitor Center** in the easygoing beach town of Ventura, consider booking one of the several cruises out to the islands through **Island Packers** or a kayaking excursion with **Santa Barbara Adventure Company**. In downtown **Ventura**, go window-shopping among the cool antiques and vintage shops that line Main Street.

Follow Hwy 1 south through downtown **Oxnard** and then to where it rejoins the coast at **Point Mugu** at the western edge of the **Santa Monica Mountains National Recreation Area,** a 156,000-acre tract of mountain and coastal parks and preserves that helps keep LA's ruthless sprawl in check. The road edges the coastline and offers several appealing stops for beachcombing, including uncrowded Point Mugu Beach and—on the west side of the celebrity-studded beach town of **Malibu**—El Matador Beach, which is famous for its cool beach boulders and sea stacks. You've now entered the western reaches of America's second largest metropolis, Los Angeles. Hwy 1 continues beneath the rarefied campus of **Pepperdine University**, through affluent **Malibu Village**, and past the see-and-be-seen sands of **Malibu Lagoon State Beach.** Appealing eateries abound: you can walk out to the end of Malibu Pier for lunch at trendy Malibu Farm Pier Cafe or sup on amazing sushi at one of the ultimate A-lister haunts in town, Nobu, inside the sleekly elegant **Nobu Ryokan Malibu** resort.

Continue east to one of the great cultural treasures of the coast, the **Getty Villa**, whose collection contains nearly 50,000 Roman, Greek, and Etruscan antiquities—it's the cousin of the newer Richard Meier–designed **Getty Center**, which exhibits masterworks from the past 400 years, 15 miles away in the hills above **Brentwood**. The road soon enters **Pacific Palisades** and runs alongside **Will Rogers State Beach**, a stretch of sand famous with everyone from aspiring models and actors to LGBTQ folks, before entering the LA-adjacent city of **Santa Monica**. Here you can walk out on arguably the most famous pier in California (it's appeared in countless movies, including *Forrest Gump* and *The Sting*), and kids love riding on the solar-powered Ferris wheel and thrilling rollercoaster before viewing creatures in the terrific little **Heal the Bay Aquarium**. Head just inland to Santa Monica's attractive downtown, where you can shop for fresh produce and light meals at the popular farmers' market (held Wednesday and Saturday mornings) in the car-free **Third Street Promenade**.

SIDETRACK

From LA, Hwy 1 continues 45 miles south through Orange County to Capistrano Beach, where it ends at I-5. If you started this trip way up north in Leggett and you're a completist, then by all means drive this final stretch. It passes through some inviting towns and is also a gateway for venturing inland to **Disneyland** and **Anaheim**'s other theme parks. But I typically skip this final stretch of Hwy 1, which is mostly four lanes, has lots of traffic signals, and offers less natural scenery. Even where it hugs the coast—for 10 miles in **Huntington Beach** as well as stretches of Laguna Beach—it's still a fairly commercial road. These drawbacks notwithstanding, it does offer some cool diversions. In the underrated LA County city of **Long Beach** (pop 467,000), cut away from Hwy 1 to visit the lively downtown, which is home to the outstanding **Aquarium of the Pacific**, the terminal for ferries out to beautiful **Catalina Island**, and the *Queen Mary*, a stately 1930s ocean liner. It's presently undergoing renovations but is expected to resume operations as a hotel with restaurants and below-deck tours. Sweeping, beautiful beaches with world-class surfing line the route through coastal Orange County, with the charming downtown of artsy **Laguna Beach** a standout for gallery-hopping and oceanfront dining on breezy terraces at hip restaurants like Splashes and The Cliff. You'll also find some snazzy spa resorts in these parts, such as **Montage Laguna Beach** and Dana Point's **Waldorf Astoria Monarch Beach**. The route ends just beyond lovely **Doheny Beach State Park**, with its scenic boardwalk and trails. Just 4 miles up Del Obispo Street, the famed **Mission San Juan Capistrano** was the first of nine California 18th-century missions established by Father Junípero Serro. The mission and the surrounding town are known for the orange-tailed cliff swallows, which arrive here by the thousands in early spring after having wintered in Argentina.

Opposite Cows grazing on the Sonoma Coast

City View
Los Angeles

Sprawling across roughly 500 sq miles, LA is the home of America's entertainment industry and the site of countless instantly recognizable attractions—the Hollywood sign, Griffith Observatory, Rodeo Drive in Beverly Hills, the Venice Beach Boardwalk. Fully explorable by car and packed with diversions, it's a perfect place to end this road trip, whether you have a few hours or a few days.

Car-friendly rating: Good. Laced by freeways and abundant with street, garage, and valet parking, LA was designed with the automobile in mind and continues to be one of the country's most car-centric places. The main drawback is that the sheer number of people and cars results in often daunting traffic jams, especially at rush hour but potentially any time of day or night. Also, most hotels do charge for parking, although it's usually less costly than in more densely settled cities.

What to see in a day: Deciding where to devote your energy in LA can feel overwhelming, especially if you have only a day or two. Given the significant distances between neighborhoods and likelihood of traffic, it's smart to focus on one area each day, perhaps **Hollywood** with its film industry-related attractions (the **Hollywood Walk of Fame**, the **Paramount Pictures** studio tour, the **Hollywood Museum**) if you're a movie buff or **Mid-Wilshire** (home to the **LA County Museum of Art**, **Petersen Automotive Museum**, and **La Brea Tar Pits**) if you're more of a culture vulture. Another option, especially if you're planning to continue into Orange County, is following Hwy 1 south through the colorful coastal neighborhoods and towns of **Venice Beach**, **Manhattan Beach**, and **Redondo Beach**, then cutting south and west along Palos Verdes Drive around the exclusive and beautiful **Palos Verdes Peninsula**, and ending at the excellent **Cabrillo Marine Aquarium** in **San Pedro**.

Where to stay: Unless you're planning to spend extra days in Los Angeles proper, in which case you might consider a more central lodging, like the opulent and historic **Millennium Biltmore** or the ultra-stylish **Ace Hotel**, it makes the most sense to stay in a coastal neighborhood or adjacent town. In Santa Monica, consider the intimate **Palihouse** or the posh **Shutters on the Beach**. The hip **Hotel Erwin** is a fun option steps from the beach and boardwalk in Venice, while the trendy **Beach House** is a favorite accommodation near the pier in laid-back Hermosa Beach.

Top Skateboarder at Venice Beach *Bottom* Griffith Park and Observatory is a short drive from Hollywood

BEST EATS

- **Trillium Cafe** Set in a fetching clapboard house in Mendocino, this casually sophisticated farm-to-table restaurant serves exquisite lunch and dinner fare in an airy dining room or aromatic garden. Three cozy guest rooms are available for overnight stays. 707-937-3200, trilliummendocino.com.

- **Harbor House Inn** Book ahead at this intimate ocean-view dining room helmed by young Michelin-starred chef Matthew Kammerer, who presents daily-changing multicourse tasting menus that showcase the local bounty of coastal Mendocino County. The inn has 11 lovely rooms and cottages. Elk, 707-877-3203, theharborhouseinn.com.

- **Hog Island Oyster Company** From the picnic tables of this famous shellfish purveyor's oyster bar near Point Reyes National Seashore, you can soak up grand views of Tomales Bay, the very source of the bivalves that appear on the menu—try them raw or barbecued before tucking into a plate of halibut crudo or local cheeses with fig jam. 415-663-9218, hogislandoysters.com.

- **Dad's Luncheonette** Kids love eating in this bright-red caboose in Half Moon Bay, and discerning adults appreciate the amazing food prepared by a celebrated chef who honed his craft at San Francisco's esteemed Saison. The short menu features local and organic fare, including burgers topped with a soft egg and herb salads with Meyer lemon vinaigrette. 650-560-9832, dadsluncheonette.com.

- **Shadowbrook** Getting to this romantic 1947 restaurant overlooking a creek just east of Santa Cruz is part of the fun: you descend a steep hillside in a small funicular. Steaks and local seafood grills star on the menu, and there's an extensive wine list. Capitola, 831-475-1511, shadowbrook-capitola.com.

- **Phil's Fish Market** Fragrant seafood cioppino and fire-roasted artichokes with aioli have long been a great reason to pull off Hwy 1 for a meal at this unassuming market and eatery with views of sea lions and otters gamboling in the waves of Monterey Bay. Moss Landing, 831-633-2152, philsfishmarket.com.

- **Wild Fish** Sustainable seafood, from house-smoked sablefish to whole-roasted rockfish with chimichurri, is the name of the game at this charming, contemporary bistro on Pacific Grove's restaurant row. Save room for the sticky toffee pudding. 831-373-8523, wild-fish.com.

- **Big Sur Taphouse** With an enchanting patio nestled beneath a canopy of leafy trees in Big Sur, this roadhouse is a reasonably priced option for tacos, cheesesteaks, barbecue pulled-pork sandwiches, and other well-prepared comfort fare. Note the extensive wine and craft-beer selection and the deli proffering tasty picnic supplies. 831-667-2197, bigsurtaphouse.com.

- **Madeline's** At this romantic candlelit Cambria dining room, sample the restaurant's own well-crafted wines; there's a second tasting room by Moonstone Beach at the Cambria Shores Inn. Lunches and dinners feature French-influenced California fare, such as pan-seared lamb porterhouse with a Dijon beurre blanc. 805-927-4175, madelinescambria.com.

- **Caruso's** For a magical meal of refined Italian cooking with views that evoke the Italian Riviera, take a seat overlooking the sea at this chic, open-air restaurant at Santa Barbara's chichi Rosewood Miramar Beach hotel. 805-900-8388, rosewoodhotels.com.

- **Cassia** This chic spot in downtown Santa Monica serves contemporary Vietnamese, Thai, and Chinese food using local, mostly organic ingredients. Consider raw spicy scallops with dried shrimp and chili oil, followed by grilled lamb breast seasoned with Sichuan peppercorns, sambal, and sesame sauce. 310-393-6699, cassiala.com.

Top A cottage at Nick's Cove, in Marin County

BEST SLEEPS

- **Little River Inn** With a splendid bluff-top setting overlooking Mendocino's Van Damme State Beach, a beautifully designed golf course, and an inviting restaurant with a well-curated local wine list, this 1930s mini-resort has 65 rooms that range from cheerfully simple to quite cushy. Tennis courts, a spa, and hiking trails round out the amenities. 707-937-5942, littleriverinn.com.

- **Wildflower Boutique Motel** Steps from Point Arena's historic movie theater and acclaimed Bird Cafe, this attractive eco-chic motel features organic bedding, breakfasts with local produce and cheeses, and universal car chargers. 707-207-6665, wildflowermotel.com

- **Timber Cove Resort** This tranquil and secluded 46-room hotel in Jenner is set along a breathtaking 25-acre headland on the Sonoma Coast. The vibe is decidedly vintage cool, right down to the Crosley LP players and vinyl records, pour-over coffee setups, and old-school Smeg refrigerators in each room. 707-847-3231, timbercoveresort.com.

- **Nick's Cove Cottages** It's a joy awakening to views of peaceful Tomales Bay and the northern tip of Point Reyes from the stylishly converted fishing cottages—each with wood-burning fireplaces and heated ceramic floors—at this romantic hideaway on the Sonoma-Marin border. I love dining in the hunting lodge-inspired restaurant and oyster bar. 415-663-1033, nickscove.com.

- **Beach House** This airy, three-story oceanfront hotel in Half Moon Bay has spacious suites with sitting areas, fireplaces, and either balconies or patios—most face the water. With free parking and a convenient Hwy 1 location, it's a good base for day trips into San Francisco. 650-712-0220, beach-house.com.

- **Chaminade Resort** Enjoy the peaceful setting, spacious rooms, first-rate restaurant, and extensive amenities at this contemporary, family-welcoming resort on a 300-acre hilltop compound in Santa Cruz. Hike on the property's wooded trails, swim in the pool, play bocce ball or disc golf on the lawn, or relax with a treatment in the spa. 831-475-5600, chaminade.com.

- **Tickle Pink Inn** A few miles south of Point Lobos State Natural Reserve at the northern edge of Big Sur, this casually elegant 35-room inn sits high on a hilltop and has well-appointed rooms with ocean-view balconies. Watch the glorious sunsets during the complimentary wine and cheese hour. 831-624-1244, ticklepinkinn.com.

- **White Water** Across the street from Cambria's spectacular Moonstone Beach and boardwalk, this sleek boutique lodge has spacious, sophisticated rooms and offers free bike loaners to pedal around town. 805-927-1066, whitewatercambria.com.

- **Anderson Inn** From your balcony at this intimate, upscale boutique inn, enjoy views of Morro Bay and the sea lions, harbor seals, and otters cavorting in the surf. Premium rooms have gas fireplaces and jetted tubs, and several popular restaurants are within walking distance. 805-772-3434, andersoninnmorrobay.com

- **Madonna Inn** All 110 rooms at this legendary, family-friendly 1950s motor lodge in San Luis Obispo have over-the-top themes and colorful, often campy furnishings—favorites include the Alps-inspired Austrian Suite and the Caveman, with animal-print fabrics, stone walls, and a rock waterfall shower. Amenities include a large pool and sundeck, a day spa, and a retro-swanky steakhouse and cocktail bar. 805-543-3000, madonnainn.com.

- **Kimpton Canary Hotel** Set amid the Spanish Colonial-style buildings of historic downtown Santa Barbara, this posh Mediterranean-inspired hotel has 97 smartly appointed rooms and a sweet roof deck and pool with views of the ocean and Santa Ynez Mountains. Finch & Fork restaurant serves exceptional modern American food. 805-884-8153, canarysantabarbara.com

---

CAMPING

The good news for camping enthusiasts is that there are dozens of absolutely stunning locales along Hwy 1, from pristine parks to cool glamping compounds like Treebones Resort in Big Sur and AutoCamp, a collection of vintage Airstreams in western Sonoma County's Russian River. The bad news is that campgrounds can be fully booked weeks in advance in summer and on weekends, so reserve as early as possible. Here's a sampling of memorable places to sleep under the stars: Mendocino Headlands is set on dramatic sea cliffs within walking distance of downtown, while farther down the coast, you'll find lovely settings at Gualala Point Regional Park, Sonoma Coast State Park, Wright's Beach, and Tomales Bay State Park (adjacent to Point Reyes National Seashore). Along the Central Coast, favorites include Santa Cruz North/Costanoa KOA near Año Nuevo State Park, Pfeiffer Big Sur, Kirk Creek toward the southern end of Big Sur, San Simeon Creek near Hearst Castle, Morro Bay State Park, Gaviota State Beach near Santa Barbara, and Sycamore Canyon near Malibu.

Opposite Vineyards at sunrise, Paso Robles

California Wine Country ★

Napa and Sonoma are indeed delightful places to sip vino, but they're just two exemplary spots on this tour through California's spectacularly scenic and diverse wine regions.

HOW LONG?

7 days; add an extra day each to see more of Santa Barbara, Oakland and Berkeley, or Santa Rosa and Healdsburg.

WHEN TO GO

Given that summer can be pricey, busy, and sometimes hot in the inland valleys, this region is most pleasant March to May and September to November. Barrel-tasting weekends add to the fun in spring, while harvest weekends and grape stomps are a tradition in the fall. Winter can be cool and damp, but also a time for more personal and relaxed tasting room experiences and good hotel deals.

NEED TO KNOW

It goes without saying that driving while tasting is dangerous and, when your blood-alcohol level exceeds .08%, illegal. Consider hiring a guide if visiting a lot of wineries, and remember that spitting out your wine during a tasting is completely acceptable—in fact, it's what most of the pros do.

→ Distances
Total distance, one-way: 550 mi (885 km)
- Santa Barbara to Paso Robles: 125 mi (201 km)
- Paso Robles to Oakland: 215 mi (346 km)
- Oakland to Calistoga: 100 mi (161 km)
- Calistoga to Philo: 95 mi (153 km)

Daytime Temperatures
January: 58-65°F (14-18°C)
July: 75-90°F (24-32°C)

More information
- Santa Barbara tourism, santabarbaraca.com
- San Luis Obispo tourism, slocal.com
- Monterey tourism, seemonterey.com
- San Jose tourism, sanjose.org
- Oakland tourism, visitoakland.com
- Berkeley tourism, visitberkeley.com
- Sonoma tourism, sonomacounty.com
- Napa tourism, visitnapavalley.com
- Mendocino tourism, visitmendocino.com

◉ SNAPSHOT

When it comes to winemaking, California's sweet spots are its valleys just inland from the coast, where ocean breezes, dry weather, cool nights, and hot summer days provide perfect growing conditions. This verdant, undulating terrain, which is dotted with hundreds of tasting rooms, is also gorgeous to drive through. And from Mendocino County down to Santa Barbara, you'll find world-class restaurants, bakeries, and cafes in communities large and small.

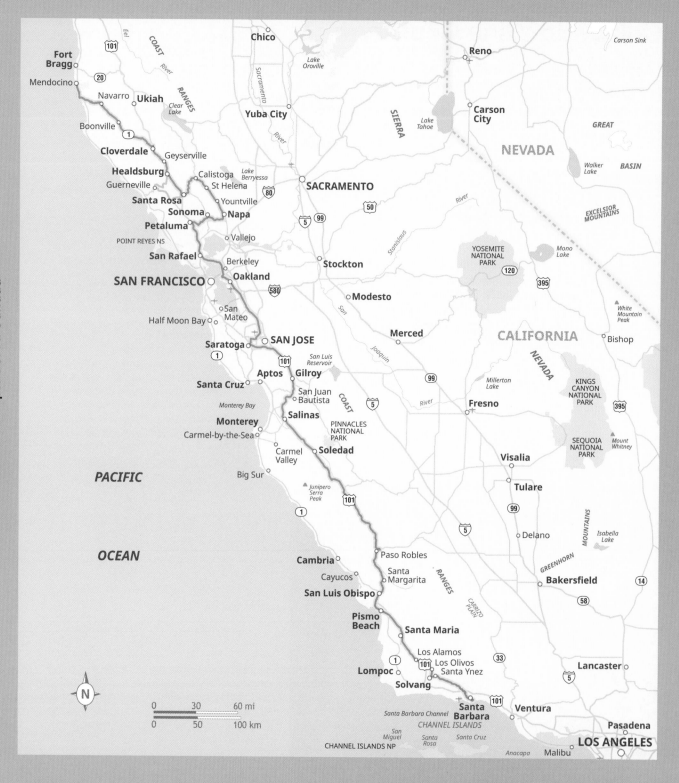

SANTA BARBARA TO PASO ROBLES

Outside of Napa and Sonoma, **Santa Barbara County** is California's most celebrated wine region. Its reputation skyrocketed in 2004 following the popularity of the cult movie *Sideways*, and in recent years, this affluent south-facing coastal region just 100 miles from Los Angeles has become only more desirable as a place to live and vacation. Most of the county's 200 wineries are in the hilly agrarian towns to the north and west, but a growing crop of often young and experimental winemakers have opened facilities in **Santa Barbara** itself, especially in the trendy **Funk Zone**, a roughly 10-block quadrant of food-related businesses nestled between downtown and the **West Beach** waterfront. It's home to venerable venues like Loquita for Spanish food, Figueroa Mountain Brewing for craft ales, and Helena Avenue Bakery for brunch and coffee. And the neighborhood's tasting rooms, such as **Margerum**, **Riverbench**, and **Jaffurs**, showcase the Pinot Noirs, Chardonnays, Rieslings, and Rhone wines that are a specialty of this region with breezy, foggy coastal vineyards that are perfectly suited to growing cooler-weather grapes as well as warmer inland areas that excel with heat-happy, fuller-body Syrahs, Grenaches, and Cabernet Sauvignons.

As you venture deeper into the county's wine country, stop to walk around the garden grounds and late-18th-century adobe buildings of **Mission Santa Barbara**, which contains a phenomenal art collection as well as a beautiful altar and tabernacle made by Indigenous Chumash inhabitants. Next set aside an hour or so for an amble around the 78-acre **Santa Barbara Botanic Garden**, which is nestled in the foothills of the Santa Ynez Mountains—I like walking up to the contemporary Pritzlaff Conservation Center, which has rotating art exhibits and panoramic ocean views. Then take scenic Hwy 154 northwest, stopping for lunch at the Cold Spring Tavern, an antiques-filled 1860s stagecoach stop serving hearty comfort fare.

Shortly after passing the curvaceous shore of **Cachuma Lake**, you'll enter the heart of Santa Barbara's wine country, which centers on **Los Olivos**, **Santa Ynez**, and—with colorful timber-stucco buildings, windmills, and shops that evoke the community's Danish heritage—**Solvang**. Treat yourself to a custard-filled kringle at Olsen's Danish Village Bakery before checking out Solvang's tasting rooms. Much of *Sideways* was filmed here, and most key sites—like **Sanford** and **Fess Parker** wineries and the old-school Hitching Post II steakhouse—are still going strong. Charming Los Olivos has

a bounty of exceptional tasting rooms—including **Stolpman** and **Carhartt Family Wines**—within walking distance as well as several appealing eateries, such as Los Olivos Cafe and Wine Merchant and Panino gourmet sandwich shop. There's also great dining in nearby **Los Alamos**, an old-fashioned Western-style ranching town that has morphed into a lauded restaurant destination—check out Bob's Well Bread bakery, Full of Life Flatbread, and the upscale French bistro Bell's. Continuing north toward the small city of **Santa Maria**, bypass US 101 and instead drive along Zaca Station and Foxen Canyon roads to explore several stunning wine estates. With glorious grounds and first-rate wines, **Zaca Mesa** (favoring Rhone wines) and **Foxen Vineyards** (amazing Pinot Noir and Chenin Blanc) are two of the best.

From Santa Maria, follow US 101 into **San Luis Obispo County**, whose winegrowing prowess has exploded over the past 25 years. Head north on Hwy 227 in **Arroyo Grande**, and then east on Biddle Ranch Rd to reach Orcutt Rd— **Wolff** and **Edna Valley** wineries are a couple of stellar spots with patios that offer dazzling vistas of the sunny surrounding hills. Continue into downtown **San Luis Obispo** (aka SLO), which is famous for its Thursday night farmers' market and offers a wealth of excellent restaurants. To sample mouthwatering oak-wood-smoked tri-tip beef barbecue, a delicacy of the Central Coast, snag a table at the sleek **Old San Luis BBQ**.

Follow US 101 as it climbs steeply over 1530 ft **Cuesta Pass** toward Paso Robles, stopping in miniscule **Santa Margarita** for a tasting at superb **Ancient Peaks Winery**. Across the street, take an exhilarating zip line tour at **Margarita Adventures** for a bird's-eye view of the area's vineyards. About 25 miles north, **Paso Robles** has a varied terroir and generally warm climate that's ideal for turning out exceptional Cabernet Sauvignon, Zinfandel, Merlot, and Petite Sirah, as well as Italian-style wines. Many of the top vineyards—there are more than 200—are in the gently rolling **Westside** hills on and around Hwy 46. They include beautiful **Halter Ranch**, Zinfandel-focused **Peachy Canyon**, and venerable **Adelaida**, a Paso Robles pioneer that launched back in 1981. For enjoyable wine-touring on foot, park near gracious **City Park** and pop inside a few downtown tasting rooms, such as **LXV**, a stylish, art-filled space founded by India transplants Kunal and Neeta Mittal, and **Justin**, a highly respected maker of expressive Bordeaux-style wines.

PASO ROBLES TO OAKLAND

Follow US 101 north through the vast and arid **Salinas Valley**, passing through eastern Monterey County's renowned **Santa Lucia Highlands** wine country. Most of the county's tasting rooms are in the coastal downtowns of **Carmel-by-the-Sea** and **Monterey** (*see* California Highway 1 chapter p. 56), but you will find a handful of excellent wine estates in this rural, arid valley, especially around **Soledad**—top-rated vintners here with lovely patios include **Hahn Estate** and **Wrath Wines**.

You'll soon reach small, prosaic **Salinas**, which has undergone a bit of a renaissance of late and has long been associated with celebrated author and native son John Steinbeck, who set his most famous novels—*East of Eden, Of Mice and Men*—in the Salinas Valley. Explore his legacy through the archives and exhibits at the **National Steinbeck Center** and enjoy lunch in the Steinbeck House Restaurant, an elegant turreted Queen Anne Victorian that the author grew up in. You can also detour northwest about 30 miles to **Aptos** to visit some of the excellent **Santa Cruz County**

vintners that thrive amid cool ocean breezes of the **Corralitos Wine Trail**, a highlight of which is **Storrs Winery**, where you can luxuriate on the patio or play bocce while savoring a glass of Chardonnay or Pinot Noir.

US 101 snakes north from Salinas past **San Juan Bautista**, where you can explore the largest of California's (it appeared famously in Hitchcock's *Vertigo*) and the buildings that make up **San Juan Bautista State Historic Park**. When you reach **Gilroy**, roll down the windows and inhale deeply through your nose: yup, that's garlic you smell. The "Garlic Capital of the World" produces the majority of the country's garlic and hosts the famous Gilroy Garlic Festival each July. Stop by the stinky-delicious **Garlic World** store to stock up on garlic-infused oils, dips, olives, and other gourmet goods.

Just south of San Jose, turn west onto Hwy 85 to reach one of the state's better kept winemaking secrets, the **Santa Cruz Mountains**, which are centered around the dapper town of **Saratoga** and are, to the surprise of even many who live in adjacent tech-driven **Silicon Valley**, one of California's oldest wine regions. Legendary French vintner Paul Masson bought nearly 600 acres on the site of what is now **Mt Eden Vineyards**, and today you'll find a dozen or so accomplished wine operations in the area. Other good stops include **Cooper-Garrod Estate**, an organic vineyard on a farm that's been in the same family since 1893, and—nearby in the foothills above Cupertino—**Ridge Vineyards**, which also produces fine Cabernet Sauvignon and Zinfandel in Sonoma County. Saratoga's other great draw is peaceful **Hakone Japanese Gardens**, which was built in 1917.

Make your way down into **San Jose**, the state's third largest city. Stop for a nosh among the stellar vendors at **San Pedro Square Market** before spending a head-scratching hour or two touring the **Winchester Mystery House**, a bizarre 160-room Victorian mansion with false staircases, dark hallways, 37 fireplaces, and plenty of other confounding features. And if time allows, also check out the excellent **Rosicrucian Egyptian Museum.**

Next head 40 miles up I-880 to **Oakland**, a vibrant and diverse city of around 425,000, and a hub of creativity, in part because of its lower cost of living—at least compared with crazy-expensive San Francisco across the bay—makes it attractive to entrepreneurs and artists. There's much to see around the **Jack London Square** waterfront, once a magnet of mostly forgettable chain restaurants that has recently transformed into a hub of legit restaurants, hip drinkeries, and buzzy urban wineries, among them Crooked City Cider Tap House, Brooklyn West Winery, and the vegan soul food spot Souley. Farther afield, neighborhoods like **Rockridge**, **Piedmont Ave**, and **Temescal** showcase Oakland's white-hot food and retail scenes.

SIDETRACK

From Soledad, it's a 12-mile drive via Hwy 146 through rolling, sun-kissed fields to the west side of **Pinnacles National Park**, an underrated 26,600-acre park that's famous for its jagged volcanic peaks and talus caves. From the park's west entrance, in just a few hours you can hike the **Balconies Cliffs**, **Juniper Canyon**, and **High Peaks** trails, and in a full day you can make it over to the stunning vistas on the park's east side, along with **Bear Gulch Cave**. Note that the park's two sides are divided by steep terrain and aren't connected by road; the east entrance, which accesses the main **Pinnacles Visitor Center**, is reached by paved roads south or north around the park, or if you're feeling adventurous, you can take unpaved but well-maintained and incredibly scenic La Gloria Rd across the northern edge of the park to Hwy 25. Unless you're spending a night in the area (lodging options are few and generally pretty basic), it makes the most sense to explore the park from just the western side.

Park road, Pinnacles National Park *Opposite* Epiphany Cellars tasting room, in Los Olivos, Santa Barbara County

OAKLAND TO CALISTOGA

Due north of Oakland, the smaller but similarly hilly East Bay city of **Berkeley** is one of the pillars of America's late-20th-century culinary revolution. Alice Waters, the iconic chef-proprietor of still-thriving Chez Panisse, helped introduce the now ubiquitous concept of locally sourced, artfully presented, farm-to-table cuisine. Her restaurant on Shattuck Ave, a few blocks from the leafy campus of prestigious **University of California Berkeley**, became the focal point of the **Gourmet Ghetto**, a food-revered neighborhood that remains a mecca for culinary adventurers. Still-beloved neighbors include Saul's Delicatessen, with

its savory Jewish deli favorites, and the Cheese Board, a cult favorite for fine cheeses and baked goods as well as delectable pizzas topped with seasonal local veggies. Before leaving town, go for a walk around the colorful and fragrant **UC Botanical Garden at Berkeley**.

Follow I-580 west over the Richmond Bridge to US 101, and head north to **Petaluma**, the southern portal to the **Sonoma Wine Country**, an 1800 sq mile tract of world-renowned wineries. With more than 60,000 acres of planted vineyards that produce first-rate versions of just about every major type of wine—from Albariño to Zinfandel—the **Sonoma Valley** is an oenophile's wonderland. Petaluma's charming, all-American downtown—featured in films like *Peggy Sue Got Married*, *American Graffiti*, and *Pleasantville*—abounds with great eateries. Drop by Stockhome to browse sleek Scandinavian housewares and fill up on Swedish-inspired street food or Della Fattoria Downtown for ethereal baked goods, then continue east along Hwy 116 across the undulating grassy hills north of San Pablo Bay, and then north up Hwy 12 to the sophisticated little town of **Sonoma**. It's anchored by a gracious plaza and **Mission San Francisco de Solano**, site of the 1846 Bear Flag Revolt, which led to California's brief (25-day) stint as a sovereign, if never formally recognized, republic. Built in 1823, it's also the last and northernmost of the state's Spanish missions. You can tour some of the country's oldest and most venerable wineries east of town, including **Buena Vista** and **Gundlach Bundschu**, which both date to 1857.

From Sonoma follow Hwy 12, stopping for fried chicken and waffles, a barbecue brisket sandwich, or a Mexican chocolate milkshake on the patio of cheerful Lou's Luncheonette, before continuing into **Napa**, the seat of **Napa County**, which has more than 400 wineries and produces some of the world's finest vinos—Cabernet Sauvignon and Chardonnay are the standouts here. Napa has a deserved reputation for uber posh resorts (**Auberge du Soleil**, **Bardessono**, **Solage**), Michelin-star restaurants (including La Toque, Kenzo, and Thomas Keller's renowned French Laundry), and spendy wineries with cult followings (**Screaming Eagle**, **Harlan Estate**, and **Grace Family Vineyards**). I'm partial to country drives and low-key, intimate tasting rooms, so I tend to bypass the valley's main route, busy and somewhat overdeveloped Hwy 29, in favor of the slower and more scenic **Silverado Trail**, which was laid out in the 19th century as a trail for silver miners. First, though, have a walk around pretty downtown Napa, and stop for a bite to eat among the trendy eateries at **Oxbow Public Market**, which include Gott's

Roadside for burgers, the Fatted Calf for charcuterie, and Anette's Chocolates for artisanal truffles and brittles.

Follow the Silverado Trail north through the eastern foothills of **Yountville, Rutherford,** and **St Helena.** Notable wine-tasting experiences along this route include stone-walled **Krupp Brothers,** which produces critically adored Viognier and Bordeaux red blends, and **Mumm,** a standout for its crisp, complex sparkling wines. You'll soon reach captivating **Calistoga,** which feels less commercial and more relaxed than, if still every bit as monied as, the rest of Napa Valley. It also offers an enticement beyond great wine: curative mineral springs, of which you can partake at several local spas and hotels. Sadly, a number of the area's wineries and several famous hotels (**Calistoga Ranch, Meadowood**) were lost in the Glass Fire of 2020. Many stellar wineries still excel here, however, including **Castello di Amorosa,** which is modeled after a 13th-century Tuscan castle and produces nicely balanced Italian-varietal wines, and **Tank Garage,** which occupies a smartly restored 1930s service station and is as known for its artful, outré wine labels as for the precious liquids inside the bottles.

CALISTOGA TO PHILO

The final leg of the trip leads you from Calistoga back into Sonoma County via rural and winding Petrified Forest and Calistoga roads. **Santa Rosa,** the region's largest city, features a pleasant downtown and a wealth of excellent restaurants, hotels, and tasting rooms. Turn south and follow Hwy 12 several miles to experience the pastoral wine estates of **Kenwood** and **Glen Ellen–Benziger,** with the added bonus of visiting with cute farm animals, and **Kunde Family Winery,** which offers a hike-and-tasting package. Then stretch your legs with a longer trek on the trails at **Jack London State Historic Park,** which preserves buildings that the noted writer and adventurer lived in during the early 1900s. Back in Santa Rosa, tour the lush gardens and greenhouses of **Luther Burbank Home** and **Gardens** and check out the **Charles M. Schulz Museum,** which is dedicated to the *Peanuts* creator and contains dozens of original comic strips.

Just north of Santa Rosa and anchored by a picture-perfect, tree-shaded plaza surrounded by upscale cafes, fine galleries, and elegant tasting rooms, **Healdsburg** has a touch of Napa's fancy vibe but with a slightly mellower personality. Excellent wineries in town include highly regarded Zinfandel makers **Seghesio** and **Stephen & Walker.** Order a scoop of Thai tea ice cream or a peach–brown-butter cupcake at Noble Folk,

before heading up US 101 through the prestigious **Dry Creek Valley,** home to venerable wine estates like **Passalacqua** and **Francis Ford Coppola** (check out the cool displays of the director's film memorabilia).

After passing through charming and easygoing **Geyserville** and **Cloverdale,** pick up Hwy 128, a picturesque, winding road that meanders up into **Mendocino County's** sunny **Anderson Valley.** A number of talented vintners, including the sensational sparkling wine producers **Roederer Estate** and **Scharffenberger,** have turned this region into one of the state's most exciting wine destinations. A wide range of wines are produced here, including Petite Sirah (try **Lee's Theopolis Vineyards**), Alsace-style Gewürztraminer (**Navarro Vineyards** is a good bet), and—most notably—Pinot Noir (consider **Drew Family Cellars** and **Baxter**). My favorite way to enjoy a visit here: order a cheese plate on the patio overlooking acres of colorful gardens and vineyards at picturesque **Goldeneye** estate.

Opposite top Full moon over the High Peaks, Pinnacles National Park *Opposite bottom* Tasting at Buena Vista Winery, Sonoma

BEST EATS

- **Yoichi's** Seven-course, kaiseki-style feasts of exquisite Japanese fare, with seafood flown in from Tokyo's famed Tsukiji Market, draw foodies to this stone bungalow in downtown Santa Barbara. Even more impressive than the well-chosen wine list is the selection of fine sakes. 805-962-6627, yoichis.com.

- **S.Y. Kitchen** The farm-fresh northern Italian food—roasted cauliflower with burrata and salsa verde, salmon puttanesca—pairs perfectly with Santa Barbara County's Mediterranean vibe and terroir-driven wines. The owners also run the terrific Nella Kitchen & Bar in Los Olivos. Santa Ynez, 805-691-9794, sykitchen.com.

- **Ember** This inviting Arroyo Grande bistro with a rustic wood-beam interior is run by Chez Panisse alum Brian Collins, who turns out phenomenal shishito pepper-sweet corn pizzas, blackened albacore, and filet mignon from a wood-fired oven. You'll also find one of the best cocktail lists in San Luis Obispo County. 805-474-7700, emberwoodfire.com.

- **La Cosecha** With sidewalk tables overlooking Paso Robles' City Park, this Latin American-Spanish restaurant serves consistently superb farm-to-table cuisine, including pan-seared scallops with a Manchego cheese sauce. 805-237-0019, lacosechabr.com.

- **Sidecar Modern Tavern** Amid the swanky expense-account restaurants in the Silicon Valley foothills, this chill neighborhood spot with plush seating specializes in inventive cocktails, boozy weekend brunches, and delish international tapas. Los Gatos, 408-399-5180, sidecar7.com.

- **Mago** Oakland's diversity shines through in its remarkably varied food scene. Case in point, this airy, contemporary Colombian restaurant on lively Piedmont Avenue. The menu changes weekly but might feature arepas with ancho-braised chicken or sturgeon glazed with black garlic and pumpkin seeds. 510-344-7214, magorestaurant.com.

- **Fish & Bird Sousaku Izakaya** On the downtown side of Berkeley's Gourmet Ghetto, this casually trendy go-to for Japanese bar food has a superb cocktail program. The panko-crusted shrimp "burger" with shiso ume tartar sauce is a revelation. 510-705-1539, fishbirdizakaya.com.

- **The Girl & the Fig** Sandra Bernstein's country French restaurant on Sonoma's gorgeous plaza has been an exemplar of California Wine Country dining since it opened in the late '90s. Tuck into classics like pastis-scented moules-frites and duck confit with bacon and roasted Brussels sprouts. 707-938-3634, thegirlandthefig.

- **Gran Electrica** Begun in Brooklyn and specializing in boldly conceived modern Mexican cuisine—queso fundido with poblanos and huitlacoche, tequila-battered Ensenada fish tacos—this cool space in bustling downtown Napa boasts acclaimed wine and mezcal lists. 707-258-1313, granelectrica.com.

- **Pizzeria Tra Vigne** Fabulous fig-gorgonzola and capicola-sausage pizzas are the pride of this beloved trattoria in Napa Valley's St Helena, but don't overlook the bountiful salads and hearty pastas. On warm days, dine on the pet-friendly, hedge-lined patio. 707-967-9999, pizzeriatravigne.com.

- **Valette** With a mission to showcase Sonoma's amazing produce, game, and wine, this stylish Healdsburg bistro is perfect for a romantic evening. Start with house-cured charcuterie and local cheeses before graduating to crispy-skinned striped bass or honey-brined pork Porterhouse. 707-473-0946, valettehealdsburg.com.

- **Catelli's** You'll find perfectly prepared red-sauce favorites like spaghetti and clams and chicken piccata at this Geyserville restaurant opened in 1936 by Italian immigrants. The reasonably priced list of Sonoma wines is superb. 707-857-7142, mycatelllis.com.

- **Albion River Inn** For a special ending to a day of Anderson Valley wine-touring, drive out to Hwy 1 for an incredible meal at this dapper country inn overlooking Albion Cove. A James Beard Award-winning chef prepares sublime locally sourced fare, with an emphasis on seafood. 707-937-1919, albionriverinn.com.

BEST SLEEPS

- **Hotel Californian** This opulent 1925 Spanish Colonial grande dame reopened in 2017 after years of neglect with a gorgeous Moroccan-inspired look. Steps from the Santa Barbara Funk Zone, the 121-room property has a cushy spa and a snazzy rooftop pool and bar with panoramic ocean and mountain views. 805-882-0100, hotelcalifornian.com.

- **Ballard Inn** Famed for its vaunted Gathering Table Restaurant (book well ahead for a meal here), this rambling, upscale hideaway is in the heart of the Santa Ynez Valley Wine Country; many of the 15 rooms have fireplaces and balconies. Ballard, 805-688-7770, ballardinn.com.

- **Skyview** This unassuming mid-century-modern motel in food-centric Los Alamos, an easy hop from the wineries of Los Olivos and Foxen Valley, has been given a cool update, with custom-designed furnishings and textiles, a terrific restaurant with patio seating and valley views, and a heated pool that begs you to linger. 805-344-0104, skyviewlosalamos.com.

- **Hotel Cerro** Highlights of this 65-room retreat include a gorgeous rooftop pool, a soothing spa, and great location in downtown San Luis Obispo near the famed Thursday-evening farmers' market. Stellar SLO Brasserie specializes in French-California coastal cuisine. 805-548-1000, hotelcerro.com.

- **Stables Inn** In leafy downtown Paso Robles, this handsomely retrofitted mid-century-modern motel offers 19 sleek rooms with whitewashed walls and modern Western-style decor; larger bunkhouse rooms are perfect for families. The same owners run the posh Hotel Cheval. 805-296-3636, stablesinnpaso.com.

- **Inn at the Pinnacles** Enjoy peace, quiet, and magical sunsets at this secluded six-room B&B on the western edge of Pinnacles National Park and surrounded by 160-acre Brosseau Vineyard. Soledad, 831-678-2400, innatthepinnacles.com.

- **Inn at Saratoga** The airy, spacious rooms at this stylish Tapestry Collection by Hilton property have balconies overlooking leafy Wildwood Park and Saratoga Creek. Historic downtown Saratoga's tony shops and eateries are within a short walk. 408-867-5020, innatsaratoga.com.

- **Claremont Club and Spa, a Fairmont Hotel** Near the Oakland border in Berkeley's picturesque Claremont Hills, this venerable 1915 hotel with a distinctive turret (it has its own suite with a private outdoor deck) exudes charm. Play tennis, enjoy a treatment in the spa, or relax over a leisurely brunch on the deck of Limewood Restaurant. 510-843-3000, fairmont.com.

- **MacArthur Place** Serene pathways wind through the 6 acres of flowering trees and fragrant gardens at this unfussy but classy boutique resort in downtown Sonoma. It's home to one of the region's loveliest spas and most inviting hotel restaurants. 707-938-2929, macarthurplace.com.

- **Archer Hotel Napa** The 183 rooms at this upmarket, contemporary hotel are decorated with soothing natural wood and porcelain materials and have pebble-stone showers. The rooftop bar has sweeping views of the surrounding hills, and just off the lobby, Charlie Palmer Steak is a carnivore's delight. 707-690-9800, archerhotel.com.

- **Indian Springs Calistoga** Soak in the curative mineral pools, fed by four natural thermal geysers, during your stay at this historic Mission Revival-style compound spread across 17 pastoral acres in northern Napa Valley. A beautifully designed spa offers an array of treatments. 707-709-8139, indianspringscalistoga.com.

- **Kenwood Inn and Spa** With a perfect location for exploring the many exceptional wineries of Kenwood and Glen Ellen, this classic Mediterranean-style retreat has 29 rooms and suites with fireplaces, plush featherbeds, and private patios or balconies. Swim or soak in the two palm-shaded pools and enjoy an extensive complimentary full breakfast each morning. 707-833-1293, kenwoodinn.com.

- **Farmhouse Inn** Even by the snazzy standards of Sonoma County, this 25-room hotel on the edge of the Russian River Valley stands out for its sheer cushiness and its Michelin-star restaurant. Accommodations have vaulted ceilings, giant fireplaces, jetted tubs, and saunas or steam showers. Forestville, 707-887-3300, farmhouseinn.com.

- **The Madrones** Comprising two distinct accommodations—the classically plush Guest Quarters suites and the secluded, redwood-shaded Brambles cabins—this tranquil Anderson Valley retreat is also home to three small-batch wineries and a superb restaurant, Wickson. 707-895-2955, themadrones.com.

CAMPING

California's wine regions offer a number of rustic-chic glamping spots, including El Capitan Canyon in Santa Barbara, Mendocino Grove near the Anderson Valley, Wildhaven Sonoma in Healdsburg, Autocamp in the Russian River, and Safari West in Santa Rosa, which has luxury tents on a 400-acre preserve with hundreds of wild animals. You'll find plenty of more conventional venues with tent sites, too. Consider Cachuma Lake Recreation Area outside Santa Barbara, Paso Robles RV Ranch & Campground in northern San Luis Obispo County, San Francisco North/Petaluma KOA and Sugarloaf Ridge State Park in Sonoma County, and Robert Louis Stevenson State Park in northern Napa County.

Jack London Square and marina, Oakland

California's Sierras ★

Home to the loftiest mountain peaks in the contiguous US as well as the deep-blue majesty of Lake Tahoe, interior California abounds with thrilling natural wonders, from Yosemite's Half Dome to the massive trees of Sequoia National Park.

HOW LONG?

7 days; add an extra day each to see more of Sequoia and Kings Canyon, Yosemite, and Lassen Volcanic national parks, and Lake Tahoe.

WHEN TO GO

Early June, by which time Lassen Volcanic's main road and Yosemite's Glacier Point (and often Tioga Road) have usually reopened, offers a perfect sweet spot of clear and sunny skies and relatively few crowds. Autumn can be just as alluring but is also prone to wildfires. Intense crowds, steep hotel rates, and fires are three reasons to avoid summer. Conversely, winter is gorgeous but snowy, which is great for skiing in Tahoe and Mammoth Lakes but results in limited access to parts of national parks.

NEED TO KNOW

Yosemite implemented a reservation system to limit crowds in 2021 and may make this a permanent feature, so check these policies in advance. In winter, always carry chains, extra food and blankets, and a first-aid kit when driving to and around Tahoe or in the mountains.

➜ Distances
Total distance, one-way: 1000 mi (1609 km)
- Bakersfield to Kings Canyon NP: 150 mi (241 km)
- Kings Canyon NP to Yosemite NP: 190 mi (306 km)
- Placerville to Lassen Volcanic NP: 205 mi (330 km)
- Lassen Volcanic NP to South Lake Tahoe: 185 mi (298 km)
- South Lake Tahoe to Mammoth Lakes: 140 mi (225 km)

🌡 Daytime Temperatures
January: 40-60°F (4-16°C)
July: 80-95°F (27-35°C)

ⓘ More information
- Sequoia and Kings Canyon National Park, nps.gov/seki
- Yosemite National Park, nps.gov/yose
- Gold Country tourism, visitgoldcountry.com
- Lassen Volcanic National Park, nps.gov/lavo
- North Lake Tahoe tourism, gotahoenorth.com
- South Lake Tahoe tourism, tahoesouth.com
- Mammoth Lakes tourism, visitmammoth.com

👁 SNAPSHOT

About California's high Sierra Mountains the great naturalist John Muir wrote, "Climb the mountains and get their good tidings. Nature's peace will flow into you as sunshine into trees." Throughout the 1880s, Muir's campaigns to protect the region's natural beauty would help to spur the designation of Yosemite National Park. A journey through inland California reveals not only the jaw-dropping vistas of Yosemite but countless other rugged mountainscapes and azure-hued alpine waters, from Sequoia and Lassen Volcanic national parks to the festive year-round recreation hubs of Lake Tahoe and Mammoth Lakes.

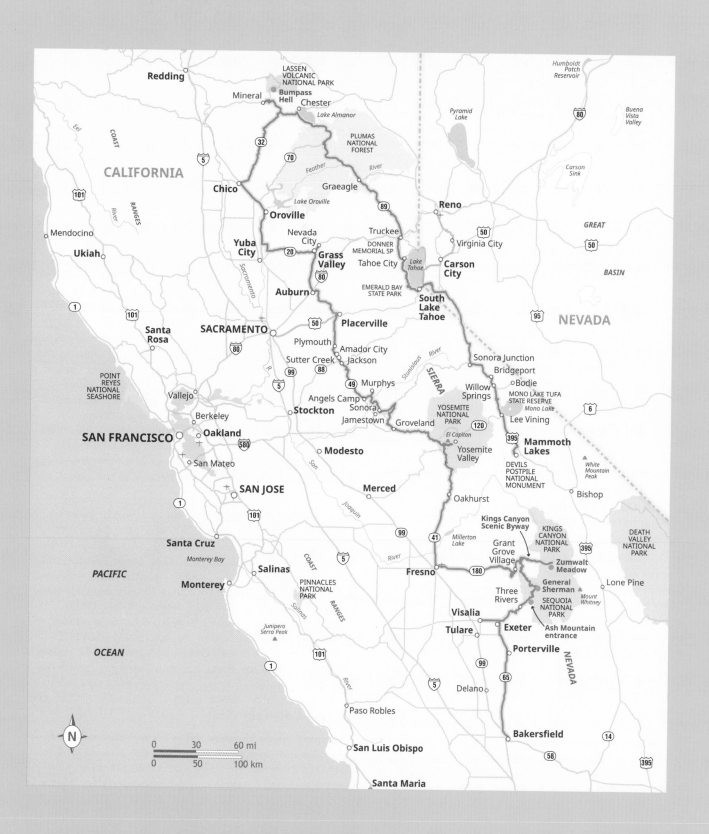

BAKERSFIELD, CA TO YOSEMITE NATIONAL PARK, CA

With a mid-size airport served by all major airlines and a convenient location at the southern end of central California's vast San Joaquin Valley, sunny **Bakersfield** is ideal for beginning this drive. I confess to usually wanting to hightail it to the mountains, but I always enjoy myself when I make the effort to explore this underrated city of about 400,000. Bisected by the Kern River, many of Bakersfield's best attractions are along this meandering waterway, including the excellent **California Area Living Museum**—where you can see barn owls, bobcats, San Joaquin kit foxes, and other native animals along with gardens and natural history exhibits—and the impressive open-air **Kern County Museum**, which contains more than 50 historic buildings that tell the story of the Central California Valley.

I suggest the scenic route north through the picturesque east side of the valley, up Hwy 65, through **Porterville** and **Exeter**, which has several noteworthy antiques shops as well as about 30 downtown buildings painted with colorful murals that depict the region's rich agricultural heritage. A popular and attractive base for exploring the Sierras, **Visalia** has a number of reasonably priced chain hotels and a historic, walkable downtown with a striking 1930s Spanish Mission-style **Fox Theatre** and several fine food and drink options, including convivial Sequoia Brewing and casual Quesadilla Gorilla, which is beloved for its fast, filling, and creative Mexican fare. Head east on Hwy 198 through the foothills village of **Three Rivers** to the Ash Mountain Entrance of **Sequoia National Park**. Although Sequoia and adjacent Kings Canyon are technically two separate parks, they're administered as one, and the $35 admission is good for both.

The park's main road, Generals Highway climbs through a series of dramatic curves and switchbacks into a landscape dominated by the world's largest trees. In October 2021 my partner and I hiked among these humungous sequoias hours before authorities closed the park in order to fight the devastating KNP Complex wildfire. Although it and the Windy Fire of 2020 caused extensive damage (nearly 20% of the world's sequia trees were destroyed) the park still contains thousands of these incredible trees, which can reach heights of over 300 ft and widths of 100 ft—the oldest ones have been alive for more than 3000 years. They're slightly shorter than California's coastal redwoods (which top out around 380 ft), but they have greater masses, weighing as much as 2.7 million pounds (or about the weight of 45 adult gray whales). About midway into the park, make the signed right-hand turn for the short road to **Moro Rock**—this half-mile trail leads up

370 steps to the domed 6725 ft peak of this awesome granite monolith, affording some of the grandest views in the Sierras. Along this same side road, drive through the famed **Tunnel Log**, a fallen sequoia with a car-size opening carved in its massive trunk. Back on Generals Highway, stop by the **Giant Forest Museum**, which occupies a 1928 former market building and contains engaging exhibits on the park's ecology, and then venture out for a hike along the interpretative trails that meander through the **Giant Forest**. A short drive north, hike the 1.3-mile loop to the park's most imposing tree, **General Sherman**, which has a whopping 36.5 ft diameter and rises 275 ft above the forest floor.

Continue another 30 miles north to **Kings Canyon National Park**, stopping in **Grant Grove Village** to get a park overview at the visitor center and stroll through the 130 acres of sequoias, a highlight of which is the hulking **General Grant Tree** (which is even thicker than General Sherman at its base). To get a full perspective on this park's glacially carved canyon—which is even deeper than the Grand Canyon—drive the 30-mile section of Hwy 180 known as the **Kings Canyon Scenic Byway**, taking in sweeping vistas of sheer rock cliffs and rushing rivers and cascades. There are numerous pullouts, including **Junction View Overlook** and **Canyon View**, before the road ends at glorious **Zumwalt Meadows**, where a 1.5-mile round-trip trek offers breathtaking views of wildflower-dotted meadows and the frothy Kings River. Allow about two to three hours round-trip for this drive, depending on how many stops you make.

Follow Hwy 180 west out of the park and down through the western Sierra Nevada into the San Joaquin Valley's largest city, **Fresno** (pop 538,000), which has the region's best selection of budget- and mid-priced hotels. Explore the cool eateries and shops of the bustling **Tower District**, and take a guided tour of the intriguing grottos, passageways, and landscaped courtyards of **Forestiere Underground Gardens**. On your way out of town, pick up some healthy hiking snacks—dried fruit, nuts—at **Simonian Farms**, a colorful farmstand that's been run by the same family since 1901. Take Hwy 41 up through **Oakhurst**, a good base for visiting **Yosemite National Park**, the South Entrance of which lies another 15 miles north. Just after entering the park, walk through Yosemite's largest and most spectacular stand of giant sequoias, **Mariposa Grove**.

Unquestionably, **Yosemite Valley** is the park's focal point, but this narrow, dramatic slice of greenery bisected by the Merced River and framed by 3500 ft cliffs can get crowded. After admiring the exhibits at the **Yosemite Valley Visitor**

Center, and checking out the original black-and-white landscape photos at the **Ansel Adams Gallery**, have lunch at one of the national park lodges (the patio of the magnificent Ahwahnee Bar is my favorite, but Curry Village Pizza Patio is quicker and simpler). Then head for higher ground. There are two main ways to get to the park's most famous observation area, **Glacier Point**: you can hike the arduous but highly rewarding **Four Mile Trail**. It's actually 4.8 miles each way, and it took us about six hours round-trip to complete this 3200 ft climb on a recent 98° summer day (but we loved every second of it). Or make the hour-long, 30-mile drive out of the valley and up **Glacier Point Road** to this awe-inspiring promontory, from which you'll be treated to panoramic views of America's highest cascade, 2425 ft **Yosemite Falls**, as well as the world's largest hunk of granite, massive **El Capitan**. You can see evidence of glaciation in every direction, most famously the distinctive **Half Dome** monolith.

If you have a second day in park or you want to make a scenic shortcut across the Sierras to Mammoth Lakes, you can drive east through Yosemite via **Tioga Road**, a generally less crowded 60-mile route that reveals many of the park's less famous but still arresting features, among them **Olmsted Point** (which offers you a different perspective on Half Dome), azure **Tenaya Lake** (lovely for swimming on a warm day), and grand **Tuolumne Meadows**. Just before reaching **Tioga Pass Entrance Station**, you'll find the trailhead for several fantastic hikes, including the steep but worthwhile 3.7-mile round-trip jaunt to **Great Sierra Mine** by way of rippling **Middle and Upper Gaylor Lakes**. Tioga Road closes early fall to late spring, depending on snowfall.

YOSEMITE NATIONAL PARK TO PLACERVILLE

Make your way out of Yosemite via Big Oak Flat Road to Hwy 120, stopping in quirky **Groveland**, where you might pause for a chocolate-raspberry cheesecake bar at Tangled Hearts Bakery. This is the edge of California's **Gold Country**, a nine-county swatch of friendly mountain towns that hopeful prospectors and adventurers swarmed following the 1849 Gold Rush. Appropriately, the region's main route is Hwy 49, which you can pick up west of Groveland after driving down the steep and scenic Priest Grade section of Hwy 120. Continue through a series of villages—**Jamestown, Angels Camp, Jackson**—known as much for their colorful gold-mining legacies as for their current treasures: antiques shops, art galleries, and a growing number of wineries. Several attractions preserve the region's mining history and offer visitors the chance to pan for gold (you're not going

Top Sequoia National Park *Bottom* Alwahnee Hotel, Yosemite National Park

to strike it rich this way, but it's a lot of fun for kids) and talk with docents demonstrating the trades of the day. Good ones, as you move north, include **Columbia State Historic Park**, **Gold Bug Park** in Placerville, and **Marshall Gold Discovery State Historic Park** in Coloma.

At Angels Camp, the seat of **Calaveras County**, turn northeast on Hwy 4 to the Sierra Nevada foothills town of **Murphys**, a star of this area's winemaking. The varietals best represented here include Italian and Spanish grapes like Barbera, Tempranillo, and Nebbiolo as well as old vine Zinfandel—**Ironstone** and **Twisted Oak** are a couple of my favorites for tasting. Continue to another highly acclaimed wine region, **Amador County**, which is home to acres of gnarled grape vines that produce some of the world's best Zinfandel. Most of the area's 40 or so wineries—including stalwarts like **Turley**, **Cooper**, and **Sobon Estate**—are in the towns of **Sutter Creek** and **Plymouth**. For a quick lunch, consider **Amador City**'s intimate Small Town Food & Wine, which turns out simple but stellar roasted-chicken-brie-pesto sandwiches and crispy flatbread pizzas. Continue north into picturesque **Placerville**, one of the largest and most prolific hubs of the Gold Rush era, as evidenced by its well-preserved Victorian buildings.

PLACERVILLE TO LASSEN VOLCANIC NATIONAL PARK

Follow Hwy 49 northwest, crossing I-80, and continue to the small Gold Rush towns of **Grass Valley**, where you can tour the **Empire Mine State Historic Park**, and **Nevada City**, with its lovingly restored Victorian buildings that today contain distinctive shops, inns, and restaurants, such as the 1940s-era Willo Steakhouse. Both towns have blossomed into vibrant arts colonies, and numerous galleries and community spaces present shows and exhibits, including the beautiful **Miners Foundry Cultural Center**, which occupies an 1850s ironworks.

Allow about three hours for the drive north by way of **Chico** to reach the Southwest Entrance to **Lassen Volcanic National Park**, which I consider to be almost criminally underappreciated. This immense wilderness boasts much more than the 10,457 ft peak for which it's named, including rippling lakes, rushing waterfalls, and pine-scented forests, many of them reached via the 30-mile **Lassen Volcanic National Park Highway**. But let's start with that peak: it last erupted in 1921, causing widespread destruction—much of it still visible in the park today. Give yourself at least two hours to explore **Bumpass Hell**, where boardwalks lead you safely through 16 acres of belching mud pots, hissing

From Placerville it's an easy one-hour drive west on US 50 to **Sacramento**, the state capital and a somewhat overlooked city of about 530,000 with a wealth of impressive attractions, an unpretentious vibe, and several acclaimed locavore-minded restaurants, such as Ella Dining Room, Localis, The Kitchen, and Mulvaney's. Visit the riverfront **Old Sacramento** district to learn about the city's colorful Gold Rush heritage—kids love clambering about the **California State Railroad Museum**'s vintage 1860s trains, and you can even spend the night on the century-old **Delta King Riverboat**, now a hotel with a pair of convivial restaurants. In **Midtown**, you'll find striking street murals, cool galleries, and hip bars and cafes—try Temple Coffee Roasters and The Cabin cocktail bar—and streets lined with neatly restored craftsman homes. Go for a walk among the camellia trees, cacti, and some 1200 rose bushes that dot the 40-acre lawns and gardens surrounding the 1869 **California State Capitol**, with its soaring 128 ft dome (it was modeled after the US Capitol). Nearby must-visits include the exceptional **Crocker Art Museum**, with works depicting the state's breathtaking landscapes by Ansel Adams, Georgia O'Keeffe, and Dorothea Lange; and the **California Museum**, which presents well-designed exhibits and oral histories that relate the stories of the state's diverse communities, including native tribes, Chinese Americans, and Latinx.

Top Bumpass Hell, Lassen Volcanic National Park
Opposite Bright lights of Reno

steam vents, and simmering hot springs, all set against an eerie badlands vista of rust- and mustard-colored geological formations. Lassen Volcano may technically be dormant, but the surrounding landscape gregariously—and aromatically (note the waft of hydrogen sulfide, reminiscent of rotten eggs)—assures us that it's extremely active. If you have extra time, I highly recommend making the roughly 90-minute drive into **Warner Valley**, which offers less crowded trails to similarly dramatic geothermal features, including the fumaroles and steam vents of **Devils Kitchen** and the strange milky-green waters of **Boiling Springs Lake.** You can even spend the night at the only lodging inside the park, the historic **Drakesbad Ranch**, which offers horseback rides through this rugged wilderness.

LASSEN VOLCANIC NP TO SOUTH LAKE TAHOE

From Lassen, you'll pass through **Chester**, which offers a handful of hearty dining options, and along the shore of beautiful **Lake Almanor,** and then continue south for about 2.5 hours through the eastern reaches of pristine **Plumas National Forest** to historic **Truckee.** This town near the north end of Lake Tahoe is synonymous with the tragic story of the ill-fated Donner party, which was stranded here by relentless blizzard conditions during the winter of 1846–47. Nearly half of the group of 87 westward-bound settlers perished. With its artsy shops and fashionable eateries, it's a little hard to imagine Truckee as such an inhospitable place today—that is unless you visit during one of the region's legendary snowstorms. You can learn about the ordeal of the ill-fated pioneers at the **Donner Memorial State Park and Emigrant Trail Museum.**

At nearly 200 sq miles, **Lake Tahoe** is North America's largest alpine lake and the nation's second deepest at 1645 ft. Flanked by towering mountains that support several hugely popular ski resorts—**Heavenly, Palisades, Northstar, Sierra**—Tahoe is a world-class vacation destination. The western two-thirds of the lake are in California, and the rest is in Nevada, where you'll find about a dozen glitzy casinos. From **Truckee**, drive south on Hwy 267 to **Kings Beach,** which overlooks stunning **Agate Bay.** It takes about two hours to drive entirely around this gorgeous, deep-blue lake, which is fringed with interesting stops, but if time is short, I suggest driving down the less developed western shore, from Hwy 28 to Hwy 89 to US 50. For a memorable hike, stop at **Emerald Bay State Park** and take the 2-mile out-and-back trail to **Eagle Falls,** a rocky climb with fantastic lake and mountain views.

SIDETRACK

It's an hour from South Lake Tahoe via several scenic routes to reach northern Nevada's largest city, **Reno**— or as local boosters might refer to it, "The Biggest Little City in the World." Developed as a silver-mining boomtown and railroad center in the 1860s, Reno grew into a center of gaming in the 20th century and has become increasingly popular as a reasonably priced place to live and vacation. The **Truckee River**, which is lined with walking paths and anchored by a small island containing **Wingfield Park**, is a fun spot for rafting, kayaking, and swimming. A half block from the river, the **National Automobile Museum** showcases an incredible collection of 220 vintage autos, including cars once owned by James Dean, Elvis Presley, and President John F. Kennedy. On the drive back to South Lake Tahoe, detour along Hwy 341 through **Virginia City**. This mountainous mining town mushroomed into a genuine boomtown in 1859 upon the discovery of the country's first major silver deposit, the Comstock Lode. A young reporter named Samuel Clemens, later to be known as Mark Twain, once walked among the vintage brick and wood-frame buildings that now house endearingly touristy saloons and souvenir shops on historic C Street.

SOUTH LAKE TAHOE TO MAMMOTH LAKES

The liveliest section of lakeshore, the twin towns of **South Lake Tahoe** in California and **Stateline** in Nevada serve as the base camp for famed **Heavenly Ski Resort**. During the warmer months you can take a scenic 2.4-mile ride on the gondola to the **Observation Deck**, maybe breaking for lunch at Cafe Blue, before going hiking or mountain-biking. Down on the lakeshore, rent jetskis, kayaks, and other watercraft at **Timber Cove Marina**, swim and sunbathe at **Regan Beach**, or book a 2.5-hour sightseeing cruise at **Zephyr Cove** on the **M.S. *Dixie II*** paddle wheeler.

From South Lake Tahoe, cross into Nevada and take Hwy 267 on a curving ascent up Kingsbury Grade and then across the Carson Valley to US 395. Follow it south into California at beautiful **Topaz Lake** and continue down through the sparsely populated eastern Sierras by way of **Bridgeport**. About 7 miles south in **Willow Springs**, detour east on Hwy 270 for 13 miles to the fascinating old ghost town of **Bodie**, which is now a state historic park containing some 100 buildings that date back to the short but sweet gold-mining boom in the late 1870s. Situated at 8400 ft above sea level, Bodie is unrestored and uninhabited, and it's a fun family-friendly destination to wander about and imagine what it must have looked like when it burst at the seams with 10,000 residents.

Returning to US 395, you'll come to a sharp bend in the road with an overlook offering stunning views of **Mono Lake**. This natural salt lake formed some 750,000 years ago and is dotted with strange, calcified limestone spires, known as tufa. You can hike out to view the tufa at **Mono Lake Tufa State Natural Reserve** and gaze out at Paoha Island, which rises on the horizon in the center of the lake. The view is especially impressive up the hill from the patio at contemporary **Mono Basin Scenic Area Visitor Center**.

A few miles south in **Lee Vining**, you'll come to the turnoff for Hwy 120 (Tioga Road), which leads to the summer-only Tioga Pass Entrance to Yosemite National Park. At this same intersection, you can fuel up on carnitas tacos, buffalo meatloaf, and craft beer at the cafe inside Whoa Nellie Deli. Unless you're headed into the park, stay south on US 395 for about 20 miles, then turn right onto **Mammoth Scenic Loop**, which climbs up to the upscale resort town of **Mammoth Lakes**, a year-round recreation destination with skiing and snowboarding in winter and hiking and biking during the warmer months. Continue west on Hwy 203, taking the short side road to **Minaret Vista Overlook**

Top Hiking the Four Mile Trail, Yosemite Valley *Opposite* Lassen Volcanic National Park

for a view of the granite sawtooth mountains that frame the region. Then follow the road up and around a sharp bend to **Devils Postpile National Monument**, which features a 60 ft high wall of hexagonal basalt columns formed by a heady combination of volcanic lava flow and glacial ice melt. You can make the short .8-mile hike to the base and then up to the top of the formation. Also rewarding is the relatively easy 5-mile round-trip trek to 101 ft **Rainbow Falls**.

Although this tour ends at Mammoth Lakes, keep driving down US 395 if you're enjoying the scenery, as the views of the mountains—including the Lower 48's highest peak, 14,505 ft **Mt Whitney**—are stupendous. Continue through the towns of **Bishop** and **Lone Pine**, which is perhaps best known for its **Museum of Western Film History**. From here you can head east into **Death Valley National Park** (*see* The Desert Southwest chapter p. 87) or continue south on US 395 another 70 miles to Hwy 178, which you can then follow west over the mountains, past **Lake Isabella**, and back to Bakersfield.

BEST EATS

- **Nuestro Mexico** The San Joaquin Valley abounds with stellar Mexican food, and this cute and colorful restaurant near Bakersfield's Mill Creek Park is one of the best—try the chilaquiles with red sauce, shrimp aguachiles, and steak *encervezado*, stewed in beer and vegetables. 661-637-1343, nuestromexico.online.

- **Vintage Press** Since 1966, downtown Visalia's top spot for a special meal has been this dimly lighted dining room with crisp linens, stained glass, and elegant murals. Enjoy modern takes on old-school Continental favorites—escargot with garlic and ginger, blackened Pacific snapper with lime and jalapenos. 559-733-3033, thevintagepress.com.

- **June Bug Cafe** For some of the tastiest food in the region, make the 30-mile drive south from Yosemite to this cheerful restaurant in the Yosemite Bug Rustic Mountain Resort. The menu always features healthy options, such as yogurt-marinated tandoori chicken and vegan white bean, eggplant, and mushroom cassoulet. Midpines, 209-966-6666, yosemitebug.com.

- **Alchemy** The menu at this lively Murphys wine bar blends comfort food sensibilities with contemporary twists—think fried chicken with a sweet Asian-spiced chile glaze or mac-and-cheese with lump crab meat. It's a great place to sample vino from surrounding Calaveras County. 209-728-0700, alchemymurphys.com.

- **Three Forks Bakery & Brewing** First-rate craft beers and ethereal wood-fired pizzas are the draw at this easygoing hangout in historic downtown Nevada City. The desserts— almond polenta cake with caramelized oranges—are worth saving room for. 530-470-8333, threeforksnc.com.

- **Trokay** This romantic stone-walled Truckee bistro presents prix-fixe meals of delicious modern American cuisine— tempura soft-shell crab, dry-aged New York strip steak, along with optional wine pairings. Cooking classes are offered, too. 530-582-1040, restauranttrokay.com.

- **Wolfdale's** Book a table at this upscale Tahoe City restaurant—some tables have lake views—to feast on flavorful Asian-influenced cuisine. You might start with ahi and hamachi sashimi before graduating to tamarind seafood stew with scallops, crab, and lobster tail. 530-583-5700, wolfdales.com.

- **Himmel Haus** Kids and adults enjoy the colorful murals, convivial ambience, and hearty German food at this Alps-style restaurant in South Lake Tahoe at the base of Heavenly's aerial tram. After a day of skiing or hiking, enjoy a stein of weissbier and a plate of bockwurst and mashed potatoes or sauerbraten. 530-314-7665, himmelhausslt.com.

- **The Warming Hut** An affordable Mammoth Lakes option for breakfast, lunch, and dinner, this airy lodge with pitched timber ceilings and a big stone fireplace is ideal for fueling up before or after a day of outdoor adventures. Try Benedict hash with ham and dill-hollandaise sauce. 760-965-0549, thewarminghutmammoth.com.

Mono Lake

BEST SLEEPS

- **Padre Hotel** Bakersfield's stately eight-story Spanish Colonial grande dame dates to 1928 and has rooms decorated with dashing mid-century furnishings. The mural-filled lobby is a grand place to relax before dining in the swanky Belvedere Room. 661-427-4900, thepadrehotel.com.

- **The Darling Hotel** Set inside downtown Visalia's stately 1930s former courthouse annex, this gorgeous property has been meticulously restored to its original Art Deco splendor. The 32 high-ceilinged rooms are beautifully furnished, and common features include a snazzy rooftop restaurant and a relaxing pool. 559-713-2113, thedarlingvisalia.com.

- **Sequoia and Kings Canyon National Park lodgings** The only hotel inside Sequoia National Park, the light-filled and contemporary 102-room Wuksachi Lodge is a standout for its grand vistas of the surrounding forest and mountain peaks. You have three options in Kings Canyon: modern and comfortable John Muir Lodge, older and more rudimentary wood-panel Grant Grove Cabins near the park's main entrance, and rustic 21-room Cedar Grove Lodge, which enjoys a peaceful setting on the South Fork Kings River. 866-807-3598, visitsequoia.com.

- **Yosemite National Park lodgings** With its awesome Yosemite Valley setting and stunning Native American interior design elements, the vaunted 1920s Ahwahnee is one of the country's most iconic—and expensive—national park hotels. The casually elegant 1915 Yosemite Valley Lodge and simple but less spendy Curry Village (with standard motel rooms, cabins, and canvas tent cabins) have the same stunning and central locations but don't overlook the old-timey Wawona Hotel, with its modest rooms (half of them have shared baths) and tranquil setting near the soaring sequoias of the Mariposa Grove. 602-278-8888, travelyosemite.com.

- **Groveland Hotel** Offering proximity to Yosemite's Hetch Hetchy Entrance, this former trading post in the Gold Country town of Groveland was built in 1849 and now contains 18 simple but smartly updated hotel rooms and a rollicking taproom and barbecue joint with a big back patio. 209-962-4000, groveland.com.

- **National Exchange Hotel** At the foot of Nevada City's colorful main drag, this 1850s redbrick Victorian reopened in 2021 following an ambitious top-to-bottom renovation. Inviting features include a grand lobby with comfy seating, farm-to-table-focused Lola Restaurant, and high-ceilinged rooms that blend period-style decor with modern amenities. 530-362-7605, thenationalexchangehotel.com.

- **Highlands Ranch Resort** From the hot tub or big windows of your luxurious suite or cottage at this contemporary 175-acre property near the southern entrance to Lassen Volcanic National Park, gaze out at the cattle, migratory birds, and even the occasional bear meandering in the surrounding meadows. The elegant restaurant specializes in steaks and seafood. Mill Creek, 530-595-3388, highlandsranchresort.com.

- **Cedar House Sport Hotel** Just outside historic downtown Truckee and a 15-minute drive from Lake Tahoe's north shore, this stylish 40-room ski chalet-inspired hotel abounds with family-friendly features: free cruiser bikes, rooms with kitchenettes and modular furniture that can be converted into twin beds, and a convivial restaurant with garden patio seating. 530-582-5655, cedarhousesporthotel.com.

- **Coachman Hotel** This rustic-chic reimagining of two 1960s South Lake Tahoe motels has sleek, uncluttered rooms with custom-built plywood furnishings, plus an inviting lobby coffee bar and a seasonal pool and hot tub. It's a short walk from Lakeside Beach, Heavenly ski resort, and the Nevada casinos. 530-545-6460, coachmantahoe.com.

- **Tamarack Lodge and Resort** Overlooking Twin Lakes and just off the popular Lakes Basin Bike Path, this historic compound near Mammoth Mountain Ski Resort offers a wide range of accommodations, from cozy knotty-pine rooms with shared bathrooms to well-outfitted three-bedroom California craftsman-style cabins built in the 1920s. 760-934-2442, tamaracklodge.com.

CAMPING

You'll find plenty of tent and RV camping in this part of the state. The national parks have some of the most beautiful campgrounds, but you need to reserve well in advance. In Yosemite, consider Bridalveil Creek near Glacier Point and Wawona near Mariposa Grove; Manzanita Lake and both Summit Lake campgrounds are lovely, centrally located options at Lassen Volcanic; and at Sequoia and Kings Canyon, good bets include Lodgepole Campground in Sequoia and Azalea (more central) and Sentinel (deep in the park, closer to Zumwalt Meadows) in Kings Canyon. Also consider some cool glamping venues near Yosemite, such as AutoCamp, with its sleek Airstream trailers and posh tent platforms, or Yosemite Pines, where you can overnight in modernized Conestoga-style covered wagons. In the Gold Country, reliable options include Placerville KOA, Angels Camp RV and Camping Resort near Jamestown, Gold Country Campground Resort near Jackson, and Willow Creek Campground near Grass Valley and Nevada City. On the east side of the Sierras, Fallen Leaf has a lovely location near South Lake Tahoe, and Twin Lakes has a beautiful waterfront setting in Mammoth Lakes.

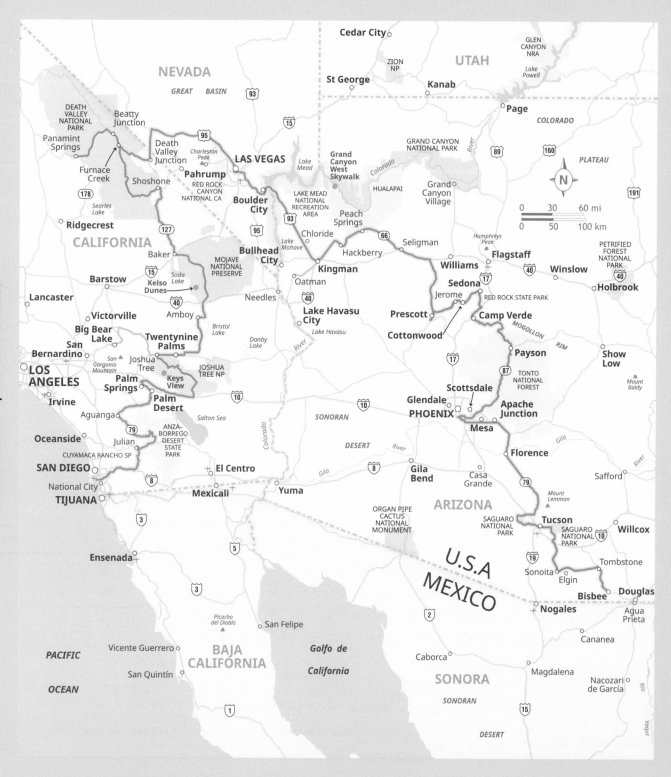

The Desert Southwest ★

Punctuated by the modern cities of Las Vegas and Phoenix, this epic, arid journey traverses a brilliant desert landscape of otherworldly flora, fauna, and geological formations, not to mention a trove of dusty little towns frozen in time.

HOW LONG?

10 days; add an extra day each to see more of San Diego, Palm Springs and Joshua Tree National Park, Las Vegas, Phoenix, and Tucson.

WHEN TO GO

Avoid making this trip in summer—even September and May can be sizzling, and June to August can actually be unsafe for daytime hiking. Winter temperatures are ideal—it can even get a bit chilly in higher elevations, such as Sedona and Tucson. March to April and October to November offer perhaps the best balance of comfortable weather, flowering cacti in spring and foliage in fall, and manageable crowds.

NEED TO KNOW

Some hotels, restaurants, and attractions—especially inside the national parks—close or limit hours in summer. Conversely, winter is high season, and hotels often book up way in advance. It's possible to drive for long stretches through rugged, unforgiving terrain without passing a gas station or having cell service, so keep your tank topped and travel with extra water, food, and basic first-aid supplies.

⊙ SNAPSHOT

One of the delightfully unexpected joys of the three—Colorado, Mojave, and Great Basin—deserts of the Southwest is the wildly varied landscape. With their fantastic shapes and proportions, Joshua trees and saguaro cacti appear almost cartoonlike. As you travel from low hot basins to towering craggy peaks, you'll spy pink sand dunes, ochre and teal badlands, and crimson canyons. And these remote locales offer pitch-black skies that are perfect for stargazing.

→ Distances

Total distance, one-way: 1650 mi (2655 km)
- San Diego, CA to Palm Springs, CA: 225 mi (362 km)
- Palm Springs, CA to Panamint Springs (Death Valley), CA: 435 mi (700 km)
- Panamint Springs (Death Valley), CA to Las Vegas, NV: 185 mi (298 km)
- Las Vegas, NV to Sedona, AZ: 340 mi (547 km)
- Sedona, AZ to Phoenix, AZ: 175 mi (282 km)
- Phoenix, AZ to Bisbee, AZ: 225 mi (362 km)

⊙ Daytime Temperatures

January: 58-70°F (14-21°C)
July: 85-118°F (29-48°C)

ⓘ More information

- San Diego tourism, sandiego.org
- Anza-Borrego Desert State Park, parks.ca.gov/anzaborrego
- Palm Springs tourism, visitgreaterpalmsprings.com
- Joshua Tree National Park, nps.gov/jotr
- Death Valley National Park, nps.gov/deva
- Las Vegas tourism, visitlasvegas.com
- Sedona tourism, visitsedona.com
- Phoenix tourism, visitphoenix.com
- Tucson tourism, visittucson.org
- Bisbee tourism, discoverbisbee.com

City View
San Diego

America's eighth largest city makes a fine start to a coastal road trip, but a desert adventure, you ask? Strangely enough, yes. Although San Diego enjoys mild, ocean-cooled temperatures, it actually has a semi-arid climate, and the eastern side of the county is pure desert. This attractive metropolis by the sea offers surfing and strolling in the beach districts and a heady mix of museums and cultural institutions in Balboa Park. And there are several famous family attractions, including LEGOLAND (in nearby Carlsbad), SeaWorld, and the incomparable San Diego Zoo.

Car-friendly rating: Good. Most of San Diego is easily navigated by car, including the beach communities and the neighborhoods that fringe Balboa Park, which have ample free or inexpensive street or lot parking. Downtown is the one challenge; it has plenty of lots and garages, but rates at downtown hotels can exceed $40 a night.

What to see in a day: A verdant 1200-acre hilltop oasis in the center of the city, **Balboa Park** is a joy to explore, but it's also huge, so budget your time realistically; just visiting the **San Diego Zoo** usually takes me a half day. Other highlights include the **Japanese Friendship Garden**, the **1915 Botanical Building**, the tiny but impressive **Timken Museum**, and the folk art-focused **Mingei International Museum**. On the coast, visit the cliffs of **Cabrillo National Monument** for a gorgeous view of the bay, then venture for people-watching and swimming by the pier in **Ocean Beach**, near the boardwalk in **Mission Beach** and **Pacific Beach**, and around the cove in **La Jolla**, with its tony boutiques and restaurants. Be sure to stop for Baja-style fish tacos—and a pint or two of San Diego's famous craft beer—at Pacific Beach Fish Shop or La Jolla's Galaxy Taco.

Where to stay: One of the world's largest wood-frame buildings, the grand 1888 **Hotel del Coronado** offers a splendid beachfront setting, eight restaurants, and an indulgent spa. Fringing a coastal nature reserve north of La Jolla, the romantic Arts and Crafts-style **Lodge at Torrey Pines** has a stellar restaurant and an acclaimed golf course. Less expensive properties with distinctive personalities and winning locations include the **Hotel Indigo** in downtown's Gaslamp Quarter, the **Pearl Hotel** in Point Loma, and the **Lafayette Hotel, Swim Club and Bungalows** in historic University Heights.

Top The Botanical Building, Balboa Park *Bottom* Ocean Beach

SAN DIEGO, CA TO PALM SPRINGS, CA

From San Diego head east on I-8 to Hwy 79, which climbs up through the coniferous forests and wildflower meadows of **Cuyamaca Rancho State Park** into the former mining town of **Julian**, which is better known today for its apple orchards. Enjoy a slice of apple pie at Mom's Pie House or Julian Pie Company, or for a refined, leisurely lunch, book a table at Jeremy's on the Hill. Turn east onto Hwy 78 and descend down sheer and twisty Banner Grade into the breathtaking desert valley centered on 600,000-acre **Anza-Borrego Desert State Park**, where you can hike the beautiful 3.3-mile **Palm Canyon** loop to an oasis of stately fan palms (watch for bighorn sheep). Then drive through **Galleta Meadows** to check out the 130 hulking, whimsical sculptures—they include sloths, scorpions, dinosaurs, and a 350 ft long sand serpent—created with scrap metal by Mexican-American artist Ricardo Breceda. Anza-Borrego is famous for its clear, jet-black night skies, especially during midsummer's Perseid meteor shower. A few companies offer star-gazing tours.

Follow Hwy S22 west out of the valley and then drive north through the mountains to **Coachella Valley**, with its laid-back desert vibe and fancy resort communities, including retro-cool **Palm Springs**. This playground of celebrities in the 1930s has blossomed into a vibrant center of art and design, a relaxing place to laze by the pool, and one of the world's top gay vacation destinations. Try to visit during one of the region's countless annual events, which include several film festivals and LGBTQ parties, the internationally acclaimed **Modernism Week** in February, and the renowned **Coachella Valley Music and Arts Festival** in April. My favorite pastime here is exploring the city's mid-century-modern architecture. View exhibits and book house tours at the **Palm Springs Art Museum Architecture and Design Center**, which occupies a low-slung mid-century bank building, and then browse for cool furnishings among the city's many galleries and vintage design shops, such as **Pelago** and **Modernway**. For outdoor recreation, hike the lush waterfalls of **Indian Canyons** nature reserve, which is on land owned by the Agua Caliente tribe. And don't miss the **Palm Springs Aerial Tramway**, which rotates slowly as it rises 2.5 miles above the desert floor to an 8516 ft perch in the San Jacinto Mountains, where miles of trails through a cool-aired piney forest await you.

PALM SPRINGS, CA TO DEATH VALLEY NATIONAL PARK, CA

Head east on I-10 to the South Entrance of **Joshua Tree National Park**. This 1235 sq mile desert preserve is named for the peculiar-looking plants—they're a form of yucca that can reach heights of 40 ft—that dominate the landscape, but it's also popular for rock climbing and hiking. I like to follow Pinto Basin Road northwest, stopping to snap a photo at **Cholla Cactus Garden**, before continuing to the Jumbo Rocks area to scamper among the wonderfully weird rock formations along the 1.8-mile **Discovery Trail**, home to ominous-looking **Skull Rock** and vertically cleaved **Split Rock**. At **Cap Rock**, make the 11-mile round-trip drive south to **Keys View** overlook for its far-reaching panoramas; on clear days you can see into Mexico. Continue northwest on the park road, stopping for the family-friendly, mile-long hike amid the boulders strewn throughout **Hidden Valley**. Then depart through the West Entrance into the small town of **Joshua Tree**, where you can view more than 100 sculptures fashioned out of reclaimed materials and household items at **Noah Purifoy's Outdoor Desert Art Museum**.

Follow Hwy 62 east through **Twentynine Palms**, whose downtown features more than two dozen striking murals, and continue northeast 50 miles to tiny **Amboy** to make the 4-mile round-trip hike to **Amboy Crater**, an extinct volcanic cinder cone that's some 1500 ft in diameter. Then cross I-40 and continue into **Mojave National Preserve**, a 1.5-million-acre wonderland of lava flows and limestone caverns. Stop at **Kelso Depot**, a 1920s railway station that now contains the park's visitor center, and explore **Kelso Dunes**, which rise as high as 600 ft in places. Continue to **Baker**, a good place to fill your gas tank, and take Hwy 127 north.

Nearly the size of Connecticut, 160 mile long **Death Valley** is the largest national park in the lower 48 states. In this land of extremes, the highest temperature on earth (134°F) was recorded in 1913, not far from the lowest point in North America (282 ft below sea level), Badwater Basin. Before my first visit, I envisioned a bleak landscape, and although Death Valley can be harsh and searing hot, it also features a wonderfully colorful and eclectic landscape of brightly hued rock formations and badlands, pine-covered mountains that rise as high as 11,000 ft, and fascinating mining ruins, such as **Harmony Borax** and **Eagle Borax Works**.

With limited time, focus on the park's relatively compact southeastern quarter. Enter from tiny **Shoshone**, stopping for a bite to eat at the merry Crowbar Cafe and Saloon, then

From Joshua Tree, head west to **Yucca Valley**, and then take Hwy 247 north through **Landers**, an idiosyncratic high-desert haven of artists and free spirits that has several unusual art installations, including **The Integration** sound chamber and the **Dream Wanderer** virtual reality bus, as well as a remarkable natural feature, 70 ft tall **Giant Rock**. Follow Hwy 18 as it gains about 3500 ft in elevation on its way into the **San Bernardino Mountains**, where it's better known as the **Rim of the World Scenic Byway**, owing to its sweeping views of the surrounding desert. The cute alpine town **Big Bear Lake** is my go-to for cool relief from the desert heat—this four-season recreation hub offers great skiing in winter and hiking in summer. Make the 2-mile hike up to **Castle Rock** for views of the crystalline blue lake.

Whether you're an ardent fan of Route 66 culture or you just have a penchant for quirky little desert towns, head southwest on Hwy 10, off I-40 southwest of Kingman. This narrow, lonely, but picturesque road through the rugged Black Mountains is one of the better preserved stretches of the original **Historic Route 66** (much of the rest of the 2448-mile "Mother Road" from Chicago to Los Angeles has been replaced with cookie-cutter interstate highways). Stop in colorful **Oatman**, which has just over 100 year-round residents along with a sizable population of friendly braying burros who mill around happily, sometimes blocking traffic. After the discovery of a massive gold vein in 1915, this speck of a village grew practically overnight into a boomtown of 3500, complete with brothels and saloons. The mines were exhausted by World War II, and soon the interstate highway bypassed the town many miles to the south, rendering this stretch of Route 66 obsolete and Oatman a virtual ghost town. These days you'll find a few endearingly dusty cafes and galleries, a trove of memorabilia in the **Oatman Jail and Museum**, and juicy burgers at the creaky old **Oatman Hotel** tavern, whose walls are papered over with signed dollar bills.

take Hwy 178 around the Black Mountains to **Badwater Basin**. Walk out on the boardwalk across a pool of intensely salty groundwater and through crusty salt flats, and look up at the hills high above to see a sign that marks the point of sea level. Back on Hwy 178, you'll come to the park's must-see feature, 9-mile **Artists Drive**, a narrow one-way ribbon of blacktop that snakes through an eerie badland streaked with a kaleidoscope of oxidized hues; from the parking area, you can hop out for a scramble through this otherworldly place.

At the junction with Hwy 190, **Furnace Creek Village** contains historic restaurants and hotels as well as the main visitor center. From here you can venture much deeper into the park—perhaps out west to **Panamint Springs** and **Father Crowley Vista Point** or south to the **Charcoal Kilns** and **Mahogany Flat**. At the very least, drive the 20 miles to **Mesquite Flats Sand Dunes** to hike through these rolling, rippling mountains of golden grains. Back at Furnace Creek, head east on Hwy 190 to **Zabriskie Point** overlook. Amazing scenery greets you in every direction: pink-rock badlands, wavy sand dunes, sweeping desert valleys, and the lofty peaks of the Panamint Mountains. Just before you exit the park, a side road leads to another stunning park overlook, 5475 ft **Dante's View**. Exit the park, and at Death Valley Junction, take Hwy 373 north and then US 95 east through the southern Nevada desert to Las Vegas.

DEATH VALLEY NATIONAL PARK, CA TO PHOENIX, AZ

From Las Vegas it's a long but relaxing and generally traffic-free 300-mile drive through the Mojave Desert to north-central Arizona. First pass around the southern edge of **Lake Mead** and have a look at a truly remarkable feat of engineering, **Hoover Dam**—I-11 bypasses the dam via a new and high bridge across the Colorado River, but I like to exit the freeway for a closer look, or even to take a tour of this 726 ft tall monolith completed in 1936. On US 93 about 20 miles before Kingman, turn left onto Hwy 125 to visit the eccentric little ghost town of **Chloride**, where a rough (take it slowly) dirt road leads 1.5 miles to whimsical murals painted on a huge rock by artist Roy Purcell in 1966. In **Kingman**, drive through the historic downtown and stop by the **Powerhouse Visitor Center**, which occupies a 1907 power plant and contains a Route 66 museum and photo gallery. Kids enjoy the drive through the goofy but fun **Route 66 Arch** for a photo op, and then feasting on cheeseburgers and root beer floats at '50s-style Mr. D'z Route 66 Diner.

Opposite Mr. D's Route 66 Diner, Kingman

Back in Kingman, skip the interstate and instead driving east along another picturesque stretch of Historic Route 66, which meanders for about 85 miles through the evergreen hills south of the Grand Canyon. The road passes through **Peach Springs**, the tribal capital of the **Hualapai** Native American reservation and also a gateway for visiting **Grand Canyon West**, and the tribally owned **West Rim of the Grand Canyon**, whose signature attraction is the 4000 ft high **Skywalk** glass bridge. The colorful old railroad town of **Seligman** offers a neon-lit slice of Route 66 Americana, with its several restored motels, shops, and diners. I'm partial to Westside Lilo's Cafe, which serves tasty diner fare but is especially famous for carrot cake—it's doled out in gargantuan slices big enough for four people to share.

Take I-40 to **Ash Fork**, and then head south about 50 miles to **Prescott**, an attractive mile-high city of about 44,000 nestled in the Bradshaw Mountains. It served briefly in the 1860s as Arizona's territorial capital and is today a popular recreation base known for its superb **Phippen Museum**, which is devoted to Western art and pioneer and ranching history; the engaging and interactive **Museum of Indigenous People;** and **Whiskey Row**, a strip of lively eateries and bars, including the colorful Palace Restaurant and Saloon. Head

east on Hwy 89A over the Black Hills to diminutive **Jerome**, which clings to the steep slopes of Cleopatra Hill. When the town's once-prolific copper mines closed in the early 1950s, Jerome faded into oblivion before eventually becoming fashionable with artists and bohemians. At the **Gold King Mine and Ghost Town,** kids love wandering amid 180 old autos and motorcycles, vintage mining equipment, and a petting zoo. It's a delight walking the town's narrow streets and precipitouos staircases, dropping inside convivial bars, wine tasting rooms, and galleries and taking in the astounding views across the **Verde Valley**.

Follow Hwy 89 across the valley by way of historic **Clarkdale** and **Cottonwood**, stopping to explore the 1000-year-old Sinaguan pueblo ruins at **Tuzigoot National Monument** and perhaps to a winery or two—**Provisioner Wines and General Store** and **Oak Creek Vineyards** are good choices. The road continues through the red rock canyons and buttes that dominate **Sedona**, which has blossomed over the past half century into a world-famous hub of New Age spirituality—some attribute this development to the incredible surrounding beauty, and others to the presence of four energy vortexes, which are said to release positive, healing energy. Whatever the cause, you'll find more holistic

City View
Las Vegas

Cacophonous casinos, shimmering shopping malls, and glamorous resort hotels with celebrity-affiliated restaurants are the main draws in glitzy Las Vegas, a city that's more about gaming, partying, and attending conventions than road-tripping. Still, with its proximity to Death Valley, Zion, and the Grand Canyon, it's an excellent place to spend a night or two as you explore the Southwest, and even if just passing through for 24 hours, it's easy to pack in a lot of excitement.

Car-friendly rating: Excellent. This modern, sprawling city was designed for cars. Most hotels have free or very cheap parking. The only downsides are occasional traffic jams during rush hour and during weekend evenings on the Strip, and that Las Vegas is a pretty bland—in some places downright ugly—city to drive in.

What to see in a day: Whether or not you're a fan of casinos, experiencing the neon signs, replica landmarks (the Eiffel Tower, the Empire State Building), and animated crowds of the **Las Vegas Strip** is a trip. Drive this eight-lane, 4.3-mile road at night for the best views and people-watching, and if you're up for a wonderfully bizarre immersive arts experience, head just across I-15 to **AREA15**, an outpost of Santa Fe's famous Meow Wolf. My favorite part of Vegas is **Downtown**, which you can mostly explore on foot. Start in the **Arts District**, with its several blocks of hip eateries, coffeehouses, and shops and dozens of cool and colorful murals. Continue north to the older cluster of casino hotels on **Fremont Street**, a pedestrianized, covered entertainment zone that's close to a pair of intriguing attractions: the **Mob Museum**, which occupies a 1930s former courthouse and tells the fascinating story of the city's long and sordid relationship with organized crime, and—a short drive north—the **Neon Museum** offers nearly 3 acres of vintage, often iconic, signs. For some of the best food in Las Vegas, skip the Strip—which is sadly prone to overpriced and overhyped celebrity restaurants—and head a few miles west to **Spring Mountain Road**, which locals refer to as **Chinatown**. But it's really a pan-Asian mash-up of international eateries and markets with dozens of exceptional options, including Lamoon (Japanese-Thai), District One (Vietnamese), Cafe Sanuki (Japanese), Chengdu Taste (Chinese), and Hobak (Korean).

Where to stay: You'll find a huge selection of hotels, from indies to chains, in every price range, with the most famous ones attached to Strip casinos. My favorite of these is the stylish **Venetian Resort**, which has excellent restaurants, a superb spa, and free parking (the garage for the swanky Palazzo Tower is conveniently right below the building, a rarity on the Strip). Some of the most appealing lodgings are away from the Strip, however, and include the posh **JW Marriott Las Vegas Resort and Spa** in Summerlin, Downtown's mid-century cool **Cabana Suites** at the historic **El Cortez Hotel**, and the new **English Hotel**, a 74-room boutique property in the Arts with a restaurant by famed chef Todd English.

Fremont Street

spas and wellness centers here than you can shake a smudge stick at. There are also plenty of swanky resorts, including **Enchantment**, **Kimpton Amara**, and **L'Auberge de Sedona** (its Cress on Oak Creek restaurant is fantastic). The breathtaking landscape is a hiker's paradise. My favorite treks include the 5 miles of trails at **Red Rock State Park**, which is bisected by beautiful Oak Creek, and the 4-mile **Courthouse Butte Loop Trail**, from which you can scramble up a crimson palisade for a close view of Bell Rock.

Head south to **Camp Verde** for a look around **Montezuma Castle National Monument**, with its eye-popping five-story cliff dwelling built by the Sinagua people around AD 1200 (and erroneously named by early Europeans who believed it had been constructed by the Aztec emperor Montezuma). Via I-17 it's about 75 minutes to Phoenix, but I favor taking Hwy 260 east through **Tonto National Forest** and along the rugged Mogollon Rim to **Payson**, and then following Hwy 87 south. It takes only 20 minutes longer.

Zabriskie Point, Death Valley National Park

PHOENIX, AZ TO BISBEE, AZ

From Phoenix, allow 2.5 hours via the scenic but slightly longer route through **Apache Junction** and **Florence** to **Tucson**, a sprawling, hilly university city with a population of 540,000 and a dramatic natural setting. Amid its cactus-studded foothills, you'll find several luxurious spa resorts, among them the **Ritz-Carlton Dove Mountain**, **Canyon Ranch**, and the **Loews Ventana Canyon**. Arrive from the north via Hwy 77 and stop at **Catalina State Park** for a quick ramble on the **Romero Ruins** loop, which leads past remnants of both AD 800 Hokokam communities and an abandoned 19th-century ranch home. About 8 miles south, stop for a walk among the plant life of **Tohono Chul Park**, a beautiful high-desert garden anchored by a Santa Fe–style adobe house that now contains art exhibits as well as an inviting bistro set amid wildflowers.

From *Wile E. Coyote and the Road Runner* cartoons to classic Western movies like the *Gunfight at the O.K. Corral*, the towering, multipronged cactuses that gave **Saguaro National Park** its name have been depicted in popular culture for generations. Tucson is the epicenter of their Sonoran Desert range and it lies between this national park's two parcels, the **West (Tucson Mountain) District** and the **East (Rincon Mountain) District**, which are about an hour's drive apart. Although designated first and foremost to preserve the habitats of these distinctive plants, which can live for a couple of centuries and grow as tall as 45 ft, Saguaro National Park also protects some 25 other types of cactus as well myriad flora and fauna.

From Tohono Chul Park, drive 20 minutes to the West District's contemporary **Red Hills Visitor Center**, which presents a short film on the park's flora and fauna, has excellent natural history exhibits, and offers stunning mountain views. Nearby, drive the 6-mile **Bajada Loop** to see prolific stands of saguaro cactus, stopping at **Signal Hill** for a quick look at the well-preserved petroglyphs carved at least 900 years ago by Ancestral Puebloans. Exit the park southeast on North Kinney Rd, then tour of the superb 98-acre **Arizona-Sonora Desert Museum**, a remarkable zoo, aquarium, art gallery, botanical garden, and natural history museum that's a favorite with visitors of all ages.

Continue east along windy and beautiful Gates Pass Rd through **Tucson Mountain Park** and into Tucson's bustling downtown, a lively quadrant of both historic Spanish Colonial and contemporary architecture and trendy eateries, craft breweries, and indie shops. Much of the action is along **East Broadway** and **Congress St**, and then north along **Historic 4th Ave**. Tucson has a number of notable attractions, including the extensive anthropological collections at the venerable **Arizona State Museum** on the pretty campus of the **University of Arizona** and the massive open-air **Pima Air and Space Museum**, with its nearly 400 aircraft. In **South Tucson**, 4th Ave is the historic heart of the city's Mexican-American community—it's home to renowned Sonoran-style Mexican eateries, such as Guillermo's Double L and Mi Nidito.

As you depart Tucson, make a quick stop in Saguaro National Park's East District to travel **Cactus Forest Drive**, an 8-mile scenic loop with numerous turnouts offering fantastic photo ops. Head south to Hwy 83 and continue in that direction through the Santa Rita Mountains and to the small towns of **Sonoita** and **Elgin**, which lie at the heart of southern Arizona's well-regarded wine country—**Dos Cabezas**, **Callaghan**, and **Deep Sky Vineyard** are among the several notable tasting rooms. Turn east onto Hwy 82 and continue through the open high desert to **Tombstone**. A lucrative silver boom in the late 1870s led to the town's founding and contributed to a series of ugly scrapes involving Wyatt Earp and his brothers Virgil and Morgan, Doc Holliday, and the

Clanton and McLaury brothers. Just about every business in Tombstone commemorates these raucous showdowns, including the infamous Gunfight at the O.K. Corral. Shootouts are reenacted daily outside this rambling old livery. With its stagecoach rides, ghost tours, and rollicking saloons and souvenir shops, Tombstone is especially enjoyable for kids and history buffs.

Just 20 miles southeast, with its steep, narrow streets and offbeat countercultural vibe, **Bisbee** bears a resemblance to Jerome and was a hub of silver, gold, and copper mining throughout the first century of its roughly 140-year history. Many of the town's colorful Italianate, Renaissance Revival, and Art Deco buildings now house cozy B&Bs and inns, acclaimed art galleries, and spirited saloons and restaurants like Screaming Banshee Pizza, St Elmo Bar, and—a little southeast of town—the original location of Arizona's acclaimed Bisbee Breakfast Club empire. You can learn about the area's booms and busts at downtown's Smithsonian-affiliated **Bisbee Mining and Historical Museum** or by taking an underground hard-hat tour through the legendary **Copper Queen Mine**—excursions led by retired miners descend some 1500 ft into this enormous mine that was once the most prolific in Arizona.

City View
Phoenix

Having more than quadrupled in size since 1960, America's fifth largest city also borders fast-growing Tempe, Mesa, Chandler, Glendale, and Scottsdale. The metro region is famed for its swanky golf and spa resorts but also has a number of notable museums and several stunning desert mountain parks—McDowell Mountain, South Mountain, and Camelback Mountain among them.

Car-friendly rating: Excellent. Metro Phoenix has a well-designed grid of freeways and broad surface roads, and although you can sometimes encounter LA-caliber traffic jams, it's generally easy to drive in and offers plenty of free or cheap parking. Its numerous strip malls and subdivisions diminish the city's curb appeal, but impressive mountain views help compensate.

What to see in a day: Spend the morning downtown at the superb **Heard Museum**, which contains comprehensive collections of Native American art and artifacts, from Navajo rugs to Zuni jewelry. The nearby **Phoenix Art Museum** is also excellent, and in the thriving **Roosevelt Row Arts District**, the **Churchill** comprises about a dozen eateries and shops housed in converted shipping containers set around a breezy courtyard. Head east to **Old Town Scottsdale**, with its dozens of acclaimed art galleries and tony shops, and visit the stellar, Smithsonian-affiliated **Western Spirit: Scottsdale's Museum of the West**. Dine someplace trendy, such as FnB Restaurant and Virtu Honest Craft. Drive north to tour the world-famous campus of Frank Lloyd Wright's **Taliesin West**, where the cantankerous but brilliant architect spent his final years. Then visit the **Musical Instrument Museum**; set inside a stunning contemporary building, it contains more than 15,000 instruments from all over the world, and kids enjoy listening to every imaginable genre of music through wireless headphones.

Where to stay: In downtown Phoenix, the sleek **Kimpton Hotel Palomar** stands out for its rooftop pool, smartly designed rooms, and great restaurant. In the shadows of Phoenix Mountains Preserve, the elegant **Arizona Biltmore** resort was designed in 1929 by a protégé of Frank Lloyd Wright and has beautifully appointed rooms and fantastic dining options. Scottsdale has dozens of fancy resorts, many with world-class spas and golf courses—standouts include the **Andaz Scottsdale** and the **Westin Kierland Resort**, with its kid-approved Adventure Water Park. My favorite area lodging is the mid-century-modern **Hotel Valley Ho**, a swanky urban resort on the edge of Old Town Scottsdale.

Top **Heard Museum** *Bottom* **Downtown Phoenix** *Opposite* **Bisbee**

BEST EATS

- **Red Ocotillo** This cheerful Borrego Springs cafe with a covered patio stands out for its cinnamon French toast and smoked salmon Benedicts in the morning but serves tasty lunch and dinner fare and creative cocktails, too. 760-767-7400, redocotillo.com.

- **Rooster and the Pig** Tuck into shareable plates of boldly flavored Vietnamese fusion—caramelized-fish-sauce wings, lemongrass pork-date rolls, sweet potato noodles with shishito peppers—at this industrial-cool bistro in a discreet Palm Springs shopping center. 760-832-6691, roosterandthepig.com.

- **Farm** At this intimate, Provençal country house-inspired space in Palm Springs' charming La Plaza, enjoy delicious French classics, from wild-mushroom-and-Gruyere crepes to roasted pheasant with a juniper berry sauce. 760-417-4471, farmpalmsprings.com.

- **Pappy and Harriet's Pioneertown Palace** Nestled amid the desert hills of a historic movie ranch west of Joshua Tree, this quirky saloon with a big patio serves up well-crafted bison burgers, baby-back ribs, and veggie nachos, plus cocktails in Mason jars. Notable rock, country, and blues concerts take place several times a month. Pioneertown, 760-228-2222, pappyandharriets.com.

- **Atmesfir** Set in a cozy storefront space in downtown Prescott's colorful Whiskey Row, this hip neighborhood bistro offers beautifully presented, farm-to-table modern American fare. Consider the line-caught halibut with bacon and grapefruit or seared duck breast with a mushroom ragout. 928-445-1929, atmesfir.com.

- **Cowboy Club Grille** Breathe in views of red-rock peaks and the savory scent of wood-fired elk chops and cast-iron cornbread at this beloved tavern in Sedona's lively Oak Creek neighborhood. 928-282-4200, cowboyclub.com.

- **Anello** Thin, blistered-crust pizzas with fresh, simple toppings—wood-roasted peppers, smoked mozzarella, artisanal sausages—are the star at this sleek contemporary spot on the edge of Tucson's lively Fourth Ave District. No phone, anello.space.

- **Tito and Pep** This stylish but laid-back neighborhood cantina in Midtown Tucson serves perfect margaritas and mezcal cocktails, as well as delicious contemporary Southwestern fare, like steak skewers with chipotle-tomatillo salsa and Baja shrimp in a seafood broth with masa dumplings. 520-207-0116, titoandpep.com.

- **Cafe Roka** One of Bisbee's most romantic destinations for refined, creative cooking, this lovely Italian bistro occupies a handsome Victorian building with high pressed-tin ceilings and exposed brick walls hung with local artwork. The boneless short ribs are a specialty. 520-432-5153, caferoka.com.

BEST SLEEPS

- **Borrego Valley Inn** With two swimming pools and rooms with private patios, fireplaces, and garden views, this 15-unit oasis near the entrance to Anza Borrego State Park makes for a tranquil desert hideaway. 760-767-0311, borregovalleyinn.com.

- **Korakia Pensione** This quietly posh inn with gorgeous Moroccan-style furnishings and design elements occupies two fabulous 1920s villas. Nestled against the foothills but within walking distance of downtown Palm Springs, Korakia has spacious suites with beamed ceilings and French doors and two heated pools. 760-864-6411, korakia.com.

- **Spring Resort and Spa** After a day of hiking around nearby Joshua Tree or the San Jacinto Mountains above Palm Springs, soak your bones in the mineral pools or book a Swedish massage or marine mud wrap at the spa of this peaceful boutique resort in the hills of Desert Hot Springs. 760-251-6700, the-spring.com.

- **29 Palms Inn** A short drive from the Twentynine Palms entrance to Joshua Tree National Park, this sun-kissed 70-acre property has a wide range of tasteful rooms set in mid-century bungalows and casitas. The inn's restaurant serves healthy, locally sourced dinners. 760-367-3505, 29palmsinn.com

- **Death Valley National Park lodgings** Given the size of Death Valley and the dearth of accommodations near the park, it's worth staying inside the park. A gracious, high-end adobe hotel built in the 1920s, the Inn at Death Valley is the park's signature property—it has a wonderful restaurant, stunning views, and a convenient location in Furnace Creek Village. This is also home to the slightly less spendy Ranch at Death Valley, where you'll find both elegantly renovated motel rooms and 80 newly constructed cottages. More affordable options include basic but pleasant Stovepipe Wells Village, near Mesquite Flat Sand Dunes, and Panamint Springs Resort, on the far west side of the park. nps.gov/deva.

- **Jerome Grand Hotel** Set high on a promontory overlooking Jerome and the dramatic Verde Valley beyond, this red-roofed 1920s former hospital has beautiful period-decorated rooms, many with balconies. The elegant Asylum Restaurant serves rarefied American and European cuisine. 928-634-8200, jeromegrandhotel.com.

- **El Portal** Arts and Crafts-style handcrafted furniture, recycled 200-year-old wood, stained-glass panels, and distinctive architectural accents imbue this laid-back but sophisticated 12-room adobe inn with a warm and inviting Frank Lloyd Wright vibe. It's a short stroll from Sedona's Tlaquepaque gallery and shopping village. 928-203-9405, elportalsedona.com.

- **Arizona Inn** Family-owned since it opened in 1930 near the University of Arizona, this enchanting compound with 89 warmly appointed rooms and suites has pleasing amenities, including a pool, neatly maintained gardens, tennis courts, and loaner bikes. The old-world restaurant and Audubon Bar are delightful. 520-325-1541, arizonainn.com.

- **El Dorado Suites** Steps from Old Bisbee Brewing and several other colorful bars, this handsomely restored 1914 building has roomy apartment-style one- and two-bedroom accommodations with full kitchens, large verandas, showers with original clawfoot tubs, and sweeping views of the countryside. 520-432-6679, eldoradosuitesbisbee.com.

—

CAMPING

Tenters and RVers have many wonderful options to choose from in the Southwest's vast parks. Anza Borrego has gorgeous campsites at the mouth of Palm Canyon, while in Mojave National Preserve you can fall asleep under a canopy of stars at Hole-in-the-Wall Campground. Surrounded by cool geological formations, Jumbo Rocks and White Tank are favorites among Joshua Tree National Park's seven campgrounds, while Death Valley's Furnace Creek and Texas Spring sites offer similarly astounding views. There's no drive-up camping at Saguaro National Park (just some primitive backcountry sites that require several miles of hiking), but Tucson/Lazydays KOA Resort is a good central Tucson option. Sam's Family Spa and Hot Water Resort (only for RVers) and Palm Springs/Joshua Tree KOA are great facilities in Desert Hot Springs (near Palm Springs). Close to but peacefully west of the glare of Las Vegas, Red Rock Campground has simple tent and RV sites. In Sedona and Verde Valley, try Crescent Moon Ranch and Dead Horse Ranch State Park, and in metro Phoenix, consider Cave Creek Regional Park. The Shady Dell Vintage Trailer Court is a fun option in Bisbee.

Opposite top Galleta Meadows, Anza-Borrego Desert State Park
Opposite middle Sedona *Opposite bottom* Joshua Tree National Park

Utah's Mountains and Canyons ★

Home of five of the country's most celebrated national parks and several world-famous ski areas that double as hiking meccas in summer, Utah is a year-round paradise for outdoor adventurers.

HOW LONG?

7 days; add an extra day each for more hiking, skiing, or spa-going in Park City and exploring more of the bigger national parks, such as Canyonlands, Zion, and possibly Capitol Reef.

WHEN TO GO

Although Utah is gorgeous year-round, a winter trip differs greatly from the rest of the year in that Salt Lake and Park City draw skiers and snowboarders, and parts of some of the national parks are either closed or harder to reach. Summer is hugely popular, which means more crowds and also hot temperatures, especially in southern Utah. That makes April to May and September to October the ideal times for this drive, as you'll encounter fewer fellow tourists and milder temperatures.

NEED TO KNOW

Especially around Salt Lake and Park City, snowy weather can result in road closures in winter. In summer, overcrowding has become a big issue in many of the state's national parks, Arches—which now requires timed-entry reservations—and Zion in particular. Try to visit on weekdays and arrive at trailheads or key park sites either very early in the morning or late in the day. Distances between services can be considerable in southern Utah, so top off your gas tank regularly.

➜ Distances
Total distance, one way: 975 mi (1571 km)
- Salt Lake City to Moab (via Park City): 280 mi (451 km)
- Moab to Torrey (via both units of Canyonlands NP): 375 miles (604 km)
- Torrey to Kanab (via Bryce Canyon NP): 220 miles (354 km)
- Kanab to St George: 90 mi (145 km)

🔅 Temperatures
January: 35-55°F (2-13°C)
July: 82-100°F (28-38°C)

ⓘ More information
- Utah tourism, visitutah.com
- Salt Lake City tourism, visitsaltlake.com
- Arches National Park, nps.gov/arch
- Canyonlands National Park, nps.gov/cany
- Capitol Reef National Park, nps.gov/care
- Bryce Canyon National Park, nps.gov/brca
- Zion National Park, nps.gov/zion
- St George tourism, greaterzion.com

👁 SNAPSHOT

Immortalized over the years in countless Hollywood movies, the red rock canyons and lofty snowcapped mountains of this mecca for skiing, hiking, mountain-biking, and nature photography bring together the best features of the dramatic desertscapes of the US Southwest and the soaring, emerald mountainscapes of the Rockies. Whether you're an extreme adventurer behind the wheel of a jeep or merely an occasional hiker with a love of capturing the perfect sunset against a multihued rock formation, driving through Utah will excite your senses; every mile of this itinerary yields eye-popping views.

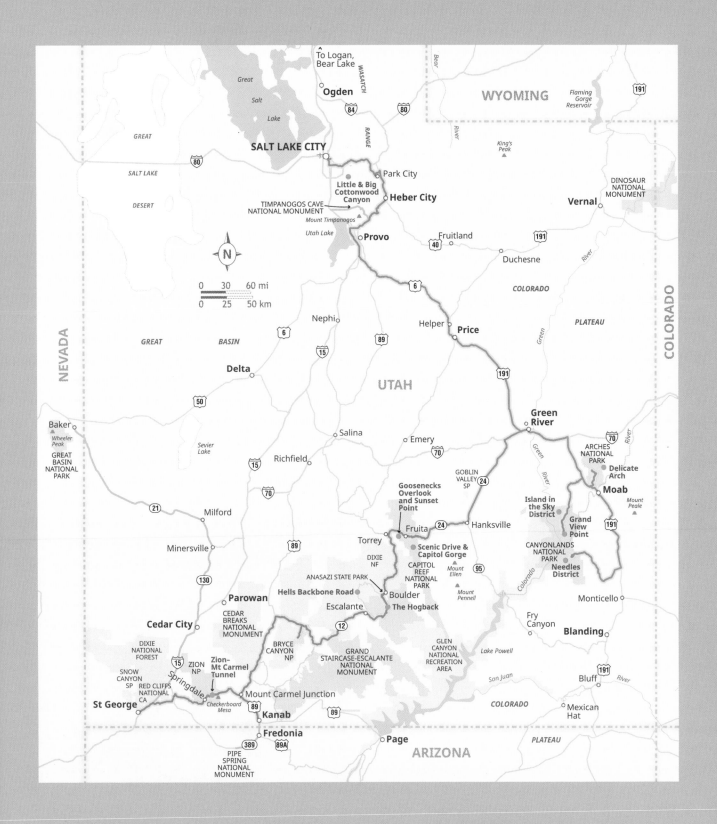

SALT LAKE CITY TO PARK CITY

Bisected by two major interstate highways and home to a major international airport (it's a Delta Airlines hub), **Salt Lake City** is a true crossroads and an optimal place to begin a tour of Utah, of which it's the capital. With a population of about 200,000 (though 1.3 million in the greater region), it's also the largest metropolis. One reason people love living here is that the city lies within 10 miles of amazing ski and hiking terrain. The resorts here and in nearby Park City are famous the world over, especially since hosting the Winter Olympics in 2002, for receiving buckets of fluffy, dry, powdery snow each winter.

To get a feel for this friendly, outdoorsy city near the southern shore of the Great Salt Lake and on the western slopes of the Wasatch Mountains, start downtown at 10-acre **Temple Square**, which is the historic heart of both the city and the Church of Jesus Christ of Latter-day Saints. It contains a pair of visitor centers, pretty gardens and a reflecting pool, the church's imposing 1893 temple, with its ornate exterior and six spires, and the even older **Salt Lake Tabernacle**, where the famed Tabernacle Choir performs. Although it was founded by Mormon pioneers and is still closely associated with the church, Salt Lake City itself has become increasingly diverse and secular over the years, as new residents move here from other parts of the country; the city is now majority non-Mormon and leans heavily Democrat (in contrast to most of the rest of the state).

Fanning south and west from Temple Square, downtown has a lively entertainment district with an impressive international dining scene, from the Japanese rolled-ice-cream and dessert parlor Doki to Arempa's for boldly flavored Venezuelan fare. HallPass, a lively food hall decorated with cool murals in downtown's **Gateway** retail plaza, has several excellent food stalls—Blaze of Thunder for Nashville-style hot chicken, Graffiti Bao for pan-Asian fare—and a full bar with a comprehensive selection of Utah craft brews.

Head northeast up State St, passing by the monumental **Utah State Capitol** and up into the hilly **City Creek Natural Area**, with its impressive views of the surrounding valley and mountains and some short, pretty hiking trails. Take Bonneville Blvd south into **The Avenues**, a historic residential neighborhood, and continue east into the city's **East Bench**, a picturesque area dominated by the **University of Utah** campus. It climbs into the foothills of the Wasatch Mountains, where you'll find more great trails. Visit the superb **Natural History Museum of Utah** and **Red Butte**

SIDETRACK

This 125-mile trip through dramatic mountain passes to 109 sq mile **Bear Lake** is a rewarding sidetrip, but also an interesting way to travel between Salt Lake and Wyoming's Jackson Hole. From Salt Lake City, take I-15 north—stopping briefly to check out the historic downtown of **Ogden**—and then US 89 to **Brigham City**. Continue along US 89, which climbs through the Wellsville Mountains and down into Cache Valley en route to the pretty college town of **Logan**, home both to Utah State University and the superb summer **Utah Opera and Musical Theatre Festival**. Grab lunch at Crumb Brothers Artisan Bread, which serves a delicious croque madame, then continue on US 89 northeast through majestic **Logan Canyon**. Some great hikes along this route include 4-mile **Wind Cave Trail** and 3.5-mile **Highline Trail**. After crossing 7818 ft **Bear Lake Summit**, US 89 winds down into **Garden City**, the small vacation hub for visiting **Bear Lake**, with its brilliant turquoise waters (the lake gets its dramatic color from the way light refracts off of calcium carbonate deposits). You can laze on the beach, rent kayaks and jet skis, or drive around the entire lake, half of which is in Idaho, in about 75 minutes. End your adventure with a burger and fresh raspberry milkshake at LaBeau's.

Bryce Canyon National Park *Previous* Canyonlands National Park

Garden, a lush 21-acre arboretum laced with walking paths. Follow rural **Emigration Canyon Rd** east along a gurgling creek into the meadowy, rolling foothills, stopping for a crisp pale ale and Bavarian-style pretzel at Emigration Canyon Brewing Co. or "Grandma Claire's" baked mac-and-cheese followed by a slice of peach-and-blueberry cobbler at old-fashioned Ruth's Diner. After passing over Little Mountain Summit, turn right onto Hwy 65 and follow it south around Little Dell Reservoir to I-80 to return to the city.

Even more visually dramatic than the East Bench are Little Cottonwood and Big Cottonwood canyons, which begin about a 20-minute drive southeast of the city center. Hwy 210 climbs 7 miles east into **Little Cottonwood Canyon**, dead-ending at Snowbird and Alta ski resorts. The road through parallel **Big Cottonwood Canyon**, Hwy 190 twists and turns beneath sheer rock cliffs and along a frothy creek for 14 miles to the Solitude and Brighton ski areas, where it also dead-ends in winter. My favorite hike in the area is the moderately challenging but gorgeous 4.5-mile round-trip trail from Brighton's base up around pristine **lakes Mary, Martha, and Catherine**. Gazing down upon these rippling waters, it's hard to imagine you're in the outskirts of a good-size city.

In summer, just before you reach Brighton Resort, you can make a left turn onto **Guardsman Pass Road** and continue another 10 miles on a breathtaking alpine adventure that is by far the most rewarding way to get to **Park City**. The road takes you over 9700 ft Guardsman Pass, where you can hike the fairly easy and quite stunning 2.7-mile (out and back) trail through groves of quaking aspens to **Blood Lake**. Back on Guardsman Pass Road, when you reach Hwy 224, turn left and follow it north as it descends steeply down through the **Deer Valley** ski area and deposits you into the center of this posh ski town. When snow closes Guardsman Pass, usually from about mid-October to mid-May, you can get to Park City via the less interesting but more direct I-80 to Hwy 224 south.

PARK CITY TO MOAB

When Park City, nestled in the Wasatch Mountains just 20 miles east of Salt Lake City, was established in 1884, it was famous for its silver mines. Today, many of its colorful buildings—including more than 60 on Main St—date back to that boomtown era. During the mid-20th century, as the mining riches dwindled, so too did Park City's population. But during this period, a ski area opened atop the abandoned mines, and the town has been booming again ever since. This affluent town is home to two acclaimed and very

SIDETRACK

When you get to **Wildwood** on US 189 in Provo Canyon, turn right onto Hwy 92, aka the **Alpine Loop Scenic Hwy**, to visit the renowned **Sundance Mountain Resort**, a ski area and upscale hotel founded by Robert Redford in the 1970s and the site of many screenings during the Sundance Film Festival, which Redford launched in 1979. It's an inviting place to spend the night, go hiking, or simply enjoy a meal in the rustic-chic Foundry Grill. Continue along this narrow, stunning route as it curves around massive 11,749 ft **Mt Timpanogos**, aka the Timp. You can hike 3.5 miles to **Stewart Falls**, a ravishing 200 ft cascade, or go spelunking on a guided tour of the fascinating, though frigid, caverns of **Timpanogos Cave National Monument**. From here you can backtrack the way you came or get to Provo by continuing west and then south on Hwy 146 and I-15.

family-welcoming ski areas, including Deer Valley and massive (the largest in the country) **Park City Mountain**, and each January to the buzzy **Sundance Film Festival**. People come to Park City chiefly for recreation. In summer the ski areas welcome hikers and mountain-bikers, and downtown hosts well-attended festivals, including the weekly **Park Silly Sunday Market**, featuring arts and crafts, food, music, and great people-watching. Along Main St, you'll find dozens of mostly upscale shops, galleries, restaurants, and bars as well as the excellent **Park City Museum**, which contains the city's old jail and mining exhibits. With plenty of snazzy resort hotels, fine restaurants, and sybaritic spas, it's also a wonderful little town for pampering yourself.

Follow Hwy 248 east and then US 189 south, which curves along the eastern side of the Wasatch Mountains past Jordanelle Reservoir, through the laid-back but fast-growing mountain town of **Heber City**, and then alongside Deer Creek Reservoir and down through Provo Canyon to **Provo**, the home of Brigham Young University. Then pick up US 6 east back over a dramatic stretch of the Wasatch Range to **Price**.

US 6 climbs dramatically over the mountains and down through the old railroad and coal-mining towns of **Helper** and **Price**. Continue two hours south on US 191 to **Moab**, one of the Southwest's magnets for outdoor recreation, from relatively easy hiking, rafting, and road biking to more extreme pursuits like rock climbing, off-road ATVing, and mountain-biking. The town is also home to incredibly beautiful and popular Arches and Canyonlands national parks. It's possible to see the best parts of these places in either a long day or parts of two days, but Canyonlands is enormous (almost five times the size of Arches) and is ideally explored over two days, especially if you visit the more remote Needles District.

Relatively compact and accessible via a single 18-mile park road, **Arches National Park** fringes the Colorado River and contains more than 2000 red- and rust-hued sandstone arches, fins, and spires formed by millions of eons of erosion. Notable stops include **Park Avenue and Courthouse Towers** (which are also connected by a 1-mile hike), **Balanced Rock**, **the Windows**, and—at the end of the road—**Devils Garden**, which contains some of park's best hikes. Try to arrive at the trailhead for the park's most iconic features, **Delicate Arch**, about 60 to 90 minutes before sunset; after hiking the slightly steep 1.5-mile trail to the natural amphitheater overlooking this 46 ft tall arch, just sit back, relax, and watch the setting sun illuminate it brilliantly.

Allow two to four hours to explore Canyonlands' northern **Island in the Sky** section, which is just north of Moab via Hwy 313. Stop at **Sky Visitor Center** to check out the natural history exhibits and learn what ranger programs are offered that day. The road continues along a sweeping, sagebrush- and piñon-dotted mesa, offering several turn-offs with astounding vistas, before ending at **Grand View Point**, from which you can see for miles across the park's dazzling landscape of deep red-rock canyons, including the biggest one of all, the confluence of the Green and Colorado rivers 2000 ft below. I like to follow the 1.8-mile round-trip trail that curves along the rim to the right, ending at a rocky promontory with spectacular vistas, especially at sunset.

Visiting the park's **Needles District** requires a three-hour round-trip drive south from Moab's cute and compact downtown, which is close to the Colorado River and has interesting little shops and galleries as well as the best restaurant scene in southeastern Utah—good bets include hip Moab Garage Co. for breakfast and the brightly painted food truck Quesadilla Mobilla for lunch. After stopping by the visitor center in Needles, continue another 7 miles to where the road dead-ends near the **Slickrock Foot Trail**, an easy to moderate 2.5-mile loop that takes two or three hours to hike and offers great views of Big Spring and Little Spring canyons. Another rewarding diversion is driving the narrow road to **Elephant Hill**, which is famous for off-road four-wheeling. In a conventional vehicle, you can go as far as the Elephant Hill Trailhead, but—as long as you're careful to avoid passing ATVs and mountain bikes—you can walk up Elephant Hill to get a sense of the skill and courage it takes to drive this hair-raising road. Also leading from that trailhead is a network of hiking trails through some of the park's most eye-popping terrain.

MOAB TO TORREY

From Moab backtrack up US 191 and across I-70, stopping in **Green River**, home to the **John Wesley Powell River History Museum**—which overlooks a pretty stretch of this 730-mile main tributary of the Colorado River—and, just across with the same river views, Tamarisk Restaurant, where you can dine on tasty elevated-diner fare. Continue to Hwy 24 and follow it south through the open desert, stopping to traipse among the mushroom-shaped sandstone hoodoos, or "goblins," at **Goblin Valley State Park**. In tiny Hanksville, Stan's Burger Shack is a funky little wayside eatery that's known for its two-fisted double-cheeseburgers. About 30 miles west, you'll enter what I believe is the underrated treasure among the state's five national parks, **Capitol Reef**.

The road flanks the Fremont River as it passes through an astonishing (even after having visited Moab) red rock landscape to **Fruita**, where there's a visitor center, a tranquil tree-shaded picnic area, and a handful of historic buildings that date back to when this fertile desert oasis thrived as a grower of apricots, apples, cherries, and other fruit trees. The 2-mile round-trip **Hickman Natural Bridge** hike offers a nice chance to stretch your legs. Set aside an hour or two for 8-mile **Scenic Dr** (the last section—through steep-walled, boulder-strewn **Capitol Gorge**—is unpaved but well maintained). At the end of the road, continue on foot through this dramatic gorge as far as the natural water cisterns, known as "the tanks." Back on Hwy 24, as you continue west stop at **Goosenecks Overlook** and **Sunset Point**, which are reached via a short side road, and hike the 3.3-mile **Chimney Rock Trail** loop, which climbs about 750 ft over a mesa and offers dazzling views in all directions. Just outside the park's western entrance, you'll come to **Torrey**, which has a good range of hotels and restaurants.

TORREY TO KANAB

In a state with endless stunningly scenic byways, the 140-mile drive south on Hwy 12 from Torrey to US 89 is arguably the most spectacular. It passes through a portion of **Grand Staircase–Escalante National Monument** and leads to mesmerizing Bryce Canyon National Park. I recommend spending a night along this drive to fully appreciate the incredible scenery. From Torrey, Hwy 12 winds south and offers great views into Capitol Reef and surrounding Dixie National Forest. You'll soon pass through **Boulder**, which is really just a remote sprinkling of homes and a few businesses. Pause at **Anasazi State Park Museum**, which preserves and interprets a partially excavated Ancestral Puebloan community that thrived in the 12th century, and dine at the renowned Boulder Mountain Lodge. A few miles farther, you have a choice: stay on Hwy 12, which soon enters **Grand Staircase–Escalante National Monument** and descends through a series of wild, narrow curves, called **the Hogback**; here I suggest hiking all or a part of the gorgeous 6-mile round-trip **Lower Calf Creek Falls** trail. Or instead you can take the famous alternate route, **Hells Backbone Road** (officially Hwy 153), a thrilling gravel road and marvel of highway engineering built by the Civilian Conservation Corps (CCC) in the 1930s. It twists and turns precipitously for 38 miles before rejoining Hwy 12.

Both routes lead to **Escalante**, a once-forgotten ranching town that has grown substantially in recent years with inns, eateries, and recreation outfitters that serve the growing crowds drawn to the national monument (which was designated only in 1996). Continue another 50 miles and turn left onto Hwy 63 to reach **Bryce Canyon National Park**, a 55 sq mile tract of dramatic natural amphitheaters dotted with thousands of sedimentary-rock hoodoos and bizarre, red-orange pinnacles that at times resemble giant pipe organs, along with arches, gray-white cliffs, and other fantastic features. Drive the 18-mile park road, stopping first at the visitor center, which has excellent exhibits on the park's geology and presents an informative movie. Then park near either **Sunrise or Sunset points**, which are connected via an easy, level trail along the canyon rim. The somewhat steep **Queen's Garden Trail** leads a mile down into the canyon from Sunrise Trail and connects with a veritable maze of side trails. Back up on the rim, stroll over to the **Lodge at Bryce Canyon**, a classic 1925 national park lodge with a casual restaurant that's perfect for a post-hike meal. If you have another hour or two, follow the park road to the end, pausing for photos at **Bryce Point** and **Ponderosa Canyon**, and then hiking the quarter-mile loop around **Yovimpa Point**, the summit of a massive vermilion-and-white limestone palisade that offers 100-mile views to the south.

Back on Hwy 12, continue west and then south on US 89 to **Kanab**, a beautifully situated town surrounded by colorful rock formations that lies just 3 miles north of the Arizona

SIDETRACK

Head south from Kanab into tiny **Fredonia, AZ**, and then drive west on Hwy 389 to reach **Pipe Spring National Monument**, an interesting and less visited park that's nestled beneath a rocky rampart on a site that's been occupied variously by Puebloan and Paiute peoples and then Spanish and Mexican settlers. You can tour the late-1800s buildings and make a nice little half-mile hike up along a desert ridge, taking in views of the massive plateau known as the Arizona Strip. For an even bigger detour, it's just 75 miles to reach the **North Rim** of the **Grand Canyon**.

border, making it an excellent base for exploring not only Zion National Park but also the North Rim of the Grand Canyon. Dozens of famous Westerns were shot around Kanab during Hollywood's Golden Age, including *Mackenna's Gold*, *How the West Was Won*, and *The Outlaw Josey Wales*.

Hiking the Lakes Mary, Martha, and Catherine Trail, Big Cottonwood Canyon, Salt Lake City

KANAB TO ST GEORGE

It's a gorgeous drive to Utah's most visited national park, **Zion**. From **Carmel Junction**, continue along a sagebrush plateau to the park's East Entrance (you must pay the $35 entrance fee to continue on Hwy 9, even if you're just passing through the park without stopping). Almost immediately the curious crack pattern of sandstone **Checkerboard Mesa** will come into view, and then you'll come to the trailhead for the short 1-mile-long trail to **Zion Canyon Overlook**, where you're treated to an amazing view from a dramatic perch more than 1000 ft above the valley floor. Parking is limited, but it's worth persevering.

Continue through the low and narrow **Zion–Mount Carmel Tunnel**, a remarkable engineering feat designed in 1930, after which the road switchbacks down into the canyon. From mid-March through October (and also weekends in November), private cars can't turn onto **Zion Canyon Scenic Road**, so continue on Hwy 9 to the excellent **Zion Human History Museum**, with its fascinating exhibits, or the large parking lot at **Zion National Park Visitor Center**. Here or in the neighboring town of **Springdale** you can catch one of the frequent shuttle buses to explore Zion Canyon Scenic Road, whose highlights include **Temple of Sinawava**, **Angels Landing**, and the **Emerald Pools**.

Drive west on Hwy 9, stopping briefly to look around the ghost town of **Rockville**, and then about 35 miles to **St George**, a fast-growing city of about 90,000 that's the largest metropolis between Las Vegas (two hours south) and Salt Lake (4.5 hours north). It's is a good place to stock up on supplies or tack on an extra day or two. **Red Hills Desert Garden** is a beautiful park landscaped with flora that thrives in the Southwest, and the surrounding **Red Cliffs National Conservation Area** and **Snow Canyon State Park** offer miles of well-marked trails through stunning high-desert terrain.

SIDETRACK

Great Basin National Park is just over the Utah border in eastern Nevada, and it's a relatively easy side trip from St George, especially if you were already headed back up to Salt Lake City. From St George, take I-15 north to the picturesque college town of **Cedar City**, then meander up through **Minersville** to **Baker, NV**, the park's headquarters. The best strategy for a half-day visit is driving **Wheeler Peak Scenic Road** on its 12-mile climb from 6800 to 10,000 ft. It ends in the "great basin" beneath 13,063 ft Wheeler Peak, which is Nevada's second-highest summit. From here, take the 4.5-mile **Bristlecone Pine Glacier Trail**, which first climbs through a grove of bristlecone pines. Looking a bit like the fighting trees in *The Wizard of Oz*, these gnarled conifers have been determined to be the oldest living things on the planet, some of them dating back 5000 years. The trail ends in a rocky valley and a majestic overlook of one of the southernmost glaciers in the United States. Back in Baker, Kerouac's Restaurant and Sugar, Salt and Malt are great places for lunch or dinner.

BEST EATS

- **SLC Eatery** Beneath exposed air ducts and Edison bulbs, feast on some of Utah's most creative and beautifully plated contemporary cuisine, prepared from a seasonally changing menu. There's also a fabulous weekend brunch. Salt Lake City, 801-355-7952, slceatery.com.
- **Bombay House** In a city with a rich variety of international cuisine, this wood-paneled Indian restaurant in Salt Lake City's East Bench neighborhood might just be the best. The savory lamb, chicken, shrimp, and vegetarian dishes are authentically prepared. 801-581-0222, bombayhouse.com.
- **Handle** This scene-y Park City restaurant focuses on locavore-driven American fare, such as bone-in rib-eye and bucatini pasta with mushroom Bolognese and truffled mascarpone. The craft cocktail list is superb. 435-602-1155, handleparkcity.com.
- **Firewood** Set in a rustic-chic timber-and-brick dining room on Park City's Main St, this buzzy bistro specializes in locally sourced food prepared over a wood fire—think oxtail crepinettes and bison short-rib stroganoff with house-made pasta. 435-252-9900, firewoodonmain.com.
- **Lakehouse at Deer Creek** With grand views across Heber City's Deer Creek Reservoir, this is a heavenly place to stop for lunch on your drive toward Provo Canyon or Sundance. Try the sliced tri-tip steak sandwich. 435-210-7474, thelakehousedeercreek.com.
- **Trailhead Public House and Eatery** Fuel up after hiking at this boisterous bilevel gastropub in downtown Moab. Hearty favorites include green-chile pork poutine, and wagyu burgers topped with house fire-roasted chiles, cheddar, and bacon. 435-355-1782, moabtrailhead.com.
- **Hunt and Gather** A short drive from Capitol Reef National Park, this worldly but unpretentious restaurant overlooking the red rock mountains specializes in the regional bounty— elk loin, foraged wild mushroom risotto, red-rainbow trout. 435-425-3070, huntandgatherrestaurant.com.
- **Burr Trail Grill** Folks drive for miles to tiny Boulder to sample the sensational modern American fare at this quirky roadhouse known for in "burgers, beer, and homemade pie." The lamb burger is a favorite. Save room for caramel-apple-cardamom pie. 435-335-7511, burrtrailgrill.life.
- **Rocking V Cafe** Tiny Kanab has developed an impressive little dining scene, with this lively storefront bistro leading the charge. The eclectic menu offers vegan burgers, chargrilled pork chops with apple-cranberry compote, and bread pudding with an ever-changing array of flavors. 435-644-8001, rockingvcafe.com.

- **King's Landing Bistro** On Springdale's cute main drag, this art-filled restaurant overlooking Zion's dramatic rocky buttes turns out artfully prepared food, too. Consider the heirloom tomatoes with burrata, and king salmon with saffron couscous. 435-772-7422, klbzion.com.
- **Xetava Gardens Cafe** The culinary centerpiece of the Kayenta arts colony just outside St George, this hip brunch and lunch spot has seating in a beautiful xeriscape courtyard with stunning views of red rock mountains. Belgian waffles, green-curry mahi-mahi, and bacon-blue cheese burgers are standouts. 435-656-0165, xetava.com.

BEST SLEEPS

- **Kimpton Hotel Monaco** This stylish boutique hotel in a 1920s bank building in Salt Lake City has spacious rooms with bold patterns and colors, many of them facing the snowcapped Wasatch Mountains. Bambara serves exceptional contemporary American cuisine. 801-595-0000, monaco-saltlakecity.com.
- **Washington School House Hotel** All 12 rooms and suites in this stunningly transformed 1889 limestone schoolhouse in downtown Park City have been individually outfitted with custom-designed beds, well-chosen antiques, and thoughtful amenities like French press coffeemakers, slippers, and robes. There's a heated pool, too. 435-649-3800, washingtonschoolhouse.com.
- **Montage Deer Valley** For a luxurious Park City splurge, stay at this plush ski-in, ski-out resort amid the rarified mountain air of Empire Pass in Deer Valley. Diversions include five superb restaurants, a bowling alley, and a fabulous spa. 435-604-1300, montagehotels.com.
- **Red Cliffs Lodge** With a breathtaking location alongside the Colorado River near Moab, this historic property served originally as a filming locale for Hollywood Westerns (there's a cool film museum). It has a great restaurant and inviting rooms with tile baths, and chunky hand-hewn wooden furniture; some cabins have decks on the river. 435-259-2002, redcliffslodge.com.
- **Gonzo Inn** Bright color schemes, contemporary art and furniture, and enchanting balconies or patios are standout features at this quirky condo-style hotel within walking distance of downtown Moab restaurants. Suites have fully stocked kitchens. 800-791-4044, gonzoinn.com.
- **Austin's Chuckwagon Hotel** A short drive west of Capitol Reef National Park, this compound comprising a rustic log cabin-style motel and several two-bedroom cabins includes a pool with hot tub as well as a deli. 435-425-3335, austinschuckwagon.com.

- **Boulder Mountain Lodge** This gorgeous 11-acre spread that's home to the celebrated Hell's Backbone Grill is reason alone to spend an extra night between Capitol Reef and Bryce Canyon. The high-ceilinged rooms overlook wetlands and a migratory bird sanctuary and many have kitchens. Boulder, 435-335-7460, boulder-utah.com.

- **Stone Canyon Inn** On the outskirts of Tropic, this compound of elegant, contemporary cabins, bungalows, and guest suites is adjacent to Bryce Canyon. You can see amazing rock formations from the property's expansive deck, which extends from romantic Stone Hearth Grill. 435-679-8611, stonecanyoninn.com.

- **Lodge at Bryce Canyon** With its steep green-shingle roof, stone and timber frame, and idyllic setting, this 1925 structure is steps from glorious Sunrise and Sunset points. It contains just four guest rooms but also has a rustic restaurant and inviting common spaces. Adjacent are a pair of newer motel-style buildings and—my favorite place to stay in Utah—several historic stone-and-log cabins with fireplaces and lodgepole pine walls. 435-834-8700, brycecanyonforever.com.

- **Parry Lodge** The simple, economical rooms in this 1920s Kanab motor lodge are named for illustrious actors who stayed here while filming movies, among them Lana Turner, and Clint Eastwood. 435-644-2601, parrylodge.com.

- **Canyons Boutique Hotel** Part of a trio of artfully appointed, cozy inns, all within walking distance of downtown Kanab, this 28-room property has a pair of outdoor pools, and guests can borrow bicycles to pedal around town. 435-644-8660, thecanyonscollection.com.

- **Zion Lodge** Surrounded by soaring canyon walls and mountain peaks, this meticulously detailed 1990 reconstruction of the original 1924 lodge, which was lost in a fire in 1966, is along the park's scenic road and contains 80 warmly appointed rooms and the excellent Red Rock Grill. Many historic 1920s buildings still surround the lodge, including 40 guest cabins, each with gas-log fireplaces and private porches. Zion, 435-772-7700, zionlodge.com.

- **Cable Mountain Lodge** This chic Springdale lodge is just across the Virgin River from Zion National Park's visitor and is the perfect place to unwind after a day of hiking or driving, as the resort's soothing spa offers a slew of treatments. 435-772-3366, cablemountainlodge.com

- **Inn on the Cliff** This two-story, 27-room boutique hotel sits high on a ridge overlooking St George and the miles of beautiful red rock cliffs beyond. You can drink up the scenery from your room's private balcony while sunning by the pool, or during lunch or dinner in the classy restaurant. 435-216-5864, innonthecliff.com.

CAMPING

With a sunny high-desert climate, well-developed national and state parks, and spectacular views in every direction, Utah is a fantastic state for camping, especially if you love backcountry adventures far from the crowds. But fans of car camping and RVing will find loads of options, too. All five national parks have at least one developed campground; you'll also find commercial RV and tent campgrounds in many nearby towns—these include Moab Valley RV Resort, Wonderland RV Park in Torrey, Ruby's Inn RV Park near Bryce, Dark Sky RV Campground in Kanab, and Zion Canyon RV Resort in Springdale. Redman Campground is a great option during the summer months in Big Cottonwood Canyon—it's close to both Salt Lake City and Park City.

Top Arches National Park *Opposite* Antelope House Overlook, Canyon de Chelly National Monument *Previous* The trail to Delicate Arch, Arches National Park

The Four Corners ★

The piney slopes of the Rocky Mountains and the painted high deserts of the Southwest intersect along this wide-open journey through the Grand Canyon, Monument Valley, and Indigenous communities that trace their roots back more than 1500 years.

HOW LONG?

7 days; add an extra day to explore more of Flagstaff, the Grand Canyon, and Mesa Verde.

WHEN TO GO

Spring and fall are just about perfect in these parts, offering cool to mild temperatures, plenty of sunshine, and moderate crowds. Summer brings sometimes unbearable crowds to the Grand Canyon and some of the region's other top draws. In winter I love seeing the contrast of snow against the region's red rocks and evergreen forests, but parts of the Grand Canyon, Mesa Verde, and other attractions are closed then.

NEED TO KNOW

Exercise caution using GPS in this region of often isolated communities and rural, unpaved roads—stick with well-established routes. It's possible to go long distances between gas stations, so top off your tank regularly.

→ Distances

Total distance, one-way: 1050 mi (1690 km)
- Flagstaff, AZ to Page, AZ: 220 mi (354 km)
- Page, AZ to Durango, CO: 290 mi (467 km)
- Durango, CO to Gallup, NM: 220 mi (354 km)
- Gallup, NM to Winslow, AZ: 270 mi (435 km)

⬇ Daytime Temperatures

January: 36-45°F (2-7°C)
July: 84-98°F (29-37°C)

ⓘ More information

- Flagstaff tourism, flagstaffarizona.org
- Grand Canyon National Park, nps.gov/grca
- Monument Valley, navajonationparks.org
- Mesa Verde National Park, nps.gov/meve
- Durango tourism, durango.org
- Canyon de Chelly National Monument, nps.gov/cach
- Petrified Forest National Park, nps.gov/pefo

◉ SNAPSHOT

I find the purest joy of driving through the Navajo and Hopi lands of the Southwest comes from simply gazing out the car window at some of the nation's most awe-inspiring canyons and mountain peaks. There are no traffic jams or urban sprawl to contend with in this sparsely populated junction of four states famed for their awesome untamed beauty. Arizona, Utah, Colorado, and New Mexico.

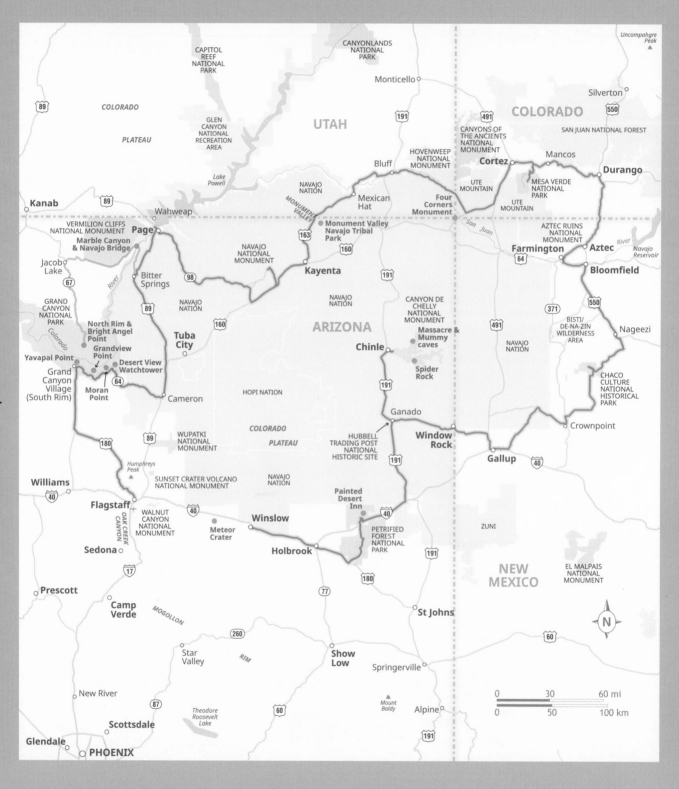

FLAGSTAFF, AZ TO PAGE, AZ

With about 78,000 residents plus another 28,000 students enrolled at Northern Arizona University, sunny and outdoorsy **Flagstaff** sits at an elevation of nearly 7000 ft and is one of the major crossroads of the Southwest (it has more than 100 motels and hotels). It's a major gateway to both the Grand Canyon and—just 30 miles down through beautiful Oak Creek Canyon—Sedona (*see* The Desert Southwest chapter p. 87). Surrounded by so many alluring attractions, it's a destination that can test your ability to prioritize your time. Fascinating tours are available at **Lowell Observatory**, which was established in 1894 and is where astronomer Clyde Tombaugh discovered the dwarf planet Pluto in 1930. And 12,633 ft **Humphreys Peak** and the **Arizona Snowbowl**, whose popular hiking trails you can access from the gondola at Snowbowl ski resort, are good choices for hikers (and they're en route to the Grand Canyon). Of the area's three national monuments, both **Walnut Canyon** and **Wupatki** preserve ancient Puebloan structures, and although they're both fascinating, you're going to see many more of these dwellings on this tour. So I'd make **Sunset Crater Volcano** a priority—it's a significant and impressive example of a cinder cone, and it's close enough to Wupatki to easily combine the two.

Also try to explore on foot the shops, eateries, and vintage early- to mid-20th-century architecture of Flagstaff's **Historic Downtown and Railroad District**, which is bisected by a colorful span of Old Route 66. Fans of the Arts and Crafts design shouldn't miss **Riordan Mansion State Historic Park**. Start the day with breakfast at quirky Tourist Home All Day cafe and bakery or MartAnne's Burrito Palace (the scrambled eggs with house-made chorizo are delicious and substantial). Later in the day, stop for drinks and apps at Mother Road Brewing or the Rendezvous bar inside the rambling (and haunted) 1926 **Hotel Monte Vista**. As you depart town northwest via US 180, visit the **Museum of Northern Arizona**, with its wooded campus of 1930s Pueblo Revival and Mission Revival buildings housing a stellar collection of Hopi and Navajo textiles, jewelry, and art as well as nicely designed natural history exhibits. When you reach Hwy 64, it's another 30 miles up to **Grand Canyon National Park**'s **South Rim**, the far more visited side of this 18-mile-wide, 277-mile-long, mile-deep gorge and the only rim that's accessible year-round. Start in **Grand Canyon Village**, a collection of turn-of-the-20th-century buildings, first by stopping inside the Mission-style **Verkamp's Visitor Center** and park store. Then walk along the level (it's suitable even for young kids) **Rim Trail** to take in the mesmerizing vistas

SIDETRACK

About 55 miles north of Cameron at **Bitter Springs**, US 89A leads 100 miles to the **North Rim** of the Grand Canyon. Keep in mind that it's a nearly four-hour round-trip drive, so I recommend making this detour only if you have at least a half day to spare. Also, the park road to the North Rim is closed due to snow from about late October to mid-May. That said, this trip has plenty of thrills, starting with the drive across **Marble Canyon**. It's spanned by the **Navajo Bridge**, which at 467 ft tall was the highest steel arch bridge in the world when it was completed in 1929. A newer bridge parallels the earlier bridge, which is open for pedestrians and adjoins a stately stone visitor center and bookstore. US 89A ascends some 4500 ft in elevation through stunning red rock ramparts that form the southern boundary of **Vermilion Cliffs National Monument**. At **Jacob Lake**, Hwy 67 leads about 40 miles across the Ponderosa pine-dotted Kaibab Plateau to the North Rim, which rises some 1000 ft higher than the South Rim. My perfect day here consists first of driving 20-mile **Cape Royal Road** and stopping at the **Vista Encantada** and **Walhalla** overlooks to gain a very different perspective on the canyon, and then hiking the 4-mile out-and-back **Cape Final Trail**—the view at the end is one of the most awesome in the park. Then visit **Grand Canyon Lodge**, an impressive limestone-and-timber building designed by Gilbert Stanley Underwood in 1928. As sunset approaches, make the easy 1-mile round-trip hike to **Bright Angel Point**, and then return to enjoy dinner in the main dining room. Consider overnighting at Grand Canyon Lodge or possibly even the Jacob Lake Inn, keeping in mind that the few accommodations near the North Rim can book up months in advance.

across the canyon; I like to start by walking west and visiting the Mary Colter–designed **Hopi House**, with its extensive collections of regional Native American art, and the 1904 **Kolb Studio**, where you can view engrossing photography exhibits and antique equipment. Break things up with a bite to eat—maybe a casual meal at Fred Harvey Burger or a more elegant repast in the dining room of the park's flagship 1905 hotel, El Tovar.

In the afternoon, walk east along the canyon rim from Verkamp's Visitor Center for 1.4 miles to **Yavapai Point and Geology Museum**, or get your blood flowing by descending into the canyon via **Bright Angel Trail**. If time is tight, turn around after the first half hour or so (remember that it will take you twice as long to hike back out of the canyon). Otherwise, continue to the **1.5-Mile Resthouse** before returning. Late in the afternoon, take the free shuttle bus (from December through February, you can drive your own vehicle) on a 7-mile scenic ride along **Hermit Rd**, stopping at the amazing **Hopi Point** and **Mohave Point** overlooks. At the end you'll reach **Hermits Rest**, where a short stroll leads to an incredible sunset vista.

Leave the park via **Desert View Dr**, a 22-mile scenic route with numerous pullouts, including **Grandview Point** and **Moran Point**. Near the exit, ascend the five-story Pueblo Revival–style **Desert View Watchtower**, another of acclaimed architect Mary Colter's designs. Note the interior murals by Hopi artist Fred Kabotie. Continue to US 89, then turn north and stop in the small Navajo village of **Cameron** to fill your gas tank and buy souvenirs and crafts at **Cameron Trading Post**, which was built in 1916 and also features a casual restaurant filled with striking Native American art and serving pretty good food, like Navajo-style French dip fry bread sandwiches and prickly pear–barbecue pork ribs. You can also walk over to view the dramatic **Cameron Suspension Bridge**, which spans the Little Colorado River. From here, it's an 80-mile drive north through the high desert to Page.

PAGE, AZ TO DURANGO, CO

With its neat rows of single-story homes and grassy lawns, **Page** looks oddly suburban for a town surrounded by a wilderness of brilliant red rock canyons and mesas. Indeed, it's a young company town that was established in 1957 to house the workers who built Glen Canyon Dam, the nation's fourth largest. You can view and learn about the controversial (many environmentalists continue to lobby for its removal) construction of this remarkable 710 ft tall structure at the **Carl Hayden Visitor Center**. Then drive a few miles north to **Wahweap Marina**, which overlooks a relatively small section of **Lake Powell**, the body of water created by this massive hydroelectric project. This 254 sq mile lake (it's about 25% larger than Lake Tahoe) extends many miles east through a series of narrow and steep canyons that form **Glen Canyon National Recreation Area**. The best way to see the lake is by taking a two-hour sunset boat ride through **Lake Powell Boat Tours** at Wahweap Marina, which is part of **Lake Powell Resort** and includes a hotel and several restaurants. Have dinner at the Rainbow Room, which has panoramic views of the lake.

Page is also a popular base for nature photographers, as there are several incredible venues relatively nearby that shutterbugs flock to, including the dramatic U-shape turn in the Colorado River known as **Horseshoe Bend** and the **Upper and Lower Antelope Canyons**, a pair of dramatic red-sandstone slot canyons that are illuminated by beams of overhead sunshine and can be visited only on a tour with an official Navajo guide (**Antelope Canyon Tours** and **Ken's Tours** are both reliable). From Page follow Hwy 98 through a sparse wilderness and into the western side of Navajo Nation, a 27,413 sq mile Indigenous tribal land that's slightly larger than the state of West Virginia. At US 160 continue to **Kayenta**, stopping briefly to see the **Navajo Code Talkers Exhibit**, which—believe it or not—is set inside a Burger King. With memorabilia, photos, and documents, it's a fascinating place that shines a light on the valiant and important efforts of 29 men who used their fluency with the Navajo language—which the Japanese were never able to decipher—to send and receive hundreds of coded messages on behalf of the US Marines during World War II. This small town with a handful of hotels and eateries marks the southern end of **Monument Valley**, a roughly 30 sq mile tract of beguiling sandstone buttes and boulders that rank among the world's most recognizable rock formations—this iconic landscape has appeared in dozens of Hollywood films, including *The Searchers*, *2001: A Space Odyssey*, and *Forrest Gump*, and it was even re-created in the animated movie *Cars*.

Drive north on US 163 and, just after crossing the Utah border, turn right to reach **Monument Valley Navajo Tribal Park**, stopping first at the visitor center, where you'll find exhibits on the area's natural and human history and an observation deck that takes in the jaw-dropping scenery. There's also a trading post and restaurant, and next door is the modern **View Hotel**. You can also make the 17-mile scenic loop drive through the valley. I've done this once

Bright Angel Trail, Grand Canyon National Park
Previous Monument Valley

and am glad I did, but I wouldn't say it's a must, especially if you're limited on time. The drive takes two to four hours along a rough road, but if you'd rather not subject your own car to this undertaking, you can also book a tour with an official Navajo guide (I recommend the knowledgeable team at **Monument Valley Safari**). Consider heading just west across US 163 to **Goulding's Trading Post**, a 1920s lodge and museum set beneath a sheer red-rock monolith that also has a festive restaurant with terrific views. Continue north up US 163 over a high ridge with dazzling valley views, and then down across the San Juan River into the tiny speck of a village known as **Mexican Hat**, which takes its colorful name from a curious sombrero-shaped rock formation on the side of the road.

Follow the road east to **Bluff**, an attractive pioneer town with a handful of picturesque lodgings and restaurants, including Twin Rocks Trading Post, a friendly diner and colorful crafts shop—kids are often awed by its improbable setting beneath sandstone pillars. Continue southeast into Colorado. At US 160, you can detour 6 miles southwest to **Four Corners Monument** and delight your Instagram followers by posting a photo of yourself with each of your arms and legs anchored in a different one of the four states— Arizona, Utah, Colorado, and New Mexico—that meet at this point. The park also marks the boundary between the Navajo Nation and Ute Mountain Ute Reservation. Head northeast to **Cortez**, a friendly town of around 8800 residents that's surrounded by some of the Southwest's most important prehistoric archaeological sites. Some of these—**Hovenweep** and **Canyons of the Ancients** national monuments, in particular—require a good bit of time and effort to explore. Skip them if you're short on time, but 10 miles east, **Mesa Verde National Park** is a must. Established in 1906, it

contains an incredible 600 different cliff dwellings that were constructed by the Ancestral Puebloan people, who inhabited this region between about 600 and the early 1300s.

View the exhibits at the strikingly contemporary LEED-certified **Mesa Verde Visitor and Research Center**, where you can also purchase tickets to see the several park cliff dwellings that can be visited only on a ranger-led tour; these tours often sell out quickly, but you can buy tickets at recreation.gov up to 14 days in advance. Follow the steep and hilly road up atop the mesa, and just past the park's only accommodation—the **Far View Lodge**—you'll reach the turnoff for **Wetherhill Mesa**, the more remote of the park's two main collections of cliff dwellings. Unless I've got a full day to explore Mesa Verde, I usually skip this 25-mile side excursion and instead continue south to drive both the **Cliff Palace Loop** and **Mesa Top Loop**. Start at the **Chapin Mesa Archaeological Museum**, a fascinating early 1920s building that shows an excellent film about the park. Then set out on a short self-guided (no tickets required) walk along the half-mile trail to view **Spruce Tree House**, an impressive circa-mid-1200s dwelling tucked into a long sandstone ledge and containing some 130 rooms—it's the third largest Puebloan structure in the park. Although you will need tickets to two of the park's most majestic dwellings, **Cliff House** and **Balcony House**, you can get a view of Cliff House from the **Sun Point View** lookout on Mesa Top Loop.

Back on US 160, continue east through **Mancos**, which has a handful of one-of-a-kind shops and eateries, including the sophisticated contemporary American restaurant Olio and the more casual Mancos Brewing Company. The road then rises up through the southern edge of conifer-shaded **San Juan National Forest** and into the arresting little city of **Durango** (pop 19,000). More than 150 miles from the nearest interstate highway, this relatively secluded slice of southwestern Colorado wilderness is popular for skiing and hiking and also boasts a charming downtown abundant with stylish yet laid-back hotels, restaurants, and taverns. The town's main attraction is the **Durango and Silverton Narrow Gauge Railroad and Museum**, which offers 10-hour round-trip rides (including a two-hour layover) in vintage rail cars through magnificent alpine scenery to **Silverton**. Bear in mind, though, that you can also explore this same mountainous corridor by driving north up US 550 (*see* The Colorado Rockies chapter p. 117 for more on Silverton and Ouray). For a spectacular view of downtown Durango and the verdant Animus River Valley, drive up to the pretty campus of **Fort Lewis College** and turn onto Rim Drive.

DURANGO, CO TO GALLUP, NM

Head south from Durango on US 550, crossing into New Mexico and stopping in the village of **Aztec** to visit the compact and easily accessible Ancestral Puebloan ruins of **Aztec National Monument**, an extensive and misnamed (by 19th-century pioneers) network of 13th-century structures. Head southwest through the comparatively modern oil-and-gas town of **Farmington**, breaking for a burger and a beer at genial Three Rivers Brewery and to admire the eclectic artwork at **Artifacts Gallery**. For a view of one of the strangest landscapes in the Southwest, head south about 40 miles to Hwy 7297, which leads to the main parking area for the mesmerizing badlands of the **Bisti/De-Na-Zin Wilderness**. I love to walk amid these bizarre and colorful hoodoos, spires, and mounds of sand layered in rusty-red, jet-black, burnt-orange, and yellowish-gray hues, but I always bring a compass and download a map on my phone for any longer treks—it's easy to get disoriented.

Back in Farmington, follow US 550 southeast to the small Navajo village of **Nageezi**, and then take the turnoff for **Chaco Culture National Historical Park**. So begins a bumpy—and sometimes treacherous after heavy rains—21-mile unpaved drive to one of America's most remarkable archaeological sites. Before you attempt visiting, though, while you're still in Farmington call the visitor center to ask about the latest road conditions. If the road isn't passable (you'll fare better in a four-wheel-drive vehicle), bypass Chaco and continue to Gallup via Hwy 371 instead of US 550. If you go to Chaco, start at the visitor center, which has excellent exhibits about this ancient city that stood at the center of a vast trade network and was the home to thousands

of Ancestral Puebloans from roughly 850 to 1250. This is a primitive park with no lodging or dining facilities, but the rangers are extremely knowledgeable, and part of what's wonderful is the lack of crowds (about 40,000 people visit annually compared with around 600,000 to Mesa Verde). Follow the 8-mile, one-way scenic loop, hopping out to hike the interpretive trails that lead through the largest of these formidable multiroom sandstone buildings, including **Pueblo Bonito**, **Chetro Ketl**, and **Casa Rinconada**. Exit the park by driving southwest on Hwy 57, crossing through the Navajo settlement of **Crown Point** on Hwy 371, and then across the sweeping high desert through **Standing Rock** and down to **Church Rock** to Gallup.

GALLUP, NM TO WINSLOW, AZ

Founded in 1881 as a railroad hub, **Gallup** later became a favorite overnight stop on Historic Route 66. This small city is also on the edge of the Navajo Nation and Zuni Pueblo, and nearly half of its 21,700 residents identify as Native American. You'll find venerable trading posts, including **Bill Malone** and **Richardsons** (which dates back to 1913), and an array of down-home eateries serving up tasty New Mexican fare—Jerry's, Route 66 Railway Cafe, and Sandra's Place are all great. Also check out the **Gallup Cultural Center**, which is inside the 1918 Santa Fe Rail depot and contains a small but excellent museum devoted to the region's vibrant Native American heritage. For me, no trip to Gallup is complete without a visit to the **El Rancho Hotel**, with its fabulous neon sign and walls hung with framed photos of the many movie stars—William Holden, Kirk Douglas, Errol Flynn— who stayed here while filming classic Westerns like the *Streets* *of Laredo* and *Ace in the Hole*. There's nothing fancy about either the funky old rooms or the rollicking restaurant, but the old-school vibe is unbeatable.

Head north and then west through the southern end of the Navajo Nation, crossing into Arizona and stopping briefly in **Window Rock**, the Nation's administrative center, to view the engaging exhibits and fine artwork at the **Navajo Nation Museum**. Continue west on Hwy 264 through **Ganado** to browse the hand-woven Navajo rugs sold in the shop at **Hubbell Trading Post National Historic Site**, one of the oldest continuously operated trading posts in the country (it dates back to 1876). US 191 leads 33 miles to **Chinle**, the site of what I consider to be the most majestic national monument in the country, **Canyon de Chelly**. Entirely within the Navajo Nation, it's the only national park property managed in partnership with a Native nation, and visitors may enter the interior of the park only with a Navajo guide or park employee (you can drive the park's canyon roads on your own). The 131 sq mile park consists of three spectacular canyons with sheer sandstone walls that rise as high as 1000 ft. I recommend spending the night inside the park at the mid-century **Thunderbird Lodge**. In the morning, stop by the small visitor center and head out on **North Rim Drive** to visit the **Massacre Cave** and **Mummy Cave** overlooks and take a short hike out to see the **Antelope House Overlook**. Return to grab lunch at the Thunderbird Lodge, and then spend the afternoon exploring the views along **South Rim Drive**, including the **White House Overlook**, where you can hike down to an impressive ruin. End your visit at the overlook for **Spider Rock**, a spectacular red-rock spire that rises some 700 ft above the canyon floor.

Backtrack to Ganado and continue south to I-40 and then west to the main entrance to **Petrified Forest National Park**, a 221,390-acre tract of high-desert badlands and sweeping, shrubby mesas dotted with trunks of trees from the Late Triassic period (about 230 million years ago) that have become petrified—or fossilized into quartz crystals. The park closes to visitors around sunset, so always check hours. Also, the park has one basic cafeteria-style restaurant (at the main **Painted Desert Visitor Center**) and no accommodations—I usually bring picnic supplies to enjoy at one of the many pretty overlooks. **Painted Desert Visitor Center** and its adjacent buildings are an overlooked architectural treasure; they were designed in 1958 by the Austrian American architect Richard Neutra, a founder of California Modernism, and they're one of the most impressive representations of mid-century architecture in the National Park system. Along

the park road, you'll come to another striking structure, the **Painted Desert Inn**. This Pueblo Revival–style building was built in the 1930s by the Civilian Conservation Corps (CCC), renovated by famed architect Mary Colter—with interior murals by Hopi artist Fred Kabotie—in the 1940s, and operated as a park lodging for another couple of decades. The view from the terrace across the Painted Desert badlands is incredible. And we haven't even gotten to the park's namesake petrified wood, which you can see and even touch at numerous points along the 28-mile park road. Notable pull-offs include remnants of where the original Route 66 passed through the park (just north of where present-day I-40 does today), the 600-year-old petroglyphs **Puerco Pueblo** and **Newspaper Rock**, and the prolific petrified wood visible in Crystal Forest and along the **Giant Logs Interpretive Loop Trail**, which is adjacent to the **Rainbow Forest Museum**. If you have time for just one short hike, make it **Blue Mesa**, where a paved 1-mile loop trail descends through a valley of distinctive formations, petrified wood trunks, and blue-hued bentonite clay hills. Don't ever remove so much as a sliver of petrified wood from the park (doing so will result in a steep fine). If you must own a piece, stop by **Jim Gray's Petrified Wood Co.** in Holbrook, which sources its wood from land it owns outside the park.

Exiting through the south entrance, head west on US 180 to quirky **Holbrook**, which is famous for its **Wigwam Motel**, a still-operating 1949 motor court with rooms inside cement "teepees"—cars from the '50s and '60s are parked throughout the property. Stop by Bienvenidos Restaurant for a hearty platter of chicken-fried steak or a barbecue brisket sandwich. Then continue west 30 miles to **Winslow**—yes, the very Winslow, Arizona immortalized in the classic Eagles song "Take It Easy." There's even a statue of a musician strumming a guitar downtown in **Standin' on the Corner Park**. Another stately Mary Colter creation, the 1929 **La Posada Hotel**, sits on the edge of downtown and is wonderful for lunch, dinner, or simply strolling amid the art-filled common rooms and flowery gardens. It's just an hour's drive to Flagstaff. Along the way, you could stop for a tour of **Meteor Crater and Barringer Space Museum**, the site of a 560 ft deep crater from a meteor that crashed here about 50,000 years ago. The $20 per person admission to visit this privately owned wonder is a bit steep, but it does make for an appropriately dramatic final stop on this tour of the otherworldly Four Corners region.

Opposite The View Hotel, Monument Valley

BEST EATS

- **Tinderbox Kitchen** This casually stylish downtown Flagstaff bistro serves some of the tastiest food in town—think seared sea scallops in a red curry sauce with pineapple and sesame. The wine list is terrific, too. 928-226-8400, tinderboxkitchen.com.

- **El Tovar Dining Room** Only a handful of tables at this rustic 1905 lodge have (somewhat distant) views of the Grand Canyon, but this warmly appointed space with native stone and timber walls as well as murals depicting Hopi, Apache, Mojave, and Navajo life is a genuinely special place. Reservations are an absolute must, and if you can't make it for dinner, come during the less-crowded breakfast and lunch hours. 928-638-2631, grandcanyonlodges.com

- **Sunset 89** Both the dining room and the terrace of this airy restaurant in Page have splendid views—especially at sunset—of Lake Powell and Glen Canyon Dam. It serves superb Asian and Hawaiian cuisine. 928-608-5562, sunset89.com

- **Farm Bistro** This dapper dining room with pressed-tin ceilings and polished wood floors stands out among a few good restaurants in the laid-back Cortez near Mesa Verde National Park. Cast-iron skillets play a central role in the preparation of several dishes, including Moroccan-style lamb meatballs. 970-565-3834, thefarmbistrocortez.com.

- **El Moro Tavern** With soft lighting, exposed-brick walls, and a long old-fashioned bar, this cozy and convivial Durango gastropub features a finely curated charcuterie and cheese list and internationally inflected dishes like green-curry mussels and pickled-shiitake ramen. 970-259-5555, elmorotavern.com.

- **James Ranch Grill** It's a beautiful 15-minute drive north of Durango to this handsome wood-frame restaurant set in the middle of a verdant 400-acre ranch. The kitchen turns out farm-fresh organic dishes, such as grass-fed burgers and chopped-kale salads with roasted butternut squash. 970-764-4222, jamesranch.net

- **Jerry's Cafe** This cozy adobe-brick storefront diner with an iconic red, blue, and yellow neon sign serves fantastic home-style New Mexican fare. Arrive hungry for massive portions of flavorful guacamole cheeseburgers, chiles rellenos, and beef-and-bean-stuffed sopaipillas (which are essentially puffy pillows of fried dough and a New Mexico specialty). 505-722-6775, no website.

BEST SLEEPS

- **Starlight Pines B&B** A stylishly appointed, romantic alternative to the scads of motels and chain properties in Flagstaff, this cheerful blue farmhouse has four spacious, light-filled rooms, a long verandah that's perfect for relaxing on a warm afternoon. 928-527-1912, starlightpinesbb.com.

- **Grand Canyon National Park lodgings** You have plenty of accommodations to choose from, including no-frills properties (Yavapai and Maswik Lodge) and one of the most celebrated national park buildings, the 1905 El Tovar Hotel. If you're willing to share a bath, the tiny and simple rooms in the stone-and-log Bright Angel Lodge, which Mary Colter designed in 1935, are a bargain—some have canyon views and all are steps from the South Rim. Built in the 1960s, the nearby Kachina Lodge and Thunderbird Lodge also have rooms with partial canyon views, and all have private baths. On the North Rim, the stately 1928 Grand Canyon Lodge has cabins and traditional hotel rooms near the canyon. 888-297-2757, grandcanyonlodges.com.

- **The View Hotel** I am not a morning person. But every time I've been fortunate enough to snag a room in this three-story contemporary hotel perched on a ledge in Monument Valley Navajo Tribal Park, my excitement has helped me awaken for sunrise. Watching the sun slowly climb over the iconic Mittens sandstone buttes is a magical experience, and at night you'll be treated to incredible stargazing. 435-727-5555, monumentvalleyview.com.

- **Bluff Dwellings Resort** About a 45-minute drive northeast of Monument Valley, this luxurious and contemporary Pueblo Revival-style hotel is surrounded by sheer 200 ft cliffs and makes a great base for exploring Mesa Verde, Canyonlands, and Arches national parks. 435-672-2477, bluffdwellings.com.

- **Far View Lodge** The lone lodging inside Mesa Verde National Park didn't get its promising name for nothing; each of the 150 rooms in this low-slung late-1960s hotel have private balconies with vistas as far as 100 miles on clear days. The rooms themselves have few frills, but they're comfortable, and there are a couple of restaurants on-site. 800-449-2288, visitmesaverde.com.

- **Rochester Hotel** My favorite Durango property is this 1890s former boarding house with 15 smartly appointed rooms and decorative themes based on movies that have been filmed in the area (*City Slickers, Butch Cassidy and the Sundance Kid*). 970-764-0035, rochesterhotel.com.

- **Casa Blanca Inn and Suites** Set on a hilltop overlooking downtown Farmington, this peaceful Spanish Colonial inn surrounded by fragrant gardens and courtyards offers nine spacious rooms and suites. It's an ideal base for exploring Chaco Canyon and the Bisti Badlands. 505-327-6503, casablancanm.com.
- **Thunderbird Motel** This comfy and cozy Navajo owned and operated mid-century motor court inside Canyon de Chelly National Monument has rooms for less than $100 nightly. It's spotless and warmly furnished and has a simple restaurant. 928-674-5842, thunderbirdlodge.com.
- **La Posada Hotel.** One of my favorite hotels in the Southwest, this rambling 1920s Fred Harvey railroad hotel with a red-tile roof and gorgeously decorated guest rooms and common spaces is surrounded by pretty gardens and tranquil courtyards. Winslow, 928-289-4366, laposada.org.

CAMPING

With some of the most scenic tent and RV sites in the country, the sparsely populated Four Corners is a paradise for fans of camping. Of the region's national parks, only Petrified Forest lacks campgrounds, but popular Holbrook/Petrified Forest KOA is within a half-hour drive. The Grand Canyon has myriad options, including sites right by the edge or inside the canyon: Indian Garden and Desert View at the South Rim and North Rim Campground on the other side. Mesa Verde has one option: the peaceful and picturesque Morefield Campground. And at Canyon de Chelly National Monument, there's Cottonwood Campground, which is close to the park restaurant and visitor center. There are also basic (no hookups) tent and RV sites with a wonderfully tranquil setting beneath the stars at remote Chaco Culture National Historical Park. Other great options include Woody Mountain and Flagstaff KOA in Flagstaff, Wahweap and Lone Rock Beach on Lake Powell just outside Page, and both The View and Goulding's Resort at Monument Valley.

Top Painted Desert Inn, Petrified Forest National Park
Bottom La Posada Hotel, Winslow

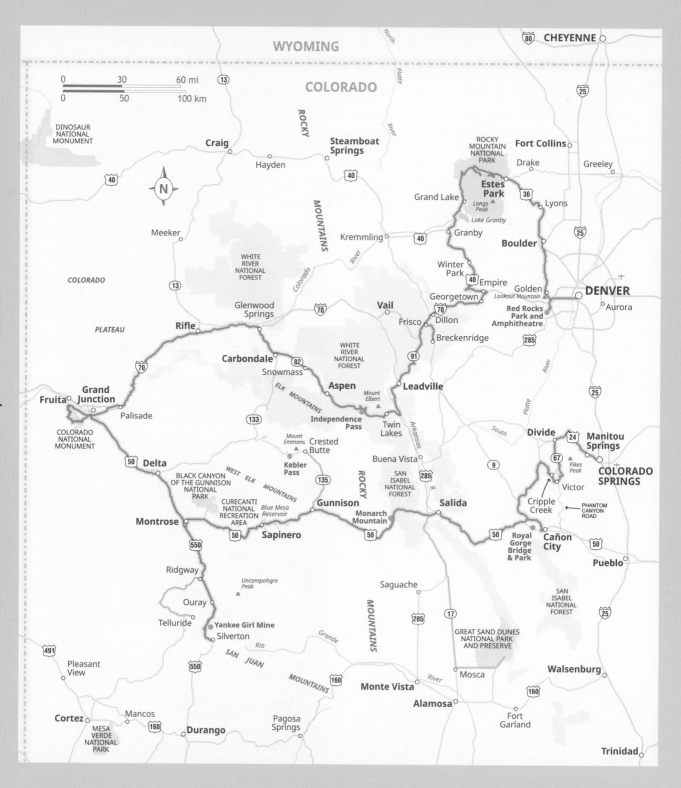

The Colorado Rockies ★

Traversed by some of the highest roads in the country, Colorado is the ideal destination if you love spying snowcapped mountain peaks and wildflower-strewn meadows out your car window.

HOW LONG?

7 days; add an extra day each to see more of Denver and Rocky Mountain National Park or to feel less rushed on the Telluride and Great Sand Dunes National Park sidetracks.

WHEN TO GO

Yes, the Colorado Rockies rank among the world's leading ski destinations, but the snowy season from mid-November to late April isn't a great time for a road trip. You won't be able to drive fully across Rocky Mountain National Park, nor will you be able to get from Leadville to Aspen via stunning Independence Pass. Summer is lovely because the high elevations offer cool relief, but you'll also encounter lots of fellow travelers. My favorite times for this drive are late spring—when wildflowers bloom everywhere—and early fall—when aspens, cottonwoods, and other deciduous trees display their brilliant foliage. Hotel rates tend to be lower, too.

NEED TO KNOW

This route traverses some of the nation's highest terrain, and snowstorms can occur even in summer. Check cotrip.org for current road conditions, and be aware that wildfires can hamper travel in summer and autumn. Pack layers to prepare for the sometimes extreme temperature swings between day and night and among different parts of the state.

→ Distances
Total distance, one-way: 975 mi (1569 km)
- Denver to Winter Park: 150 mi (241 km)
- Winter Park To Grand Junction: 335 mi (539 km)
- Grand Junction to Gunnison: 245 mi (394 km)
- Gunnison to Colorado Springs: 230 mi (370 km)

ⓘ Daytime Temperatures
January: 30-50°F (-1-10°C)
July: 72-94°F (22-34°C)

ⓘ More information
- Denver tourism, denver.org
- Boulder tourism, bouldercoloradousa.com
- Rocky Mountain National Park, nps.gov/romo
- Grand Junction tourism, visitgrandjunction.com
- Black Canyon of the Gunnison National Park, nps.gov/blca
- Colorado Springs tourism, visitcos.com

◉ SNAPSHOT

This sometimes topsy-turvy and consistently breathtaking drive through the Colorado Rockies, which claims no fewer than 58 peaks exceeding 14,000 ft in elevation, offers endless views of rugged alpine scenery. And although this part of the continent is catnip for fans of hiking through sheer canyons and over conifer-dotted ridges, it also begins and ends in a pair of laid-back but urbane cities and passes through several sophisticated—and in some cases downright ritzy—resort towns. Those who appreciate high-end shopping and plush spa hotels will not be disappointed.

City View

Denver

At the junction of I-25 and I-70 and with an airport that serves as a hub of both United and Frontier airlines, the Mile High City is a great place to begin a cross-Colorado journey for logistical reasons, but this vibrant metropolis of about 750,000 is a terrific city in its own right—I recommend spending a couple of days here if you can. Sunny with relatively milder temperatures than the higher elevation Rocky Mountains to the west, Denver has superb museums, leafy parks and bike paths that make it a recreation paradise, and enough first-rate craft breweries, third-wave coffeehouses, and farm-to-table restaurants to keep foodies sated for days.

Car-friendly rating: Good. With the exception of densely developed downtown, where nightly parking rates can exceed $40 at hotels or in lots, most of Denver is easy to explore by car, including many of its interesting outer neighborhoods, which often have free or inexpensive street or garage parking.

What to see in a day: Denver is very much a city of neighborhoods, and the best plan for appreciating it is to venture beyond downtown. I like starting in **LoDo** (Lower Downtown), a district of handsome late-Victorian warehouses and buildings that now contain beloved galleries, buzzy eateries, and indie shops—Tattered Cover bookstore and Wynkoop Brewing among them—plus stunningly restored **Union Station**, where you can dine at trendy Stoic & Genuine or Ultreia. Across the South Platte River in **Denver Highlands** and a few blocks away in **RiNo** (River North Art District), the variety of superb restaurants, bars, and retailers increases almost exponentially. Just south of downtown and the gilt-domed **Colorado State Capitol**, you'll find some top cultural institutions along Broadway, including the beautifully designed **Denver Art Museum** and smaller gems like the **Clyfford Still Museum** and **Kirkland Museum of Fine and Decorative Art**. One last area I always make a point of visiting, especially around dusk, is stately **Cheesman Park**, with its lush **Denver Botanic Gardens** and sweeping westward views of the Rockies. Kids love getting an up-close view of lion and elephants at the nearby **Denver Zoo**, with its carousel and miniature railroad, and roaming among the interactive exhibits at the adjacent **Denver Museum of Nature & Science**, with its IMAX 3D theater.

Where to stay: Denver doesn't lack distinctive, smartly designed hotels, the majority of them downtown—and thus with pricey parking. If that's not a deal-breaker, I recommend a couple of LoDo properties: the historic **Oxford Hotel** for its abundance of charm and stylish Art Deco Cruise Room bar and the swanky **Crawford Hotel**, which is set inside the restored terminal at Union Station. Elsewhere, you'll find cheaper or free parking and a more car-friendly vibe at the modern **Source Hotel** in RiNo, the **Art Hotel Denver** beside the Denver Art Museum in South Broadway, and **The Jacquard** in the retail hub of Cherry Hill.

Red Rocks Amphitheatre

DENVER TO WINTER PARK

Depart the city via 900-acre **Red Rocks Park and Amphitheatre**, where you can hike a 6-mile loop through striking geological formations with fantastic views of Denver's skyline. The real showstopper, pardon the pun, is the 9500-seat amphitheater that's built directly into these red rock monoliths—I've seen a half dozen concerts here over the years, from Depeche Mode to Stevie Nicks, and the acoustics and setting are second to none. Head north through **Golden**, a hilly suburb set snug against the Fort Range, with an inviting historic downtown. It's the headquarters for an interesting mix of organizations and companies, ranging from the National Renewable Energy Laboratory to Coors Brewing. My favorite childhood candy, Jolly Ranchers, were introduced here in 1949 (Hershey has since bought and relocated them). Don't miss the **Buffalo Bill Museum and Grave**, in part because the exhibits about this legendary Western showman are quite interesting, but even more because it's located atop 7377 ft **Lookout Mountain**, which has an observation deck with impressive views.

Continue north up to **Boulder**, a bustling college town and center of art, progressive politics, and outdoor recreation (**Boulder Canyon**, **Wonderland Lake**, and **Chautauqua Park** are among several beautiful venues for hiking). The city is centered around the attractive campus of the **University of Colorado** and its distinctive Tuscany–meets–The Rockies architecture as well as downtown's **Pearl Street Mall**, a landscaped pedestrian promenade lined with colorful eateries, shops, and public art installations. **Avanti F & B** food hall opened near the mall in 2020 and has become a top stop for tasty international fare; I like the modern Taiwanese food at Pig and Tiger and the bagels and Jewish deli items at the Rye Society. The rooftop seating has fantastic sunset views. Save room for a dish of brown butter pecan or lavender poppy next door at Gelato Boy.

Take US 36 northwest from Boulder for the hour-long trip up to **Estes Park**, the primary base camp for the Rocky Mountain National Park. This alpine community is anchored by serene **Lake Estes** and a downtown with an eclectic mix of T-shirt, outdoor gear, and crafts shops and galleries. It's also famous for the 1909 **Stanley Hotel**, which is the inspiration for the Overlook Hotel in Stephen King's *The Shining*, but fans of the Stanley Kubrick film adaptation may be disappointed to learn that it doesn't appear in that movie (it did, however, star in the less critically acclaimed 1997 TV miniseries). You can tour the grandiose and touristy Colonial Revival hotel for $24 per person, park for $10 to dine or walk around on your own, or spend the night in one of the 140 rooms, but the rates are hefty for a property that's greatly in need of some TLC. A better investment of time is taking the **Estes Park Aerial Tramway** for a swift five-minute climb to the top of 8700 ft Prospect Mountain, offers spectacular vistas of the national park.

Established in 1915 and covering 415 sq miles that include dozens of mountains higher than 10,000 ft, **Rocky Mountain National Park** spans the Continental Divide and offers both relatively easy hikes to stunning alpine lakes and more extensive backcountry treks. Start with the exhibits in the architecturally striking **Beaver Meadows Visitor Center**, which was designed in 1964 by the Frank Lloyd Wright–established Taliesin Associated Architects. Because of the park's immense popularity, a reservation system is in effect from late May through mid-October. A must-visit is 9.5-mile **Bear Lake Road**, which offers glorious scenery and the best bang-for-your-buck hikes in the park, including both **Emerald Lake** and lily-pad-covered **Nymph Lake**. Keep in mind that Trail Ridge Road (US 34), which traverses the park from east to west, is closed due to snow from about mid-October to late May; if driving this itinerary during these months, detour around the south side of the park, via I-70.

When Trail Ridge Road is open, follow it through the park's highest peaks—stopping for photos at the **Many Parks Curve** and **Rainbow Curve** overlooks. After crossing the **Trail Ridge Road Summit** (elevation 12,183 ft), stop at Alpine Ridge Visitor Center, then hike the easy half-mile round-trip **Alpine Ridge Trail** for a sweeping view—you can see the grassy plains of southern Wyoming on clear days. You could have lunch here at the park's only eatery, the modest and often crowded Cafe at Trail Ridge, but I prefer the food (try the Colorado lamb meatballs) at the Huntington House Tavern inside the rustic **Grand Lake Lodge** by the park's southwestern entrance. Continue to the **Colorado River Trailhead**, from which it's an easy half-mile trek along the banks of this iconic river to its source at La Poudre Pass Lake. Seeing this gentle, narrow stretch that you could easily skip a stone across, it's hard to imagine that it flows for another 1450 miles through the Grand Canyon and eventually to Mexico's Gulf of California. Follow US 34 south into the small mountain resort community of **Grand Lake**, which overlooks a rippling body of water by that same name as well as neighboring Shadow Mountain Lake, and onward to US 40, through laid-back **Granby**, and to the modern ski town of **Winter Park**, which offers a nice selection of hotels and restaurants.

WINTER PARK TO GRAND JUNCTION

From Winter Park follow US 40 down a series of hairpin turns through **Empire** and then head west on I-70, pulling off soon after to admire the well-preserved Victorian architecture of the 1880s silver-mining boomtown **Georgetown**. Continue through **Eisenhower Tunnel** (which at 11,158 ft is the highest point in the country's network of interstate highways) and past the ski towns of **Dillon** and **Frisco**. At Hwy 9 drive south to **Breckenridge**, especially if you're hungry, as this acclaimed ski town with a nosebleed-inducing altitude of 9600 ft has terrific options for lunch or an early dinner, including Sancho taqueria and Breckenridge Distillery Restaurant (the bourbon-style whiskies are outstanding).

Return to Frisco and continue 7 miles, but before you exit south onto Hwy 91, make sure Independence Pass is open (heavy snows shut it down late October to late May). This vertiginous road winds through rugged coniferous forests to **Leadville**, elevation 10,151 ft (hence its nickname, the Two-Mile-High City), which was founded in 1877 as another pivotal silver-mining hub—you can learn about this rich legacy at the **National Mining Hall of Fame and Museum**. (If Independence Pass is closed, your best route west is I-70.)

South of Leadville, make a left turn onto Hwy 82. Shortly after at **Twin Lakes**, stop by the **Red Rooster Visitor Center**, which was built as a dance hall in the 1870s and is a good place to pick up maps and hiking advice, or enjoy a picnic overlooking a crystalline lake. The drive continues 18 miles, rising higher and higher until traversing 12,095 ft **Independence Pass**, one of the loftiest paved roads in the Rockies. The road steadily descends through verdant forest and narrow, deep canyons before entering the rarefied—in both elevation and per-capita income—resort town of **Aspen**, known for its uber-posh hotels, see-and-be-seen restaurants, and glamorous boutiques proffering everything from ski gear to fur coats. Even outside of ski season, the so-called Glitter Gulch is a bit of a trip—the people-watching can entertain you with people-watching (celeb regulars include Goldie Hawn and Kurt Russell, Melanie Griffith, and Kevin Costner) and there's great hiking, especially in the **Maroon Bells** area about 10 miles south on Hwy 13. The town's chic reputation accounts for an impressive array of stellar restaurants, too—try Matsuhisa for sushi, or for a simple and healthy lunch, have a seat at Pyramid Bistro in the cozy space above Explore Booksellers.

Follow Hwy 82 northwest through **Roaring Fork Valley**, passing the modern ski-resort developments at **Snowmass**

and through cute and eminently walkable **Carbondale**. Just beyond, the Victorian spa town of **Glenwood Springs** has long been an oasis for its abundance of mineral hot springs. You can go for a soak in what's reputed to be the largest mineral pool in the world at **Glenwood Hot Springs Resort** or at **Yampah Spa** you can relax on a marble bench inside the underground "vapor caves." The interstate borders the Colorado River down through western Colorado's **Roan Plateau**, a fertile agricultural region famous for its pear, peach, and apricot orchards.

The 20 miles between **Palisade** and **Grand Junction** is one of the nation's fastest-emerging wine regions. Nearly 30 wineries offer tastings in the **Grand Valley**—top grapes include Cabernet Sauvignon, Merlot, and Syrah, and **Two Rivers Winery** and **Colterris** are a couple of top vineyards. I usually pick up a few bottles of wine when I'm in the area, but I *never* leave Grand Junction without a box of almond toffee from family-owned **Enstrom Candies**, which has been a bane of dentists since 1960. Grand Junction is a sunny high-desert city of about 65,000 that's just over 100 miles from Moab, UT. Downtown is rife with engaging shops and cafes as well as the exhaustive trove of historical artifacts at the **Museum of the West**, and nearby you can explore impressive **Colorado National Monument**, where the breathtaking park road **Rim Rock Drive**, built by the Civilian Conservation Corps in the 1930s, wends 23 miles through a series of soaring sandstone and granite-gneiss canyons and buttes. I think it's prettiest if you start at the **West (Fruita) Entrance** and follow it southeast to the **East (Grand Junction) Entrance**. Top stops for memorable photo ops include **Balanced Rock View**, **Otto's Trail**, **Artists Point**, and **Devil's Kitchen**, where you can hop out and scamper among the red rocks on a 1.2-mile round-trip trail.

GRAND JUNCTION TO GUNNISON

Grand Junction forms the western edge of this boomerang-shaped journey. Follow US 50 southeast through the farming and ranching towns of **Delta** and **Montrose**. The latter is home to a pair of small but excellent regional history sites, the **Museum of the Mountain West** and the **Ute Indian Museum**. It's also the start of the **Million Dollar Highway**, which allegedly earned its name because it cost a million dollars per mile to construct in the 1920s. This 25-mile stretch of US 550 climbs through majestic mountainous terrain as well as the atmospheric old mining towns of **Ouray** and **Silverton** (where you could continue another beautiful 48 miles south to Durango; *see* The Four Corners chapter p. 107). Ouray is one of the country's top destinations for rock- and ice-climbing and also for tours and gold-panning at the once-prolific **Bachelor Syracuse Mine**. It may sound odd, but the **Ouray Alchemist Museum** is fascinating—it's filled with more than 700 antique pharmacy bottles (quite a few of them still contain drugs) as well as dozens of containers of bogus medicinal treatments sold back in the day by unscrupulous traveling salesmen. As you follow the route south through the **San Juan Mountains**, stop at the observation platform to watch **Bear Creek Falls** rushing beneath the road bridge and then by **Yankee Girl Mine**, which was one of the most valuable silver mines of the late 19th century—you can walk around the old buildings and take in impressive views of **Red Mountain**. After another 12 miles you'll reach Silverton, a small 9318 ft high mining town with a lively main street of colorfully painted buildings that house rambling old hotels, craft breweries, and galleries.

SIDETRACK

On your way back up US 550 toward Montrose, make a left turn in **Ridgeway** for the 40-mile drive to **Telluride**, another celebrity-studded ski town (Tom Cruise, Oprah Winfrey, and Jerry Seinfeld have homes here). With its intimate downtown of neatly restored Victorian houses and storefronts, the wonderfully inviting 1895 **New Sheridan Hotel**, and jaw-dropping mountain views, Telluride feels a bit less shiny and commercial than Aspen, although we're talking a matter of degree here. The ski area and its Alps-inspired condos and hotels are reached via a free gondola from town. For a memorable meal en route, hop out when the gondola reaches **San Sophia Station** and have an early dinner at Alfred's Restaurant, with its tall windows and magnificent views. Continue down into the heart of the modern village that is **Telluride Ski Resort**, where you can access dozens of hiking and mountain-biking trails in summer. My preference for visiting Telluride is to make a 250-mile loop that starts and ends in Ridgeway and passes southwest through Cortez and then across to Durango and back up through Silverton and Ouray, but this adventure really only makes sense if you can tack on another day or ideally two to your trip.

Top The Million Dollar Highway, between Ouray and Silverton
Bottom Kebler Pass, Crested Butte

From Gunnison, Hwy 135 winds through a wide sunny valley to **Crested Butte**, a laid-back Western ski town that came close to being transformed into a molybdenum mining center in the mid-1970s. Mayor W Mitchell (full disclosure: he's my uncle) spearheaded a campaign to keep AMAX mining company from turning massive 12,401 ft Mt Emmons into a mining site, and some have speculated that this story helped to inspire part-time Crested Butte resident James Cameron's sci-fi blockbuster *Avatar* (whose protagonist, Jake Sully, is—like W Mitchell—a paralyzed Marine veteran). During the warmer months, this friendly, picturesque village is a great place for a backcountry drive on Hwy 12 over the West Elk Mountains and 10,000 ft **Kebler Pass** to view wildflowers in the spring and spectacular groves of bright-yellow quaking aspens in the fall. You can drive the first 20 miles west to take in the best of the scenery and then return to Crested Butte. Or follow the road another 10 miles to Hwy 133, where a right turn leads north to Carbondale. Most of Hwy 12 is unpaved, but it's well-maintained and suitable even for standard passenger vehicles; it does close due to snow November to May.

Back in Montrose, drive east 7 miles and then take Hwy 347 another 5 miles up to the **South Rim** entrance of **Black Canyon of the Gunnison National Park**. This 31,000-acre tract of wilderness is bisected by the Gunnison River and a 12 mile long stretch of sheer palisades. At the contemporary **South Rim Visitor Center**, view exhibits about the park's unique geology and flora and then walk out to **Gunnison Point Overlook** for a grand view of this 2250 ft deep canyon. Then drive 6 miles west to **High Point**, stopping at **Pulpit Rock**, **Chasm View**, and **Cedar Point** overlooks. At High Point give yourself about an hour for the 1.5-mile round-trip ramble to **Warner Point** for an amazing view west (especially at sunset). If you have more time, drive **East Portal Rd** (it's closed roughly November through April), which drops some 2000 ft on its 5-mile journey down to the river—you can get a good view at the East Portal picnic area and campground. Continue east to **Sapinero**, a dammed section of the Gunnison River that forms **Blue Mesa Reservoir** and is part of western edge of **Curecanti National Recreation Area**. From here it's another 25 miles to the laid-back western town of **Gunnison**.

Top Black Canyon of the Gunnison National Park
Middle Downtown Aspen *Bottom* Downtown Silverton

GUNNISON TO COLORADO SPRINGS

From Gunnison drive east 65 miles up over **Monarch Mountain** and then down into one of my favorite Colorado towns, **Salida**, which offers a wonderful balance of sophisticated but easygoing eateries, shops, and art galleries and is surrounded by impressive mountain peaks and flanked by a roaring stretch of the Arkansas River.

Back in Salida follow US 50 east to Hwy 3A, the turnoff to **Royal Gorge Bridge and Park**, a beloved tourist attraction that developers created in 1929 by constructing a steel, wooden-deck suspension bridge 955 ft above the Arkansas River (until 2001 it was the highest bridge in the world). Since then, the attraction has expanded with all sorts of new family-friendly draws, including an aerial tram, a zip-line crossing, and a Skycoaster. At a minimum, walk out on the **Overlook Trail**, which is free, to view this impressive structure. Nearby **Canon City** has a dapper downtown historic district. As you approach town, exit US 50 and drive the last 2.5 miles on narrow and dramatic **Skyline Drive**. Be sure to visit the unusual and engrossing **Museum of Colorado Prisons**. It's inside a former women's prison and is adjacent to the Colorado Territorial Correctional Facility, which has operated continuously as a prison since 1871. The museum displays memorabilia and photos that trace the facility's 150-year span—you can also visit former jail (and isolation) cells, the old kitchen and dining room, and other eerie spaces. Also worth a visit is the **Winery at Holy Cross Abbey**, which occupies a beautifully adapted 1895 monastery and boarding school.

Backtrack on US 50 to just west of Royal Gorge, and follow Hwy 9 and then Hwy 11 on a winding backcountry trip through the Rockies to itty-bitty **Cripple Creek**, a colorful late-19th-century mining community whose most prominent old buildings now contain casino hotels. More interesting is the even tinier village of **Victor** (pop 432), which lies south a few miles and has been barely touched by commercialism. Go for a walk along the precipitous streets to admire the gracious old buildings, stopping for lunch at rollicking Mining Claim 1899 Saloon. Note you can also get to Victor from Canon City via unpaved **Phantom Canyon Road**, a nearly 30-mile route that follows a retired 1894 railroad line and passes through stone tunnels and over historic wooden bridges. The spectacular drive can be driven in a standard car, but it is bumpy in places, especially after rain, can easily take a couple of hours, and becomes impassable when there's snow. From Victor head north, stopping to hike around the abandoned buildings of the old **Vindicator Gold Mine**, which employed

SIDETRACK

You'll need a half day for this detour from Salida south to **Mosca** and then east to **Great Sand Dunes National Park**, but this is one of Colorado's more unusual and impressive sights. Stop at the main visitor center to learn about this 232 sq mile tract of dunes, some rising 750 ft, and then drive a short way to the parking area to explore. It takes fewer than 15 minutes to find yourself traipsing amid these massive, constantly shifting forms. Looks can be deceiving, and what may look like an easy stroll may actually entail a several-hour hike up steep and challenging terrain, so pace yourself.

some 350 workers during its peak in the early 1910s. The route winds north through rugged ranching country up to US 24, which leads east to Manitou Springs. On the way, consider detouring onto **Pikes Peak Toll Road**, a 38-mile round-trip journey up through the Front Range of the Rockies to the summit of **Pikes Peak**, the imposing 14,115 ft peak. Author and poet Katharine Lee Bates felt so moved by the view she penned the lyrics to "America the Beautiful."

Manitou Springs, a western suburb of Colorado Springs, has an endearing small-town vibe and a wealth of romantic Victorian inns and eateries—pleasant stops to eat include Red Dog Coffee and Swirl Wine Bar. Just northeast of town, explore the region's most celebrated attraction, the **Garden of the Gods**. Occupied over the centuries by several Native communities, the Ute people in particular, this tract of soaring rock formations and overlooks is laced with trails and is especially striking in the morning and late afternoon, when the sun brilliantly illuminates the red stone. Famous as the home of both the **US Air Force Academy** and the sprawling and luxurious **Broadmoor** golf and spa resort, **Colorado Springs** has grown rapidly over the past half century—the population is just under a half million. The lively **Old Colorado City** historic area teems with restaurants and shops. Great family attractions include the outstanding **Cheyenne Mountain Zoo** and the Air Force Academy (guided tours are available). The related **National Museum of World War II Aviation** also has outstanding exhibits, and there's plenty of great hiking in the area, from **Red Rock Canyon** to the catwalks and viewing platforms that lead through **Seven Falls**. From downtown it's just a 75-minute drive north to Denver.

BEST EATS

- **Frasca** Specializing in flavorful charcuterie, fish, and game of northeastern Italy's Friuli Venezia Giulia region, this acclaimed Boulder restaurant is perfect for celebrating a romantic evening. 303-442-6966, frascafoodandwine.com.

- **Rock Inn Mountain Tavern** Less than a mile from Rocky Mountain National Park's Beaver Meadows Visitor Center, this beloved 1930s restaurant and music club has a patio with sweeping views of the region's peaks. 970-586-4116, rockinnestes.com.

- **Pepe Osaka's Fish Taco** The name of this colorful and casual Winter Park restaurant hints at the kitchen's unusual fusion of Mexican and Japanese cooking, from spicy tuna nachos with smoky yum-yum sauce to steak tataki tacos. 970-726-7159, pepeosakasfishtaco.com.

- **Bosq** A favorite of A-listers and gourmands, chef Barclay Dodge's stylish Aspen bistro turns out exquisitely plated Rocky Mountain fare, such as local lamb loin with green coriander and pistachio. 970-710-7299, bosqaspen.com.

- **Bin 707** Sample wines from Colorado but also from some of the world's top regions at this inviting Grand Junction neighborhood bistro that also stands out for its impressive beer selection and creative American fare. 970-243-4543, bin707.com.

- **Blackstock Bistro** Hearty bowls of pork-belly and creamy soba-shrimp ramen are the specialty of this easygoing Gunnison eatery that also serves diverse international dishes, from IPA-battered fish and chips to pineapple red curry. 970-641-4394, blackstockbistro.com.

- **The Fritz** After a day of rafting or hiking, have a seat at this warmly lighted, high-ceilinged Salida gastropub and savor such soul-warming dishes as bratwurst with curry ketchup and a sharp-cheddar burger topped with house-fermented kimchi. 719-539-0364, thefritzsalida.com.

- **The Rabbit Hole** You really do descend down through a rabbit hole of sorts—a narrow, neon-lighted staircase—to reach this art-filled subterranean lair in downtown Colorado Springs. Meat and veggie boards and artful salads are on offer. 719-203-5072, rabbitholedinner.com.

BEST SLEEPS

- **Hotel Boulderado** This landmark 1909 lodging—with its tall windows, Italian Renaissance details, and green gabled roofs—is just a stone's throw from Boulder's Pearl Street pedestrian mall. 303-442-4344, boulderado.com.

- **Grand Lake Lodge** This genial 1920s compound of handsomely outfitted cabins and bungalows is just outside of Rocky Mountain National Park. Amenities include the inviting Huntington House Tavern and a fireside deck and pool. 970-627-3967, grandlakelodge.com.

- **Hotel Jerome** For the ultimate splurge in a town of unbridled opulence, check into this 1889 redbrick stunner that hosted celebrities during its early years, devolved rather charmingly into a $5-a-night ski-bum hideaway in the early 1970s, and has become steadily swankier in recent years. 970-920-1000, aubergeresorts.com.

- **Distillery Inn** This upscale but unpretentious five-suite inn sits directly above acclaimed Marble Distillery in bustling Carbondale. You can saunter down to the tasting room to sample the fine spirits or order craft cocktails delivered to your room, where you sip them on your private balcony. 970-963-7008, marbledistilling.com.

Top The modern Taiwanese food at Pig and Tiger, Boulder
Opposite top Inside the historic Hotel Boulderado
Opposite bottom Grand Lake Lodge, Rocky Mountain National Park

- **Hotel Maverick** On the leafy campus of Grand Junction's Colorado Mesa University, this contemporary boutique hotel offers airy and tasteful accommodations and a raft of pleasing amenities, including a spacious outdoor terrace and a rooftop restaurant and bar. 970-822-4888, thehotelmaverick.com.

- **Hotel Ouray** This refined 1890s inn in charming Ouray is a perfect roost for exploring the famously stunning Million Dollar Highway or even Black Canyon of the Gunnison National Park, an hour north. The 14 rooms range from cozy and economical to roomy and romantic. 970-325-0500, hotelouray.com.

- **Amigo Motor Lodge** The perfectly curated Southwestern decor and mid-century-modern vibe of this cool little Salida motel are perfect for social media postings, but the rooms and restored Airstreams are also wonderfully comfortable. 719-539-6733, amigomotorlodge.com.

- **Cliff House at Pikes Peak** From this Victorian wedding cake of a hotel, it's a few minutes' stroll to the inviting boutiques and eateries of Manitou Springs and a 19-mile drive to the lofty summit of the famous mountain for which the hotel is named. 719-785-1000, thecliffhouse.com.

- **The Broadmoor** Practically a city within the city of Colorado Springs, this elegant 5000-acre resort boasts world-class dining, golf, and spa facilities and impeccably appointed rooms. My favorite parts of the property are the Wilderness Accommodations, which include Cloud Camp, a magical, all-inclusive compound set 3000 ft above the main resort. 719-623-5112, broadmoor.com.

CAMPING

With fantastic national and state parks and plenty of rugged scenery, Colorado is one of the best states in the West for camping. Just west of Denver along the Front Range there are wonderfully scenic sites at Clear Creek RV Park in Golden and Boulder County Fairgrounds Campground in Longmont. Rocky Mountain National Park has five camping areas, with Aspenglen (close to Estes Park) and Timber Creek (close to Grand Lake) among the most appealing. As you make your way across the mountains west to Grand Junction, consider Carbondale/Crystal River KOA Holiday in the Roaring Fork Valley and Saddlehorn Campground inside Grand Junction's Colorado National Monument. Ouray RV Park and Cabins has beautiful sites south of Montrose, and South Rim Campground is a favorite in Black Canyon of the Gunnison National Park. Other notable options include Gunnison KOA Journey, Mountain View RV Resort in Canon City, and Garden of the Gods RV Resort in Colorado Springs.

Northern New Mexico:
Santa Fe and Taos ★

Bisected by the dramatic Rio Grande Gorge and crowned with dramatic snowy peaks, northern New Mexico offers breathtaking scenery at every turn and the chance to explore world-class art galleries and stay in rambling 200-year-old adobe inns.

HOW LONG?

5 days; add an extra day to see more of Santa Fe, Taos, and Albuquerque.

WHEN TO GO

Northern New Mexico has its charms any time of year, even winter, which though very cold in these high elevations, warms the soul with its majestic snowy landscapes and the smell of piñon burning in fireplaces. Summer is gorgeous and usually not too hot, thanks to the regular appearance of dramatic late-afternoon thunderstorms. Fall has the most consistently sunny, dry, and pleasant weather. The only less-than-ideal period is March and April, which are still chilly and also often unpleasantly windy.

NEED TO KNOW

Elevations in northern New Mexico range from 5000 to 8000 ft, so go easy the first day or two as you acclimate—keep hydrated, drink less alcohol, and avoid planning any super strenuous hikes. Big events, like the Albuquerque Balloon Fiesta in October and various art markets throughout summer in Santa Fe and Taos, can result in sky-high hotel rates, so plan accordingly.

→ Distances
Total distance, one-way: 500 mi (805 km)
- Albuquerque to Abiquiu: 140 mi (225 km)
- Abiquiu to Taos: 75 mi (121 km)
- Taos to Santa Fe (with Enchanted Circle): 160 mi (257 km)
- Santa Fe to Albuquerque: 75 mi (121 km)

Daytime Temperatures
January: 37-50°F (3-10°C)
July: 75-93°F (24-34°C)

More information
- Albuquerque tourism: visitalbuquerque.org
- Bandelier National Monument: nps.gov/band
- Taos tourism: taos.org
- Santa Fe tourism: santafe.org

👁 SNAPSHOT

As you drive across far-reaching high desert mesas beneath New Mexico's soaring Sangre de Cristo Mountains, you'll be following in the footsteps of Ancestral Puebloans who have inhabited this land continuously for more than 1000 years, along with 17th- and 18th-century Spanish conquistadors and settlers, 19th-century Anglo traders, and 20th-century artists, musicians, and other creative spirits. This tri-cultural region with its own distinct artistic, musical, and culinary beats offers a rich mix of world-class museums and breathtaking natural landscapes.

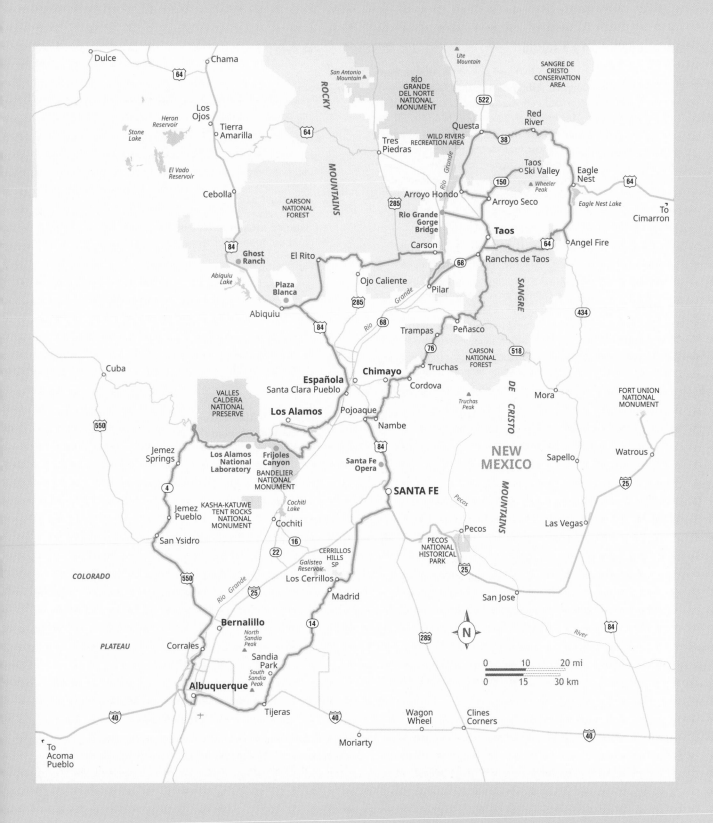

ALBUQUERQUE TO ABIQUIU

At the junction of I-25 and I-40 and served by Amtrak and the state's largest airport, **Albuquerque** (pop 565,000) is the best place to start and end your journey. Straddling the Rio Grande, New Mexico's largest city spreads out in all directions, pushing up against the 10,700 ft Sandia Mountains to the east, giving way to vast high-desert plateaus to the west, and extending into cottonwood-shaded river valleys to the north and south. Although much of modern Albuquerque has a suburban vibe, the city's historic central neighborhoods abound with cultural attractions and distinctive restaurants and galleries.

Begin in the bustling **Nob Hill District**, along **Central Avenue**, which is one of the more colorful stretches of **Historic Route 66**. Lined with colorful vintage motels and retro-style bars and eateries mixed in with more contemporary establishments, the neighborhood really pulses from San Mateo Blvd west to the campus of the **University of New Mexico**, which is anchored by a cluster of classic Pueblo Revival buildings that exemplify the state's early-20th-century architectural style. Stop for coffee and a bite to eat at Flying Star Cafe or a local craft beer and tasty pub fare at Bosque Brewing, and on campus, visit the excellent **University of New Mexico Art Museum** and the **Maxwell Museum of Anthropology**.

Head west on Central Ave through downtown, noting the flamboyantly designed Art Deco–Pueblo Revival 1927 **KiMo Theatre**, and continue to Old Town, which has several adobe buildings that date to the city's 1706 founding, numerous galleries and trading posts, and a cluster of exceptional museums—I recommend the **Albuquerque Museum of Art and History**. It's just a few minutes' drive to the **Indian Pueblo Cultural Center**, a museum and educational-arts space with exhibits about each of the state's 19 Indigenous Pueblo communities as well as a restaurant serving both traditional and contemporary Puebloan fare, including Feast Day red-chile beef-bone pozole and juniper-braised buffalo short ribs.

From Old Town, follow Rio Grande Blvd NW through the city's verdant and historic **Los Ranchos de Albuquerque** district, which is home to both **Los Poblanos Inn and Organic Farm** (there's a superb restaurant, too) and the excellent **Casa Rondeña Winery**, where you can enjoy a tasting on the gorgeous grounds. Then continue up to view the fascinating collection of hot-air-ballooning memorabilia and equipment at the **Anderson Abruzzo Albuquerque**

It's an hour drive through the wide-open mesas west of Albuquerque to reach **Acoma Pueblo**. For its setting alone, this is my top recommendation if you have time to visit only one of the state's Indigenous communities. The original village, with roughly 300 interconnected adobe buildings, is perched dramatically atop a 367 ft tall mesa with sheer cliffs on all sides and has been continuously inhabited since around AD 1100. At the base of the mesa, visit the striking **Sky City Cultural Center and Haak'u Museum**, with its excellent history exhibits and exceptional collection of both ancient and more recent Acoma pottery. Here you can book a guided 90-minute tour to the pueblo, with transportation either by bus or, if you're down for a good workout, by hiking up the rugged staircase that residents have used for centuries. There's a good restaurant in the cultural center, but for some of the tastiest green-chile cheeseburgers in the state, I prefer stopping by Laguna Burger, which is just off I-40 in the nearby **Laguna Pueblo**.

International Balloon Museum, which is on the grounds that host the world-famous Albuquerque Balloon Fiesta each October.

Drive west across the Rio Grande River, and follow Hwy 448 up through beautiful **Corrales**, which has a surprisingly rural and historic feel despite it being ostensibly a suburb of Albuquerque. Continue to **Bernalillo**, then head northwest on US 550 for 25 miles to **San Ysidro**, turning right onto Hwy 4 and following this route through **Jemez Pueblo** and a striking red rock canyon to **Jemez Springs**, where a short stroll at **Jemez State Historic Site** leads to the ruins of a 16th-century pueblo as well as a hulking 17th-century Spanish Colonial mission. Just a little farther north, you can walk over and around a series of travertine and calcium carbonate hot springs and a pretty waterfall at **Jemez Springs Soda Dam**. The town is famous for its curative hot springs, and you can book a soak in one of four outdoor mineral pools at **Jemez Hot Springs**, which also operates a couple of inviting, reasonably priced boutique accommodations in town, **Cañon del Rio** and **Laughing Lizard Inn**.

Hwy 4 climbs up through higher and greener mountains, curving around the southeast side of **Valles Caldera National Preserve**, a nearly 14 mile wide volcanic crater that's open to the public for hiking, mountain-biking, and other recreational activities. The route soon crests a high ridge before winding down around the southern edge of the vast (and high-security) **Los Alamos National Laboratory** and reaches the entrance to one of my favorite places in the region, **Bandelier National Monument**. From mid-May to mid-October, from 9am to 3pm, private cars aren't allowed in the park, and you'll need to drive 8 miles farther to **White Rock Visitor Center** and take a free shuttle bus into the park; at other times, you can drive in and park near the **Bandelier National Monument Visitor Center**, a stately 1936 Spanish Colonial adobe building with well-executed exhibits that interpret the lives of the Ancestral Puebloans who lived here, primarily from AD 1100 to 1600. An easy paved loop leads through adjacent **Frijoles Canyon**, where you can view petroglyphs. Kids and adults love climbing up the wood ladders to enter several ancient, multistory dwellings carved into sheer cliff.

Back on Hwy 4, continue east, but if you have an extra couple of hours make a detour west on Hwy 502 into **Los Alamos**, a fascinating company town created in top secret by the US government in 1943 as the location of the Robert Oppenheimer–led Manhattan Project, which developed the nuclear weapons that would ultimately be detonated over Hiroshima and Nagasaki at the close of World War II. You can learn more about the town's rather amazing and controversial history at the **Bradbury Science Museum** and the **Los Alamos History Museum**, which are both outstanding. Head east and pick up Hwy 30, which runs north through **Santa Clara Pueblo** and its famous **Puye Cliff Dwellings** (you can visit them by guided tour) to **Española**, a good town to stop for fuel or a quick snack, perhaps at Blake's Lotaburger, a New Mexico fast-food chain with tasty green-chile cheeseburgers and cherry milkshakes.

Drive north on US 285 and then US 84 to the picturesque high desert village of **Abiquiu**, which is where the renowned artist Georgia O'Keeffe resided for some 40 years until shortly before her death in 1986. You can tour the rambling adobe **O'Keeffe Home and Studio**, which sits high on a bluff overlooking the Chama River Valley—a view you may recognize from several of her paintings—and is furnished largely as she left it. These fascinating tours depart from **O'Keeffe Welcome Center** beside the **Abiquiu Inn** and should be booked as far ahead as possible.

Frijoles Canyon dwellings, Bandelier National Monument
Previous The High Road to Taos

SIDETRACK

From Abiquiu, it's a stunning one-hour drive north up US 84 through a landscape that's appeared in *City Slickers, Wyatt Earp, 3:10 to Yuma,* and many other Hollywood pictures to the old railroad town of **Chama**. On the way, you can stop by **Ghost Ranch**, a boundless 21,000-acre tract of red-rock canyons and mesas where O'Keeffe also painted and kept a home (it's not open for visits). Now a retreat center, Ghost Ranch does welcome the public (day passes cost $10) to hike its trails and visit its paleontology and anthropology museums. In the high-elevation town of Chama, the big draw is the **Cumbres and Toltec Scenic Railroad**. Here you can ride a vintage narrow-gauge train on a breathtaking 64-mile journey over the 10,015 ft Cumbres Pass to **Antonito, Colorado** (you have the choice of returning by train or—my recommendation if you're short on time—motorcoach). On your way back, stop briefly in historic **Los Ojos** to visit **Tierra Wools**, a shop and studio that preserves the northern New Mexico tradition of hand-dying and -weaving—using Rio Grande-style looms—colorful blankets, rugs, and other textiles using wool from local sheep.

ABIQUIU TO TAOS

East of Abiquiu, turn left onto Hwy 554, then make an immediate left after crossing Rio Chama and follow the signs to **Plaza Blanca**, a wonderland of pale gray-and-white striated cliffs and rock formations and badlands that's great fun to scamper around. Back on Hwy 554, continue to **El Rito**, a small Hispanic village that looks much as I imagine it did 100 years ago. I recommend dropping by El Farolito, a family-run, hole-in-the-wall cafe that serves delicious home-style New Mexican fare—order the relleno-enchilada combo "Christmas," which in the Land of Enchantment means smothered with both red and green chile sauce. Continue to Hwy 111, and then turn south on US 285 to one of the Southwest's most inviting hot springs resorts, historic **Ojo Caliente**. You can spend the night here—both simple and swanky accommodations are offered—or just enjoy a soak in the mineral-springs pool and mud baths or a blue corn–prickly pear salt scrub in the relaxing spa. The resort's Artesian Restaurant serves exceptional farm-to-table fare.

Follow US 285 north 10 miles, and then turn right onto Hwy 567, following it across a high mesa through tiny **Carson**, and then to Hwy 570, a narrow but well-maintained dirt road that descends dramatically into the Rio Grande Gorge, crossing the river and fringing it until depositing you in **Pilar**, where you should stop by the **Rio Grande Gorge Visitor Center** to pick up info about hiking, whitewater rafting, and other adventures in the surrounding **Rio Grande del Norte National Monument**. Take Hwy 68 north as it climbs up through the east side of the gorge and emerges on a plateau with eye-popping views of **Taos**, nestled beneath the snowcapped, emerald-green Sangre de Cristo Mountains.

Indigenous people have resided for more than 1000 years at **Taos Pueblo**, which is open for self-guided tours. In 1898 artists Bert Phillips and Ernest Blumenschein stopped in town when a wheel on their wagon broke. They fell completely in love with the surroundings and made Taos their home base, establishing an art colony that's still thriving today. This town of around 5800 supports around 80 galleries and several outstanding museums, plus myriad shops and studios producing handmade furniture, crafts, and other local goods.

Located at the stately 1920s Fechin House, the **Taos Art Museum** showcases works by the town's early luminaries. Another must-see, on a mesa north of town, is the **Millicent Rogers Museum**, which contains a trove of pottery, art,

SIDETRACK

Those with a little extra time can make a couple of nifty detours from the Enchanted Circle (Red River has several reliable lodging options if you'd like to tack on a night). From Questa it's a 15-mile drive through one of the most remarkable sections of Rio Grande del Norte National Monument to **Wild Rivers Recreation Area**. The views from the rim the Rio Grande Gorge are stunning, and you can also hike 3 miles—descending 1200 ft—on the **Canon Del Trail** down to the confluence of the Rio Grande and Red River. Another notable detour entails driving east from Eagle Nest on US 64 for 25 miles through breathtaking **Cimarron Canyon** to the bitty Wild West town of **Cimarron**, which is home to the famous (and allegedly haunted) **St James Hotel**, an 1870s Territorial-style adobe building whose guests have included Wyatt Earp, Buffalo Bill Cody, and Annie Oakley.

textiles, and jewelry produced by both Native American and Hispanic artists. On the south side, in historic **Rancho de Taos**, be sure to view the imposing **San Francisco de Asis Church**, a thick-walled adobe structure built in the late 18th century and immortalized in famous paintings by Georgia O'Keeffe and photographs by her husband Alfred Stieglitz and his contemporary, Ansel Adams. Taos also abounds with excellent restaurants and inns, most of them inside rambling old adobe homes. This is a town where you could easily lose yourself for days or just as Bert Phillips and Ernest Blumenschein did—for years. I became smitten myself with the area's grandeur in the late '90s and nearly moved here myself, settling instead for several years in Santa Fe (mostly so I'd be closer to an airport).

Continue north from town via US 64, turning left at the junction with Hwys 150 and 522. After about 7.5 miles of driving across what appears to be a flat, uninterrupted plateau with glorious mountain views, a very strange sight appears: the **Rio Grande Gorge Bridge**. You can pull out on either side of this towering suspension bridge and, unless you have a fear of heights, walk across it for a thrilling view of the river 650 ft below—keep an eye out for rafts carrying paddlers down the river. Backtrack to Hwy 150 and follow it into one of the prettiest little villages in the Southwest, **Arroyo Seco**, whose awesome 100-mile views across sagebrush-dotted mesas is even more impressive than Taos's. You'll find a small cache

of noteworthy galleries and restaurants—I always stop by Taos Cow for a dish of piñon caramel or Mexican chocolate ice cream. Optionally, continue on a gorgeous 10-mile drive on Hwy 150 through dense evergreen and aspen groves to **Taos Ski Valley**, a Swiss chalet–style ski village with some of the best skiing in the southern Rockies and awesome hiking in summer. I once broke in a pair of hiking boots by making the heart-pumping 8.5-mile round-trip hike, with an elevation gain of about 3000 ft, to the state's highest peak, 13,161 ft **Mt Wheeler**. The incredible views were worth the blisters.

Back in Arroyo Seco, head west on Hwy B143, which traverses a scenic mesa past vacation homes and farms and then dips down into **Hondo Arroyo**, past a beautiful adobe 1890s church, before joining Hwy 522. You could turn left here to return to Taos, but for another grand alpine adventure I suggest turning right onto Hwy 522 and driving New Mexico's famous **Enchanted Circle**, a roughly 80-mile scenic loop that rises through the sleepy village of **Questa** and then through the evergreen-shrouded ski town of **Red River** before emerging from the mountains and cutting down through the laid-back village of **Eagle Nest** and the modern ski resort town of **Angel Fire** before reentering Taos from the east.

TAOS TO SANTA FE

There are two main routes between Taos and Santa Fe. The most direct is the **Low Road**, which runs alongside the Rio Grande to Española before turning south down US 285 for the final stretch. It's a lovely 70-mile route that takes about 1.5 hours. The other option, and I consider this by far the most breathtaking, is the **High Road**, which descends through a series of high-country villages inhabited by many of the same Hispanic families for more than three centuries but also increasing numbers of artists, writers, and free spirits. This 75-mile route takes about two hours, but allow a half day for stops. Note that driving south from Taos to Santa Fe offers better views than the other way around.

Begin the High Road in Rancho de Taos, following Hwy 518 south about 15 miles over a lofty mountain pass through **Carson National Forest**, then turning onto Hwy 75 and continuing through **Peñasco**, and then following Hwy 76 through tiny **Trampas**, stopping to admire **San Jose de Gracia Church**, which dates to the 1770s and is one of the Southwest's best preserved Spanish Colonial places of worship. Stop in the stunningly situated village of **Truchas**, which you may recognize from the Robert Redford–directed 1988 movie *The Milagro Beanfield War*. Turn left onto Hwy 75

and follow it a couple of miles to take in the splendid views of the Sangre de Cristo Mountains and see couple of the better galleries in the region, **High Road Marketplace** and **Hand Artes**.

Back on Hwy 76, continue southwest, admiring the views across the Rio Grande Valley on your right and the mountain peaks on your left. Consider detouring briefly through **Cordova**, a diminutive village that's famous for its generations-old tradition of Spanish Colonial woodcarving. A few miles later, you'll reach the largest arts enclave along the High Road, **Chimayo**, where I recommend checking out the wares at **Oviedo Carvings and Bronze**, **Centinela Traditional Arts**, and **Ortega's Weaving Shop**. Make a left onto Hwy 98, breaking for a leisurely lunch on the patio of Rancho de Chimayo, which occupies a beautifully restored Spanish Colonial hacienda. Continue to the village center to see the twin-belfried, tin-roofed **Santuario de Chimayo**, an 1816 adobe church that's said to be a site of countless miracles. More than 300,000 people, many of them devoted pilgrims, visit each year, leaving behind photos, crutches, and keepsakes of loved ones in hopes of receiving a blessing that will cure whatever ails them. Hwy 98 continues south to Hwy 503, which meanders west over rolling piñon-dotted hills through the Puebloan communities of **Nambé** and **Pojoaque**. At US 285/84, turn south for the final 15 miles to Santa Fe, keeping an eye out for the majestic, open-air **Santa Fe Opera House**, which hosts the city's prestigious opera festival each summer.

The second oldest city in the United States (after St Augustine, FL), **Santa Fe** is the capital of New Mexico, despite being much smaller (pop 85,000) than Albuquerque. This New Age-y upscale center of art, music, food, spa-going snuggles up against the 12,500 ft Sangre de Cristo Mountains and is best experienced over the course of two or three days—there's lots to see. But if time is limited, I'd make a priority of visiting the family-friendly **Museum of International Folk Art**, which is on **Museum Hill**, a complex of cultural institutions that includes the gorgeous **Santa Fe Botanic Garden**. Then visit one or two sites around Santa Fe's central **Plaza**, such as the **Palace of the Governors**, the nation's oldest public building in continuous use (it dates to 1610) or the neighboring **New Mexico Museum of Art**. The Plaza and the blocks around it abound with intriguing B&Bs and both traditional New Mexican and buzzy contemporary restaurants. Rooftop Pizzeria and Draft Station is a nice perch from which to watch the goings-on around the Plaza.

Also set aside at least two hours to explore the city's eastern foothills, best accessed by driving or walking up **Canyon Road**, which is lined with superb art galleries, and following it past the imposing **Cristo Rey Church** and another 2 miles to the **Randall Davey Audubon Center**, a 135-acre birding and wildlife sanctuary laced with trails through butterfly gardens and over rocky ridges. One other important attraction that you can save for your drive out of town along strip-mall-laden Cerrillos Road is **Meow Wolf**, an interactive must-be-seen-to-be-understood art installation set inside a former bowling alley.

SANTA FE TO ALBUQUERQUE

It's an easy one-hour drive south from Santa Fe to Albuquerque on I-25, although you could potentially add a side adventure to hike through a slot canyon amid striking rock formations at **Kasha-Katuwe Tent Rocks National Monument**. I suggest getting to Albuquerque via Hwy 14, aka **Turquoise Trail**, which takes about 90 minutes without stops. In southwest Santa Fe, follow the road south—stopping if you're hungry for a delicious brunch at the funky San Marcos Cafe and Feed Store—through the sweeping hills to **Los Cerrillos**, a funky old turquoise-mining hub whose heritage you can learn about at **Cerrillos Hills State Park**. Back on Hwy 14, it's just a few miles further to **Madrid** (the emphasis is on the second syllable), which boomed as a coal-mining center during the late 1800s. Developed as a company town with mostly wood-frame buildings, Madrid fell on hard times once the mines were depleted, became something of a counterculture hideout in the 1960s and '70s, and has more recently become another prolific arts colony. The main drag is lined with studios and galleries, and at the historic Mine Shaft Tavern, you can savor a burger and a margarita, watch a show in the **Engine House Theater**, and learn about Madrid's checkered history in the small museum.

Hwy 14 continues south through another quiet, old mining town, **Golden**, and then to **Sandia Park**, where you can take Hwy 536 for 13 topsy-turvy miles west to 10,679 ft Sandia Crest. Here I recommend hiking the 1.5-mile trail along the ridge to the terminus of **Sandia Peak Aerial Tramway**, the longest such tram in the Western Hemisphere. There's an observation deck here as well as a restaurant, TEN 3, with stunning views over Albuquerque and the hills beyond. (You can also get here by riding the tram from its base in northeast Albuquerque.) Returning to Hwy 14, stop if you have a half hour or poke around the quirky folk-art collections at the **Tinkertown Museum** before continuing 6 miles south to I-40, which leads west back into Albuquerque.

Dining at Los Poblanos Inn, Albuquerque
Previous Arroyo Seco village

SIDETRACK

Modern I-25 follows a good bit of the historic **Old Santa Fe Trail** from Santa Fe down around Glorieta Pass and then up through the bustling railroad town of **Las Vegas** and to **Fort Union National Monument** on its way up toward Colorado. Although driving the interstate may not sound too exciting, I'm always blown away by the tremendous mountain panoramas along this route. About 15 miles past Santa Fe, take Hwy 50 to **Pecos National Historical Park**, where you can explore well-preserved ruins that tell the stories of several groups that have lived on this site, from Ancestral Puebloans in the 12th century to Spanish missionaries in the early 17th century. Continue to **Las Vegas**, which was established in 1835 as an important stop along the Old Santa Fe Trail and contains a beautiful downtown filled with both adobe-style and Victorian buildings and anchored by a tree-shaded plaza. Here you'll find the handsome Italianate-style **Plaza Hotel**, which appeared prominently in the Coen brothers' 2007 film, *No Country for Old Men*. On the other side of town, next to the turn-of-the-20th-century train station, the owners of the Plaza Hotel have painstakingly restored the **Castañeda Hotel**, a lavish property built in 1898 as the first cog in the renowned Fred Harvey lodging dynasty; the hotel's terrace restaurant is wonderful for lunch or cocktails.

BEST EATS

- **Farm & Table** The name of this casually sophisticated restaurant in Albuquerque's pastoral North Valley reflects the kitchen's locavore-minded culinary approach. On warm evenings, dine on the gracious patio. 505-503-7124, farmandtablenm.com.

- **Range Cafe** Whimsical folk art, vintage signs, and hefty portions of classic New Mexican and American fare are hallmarks of this local chainlet with an original location in Bernalillo but several outposts throughout Albuquerque, including one downtown in a neatly renovated 1930s gas station. Try the tender carne adovada huevos rancheros or the blue-corn pancakes with blueberries and toasted pine nuts. 505-243-1440, rangecafe.com.

- **Pig & Fig** Perfect for a meal before or after exploring nearby Bandelier National Monument or Los Alamos, this contemporary bistro specializes in creative gastropub fare, including seasonally inspired quiches and sandwiches. White Rock, 505-672-2742, pigandfigcafe.com.

- **El Paragua** Easily reached from both the Low Road and the High Road to Taos, this lively Española restaurant with cozy wood-and-stone dining rooms serves up tasty steaks, chile-smothered chicken enchiladas, and other old-school Mexican fare. 505-753-3211, elparagua.com.

- **Lambert's of Taos** Set in a 19th-century adobe, this romantic and refined restaurant stands out for its knowledgeable service, extensive wine list, and artful contemporary Southwestern cuisine. 575-758-1009, lambertsoftaos.com.

- **Farmhouse Cafe & Bakery** Stop for breakfast or lunch at this laid-back eatery with a patio surrounded by peaceful gardens, outdoor sculptures, and commanding views up toward the ski valley and Wheeler Peak. The kitchen uses local, organic ingredients. El Prado, 575-758-5683, farmhousetaos.com.

- **Aceq** Steps from the colorful galleries of Arroyo Seco, this intimate bistro with inviting indoor and outdoor seating presents a rotating menu based on what's fresh and available. Tuck into beer-braised meatballs in a hearty green-chile gravy or an ahi tuna poke bowl. 575-776-0900, aceqrestaurant.com.

- **Sugar Nymphs Bistro, Peñasco** When driving the High Road, I always try to stop in rural Peñasco at this funky restaurant painted with vibrant murals. Run by the founders of the famous San Francisco vegetarian restaurant Greens, this cozy spot turns out terrifically tasty salads, burgers, and baked-from-scratch pies and cakes. 575-587-0311, sugarnymphs.com.

- **Geronimo, Santa Fe** Within the thick adobe walls of this mid-1700s ranch house on Santa Fe's art gallery-lined Canyon Road, sample worldly dishes like wagyu beef carpaccio, tellicherry-rubbed elk tenderloin, and green miso sea bass. 505-982-1500, geronimorestaurant.com.

- **La Choza, Santa Fe** In Santa Fe's hip and lively Railroad District, this casual spot with a convivial patio serves stellar New Mexican fare—including pork posole with red chile, Frito pie, and margaritas. 505-982-0909, lachozasf.com.

- **Harry's Roadhouse** Since 1992 this off-the-beaten-path Santa Fe restaurant with a charming back courtyard has been a local favorite for eclectic American, international, and Southwestern fare, from Tres Leches French toast to wild-mushroom pizzas to Moroccan lamb tagine. 505-989-4629, harrysroadhousesantafe.com.

BEST SLEEPS

- **Hotel Parq Central** This elegant yet quirky hotel along Route 66 in Albuquerque's hip EDo neighborhood dates to the 1920s. From the rooftop Apothecary Lounge, the sunsets and mountain views are stupendous. 505-242-0040, hotelparqcentral.com.

- **Los Poblanos Historic Inn** The 50 rooms at this chic 1930s property in Albuquerque's agrarian North Valley have handcrafted furnishings and kiva-style fireplaces, and the pastoral grounds feature fields of lavender and a superb restaurant. 505-344-9297, lospoblanos.com.

- **Abiquiu Inn** Beneath the visitor center for tours to Georgia O'Keeffe's nearby home and studio, this cheerful mid-priced boutique hotel has 25 pleasantly furnished rooms and a great restaurant. 505-685-4378, abiquiuinn.com.

- **Adobe & Pines Inn** Parts of this rambling adobe B&B in historic Ranchos de Taos date back to the 1830s. The rooms and casitas are decorated with well-chosen Southwestern antiques and art, and rates include a generous full breakfast. 575-751-0947, adobepines.com.

- **Historic Taos Inn** Possibly haunted and at the very least possessing a storied past, this colorful 1880s hotel is within walking distance of Taos Plaza. The Adobe Bar is a fabulous spot to enjoy a margarita and some tasty appetizers. 575-758-2233, taosinn.com.

- **Rancho de Chimayó Hacienda** The seven economical rooms in this gracious 1800s adobe farmhouse across the street from the venerable restaurant of the same name have traditional beam ceilings and Spanish Colonial furnishings. There's neither Wi-Fi nor TVs, but it's utterly tranquil here. Chimayó, 505-351-2222, ranchodechimayo.com.

- **Ten Thousand Waves** The 14 hillside casitas at this serene spa resort in Santa Fe's picturesque foothills have a minimalist Japanese aesthetic. Rates include an excellent breakfast as well as access to the communal soaking tubs, and restaurant Izanami serves superb izakaya fare. 505-982-9304, tenthousandwaves.com.

- **Inn of the Governors** The rare downtown Santa Fe hotel that offers free parking, this handsomely updated motor lodge is within walking distance of the Plaza and several museums. 505-982-4333, innofthegovernors.com.

- **El Rey Court** At this happily idiosyncratic 5-acre vintage 1930s motor court in Santa Fe, you can park right outside your room or casita. Although situated on a busy road, the grounds are quiet and include a gym, sauna, and a good-sized pool. 505-982-1931, elreycourt.com.

CAMPING

Both RVing and backcountry camping are popular activities in this part of the world. You'll find great commercial campgrounds in Albuquerque (KOA Journey), Santa Fe (Santa Fe Skies), and Taos (Taos Monte Bello), but if you're seeking a more tranquil experience in the wilderness, where you can fully appreciate northern New Mexico's dark, starry nights, consider Jemez Falls, Aspen Basin near Santa Fe's ski area, Orilla Verde Recreation Area in the Rio Grande Gorge south of Taos, Riana Campground at Abiquiu Lake, and the backcountry of Bandelier National Monument.

Kasha-Katuwe Tent Rocks National Monument
Opposite San Francisco de Asis Church, Taos

West Texas and Southern New Mexico ★

Explore the expansive, alluring desert and mountain landscapes along the US-Mexico border, from Big Bend and Carlsbad Caverns national parks to offbeat arts enclaves like Marfa and Silver City.

HOW LONG?

7 days; add an extra day or two to explore more of Big Bend and Guadalupe Mountains national parks.

WHEN TO GO

This is potentially a year-round itinerary, but with some caveats: the Rio Grande Valley can be searingly hot (though fairly dry) in summer, and higher elevations—Cloudcroft especially—can be frigid and even snowy (but beautiful) in winter. That leaves spring and fall as the ideal seasons for this trip. Whatever time of year you go, temperatures will range greatly throughout the region, so pack lots of layers.

NEED TO KNOW

There are a few points where you can cross the border into Mexico, so carry your passport. If visiting Mexico briefly, there's no need to obtain Mexican pesos; many businesses accept credit cards, and most cash-only establishments along the border happily accept greenbacks.

⊙ Distances

Total distance, one-way: 1100 mi (1770 km)
- El Paso, TX to Silver City, NM: 165 mi (266 km)
- Silver City, NM to Carlsbad, NM: 360 mi (579 km)
- Carlsbad, NM to Marfa, TX: 195 mi (314 km)
- Marfa, TX to Marathon, TX: 315 mi (507 km)

⊙ Daytime Temperatures

January: 42-60°F (6-16°C)
July: 72-100°F (22-38°C)

ⓘ More information

- El Paso tourism, visitelpaso.com
- Silver City tourism, visitsilvercity.org
- Las Cruces tourism, lascrucescvb.com
- White Sands National Park, nps.gov/whsa
- Carlsbad Caverns National Park, nps.gov/cave
- Guadalupe Mountains National Park, nps.gov/gumo
- Big Bend tourism, visitbigbend.com
- Big Bend National Park, nps.gov/bibe

⊙ SNAPSHOT

I'm amazed by how many travelers zip through the Borderlands region of West Texas and southern New Mexico without venturing more than a few miles from bland I-10. This enormous area offers a visual buffet of striking contrasts: piñon-dotted 9000 ft mountain peaks, rolling meadows bursting with wildflowers, stony cliffs flanking the Rio Grande, and vast deserts of yuccas, agaves, and ocotillos. The region's towns and cities—from quirky gallery-filled villages to the bustling binational El Paso-Ciudad Juárez-Las Cruces borderplex—also abound with superb museums, grand historic hotels, and cheerful restaurants.

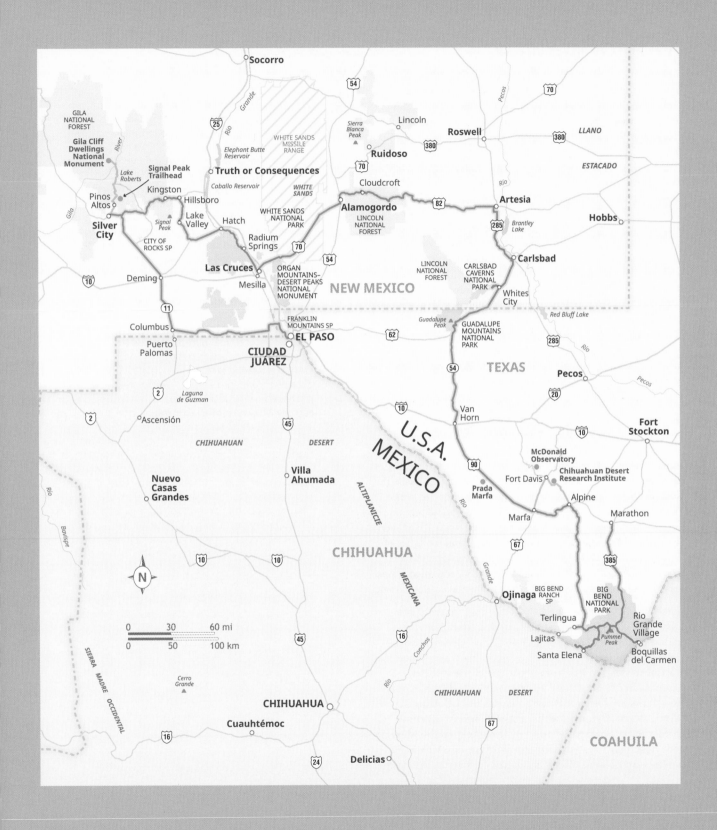

EL PASO, TX TO SILVER CITY, NM

Many visitors are surprised by how many cool things there are to see and do in **El Paso**. It's pretty remote—an eight-hour drive from San Antonio and a four-hour drive from Albuquerque—yet with its Mexican neighbor **Ciudad Juárez**, it forms the largest binational city in the Western Hemisphere (with 2.7 million residents, about a third of them in El Paso). Of course, the Rio Grande and a heavily fortified border wall divide the two cities, but many residents flow freely back and forth each day for work, school, and errands. Nestled against the border, El Paso's compact downtown is filled with handsome 19th- and early 20th-century buildings, a beautiful minor league baseball stadium, and a mix of lively cocktail bars, restaurants, colorful shops carrying regional arts and crafts, and stylish hotels. Along Santa Fe St you'll find the exceptional **El Paso Museum of Art** and **El Paso Museum of History**, which anchor the Downtown Arts District. Several blocks east at **Magoffin Home State Historic Site**, you can tour an 1877 Spanish Colonial–Territorial-style adobe hacienda to get an intimate sense of what it would have been like at the time to live in the then-tiny frontier settlement of El Paso.

As you head north from downtown, take curving **Scenic Drive** west over a steep ridge, stopping at the overlook to behold both cities and the dramatic Chihuahuan Desert mountains to the west. Continue down to Mesa St, which is lined with trendy eateries popular with artists, entrepreneurs, and students from nearby University of Texas at El Paso—the Hoppy Monk is a great spot for regional craft brews, while Yamaguchi Ramen serves boldly flavored Japanese fare. For an outdoor adventure, head to northern El Paso's 25,000-acre **Franklin Mountains State Park**, which contains miles of beautiful trails. If it's late in the day, follow the main park road to the end. Here the Upper Sunset-Tom Mays loop is an easy kid-appropriate hike that offers tremendous sunset vistas.

Leaving El Paso, cross the state border into southeastern New Mexico and head west on Hwy 9, a 60-mile lonely desert road that loosely parallels the New Mexico–Mexico international border and offers far-reaching desert panoramas. In **Columbus** you can learn about one of the stranger episodes in US-Mexico relations: the 1916 raid by Mexican Revolutionary General Pancho Villa on the US Army's 13th Cavalry Regiment, which was stationed in this tiny border town. Seventy-five men, most of them on the Mexican side, lost their lives in this messy skirmish in which Villa and his troops were ultimately chased back across the border.

SIDETRACK

Although plagued by drug violence in the early 2010s, **Ciudad Juárez** has become safer in recent years, especially in the areas where tourists tend to venture, and even just a brief stroll around the downtown (**El Centro**) of this friendly, art-filled city provides an interesting perspective on the hybrid US-Latinx culture and history of the borderplex region. I don't recommend driving across, as you'd need to buy separate auto insurance in Mexico and deal with potentially long lines at customs. But walking across the border bridge from downtown El Paso to Avenida Benito Juárez is a breeze (bring your passport and 50 cents for the toll each way). Walk 10 minutes south to the excellent **Museum of the Revolution at the Borderland**, which occupies the palatial 1880s customs house and tells the turbulent though colorful story of US-Mexican relations throughout the 1910s, during the Mexican Revolution. Walk around the cathedral and **Plaza de Armas Park**, and if you're game to explore a bit further, call an Uber (this service is inexpensive and reliable in Juárez). Notable attractions within a short drive include the excellent **Art Museum Ciudad Juárez**, the **Archaeology and History Museum of El Chamizal,** and such stellar restaurants as Maria Chuchena and Flor de Nogal, which showcase creative regional Chihuahuan cuisine crafted by world-class chefs. On your walk back to the border bridge, drop by the World Famous Kentucky Bar and Grill for a margarita and a plate of shrimp in garlic sauce. Do I believe the claims that this colorful, century-old bar invented the margarita cocktail? No, there's pretty good evidence the drink was concocted earlier, elsewhere (my money's on Tijuana). But I still get a kick out of this place.

Opposite Santa Elena Canyon, Big Bend National Park
Previous Murals, Alpine

The drive north from Silver City along Hwy 15 is one of the prettier journeys in southern New Mexico. After 8 miles you'll reach the once-rollicking alpine village of **Pinos Altos**, famed since the 1860s for its Buckhorn Saloon and Opera House, which still serves up great live music, juicy rib-eye steaks, and green-chile chicken Alfredo. The road snakes north through the dense stands of Douglas fir, ponderosa pine, and juniper in **Gila National Forest**. For a brisk workout, park at the trailhead for **Signal Peak** and hike 4.4 miles (round-trip) to a fire tower, from which you can see as far south as Mexico on clear days. It's another 30 scenic miles to fascinating **Gila Cliff Dwellings National Monument**, which was established in 1907 to protect and interpret five cave dwellings that were carved into the soaring stone palisades roughly 700 years ago. From the small visitor center and museum, an easy 1-mile round-trip trail leads into the 46 rooms spread among these dwellings. You can return the way you came, or to join this itinerary farther east, when you get to **Lake Roberts**, turn onto Hwy 35 and follow this south to Hwy 152.

Pancho Villa State Park preserves the encampment and battle site and has a great museum filled with memorabilia about the Battle of Columbus, and if you scamper up atop Cootes Hill, you can see into **Puerto Palomas**, Mexico, just 3 miles away. For a more immersive experience, park your car at the international border crossing and stroll into this small, laid-back village, stopping to browse the enormous selection of Mexican crafts and housewares at the **Pink Store**, which also has a spirited restaurant serving steaks, enchiladas, and margaritas on a lovely, covered terrace.

From Columbus take Hwy 11 about 35 miles north to **Deming**, a former railroad hub that's home to the impressive **Deming Luna Mimbres Museum**. It contains three big buildings of art and artifacts—including priceless Mimbres pottery, restored antique cars, and vintage ranching supplies. Afterward stop for lunch at convivial Elisa's House of Pies, which serves up flavorful soul food (pork ribs, fried catfish, candied yams) and—naturally—delicious desserts, including shoofly pie and sweet-potato pies. Head northwest on US 180. Your kids will thank you for making a brief foray to climb among the massive boulders and crazy spires of the massive boulders and spires of **City of Rocks State Park**. Continue to **Silver City**, an inviting arts colony and college town (Western New Mexico University) known for its brightly painted Victorian and Spanish Colonial buildings, many of them housing galleries. Break up your explorations with a burger and a well-crafted IPA at Little Toad Creek Brewery and Distillery or an iced coffee at offbeat Tranquilbuzz Coffee House.

SILVER CITY, NM TO CARLSBAD, NM

From Silver City head east on Hwy 152, which traces a significant—and I think the most dramatic—section of the **Geronimo Trail Scenic Byway**. The road passes through a pair of tiny, scenic 1880s mining villages, **Kingston** and **Hillsboro**. Here, a right turn onto Hwy 27 leads south to **Lake Valley**, a curious, privately owned ghost town that you're welcome to explore on foot, as long as you take care not to disturb the sometimes-rickety old buildings, rusting cars, and abandoned mining equipment. The contrast of these dilapidated buildings against the sagebrush desert and deep-blue sky makes for some dramatic photo ops. Continue southeast to **Hatch**, the self-proclaimed "Chile Capital of the World." Each Labor Day weekend more than 30,000 heat-seeking chile connoisseurs attend the annual Hatch Chile Festival. Several shops and casual eateries in town sell roasted chiles or serve chile-smothered food—the Pepper Pot and

Playing on the dunes, White Sands National Park

Sparky's Burgers are good bets. Continue south along the Rio Grande to **Radium Springs** and stop for a quick 30-minute walk around the remains of an adobe Confederate Civil War fortification at **Fort Selden Historic Site**.

Hwy 115 soon leads you into southern New Mexico's largest city, **Las Cruces** (pop 105,000), the home of New Mexico State University and the third prong of the Borderland metro region made up of El Paso and Ciudad Juárez, which are only 45 miles south. Detour west briefly to the Scenic Overlook Rest Area to view the massive **Roadrunner Sculpture** constructed in 1993 of recycled metal. It's a wonderfully odd piece of roadside art. Las Cruces has a lively downtown centered on several blocks of North Main St, which is lined with indie shops and eateries, such as Zeffiro Pizzeria and Broken Spoke Taphouse. On the southside of town, explore **Mesilla**, a village founded in 1848 that was part of Mexico until the Gadsden Purchase a few years later. In the town's courthouse in 1881, notorious outlaw Billy the Kid was convicted of murder and sentenced to hang (he would famously escape from the town jail in Lincoln, NM, kill two sheriff's deputies in the process, and then be tracked down and shot dead by Sheriff Pat Garrett). The many neatly preserved adobe buildings house galleries and restaurants, including the Double Eagle, an ornately decorated and allegedly haunted eatery that dates to the town's founding.

Leave town east along Dripping Springs Rd, stopping to tour the extensive and beautifully designed, kid-friendly exhibits at the **New Mexico Farm and Ranch Heritage Museum**, where you can watch saddle-making demonstrations, tour the sheep and goat barns, and view a re-created colonial New Mexican home. Continue 9 miles east to **Dripping Springs Natural Area** to view the natural history displays in the main visitor center of **Organ Mountains–Desert Peaks National Monument**, a 776 sq mile expanse of mountain wilderness centered on a range of 9000 ft rock spires that resemble a giant pipe organ. Designated as a national monument in 2014, it's a beautiful place for hiking, wildlife viewing, and photography. At Dripping Springs you can hike 3 miles round-trip to a waterfall that's especially photogenic after the rains of New Mexico's summer monsoon season. My favorite part of the park is east of the mountains' spine, reached by taking US 70 over St Augustine Pass and then turning right onto Aguirre Springs Rd and following it to the trailhead for the 4-mile **Pine Tree Loop** or 4-mile out-and-back **Baylor Canyon Pass** trek. Both offer dazzling views of the monument's soaring peaks as well as White Sands National Park to the east.

Back on US 70 it's an easy 40-mile drive through a portion of massive (it's larger than the state of Delaware) White Sands Missile Range to reach the adjacent **White Sands National Park**, one of the Southwest's most visually striking places. Stop at the handsome Spanish Colonial–style visitor center, which was built by the WPA in the 1930s and contains several informative exhibits that explain the unique geology of this park that covers about 40% of the world's largest (275 sq miles) field of gypsum sand dunes. Then drive the 16-mile park loop road; as you venture deeper into this expanse of dunes, the landscape becomes whiter and whiter, to the point that even on the hottest summer day, it feels as though you've entered a snowy winter wonderland. Stop at several turnouts to run and even roll down the dunes, which rise as high as 50 ft. I like to park near the end of the road, walking a short portion of the 4.8-mile **Alkali Flat** loop (follow the signposts carefully, as winds can blow the sand and disorient you). You can even buy a waxed plastic saucer at the visitor center gift shop to go sledding down the steeper dunes. In my experience, kids have far better success at this endeavor than adults.

US 70 continues into the small high-desert city of **Alamogordo**, a largely military town that's home to the very interesting **New Mexico Museum of Space History**, where you can view exhibits on humanity's explorations of the solar system and gawk at spacecraft, including the 86 ft *Little Joe II* rocket. The gorgeous 150-mile drive to Carlsbad crosses over the lofty Sacramento Mountains and through verdant **Lincoln National Forest**. From Alamogordo, US 82 climbs swiftly up a series of switchbacks, rising some 4300 ft in about 15 miles en route to the cheerful mountain village of **Cloudcroft**. Here you can look back across the valley—and a formidable 1899 wooden railroad bridge—from the overlook at **Mexican Canyon Trestle Overlook** and check out the cute, if touristy, saloons and gift shops tucked behind traditional Western facades along Burro Ave. US 82 meanders through the forest and then plunges down into the sunny and fairly flat Chihuahuan Desert and Pecos River Valley. At the first good-size town, the petroleum-refining hub of **Artesia**, turn right and follow US 285 south to Carlsbad, another prolific oil refinery town that's also the gateway to Carlsbad Caverns National Park.

CARLSBAD, NM TO MARFA, TX

Before you make a beeline to the famous caverns, keep in mind they're a 45-minute drive from **Carlsbad** proper. I recommend exploring the town itself before you continue to the national park and then onward into West Texas. At a minimum, drive up to the **Living Desert Zoo and Gardens State Park**. Set high on a hill with far-ranging views of the desert, the paths through this scenic park offer an up-close look at flora and fauna native to the Chihuahuan Desert,

including burrowing owls, black bears, and javelinas, as well as myriad cacti. If you have more time, walk around the attractively landscaped parkland along downtown's short but pretty stretch of the 925-mile Pecos River, and visit the small but excellent **Carlsbad Museum and Art Center**, which showcases both classic and contemporary artwork by a number of exceptional New Mexican artists. Also note that the few food options in or near Carlsbad Caverns are mediocre, and there is no food available in neighboring Guadalupe Mountains National Park, so eat or buy picnic supplies in Carlsbad, which has several good restaurants, including Red Chimney Pit Bar-B-Q and Blue House Bakery and Cafe.

Take US 62/180 southwest to **Whites City**, a small, ragtag collection of businesses that caters to park visitors. I've stayed at the no-frills **Whites City Cavern Inn** enough times to feel that the pros (low rates and close park proximity) outweigh the cons (it's very basic and there's no good dining nearby). From Whites City, Hwy 7 enters **Carlsbad Caverns National Park** and snakes for about 7 miles through a picturesque canyon up to the main visitor center, which contains modern, interactive exhibits about the park's roughly 120 limestone caves (discovered so far). Amazingly, the main cave open to visitors extends for about 30 miles, but the largest (and deepest) cavern, Lechuguilla, extends a whopping 140 miles. It costs nothing to enter the park and view the exhibits, but in the visitor center you'll need to purchase a $15 ticket to enter the caverns, which you reach either by descending 754 ft in a somewhat cozy elevator or walking through the **Natural Entrance** and hiking about 1.3 miles down. I'm a bit claustrophobic about that elevator and prefer hiking in and out of the Natural Entrance, which also offers dramatic scenery. However when you get down to what's known as the 8.2-acre **Big Room**, prepare to be dazzled as you walk along a paved loop past well-lit stalactites, stalagmites, and other curious rock formations. It's a lot of fun to leave the cavern shortly before sunset so that you can watch the nightly ritual of as many as half a million Brazilian free-tailed bats emerging from the Natural Entrance and out into the night sky.

Back on US 62/180, it's a half-hour drive southwest to **Guadalupe Mountains National Park**, which is one of the lesser known jewels of the US National Park system. It's a majestic park with some incredible hiking, but it takes time and energy to explore its interior, which is home to the highest point in Texas, 8751 ft Guadalupe Peak. In an afternoon, however, you can experience **Frijole Ranch**, a crude 1876 homesteader's house that contains photos and artifacts about West Texas frontier life and the remains of the 1858 **Pinery Butterfield Stagecoach Station**. At the main visitor center, after viewing the natural history displays, venture out for one of the park's shorter hikes. I'm partial to the 3.8-mile round-trip scramble into **Devil's Hall**, a narrow slot canyon with sheer 100 ft walls that passes in the shadows of some of the park's highest peaks. Another favorite is the easy but pretty 1-mile nature loop in **McKittrick Canyon**, which is especially ravishing in October and November when its oak and maple trees explode with color. From the park follow Hwy 54 and then US 90 south-southeast about 140 miles through the sparsely settled West Texas high desert to Marfa. About 36 miles south of **Van Horn**, keep an eye out for **Prada Marfa**, a much-Instagrammed art installation in the middle of a vast grassy plain that was created in 2005 to look like a genuine Prada store facade.

MARFA, TX TO MARATHON, TX

The strangely wonderful little art town of **Marfa** first burst onto the pop-culture scene with the release in 1956 of the epic movie *Giant*, starring James Dean, Rock Hudson, and Elizabeth Taylor. It was filmed almost entirely around what was then a sleepy railroad town and seat of Presidio County, and the film crew stayed at the still stately **Hotel Paisano**. In the early 1970s, minimalist modern art visionary Donald Judd moved to town and began buying up land, empty warehouses, downtown storefronts, and an old army base, converting them into often massive art spaces. Judd passed away in 1994, but his legacy continues at the 340-acre campus of the **Chinati Foundation** contemporary art museum, which offers guided and self-guided tours. Marfa now hums with often unconventional galleries and eateries, giving it something of the feel of a miniature Austin in the wilderness. For a bite to eat, try cozy Aster for creative breakfast and lunch fare and baked goods, or head just to the west of downtown to Convenience West, which serves mouthwatering barbecue.

Drive east toward Alpine, pulling over about 9 miles from town at the overlook for the eerie, mysterious, or maybe just apocryphal **Marfa Lights**, unexplained night-time phenomena described by those who claim to have witnessed them as bursts of light dancing on the horizon. **Alpine** has a downtown that's every bit picturesque as Marfa's, albeit minus the minimalist-chic aesthetic. Many of its Victorian and early-20th-century buildings have colorful murals, and you'll find a mix of shops and eateries, including well-stocked Front Street

SIDETRACK

From Marfa or Alpine, it's a 20- to 30-minute drive north to **Fort Davis**, a historic town centered around a late-19th-century military garrison and home to the beautifully restored **Hotel Limpia**. At **Fort Davis National Historic Site**, you can learn more about the area's compelling history, including its role in stationing several all-black "Buffalo Soldier" regiments. Other notable attractions include **McDonald Observatory**, with its Frank N. Bash Visitors Center and its astronomical exhibits and telescopes, and the **Chihuahuan Desert Research Institute**, which offers 20 acres of botanical gardens.

Books, behind which Cedar Coffee Supply brews exceptional java. On the campus of **Sul Ross State University**, tour the outstanding **Museum of the Big Bend**, with its extensive collections of art and historical exhibits related to this scenic region.

And now for the pièce de résistance of this road trip: **Big Bend National Park**, a somewhat underrated 1252 sq mile wilderness that encompasses everything from 7825 ft high pine-shaded mountain peaks to 118 miles of Rio Grande riverfront along the Mexican border.

Big Bend offers just about everything you could want from a national park, including vast expanses of untrammeled nature, stunning scenic drives, and 19th-century buildings with captivating stories. From Alpine it's an 82-mile drive south to the **Maverick Junction** entrance. Just before you reach the park, a right turn onto Hwy 170 leads west through the quirky ghost town of **Terlingua** and its small cache of oddball dining and lodging options. Continue farther, if you wish, to reach the bitty resort town of **Lajitas** and the eastern edge of **Big Bend Ranch State Park**, which is itself a marvel and—at 311,000 acres—larger than many national parks.

Try to enter the park in the morning so you'll have time for at least a brief foray into its three key regions. First, take 30-mile **Ross Maxwell Scenic Drive**, which threads a lush valley with several short turnoffs that access abandoned ranches and offer stunning vistas. The big prize lies at the end of the paved road, where you can follow a 1.5-mile round-trip trail into **Santa Elena Canyon**, a monumental stretch of the Rio Grande that's bracketed by 1500 ft tall stone cliffs.

You can take in the bigger view from the roadside at **Santa Elena Canyon Overlook**, but hiking into the canyon itself is well worth the effort.

Return back up Ross Maxwell Scenic Drive, turn right, and continue to the park's main **Panther Junction Visitor Center**, which has interesting exhibits and a short nature trail with signs identifying local flora. Next, take the road south as it climbs 1700 ft into the park's dramatic mountains, where you can eat lunch with incredible vistas at Chisos Mountains Lodge (the view is far superior to the food), and then go for a short hike out to the **Window Overlook**. Several longer hikes depart from the lodge, but by far my favorite trek in the vicinity is the Lost Mine Trail. Parking is limited, but if you can snag a spot at the trailhead, make this 4.8-mile round-trip hike to a lofty promontory with million-dollar views and giant rock formations. Next drive east past Panther Junction and continue 20 miles to **Rio Grande Village** to hike the 1-mile loop to soak in the soothing 105-degree hot springs, or in the other direction, walk 1.2 miles round-trip into Boquillas Canyon, another dramatic steep-walled expanse of the Rio Grande. If you have time, take a short row-boat ride ($5 round-trip) across the river into **Boquillas del Carmen**, Mexico, a little hiccup of a hamlet with a couple of friendly cantinas. Note that this is an official border crossing, and you'll need your passport to clear customs at the Boquillas Crossing port of entry, which has limited hours (confirm before crossing). From Panther Junction, it's a 70-mile drive north on US 395, through Big Bend's **Persimmon Gap Entrance**, to end your adventure in the little town of **Marathon**, famous for its historic **Gage Hotel**.

Commemorating the filming of *Giant* in Marfa

BEST EATS

- **Taft Díaz** Named for the US and Mexican heads of state who convened at the border in 1909, this sophisticated restaurant in El Paso's arty Stanton House Hotel features a tantalizing marriage of inventive American and Mexican cuisine. 915-271-3600, stanton-house.com.

- **Revel** This standout among several excellent eateries in downtown Silver City sources ingredients from area farms to create flavorful international dishes like beef braised in an Indian pumpkin curry and Creole-style crab-and-shrimp étouffée. 575-388-4920, eatdrinkrevel.com.

- **Sparky's** Order a green-chile cheeseburger (I'm partial to the Oinker version topped with pulled pork) from this kitschy joint festooned with vintage signs and figurines of pop-culture icons. It's right in Hatch, New Mexico's famed green-chile capital. 575-267-4222, sparkysburgers.com.

- **Salud de Mesilla** On the edge of the Spanish Colonial Mesilla, this smart-casual bistro is a cheerful go-to for weekend brunch, late-afternoon wine and tapas, or a romantic dinner. 575-323-3548, saludmesilla.com.

- **Mad Jack's Mountaintop BBQ** It's worth braving long lines at this Cloudcroft eatery for the legit phenomenal Texas-style barbecue, which includes tender chopped brisket, green-chile sausages, and sliced turkey. 575-682-7577, facebook.com/madjacksbbqshack.

- **Carnicería San Juan de los Lagos** Grab a picnic table inside this bustling butcher-market-cafe in Carlsbad. The Sonora-style Mexican food is authentic and flavorful, from pork carnitas tortas to shrimp tacos. 575-887-0034, carniceriasanjuandeloslagos.com.

- **Cochineal** This buzzy bistro with an intimate patio captures Marfa's arty, Instagrammable aesthetic while also showcasing the town's outsized culinary bona fides. Try the Texan elk osso bucco with red wine risotto. 432-729-3300, cochinealmarfa.com

- **Reata** Set in a charming Alpine house with a tin roof, this refined restaurant with an equally famous sister restaurant in Fort Worth serves up hearty Texan fare with modern twists. 432-837-9232, reata.net.

- **Starlight Theatre Restaurant** For the best cooking near Big Bend National Park, snag a table at this funky old restaurant, saloon, and music venue in the eccentric ghost(ish) town of Terlingua. The Tex-Mex fare is tasty—try the smoked-brisket queso or the antelope burger topped with green chiles. 432-371-3400, thestarlighttheatre.com.

Top Silver City *Middle* El Paso Museum of History
Bottom Frijole Ranch, Guadalupe Mountains National Park
Opposite The Lodge Resort, Cloudcroft

BEST SLEEPS

- **Hotel Paso del Norte** Reopened in 2020 after a long dormancy and a massive renovation, this 1912 tower in El Paso's bustling Downtown Arts District offers 351 warmly appointed rooms, a full-service spa, and an array of bars and restaurants. 915-534-3000, marriott.com.

- **Bear Mountain Lodge** As much as I like staying in Silver City's colorful gallery district (the neighboring Palace and Murray hotels both have a lot of character), this 11-room hideaway is my top choice for its gorgeous setting in the Gila Mountains and its 1920s Spanish Colonial-Pueblo architecture. 575-538-2538, bearmountainlodge.com.

- **Hotel Encanto** This handsome Spanish Colonial-inspired hotel, provides a sense of warmth and luxury thanks to its beautiful pool area and elegant old-world lobby and restaurant. 575-522-4300, hotelencanto.com.

- **The Lodge Resort** Set at an elevation of nearly 9000 ft in woodsy Cloudcroft, this allegedly haunted 1899 hotel with a colorfully painted central tower has one of the coolest—literally and figuratively—settings in New Mexico. Amenities include a restaurant, spa, and nine-hole golf course. 575-682-2566, thelodgeresort.com.

- **Trinity Hotel** This luxurious nine-room boutique hotel fashioned out of an 1892 bank building is the most interesting lodging near Carlsbad Caverns. Dine in the superb Italian restaurant and sample wines from the property's Balzano Vineyards. 575-234-9891, thetrinityhotel.com.

- **Hotel El Capitan** Designed in 1930 by the celebrated architect who designed the similar Hotel Paisano in Marfa, this 49-room beauty has reasonably priced rooms with charming period details and a convivial restaurant. It's an hour south of Guadalupe Mountains National Park. 432-283-1220, thehotelelcapitan.com.

- **Hotel Saint George** Marfa's largest and most contemporary hotel is also its swankiest, and with its sleek decor and plush amenities—including a good-size pool and a lively bar, a scene-y restaurant, it feels pretty urbane for a small town. But then again, Marfa is no ordinary small town. 432-729-3700, marfasaintgeorge.com.

- **Chisos Mountains Lodge** The only accommodation inside Big Bend National Park consists mostly of prosaic motel rooms, along with a handful of more atmospheric lodge rooms and stone cottages, but they all have absolutely breathtaking views of the mile-high Chisos Basin. 432-477-2291, chisosmountainslodge.com.

- **Gage Hotel** Since it opened in the late 1920s, this beloved lodging in tiny Marathon—40 miles north of Big Bend—has added increasingly posh accommodations (I still prefer the one-of-a-kind rooms in the original main building). The Gage has some of the best dining in West Texas, plus a cushy spa and heated saltwater pool. 432-386-4205, gagehotel.com.

CAMPING

This is a great adventure for fans of RVing or tent camping, as there are myriad options with dramatic scenery. Franklin Mountains State Park outside El Paso and Silver City KOA Holiday are both great. From Aguirre Spring Campground in Organ Mountains-Desert Peaks National Monument, you're treated to amazing views across the valley toward White Sands National Park, which has only primitive backcountry camping sites; however, you'll find 44 sites at Alamogordo's gorgeous Oliver Lee Memorial State Park. Farther east, consider Deerhead Campground near Cloudcroft, Carlsbad RV Park, and Pine Springs Campground inside Guadalupe Mountain National Park. At the hip El Cosmico resort in Marfa, you can pitch a tent or rent all sorts of fun glamping structures, from restored vintage trailers to yurts and safari tents. Big Bend has several appealing campgrounds, and Chisos Basin has amazing views and cooler weather, while Rio Grande Village offers a wide range of amenities and access to some wonderful hikes.

Montana and Wyoming ★

This spectacular journey through the northern Rockies should be on any national park lover's bucket list, and culture vultures will appreciate the region's several hip and artsy resort towns.

HOW LONG?

10 days; add an extra day each for a deep dive into Grand Teton, Yellowstone, and Glacier national parks.

WHEN TO GO

Mid-June to mid-September offer the best weather but the national parks can be swarmed with visitors. The mid-May to mid-June and mid-September to mid-October shoulder seasons are a wonderful time to visit, with more availability and fewer crowds; spring features roaring waterfalls and colorful wildflowers, and fall is perfect for viewing gorgeous foliage. Although snow sports are popular in winter, it's not a good time for road-tripping; some roads are closed during this period, as are many park facilities.

NEED TO KNOW

The wildfire season in the West has gotten longer and more intense in recent years, so be prepared for smoke, haze, and even potential road or park closures from July through October. In this remote, rugged region where wildlife encounters are common, always come prepared: pack appropriate gear and attire, carry bear spray, and pay attention to park regulations and bulletins.

→ Distances
Total distance, one-way: 1300 miles (2092 km)
- Jackson, WY to Cody, WY: 230 mi (370 km)
- Cody, WY to Bozeman, MT: 215 mi (346 km)
- Bozeman, MT to Missoula, MT: 210 mi (338 km)
- Missoula, MT to East Glacier Park Village, MT: 192 mi (309 km)
- East Glacier Park Village, MT to Kalispell, MT: 115 mi (185 km)
- Kalispell, MT to Spokane, WA: 245 mi (394 km)

Temperatures
January: 25-35°F (-4-2°C)
July: 75-85°F (24-29°C)

More information
- Jackson Hole tourism, visitjacksonhole.com
- Grand Teton National Park, nps.gov/grte
- Yellowstone National Park, nps.gov/yell
- Bozeman tourism, bozemancvb.com
- Missoula tourism, destinationmissoula.org
- Glacier National Park, nps.gov/glac
- Spokane tourism, visitspokane.com

◉ SNAPSHOT

The otherworldly geothermal features and eye-popping scenery of Yellowstone inspired the formation of the US National Parks system, and this trip through the northern Rockies includes two more gems, Glacier and Grand Teton. Montana and Wyoming teem with bison, bears, elk, and other larger-than-life animals, and this route through the junction of America's high plains and most iconic mountain range offers endless oohs and aahs, as well as hikes for all ages and abilities.

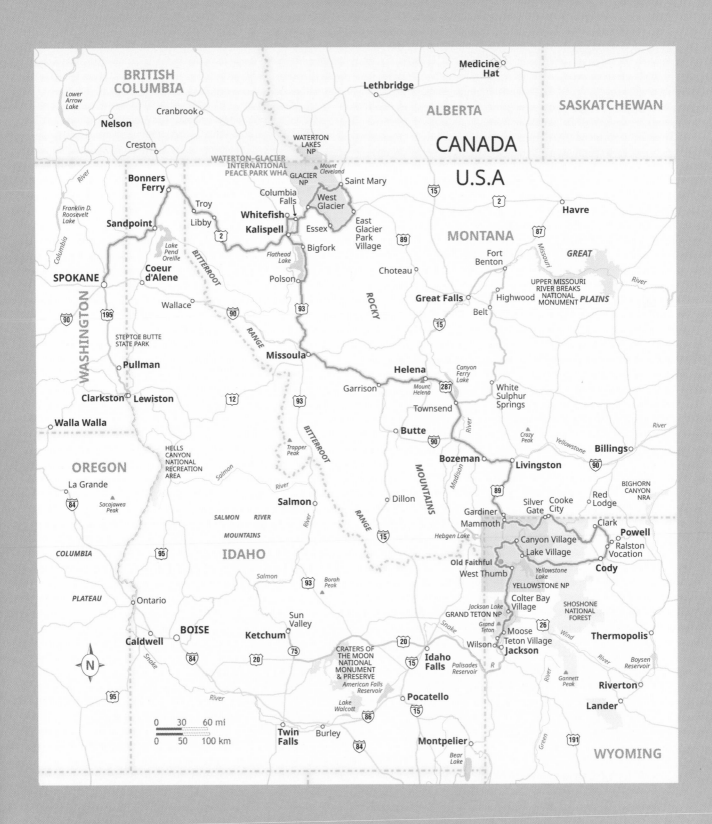

In **Jackson**, a conspicuously affluent yet friendly mountain town adjacent to Grand Teton National Park, spend time perusing downtown's tony galleries and bespoke clothiers and people-watching at the countless trendy restaurants and bars. Then head west to tiny **Wilson** to stock up on picnic supplies and colorful keepsakes at 70-year-old **Hungry Jack's General Store**, before turning north up Hwy 390 through the Snake River Valley to the famous ski area, **Teton Village**.

Hwy 390 continues into the Granite Canyon section of **Grand Teton National Park**, where it becomes a winding and partly unpaved (but well-maintained) stretch of road that leads to the **Laurance S. Rockefeller Preserve**. Here kids and adults enjoy the tactile and auditory interactive nature exhibits in the eco-friendly interpretive center. Several excellent trails lead from the preserve, including the easy 3-mile **Lake Creek–Woodland Loop**, which circles the southern shore of Phelps Lake. The road continues to **Moose**, where you can learn more about the region's history and terrain at the strikingly contemporary **Craig Thomas Discovery and Visitor Center** and visit the interesting early 1900s buildings that make up the **Menors Ferry Historic District**, including the **Chapel of the Transfiguration**, a 1925 log structure with stained glass windows. Moose is one of the park's main service hubs, offering a gas station and family-friendly Dornan's Pizza and Chuckwagon restaurants.

Continue north through the park, allowing at least an hour and ideally half a day at **Jenny Lake**, a gorgeous body of water fringed by hiking trails. A beautiful picnic area frames the massive peaks (or *tetons*, in French) for which this park is named. You can take a quick ferry ride across the lake to access the fantastic and fairly easy trails to **Hidden Falls** and the **Inspiration Point** overlook. Then drive around the east side of the park's largest body of water, **Jackson Lake**, taking a 4-mile side road up to one of the park's best overlooks, **Signal Mountain**. Continue north on US 89/287/191 through the park's northern reaches and then up into Yellowstone National Park.

Established in 1872 as the world's first national park, **Yellowstone** is also the second largest in the continental United States, covering 3437 sq miles. My advice is to allow at least two full days here just to visit the must-see features. If you can (you'll need to book weeks or even months in advance), spend one night inside the park. If that's not possible, stay at one of Cody's many hotels your first night. Following the park's figure-eight-shaped road network, enter

It's a relaxing, traffic-free three-hour drive west from Jackson, via US 26 and US 20, to Idaho's striking **Craters of the Moon National Monument**, the nation's largest (753,000-acre) basaltic lava field, which you can explore on short hiking trails and a scenic road. It's a 90-minute drive northwest via US 20 and Hwy 75 to **Sun Valley** and its neighbor **Ketchum**. An attractive winter ski area resort, Sun Valley offers great hiking and biking in summer. In Ketchum view the memorial to Ernest Hemingway, who spent his final two years in this alpine village before taking his own life in 1961. Note that you could combine visiting this part of Idaho with Hells Canyon (see below, for the Sidetrack from Spokane), thereby turning this chapter's entire itinerary into one big scenic loop—it's a picturesque seven- to eight-hour drive via Boise from Sun Valley to Hells Canyon.

from Grand Teton through the South Entrance. I suggest making your way to the legendary **Old Faithful** section first, where in addition to viewing the iconic geyser—which soars nearly 200 ft roughly 20 times a day—and then stepping inside the classic **Old Faithful Inn**, you can make the 2.5-mile **Geyser Hill Loop** up to **Observation Point** for a view of this basin filled with amazing hydrothermal features.

Drive a bit farther, stopping to walk the short boardwalk around the brilliant turquoise, emerald, ochre, and copper waters of **Grand Prismatic Spring**, then turn east at **Madison Junction** and continue to **Canyon Village**, where from several different viewing areas (**Artist Point** is a favorite), you can take in the mesmerizing views of **Yellowstone Falls** and the most dramatic section of the 24 mile long **Grand Canyon of the Yellowstone**, with its precipitous walls that rise to 1200 ft in places. Drive south through **Hayden Valley**, where you might see bison roaming in the morning or early evening, and stop for lunch or dinner at the grand Victorian **Lake Yellowstone Hotel**. It's a little under a two-hour drive skirting the north shore of massive **Lake Yellowstone** and then driving east through **Shoshone National Forest** to the rollicking Wild West town of **Cody**.

If you arrive in time, attend the **Cody Night Rodeo**, a family-friendly event that takes place nightly all summer. The next day, take at least two hours to explore the exceptional **Buffalo Bill Center of the West**, a Smithsonian-affiliated museum complex with five sections: Buffalo Bill,

Plains Indian, Cody Firearms, Draper Natural History, and Whitney Western Art. They're all world-class, but if you're short on time, I would skip the firearms and Buffalo Bill museums. Drive northeast via US Alt 14 to the poignant **Heart Mountain Interpretive Center**, a museum and a tribute to the hardships endured by Japanese Americans who were forced from their homes in California and detained here from 1942 to 1945. This was one of 10 "relocation camps" established by President Franklin D. Roosevelt, and as much as they're a tragic mark on the nation's legacy of xenophobia and human rights violations, the center also highlights the spirit and vitality of the nearly 14,000 US citizens of Japanese descent who endured in this unjust detention.

CODY, WY TO BOZEMAN, MT

Turn north onto Hwy 214 and follow Hwys 120 and 296 to US 212, the **Beartooth Highway**, for a spellbindingly gorgeous drive back through the formidable mountain range for which the road is named, returning to Yellowstone National Park through its Northeast Entrance. Just before the entrance, the spirited twin villages of Cooke City and Silver Gate are good places to fuel up and have lunch.

Re-entering Yellowstone National Park, follow the park road west through the broad **Lamar Valley**, one of the best places in North America to view bison grazing and sometimes running—they can reach speeds of 35 mph—through the grasslands, along with pronghorn, brown bears, and gray wolves. Continue to **Mammoth Hot Springs**, where you can walk along a boardwalk trail through surreal-looking natural travertine terraces with steaming pools and cascades of mineral water. The historic village contains the park's headquarters, the handsomely restored barracks and buildings of 1890s Fort Yellowstone, and a popular park lodge and restaurant.

Depart Yellowstone through the small town of **Gardiner**, which has several popular restaurants with patios overlooking the Yellowstone River—the Iron Horse Bar and Grill is a reliable option. Continue north for 55 miles through the grand **Yellowstone River Valley** to enchanting **Livingston**, with its historic district of colorfully painted Victorian buildings, many containing fine shops and eateries. It's just a half-hour drive west to fast-growing **Bozeman**, a lively college town and outdoor recreation hub that's a good base both for Yellowstone and the acclaimed Big Sky ski area. Near the Montana State University campus, check out the superb **Museum of the Rockies**. Kids will love seeing life-size bronze sculpture of *Big Mike*, a Tyrannosaurus Rex whose

Grand Prismatic Spring, Yellowstone National Park
Previous Hidden Lake, Glacier National Park

fossilized remains were found in eastern Montana in 1988, and exploring the adjacent living history farm. Evidence of Bozeman's rapid boom (the population has doubled since 2000 to more than 54,000) is visible throughout the city, from the sleek new apartment buildings to trendy farm-to-table eateries and third-wave coffeehouses. It feels a bit like a miniature Denver.

BOZEMAN, MT TO MISSOULA, MT

There are a few ways, all of them quite scenic, to get from Bozeman to Glacier National Park. My favorite is by way of the state's attractive capital, **Helena**, where you can stop at the engaging **Montana Historical Society Museum** and the remarkable **Cathedral of St Helena**, an imposing 1908 structure modeled after Vienna's Votivkirche. Or get a bird's-eye view of the city by taking one of the relatively short but steep (there's a 1000 ft gain) trails to the top of **Mt Helena**. Continue west on US 12 to **Missoula**, an upbeat, progressive college city (pop 73,500) that's home to the University of Montana and has an attractive downtown with pathways along the Clark Fork River.

Whether as a detour or a less direct but interesting alternate route to Glacier National Park, cut east from **Townsend**—between Bozeman and Helena—on US 12 to **White Sulphur Springs** and then up through the small towns of **Belt** and **Highwood** to **Fort Benton**, the second oldest town in Montana and the western gateway to **Upper Missouri River Breaks National Monument**. The Lewis and Clark expedition paddled this stretch of river; you can learn about their adventures as well as the experiences of early homesteaders and fur traders at the several units that make up the **Fort Benton Montana Museums and Heritage Complex**. I like stopping by the handsome redbrick **Grand Union Hotel**—a wonderfully atmospheric place to stay—for dinner on the riverfront garden patio of the outstanding restaurant. Head southwest on US 87 to the state's third largest city, **Great Falls**, stopping at the excellent **C.M. Russell Museum**, which is devoted to the legendary Western painter and sculptor. You can then either follow I-15 to Helena or skip Helena and Missoula and drive 2.5 hours northwest via **Choteau** to the east side Glacier National Parks.

MISSOULA, MT TO GLACIER NATIONAL PARK, MT

From Missoula follow US 93 north to **Polson**, a cute vacation town overlooking the southern shore of mammoth **Flathead Lake**, which is roughly the size of Lake Tahoe. Lively resort communities surround this beautiful lake, and numerous marinas rent boats and kayaks, and some offer scenic cruises. You can follow the lake's eastern or western shore—both are beautiful; I like the eastern route on Hwy 35 in the morning, when the sun shines across the lake and illuminates the mountains to the west. Either way, you eventually pass through the region's largest community, **Kalispell**, and then the tony ski and lake town of **Whitefish**. Both are popular bases for exploring **Glacier National Park**. As with Yellowstone and Grand Teton, the most magical overnight experiences are in one of the historic lodges in the park, but you'll need to book far in advance.

Give yourself at least a full day, and ideally two, to fully appreciate the grandeur of America's eighth oldest national park. From Whitefish or Kalispell it takes about 45 minutes to reach the park's entrance at **Apgar Village**, where you then turn onto one the most majestic park drives in North America, **Going to the Sun Road**. This route can get crowded, and in high season, the park requires reservations—which you must book online and as well in advance as possible. The first must-see along this road is glacially carved, and almost shockingly clear, **Lake McDonald**, which you can view from the chalet-style 1913 **Lake McDonald Lodge**—scenic cruises are offered from the dock.

An incredible feat of engineering that took 11 years to complete in 1932, narrow Going to the Sun Road zigzags some 3300 ft up through the park's vertiginous **Garden Wall** section before summiting over the Continental Divide at **Logan Pass**, where you'll find a distinctive mid-century-modern visitor center that also serves as a trailhead for several great hikes, including the moderately challenging, though often crowded, 3-mile jaunt to **Hidden Lake Overlook**. I prefer hiking the **Highline Trail**, which clings narrowly to the Garden Wall (it's not a good choice if you're uneasy about heights), paralleling Going to the Sun Road beneath it. Although it takes all day to hike the entire 15-mile route, you can enjoy dazzling vistas by hiking 30 or 45 minutes before turning around.

Continue to Lake St Mary, a route that will look instantly familiar if you've ever watched the hauntingly beautiful opening credits of Stanley Kubrick's horror masterpiece, *The Shining*. Exit the park into tiny **St Mary**, which has a clutch of gas stations, restaurants, and hotels. From here drive north on US 89 to **Babb**, and then turn west to re-enter the park and visit the breathtaking **Many Glacier** section. Here you'll find the trailhead for several amazing hikes, including the 9.8-mile round-trip trek to **Iceberg Lake**, which is one of the park's true gems. Try to end your hike early enough to enjoy a sunset dinner at the Swiss chalet–style **Many Glacier Hotel**, whose dining room offers awe-inspiring views across Swiftcurrent Lake and toward the jagged granite peaks beyond.

GLACIER NATIONAL PARK, MT TO SPOKANE, WA

From Many Glacier it's a nearly three-hour drive back to the Whitefish-Kalispell area, so you may wish to spend the night on the east side of the park, either in a park lodge, St Mary or, farther south, **East Glacier Park Village**. If driving all the way back to Whitefish at night, avoid tortuous Going to the Sun Road and instead take US 2 around the southern end of the park.

Take US 2 west from Kalispell through western Montana's peaceful, forested mountains to **Bonners Ferry**, ID, and then south 30 miles to **Sandpoint**, a pleasing patch of lakeside bliss in northern Idaho's panhandle. It's a great place to chill out at a spa or in a little cottage overlooking **Lake Pend Oreille**. US 2 continues along the Priest River and then down through eastern Washington's Selkirk Mountains to **Spokane**, a rugged and friendly city of about 220,000. The historic downtown is anchored by 100-acre **Riverfront Park**, which comprises several islands in the Spokane River and was the site of the 1974 World's Fair; you'll find a slew of engaging, kid-approved diversions, including an IMAX theater, a working antique carousel, and an aerial gondola that glides across the roaring Spokane Falls. Just steps away are the excellent **Mobius Discovery Center**, which contains a fantastic kid-centric science museum, and the **Cork District**, where you can venture into tasting rooms of more than a dozen acclaimed Washington wineries.

Opposite Hiking around Jenny Lake, Grand Teton National Park

SIDETRACK

Since 1932, Glacier has been part of **Waterton-Glacier International Peace Park**, a UNESCO World Heritage site and the world's only bi-national park, with its shared 19-mile border with southern Alberta's **Waterton Lakes National Park**. From St Mary, MT it's a 40-mile drive to Waterton's entrance on Hwy 5 by **Maskinoge Lake**. Just one-eighth the size of Glacier, and with its main activities centered around the small town of **Waterton Park**, it's relatively easy to explore in a day, although I recommend spending the night at the marvelous **Prince of Wales Hotel**, a 1927 stunner set high on a bluff overlooking Alberta's deepest body of water, **Waterton Lake**. Framed by massive rocky peaks, the lake stretches 10 miles south, with the southern tip dipping back across the US border. You can take a scenic boat cruise down the lake and then go for a hike, either the 2-mile round-trip trek to **Goat Haunt Lookout** or the 5.5-mile jaunt to **Kootenai Lakes**. The park also has paved bike paths as well as mountain biking trails, and there are several good hikes that start in Waterton. Be sure to check both park websites for details on clearing customs as you travel back and forth across the US-Canadian border.

SIDETRACK

From Spokane, it's a two-hour drive to **Hells Canyon National Recreation Area**, which contains the deepest river gorge on the continent (about 8000 ft deep). The Snake River cuts through this natural wonder on its nearly 1100-mile journey from Yellowstone National Park to the Columbia River. Follow US 195 south, stopping for a scenic view of eastern Washington's rolling Palouse grasslands from the 3612 ft bluff at **Steptoe Butte State Park**. You'll soon come to the neighboring college towns of **Pullman** (Washington State University) and—just across the state line—**Moscow** (University of Idaho), which have appealing downtowns rife with good places to eat and drink. Continue to **Clarkston**, WA, and **Lewiston**, ID, small twin cities bisected by the Snake River, where you can book exhilarating jet-boat tours into Hells Canyon. From here, instead of returning to Spokane, you could end your journey in **Tri-Cities**, WA (130 miles west) or **Boise**, ID (270 miles south), both of which have airports served by most major airlines. Returning all the way to Jackson, WY—a 10- or 11-hour journey, depending on the route—is also an option, but with an overnight along the way.

BEST EATS

- **Handfire Pizza** Part of the fun of this family-friendly Jackson eatery is the space itself, a cleverly and strikingly reimagined Art Deco movie theater. But the food is great, too: wood-fired pizzas with interesting toppings like burrata, prosciutto, and arugula. 307-733-7199, handfirepizza.com.

- **Gather** In this sleek restaurant with a curved wall of windows and banquette seating, tuck into plates of locally sourced, globally inspired fare like Bolognese with elk, bison, and wagyu steak. 307-264-1820, gatherjh.com.

- **Jenny Lake Lodge Dining Room** The shining star of Grand Teton National Park's several restaurants, this upscale log-cabin space has huge picture windows with incomparable panoramic views of alpine peaks. Dinner is an elaborate five-course, prix-fixe adventure with pairings from a well-curated wine list. 307-543-3351, gtlc.com.

- **Lake Yellowstone Hotel Dining Room** This elegant restaurant with high ceilings and waterfront views is Yellowstone National Park's most memorable dining venue. The menu specializes in local game and fish. 307-344-7311, yellowstonenationalparklodges.com.

- **MontAsia** This wonderful eatery just outside Yellowstone's Northeast Entrance specializes in both Montanan and Malaysian food. Everything is delicious, from bison burgers and a yak variation of Sloppy Joes to chicken curry and sashimi salmon. 406-838-2382, montasia.ninja.

- **Plonk** Pressed-tin ceilings, exposed-brick walls, and soft lighting create a comfy ambience at this trendy Bozeman wine and tapas bar with a second location in Missoula. 406-587-2170, plonkwine.com.

- **Whistle Pig Korean** Head to this hip and cozy Bozeman space for stellar Korean fare, including scallion dumplings with tofu and a gochujang chili sauce and beef bulgogi. 406-404-1224, whistlepigkorean.com.

- **Notorious Pig BBQ** This playfully named barbecue joint near Missoula's Clark Fork River specializes in St Louis-style ribs, but regulars also rave about the brisket and smoked turkey. 406-926-1461, thenotoriouspigbbq.com.

- **Whitefish Handcrafted Spirits** This small-batch Kalispell distillery produces superb botanical gin and huckleberry liqueur, and features an extensive menu featuring tasty tapas. 406-890-2300, whitefishspirits.com.

- **The Wich Haus** Near Whitefish's popular lakefront beach, this beloved cafe serves phenomenally good farm-to-table sandwiches on fresh-baked bread—consider the fried chicken thigh with spicy pickled peaches and charred jalapeno mayo. 406-730-2018, thewichhaus.com.

- **Bonsai Brewing** This welcoming brewpub is known for well-crafted brews with fun names (like the Miss Thang habanero-ginger blond ale). The kitchen turns out tasty ahi bowls, beet-goat cheese salads, and brisket burgers. 406-730-1717, bonsaibrew.com.

- **Trinity at City Beach** Great live music, ample deck seating, and well-prepared comfort food—Cajun-style mac-and-cheese, fish and chips—are the hallmarks of this popular lakefront restaurant by Sandpoint City Beach Park. 208-255-7558, trinityatcitybeach.com

- **Mizuna** Near Spokane's Riverfront Park, this handsome space with stained-glass windows showcases the exceptional local wines and veggie-friendly food. Save room for the caramelized pear-pecan bread pudding. 509-747-2004, mizuna.com.

BEST SLEEPS

- **Wort Hotel** Steps from Jackson's bustling town square, this upscale but unfussy hotel with a world-class collection of Western art has attracted celebs and dignitaries since it opened in 1941. Listen to local bands in the rollicking Silver Dollar Bar. 307-733-2190, worthotel.com.

- **Elk Refuge Inn** Reasonably priced for Jackson Hole, this attractive motel overlooking the National Elk Refuge is a short drive from downtown and Grand Teton. The sweet and simple rooms all have balconies or patios with sweeping views. 307-200-0981, elkrefugeinn.net.

- **Grand Teton National Park lodgings** Among the park's several hotels and cabin compounds, which are open late spring to early autumn, the crown jewel is the intimate Jenny Lake Lodge, whose handsomely kitted cabins feel right out of a Western fairy tale. With 385 rooms, the stately Jackson Lake Lodge is a hive of activity with gargantuan floor-to-ceiling windows overlooking the water. Offering a full-service marina with boat rentals and three restaurants, the Signal Mountain Lodge is an underrated favorite that doesn't usually book up so fast. 307-543-2811, gtlc.com; 307-543-2831, foreverresorts.com
- **Yellowstone National Park lodgings** The nine park accommodations each have slightly different seasons but most close by late October until mid-May. The handsome Mammoth Hot Springs Hotel stays open longest. Even more special is the Lake Yellowstone Hotel, a massive yellow Greek Revival grande dame with sterling water views and the Old Faithful Inn, arguably the most iconic lodging in any national park. 307-344-7311, yellowstonenationalparklodges.com.
- **Chamberlin Inn** A block from Cody's colorful main drag, this cozy redbrick former boardinghouse and later hotel that Hemingway stayed in for a time contains 21 warmly decorated rooms, suites, and cottages, some with fireplaces and clawfoot soaking tubs. 307-587-0202, chamberlininn.com.
- **Murray Hotel** With a glowing three-story red neon sign, this 1904 hotel built to accommodate rail passengers anchors beautiful little Livingston. One of the 25 charmingly furnished rooms and suites is named for legendary director and one-time hotel resident Sam Peckinpah. 406-222-1350, murrayhotel.com.
- **RSVP Hotel** This mid-century-modern lodging in Bozeman has sleek rooms with contemporary art, a lovely pool, and a cool little cafe. 406-404-7999, rsvphotel.co.
- **Kimpton Armory Hotel** In Bozeman's bustling, historic center, this sophisticated 9-story design-driven hotel sits atop the city's Art Deco armory building and offers superb dining in trendy Fielding's restaurant and a rooftop pool, in-room yoga mats, and loaner bikes. 406-551-7700, armoryhotelbzn.com.
- **Glacier National Park lodgings** Glacier has some simpler vintage motor courts that tend to have more availability and a couple of more distinctive and historic Swiss chalet-style hotels on the water—the Lake McDonald Lodge on Going to the Sun Road and the more remote Many Glacier Hotel. Just outside the park is the stately 1913 Glacier Park Lodge in East Glacier. Properties tend to be open from around late May to late September. 303-265-7010, glaciernationalparklodges.com; 406-226-5600, glacierparkcollection.com.

- **North Forty Resort.** Set on 40 evergreen-shaded acres between Whitefish and Glacier's West Entrance, this friendly, family-run compound offers comfortably outfitted log cabins with gas fireplaces and kitchens. Columbia Falls, 406-862-7740, northfortyresort.com
- **Pine Lodge on Whitefish River** This mid-priced hotel with a scenic riverfront setting is near downtown Whitefish and offers a slew of family-oriented amenities, including an indoor/outdoor pool, a game room, and kayaks, SUPs, and bikes. 406-204-4519, thepinelodge.com.
- **Lodge at Sandpoint** With a majestic setting on Lake Pend Oreille, this contemporary lodge near downtown Sandpoint has dramatic water and mountain views from every room. There's a private beach and two restaurants. Sagle, 208-263-2211, lodgeatsandpoint.com.
- **Historic Davenport** Steps from Riverfront Park and the Cork District's wineries, this imposing 1914 Spanish Colonial-Mission Revival property stands out among Spokane's several historic downtown hotels. 509-455-8888, davenporthotelcollection.com.

—

CAMPING

The three national parks have beautiful campgrounds, although they fill up fast in summer. For campgrounds that accept reservations, you can book a site up to six months in advance. All of the parks have some camping available on a first-come, first-served basis; these also fill up fast, so arrive in the morning. Good bets in Yellowstone include Norris to be near cool geyser activity, Grant Village for being near the lake and lots of services, and Slough Creek for a more remote setting. Jenny Lake is a top option in Grand Teton; also consider Signal Mountain on Jackson Lake and shady Gros Ventre. In Glacier the camping areas that overlook beautiful lakes—Apgar, St Mary, Two Medicine Lake—rank among my favorites. Outside of the parks, notable options include Buffalo Bill State Park in Cody, Livingston/Paradise Valley KOA, Polson/Flathead Lake KOA, Sandpoint City Beach Park, and Riverside State Park near Spokane.

Opposite Fielding's restaurant, Kimpton Armory Hotel, Bozeman

The Dakota Badlands ★

The extreme, strangely eroded landscapes of the badlands can leave you feeling like you're driving across another planet, while the verdant pine forests and vast grasslands around Mt Rushmore and Deadwood enchant hikers and Wild West history seekers.

HOW LONG?

6–7 days.

WHEN TO GO

May to October is ideal, as frigid, snowy weather can make winter travel a challenge, and many businesses close or reduce hours at this time. You'll find milder temperatures in spring and fall, but even summer weather is usually pretty comfortable, and crowds are fewer than in the Rockies to the west.

NEED TO KNOW

Smoke from forest fires in the Rockies can lead to hazy skies from July through October. The drive north from Devils Tower through eastern Montana and around Theodore Roosevelt National Park is fairly remote, sometimes with few services in between towns, so always keep your gas tank at least half full.

⊙ Distances

Total distance, one-way: 700 mi (1127 km)
- Badlands National Park, SD to Rapid City, SD: 100 mi (161 km)
- Rapid City, SD to Deadwood, SD: 160 mi (257 km)
- Deadwood, SD to Devils Tower National Monument, WY: 75 mi (121 km)
- Devils Tower National Monument, WY to Watford City, ND: 305 mi (491 km)

⊙ Temperatures

January: 22-35°F (-6-2°C)
July: 85-92°F (29-33°C)

ⓘ More information

- Badlands National Park, nps.gov/badl
- Black Hills and Badlands tourism, blackhillsbadlands.com
- Wind Cave National Park, nps.gov/wica
- Devils Tower National Monument, nps.gov/deto
- Theodore Roosevelt National Park, nps.gov/thro

◎ SNAPSHOT

Three underrated national parks, iconic sites like Mt Rushmore and historic Deadwood, and dramatic landscapes are among the reasons to explore this sparsely populated region that played a central role in the nation's westward expansion and in turn has a tainted legacy concerning the unjust treatment of Native Americans. You can learn about this complicated history at several excellent museums.

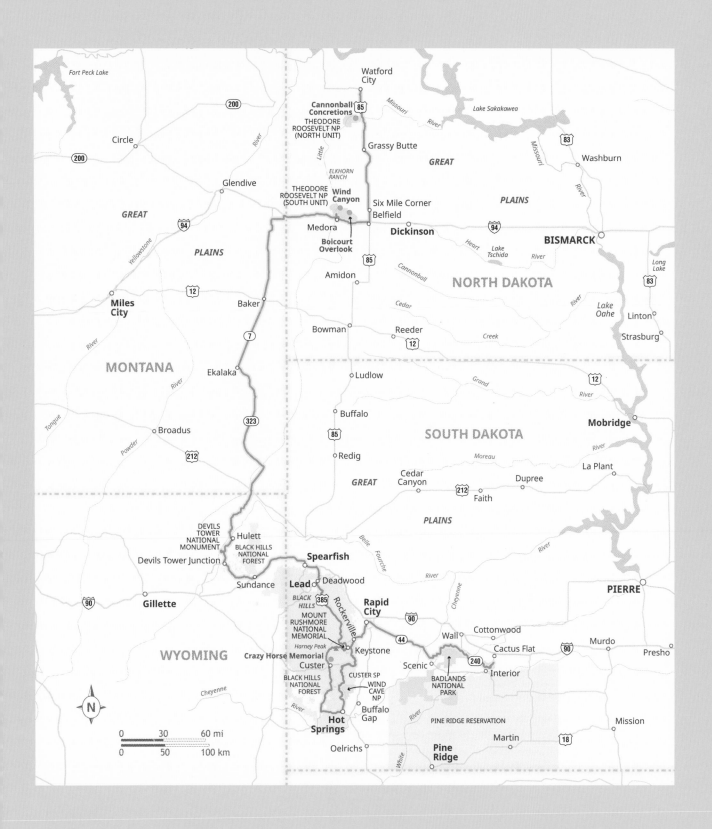

BADLANDS NATIONAL PARK, SD TO RAPID CITY, SD

There aren't many services around **Badlands National Park**, a place that's named for its spectacular, but not especially hospitable or fertile, landscape. Because it's fairly remote, you may want to stay and eat in Rapid City, which is only an hour west via I-90 and not much farther via more picturesque Hwy 44. My preference, though, is always to spend at least one night in one of the small towns near the park. The best option is tiny **Interior**, which is home to the main (Ben Reifel) visitor center, and the only hotel and restaurant inside the park, **Cedar Pass Lodge**. Interior has only a few businesses, but there is a small grocery and a fun tavern—the Wagon Wheel Bar, with decent burgers and pizzas, a pool table, and a great beer selection. Staying in Interior puts you right within view of the park's dramatic landscape and just off the main scenic route, Badlands Loop Rd (Hwy 240). Or just 8 miles from the park's northern Pinnacles Entrance and just off I-90, the small town of **Wall** has several budget chain motels and eateries, a ranger office and visitor center for the US Forest Service's National Grasslands (which consist of 20 tracts of land around the country, including several in the Dakotas), and one of the more famous roadside attractions in the Plains, **Wall Drug Store**, a nearly 80,000 sq ft compound consisting of Wild West–themed souvenir stands and gift shops, down-home restaurants (it's a good bet for a greasy-spoon breakfast and doughnuts), and a sculpture of an 80 ft brontosaurus. This 1931 institution contains an actual pharmacy (I once bought pain reliever for an abscessed tooth, somewhat to the surprise of a jaded clerk). It's a tourist trap, but a fun one.

Badlands National Park consists of two units, but as the southern section is quite remote (it's located within the Oglala Lakota tribe's Pine Ridge reservation), this itinerary focuses on the much more accessible **North Unit**. After viewing the natural history exhibits at the **Ben Reifel Visitor Center**, hop onto **Badlands Loop Rd** (Hwy 240), and follow it west as it curves through White River Valley and gradually ascends to the valley rim; just past **Pinnacles Overlook**, turn left onto Sage Creek Rim Rd (which is partly unpaved but well maintained) and follow it southwest to the small and aptly named town of **Scenic**, from which it's a 45-mile drive on Hwy 44 west to Rapid City.

Allow at least two hours to drive through the park and pause at a few of the many well-marked overlooks along the way: the views of striated, multicolor hoodoos, soaring spires, eroded buttes, and sweeping prairies will inspire you to stop often for photos and short strolls. And especially once you reach the rim of the valley, you're likely to see bison, prairie dogs, and raptors, and possibly bighorn sheep, pronghorns, and black-footed ferrets. **Panorama Point**, **Conata Basin**, and **Sage Creek Basin** are my favorite vista points. Near the eastern end of Badlands Loop Rd, by the short but interesting **Fossil Exhibit Trail**, you can also access one of the best hikes in the park, the **Castle Trail**. It's a 10-mile there-and-back trek that's fairly level and takes about 5 hours to complete, but if time is short, it's still well worth hiking just part of it. It's best to start from the east (by the **Notch Trailhead** on Hwy 240), as relatively quickly you'll pass prairies, wildflower meadows, and rock formations.

RAPID CITY, SD TO DEADWOOD, SD

The steadily growing gateway to the **Black Hills** and badlands of the Dakotas, **Rapid City** (pop 78,000) is the biggest place you'll visit on the itinerary and thus a good place to stock up on supplies and to fly in and out of. And because it's within day-tripping distance of Badlands and Wind Cave national parks, Mt Rushmore, and other key attractions, it can also work as a base camp for exploring the area before you head northwest into Wyoming. There's also a lively downtown with a good mix of indie shops and eateries as well as a promenade along Main St with life-size statues of every US president.

The drive south through the Black Hills to Wind Cave National Park and then back up to Deadwood is best enjoyed as a near loop, and depending on how much time you have as well as your appetite for kitschy attractions, it could take five hours, or you could break it up over two days, spending a night in Hot Springs or Custer. As you make your way south on US 16, you'll pass family-friendly amusements like **Reptile Gardens**—a zoological park with plants and animals—and **Bear Country USA**, a hugely popular drive-through wildlife center. At the town of **Rockerville**, make a left on South Rockerville Rd and follow this winding, quiet mountain road that's usually almost entirely free of traffic south, turning briefly east (left) onto US 40 and then right onto similarly scenic Playhouse Rd, which winds south to US 16A, part of the **Peter Norbeck National Scenic Byway**. A left turn leads southeast to one of South Dakota's most beautiful wildlife preserves, **Custer State Park**, a huge tract of grasslands and rocky spires with an excellent natural history museum and a scenic wildlife loop road that's great for viewing bison and other local fauna.

Follow US 16A as it curves west out of the state park and intersects Hwy 87, aka the **Needles Highway**. A left turn leads south into **Wind Cave National Park**, but if you have an extra hour or two, consider following Hwy 87 north along the most spectacular stretch of the Needles Highway, at least as far as pretty **Sylvan Lake**, and even to its northwestern terminus with US 385 if you're really enjoying yourself. Along this route through pristine spruce groves you'll squeeze through the dramatic **Needles Eye Tunnel** (as long as your vehicle is narrower than 8 ft and shorter than 12 ft) and drive beneath some eye-popping granite spires. You can then backtrack to the northern entrance of Wind Cave the way you came or via the town of Custer (more on that later).

Although famed for its 149-mile network of caverns, Wind Cave is also beautiful to explore above-ground. Soon after you enter the park on Hwy 87, stop to amble along the 1-mile **Rankin Ridge Interpretive Trail**, which offers sweeping views of surrounding grasslands and mountains. The drive continues south through a pine forest dotted with rocky outcroppings and soon descends into wide-open wildflower meadows inhabited by bison and other native wildlife. At the south end of the park, stop by the **Wind Cave Visitor Center**, where exhibits tell the story of what's been described as the world's densest cave network. Here you can also book one of a few ranger-guided cave tours—the hour-long Garden of Eden Tour offers a good intro to the park's subterranean wonders. Note that tours book up early, so if your heart is set on one of these, try to arrive by noon, as they're on a first-come, first-serve basis.

From the park it's a 10-mile straight shot down US 395 through the open prairie to the town of **Hot Springs**, which is a good bet for a bite to eat. Both Mornin' Sunshine Coffee House and Upper Crust Bakery are tasty options. From here jog west on US 18 and then north on Hwy 89 and US 385 through the town of **Pringle** and up to one of the cuter communities in the region, **Custer**, which is a popular regional base for exploring Black Hills attractions, including yet another amazing network of caverns (the world's third longest system), **Jewel Cave National Monument**. It's 13 miles west via US 16 and can also be explored via a few different ranger-guided tours.

From Custer head north on US 385, stopping to visit the **Crazy Horse Memorial**, a hugely ambitious undertaking on private land that involves the construction—begun in 1948—of what will become North America's largest statue when it's completed (many years from now), a 641 ft long and 563 ft high depiction of the Oglala Lakota chieftain Crazy Horse. The visitor campus includes the **Indian Museum of North America**, the studio and home of the late Korczak Ziolkowski (who designed and began work on the sculpture), a restaurant, and a few other interesting diversions.

About 8 miles north on US 385, shortly after passing the previously described western entrance to the Needles Highway (Hwy 87), you'll make a right turn onto Hwy 244, which leads 9 miles to the iconic site that upon its completion in 1941 helped turn the Black Hills into an internationally recognized tourist draw, **Mt Rushmore National Memorial**. Carved out of a granite cliff by Gutzon Borglum and his son Lincoln over about 15 years, the 60 ft tall heads of US presidents Washington, Jefferson, Theodore Roosevelt, and Lincoln rise grandly above the wooded hills and draw more than two million visitors annually. You'll probably be in the majority if all you do is park in the massive underground garage, stroll to the viewing platform, and snap a few selfies, but you can also view exhibits in the visitor center, tour Borglum's studio, and enjoy a burger or a bowl of ice cream with views of the presidential faces in the park's Carvers' Cafe. You'll also find several restaurants just east of the park in the touristy little town of **Keystone**, from which it's about an hour's drive north to Deadwood.

Devils Tower National Monument
Previous Wild horses, Theodore Roosevelt National Park

DEADWOOD, SD TO DEVILS TOWER NATIONAL MONUMENT, WY

Don't come to **Deadwood** expecting the dusty, rough-and-tumble hamlet of roguish Wild West characters you got to know by watching the TV series of the same name. The modern town of Deadwood, though retaining its historic flair and enjoying a gorgeous alpine setting surrounded by **Black Hills National Forest,** feels unabashedly touristy with its casinos, saloons, and souvenir shops. Although the population has shrunk from as many as 25,000 during the Black Hills Gold Rush days of the 1870s—when Calamity Jane, Wild Bill Hickok, and Wyatt Earp lived here—to about 1300 year-round residents today, Deadwood feels much larger with its thousands of tourists. Still, if you can appreciate a good Disney-meets-Vegas take on western Americana, Deadwood has a few attractions that do channel the town's wild and wooly past, such as **Mt Moriah Cemetery** (where Wild Bill and Calamity Jane are interred) and the **Adams Museum,** which contains a trove of memorabilia.

The Black Hills extend into northeastern Wyoming and stretch right to the base of yet another cornerstone of Hollywood pop culture, the tapered 1267 ft tall igneous-rock monolith known as **Devils Tower,** which captured the imagination of filmgoers in Steven Spielberg's sci-fi thriller *Close Encounters of the Third Kind*. The centerpiece of America's first national monument (established by Teddy Roosevelt in 1906), the tower can be seen from miles away, and you can drive practically right up to its base, which you can circumnavigate via a paved 1.3-mile trail. Very few visitors ascend to the top—this is an arduous, technical climb. Keep an eye out, and you'll likely spy some climbers during your visit. Even from the base, though, though, this massive tower is awe-inspiring.

Opposite Badlands National Park

DEVILS TOWER NATIONAL MONUMENT, WY TO THEODORE ROOSEVELT NATIONAL PARK, ND

For the final leg of this itinerary, I like to download some good music and podcasts, and then sit back and enjoy the wide-open prairies on the 3.5-hour drive to Medora, ND, the southern gateway to **Theodore Roosevelt National Park.** The most direct route entails driving north through **Hulett,** WY and then **Ekalaka** and **Baker,** MT and then turning east on I-94.

Consisting of two main units and one smaller remote one, **Elkhorn Ranch,** which is roughly in between this somewhat overlooked park, was established in 1978 in honor of national park proponent Teddy Roosevelt, and on the surface it offers a landscape and other features relatively similar to Badlands National Park: miles of striking rock formations and rugged peaks and grassy prairies populated by bison. A good percentage of visitors stop only to take in the view of the park's **Southern Unit** from **Painted Canyon Visitor Center,** which is just off the interstate, but the best rewards await those who venture deeper into the park.

From cute if commercial **Medora,** which has a walkable little downtown with several restaurants and hotels, explore the park's Southern Unit by driving the 36-mile **Scenic Loop Rd**—keeping an eye out for wild horses, roaming bison, and scurrying prairie dogs—and stopping at the various overlooks to view the sweeping badlands and the curving Little Missouri River. Stop just beyond the park visitor center to walk around the restored **Maltese Cross Cabin,** where Theodore Roosevelt encamped for a while in the 1880s, and set aside a half hour or so for a couple of excellent short hikes, such as **Wind Canyon** and **Boicourt Overlook.**

You'll encounter an even more tranquil vibe and almost no crowds in the park's **North Unit,** 70 miles north a 14-mile there-and-back scenic road climbs through an undulating canyon alongside the Little Missouri River and then steadily rises to a high plateau with a spectacular—especially when wildflowers bloom in spring and trees change color in autumn—view of the river. There are a few short and enjoyable trails just off this road (**Caprock Coulee** and **Sperati Point** among them), but my must-see recommendation is the **Cannonball Concretion** pullout, named for the strange round (almost egglike) rocks scattered throughout the surrounding sandy badlands canyon. It's about a 15-mile drive to the fast-growing oil boomtown of **Watford City,** which has several lodging and dining options, including an excellent little coffeehouse, Door 204.

BEST EATS

- **Harriet and Oak** In an industrial-chic space with a vintage blue Volkswagen bus, this hip downtown Rapid City coffee roaster is a lovely place to fuel up on healthy breakfast fare. 605-791-0396, harrietandoak.com.

- **Juniper** At this sophisticated wine bistro near Rapid City's Founders Park, snag a table on the patio and savor inventive farm-to-table cuisine, such as scallops over mushroom risotto. 605-484-8593, facebook.com/juniperlocalcuisine

- **Powder House** This log-cabin-style dining room at a rustic resort near Mt Rushmore is one of the region's standout steakhouses. Wild game, including barbecue buffalo short ribs and elk medallions, is a specialty. Keystone, 605-666-4646, powderhouselodge.com.

- **Skogen Kitchen** This upscale but unpretentious eatery in historic downtown Custer serves exceptional, artfully plated contemporary fare with global influences. Consider the local goat sausage steam buns with hoisin sauce and Ibérico pork chops with green-gooseberry sauce. 605-673-2241, skogenkitchen.com.

- **Jacobs Brewhouse and Grocer** Set in a converted 1895 grocery store in Deadwood, this friendly spot turns out expertly crafted ales and pub fare, including brisket nachos and bacon buffalo burgers. 605-559-1895, jacobsbrewhouse.com.

- **Devils Tower Gulch** Soak up impressive views of the namesake rock formation from the deck of this down-home bar and grill decked with Wild West art and memorabilia and known for hefty burgers and chicken-fried steaks. 307-467-5800, facebook.com/devilstowergulch.

- **Medora Uncork'd** This cheerful wine bar and eatery outside the South Unit of Theodore Roosevelt National Park earns high marks for friendly service, shareable small plates (charcuterie, caprese salad, Thai chicken flatbread pizzas), and interesting vino by the glass or bottle. 833-623-2675, medorauncorkd.wine.

- **Stonehome Brewing** End a day of hiking around the North Unit of Theodore Roosevelt National Park with a meal nearby in Watford City at this modern, attractive craft brewery that serves tasty pastas and stone-baked pizzas. 701-444-5000, stonehomebrewing.com.

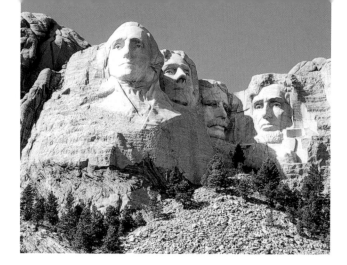

Top Mt Rushmore National Memorial *Bottom* Theodore Roosevelt National Park *Opposite* Nelson-Atkins Museum of Art, Kansas City

BEST SLEEPS

- **Cedar Pass Lodge** Awakening in one of the modern, eco-friendly cabins inside Badlands National Park, with views of peaks and spires in the distance, is a treat. The cabins were built in 2013 to resemble their 1920s predecessors and there's a restaurant on-site. Interior, 605-433-5460, cedarpasslodge.com.

- **Hotel Alex Johnson** The most urbane lodging in the Black Hills, this 143-room Tudor Revival tower in downtown Rapid City dates to 1927 and offers stylishly updated rooms. Common spaces include a rooftop bar with firepits and an old-school Irish pub. 605-342-1210, hilton.com.

- **Buffalo Rock Lodge and Cabins** A short drive from Mt Rushmore (which you can actually see in the distance) and Custer State Park, this smartly designed B&B has rooms in the main lodge and private cabins. Keystone, 605-666-4781, buffalorock.net.

- **Historic Log Cabins** This economical 1920s tourist camp with 17 cozy post-and-beam cabins, some with kitchenettes, is just outside Hot Springs and near Wind Cave National Park. 605-745-5166, historiclogcabinsinc.com.

- **Bavarian Inn, Black Hills** This spotlessly clean chalet-style mini-resort on the north side of Custer offers a nice range of amenities, including a breakfast cafe, indoor and outdoor pools, and a game room and playground for kids. The spacious, modern rooms have grand views. 605-961-0203. bavarianinnsd.com

- **Martin Mason Hotel** This elegant Deadwood Victorian inn has eight rooms decorated with period-style furnishings and plush bedding. The adjoining Lee Street Station Cafe, serves tasty diner fare. 605-722-3456, martinmasonhotel.com.

- **Devils Tower Lodge** You can't get much closer to the iconic butte than by staying at this inviting six-room B&B set on 21 wooded acres beside the national monument. A hearty full breakfast is included. 307-467-5267, devilstowerlodge.com.

- **Rough Riders Hotel** A short stroll from the main visitor center in the South Unit of Theodore Roosevelt National Park, this attractive 76-room Western-style lodge with a sunny patio is right in the center of Medora, offering its own upscale restaurant as well as close proximity to several others. 701-623-4444, medora.com.

- **Roosevelt Inn and Suites** A comfy, modern lodging that's just a 20-minute drive from the North Unit of Theodore Roosevelt National Park, this downtown Watford City hotel is also filled with photos, documents, and memorabilia related to Teddy Roosevelt. 701-842-3686, rooseveltinn.com.

CAMPING

The wide-open landscapes of the western Dakotas abound with both developed and backcountry campsites. You may recognize the tent sites and picnic shelters set against pointy rock formations in the heart of Badlands National Park—it's where Frances McDormand's character works for a stint in the 2020 Oscar-winning film *Nomadland*. Sage Creek is another popular camping area in the park, while Cottonwood and Juniper are favorite areas in Theodore Roosevelt National Park, and Elk Mountain is a great choice in Wind Cave National Park. You'll also find a number of excellent options throughout the Black Hills, including American Buffalo Resort southwest of Rapid City, Spokane Creek near Custer State Park, Mt Rushmore KOA, Deadwood/Black Hills KOA, and Devils Tower/Black Hills KOA Journey.

The Great Plains ★

This relaxing journey across America's broad prairies and grasslands includes a hilly foray into the lush Ozarks and tours through the stately Art Deco towers, impressive museums, and bustling arts districts of several dynamic cities.

HOW LONG?

8 days; add an extra day to see more of Oklahoma City, Kansas City, and the Ozarks.

WHEN TO GO

I try to avoid the hot summers and windy winters. (I've learned to heed blizzard warnings more seriously since spinning out into a snowbank near Sioux Falls and having to take refuge in the home of a kindly local minister.) Spring and fall offer pleasant weather, especially October, when the leaves change color in the Ozarks.

NEED TO KNOW

About that snow—even a few inches of it can result in white-out conditions and deep snowdrifts in the windy Plains. This is also tornado country. So pay close attention to weather forecasts, and don't take chances. This itinerary is one of the longest in the book, but it's also an easy one to tailor to your own interests by cutting out some portions or choosing interstates over local roads

→ Distances

Total distance, one-way: 1850 mi (2978 km)
- Oklahoma City, OK to Hot Springs, AR: 300 mi (483 km)
- Hot Springs, AR to Kansas City, MO: 490 mi (789 km)
- Kansas City, MO to Omaha, NE: 320 mi (515 km)
- Omaha, NE to Sioux Falls, SD: 260 mi (418 km)
- Sioux Falls, SD to Iowa City, IA: 460 mi (740 km)

ⓘ Daytime Temperatures

January: 25-50°F (-4-10°C)
July: 85-95°F (29-35°C)

Ⓘ More information

- Oklahoma City tourism, visitokc.com
- Hot Springs National Park, nps.gov/hosp
- Kansas City tourism, visitkc.com
- Omaha tourism, visitomaha.com
- Sioux Falls tourism, experiencesiouxfalls.com
- Des Moines tourism, catchdesmoines.com

◉ SNAPSHOT

Although my general leanings don't match up very well with the flat, landlocked—and pretty conservative—Plains states (I'm a left-leaning gay guy who loves the ocean and the mountains), I always have a great time exploring this vast sweep of emerald prairies in the east and expansive, virtually treeless plains in the west. The terrain is relaxing to drive in, and the hilliness of the beautiful Ozarks provides a welcome contrast. Moreover, the region's friendly cities and progressive college towns offer a wealth of world-class museums, artfully restored historic hotels, and exciting—and generally affordable—arts and culinary districts, from Film Row in Oklahoma City to the East Village in Des Moines.

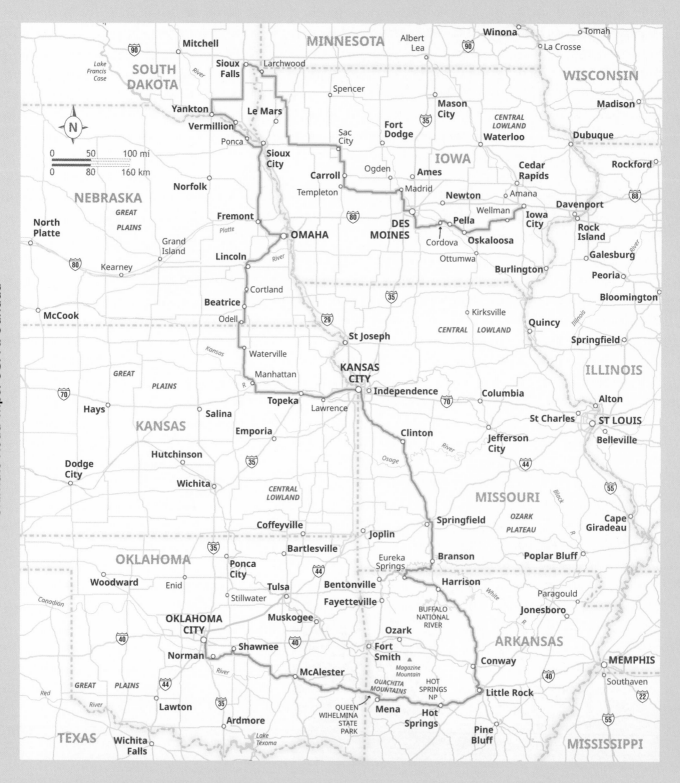

Ultimate Road Trips: USA & Canada

OKLAHOMA CITY, OK TO HOT SPRINGS, AR

The state's largest metropolis, sprawling **Oklahoma City** (pop 681,000) embodies the frontier look and personality of the Plains. It was founded in 1889 and immediately boomed with homesteaders seeking new opportunities, and the money that funded downtown's clutch of modern office towers has come significantly from oil and energy. OKC has a number of attractive residential neighborhoods and some excellent museums, including the impressive **National Cowboy and Western Heritage Museum** and the **Oklahoma City Zoo and Botanical Garden**, but the most remarkable site here is the **Oklahoma City National Memorial**. It sits on the site of the Alfred P. Murrah Federal Building, which was destroyed in a brazen act of domestic terrorism in 1995. The outdoor memorial consists of 168 chair sculptures, one for each person killed in the attack, arranged across a green lawn and overlooking a reflecting pool, and walking through this 3.3-acre site is a solemn, moving experience.

Notable neighborhoods include the **Paseo Arts District**, with its 20 galleries and several excellent restaurants, and **Bricktown**, a former industrial area that's been reinvented into a lively warren of sports and music venues, nightclubs, and hotels. My favorite area is **Film Row**, which was developed as a Hollywood movie distribution hub in the 1930s and has in recent years morphed into a cool design district. It's anchored by the **21C Museum Hotel**, which like other properties in this emerging boutique hotel brand has extensive common spaces that exhibit cutting-edge contemporary art. I like the lattes and chorizo-egg bowls at plant-filled Stitch Cafe West Village and the cocktails at natty Bar Arbolada. Speaking of eating, one of the city's strengths is authentic Vietnamese food—good bets for amazing pho and banh mi include inexpensive and casual Banh Cuon Nhu Lan and stylish and Riviere Modern Banh Mì.

It's a half-day drive from Oklahoma City to western Arkansas, and although the interstate may look fastest, taking a more scenic and eclectic route south through the bustling University of Oklahoma town of **Norman** and then diagonally southeast through **McAlester** adds only an hour or so to the journey. If you're not in a huge rush, stop for a tasty lunch on Norman's lively Main St at Scratch Kitchen, and check out the historic downtown of **Shawnee**, with its imposing **Santa Fe Depot** and the engaging **Citizen Potawatomi Nation Cultural Heritage Center**. After crossing into rugged **Ouachita Mountains** in western Arkansas, stretch your legs with the 1.1-mile **Lover's Leap Trail** loop in **Queen Wilhelmina State Park**—there's an impressive panorama of the countryside at the top. Follow Hwy 88 and US 270 east through ever loftier mountains and then down into **Hot Springs National Park**, which was established in 1921 and differs from other US national parks in that it preserves and celebrates the town's thermal springs, whose curative powers Native Americans had harnessed for several millennia. The park's focal point is **Bathhouse Row**, which is lined with ornately designed bathhouses that were built from the 1890s to the early 1920s. **Fordyce Bathhouse** serves as a museum and contains the park visitor center, and **Superior** (which also has an excellent restaurant and brewery that uses the thermal springs to produce its acclaimed beers) and **Buckstaff** are a couple of the most popular facilities still offering soaks and spa services. The hilly 5550-acre park also has a scenic drive and several hikes; I like the 2.6-mile round-trip **Peak Trail**, which starts on Bathhouse Row and climbs nearly 500 ft to a gorgeous viewpoint atop **Hot Springs Mountain**.

SIDETRACK

I've always been blown away by the cache of Art Deco treasures in Oklahoma's second largest city, **Tulsa**. Some of my favorites in this handsome city 110 miles northeast of OKC are 225 ft tall **Boston Avenue Methodist Church**, **Tulsa Union Depot**, and the **Philcade Building**, which has a small but interesting deco museum in the lobby. But as you explore the city, keep an eye out even in residential neighborhoods. Great areas for indie eats and retail include the **Brady Arts** and **Blue Dome** districts, and historic **Greenwood**, which held one of the nation's most prolific African American business districts (known as Black Wall Street) until a mob of white citizens decimated the neighborhood—and murdered 100 to 300 residents—during the Tulsa Race Massacre of 1921. You can learn about this tragic event at the **Greenwood Rising Black History Museum**, a stunning contemporary space with outstanding interactive exhibits that opened in 2021, and by viewing the neighborhood's several black history murals as well as the **Black Wall Street Memorial** across from historic Vernon AME Church. The city also boasts the superb **Philbrook Museum of Art**, a Renaissance Revival villa once owned by Phillips 66 oil magnate Waite Phillips that's packed with classical and Asian art and sculptures and is surrounded by 23 acres of formal gardens, and the **Gilcrease Museum**, which exhibits the world's largest collection of Native American and Western art.

HOT SPRINGS, AR TO KANSAS CITY, MO

Continue about an hour to the state's capital, **Little Rock**, a rolling river city that's home to the excellent **William J. Clinton Presidential Library**, next to which you can stroll along the verdant Arkansas River Trail, taking this path across the stately 1899 **Clinton Presidential Park Bridge**, which in its previous life carried Choctaw and Memphis Railroad trains. The other essential stop here is **Little Rock Central High School National Historic Site**, a Gothic Revival building that became the crux of one of the country's most contentious and important Civil Rights battles when in 1957 it refused to integrate in defiance of a 1954 US Supreme Court ruling. It's still a functioning school (and not open to the public), but you can walk around the exterior and its reflecting pool, and there's a visitor center and garden with engaging exhibits. Leave Little Rock via I-40 to Conway, and then take US 65, which winds up through the lush **Ozark Mountains**, the largest and highest range between the Appalachians and the Rockies—it's an impressive tract of densely wooded hills, steep sandstone ridges, carbonate-rock caverns (several are open for tours), and mostly man-made lakes created through flood-control dams.

You'll come to **Harrison**, whose recreational draws include **Mystic Caverns** and **Buffalo National River Park**, where a left turn on US 62 leads to **Eureka Springs**, an artsy village of about 2100 nestled among some of the region's most scenic hills. Developed as a mineral-springs health resort in the late 19th century, the town has several Victorian hotels and a wealth of romantic inns. It's also a fascinating place because it's hugely popular with two demographics that don't typically overlap: traditional devout Christians who come to attend one of the world's largest outdoor productions of the *Passion Play* and LGBTQ folks, artists, and other free spirits. Despite the potential for conflict, folks tend to get along harmoniously. As you stroll the town's steep, narrow lanes, check out the offbeat shops and galleries stocked with folk art and funky gifts. Relax with a cheese plate and a glass of wine at the convivial Stone House, or catch one of the dishy drag shows at Eureka Live. The town's most remarkable sight, other than the 65 ft statue of Christ that looms above the grounds of the Passion Play amphitheater, is **Thorncrown Chapel**, a stunning, angular structure designed in 1980 by Frank Lloyd Wright disciple E. Fay Jones. It's made of local pine and appears at first glance to be open-air but is actually clad with 425 windows.

Eureka Springs

SIDETRACK

Sam Walton opened the first Walmart in the then-tiny village of **Bentonville** in 1962. With its vintage displays of dry goods and an old-time soda fountain, the **Walmart Museum** occupies Walton's original store, but the main reason I recommend driving 40 mountainous miles from Eureka Springs to Bentonville is to see the incredible **Crystal Bridges Museum of Art**, a sleek glass-and-wood building designed by Moshe Safdie that showcases the fantastic collection of American art assembled by Walmart heiress Alice Walton. The museum campus is also home to the **Bachman-Wilson House**, a 1954 Frank Lloyd Wright Usonian dwelling moved here from New Jersey in 2014. Downtown Bentonville has a pretty town square and several excellent restaurants, including the Preacher's Son and Table Mesa Bistro, and also an outpost of the art-driven 21c Museum Hotel.

Head north and deeper into the Ozarks by crossing into southwestern Missouri and meandering around the shores of serpentine Table Rock Lake to **Branson**, sometimes referred to as "Nashville of the Ozarks," owing to its more than 50 music theaters specializing in country-western music, not to mention amusement parks, outlets shops, and other family-friendly draws. (Why is there a Titanic Museum in the middle of the Ozarks, you ask? That's a good question.) Continue north to the largest city in the Ozarks, **Springfield** (pop 170,000), whose attractive downtown is bisected by a colorful stretch of Route 66. Check out the vintage wheels at the **Route 66 Car Museum**, snap a selfie in front of the **World's Largest Fork** (why not?), and indulge in a banana-peanut butter Elvis shake at Black Sheep Burgers and Shakes before driving 167 miles northwest to Kansas City.

Hilly, laced with parks, and boasting more fountains than any place outside Rome, **Kansas City** is the point on this itinerary where I'd most strongly recommend spending an extra day. This friendly metropolis with a half-million residents abounds with great food and engaging museums. It's a physically large city, too, so consider devoting one day to the southern neighborhoods, starting in affluent and historic **Southmoreland** by touring the **Nelson-Atkins Museum of Art**, with its superb Asian and Native American art collections, striking Steven Holl–designed contemporary wing, and terraced lawns dotted with giant sculptures by Claes Oldenburg, Alexander Calder, and Henry Moore. Head west to **Country Club Plaza**, a 55-acre retail and entertainment district of ornate buildings patterned after Seville, Spain and overlooking linear **Brush Creek** park. It's home to some of the city's most elegant hotels, including **The Fontaine** and **The Raphael**. Have dinner nearby in artsy **Westport** at Canary Bar & Bistro or Q39, which serves some of the more flavorful brisket and pulled pork in a city that's famous for barbecue

On day two, stroll the gracious lawns of **Midtown's Penn Valley Park**, then continue down the hill to the 217 ft Liberty Tower, which rises above the excellent **National World War I Museum and Memorial**. Continue across the street to the gorgeously restored 1901 Beaux-Arts **Union Station**, which features restaurants, shops, and the popular **Science City** museum, then walk through the **Crossroads Arts District**, a cluster of formerly dilapidated warehouses, stopping for a bite to eat at vaunted Farina trattoria or hip Messenger Coffee Co. Walk up the hill and around the dramatic Moshe Safdie–designed **Kauffman Center for the Performing Arts**, then continue through downtown to the **River Market**

neighborhood, which is home to the myriad food stalls, cafes, and specialty grocers of Old City Market. Don't miss the fascinating **Arabia Steamboat Museum**, which displays the findings of archaeologists who in 1988 unearthed a paddle wheeler that sank into the murky depths of the Missouri in 1856, filled with perfectly preserved goods and supplies. Treat yourself to a chocolate-covered-strawberry ice cream sandwich at Betty Rae's or a cornflake-fried-chicken sandwich at Pigwich. Finish the day walking across the pedestrian bridge to the **Town of Kansas Observation Deck** for an impressive view of the Missouri River. If you have a little extra time, I recommend detouring 10 miles east to the venerable suburb of **Independence** to explore the legacy of America's 33rd president at the late-Victorian **Truman Home** and the modern **Harry S. Truman Presidential Library**.

KANSAS CITY, MO TO SIOUX FALLS, SD

Take I-70 west into Kansas, stopping in the attractive town of **Lawrence**, which is dominated by the undulating campus of the University of Kansas (KU)—excellent museums include the **Biodiversity Institute and Natural History Museum** and the **Spencer Museum of Art**. **Massachusetts St** is lined with colorful, one-of-a-kind shops and eateries. Have lunch at a sidewalk table at Ladybird Diner or a Moscow mule over happy hour at the Bourgeois Pig. Continue west to the state's capital city, **Topeka**, where you can tour the **Brown v. Board of Education National Historic Site**, which is set around an elementary school that was at the heart of the 1954 US Supreme Court case that would declare racial segregation in public schools unconstitutional. A few blocks away, the hip and historic **Cyrus Hotel** offers the most stylish accommodations in the state. Continue another hour west through the grassy **Flint Hills** region to the state's other major college town, **Manhattan**, which has a lively downtown and is home to a pair of excellent kid-friendly attractions, the **Flint Hills Discovery Center** and the intriguing—in a creepy-crawly kind of way—**Kansas State University Insect Zoo**, where you can visit with scorpions, cockroaches, and spiders and talk with a beekeeper.

Drive north on US 77 through about 135 miles of pastoral countryside to **Lincoln**, which is both the state capital and the home of the University of Nebraska. You can take an interesting tour of the **Nebraska Capitol**, which stands out for being crowned by a 400 ft Art Deco tower rather than the usual neoclassical dome. Head to downtown's bustling **Historic Haymarket District**, with its colorful shops and eateries, and then walk through the University of Nebraska

campus to visit the excellent **Sheldon Museum of Art**, which occupies a noteworthy 1963 building that iconic architect Philip Johnson described as his finest. It's an hour's drive northeast to **Omaha**, a graceful city on the banks of the Missouri River with several noteworthy attractions—it's also the hometown of a curiously diverse mix of famous Americans, including Marlon Brando, Fred Astaire, Malcolm X, Gerald Ford, Montgomery Clift, Henry Fonda, and Warren Buffet. My favorite building in Omaha is yet another Art Deco beauty (and former train station), the **Durham Museum**, which contains an eclectic collection of regional photos and historic artifacts; it's on the edge of the **Old Market**, a district of hulking redbrick warehouses, former cattle and rail yards, and cobbled streets that's now a hotbed of trendy restaurants, craft breweries, gay bars, billiards halls, and hotels, including **The Farnam**, **The Magnolia**, and **Hotel Deco**, which is my go-to for expertly poured cocktails and tantalizing charcuterie plates. One other must-see in town is the **Henry Doorly Zoo and Aquarium**, a 130-acre tract of superlatives. It features among the world's largest and most impressive indoor rainforests, deserts, and swamps.

It's about a 200-mile drive north to Sioux Falls. I recommend taking US 77, which passes through historic **Fremont** and up through wavy grasslands to **Sioux City**, IA, home to the **Lewis and Clark Interpretive Center**. This modern museum is one of the best of the many devoted to the famed 1804–06 expedition that traveled more than 2000 miles along the Missouri River. Again favoring back roads to the interstate, cross back into Nebraska and follow the river until recrossing it into **Vermillion**, home of the University of South Dakota as well as the distinguished **National Music Museum**. Continue west to **Yankton**, the engaging and historic former territorial capital that has scenic trails running along the river and over the graceful 1924 Meridian Bridge. Drive northeast about 90 minutes to **Sioux Falls**, an upbeat, rapidly growing city of about 200,000 on the scenic Big Sioux River. Start your visit in **Falls Park** to view a thrilling section of the river where frothy cascades tumble more than 100 ft down a series of rocky ramparts. Park features include walking trails, art installations, the remains of a seven-story water mill called Queen Bee, and the inviting Falls Overlook Cafe, which occupies a renovated 1908 hydroelectric plant. To the south you can visit the **SculptureWalk**, a collection of 60 public artworks set through the city's lively downtown.

SIOUX FALLS, SD TO IOWA CITY, IA

From Sioux Falls you can zigzag via any number of routes southeast to Des Moines. Driving across the sparsely populated, historically Dutch countryside of northwestern Iowa, you'll see that the scenery is pretty consistent—think broad views of cornfields, hog and cattle pastures, and colossal grain elevators. But there are three sites I always try to include on my drive: **Sac City**, because pulling up alongside the **World's Largest Popcorn Ball** (it weighs nearly 10,000 pounds) satisfies a certain joy I derive in visiting ridiculous roadside attractions; **Templeton Distillery** to sample exceptional rye whiskey in a gorgeous tasting room (and take one of the informative 1.5-hour tours if time allows); and **Madrid**, to go for a walk across the **High Trestle Trail Bridge**, a striking work of contemporary design that incorporates blue-lighted, geometric steel arches that span a half-mile-long former rail bridge rising 13 stories above the Des Moines River.

Outside of Washington, DC, perhaps no city has closer ties to American politics than **Des Moines**, the capital of the state that has long held the country's earliest election during the quadrennial primary season. Established as a frontier military outpost in the 1840s, this moderately hilly city of around 220,000 lies at the confluence of the Des Moines and Raccoon rivers. If possible, visit on a Saturday morning, when the **Downtown Farmers' Market** sets up along several blocks and proffers kombucha, hand-crafted birdhouses, apple hand pies, and other goods. Across the river the once-downcast **East Village** is a warren of hip arts spaces, boutiques, and eateries. From here stroll across **Peoples Plaza** and up the hill to the gold-domed **Iowa State Capitol**, with its ornate wood carvings, fine stenciling, and 29 kinds of marble. Heading west from downtown, stop for an horchata latte at **Ritual Cafe** to sip while you wander through **Pappajohn Sculpture Park**, an appealing 4-acre patch of greenery that's a great place for people- and pet-watching.

Head south on US 69, stopping for a sweet treat at Classic Frozen Custard, which doles out ginormous portions in rotating flavors like pumpkin and butter pecan, then drive east over serene **Lake Red Rock**—stopping to climb the 106 steps to the top of Cordova Park Observation Tower for an impressive view—and continue to **Pella**, whose windmills, canal, opera house, and annual Tulip Time Festival honor the region's Dutch heritage. Then head east through **Oskaloosa** and **Wellman**—stopping briefly, if you're a fan of *Star Trek*, for a peek inside the quirky **Voyage Home Museum** in

Riverside, which celebrates the town's future "history" as the birthplace of Captain James Kirk (in 2228). It's 15 miles north to **Iowa City,** the home of the University of Iowa (UI) and its renowned Iowa Writers Workshop, whose graduates have included Rita Dove, John Irving, Flannery O'Connor, and Michael Cunningham. My favorite of the several college towns along this route, Iowa City has a picturesque setting on the Iowa River and a lively downtown of both trendy and divy bars and restaurants—try Dandy Lion for fluffy biscuits and gravy in the morning, and Big Grove Brewery and Taproom for a crisp IPA in the afternoon. Also stop by the indie bookstore and cafe Prairie Lights, which draws some of the world's leading literary figures for readings. Downtown blends almost imperceptibly with UI's campus, highlights of which are the Greek Revival–style **Old Capitol Museum**, which was built as the state capitol in 1842 and now contains engaging history exhibits, and the striking new (set to open in fall 2022) **Stanley Museum of Art**. Cap off the afternoon with a trip into the rolling green hills east of town to pick up seasonal berries and produce and dine on flavorful barbecue at **Wilson's Orchard & Farm**.

Oklahoma City National Memorial *Opposite top* Des Moines
Opposite middle High Trestle Trail Bridge, Madrid
Opposite bottom Fordyce Bathhouse, Hot Springs National Park

BEST EATS

- **Vast** The name of this glass-walled restaurant on the 49th floor of Oklahoma City's shiny Devon Energy Center tower refers to the views it affords of the surrounding prairies. The kitchen turns out locally sourced dishes. 405-702-7262, vastokc.com.

- **Eden** Dine beneath a vaulted glass ceiling beside a leafy living wall inside the Hotel Hale, which was built in 1892, making it the oldest building on Hot Springs National Park's historic Bathhouse Row. 501-760-9010, hotelhale.com.

- **Local Flavor** The great people-watching from an umbrella-shaded deck is what first drew me to this offbeat, kitsch-filled decorated cafe on Eureka Springs' main drag, but it's the well-prepared, reasonably priced food that brings me back. 479-253-9522, localflavorcafe.net.

- **Novel** Standouts at this bistro in Kansas City's Crossroads Arts District include a savory ramen with Maine lobster, yuzu miso butter, and shiitakes and tagliatelle with a white Bolognese sauce. 816-221-0785, novelkc.com.

- **Single Barrel** Perfectly grilled steaks, smoked brisket barbecue, bacon cheeseburgers—this is the sort of carnivore-centric cooking that you'll find at this chophouse in Lincoln's trendy Graduate Hotel. 402-904-4631, thesinglebarrel.com.

- **Stirnella Bar and Kitchen** Head to Omaha's dapper Blackstone District to dine at this romantic Italian-inflected eatery set in a brick-framed storefront space with retractable garage-style windows. It's a terrific option for dinner or happy hour. 402-650-5204, stirnella.com

- **Harvester Kitchen by Bryan** In an early 1900s brick building that once sold tractors and farming equipment, this handsome Sioux Falls restaurant offers up tasty dishes from across the continent: blood-orange-glazed octopus, American wagyu steak tenderloin with onion jam. 605-271-2015, harvesterkitchensf.com.

- **Harbinger** Just west of downtown Des Moines along Ingersoll Ave's lively restaurant row, this intimate neighborhood bistro offers deftly crafted cocktails and internationally inspired cuisine. 515-244-1314, harbingerdsm.com.

- **Pullman Bar & Diner** This warmly lighted, modern take on a vintage railroad dining car serves breakfast (veggie frittatas, chicken-fried-steak burritos) all day, leisurely weekend brunches, and hearty Midwestern fare and cocktails later. 319-338-1808, pullmandiner.com.

BEST SLEEPS

- **21c Museum Hotel** At this creative hotel inside a retrofitted Ford Motors plant, I can lose myself for hours in the 14,000 sq ft of contemporary art installations. Plus there's terrific dining at the exceptional restaurant, Mary Eddy's. 405-982-6900, 21cmuseumhotels.com.

- **The Waters Hot Springs** With its towering white pilasters and ornate frieze and cornices, the facade of this 1913 building is one of the most impressive along picturesque Bathhouse Row. 501-321-0001, thewatershs.com

- **1886 Crescent Hotel & Spa** The stateliest of several Victorian spa resorts in the wooded hillsides of Eureka Springs has long verandas and a weathered stone facade. Watch the sunset over pizza and wine in the popular SkyBar. 855-725-5720, crescent-hotel.com.

- **Crossroads Hotel** From the romantic rooftop bar with expansive views of downtown Kansas City to the industrial-chic lobby, the hip public spaces in this chicly converted 1911 warehouse invite you to linger. The 131 rooms are every bit as stunning. 816-897-8100, crossroadshotelkc.com.

- **Kimpton Cottonwood Hotel** It's said that both the Reuben sandwich and butter brickle ice cream were invented (on separate occasions) at this 1916 gem. Reopened following a massive renovation in 2020, this swank hotel has 205 mid-century-modern rooms and a gracious pool and sundeck. 402-810-9500, thecottonwoodhotel.com.

- **Hotel on Phillips** Steps from bike and jogging paths along Sioux Falls' riverfront, this eight-story boutique lodging in a converted 1918 bank building offers 90 spacious and smartly designed rooms and suites plus first-rate dining in the Treasury restaurant. 605-274-7445, hotelonphillips.com.

- **The Surety** This trendy downtown Des Moines hotel occupies an elegant Beaux-Arts bank building that was the state's tallest skyscraper when it was completed in 1913. Rooms have an understated, mid-1940s vibe, and the grand common spaces include a nifty lobby and the Mulberry Street Tavern. 515-985-2066, suretyhotel.com.

- **The Highlander Hotel** Despite being a few miles from downtown, this artfully reimagined mid-century-modern property is my favorite of Iowa City's cool design hotels. Highlights include a sprawling indoor pool and patio, and colorful rooms with velvet armchairs and turntables and vintage LPs. 319-354-2000, highlanderhotel.us.

Top Sheldon Museum of Art, Lincoln *Bottom* Falls Park, Sioux Falls *Opposite* Aerial view of majestic Falls Park

CAMPING

Several state parks on this route offer pleasant camping options, from RV and tent sites to cabins. You'll also find well-maintained commercial campgrounds outside most of the area's big cities. Good bets include Lake Thunderbird State Park near Oklahoma City, Blue Springs Lake near Kansas City, Walnut Creek Recreation Area near Omaha, Ledges State Park near Des Moines, and Sugar Bottom Recreation Area near Iowa City. There are also highly rated KOA campgrounds in Hot Springs, Eureka Springs, Lawrence, and Yankton.

Heart of Texas ★

A journey through the central heart of Texas offers the chance to explore the vibrant art, design, and food scenes of some of America's most dynamic cities and the warm hospitality and gorgeous scenery of the Hill Country and Galveston Island.

HOW LONG?

5 days; add an extra day each to see more of any of the several big cities on this route.

WHEN TO GO

It can get brutally hot and humid in Texas in summer, yet winter can actually be a little chilly, especially around the Dallas–Fort Worth area (although Christmas season is a festive time to experience the San Antonio River Walk and Galveston's historic neighborhoods). For the best weather and prettiest garden and wildflower scenery, aim for mid-March through May and mid-September through December.

NEED TO KNOW

This trip connects some of the country's largest and most sprawling cities, so be prepared for heavy traffic at rush hour.

➔ Distances
Total distance, one-way: 700 mi (1127 km)
- Dallas to Fredericksburg: 285 mi (459 km)
- Fredericksburg to Austin: 190 mi (306 km)
- Austin to Galveston: 215 mi (346 km)

🕐 Daytime Temperatures
January: 55-65°F (13-18°C)
July: 88-95°F (31-35°C)

ⓘ More information
- Dallas tourism, visitdallas.com
- Fort Worth tourism, fortworth.com
- Fredericksburg tourism, visitfredericksburg.com
- San Antonio tourism, visitsanantonio.com
- Austin tourism, austintexas.org
- Houston tourism, visithoustontexas.com
- Galveston tourism, visitgalveston.com

👁 SNAPSHOT

Although central Texas is home to five of the country's dozen largest cities, it's a surprisingly great region for car touring. Houston and Dallas are true mega metropolises that you might want to visit briefly or save for another trip, but Fort Worth, San Antonio, and Austin have lower density and a wealth of world-class attractions and appealing neighborhoods that you can reach relatively easily by car. The drive from Fort Worth down into the scenic limestone hills, bountiful vineyards and orchards, and jewel-like lakes of the Texas Hill Country is one of the loveliest in the state. And this adventure ends on the pristine beaches of Galveston Island.

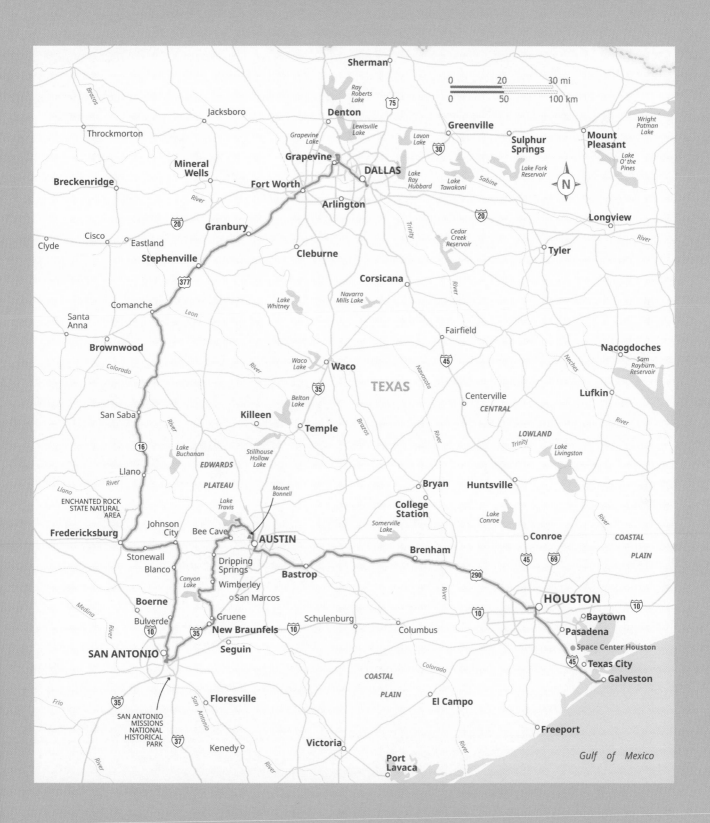

City View
Dallas

With a dramatic skyline of glitzy towers and a dense downtown core surrounded by a growing constellation of satellite neighborhoods, this cosmopolitan city of about 1.3 million has enough great things to see and do to entertain you for days, but in a short visit you can squeeze in two or three iconic attractions and eat and shop in the hip Bishop Arts District.

Car-friendly rating: Good. Like other big Sun Belt cities, Dallas is both lassoed and crisscrossed by massive freeways that can make it easy to cover large distances but can also be rife with traffic. Within the downtown core it's not hard to find metered street parking and reasonably priced garages (or even valet parking at many businesses), and in outlying neighborhoods, ample free parking is the norm.

What to see in a day: The riveting **Sixth Floor Museum at Dealey Plaza** is a true "only in Dallas" experience. Preserving the exact space in the Texas School Book Depository building from which Lee Harvey Oswald fired three shots to assassinate President John F. Kennedy, the museum contains remarkable, poignant exhibits and memorabilia about this dark day in history. Nearby, take in a spectacular 360-degree view of the skyline from the **GeO-Deck Observation Area** atop the Space Age-looking Reunion Tower. If you have a bit more time, head to the impressive **Dallas Arts District**, a 20-block tract of first-rate museums and performance venues—the peaceful, cloistered lawn of the **Nasher Sculpture Center** is my hands-down favorite, but the **Crow Collection of Asian Art** is also remarkable. You can grab lunch from a food truck at nearby **Klyde Warren Park,** before strolling over to the superb **Perot Museum of Nature and Science**, with has 11 fascinating, family-friendly halls devoted to outer space, dinosaurs, and nature—there's also a dedicated children's museum. Later in the day, drive 15 minutes southwest to the indie-spirited **Bishop Arts District**. Walk among the colorful businesses and historic homes along Bishop Ave and Davis St. My favorite eateries are Eno's Pizza Tavern, Lockhart Smokehouse (for barbecue), and Hattie's (for refined Southern fare)—wherever you go, save room for a slice of buttermilk pie at Emporium Pies.

Where to stay: This is a terrific hotel city when it comes to luxury and style. Downtown, you can go old-world posh at **The Adolphus**, artsy bespoke at **The Joule**, or boutique chic at the **Kimpton Pittman** in the lively Deep Ellum entertainment district. I like staying a little outside the hubbub of downtown at the **Warwick Melrose**, a regal 1920s hotel with upscale rooms and a gracious lobby—it's in the heart of the city's LGBTQ Oak Lawn neighborhood.

Top Dallas skyline from the Reunion Tower *Bottom* Nasher Sculpture Garden *Previous* M.L. Leddy's Boots & Saddlery,

DALLAS TO FREDERICKSBURG

The fastest way from Dallas to Fort Worth is via I-30 west, but I prefer the slightly less direct route northwest on Hwy 114 through charming **Grapevine**, which lies just north of DFW Airport at the southern tip of a massive reservoir, Grapevine Lake. Stroll along Main St, which is lined with historic redbrick storefronts housing boutiques, restaurants, and winery tasting rooms. Sample the well-balanced Cabernet Sauvignon and Chardonnay at **Messina Hof Winery**, then watch artisans craft gorgeous contemporary vases, lamps, and holiday ornaments at **Vetro Glassblowing Studio and Gallery**. At the dapper **Hotel Vin**, which also makes a good overnight base for exploring the DFW metroplex, have lunch in the bustling food hall, which is designed to echo the style of the adjacent 1880s train station. Here you can also book scenic rides to Fort Worth on the **Grapevine Vintage Railroad**.

It's about a half-hour drive southwest to the jubilant **Stockyards National Historic District** on the north side of **Fort Worth**. Established in 1890 as one of the nation's largest livestock centers, the neighborhood declined during the mid-20th century before being rebooted as a colorful tourist attraction in the 1970s. There's an endearingly hokey feel to this 98-acre tract of former animal pens, stables, meatpacking buildings, and auction houses that now contain spirited bars, souvenir shops, and steakhouses. Twice daily (11:30am and 4pm) kids love watching the Texas Longhorn cattle drive along Exchange Ave. The neighborhood's Mission Revival architecture has been beautifully preserved, and shops like **M.L. Leddy's** and **Maverick Fine Western Wear** sell beautifully crafted cowboy boots, hats, and apparel. Other highlights include dancing (and if you're brave enough riding the bucking mechanical bull) at massive Billy Bob's honky-tonk, feasting on creatively prepared steaks and contemporary Tex-Mex fare at Lonesome Dove, and examining the displays of antique gear, vehicles, and photos in the **Stockyards Museum**.

It's a 10-minute drive south to the attractive downtown of Fort Worth, an underrated city of more than 940,000 that despite its skyrocketing recent growth retains a friendly personality and has a manageable—I'd even say car-friendly—layout. It also offers a remarkable variety of attractions and inviting neighborhoods. Downtown's convivial outdoor living room of sorts, **Sundance Square** is a good place to relax with an iced latte before checking out the renowned collection of Western American paintings and sculptures at the **Sid Richardson Museum** or enjoying a meal at one of several stellar restaurants within walking distance, such as Reata

and Grace. Then drive a few miles to the city's **Cultural District**, which is home to several world-class museums designed by renowned architects. I love the clean lines and soaring windows that rise up from a reflecting pool at the **Modern Art Museum of Fort Worth**, designed by celebrated Japanese architect Tadao Ando, but the stunning **Kimbell Art Museum**, with its vaulted Louis Kahn ceilings and a remarkable Renzo Piano addition capped with a lush green roof, is a close second (and it contains an impressive collection of Asian and European masterworks).

If you have time, visit the **Amon Carter Museum of American Art**, a creation of postmodern icon Philip Johnson that showcases an extraordinary collection with works by Louise Nevelson, Grant Wood, Georgia O'Keeffe, and other luminaries. The district's **National Cowgirl Museum and Hall of Fame** is another great stop—it's filled with engrossing exhibits that honor the talented and determined women— from Annie Oakley to Temple Grandin—who've excelled at riding and rodeo. End the day with a food crawl through one of the city's hip food neighborhoods, such as **West 7th** (which has a more contemporary feel) and the **Southside**, a more vintage district whose main drag, Magnolia Ave, is lined with trendy spots like Heim Barbecue, The Usual cocktail bar, and Fixture Kitchen.

From Fort Worth, my favorite non-freeway route south to the Texas Hill Country is via US 377 southwest to Comanche, then Hwy 16 south to Fredericksburg—without stops, the drive takes about 4.5 hours. There aren't a lot of standout attractions, but this is a relaxing drive through the sunny, undulating prairies and live oak and pecan groves of central Texas, a region of ranching and farming that looks much the same as it did a century ago. The first good-size community you reach is **Granbury**, which has a dapper downtown set around a courthouse square, an elegant 1880s opera house, and one of the better craft beer makers in the state, Revolver Brewery.

As you continue, try to detour briefly from the main highways (which generally bypass the colorful downtowns) to check out the pretty centers of **Stephenville**, **San Saba**, and **Llano**. Interesting stops include Dianne's Ranch Diner, an open-air restaurant overlooking a 50-acre Stephenville ranch that's known for its hearty meatloaf and six-layer chocolate cakes. In Comanche, **Brennan Vineyards** is a pretty winery on an 1879 farmstead that produces a superb Cabernet Sauvignon and an inky, rich port-style dessert wine. And the **Llano Fine Arts Guild and Gallery** is an engaging stop in one of the region's most charming little towns. Shortly before reaching

Fredericksburg, for a terrific little side adventure, turn off of Hwy 16 onto Hwy 965, and go for a hike at **Enchanted Rock State Natural Area**, the dominant feature of which is an imposing pink-granite dome that rises several hundred feet above the arid landscape.

FREDERICKSBURG TO AUSTIN

Around San Saba, you'll enter the scenic **Texas Hill Country**, a rangy 25-county swatch of limestone and granite hills, ridges, and caverns that also forms the geographical boundary between the wetter and greener southeastern side of the state and the sunnier and tanner southwestern side. If you visit El Paso or Big Bend, Texas feels unquestionably like part of the American Southwest. If you spend time in Houston or Dallas, the state clearly seems to be an extension of the US Southeast. As you drive around the Hill County, alternating between 800 ft rocky bluffs, semi-arid stands of yucca, juniper, and live oak, and lush aquifer-fed valleys, you can fully sense being on the border of two major continental zones.

The town of **Fredericksburg** is one of the Hill Country's main gateways, and it's also an easy place to appreciate the strong German heritage that dominates much of Texas. Stretching for about 10 blocks along Main St, the downtown **Fredericksburg Historic District** is characterized by stately whitewashed or limestone buildings, many with ornate German-style wooden or iron trim—a few of these are now museums, the best being the informative **Pioneer Museum** and octagonal **Vereins Kirche Museum**. Set in a striking modern building, the **National Museum of the Pacific War**—an affiliate of the Smithsonian—contains thought-provoking exhibits. Give yourself at least half a day to explore downtown's distinctive shops and have lunch at one of several old-world German restaurants, such as the Auslander or the Old German Bakery.

Long famous for its pecan, peach, and other fruit farms and orchards, Fredericksburg is also the center of the Hill Country wine region, which is the largest and most celebrated in the state—about half of the region's more than 100 wineries are here, some downtown and others reached via picturesque drives through the rocky and rolling countryside. A few that offer a mix of striking architecture, magnificent natural scenery, and first-rate vino include **Augusta Vin**, with its 60 acres of sloping vineyards that tumble down toward the Pedernales River; **Becker Vineyards**, which is one of the region's pioneers and also offers fragrant lavender fields and tastings in a reproduction German stone barn; and **Grape Creek**, which pours its classic old-world wines in a grand Tuscan-style building and its crisp *méthode champenoise* bubblies (under the sister brand name Heath Sparkling Wines) next door.

Head east on US 290 through tiny **Stonewall**, which is famously associated with the 36th US president, Lyndon B. Johnson. You can learn about his storied, if at times controversial, life at **Lyndon B. Johnson National Historical Park**, where you can see the modest dwelling he was born in, the sprawling ranch house (known as the Texas White House) in which he spent a significant portion of his time in office, and the cemetery where he was laid to rest. About 15 miles east in **Johnson City**, you can visit the second unit of the national historical park. It contains the Victorian home that LBJ grew up in; a visitor center with exhibits about him and his wife, Lady Bird; and other buildings that belonged to his family. Continue down US 281 through the heart of the Hill Country to cute **Blanco**, which appeared prominently in the Coen brothers' acclaimed remake of *True Grit*. If it's a hot day, go for a swim in the spring-fed waters of **Blanco State Park**. Follow this with lunch at the Redbud Cafe and Pub, a vintage storefront space on the town square—order the venison burger with pepper jack cheese and grilled jalapeno mayo. Check out the owners' sturdy yet stunning stoneware pottery, which they sell in their gallery next door.

It's another 50 miles to **San Antonio**. Although this city of around 1.4 million sprawls over a 500 sq mile area, most of its key attractions lie within a narrow north-south corridor bisected by the San Antonio River. I recommend starting your explorations about 10 miles south at **Mission Espada**, which is the southernmost and oldest of five missions that were developed by the Spaniards in the late-17th and early-18th centuries. Four of these are now preserved within the linear **San Antonio Missions National Historical Park**, which leads north into downtown, where you can visit the northernmost and most famous of the group, The Alamo, which is not part of the national park. If time is limited as you drive north, I recommend skipping Mission San Juan Capistrano and going directly to **Mission San Jose**, which contains the park's visitor center and is the largest and most extensively restored of the missions. Next along the route and offering a striking contrast, **Mission Concepción** remains completely unrestored and is known for its original frescoes. As you enter downtown, drive along St Mary's Street past the ornate Victorian mansions of the **King William Historic District**, stopping perhaps for a bite at one of the hip eateries of **Southtown**, and then park around **La Villita Historic**

Arts Village, a collection of colorful galleries that's been a source of fine crafts and artwork since it was established by the WPA in 1939. Here you can access the **Downtown Reach** loop of the iconic **San Antonio River Walk**, a captivating subterranean promenade that wends through the city's heart. The downtown section is lined with somewhat touristy restaurant terraces, but its twinkly lights and colorful umbrellas are festive nonetheless, and you'll find several beguiling hotels along the route, including the funky and intimate **Hotel Havana** and the posh and contemporary **Mokara Hotel and Spa**. Emerge from the River Walk to visit **The Alamo**—exhibits relate the tale of the building's ill-fated but ultimately inspiring role in the 1836 Texas Revolution.

Follow the River Walk north through the 3-mile **Museum Reach** section. This is my favorite part—it's lined with lush greenery and whimsical public art installations. Beneath the I-35 bridge, at dusk from spring through fall you can watch a colony of about 60,000 Mexican free-tailed bats fly out from their daytime lair into the dark sky. I always break for at least an hour to visit the outstanding **San Antonio Museum of Art** before continuing north to the city's buzzy **Pearl District**, a hive of stylish eateries, shops, and a hotel that's been fashioned out of an ornately designed late-Victorian brewery complex. Try to arrive just in time to enjoy dinner at Down on Grayson or Southerleigh Fine Food and Brewery.

Follow I-35 north to **New Braunfels**, an attractive town rich in German heritage that's bisected by the Guadalupe River. Following the river a short way north, you'll come to **Gruene** (pronounced "green"), a historic village high on a bluff and teeming with spirited eateries and galleries. Continue up around the eastern shore of **Canyon Lake** and then cut northeast into picturesque **Wimberley**, where you could spend the better part of an afternoon browsing folk art, fashion, and housewares. Stop for lunch on the patio at Community Pizza and Beer Garden, then continue north past vineyards and wineries through the colorfully named towns of **Dripping Springs** and **Bee Cave**. Drive around the eastern shore of **Lake Travis**, which is actually a dammed reservoir along the 862 mile long Colorado River (not to be confused with the Colorado River that flows through the Grand Canyon).

On the western outskirts of Austin, Lake Travis is great for boating, swimming, and sunbathing. You can work up quite the adrenaline rush riding the ropes at **Lake Travis Zipline Adventures**, saunter sans-Speedo along the clothing-optional (and very LGBTQ-popular) rocky shores of **Hippie Hollow Park**, or sip margaritas and nosh on shrimp fajitas on one of

the sweeping terraces at the Oasis on Lake Travis, a rambling multistory cantina that sits high on a precipice with stunning water views. Head east into Austin via Hwy 2222, stopping to make the short but slightly strenuous trek up the 106 steps to the 705 ft summit of **Mt Bonnell** for a great view of the river.

AUSTIN TO GALVESTON

Yet another Texas city that's experienced incredibly rapid growth over the past few decades, the once-easygoing college town (University of Texas) and state capital **Austin** has doubled in population since 1990 and now has nearly a million residents. Traversed by a wide stretch of the Colorado River that's known downtown, as **Lady Bird Lake**, where it's fringed by biking and pedestrian pathways, Austin is more a place to explore neighborhoods than museums.

LBJ Presidential Library, Austin
Previous Barton Springs Pool, Austin

City View: Houston

Tremendously diverse, home to a number of world-class cultural venues, and increasingly regarded as one of America's most exciting food cities, Houston has a lot going for it. It's also remarkably friendly and easygoing for such an enormous metropolis (with 2.3 million inhabitants, it's America's fourth largest city). I love spending time here, but logistically, like Dallas, its size can make it a bit overwhelming if you're in town for just a day or two. Zeroing in on one or two key neighborhoods or attractions, however, can make for a rewarding short visit.

Car-friendly rating: Good. Everything I wrote about Dallas applies here.

What to see in a day: Easy to drive to and explore on foot, eclectic **Montrose** is west of downtown and my favorite neighborhood to explore for two reasons: it has a fantastic food and nightlife scene, much of it along Westheimer Road (Uchi sushi, Blacksmith coffeehouse, Hugo's for upmarket Mexican cuisine, and Georgia James for steaks are all terrific). And it's home to the **Menil Collection**, a striking Renzo Piano-designed contemporary art museum that adjoins a campus of compelling galleries and installations (including the **Menil Drawing Institute**, **Cy Twombly Gallery**, and **Rothko Chapel**). The other must-see area is lush Hermann Park, which anchors Houston's impressive **Museum District**—there's a lovely **Japanese Garden**, and it's a short walk north to see the extensive holdings of the **Museum of Fine Arts Houston**; the interactive **Houston Museum of Natural Science**, where kids delight in walking through the lush rainforest habitat of the Cockrell Butterfly Center; and the outstanding **Houston Museum of African American Culture**. Southeast of the city—just off the interstate en route to Galveston—**Space Center Houston** is a fascinating attraction, but you should budget at least four hours to fully experience it. There are more than 400 space-related artifacts, from moon rocks to actual spacecraft, an awesome interactive Mission Mars, and space shuttle exhibits.

Where to stay: Although it has some great properties (I like both the hip **Hotel ICON** and the old-world refined **Lancaster**), downtown Houston makes less sense for road-trippers, given that many of the best parts of the city for exploring are in outer neighborhoods. In these areas, consider the contemporary **Hotel ZaZa Museum District**, which is steps from the exceptional attractions around Hermann Park, or the arty and dashing 16-room **Modern B&B**, which is close to the Menil Collection and Montrose.

Top Houston skyline *Bottom* Reflecting pool, Rothko Chapel

That said, the imposingly austere 10-story **LBJ Presidential Library** on the tree-shaded campus of the **University of Texas** is an interesting stop for history buffs, as is the **Bullock Texas State History Museum**, whose extensive collections touch on everything from the state's rich Native American heritage to its considerable contributions to space travel. It's also worth taking a tour of the elegant Renaissance Revival–style **Texas State Capitol** building, which dates to 1885 and has a beautiful interior and grounds. On sunny days I recommend strolling amid the lovely gardens and trees of **Zilker Botanical Garden** and then taking a dip in nearby **Barton Springs Pool**, an outdoor swimming hole fed by natural underground springs that keep it at a constant temperature between 68 and 74 degrees. But the best way to experience this high-tech hub of creative design and exceptional eating and drinking is to walk around one of Austin's trendy neighborhoods, which are also home to some of the city's artfully designed boutique hotels, such as **Kimpton Hotel Van Zant** and the funky **Austin Motel**. Terrific areas for restaurant-hopping include the downtown **Warehouse District**, **Rainey Street**, **East Austin**, or—and this area also stands out for its cool boutiques—**South Congress**. If you have time for just one neighborhood, I'd go with East Austin, and specifically 6th St, where delicious options include Buenos Aires Cafe for empanadas and Argentinian fare, Gelateria Gemelli for luscious ice cream, Domo Alley-Gato for ramen and cocktails, and Suerte for delicious tacos and tamales. It's a pleasant if not especially noteworthy 2.5- to 3-hour drive via US 290 across the rolling green hills of east-central Texas to Houston.

Continue from Houston an hour down I-45 to **Galveston**, a charming early-19th-century seaport of around 50,000 that's set along a narrow 27 mile long barrier island in the Gulf of Mexico. After driving around the vast prairies, arid high desert, and dense woodlands that dominate most of the state, it feels happily surreal to pull up along the island's sweeping sandy beachfront. It may surprise you that Texas has the sixth longest coastline (367 miles) of any state. With its colorful Victorian bungalows and mansions and the stately brick architecture and wrought-iron balconies of the city center, Galveston has a bit of a New Orleans vibe. The many beach amusements are a nice diversion for any kids in your group, while the wealth of music clubs, LGBTQ bars, quirky taverns, and sophisticated wine and cocktail lounges make it fun destination for adults.

My perfect day in Galveston begins with a walk along the **Seawall**—the stretch from 13th St to **Galveston Island Historic Pleasure Pier** (with its colorful souvenir stands and boardwalk rides) is especially scenic. The city's coast faces southeast, so if you get up early enough you'll be treated to a magical sunrise. Follow this with breakfast at one of Galveston's down-home eateries, such as Mosquito Cafe, which is famous for its crab-topped scone Benedict with cheesy grits. The Sunflower Bakery and Cafe is another great option—sweet-tooths shouldn't miss the bread pudding French toast. After lunch, drive to **Moody Gardens**, a 242-acre complex comprising a golf resort, 3-D and 4-D cinemas, and three giant glass pyramids containing a hands-on science museum, an aquarium, and—my favorite—a rainforest garden that teems with colorful birds, adorable sloths and monkeys, and thousands of tropical plants and flowers. Kid alert: **Schlitterbahn Waterpark**, which boasts the tallest water coaster in the world, is next door.

Spend the rest of the day in downtown's **Strand Historic District**, with its stately Victorian buildings housing fine galleries, restaurants, and shops and shops as well as an 1894 opera house. As you walk around, note the signs on many buildings that indicate the high-tide mark during the various hurricanes that have inundated the city over the years, the most famous—and tragic—being the Great Storm of 1900, which resulted in up to 10,000 deaths. Downtown faces Galveston Bay rather than the Gulf, and here you can tour the interactive exhibits at the **Galveston Historic Seaport** and board the tall ship *Elissa*, an 1877 square-rigged iron barque. Outfitters along the bayfront offer jet-boat tours, bay cruises, and kayak and boat rentals, and you'll find several good restaurants with waterfront seating—try Katie's Seafood House or Willie G's Seafood and Steaks.

Opposite Fort Worth Stock Show and Rodeo

BEST EATS

- **Ellerbe Fine Foods** Set in a stylishly retrofitted vintage service station on Fort Worth's spirited Magnolia Ave, this welcoming bistro stands out for its artfully prepared farm-to-table fare. 817-926-3663, ellerbefinefoods.com.

- **Clay Pigeon** At this industrial-chic Fort Worth dinner house, steak frites and grilled duck breast with Fuji apples and fennel cream are among the specialties, and the wine list is first rate. 817-882-8065, claypigeonfd.com.

- **Otto's** A modern, warmly furnished take on Fredericksburg's traditional German restaurants, Otto's sources seasonal ingredients from local farms to create flammkuchen with creme fraiche and Spanish chorizo sugo, and a *wurst platte* of smoked paprika-gruyere sausage, German potato salad, and house-made sauerkraut. 830-307-3336, ottosfbg.com.

- **Curry Boys BBQ** Two food traditions dear to Texas these days—barbecue and Southeast Asian fare—are united at this simple pink takeout window with outdoor seating in San Antonio's eclectic St Mary's Strip neighborhood. The oak-smoked brisket with fragrant and spicy Thai green curry is a symphony of flavor. 210-320-0555, curryboysbbq.com.

- **Rebelle** The elegant seafood bistro inside downtown San Antonio's historic St Anthony hotel is a wonderfully refined spot for a leisurely weekend brunch of lobster Florentine, or a romantic dinner featuring a soaring seafood tower followed by blackened redfish with jalapeno-crab maque choux. 210-352-3171, rebellesa.com.

- **Gristmill River Restaurant and Bar** Part of the fun of dining at this 1880s cotton mill is the memorable setting: lushly landscaped decks and a rustic dining room with huge windows high on a bluff overlooking the Guadalupe River in the Hill Country village of Gruene. 830-625-0684, gristmillrestaurant.com.

- **Leaning Pear** In an angular contemporary building on a bluff in Wimberley, this scene-y locavore-minded restaurant serves flavorful dishes like wood-fired pizzas topped with kale and Italian sausage and grilled rainbow trout with lemon-zaatar potatoes. Save room for a slice of ginger-carrot cake. 512-847-7327, leaningpear.com.

- **El Naranjo** This handsome, modern restaurant in Austin's trendy South Lamar neighborhood serves contemporary Oaxacan fare, such as tlayudas with chorizo and chicken with a complex yellow mole. Refreshing mezcal and tequila cocktails are part of the mix. 512-520-5750, elnaranjorestaurant.com.

- **Kemuri Tatsu-Ya** Japanese food is a standout in food-forward Austin, and this cozy izakaya in boho-cool East Austin is a local star, offering delectable snacks with Texan accents. Try the cornbread taiyaki with toasted-sesame butter and local honey, followed by salmon crudo with charred green tomatoes. 512-803-2224, kemuri-tatsuya.com.

- **Truth BBQ, Brenham** On the otherwise prosaic drive from Austin to Houston, stop by this no-frills roadside shack for phenomenal Texas barbecue, including tender brisket, savory turkey breast, and piquant jalapeno-cheddar sausage links. 979-830-0392, truthbbq.com.

- **BLVD Seafood** With views of the Gulf and delicious, contemporary cuisine that's focused on red snapper, sea scallops, blue crab, and shrimp, this smart but casual spot inside a former Galveston convenience store (you'd never know it) is a fun option for lunch, dinner, or weekend brunch. 409-762-2583, blvdseafood.com.

BEST SLEEPS

- **Stockyards Hotel** This elegant 52-room lodging in Fort Worth's historic Stockyards District opened in 1907 and has been smartly updated. Countless country-western luminaries—Willie Nelson and Tanya Tucker among them—have stayed here. 817-625-6427, stockyardshotel.com.

- **The Sinclair–Autograph Collection** An Art Deco stunner on downtown Fort Worth's bustling Sundance Square, The Sinclair stands out for its spectacular rooftop bar and smartly appointed rooms. 682-231-8214, thesinclairhotel.com.

- **Dofflemyer Hotel** A perfect overnight option for breaking up the drive from Fort Worth to Fredericksburg, this distinctive and affordable six-room hotel set in a 1913 bank building in San Saba has a well-curated mercantile and cafe with local foods and gifts. 325-372-5614, dofflemyerhotel.com.

- **Lodge Above Town Creek** The 16 roomy suites in this cushy but casual Fredericksburg inn offer Jacuzzi tubs, kitchenettes, balconies, and gas fireplaces. 830-997-1615, thelodgeabovetowncreek.com

- **Hotel Emma** Set inside a magnificently transformed 19th-century brewery building that anchors San Antonio's hip Pearl District, this 146-room stunner has a fascinating steampunk-chic aesthetic. Even if you don't stay here, check out the inviting common spaces and stylish eateries. 210-448-8300, thehotelemma.com.

- **Hotel Gibbs** Considering its prime location across from The Alamo and steps from the San Antonio River Walk, this handsome boutique hotel inside the city's first "high rise" (the 1909 building has eight stories) is a bargain. There's a cool craft beer and wine bar off the lobby. 210-933-2000, hotelgibbs.com.

- **Hotel Flora and Fauna** This sleek, mid-century-modern lifestyle retreat with 12 rooms, a pool, hot tub, and fanciful wildlife murals is steps from the indie galleries and eateries of Wimberley. 512-842-9110, hotelfloraandfauna.com.

- **The Driskill** This fanciful Richardsonian Romanesque Revival 1886 grande dame in downtown Austin has hosted numerous celebrities and offers an appealing blend of the new (with its light and stylishly updated rooms) and classic (with its ornate lobby and clubby Driskill Bar). 512-439-1234, driskillhotel.com.

- **Arrive Austin** With a great location amid East Austin's buzzy food scene, this strikingly contemporary four-story hotel features 83 light-filled rooms with marble baths and low-profile custom beds. 737-242-8080, arrivehotels.com.

- **Hotel Galvez and Spa** My two favorite hotels in Galveston are this 1911 grande dame on the Gulf with gracious common areas, a beautiful spa and pool, and easy access to the beach, and its historic Victorian sister, the Tremont House, which is right in the heart of the Strand Historic District. 409-515-2154, hotelgalvez.com.

CAMPING

Although much of this drive is in densely populated areas, there are a number of appealing campgrounds just outside some of the biggest cities in Texas, such as Twin Cove Park on Grapevine Lake between Dallas and Fort Worth, Alamo River RV Resort and Campground near San Antonio, and Austin East KOA Holiday. For proximity to Houston, I recommend staying down in Galveston, either at Galveston Island State Park or Jamaica Beach RV Park. In the Texas Hill Country, you've got a number of pleasant options, including Lady Bird Johnson Municipal Park Campground in Fredericksburg and River Road Camp near Gruene.

Opposite St. Anthony Falls, Mississippi River, Minneapolis

Mississippi River Valley ★

Driving along the steep bluffs and through the fertile plains of America's longest river valley offers a fascinating look at the nation's complex history over the past 1000 years.

HOW LONG?

7 days at a brisk pace, but allow up to another week to make deeper dives into the region's several notable cities.

WHEN TO GO

The climate changes dramatically on this long north–south route, meaning winters can be bone-chillingly frigid on the northern section and summers sweltering in the South. This leaves spring and fall as relatively comfortable periods that also offer the promise of colorful autumn foliage and spring gardens.

NEED TO KNOW

From the Minnesota State Fair in St Paul to Mardi Gras in New Orleans (it's also a big deal in St Louis), the Mississippi River Valley's wealth of annual festivals can add excitement but also massive crowds and significant increases in hotel rates. Check local events calendars well in advance and plan accordingly.

→ Distances
Total distance, one-way: 1600 mi (2575 km)
- Minneapolis, MN to Galena, IL:
  290 mi (467 km)
- Galena, IL to St Louis, MO:
  400 mi (644 km)
- St. Louis, MO to Memphis, TN:
  325 mi (523 km)
- Memphis, TN to Vicksburg, MS:
  265 mi (426 km)
- Vicksburg, MS to New Orleans, LA:
  320 mi (515 km)

ⓘ Daytime Temperatures
January: 25-65°F (-4-18°C)
July: 82-92°F (28-33°C)

ⓘ More information
- Mississippi River Valley tourism,
  experiencemississippiriver.com
- Minneapolis tourism, minneapolis.org
- Quad Cities tourism, visitquadcities.com
- St Louis tourism, explorestlouis.com
- Memphis tourism, memphistravel.com
- New Orleans tourism, neworleans.com

◉ SNAPSHOT

The Mississippi River's very name, which in the Indigenous Ojibwe language translates to "long river," conjures up visions of grandeur. Driving alongside more than two-thirds of this mighty river's serpentine 2350-mile path is in many respects the quintessential all-American journey. You'll visit dynamic cities, pass beneath St Louis's enduring Gateway Arch and across dozens of dramatic bridges, and experience the unique music, literary, and culinary heritage of the Mississippi Delta and New Orleans.

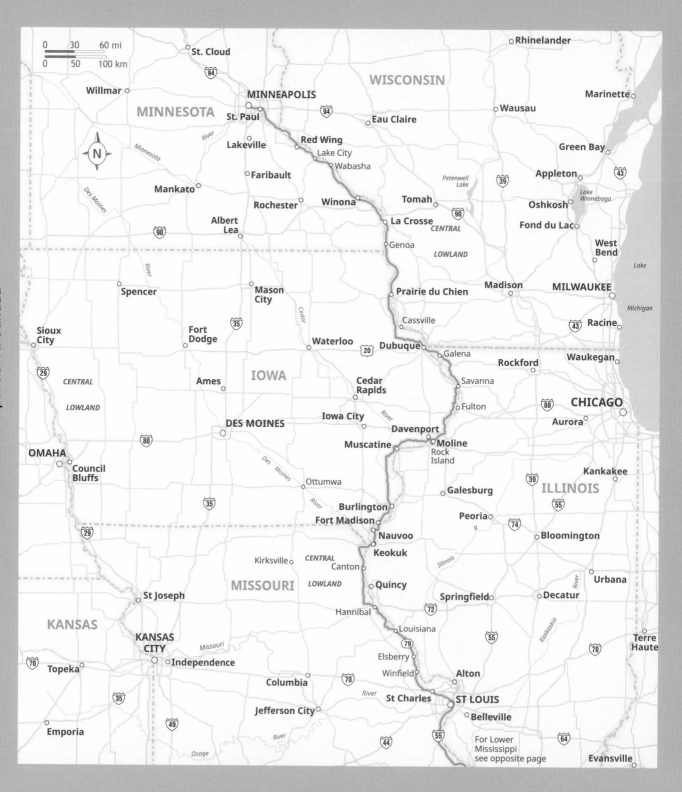

Ultimate Road Trips: USA & Canada

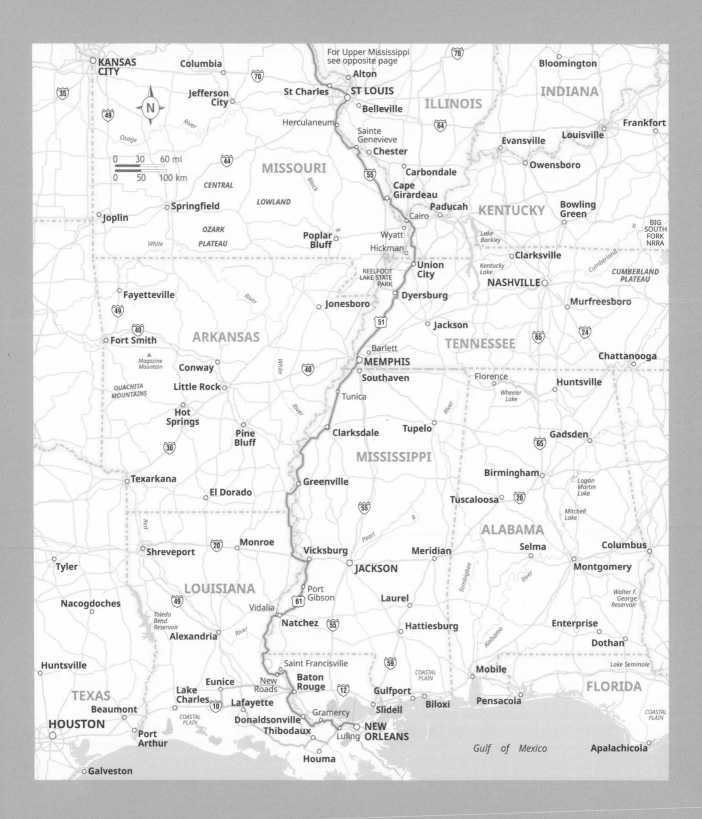

For Upper Mississippi see opposite page

This being a Mississippi River journey, why not start your explorations of **Minneapolis** right on the stretch of this mighty waterway that passes through downtown? Before we talk Twin Cities, if you're curious, the actual source of the Mississippi is **Lake Itasca**, which is a nearly four-hour drive north. It's a mere stream you could throw a stone across as it flows from this 2 sq mile glacial lake and meanders circuitously through a series of prairie towns, including **Brainerd** (which featured prominently in the darkly comic masterpiece *Fargo*) and the attractive college city of **St Cloud**. It's a pretty enough drive that lends credibility to the state's "Land of 10,000 Lakes" nickname, but I think Minneapolis makes a more interesting starting point. Specifically, I suggest beginning right on the riverfront in the **Mill District**, where vintage flour mills have been converted to condo lofts, restaurants, and the **Mill City Museum**, with its engaging history exhibits. Next door, check out the spectacular **Guthrie Theater**, a contemporary world-class performance space with a famous 178 ft long cantilevered bridge that appears to hover magically above the landscape. Walk along the riverbank and then across **Stone Arch Bridge**, an 1881 rail crossing that now serves pedestrians and bicycles and affords great views of the roaring **St Anthony Falls**. Continue along the leafy parkland on the other riverbank by **Hennepin Island** through the trendy **St Anthony Main** district (home to the celebrated restaurant Alma).

From the Mill District walk south through downtown along **Nicollet Mall**, a 12-block pedestrian-transit thoroughfare, stopping at the corner of 7th Street to satisfy your thirst for pop culture with a photo of the statue of Mary Tyler Moore as spunky TV news producer Mary Richards. (Her gracious house that appeared in her famous sitcom's opening credits is at 2104 Kenwood Parkway in the city's **Chain of Lakes** district, which is laced with scenic walking and jogging trails.) From the south end of Nicollet Mall, cut over a few blocks to leafy **Loring Park**, stopping for drinks or a bite to eat at Cafe and Bar Lurcat, and then take the angular, wood-plank pedestrian bridge across Hennepin Ave to visit the outstanding **Walker Arts Center** and walk through its adjacent **Minneapolis Sculpture Garden**.

To reach **St Paul** (the smaller of the Twin Cities and the state capital) from Minneapolis, take University Ave east a few miles from the handsome campus of the **University of Minnesota.** Just west of downtown you'll find several historic neighborhoods dotted with grand old homes (including the Victorian brownstone at 599 Summit Ave that F. Scott

Fitzgerald lived in for a time) and tree-shaded restaurant and retail strips, including **Grant**, **Summit**, and **Selby** aves. Swell dining options include the traditional Irish pub Emmett's and the inviting restaurant Revival, where you can sample some tantalizing Southern fare as a precursor to your journey toward Tennessee. Downtown St Paul has a handful of excellent museums, including the very kid-friendly **Science Museum of Minnesota**, which adjoins **Upper Landing Park**, a beautiful expanse of lawns, fountains, and paths along the Mississippi River. From here head south along the river on US 61, which marks the beginning of what's commonly dubbed the Great River Road—it more or less follows the curve of the Mississippi River for about 1400 miles south to New Orleans. Much of this itinerary does travel along US 61, but in quite a few places I've recommended different routes that either run closer to the river or offer even better scenery.

The roads along the river from southeastern Minnesota to the next major city along the route, St Louis, are known for a geological feature that visitors expecting a flat-as-a-board landscape may be surprised by: numerous limestone bluffs on either side of the river carved by glaciers during the last Ice Age, some that reach as high as 600 ft. You'll find many enjoyable hikes to these sometimes-lofty promontories along this upper stretch of the Mississippi River, extending as far south as Cairo, IL. From St Paul, driving south on US 61, one of the first dramatic overlooks you'll encounter is **Barn Bluff**, a 400 ft limestone outcropping in **Red Wing** that the Dakota tribe considers sacred because it's the site of numerous burial mounds. You can hike a 3-mile round-trip trek for dramatic views at the top. The town also has inviting indie shops, the stately **St James Hotel**, and the superb **Pottery Museum of Red Wing**. As you continue south along the Minnesota side of the river, you'll venture through several handsome river towns with notable museums, bluff hikes, or both: highlights among the latter include **Garvin Heights City Park** and **Great Bluffs State Park** in **Winona**. The two museums I'd prioritize visiting are the **National Eagle Center** in **Wabasha**, a nonprofit wildlife interpretive center that's home to several rescued bald and golden eagles and has huge windows that overlook the river banks, where many eagles in the wild make their nests, and the **Minnesota Marine Art Museum** in Winona, which is both a beautiful building (surrounded by extensive gardens and native plantings) and an impressive collection of maritime art by talents ranging from van Gogh to Emanuel Leutze (one of only two versions of his *Washington Crossing the Delaware* is here).

Crossing into Wisconsin at the small city of **La Crosse** (pop 52,000), **Grandad Bluff** is another great hike with an exceptional view, and you can also enjoy a slice of waterfront greenery at **Riverside Park** and admire an interesting collection of vintage cars (mostly Fords) at the **Dahl Auto Museum**. Drive the Wisconsin side down to **Prairie du Chien**, and then cross over into **McGregor**, IA and head down to **Pikes Peak State Park**, which has one of the highest points along the Mississippi, overlooking its confluence with the Wisconsin River. Continue south on Hwy X56, picking up US 52 in Guttenberg and then staying close to the river by taking minor roads through **North Buena Vista** and **Sherrill** to **Dubuque**, a thoroughly underrated and quite picturesque city of around 60,000 with several attractions well worth budgeting a day for, starting with the **National Mississippi Museum and Aquarium**. Other highlights include **Stone Cliff Winery**, which occupies a stately former brewery building overlooking the river, and **Fenelon Place Elevator**, a short but precipitous funicular that climbs nearly 300 ft to a hill with grand city views. At Dubuque, cross the river and take US 20 into one of the most appealing little towns along this drive, **Galena**, IL, once a prominent Mississippi River steamboat port that boasts a nearly 600-acre downtown historic district that abounds with restored redbrick Victorian buildings, many housing fine shops, galleries, and eateries—a highlight is visiting the Italianate 1859 former **home of President Ulysses S Grant**. Just outside downtown, if you're a fan of artisanal spirits, don't miss **Blaum Brothers Distilling**, which offers tours and tastings of its acclaimed oak-aged gin, bourbon, and absinthe.

GALENA, IL TO ST LOUIS, MO

Heading south from Galena, cross the striking **Savanna-Sabula Bridge** into Iowa and continue down to **Quad Cities**, the name of a two-state metroplex of, you guessed it, four cities. Of these, **Moline** has a nicely revitalized but small downtown and a pretty nature park, **Sylvan Island**, which are both enjoyable for strolling, but my favorite is **Davenport**, which has a vibrant downtown of grand old buildings, a beautifully landscaped riverfront, and an excellent regional art museum, the **Figge**. Also pay a visit to the cute and arty **Davenport Village** neighborhood, which has a number of historic homes and some great lunch spots, such as Bayside Bistro.

Continue southwest through a series of mid-sized Iowa towns that abound with late-19th- and early-20th-century architecture, pleasant waterfront parks, and the occasional odd attraction, like the **National Pearl Button Museum** in **Muscatine** and **Snake Alley**—said to be even more serpentine than San Francisco's famously crooked Lombard Street—in **Burlington**. At **Fort Madison**, cross into Illinois to visit **Nauvoo**, a small village with an outsized historical presence, as you'll immediately discern upon seeing the imposing **Nauvoo Illinois Temple**, which dates to 1846. It anchors a collection of well-preserved buildings that tell the story of one of the earliest Mormon settlements, which thrived in the mid-19th-century. This 1100-acre historic district is part of the **Mormon Pioneer National Historic Trail** and includes the homestead of the movement's founder Joseph Smith (a modern museum and visitor center is located here), the dignified 1843 **Brigham Young Home**, and several other shops and outbuildings. Adjacent **Nauvoo State Park** offers waterfront trails and has an interesting history museum.

Cross back into Iowa at the handsome hilltop town of **Keokuk**, where you can gain a sense of what it felt like to travel *on* the river at the **George M. Verity Steamboat Museum**. Continue south on US 61 to the venerable river town of Hannibal, MO, whose impressive downtown historic district includes the **Mark Twain Boyhood Home and Museum**. You can also visit some of the sites that inspired Twain's most celebrated works, such as the **Mark Twain Cave** and the **Becky Thatcher** and **Huckleberry Finn houses**. A few of the town's most impressive Victorian homes now house B&Bs, including the lavish **Rockcliffe Mansion**. Follow Hwy 79—a scenic, hilly road that passes through the attractive towns of **Louisiana** and **Clarksville**, which both have a handful of fine art galleries and antiques shops—for about 100 miles to **St Charles**. It sits astride a scenic stretch of the Missouri River about 25 miles west of its confluence with the Mississippi. Now a large (pop 65,000) suburb of St Louis, this first capital of Missouri has a charming downtown of brick-lined streets and vintage buildings that house boutiques and eateries (be sure to pick up a tin of peanut butter cookies from Grandma's Cookies). This is the town from which Lewis and Clark launched their great expedition in 1804—you can learn more about their journey at the **Lewis and Clark Boat House and Museum**.

The land that would become **St Louis** had been inhabited for generations by Indigenous Osage people when French explorers and then fur traders arrived in the late 17th and early 18th centuries. The city would flourish as an industrial center, becoming the fourth largest in the country by the time it hosted the World's Fair and the Olympics in 1904. But St Louis declined sharply in the late 20th century, and its population has plunged from nearly 900,000 to 300,000 since the early 1950s. Nevertheless, it's a wonderful place to explore, filled with gorgeous old buildings, cohesive neighborhoods, and exceptional family-friendly attractions, and its low cost of living now attracts artists and entrepreneurs. From St Charles take I-170 south to explore the lively **Delmar Loop** of **University City**, with its historic theaters and music clubs. Other neighborhoods that abound with vintage architecture, intriguing shops, and terrific restaurants include the **Central West End**, **Tower Grove South**, and **Lafayette Square**. You'll also want to visit the stately campus of **Washington University** and the beautiful grounds of **Forest Park**, which is home to the excellent **St Louis Art Museum** and the popular **St Louis Zoo**. With its 230 ft tall clock tower and regal Romanesque architecture, **St Louis Union Station** is another sightseeing highlight—kids love the aquarium and the Ferris wheel. Take Market St through downtown's clutch of gracious old buildings to **Gateway Arch National Park**, a beautifully landscaped 91-acre patch of greenery overlooking the Mississippi River and anchored by one of the country's iconic buildings, Eero Saarinen's graceful and shimmering 630 ft tall stainless-steel **Gateway Arch**.

ST LOUIS, MO TO VICKSBURG, MS

Make your way downriver, stopping at the Blue Owl Bakery in **Kimmswick** to treat yourself to a slice of the Caramel Apple Pecan Levee High Pie that Oprah Winfrey has championed, and into **Ste Genevieve**, an attractive little river town that's home to several wineries as well as the **Ste Genevieve National Historic Site**, which preserves

Missouri's earliest European settlement. Continue to **Cape Girardeau**, with its vibrant collegiate vibe. Take a walk along the downtown flood wall, which has been painted with 24 large murals that colorfully relate the region's history. Cross into Illinois and down through **Cairo** (pronounced KAIR-oh), an interesting city that's completely surrounded by levees owing to its precarious location at the confluence of the Ohio and Mississippi rivers. Then cross into Kentucky, stopping to learn about the region's Indigenous Mississippian culture at **Wickliffe Mounds State Historic Site**, before continuing into Tennessee for a scenic drive around **Reelfoot Lake State Park** and on down to Memphis.

Both a quintessential river city and a beacon of the South, **Memphis** has a fascinating and complicated past rooted in its cotton-farming and slave-trading history, its role in the Civil War, its blues and rock heritage (both W.C. Handy and Elvis found fame here), and being the site of Martin Luther King Jr.'s tragic 1968 assassination. This city of about 635,000 spawls east from its curving border with the Mississippi River, and it's along this shoreline that you'll find many of the city's most notable sites, including the pathways and gardens of **Mud Island Park**, the music clubs and the **Memphis Rock 'n' Soul Museum** amid **Beale Street**'s famed music clubs, and the site of MLK's murder, the Lorraine Motel, which has been transformed into the thoughtful and incredibly moving **National Civil Rights Museum**—the surrounding **South Main** neighborhood is now one of the city's top food and art destinations. You can explore these areas in a day, but I recommend spending a second night in order to visit some superb outlying attractions, like the legendary **Sun Studio** recording studio, the superb **Stax Museum of American Soul Music**, the indie food and retail vendors in the cool new **Crosstown Concourse** mixed-use development (it's in a retrofitted 1920s Sears distribution warehouse), and—of course—**Graceland**. Not being a particularly ardent fan of Elvis, I think I'd visited Memphis a half dozen times before ever touring this expansive campus of kitsch anchored by the fabulously garish home (and gravesite) of The King, along with his two private jets, a trove of glitzy cars, and assorted pop-culture artifacts. Now I never miss a chance to go.

Continue south down US 61 through the **Mississippi Delta**, a nearly 200 mile long alluvial flood plain that ranked among the world's cotton-production strongholds prior to the Civil War. This route also follows the **Mississippi Blues Trail**—dozens of historical markers point out key people and places that figure prominently in the uniquely American

Sylvan Island Gateway Park, Moline *Previous* Mormon Pioneer National Historic Trail, Nauvoo

music genre this region gave birth to. Stop in **Tunica**, now a sprawl of modern casino resorts, to visit the **Gateway to the Blues Visitor Center**. It occupies a restored 1890s rail depot and serves as a great intro to the region's music roots. Continue southwest to **Clarksdale**, with its scintillating and syncopating **Delta Blues Museum** as well as the **Stan Streets Hambone Art Gallery**, where you can admire the vibrant portraits of the eponymous and legendary artist. The town fervently embraces the legacy of native sons John Lee Hooker, Ike Turner, and Sam Cooke, along with musicians who resided here later in life, such as W.C. Handy and Muddy Waters. Listen to world-class music at Red's Lounge and Ground Zero, and duck into some of Clarksdale's estimable eateries, such as Levon's Bar and Abe's Bar-B-Q. At the **Shack Up Inn**, which often hosts blues workshops, you can stay in a former sharecropper's cottage.

Continue southwest to **Greenville**, which was largely razed by the Union army during the Civil War. Today it's known for pulsing blues bars as well as an important Native American archaeological park, **Winterville Mounds Historic Site**, which comprises a well-designed museum, a re-created Indigenous Natchez house, and 12 of these prehistoric earthen structures that proliferate in the Mississippi River Valley. Also stop to walk along the boardwalk trails through the serene **Greenville Cypress Preserve**, which is rife with native flora and fauna. Don't leave town without digging into a plate of traditional tamales at down-home Doe's Eat Place, which has been a fixture since 1941 in this town known as

the "hot tamale capital of the world." While I recommend driving to Greenville along Hwy 1, which hews closer to the river, you can also take US 61, US 49W, or US 49E south and then cut over west; these more interior routes pass through some intriguing small cities like **Cleveland** (where you can tour the **Grammy Museum Mississippi**), **Indianola** (home of the excellent **BB King Museum and Delta Interpretive Center**), and **Greenwood**, with its upmarket **Alluvian Hotel and Spa**. Follow US 278 west into Arkansas, and take US 65 along the river's west side down into northeastern Louisiana, passing through **Lake Providence** and **Transylvania** (fun for a photo if you're wanting a vampire-related Instagram post in Louisiana—the town's water tower features a giant bat). Then cut east back across the river to **Vicksburg**, whose pivotal role in the Civil War you can explore at the **Vicksburg National Military Park**, which is also home to the **USS Cairo**, an ironclad river ship that was sunk in 1862.

VICKSBURG, MS TO NEW ORLEANS, LA

Further south lies **Port Gibson**, a town that also figured in some key battles during the Civil War and that's famous for its eerie **Windsor Ruins**, what was once the state's largest Greek Revival mansion. All that remains today are nearly two dozen 40 ft Corinthian columns, which you may recognize from the film *Ghosts of Mississippi*. The original home burned in a fire in 1890, not the Civil War—in fact, most of Port Gibson was spared, allegedly because Gen. Ulysses S. Grant thought the town "too beautiful to burn." Drive along the gently winding **Natchez Trace Parkway** down to one of the most storied communities of the Mississippi Delta, the city of **Natchez** (pop 14,900), which was also mostly spared during the Civil War and thus retains a remarkable number of homes and plantations—constructed by generations of slave labor—that date to the early 19th and even 18th centuries. Many are now museums, including octagonal **Longwood** mansion and carefully preserved **Melrose**, which is part of **Natchez National Historical Park** and does a particularly good job providing a perspective on the diverse Indigenous, African, and European people who have lived in this region. Be sure to visit the park's **Natchez Visitor Center**, which has a commanding bluff-top setting with impressive views of the river and Natchez-Vidalia Bridge. Spend some time walking around the city's colorful downtown, where you can tour the excellent **Natchez Museum of African American History and Culture** and pop in and out of a number of excellent restaurants and music clubs. Smoot's Grocery brings in top jazz and blues acts, and the Pig Out Inn serves delicious barbecue.

From Baton Rouge, you're close to the heart of Louisiana's historically and culturally vibrant and diverse **Acadiana**, or Cajun Country. It's worth exploring this region settled largely in the late 18th century by Acadians (and their descendants), whom the British expelled from Maritime Canada. From Baton Rouge take US 190 west across the northern edge of **Atchafalaya National Wildlife Refuge**—a 15,000-acre habitat of bottomland hardwood forest and freshwater swamps that support a range of native wildlife, including black bears, alligators, great egrets, double-crested cormorants, snapping turtles, and racing snakes. Continue through colorful **Opelousas** to **Eunice** to visit the **Prairie Acadian Cultural Center**, one of several units around southern Louisiana that make up the outstanding **Jean Lafitte National Historical Park and Preserve**. This part of the park is focused especially on Cajun music and food, and attending a Rendez-vous des Cajuns music performance at the **Liberty Theater** is a must. Continue southeast to **Lafayette** (pop 120,000), Acadiana's largest city, and check out the excellent exhibits at another part of Jean Lafitte NHPP, the **Acadian Cultural Center**. This is also a fantastic city for feasting on classic Cajun food—T-Coon's and Prejean's are a couple of favorites. Then head south and east on US 90, detouring as time allows to visit some of Acadiana's more interesting small towns, such as **Breaux Bridge**, **St Martinsville**, **New Iberia**, and **Thibodaux**.

Louisiana State Capitol, Baton Rouge

Head west into **Vidalia**, LA and follow Hwys 15 and 1 south, paralleling the Mississippi and in a few instances skirting some former bends in the river that have turned into narrow lakes after the river changed course. Good examples include **Old River**, which still forms the state border, even though the Mississippi River itself now flows several miles to the east, and **False River** in **New Roads**, where you'll turn east on Hwy 10 and recross the Mississippi to visit **St Francisville**, which was the largest port on the lower portion of the river two centuries ago but is now a gentle hamlet known for its colorful shops and eateries and wealth of stately old homes, including **Rosedown Plantation State Historic Site** and the **Audubon State Historic Site**, where the renowned painter and ornithologist John James Audubon briefly resided in the 1820s. It's a 30-mile drive down US 61 to **Baton Rouge**, the state capital and home of **Louisiana State University**. With its 450 ft Art Deco tower and interesting free audio tours that relate the fascinating circumstances behind the life and 1935 assassination of charismatic governor Huey Long, the **Louisiana State Capitol** is one of my favorite attractions. But I also recommend exploring downtown's **Old State Capitol**, a castle-like 1847 structure that's now a fascinating museum of political history (which is a particularly colorful topic in Louisiana), as well as the family-popular LSU **Rural Life Museum** in the Mid-City district.

The jumble of state and county roads that flank the Mississippi River on its looping 136-mile journey south to New Orleans is famous for having some of the South's most opulent plantation homes. I have mixed feelings about touring these grandiose wedding cakes built on the backs of slave labor, especially as some of these properties—many of which are now museums, B&Bs, or both—deal with their inherently unjust origin stories less well than others. One I do appreciate visiting is **Laura**, whose thoughtful tours are based on historical accounts left by this Creole plantation's early-19th-century owners, and they do address sometimes complicated details about the family and slaves who resided here. Architecturally, my favorite site along this route is **Oak Alley**—at the very least, stop and walk the grounds, including the incredible alley of moss-draped oak trees that frames the front exterior of this 1837 Greek Revival home (it's appeared in several movies, including *Primary Colors* and *Interview with a Vampire*). Oak Alley's restaurant serves very good Cajun and Creole cuisine, too, and you can spend the night in a well-decorated cottage. I like driving along the west side of the river, which offers the better views and passes through **Donaldsonville**, a cute town with an excellent restaurant for an enjoyable lunch stopover, the Grapevine Cafe.

City View:
New Orleans

The last major stop on the Mississippi River (it empties into the Gulf of Mexico about 100 miles downstream), this storied city with its own very special food, music, style, and spirit is one of North America's most captivating places. Founded in 1718 as the territorial capital of French Louisiana, it's a captivating place to spend a couple of days (or a full week, if you ask me). My approach is simply to walk through its eclectic, history-rich neighborhoods, stopping frequently for sips and snacks. But don't overlook the several excellent museums. Keep in mind that visiting during Mardi Gras, Jazz Fest, LGBTQ Southern Decadence, or any other major annual event has pros and cons. The exuberant energy and people-watching can be incredible, but crowds, heavy traffic, and high hotel rates are serious trade-offs.

Car-Friendly Rating: Fair. Narrow streets and limited or expensive parking in central neighborhoods make car touring less than ideal in this city that is, on the other hand, fairly easy to explore on foot or by old-fashioned streetcar. But driving and parking is easier farther out, either from the Garden District upriver in Mid-City or in Bywater.

What to see in a day: Especially if it's your first time in town, the **French Quarter** is a must, despite its touristy and—at least on Bourbon Street—drunken demeanor. You can find some real gems, like Irene's for Italian food and Jewel of the South for cocktails, if you venture away from the crowds a bit. And the **Presbytere** and **Cabildo**, two compelling history museums that bookend imposing **St Louis Cathedral** on highly photogenic **Jackson Square**, are a must. Head downriver to **Frenchmen Street** in **Faubourg Marigny** and **St Claude Avenue** in **Bywater** for some of the city's best neighborhood eats and music clubs (Snug Harbor Jazz Bistro is a great bet among the latter). Fringing the **Central Business District (CBD)** and the **Warehouse District** (which is another excellent food neighborhood), the **Ogden Museum of Southern Art** and **National WWII Museum** are both outstanding. Then venture Uptown to check out the fantastic housewares stores, art galleries, and eateries on **Magazine Street** (especially the blocks in the **Lower Garden District**) and also on **Maple Street** near Loyola and Tulane universities and **Oak Street** in **Carrollton**. I've written entire articles on the best places to eat in this incredible food city—it's hard to find a bad meal here, even at the tourist traps. But I'll name five that I absolutely adore: Casamento's (for oysters), Commander's Palace (for decadently lavish Creole fare), Herbsaint (for modern Louisiana cuisine), Parkway Bakery (for po'boys), and Angelo Brocato (for Italian ice cream and

dessert). Also take time to admire the meticulously restored mansions and bungalows of the **Garden District** and the moss-draped oaks of **Audubon Park**.

Where to stay: New Orleans truly stands out for its distinctive hotels—even chains tend to be in historic buildings. When I visit with a car I try to stay outside of the congested CBD and French Quarter, although I've been known to make an exception for the old-world **Hotel Monteleone** and I'd be willing to for the hip new **Higgins Hotel**. The arty and posh **Hotel Peter and Paul** is a stunner (it occupies a mid-19th-century church) in the colorful Faubourg Marigny, a short walk from the Quarter. The swanky **Mazant** guest house in Bywater exudes modern refinement, and both the mid-century-modern **Alder Hotel** and European-style **Prytania Park Hotel** are comfortable, reasonably priced Uptown options with free parking.

Top Try po'boys at Parkway Bakery
Bottom Live music on Frenchmen Street

Top Gateway Arch National Park, St. Louis *Bottom* Tribute to Rosa Parks at National Civil Rights Museum, Memphis

BEST EATS

- **Owamni by the Sioux Chef** Owned and run by the acclaimed Oglala Lakota culinary star Sean Sherman, this contemporary glass-walled restaurant serves creative Indigenous food. Start with conifer-preserved rabbit with fermented blueberry, followed by roasted bison with a mustard greens sauce. 612-444-1846, owamni.com.

- **Sooki & Mimi** This stylishly upbeat spot in hip Uptown Minneapolis is the brainchild of James Beard-winning chef Ann Kim, and the inspired, innovative menu reflects both her Korean American upbringing and her passion for Mexican and other cuisines around the world. 612-540-2554, sookiandmimi.com.

- **Meritage** Tuck into prettily arranged plates of French bistro classics—steak tartare, moules frites, duck confit with lentils—in this warmly lighted restaurant and oyster bar in downtown St Paul. 651-222-5670, meritage-stpaul.com.

- **Lovechild** With red velvet drapes and gilt-frame mirrors, this playfully romantic La Crosse supper club serves sensational contemporary Continental fare, including fall-off-the-bone braised lamb shank. The Italian-French wine list is superb. 608-433-2234, lovechildrestaurant.com.

- **Indo** Sample stellar Southeast Asian dishes at this hip and cozy spot in St Louis's lively Tower Grove neighborhood. There's a nightly selection of nigiri sushi, plus palm sugar-glazed pork ribs and half chicken khao man gai. 314-899-9333, indo-stl.com.

- **Little Fox** This homey brick-walled neighborhood bistro overlooking St Louis's historic Fox Park serves beautifully plated modern American fare like grilled Ozarks trumpet mushrooms with a sherry vinaigrette and 'nduja-marinated pork chop with soft polenta. 314-553-9456, littlefoxstl.com.

- **The Beauty Shop** Priscilla Presley used to get her hair done in this former salon in Memphis's artsy Cooper Young neighborhood. Now a quirky restaurant serving globally inspired brunches and dinners, its decor harks back to its previous incarnation. 901-272-7111, thebeautyshoprestaurant.com.

- **The Kitchen Bistro and Piano Bar** Drop by this storefront space in Natchez to feast on sophisticated Southern cuisine and—on weekends—listen to jazz pianists. 769-355-2165, thekitchennatchez.com.

- **Parrain's** With a rustic vibe that evokes an old-time fishing shack, this Mid-City Baton Rouge favorite stands out for its boldly seasoned Cajun and Creole seafood, like crab-and-crawfish au gratin and barbecue shrimp. 225-381-9922.

BEST SLEEPS

- **Graduate Hotel** This handsome redbrick hotel with a playful collegiate design scheme is on the picturesque campus of the University of Minnesota, close to Dinkytown restaurants and shops and convenient for exploring both of the Twin Cities. 612-379-8888, graduatehotels.com.
- **Celeste St Paul** Formerly a convent and then an arts conservatory, this beautifully adapted six-story hostelry is near St Paul's Minnesota State Capitol. Ask for a top-floor room, with its high vaulted ceiling and fantastic city views. 651-222-0848, celestestpaul.com.
- **St James Hotel** Two blocks from Red Wing's riverfront, this period-furnished 1870s hotel that's hosted Mark Twain and Bob Dylan exudes old-fashioned charm and gentility. Scarlett Kitchen & Bar serves consistently good, eclectic cuisine. 651-388-2846, st-james-hotel.com.
- **Hotel Julien** A soothing spa and a fine restaurant are among the assets of this stately boutique hotel in historic downtown Dubuque, a short drive from charming Galena. 563-556-4200, hoteljuliendubuque.com
- **Hotel Blackhawk** The swanky old-world architecture and modern vibe of this downtown Davenport gem make it the most desirable lodging in the Quad Cities. Amenities include a pool, full-service spa, a retro-fun bowling alley, and martini bar. 563-322-5000, hotelblackhawk.com.
- **Angad Arts Hotel** In St Louis's Grand Center Arts District, steps from the ornate Fox Theatre, this hotel has boldly designed rooms in blue, green, red, or yellow color. The stylish Art Bar and Commonwealth restaurant are popular pre- and post-show hangouts. 314-561-0033, angadartshotel.com.
- **Central Station Memphis** By the National Civil Rights Museum, this elegantly hip hotel set in a gracious 1914 building celebrates the city's music heritage with a vinyl music collection, and an in-house DJ. Bishop Restaurant is helmed by James Beard-honored chefs. 901-524-5247, hilton.com.
- **Travelers Hotel** Established by a local nonprofit arts collective, this friendly 20-room Clarksdale lodging is filled with quilts, furniture, and artwork created by Mississippi Delta creatives. The lobby has a cool general store and a bar serving local coffee and beer. 662-483-0693, stayattravelers.com.

- **Monmouth Historic Inn** Providing a memorable way to experience one of the elegant mansions in Natchez, this lavish 1818 beauty is surrounded by carefully manicured gardens and has a refined restaurant and plush accommodations. 601-442-5852, monmouthhistoricinn.com
- **The Watermark** This stately 1920s former bank tower has chic rooms, an exceptional restaurant, and a prime location steps from the Baton Rouge riverfront and downtown museums. 225-408-3200, watermarkbr.com.

CAMPING

Parks and RV compounds line the entire Mississippi River Valley. Popular and reliable options in the upper section include Frontenac State Park near Red Wing, Pikes Peak State Park in McGregor, Palace Campground in Galena, and Buffalo Shores near Quad Cities. Farther south you'll find appealing sites at Nauvoo State Park, Mark Twain Cave & Campground in Hannibal, Trail of Tears State Park near Cape Girardeau, and Reelfoot Lake State Park north of Memphis. From the Mississippi Delta south to New Orleans, consider Hollywood Casino RV Park in Tunica, Ameristar RV Park in Vicksburg, Riverview RV Park outside Natchez, Peaceful Pines north of Baton Rouge, and New Orleans KOA Holiday.

You'll find some of the best barbecue in Memphis at Central BBQ

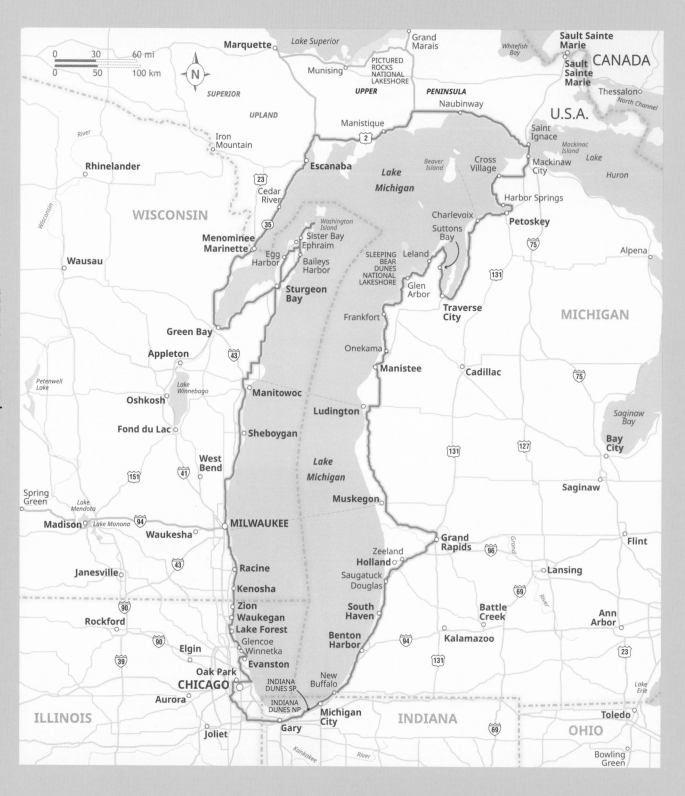

The Lake Michigan Circle ★

Soaring dunes, bustling marinas, sweeping beaches, and the striking skylines of Chicago and Milwaukee are the signature features on this drive around the only Great Lake entirely within the United States.

HOW LONG?

8 days; add an extra day or two to explore more of Chicago, Milwaukee, Door County, and Traverse City.

WHEN TO GO

Summer is prime time for the resort towns on the lake, although the heat and humidity can be stifling in the cities, and hotels are at their most expensive. The mild late spring and early autumn months are my favorite times to explore this part of the world. Winters can be relentlessly cold and snowy.

NEED TO KNOW

If time is short, you can "cheat" driving the entire lake by cutting across it on a four-hour ferry ride between Manitowoc, WI and Ludington, MI. If you do this, I recommend finding the time to skirt up the lakefront to Door County, Traverse City, or ideally both.

→ **Distances**
Total distance, one-way: 1200 mi (1931 km)
- Chicago, IL to Green Bay, WI: 365 mi (587 km)
- Green Bay, WI to Mackinaw City, MI: 260 mi (418 km)
- Mackinaw City, MI to Grand Rapids, MI: 370 mi (595 km)
- Grand Rapids, MI to Chicago, IL: 200 mi (322 km)

Daytime Temperatures
January: 25-35°F (-4-2°C)
July: 75-85°F (24-29°C)

More information
- Chicago tourism, choosechicago.com
- Milwaukee tourism, visitmilwaukee.org
- Door County tourism, doorcounty.com
- Traverse City tourism, traversecity.com
- Grand Rapids tourism, experiencegr.com
- Indiana Dunes National Park, nps.gov/indu

◉ **SNAPSHOT**

The third largest of North America's five Great Lakes forms the shore of one of the world's most celebrated cities, Chicago, and offers long stretches—mostly up north—of pristine wilderness interrupted only occasionally by fishing towns. Much of the scenic 1640-mile lakefront, especially on Wisconsin's Door Peninsula and Lower Michigan's western shore, serves as a beloved Midwest vacation destination that abounds with pretty towns, laid-back beaches, and rugged dunes. This tour is also a must for fans of Frank Lloyd Wright's singular architecture.

CHICAGO, IL TO GREEN BAY, WI

Head north up along Chicago's lakefront to **Evanston**, the first of a string of affluent and attractive suburbs known as the **Gold Coast** that hug the lakeshore. See the excellent, contemporary **Block Museum of Art** on the campus of **Northwestern University** as well as the ornate timepieces and stained-glass windows of the **Halim Time and Glass Museum**, before continuing through **Winnetka, Glencoe** (known for its spectacular **Chicago Botanic Garden**), and **Lake Forest**—towns that have appeared prominently in countless movies by John Hughes and others, including *Ferris Bueller's Day Off*, *Risky Business*, and *Home Alone*. Follow Hwys 137 and 32 north, stopping in **Zion** for a hike around **North Dunes Nature Preserve** and the acclaimed **Civil War Museum** in **Kenosha**. The small Wisconsin city of **Racine** (pop 77,000) has several noteworthy architectural attractions, including the striking Streamline Moderne **SC Johnson Headquarters** and the **Wingspread Conference Center**, which were both designed by Frank Lloyd Wright. You can also view the country's largest collection of contemporary crafts at the **Racine Art Museum**.

Continue to **Milwaukee**, an engagingly eclectic city of 587,000 that's become steadily more popular among entrepreneurs, makers, tech workers, and other creative spirits—many of them drawn to the lower cost of living compared with Chicago. Start in **Bay View**, a historically working-class neighborhood whose blocks now abound with trendy cafes and one-of-a-kind shops, and make your way up bustling South Kinnickinnic Ave into two more gentrifying warrens of grand old industrial and residentials buildings, **Walker's Point** and the **Historic Third Ward**. Sample the acclaimed barrel-reserve gin and rye whiskey at **Great Lakes Distillery** and snack on international treats at Zocalo Food Park, then cross the Menomonee River to visit the **Harley-Davidson Museum**, an industrial-chic tribute the legendary motorcycle manufacturer founded in Milwaukee in 1903.

Continue north into downtown, stopping to explore the diverse food stalls of **Milwaukee Public Market** before heading east to the city's beautiful lakefront. The seminal attraction here is contemporary Spanish architect Santiago Calatrava's nod to Frank Lloyd Wright and Eero Saarinen, the Quadracci Pavilion, which he designed as a new wing to the **Milwaukee Art Museum** in 2001. I could spend hours simply walking around the exterior of this angular concrete, steel, and glass wonder that has inspired comparisons to everything from the prow of a ship to the

SIDETRACK

From Milwaukee it's an easy 75-minute detour west on I-94 to **Madison**, the state's political and educational hub. This hilly metropolis of around 275,000, plus tens of thousands of University of Wisconsin (UW) students, enjoys an idyllic setting on a narrow isthmus between lakes Monona and Mendota. I like strolling around the picturesque **UW campus** and having a bite to eat at **Memorial Union Terrace**, a lakefront space that serves as a sort of outdoor student living room. Other notable draws include the colorful and convivial **Dane County Farmers' Market** and the verdant **Olbrich Botanical Gardens**. Madison also has a pair of buildings—**First Unitarian Society Church** and **Monona Terrace Community and Convention Center**—on the **Frank Lloyd Wright Trail**, a route of several of the architect's most celebrated public buildings. His 800-acre estate, school, and studio, **Taliesin** lies 35 miles west in **Spring Green**, a charming town on the Wisconsin River. After touring this UNESCO World Heritage Site, enjoy a meal at Riverview Terrace Cafe, which was completed by Wright's former apprentices in 1967—you can even stay at a hotel designed by his firm, the **Spring Valley Inn**.

Leon's Custard has been a must for dessert in Milwaukee since 1942 *Previous* Pictured Rocks National Lakeshore

City View: Chicago

Chicago's sensational skyline looks captivating from any vantage point, but it truly dazzles when framed by its 18-mile lakeshore. America's third largest city (pop 2.7 million) is the perfect start and end point for a road trip around Lake Michigan; it's a hub of American and Southwest airlines, and it's at the junction of several major interstates. Plus it's just a fun city with a dynamic downtown bisected by the Chicago River and bursting with fantastic museums, theaters, and hotels, many of them occupying landmark buildings. It's also a richly diverse city with a patchwork of colorful neighborhoods.

Car-friendly rating: Fair. Parking at hotels, even in outer neighborhoods, can be exorbitant enough that I often park out in the suburbs and take "the L" (rapid transit trains) downtown. Chicago has excellent public transportation and lots of pedestrian-friendly neighborhoods, and a car can be more of a hindrance than a help. You can usually find free or inexpensive street parking in less central neighborhoods.

What to see in a day: No trip to Chicago is complete without a walk around downtown, aka **The Loop**. Venture alongside the deep-blue Chicago River and admire the forest of architectural wonders, both contemporary and historic. Visit the astounding collections of the **Art Institute of Chicago**, relaxing afterward on a shaded bench in the sculpture garden, and then walk north among the tony retailers of Michigan Avenue (the **"Magnificent Mile"**) and take the elevator to the 1000 ft high observation deck of the **John Hancock Tower**. Then spend time exploring some eclectic outer neighborhoods, such as **Wicker Park**, known for its hip restaurants—I recommend Cebu for Filipino fare and Michelin-starred Schwa. **Andersonville**, a diverse district with Scandinavian roots and a hip, creative vibe, is another great area for a stroll, as is LGBTQ-popular **Lakeview**, where you can end your stroll by watching a Cubs game at legendary **Wrigley Field**. Then head south to eat your way through the Latino restaurants of **Pilsen** and **Little Village**, the Asian eateries of **Chinatown**, and soul and Southern food favorites in **Kenwood** and **Hyde Park**. Amble around the handsome campus of the **University of Chicago**, stopping for lunch at Plein Air Cafe and for a tour of the Frank Lloyd Wright-designed **Robie House**. Then walk several blocks to view the larger-than-life airplane, submarine, and space exhibits at the **Museum of Science and Industry**, which is a big hit with kids.

Where to stay: You'll find some sexy and sophisticated boutique hotels in outer neighborhoods—I like the sleekly contemporary **Hotel Zachary** across from Wrigley Field and **The Sophy**, a 98-room stunner with a swank restaurant in Hyde Park. Downtown abounds with chic options, such as the Hyatt-affiliated **Chicago Athletic Association Hotel** by Millennium Park and the **Alise**, which occupies a renowned 1890s skyscraper designed by legendary architect Daniel Burnham. Great mid-priced options include **The Robey** in Wicker Park and the **SpringHill Suites** in Chinatown.

Top **Kids leaping into Lake Michigan**
Bottom **The view from the John Hancock Tower**

wings of a giant white bird. But don't forget to go inside—the museum's 25,000 works include notable collections of German Expressionist paintings and Haitian art. You can enjoy a particularly nice view of the building from the brick terrace of Harbor House restaurant.

From Milwaukee, I-43 skirts the lake on its 80-mile path through **Sheboygan** and **Manitowoc**—where you can also take a four-hour car ferry directly across the lake to Ludington, MI—to Wisconsin's most beloved stretch of shoreline, the **Door Peninsula**. This 75 mile long finger of curving bays and family-friendly vacation towns is popular for fishing, biking, swimming, and boating—there are more than 35 beaches, several picturesque lighthouses, and countless places to launch kayaks or stand-up paddle boards. At the tip of the peninsula, you can catch a car ferry a few miles to **Washington Island**, a similarly scenic and even more relaxing summer community. On the main peninsula, the most happening villages are along the western shore and include **Egg Harbor**, **Ephraim**, and **Sister Bay**—they abound with quaint inns, waterfront lodges, U-pick orchards, and casual ice cream shops, burger joints, and seafood stands. About a third of the peninsula's 30,000 residents live in the county seat, **Sturgeon Bay**, which is worth visiting for its excellent **Door County Maritime Museum**.

GREEN BAY, WI TO MACKINAW CITY, MI

Driving southwest down the Door Peninsula leads to **Green Bay** (pop 104,000), which has the distinction of being by far the nation's smallest metro area with an NFL football franchise (or any major sports team, for that matter). Not surprisingly, the top attractions are the **Green Bay Packer Hall of Fame** and touring the team's stadium, **Lambeau Field**, although lively **Bay Beach Amusement Park** is probably the favorite draw with the under-16 set. And so begins the nearly 300-mile stretch of roads—mostly US 41 and US 2—that curve around the north end of the lake. Upon crossing the river from **Marinette**, WI, to **Menominee**, MI, you enter Michigan's rugged **Upper Peninsula**, or UP as locals refer to it, the 16,377 sq mile (it's about the size of Denmark) land mass that also borders a short section of Lake Huron along with a whopping 917 miles of Lake Superior. The UP's stretch of Lake Michigan is sparsely populated and relaxing, if lacking many noteworthy attractions. The largest town you'll pass through is **Escanaba**, which has a few lodging options and is a good place to refuel and refresh.

Continue from Escanaba through **Manistique** and the small but busy commercial fishing port of **Naubinway** to the

It's a little over an hour's drive from Escanaba to the UP's largest community, **Marquette**, a bustling college town (Northern Michigan University) with an attractive setting on Lake Superior. My recommendation is to spend at least one night here or farther east in **Munising** or **Grand Marais**, two small towns that connect the ravishing cliffs of **Pictured Rocks National Lakeshore**. Handsome and hilly Marquette has several interesting attractions, including the offbeat folk art of **Lakenenland Sculpture Park**, the lighthouse and engaging exhibits of **Marquette Maritime Museum**, and the captivating trails and natural scenery of **Sugarloaf Mountain** and **Presque Isle Park**. If you're game for an even bigger adventure, venture west along the shore and up through the quietly beautiful **Keweenaw Peninsula** to secluded **Copper Harbor**, catching the seasonal 3.5-hour ferry to explore the pristine wilderness of **Isle Royale National Park**. Then continue west to northern Wisconsin's scenic **Apostle Islands National Lakeshore** and across the Minnesota border to one of the coolest and prettiest port cities in the Midwest, **Duluth**.

The Harley-Davidson Museum, Milwaukee
Opposite Sleeping Bear Dunes National Lakeshore

majestic 5-mile bridge over the Straits of Mackinac, which separates lakes Michigan and Huron and connects **St Ignace** (on the UP) with **Mackinaw City** (on the Lower Peninsula). From either of these friendly beach towns you can take a ferry to **Mackinac** (pronounced Mackinaw) **Island**, the famously charming 4.4 sq mile isle in Lake Huron that grew from a military garrison and fur-trading and fishing hub in the late 19th century into an affluent Victorian resort favored by the some of the Midwest's wealthiest titans of industry. You can't bring your car over—the island has banned motor vehicles since the late 1890s. Visitors get around on foot, horse-drawn carriage, or bike (there are several rental shops near the ferry landing). Most visitors spend at least a couple of nights—at the old-world **Grand Hotel** or one of the smaller inns—exploring the local historic sites and beautiful parks, including Revolutionary War–era **Fort Mackinac** and the unusual **Arch Rock** geological formation, but you can see a lot on short daytrip.

MACKINAW CITY, MI TO GRAND RAPIDS, MI

From Mackinaw City cut west to **Cross Village** to begin your drive down Michigan's alluring western shore, starting with Hwy 119, aka the **Tunnel of Trees** because of its winding, picture-perfect 20-mile route along majestic coastal bluffs lined with towering hardwoods and evergreens. Midway along the route, stop at the 1930s fire-engine-red Good Hart General Store for a flaky-crust chicken pot pie or a Michigan maple snickerdoodle, then continue to **Harbor Springs**, a spirited sailing enclave with an enviable setting on pristine Little Traverse Bay. Dip your toes in the water at **Zorn Park Beach** before driving 10 miles around the bay to lively **Petoskey**, with its hilltop downtown replete with discerning boutiques and cheerful eateries, including Symons General Store and North Perk Coffee.

Continue down through the beautiful boating town of **Charlevoix** and along the east shore of Grand Traverse Bay to the classic Great Lakes vacation town of **Traverse City** (pop 14,570), which lies at the base of two scenic land masses: narrow Old Mission Peninsula and chunky Leelanau Peninsula. Famed for its weeklong National Cherry Festival in July, this bustling resort has beautiful beaches on both the east and west arms of the bay. Kids have fun with the wealth of fudge shops and outdoorsy activities, from hiking at **Boardman River Nature Preserve** to zip lining, water rides, and minigolf at **Pirate's Cove Adventure Park**, and there are plenty of great eateries on the waterfront, including hip Hexenbelle coffeehouse and colorful Little Fleet food

truck pod. Try to make time for the 20-mile drive up the enchanting **Old Mission Peninsula**, stopping to sample wine at one of the several respected tasting rooms—Bonobo and 2 Lads are standouts.

Follow Hwy 22 up and around the **Leelanau Peninsula**, breaking for an elderflower wheat ale at Farm Club brewery or dinner at the elegant and intimate Wren bistro in **Suttons Bay**. Cut across to the west side and drive through quaint **Leland** and **Glen Arbor**, and then explore the monumental landscape of **Sleeping Bear Dunes National Lakeshore**. Head into the park on **Pierce Stocking Scenic Drive**, stopping to stroll out to the **Sleeping Bear Dunes Overlook**—the view across Lake Michigan from atop these steep 460 ft dunes is astonishing.

It's a roughly 180-mile drive down the lakeshore and then slightly inland to Grand Rapids, assuming you stick close to the coast. My favorite of the small beach communities along the way is **Frankfort**, which has a colorful downtown on Betsie Lake. **Onekama** and **Manistee** are pretty stops as well, and the larger town of **Ludington** (pop 8000) is home to the gorgeous sands of **Ludington State Park Beach** and is also where you can catch the ferry across Lake Michigan to Manitowoc, WI. At the busy port city of **Muskegon**, known for its **USS *Silversides* Submarine Museum**, turn inland on I-96 for the final 40 miles to Grand Rapids.

GRAND RAPIDS, MI TO CHICAGO, IL

Michigan's second largest city (pop 200,000), **Grand Rapids** has a dapper downtown on the Grand River and is well regarded for its hopping craft brew scene and blossoming arts scene, but it's also the boyhood home of Gerald R. Ford, who later became the region's US congressman before becoming, through a series of scandals and resignations, the nation's 38th president—you can learn more about his life and legacy at the **Gerald R. Ford Presidential Museum**. The city's must-see is 158-acre **Frederik Meijer Gardens and Sculpture Park**, which is anchored by a five-story conservatory with an exceptional collection of tropical flora and also features a stunning Japanese garden and one of the country's largest children's gardens. For another brush with gorgeous greenery, take Hwy 121 rather than the interstate southwest through the Dutch-American towns of **Zeeland** and **Holland**, whose **Windmill Island Gardens** is wonderful anytime for a stroll, but especially in April and May when more than 100,000 tulips are in bloom.

Back along a splendid stretch of Lake Michigan, you'll come to the twin beach towns and arts colonies of **Saugatuck** and **Douglas**. With a stellar community performance space— the **Saugatuck Center for the Arts**—plenty of esteemed galleries and shops, and an exceptional selection of elegant B&Bs and chicly retrofitted motels, these adjoining villages are a hit with young families, LGBTQ folks, retirees, and creative spirits. Downtown Saugatuck fringes a narrow span of the Kalamazoo River, which opens into a large lake of the same name. Pick up gourmet picnic supplies in Saugatuck at Pennyroyal Cafe and Provisions or in Douglas at the Farmhouse Deli and Pantry. Then take the nation's oldest extant hand-cranked chain ferry (bikes and pedestrians only) about 300 ft across the river, walk up to the 794 ft summit of **Mt Baldhead** for a grand lake vista, and hike a half mile through a leafy forest to Lake Michigan's **Oval Beach**, where you can swim and sunbathe to your heart's content (you can also drive here).

It's easiest to continue down the shore via the interstate to **New Buffalo**, and then follow US 12 west around Indiana's north shore to **Indiana Dunes National Park**, which earned national park status in 2019. This 15,350-acre patch of shoreline borders **Indiana Dunes State Park**, which is famous for its **3 Dune Challenge**, a rigorous 1.5-mile trek over the region's three highest dunes—it's harder than it looks (I find it's easiest if you go barefoot)—with a 552 ft vertical gain, and the forested slopes hide the astounding views until

you reach the tops of these bluffs. Within the national park, you'll find many more soaring dunescapes as well as beautiful beaches, but one of the more unexpected treasures is the **Century of Progress Architectural District**, a collection of five then-futuristic homes designed for the 1933 Chicago World's Fair and then relocated to the park.

Back on the interstate, it's just 35 miles around the shore to Chicago, but en route I recommend one last detour, especially if you're an architecture fan. Head 10 miles west of the Windy City to gracious **Oak Park**, where Frank Lloyd Wright established his home and practice in 1898, residing there for 20 years. You can tour the **Frank Lloyd Wright Home and Studio** and then walk through the surrounding neighborhood, which contains several of his early Prairie School–style residential designs. End your stroll with drinks or apps at Cooper's Hawk Winery & Restaurant or a more substantial meal at Rustico. You can view several other Wright homes around town and also take a tour of the **Ernest Hemingway Boyhood Home**.

BEST EATS

- **Ardent** For a memorable meal after exploring Milwaukee's lakefront, book a table at this intimate contemporary American restaurant that's earned a raft of national honors and awards. 414-897-7022, ardentmke.com.

- **Odd Duck** You'll find some of Milwaukee's best food in quirky Bay View, including this cheerful storefront space that specializes in local cheese and charcuterie and international dishes like Brazilian moqueca (seafood stew) and Korean scallion pancakes. 414-763-5881, oddduckrestaurant.com.

- **Wickman House** On the Door Peninsula in low-key Ellison Bay, this beautifully restored 1920s former guest lodge now contains a renowned and romantic restaurant. The owners also run cozy and more casual Trixie's natural-wine bar and bistro in Ephraim. 920-854-3305, wickmanhouse.com.

- **Clover & Zot** Have a seat on the deck of this convivial gastropub on the lakefront in Baileys Harbor. Well-curated beer and wine lists complement sharable small plates (duck poutine, curried tempera artichokes) and Neapolitan pizzas. 920-839-2587, cloverandzot.com.

- **Stafford's Pier** Watch the sailboats come and go from the deck of this 1930s seafood restaurant in Harbor Springs. The menu features local (flash-fried perch with tomato-caper relish) and ocean (seared sea scallops with balsamic-sage brown butter) fare. 231-526-6201, staffordspier.com.

- **Trattoria Stella** Expertly prepared, farm-to-table Italian fare draws foodies to this Traverse City restaurant. Start with burrata or *mpanatigghi* (fried Sardinian empanadas) before graduating to wild boar agnolotti or pan-seared Atlantic hake. 231-929-8989, stellatc.com.

- **Blu** The name of this splurge-worthy restaurant just outside Sleeping Bear Dunes hints at the amazing water view. With a superb wine list and refined Continental fare, this is the ultimate spot for a special celebration. Glen Arbor, 231-334-2530, glenarborblu.com.

- **Rock's Landing** This casual beachfront cottage at Frankfort's family-friendly Chimney Corners Resort is a lovely spot for a sunset dinner on the water. The menu changes according to what's fresh. 231-399-0158, rocksoncrystal.com.

- **Brewery Vivant** Among Grand Rapids's acclaimed craft breweries, this convivial pub and beer garden stands out for its unique setting inside a LEED-certified converted funeral home. The beer is terrific (I'm a fan of the slightly tart Farm Hand saison), as is the elevated European-style comfort food. 616-719-1604, breweryvivant.com.

- **The Southerner** This cheerful, Southern restaurant overlooks the Kalamazoo River in Saugatuck. Signature dishes include the deviled crab-crawfish po'boy and Nana's Fried Chicken with a honey-butter biscuit and grits. 269-857-3555, thesouthernermi.com.

- **Stop 50** Head for this informal pizzeria near Indiana Dunes National Park for heavenly wood-fired pies with flavorful toppings—the one with wild mushroom, oregano, and mozzarella is a favorite. 219-879-8777, stop50woodfiredpizzeria.com

Top The chain ferry in dowtown Saugatuck *Bottom* Downtown Saugatuck *Opposite* Pictured Rocks National Lakeshore

Ultimate Road Trips: USA & Canada

BEST SLEEPS

- **The Iron Horse** In a redbrick converted warehouse in Milwaukee's trendy Walker's Point, this industrial-meets-convivial hotel looks across the Menomonee River at the Harley-Davidson Museum. Exposed ducts and heavy timber beams lend character to the spacious rooms. 414-374-4766, theironhorsehotel.com.

- **The Pfister** This refined 1893 Milwaukee hotel is one of the Midwest's most venerated grande dames, with a priceless Victorian art collection and ornately muraled lobby. The pool, spa, and fine restaurant are on the 23rd floor. 414-273-8222, thepfisterhotel.com.

- **Dörr Hotel** An easy stroll from the festive dining, shopping, and beachfront in Door County's Sister Bay, this upscale 47-room hotel with a clean and contemporary Scandinavian-influenced design opened to rave reviews in 2021. 844-944-0354, thedorrhotel.com.

- **Scofield House** This lovingly maintained six-room B&B in a quiet but central Sturgeon Bay neighborhood exudes romance. Several rooms have fireplaces and whirlpool tubs. 920-743-7727, scofieldhouse.com.

- **Inn at Bay Harbor** A modern upscale property designed in the style and spirit of the great Victorian resorts of yesterday, this stately 105-room spa and golf resort near Petoskey offers lovely bay views. 231-439-4000, innatbayharbor.com.

- **Chateau Chantal** With commanding vineyard and lake views from a bluff on Traverse City's narrow Old Mission Peninsula, this opulent 12-room B&B is part of an acclaimed winery. The airy rooms have whirlpool tubs. 231-223-4110, chateauchantal.com.

- **Canopy by Hilton** Close to the museums, brewpubs, and riverfront in Grand Rapids, this contemporary boutique hotel with tech-savvy rooms has a cheerful rooftop beer garden. 616-456-6200, hilton.com.

- **Lake Shore Resort** This mid-century resort offers sweeping Lake Michigan views as well as from an attractive pool and deck. The vibe is low-key but family-friendly, and amenities include bikes, kayaks, and morning yoga. 269-857-7121, lakeshoreresortsaugatuck.com.

- **Saugatuck Retro Resort Motel** My favorite of several reasonably priced Saugatuck and Douglas motor courts that have been given sleek mid-century-modern makeovers (Pines Motor Lodge is also great), this property has 22 compact rooms, a central pool and firepit, and classic Adirondack chairs to enjoy on the common patio. 269-857-8888, thesaugatuck.com.

- **Marina Grand Resort.** Overlooking a colorful marina near the Michigan-Indiana border, this upscale condo-style hotel has spacious waterfront rooms and suites—some with fireplaces—and is just a half-hour drive from Indiana Dunes National Park. 877-945-8600, marinagrandresort.com.

CAMPING

Opportunities for pitching a tent or parking an RV exist all around the lake, more so around the less populated northern half. But even within an hour of Chicago, there are lovely sites at Dunewood Campground and Lakeshore Camp Resort in and around Indiana Dunes National Park, and at Illinois Beach State Park near the Wisconsin border. Notable west shore options include Cliffside Park south of Milwaukee, Fish Creek and Wagon Trail campgrounds on the Door Peninsula, and Fayette State Park in Michigan's Upper Peninsula. On the east shore of Lake Michigan, consider Magnus Park near Petoskey, D.H. Day Campground at Sleeping Bear Dunes, National Lakeshore near Traverse City, Ludington State Park, and Holland State Park near Grand Rapids and Saugatuck.

Top The lobby of the Pfister Hotel, Milwaukee
Opposite Skyline view from the Toronto Islands

Lakes Ontario, Erie, and Huron ★ 🍁

Few of the drives in this book offer greater extremes between vibrant urban culture (Toronto, Cleveland, Detroit) and spectacular natural scenery (Niagara Falls, the Bruce Peninsula, Algonquin Provincial Park).

HOW LONG?

8–9 days; add an extra day to see more of Toronto or Detroit.

WHEN TO GO

Late spring through early fall offers the best weather, but summer can be hot and humid in the cities and crowded in the parks. In northern Ontario I recommend waiting at least until early June to avoid muddy trails and black fly season. September and October, with their brilliant autumn foliage, are perfect for this adventure.

NEED TO KNOW

The ferry from Bruce Peninsula to Manitoulin Island runs only from around May through October; the rest of the year, you could adapt this trip by returning to Toronto after visiting Bruce Peninsula and continuing along the lakeshore to Prince Edward County and Kingston.

➡ Distances
Total distance, one-way: 1475 mi (2374 km)
- Toronto, ON to Cleveland, OH: 300 mi (483 km)
- Cleveland, OH to Stratford, ON: 360 mi (579 km)
- Stratford, ON to Sudbury, ON: 365 mi (587 km)
- Sudbury, ON to Kingston, ON: 395 mi (636 km)

🌡 Daytime Temperatures
January: 17-35°F (-8-2°C)
July: 75-82°F (24-28°C)

ⓘ More information
- Toronto tourism, destinationtoronto.com
- Niagara Falls tourism, niagarafallstourism.com
- Cleveland tourism, thisiscleveland.com
- Cuyahoga Valley National Park, nps.gov/cuva
- Detroit tourism, visitdetroit.com
- Bruce Peninsula National Park, pc.gc.ca/en/pn-np/on/bruce
- Algonquin Provincial Park, algonquinpark.on.ca
- Prince Edward County tourism, visitpec.ca

👁 SNAPSHOT

This intentionally circuitous journey around the three easternmost of North America's Great Lakes offers a little something for everyone: impressive art and cuisine in cities with dramatic skylines and picturesque lakefronts, acclaimed wineries and venerable theater festivals in several smaller towns in Ontario, and the peaceful, virtually untouched wilderness around Georgian Bay and in vast Algonquin Provincial Park. Whether you're seeking nature's call or urbanity's excitement, it's easy to tailor this looping trek to your interests.

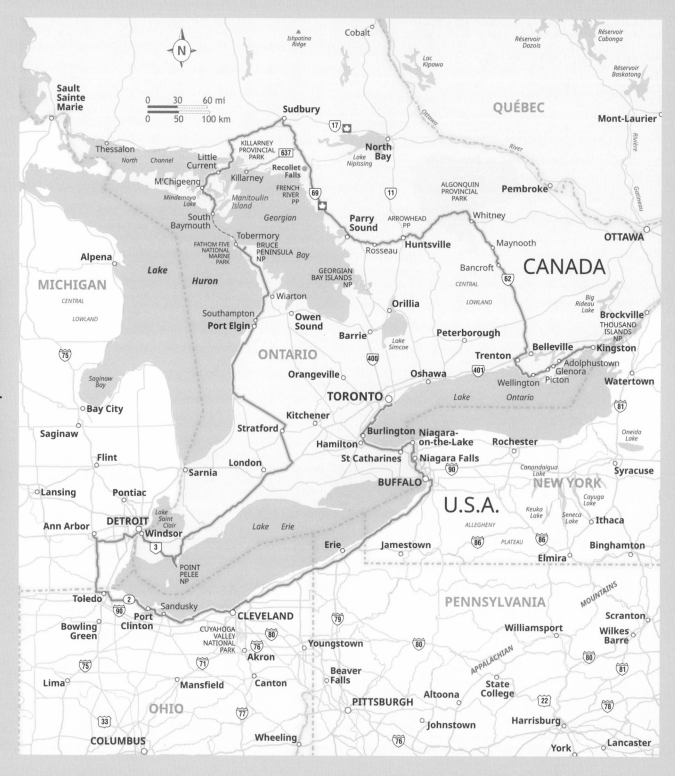

Sault Sainte Marie

Cobalt

Ishpatina Ridge

Réservoir Dozois

Réservoir Cabonga

QUÉBEC

Mont-Laurier

Réservoir Baskatong

Sudbury

Thessalon

North Channel

Little Current

KILLARNEY PROVINCIAL PARK

637

17

North Bay

Lac Kipawa

Ottawa River

M'Chigeeng

Killarney

Recollet Falls

Lake Nipissing

11

Pembroke

OTTAWA

Mindemoya Lake

FRENCH RIVER PP

69

ALGONQUIN PROVINCIAL PARK

Gatineau

South Baymouth

Manitoulin Island

Georgian

Parry Sound

ARROWHEAD PP

Whitney

CANADA

Tobermory

FATHOM FIVE NATIONAL MARINE PARK

BRUCE PENINSULA NP

Bay

Rosseau

Huntsville

Maynooth

62

CENTRAL

Alpena

Lake

Wiarton

GEORGIAN BAY ISLANDS NP

Bancroft

Big Rideau Lake

Brockville

MICHIGAN

Huron

Southampton

Port Elgin

Owen Sound

Orillia

LOWLAND

THOUSAND ISLANDS NP

CENTRAL

LOWLAND

Barrie

Lake Simcoe

Peterborough

Belleville

Kingston

75

Saginaw Bay

ONTARIO

Orangeville

400

Trenton

Adolphustown

Glenora

Picton

Watertown

Bay City

Kitchener

Oshawa

401

Wellington

Lake Ontario

81

Saginaw

Stratford

TORONTO

Oneida Lake

Flint

London

Burlington

Hamilton

Niagara-on-the-Lake

Rochester

Lansing

Pontiac

Sarnia

St Catharines

Niagara Falls

90

Canandaigua Lake

Syracuse

Ann Arbor

Lake Saint Clair

BUFFALO

U.S.A.

NEW YORK

Keuka Lake

Seneca Lake

Ithaca

DETROIT

Windsor

3

Lake

Erie

Erie

Jamestown

ALLEGHENY

PLATEAU

86

Cayuga Lake

86

Binghamton

POINT PELEE NP

Elmira

Toledo

2

Sandusky

CLEVELAND

79

PENNSYLVANIA

Scranton

90

Port Clinton

CUYAHOGA VALLEY NATIONAL PARK

80

Youngstown

80

Williamsport

Wilkes Barre

80

Bowling Green

76

Akron

Beaver Falls

APPALACHIAN

81

75

71

Canton

State College

78

Lima

Mansfield

Altoona

22

Harrisburg

OHIO

33

77

Wheeling

PITTSBURGH

Johnstown

COLUMBUS

76

York

Lancaster

City View
Toronto

With its gleaming modern skyline and renowned museums, diverse neighborhoods, and verdant islands fringing the Lake Ontario shoreline, Toronto ranks among North America's most exciting cities. With a population of 3 million, more than half foreign born, the city's international spirit shines through in its restaurants, markets, arts spaces, and music clubs.

Car-Friendly Rating Fair. For such an immense and dense city, Toronto isn't terribly difficult to navigate by car, although around downtown and the Harbourfront, parking at hotels and in garages can get very pricey. I recommend using the city's clean and efficient subway in the city center. In outer neighborhoods, parking is easier to find, but overnight street parking (where allowed; always check signs for restrictions) requires a temporary visitor permit, which you can purchase at toronto.ca. I generally find it easier to pay the C$25 to C$50 daily to park in a garage.

What to see in a day: With so much to entertain you in Toronto, I suggest focusing on downtown during the daytime, checking out the impressive artwork and kid-friendly exhibits—a dinosaur hall, a bat cave, a hands-on biodiversity gallery—at the **Royal Ontario Museum** (with its cool Daniel Libeskind addition) and the **Art Gallery of Ontario** (with its striking addition designed by native Torontan architect Frank Gehry), and then riding the glass elevator to the 1465 ft observation deck atop the **CN Tower**, which soars above Rogers Centre stadium (home of baseball's Toronto Blue Jays) and the family-friendly **Ripley's Aquarium of Canada**. Break things up with lunch at one of the dozens of great food stalls and international eateries at **Kensington Market** (near the University of Toronto campus) or historic **St Lawrence Market** (in colorful Old Toronto). During the warmer months, take the short passenger ferry from Queens Quay out to the beautiful **Toronto Islands—Centre Island** is great for all ages with gorgeous gardens and an amusement park. Dozens of fantastic neighborhoods abound with indie shops, stellar restaurants, and buzzy nightspots, including **Leslieville** (and adjacent **Little India**) on the East Side, LGBTQ **Church Street Village** a bit north of downtown, and **Ossington Avenue**, **West Queen West**, and **The Junction** on the West Side.

Where to stay: I prefer the design-driven accommodations in some of the less central neighborhoods, such as the **Gladstone Hotel** and the **Drake Hotel** on the West Side, and the chic **Broadview** on the East Side. Standout in the city center include the **Kimpton Saint George** (near the Royal Ontario Museum) and the hip **Thompson Toronto**, with its 16th-floor rooftop bar and pool.

Top Royal Ontario Museum *Bottom* Toronto skyline

You should stick mostly with freeways (Queen Elizabeth Way in Canada and I-90 in the US) for the drive around the west end of Lake Ontario and the south shore of Lake Erie. Queen Elizabeth Way passes through Toronto's western suburbs and then around the lake via the attractive neighboring cities of **Burlington** (pop 205,000), with its flourishing **Royal Botanical Gardens**, and **Hamilton** (pop 537,000), home to prestigious McMaster University and several very good museums (the **Art Gallery of Hamilton** and **Dundurn Castle** among them). When you reach **St Catharines,** follow Hwy 87 parallel to the lakeshore roughly 20 miles to **Niagara-on-the-Lake**, a charming weekend getaway in the heart of Ontario's most distinguished wine country. In addition to more than 30 acclaimed wineries—**Konzelmann Estate** and **Peller Estates** are a couple of the best—this colonial town of around 18,000 that served originally as the provincial capital is known for its renowned **Shaw Festival**, which presents a mix of classic and contemporary works in repertory from April through December. Also explore its historic historic downtown with its inviting restaurants, boutiques, and B&Bs. You can learn of the town's prominent role in the War of 1812 at **Fort George National Historic Site**.

It's a 15-mile drive south on panoramic **Niagara Parkway** to **Niagara Falls**, which is the umbrella name of the three massive waterfalls—**Horseshoe Falls** being the most famous—that span the US-Canada border, and also of the cities on each side. Each year more than 25 million people view these dramatic cascades, which have been a major tourist attraction (and source of hydroelectric power) since the mid-19th century. Geologically, they're a prominent feature of the **Niagara Escarpment**, a 650 mile long dolomitic limestone ridge that curves more or less continuously from Rochester, NY, across lower Ontario and Michigan's Upper Peninsula and then through Wisconsin's Door Peninsula (*see* The Lake Michigan Circle chapter p. 193). At about 180 ft, the falls aren't especially tall but they are—at 3950 ft—North America's widest, and they're unquestionably dramatic. The views are jaw-dropping on either side, but I find the angle from the Canadian shore more impressive. As far as the two cities go, **Niagara Falls, ON** (pop 88,000) is far more developed and has a greater array of glitzy hotels, restaurants, and attractions, but it's also crowded and over-the-top garish in places. The downtown of **Niagara Falls, NY** (pop 48,000) is quieter but a little rough around the edges. What I do recommend on this side is **Niagara Falls State Park**, a lush 221-acre patch of greenery designed by Frederick Law Olmsted and Calvert Vaux that's anchored by the 282 ft **Prospect Point Observation Tower**. You can move between the two sides by walking across the soaring **Rainbow International Bridge**—just be sure to bring your passport and $1 for the toll.

From either side of the falls, it's a 30- to 40-minute drive south to **Buffalo** (pop 279,000), the largest city in western New York and something of an underdog destination—maybe that's one reason I like it so much. Throughout the 19th century, Buffalo thrived as a railroad and shipping port. By 1901—the year it hosted the Pan-American Exposition, at which President William McKinley was assassinated (you can learn more about this event at the **Theodore Roosevelt Inaugural National Historic Site**)—it was America's eighth largest city. An economic downturn plagued Buffalo during the late 20th century, but downtown still contains dozens of impressive late 1800s and early 1900s architectural wonders, including Louis Sullivan's 1896 **Guaranty Building** and the spectacular Art Deco 1931 **City Hall**. Go for a walk along the Buffalo River in the lively **Canalside** district, which marks the start of the Erie Canal (it stretches 363 miles to the Hudson River near Albany). Elsewhere in town, check out the impressive collection of vintage cars, bikes, and motorcycles at the **Pierce-Arrow Museum**, and take a tour of Frank Lloyd Wright's early 1900s **Darwin D. Martin House**, one of the architect's most celebrated designs. Between here and downtown, the diverse **Elmwood Village** and **Allentown** neighborhoods abound with eclectic shops and restaurants.

Follow I-90 along Lake Erie's shoreline through western New York, northwestern Pennsylvania, and northeastern Ohio to **Cleveland**, which like Buffalo typifies America's so-called Rust Belt of Midwestern and Great Lakes cities that flourished as centers of industry before declining after World War II. Like many of its peers, this city of around 370,000 has improved its fortunes in recent years. It features several outstanding museums and a picturesque, elevated setting on Lake Erie's shore—my favorite place to take in the views of the water and the skyline is **Voinovich Bicentennial Park**. Afterward, walk next door to the pyramid-shaped, I.M. Pei–designed **Rock and Roll Hall of Fame**, whose interactive kiosks and colorful memorabilia—fabulous Tina Turner and Stevie Nicks concert dresses, Jimi Hendrix and Eddie Van Halen guitars—are great fun. Other cultural draws include the outstanding **Cleveland Museum of Art** and **Cleveland Museum of Natural History**, but plenty of visitors are every bit as impressed, if not more so, with the **Christmas Story House**, the late-19th-century yellow clapboard house in which Ralphie Parker and his family resided in the iconic and eponymous 1983 classic movie. Complete with a tasseled leg lamp in the front window, the house-museum is in **Tremont**, a neighborhood rife with engaging bars and restaurants. It adjoins an even more esteemed foodie district, **Ohio City,** where you can wander the aromatic halls of **West Side Market**, a grandiose 1912 Neoclassical-Byzantine structure with more than 100 vendors proffering everything from Greek pastries (Spanos Bakery) to Polish stuffed cabbage (Pierogi Palace) to sausage sticky rice (Kim Se Cambodian Cuisine). Save room for a slice of banana cream pie or caramel gingersnap ice cream down the block at Mitchell's.

CLEVELAND, OH TO STRATFORD, ON

Continuing across northern Ohio, I recommend taking US 20 through the historic western Cleveland suburbs and then US 6 along the Erie lakeshore. It's a bit slow in places, but you'll pass several pretty parks and beaches. In **Sandusky** kids can play for hours at the country's second oldest amusement park, massive **Cedar Point.** Continue northwest through **Port Clinton**, where you can visit the excellent **Liberty Aviation Museum** and tour the 1896 **Port Clinton Lighthouse.** Head west to **Toledo,** an oft-overlooked city with two legit must-see attractions: the world-class **Toledo Museum of Art** (its stunning 2006 Glass Pavilion is one of the Midwest's most acclaimed contemporary architectural works) and the **National Museum of the Great Lakes**, which features a remarkable collection of model ships and artifacts that shine a light on the fascinating maritime history of this interconnected inland ocean. It's less than an hour's drive north to **Ann Arbor**, a vibrant college town that's home to the main campus of the **University of Michigan.** Visit here when there's a college football game, and you'll struggle mightily to find a hotel room—**Michigan "Big House" Stadium** has a capacity of 108,000, making it the largest arena in the Western Hemisphere. The school's campus is beautiful—enjoy great people-watching as you amble across the central **Diag**, then explore the school's first-rate museums, the **UM Museum of Art** and **UM Museum of Natural History.** Downtown bustles with the eclectic restaurants and shops you might expect of a big college town, but Ann Arbor's most charming neighborhood is **Kerrytown**, where the historic **Ann Arbor Farmers' Market** takes place year-round on Wednesdays and Saturdays, and where you can nosh your way through the flagship location of Zingerman's Delicatessen (try the chocolate and raspberry rugelach). It's a 45-minute drive east to Detroit.

I visited **Cuyahoga Valley National Park** for the first time in summer 2021, having intended to go many times over the years. This captivating river valley is a terrific find, interesting for its cultural heritage but also for the chance to stretch your legs on some 125 miles of wooded hiking trails. The most famous is the 1.4-mile loop over **Brandywine Falls**, which is beautiful (especially with vibrant orange, red, and yellow leaves hanging over it in October), but I'm even more impressed with **The Ledges Trail**, a 2.2-mile circuit that climbs over and under a series of dramatic rock formations. Other worthwhile points of interest in this 32,572-acre park include the **Boston Mill Visitor Center**, which occupies a restored 1905 general store, and the early 1800s **Hale Farm & Village** living history museum. There are also several good spots to eat in or near the park, such as the two Trail Mix snack bars and Sarah's Vineyard winery and restaurant. Plus, the atmospheric six-room **Inn at Brandywine Falls** offers lovely overnight accommodations.

Cuyahoga Valley National Park

City View
Detroit

Famed for its automotive industry, phenomenal music heritage, and iconic art and architecture, Detroit wears its "Comeback City" status on its sleeve, promoting a creative vibe, entrepreneurial spirit, ethnic and racial diversity, and a low cost of living that's helping attract an influx of new residents. America's fourth largest city in 1920, Detroit is now at about a third (638,000 residents) of its peak population, but to me it feels as dynamic as any metropolis in the Midwest.

Car-friendly rating: Good. In deference to its powerful car manufacturers, Detroit was laid out from the start as an automobile-friendly city, with broad avenues and a phalanx of freeways (alas, the automakers also conspired to dismantle its once-impressive mass transit system). In the downtown core, street parking can be tough to come by, but garages aren't terribly expensive. You really need a car to navigate outlying neighborhoods, but fortunately it's easy to find street spaces or inexpensive lots.

What to see in a day: Of the three attractions I consider unequivocally to be must-sees, the **Motown Museum**—which occupies music magnate Berry Gordy's Hitsville U.S.A. former recording studio—was undergoing a major expansion as of this writing but is expected to have reopened by fall 2022. Another is the nearby **Detroit Institute of Arts**, a fantastic museum whose central marble court contains Diego Rivera's massive masterpiece, the Detroit Industry frescoes. The third standout, the **Henry Ford Museum of Innovation** is 15 miles away in suburban Dearborn and features an incredible trove of automobiles (from an antique Oscar Mayer Wienermobile to the '61 Lincoln that John F. Kennedy was riding in when he was assassinated) as well as countless influential and scientific artifacts. Some of these—such as the Wright brothers' home and bicycle shop and a re-creation of Thomas Edison's laboratory—are part of the adjacent **Greenfield Village** living history museum. You can also tour the neighboring **Ford Rouge** automobile factory. If you have an extra half day, I recommend exploring Detroit's east side, picking up snacks and admiring the colorful murals at the 19th-century **Eastern Market**, walking around the unusual folk-pop-recycled art installation known as the **Heidelberg Project**, and stopping by **Pewabic Pottery**, which has been producing and selling gorgeous Arts and Crafts glazed tiles and decorative housewares since 1903. If it's a nice day, head to nearby **Belle Isle**, a nearly 1000-acre park set on a leafy island in the Detroit River, less than a half mile across the water from Windsor, ON. Whatever you do, set aside time to check out the city's white-hot food scene—if you have time for just three meals, go with the sleek Thai restaurant Takoi, the Corktown izakaya Ima, and the butcher shop-cum-bistro Marrow.

Where to stay: Several of downtown Detroit's architectural landmarks now contain beautiful accommodations, my favorite being the swanky **Detroit Foundation Hotel**, which occupies a stunningly restored 1920s fire department headquarters with the inviting Apparatus Room restaurant and bar at street level. **Aloft at the David Whitney, Element Detroit at the Metropolitan**, and the **Westin Book Cadillac** also offer a pleasing mix of old-world elegance and chic contemporary style. You'll find some gracious properties in surrounding close-in suburbs, too, like **The Henry, Autograph Collection** in Dearborn, and **The Daxton** in Birmingham—the latter is a good base for exploring the vibrant Woodward Corridor, which includes the hip food and retail towns of Ferndale and Royal Oak and Bloomfield Hills, with its noteworthy art and science museums.

Takoi restaurant *Opposite* Niagara Falls

The small city of **Windsor** (pop 218,000) has the geographical distinction of being in Canada yet lying directly south of the US city of Detroit—you can get between them by tunnel or bridge. Windsor has an attractive riverfront park with walking and running trails and superb views of the Detroit skyline. Follow Hwy 3 southeast to ecologically diverse **Point Pelee National Park**, a triangular 6 sq mile (it's Canada's second smallest national park) patch of forest, beaches, and wetlands that attract nearly 400 species of birds. Stop at the visitor center, walk the picturesque **Marsh Boardwalk Trail**, then continue south to **The Tip**, a narrow wedge with a 78 ft lookout tower. Here, at a latitude of 41.96 (it's roughly the same as Providence, RI and Crescent City, CA), you're at the very southernmost point of mainland Canada.

STRATFORD, ON TO SUDBURY, ON

It's about a 2.5-hour drive via the collegiate city of **London** to **Stratford**. One of Ontario's most inviting weekend destinations, this theater-centric town of around 32,000 is famous for the **Stratford Festival**, an April–October season featuring about a dozen works, usually three or four by the Bard and the rest a mix of classic and contemporary productions, performed in repertory among four theaters. The main stage is set amid the leafy gardens of **Upper Queens Park**. It's a pleasure to stroll among the many shops, B&Bs, and eateries—some with theatrical themes or Elizabethan-inspired designs—and to stop and smell the roses in the riverfront **Elizabethan Gardens**. If you're a fan (or "Belieber") of Justin Bieber, take note: the local tourism office has produced a map of the Stratford native's favorite local spots, including the steps of the Avon Theatre, where the pop icon busked for bucks as a kid.

This itinerary becomes increasingly rural as you venture three hours north to the **Bruce Peninsula**, a narrow finger of land that juts out between Lake Huron and Georgian Bay (sometimes referred to as the sixth Great Lake—at 5792 sq miles it's only slightly smaller than Lake Ontario). The peninsula forms one of the most prominent sections of the **Niagara Escarpment World Biosphere Reserve**, and its upper tip—reached via Hwy 6—is dominated by two remarkable preserves known for their otherworldly landscapes and Caribbean-like bright turquoise waters: Bruce Peninsula National Park and Fathom Five National Marine Park. The contemporary visitor center serving both places is in the small town of **Tobermory**, which has a smattering of B&Bs and eateries (you'll find a greater selection farther down the peninsula in **Southampton** and **Port Elgin**).

SIDETRACK

Southeast of Sudbury on the Trans-Canada Hwy, turning west on Hwy 637 leads 35 miles to **Killarney Provincial Park**, an untamed 250 sq mile tract of sloping and rocky hardwood forest that fringes the northeastern shore of Georgian Bay. It's one of the province's most alluring destinations for hiking, paddling (**Killarney Outfitters** has canoe and kayak rentals), and wildlife-watching. Top treks include the moderately challenging but breathtaking 4.7-mile **Crack Trail** and the lush and easier **Cranberry Bog Trail**. Just beyond the park in the village of **Killarney**, you'll find laid-back but comfortable waterfront lodgings at **Killarney Mountain Lodge** and **Sportsman's Inn Resort** and delicious fish and chips at Herbert Fisheries.

In **Bruce Peninsula National Park**, highlights include the limestone cliffs and ancient trees of **Driftwood Cove**, the cobblestone beach at **Indian Head Cove**, the breathtaking **Grotto** sea cave, and the massive boulders of **Halfway Log Dump** (from spring through fall, you must purchase advance parking on the park website for the Grotto and Halfway Log Dump). At **Fathom Five National Marine Park**, hike the rocky and rugged 3.2-mile **Burnt Point Loop** around Little Dunks Bay, and then take a glass-bottom boat cruise to view imposing **Big Tub Lighthouse**, see well-preserved 1800s shipwrecks, and be dropped off at nearby **Flowerpot Island** to hike amid bizarre columnar rock formations with plants and trees growing out of the top.

From May through October you can take a two-hour car ferry from Tobermory to **South Baymouth** and continue your journey across 1068 sq mile **Manitoulin Island**, the world's largest freshwater island—you'll find a few casual, mid-priced lodgings here, including **My Friends Inn** and **Huron Sands Motel** (Sudbury, 2.5 hours north, has a greater selection). Take Hwys 542 and 551, stopping for lunch at the cheerful Garden's Gate Restaurant & Market. Then follow along the shore of rippling **Mindemoya Lake** and stop in **M'Chigeeng** to view the art and historical exhibits at the **Ojibwe Cultural Foundation**, which preserves and interprets the heritage of the Anishinaabe People, who have thrived on this land for centuries. North of here you can hike the 3-mile **Cup and Saucer Trail**, where you'll be treated to sweeping views of the Niagara Escarpment from 240 ft cliffs. Continue onto the mainland about 70 miles through a densely wooded wilderness to the region's largest city, **Sudbury** (pop 162,000). It's known for the **Science North** museum complex, where you can view outstanding exhibits about northern Ontario's ecosystem; a few miles away, Science North also operates **Dynamic Earth**, a museum focused on the region's prominent mining heritage—tours of the mine descend seven stories beneath the earth by elevator. The museum's 30 ft diameter **Big Nickel**—a replica of a 1951 Canadian five-cent coin—is a favorite photo op. Treat yourself afterward to a tasty cheese and charcuterie platter at downtown's La Fromagerie.

SUDBURY, ON TO KINGSTON, ON

From Sudbury head south on the Trans-Canada Hwy through the verdant eastern shore of Georgian Bay, pausing at **French River Provincial Park Visitor Centre** for an easy 1.7-mile out-and-back walk through a scenic gorge to **Recollet Falls**. Continue south about 90 minutes to **Parry Sound**, and then cut east an hour to **Huntsville**, a town of 20,000 surrounded by rolling hills and such appealing diversions as **Sugarbush Hill Maple Farm**, **Trillium Resort & Spa**, and **Arrowhead Provincial Park**, with its **Stubb's Falls** hike and oft-photographed **Big Bend Overlook**. Huntsville is also the western gateway into enormous (it's 20% larger than Banff National Park) **Algonquin Provincial Park**. Most of this spectacular but remote woodland backcountry is hard to access, but gorgeous Hwy 60 meanders some 35 miles through the park's southern reaches and leads you to a number of beautiful lakes and trails as well as a few peaceful and picturesque overnight lodges. Highlights include the **Algonquin Art Centre**, with its venerable collection of works by some of Canada's preeminent landscape and wildlife painters, and the sandy beach at **Lake of Two Rivers**. Farther east, see the natural history exhibits at the informative **Algonquin Park Visitor Centre**, and then hike the peaceful **Spruce Bog Boardwalk Trail**.

Emerging from the park to the east in **Whitney**, you can visit the **Algonquin Logging Museum**, where kids love to climb aboard the crazy-looking, steam-powered "Alligator," an amphibious tug. Then head south through the woods on Hwys 127 and 62, breaking in **Bancroft** for poutine or a burger at down-home Eagles Nest Restaurant, and continue to **Belleville** and **Trenton**, which lie along the **Bay of Quinte**, a long arm of Lake Ontario. Take Hwy 33 south into peninsular **Prince Edward County**, a fast-emerging wine region with a wealth of tasting rooms, U-pick fruit farms, and art galleries. My favorite town is **Wellington**, which boasts a small downtown with an outsized selection of excellent restaurants and arts studios. Continue east into charming **Picton** and along the south shore of **Adolphus Reach**, catching a quick ferry ride from Glenora to Adolphustown and following Hwy 33 another half-hour east to **Kingston** (pop 124,000). Established in 1673 on the north bank of the St Lawrence River near its confluence with Lake Ontario, this lively city buzzes with student life (there are two large universities). It briefly served as Canada's first capital in the early 1840s and has a handsome park-lined waterfront and several notable historic attractions, including **Fort Henry National Historic Site** and **Bellevue House National Historic Site**—the latter was the home of the country's first prime minister, John A. MacDonald. Kingston is also a base for exploring the Thousand Islands (*see* Upstate New York chapter p. 211) and a lovely place to end your adventure with a night or two of exploring. It's a three-hour drive back to Toronto, or just two hours to Ottawa.

Opposite top West Side Market, Cleveland
Opposite bottom Detroit Foundation Hotel

BEST EATS

- **Treadwell** Set in a stately redbrick house with a plant-filled patio, this wine-driven restaurant in Niagara-on-the-Lake serves exceptional farm-to-table fare. The owners also operate the posh 30-room 124 on Queen hotel next door. 905-934-9797, treadwellcuisine.com.

- **Weinkeller** Choose from three- or five-course prix fixe menus of refined contemporary Canadian cuisine at this casually elegant restaurant and winery in the heart of Niagara Falls, steps from the casino, waterpark, and Niagara SkyWheel. 289-296-8000, weinkeller.ca.

- **Allen Street Hardware** Along the bustling restaurant row in Buffalo's Allentown neighborhood, this art-filled gastropub is set in a colorfully painted former hardware store. Try the fried chicken sandwich and a well-crafted cocktail. 716-882-8843, allenstreethardware.com.

- **Vero Pizza Napoletana** After a day of hiking at Cuyahoga Valley National Park, treat yourself to a thin-crust pizza at this narrow space in charming Cleveland Heights. Carefully selected ingredients—Fior di Latte mozzarella, San Marzano tomatoes, hot honey—result in boldly flavorful pies. 216-229-8383, verocleveland.com.

- **Alea** This intimate bistro in Cleveland's trendy Ohio City offers thoughtfully curated wines and skillfully mixed cocktails, and contemporary Mediterranean dishes like sea trout crudo and black cod topped with Spanish ham. 216-912-8890, aleacle.com.

- **Miss Kim** A standout among Ann Arbor's acclaimed international, and especially Asian, restaurants, this sleek white-brick-walled space in lively Kerrytown features the artful creations of celebrated Korean chef-owner Ji Hye Kim. 734-275-0099, misskimannarbor.com.

- **Braai House** Fire plays a central role in every element of this popular pre-theater South African restaurant in Stratford whose name refers to that country's style of barbecue: there's a wood-fired grill and pizza oven, a fireplace in the stylish dining room, and fire torches on the airy patio. 519-271-5647, braaihouse.restaurant.

- **La Condesa** This hip yet homey restaurant in Prince Edward County serves locally sourced, boldly flavored Mexican fare—octopus-chorizo tostadas, cochinita pibil tacos—and artisan tequilas and mezcals. Wellington, 613-399-2007, lacondesarestaurant.com.

- **Chez Piggy** Offering seating in a gloriously renovated limestone stable and in a leafy courtyard, this downtown Kingston favorite offers globally inspired treats, from Korean kimchi pot stickers to beef tenderloin with oxtail bone marrow bordelaise sauce. 613-549-7673, chezpiggy.ca.

BEST SLEEPS

- **Riverbend Inn & Vineyard** It's hard to imagine a more romantic Niagara-on-the-Lake setting than this Georgian-style mansion on scenic Niagara Parkway. The 21 rooms are lavishly appointed, and The Oaklands restaurant serves locally sourced French cuisine. 905-468-2270, riverbendinn.ca.
- **Cadillac Motel** The '50s kitsch and vintage car-themed art are part of the charm of this reasonably priced, souped-up motor lodge in Niagara Falls, Canada. 905-356-0830, cadillacmotelniagara.com.
- **Inn Buffalo off Elmwood** This 1890s Victorian mansion with nine elegantly appointed guest rooms is within walking distance of Buffalo's lovely Delaware Park and the great restaurants of the Elmwood district. 716-867-7777, innbuffalo.com.
- **Kimpton Schofield** Steps from Cleveland's theaters and sports arenas, this dapper 122-room boutique hotel in a landmark 1902 building abounds with creature comforts and even offers loaner guitars. 216-357-3250, theschofieldhotel.com.
- **Graduate Ann Arbor** Within walking distance of the UM campus and Kerrytown, this whimsically decorated, collegiate-themed hotel has inviting guest rooms and an old-school-cool cocktail lounge. 734-769-2200, graduatehotels.com.
- **Bruce Hotel** You can walk to the Stratford Shakespeare Festival theaters from this intimate and refined 25-room boutique hotel set amid 6.5 acres of gardens and lawns. An elegant restaurant serves contemporary Canadian cuisine. 519-508-7100, thebruce.ca.
- **Algonquin Provincial Park lodgings** Given the vastness of this timber-scented preserve, it makes sense to spend a night inside it. The rustic-elegant Arowhon Pines overlooks serene Little Joe Lake. Bartlett Lodge has cozy cabins on the shore of Cache Lake, and Killarney Lodge is a 1930s all-inclusive property on a peninsula that juts into Lake of the Two Rivers.
- **Drake Devonshire Inn** The urbane sister property to Toronto's chichi Drake Hotel has sleek rooms and a see-and-be-seen restaurant overlooking Lake Ontario's shoreline in the fashionable village of Wellington. More affordable rooms can be had in the nearby Drake Motor Inn. 613-399-3338, thedrake.ca.

- **June Motel** On Picton Bay, this smartly rehabbed mid-century motel has a mod-lifestyle aesthetic, right down to the cheeky "This Might Be Wine" coffee mugs. The owners' equally inviting Sauble Beach June Motel—which was featured in the Netflix reality TV show *Motel Makeover*—overlooks Lake Huron near Bruce Peninsula National Park. No phone, thejunemotel.com.

CAMPING

Wonderfully picturesque and peaceful campgrounds abound in the more rural parts of this itinerary; Tobermory Village and Flowerpot Island at Bruce Peninsula National Park, South Bay Resort and Campground on Manitoulin Island, Arrowhead Provincial Park, Lake of Two Rivers in Algonquin Provincial Park, and the canopy A-frame cabins at Point Pelee National Park are among the most alluring venues. In more populated areas of Ontario, consider Wildwood Conservation Area near Stratford and Outlet River Campground in Prince Edward County, while Niagara Falls North/Lewiston KOA and Detroit/Ann Arbor KOA are good bets in the US.

Top Kayaking, Algonquin Provincial Park
Opposite Cornell University, Ithaca

Upstate New York ★ 🍁

*Rich in history, art, and natural beauty, the Empire
State contains some of the Northeast's most dramatic
mountain ranges and river valleys plus a heady mix
of world-class museums and enchanting small towns.*

HOW LONG?

8 days; add an extra day each to explore more of the Adirondacks,
Thousand Islands, and Finger Lakes.

WHEN TO GO

Summer greenery and fall foliage make June to mid-October the most
beautiful (but also expensive) period for touring upstate New York.
Consider late spring and just after peak autumn leaf-peeping to avoid
the crowds while still enjoying moderate weather. Unless you're keen on
snow sports, avoid the Adirondacks and western New York in winter.

NEED TO KNOW

The scenic parkways that run through the Hudson River Valley can
be narrow and curvy, so keep your eyes on the road and observe speed
limits. Some businesses in more remote lake and mountain towns shut
down in winter.

→ Distances
Total distance, one-way: 1075 mi (1730 km)
- New York City to Albany: 210 mi (338 km)
- Albany to Alexandria Bay: 350 mi (563 km)
- Alexandria Bay to Canandaigua:
  190 mi (306 km)
- Canandaigua to Cooperstown:
  255 mi (410 km)

▤ Daytime Temperatures
January: 25-40°F (-4-4°C)
July: 77-86°F (25-30°C)

ⓘ More information
- New York City tourism, nycgo.com
- Hudson Valley tourism,
  travelhudsonvalley.com
- Albany tourism, albany.org
- Saratoga Springs tourism,
  discoversaratoga.org
- Adirondacks tourism, visitadirondacks.com
- Thousand Islands tourism,
  visit1000islands.com
- Finger Lakes tourism, fingerlakes.org
- Cooperstown tourism,
  thisiscooperstown.com

◎ SNAPSHOT

Visitors are sometimes surprised by how easy
it is to find remote wilderness within about an
hour's drive of the nation's largest city. The
chance to commune with nature is just one
great reason to explore Upstate New York. You'll
encounter spectacular scenery along the glacially
sculpted shores of the Hudson River Valley, the
Thousand Islands, and the Finger Lakes and
amid the soaring peaks of the Catskills and
the Adirondacks. The region also abounds with
captivating small cities and towns, offering
museums, performance venues, and restaurants
and bars that could hold their own in Manhattan.

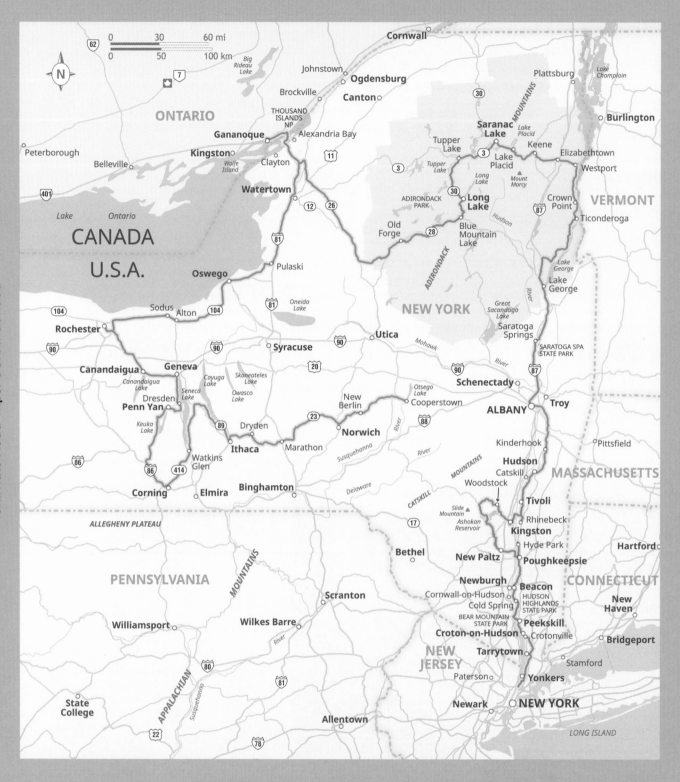

Top **Central Park** *Bottom* **Metropolitan Museum of Art**

City View
New York City

Even as a former New Yorker who rather enjoys the orderly chaos of driving in the nation's largest metropolis, I don't actually consider NYC a suitable road-tripping destination. It's too big, too dense, and too expensive. However, it *is* an incredible city with iconic cultural and culinary scenes. And with three major airports (including Newark, NJ) and two huge train stations, it can make an exciting and even practical start or end to an auto tour of the Empire State. You can save yourself a lot of money and hassle, however, by following a couple of basic guidelines: (1) Use public transit rather than driving in Manhattan. Either park your car at a commuter lot outside the city and take the train in, or if renting a car, do so upon leaving the city, ideally in a suburb where rates tend to be lower. (2) If staying in NYC with a car, stick with Brooklyn and Queens, which are easier to drive and park in; Brooklyn, in particular, has great hotels with moderately priced parking and close proximity to subway stations.

Car-friendly rating: Poor. With sky-high parking rates, exorbitant bridge and tunnel tolls, maddening rush hour traffic, and—expected to begin in 2023—congestion pricing for driving in Midtown, Manhattan is a terrible place to bring a car. The Outer Boroughs are better but still difficult to navigate. I recommend sticking with NYC's comprehensive subway and bus systems.

What to see in a day: For a short visit, focus on one or two neighborhoods. My top recommendations in **Manhattan** are **Central Park** and the **Upper East Side**'s top museums—**The Guggenheim**, the **Metropolitan Museum of Art**, the **Cooper Hewitt**, **El Museo del Barrio**, the **Museum of the City of New York**—if you're a culture vulture. I also recommend **Greenwich Village** and **Chelsea**—the **High Line** park, **Chelsea Market**, the **Whitney Museum of Art**, **Little Island**, **Washington Square**—if you're more about sidewalk strolling, cool bars and eateries, and galleries and indie retailers. But you could also skip Manhattan and focus instead on some of the captivating neighborhoods in other boroughs. **Brooklyn** is my top choice—there's **Brooklyn Heights**, with its gorgeous **Promenade** park; **Park Slope** with leafy **Prospect Park**, the **Brooklyn Botanic Garden**, and the **Brooklyn Museum**; and **Williamsburg** and **Greenpoint**, with their trendy restaurant and retail scenes. The neighborhoods of **Queens** closest to Manhattan have some impressive attractions, too, such as **MoMA PS1**, the **Museum of the Moving Image**, and the **Noguchi Museum**. Or there's upper Manhattan and **The Bronx**, where you could start with a stroll through the **Met Cloisters** and adjacent **Fort Tryon Park** before heading north to the **Bronx Zoo**, the **New York Botanical Garden**, and **Arthur Avenue**'s Italian restaurants.

Where to stay: If you have a car, staying in Manhattam doesn't make a lot of sense. In Brooklyn some appealing boutique properties with free parking are **Hotel Le Jolie** in Williamsburg, **Hotel Le Bleu** in Park Slope, and the **RL Brooklyn** in Bushwick. The **William Vale** and the **Henry Norman** are a couple of other Brooklyn gems that either charge for parking or where you'll have to park on the street, but the stunning rooms and common spaces are worth that one inconvenience. In Queens the **Boro Hotel** is a terrific option, and the **Residence Inn New York Metro Center Atrium** is a solid lodging in The Bronx.

NEW YORK CITY TO ALBANY

Technically, every square mile of state above New York City could be considered "Upstate New York," from the near-NYC suburbs of Westchester and Rockland counties to the secluded hinterlands of the rugged Adirondack Mountains, the binational Thousand Islands, and the wine-centric Finger Lakes. Throughout this geographically and culturally diverse region, you'll discover plenty of picturesque places to explore and a colorful mix of captivating roads to get there. My favorite way through the **Hudson River Valley** is via the region's scenic parkways, a network of undulating mostly four-lane roads, the brainchild of the controversial urban planner and megalomaniac Robert Moses, whose ruthless ambition and often racist and classist projects caused more harm than good (I recommend reading Robert Caro's riveting biography of Moses, *The Power Broker*). But the parkways—free of billboards and commercial vehicles, curving through woodlands, around streams and lakes, and over bridges—are his most beautiful legacy.

From **Upper Manhattan** and **The Bronx** take the Henry Hudson and then Saw Mill River parkways through **Yonkers** and **Tarrytown**, and then the Taconic and Briarcliff-Peekskill parkways to **Crotonville**, where you can hop out to stretch your legs and enjoy a lovely view of the Hudson River at 504-acre **Croton Point Park** and explore the exhibits on Native American history and the region's flora and fauna in the park's nature center. Continue up the Croton Expressway (US 9) to **Peekskill** (pop 24,600), a bustling Victorian factory town whose vintage architecture—check out the meticulously restored 1930 Paramount Hudson Valley Theater—continues to draw artists and young professionals priced out of New York City (this is a trend that's fueled urban revivals up and down the Hudson Valley). Follow US 202, which parallels the river as it snakes over a series of dramatic ridges through the mountainous Hudson Highlands, stopping at the **Bear Mountain Bridge Toll House Visitor Center**. It occupies a restored 1920s toll house and dispenses information on hikes and scenic overlooks in 8000-acre **Hudson Highlands State Park**, which comprises a series of noncontiguous preserves along both sides of the river. You'll soon spy the 360 ft towers of the **Bear Mountain Bridge**, which was the world's longest suspension bridge upon its completion in 1924—the **Appalachian Trail** follows the pedestrian walkways across this handsome two-lane bridge.

Head north on Rte 9D from the Bear Mountain Bridge. Interesting stops include **Manitoga/the Russel Wright Design Center**, the 75-acre wooded estate and striking glass-

SIDETRACK

When time allows, I like detouring across the bridge—which offers majestic panoramas up and down the river—to **Bear Mountain State Park** and driving or hiking the 3.8-mile loop trail to the 1305 ft summit of Bear Mountain. Here you can ascend to an observation deck atop the **Perkins Memorial Tower**, which was built by the CCC in the 1930s. You can also visit the park's zoo and the **Bear Mountain Inn**, a 1915 stone-and-timber lodge that now contains a restaurant and gift shop; its design inspired the rustic style of architecture that would become commonplace throughout America's national parks. From here it's just a few miles up US 9W to the imposing campus of the **US Military Academy**, better known simply as West Point, where you can tour the excellent **West Point Museum**. It's another 8 miles to **Cornwall-on-Hudson** and an enticing mountain preserve, **Storm King State Park**, as well as **Storm King Art Center**, a phenomenal 500-acre sculpture park (tickets must be purchased in advance and can sell out well ahead during peak periods). You can either continue up the west side of the river, crossing back at the small city of **Newburgh**, or return the way you came.

National Baseball Hall of Fame, Cooperstown

walled, green-roofed mid-century home of an acclaimed industrial designer, and the **Boscobel House and Gardens**, an early 1800s neoclassical mansion filled with fine decorative arts and surrounded by more than 60 acres of gardens with commanding river views. The village of **Cold Spring** has one of the valley's prettiest downtown historic districts as well as a dramatic riverfront setting. Admire the view of West Point from the town's riverfront park, have brunch or lunch at the elegant 1830s Hudson House River Inn (which also has 13 rooms and suites), and walk among the old buildings and remnants of **West Point Foundry**, an important 19th-century ironworking site that's now a 93-acre preserve. Don't leave town without breaking for a scoop of butterscotch toffee crumble or pomegranate chip ice cream at Moo Moo's Creamery. Continue alongside the river and railroad tracks up Rte 9D to **Beacon** (pop 14,600), a once-industrious manufacturing town that had more than 50 hat factories during its peak. A sharp economic decline led eventually to a renaissance precipitated by the 2003 opening of the prestigious **Dia Beacon** contemporary art museum, which is inside a 160,000 ft former Nabisco box factory. After exploring the compelling art installations and gardens, walk or drive down the hill for a riverfront stroll at **Scenic Hudson's Long Dock Park**, and then make your way to Main St, with its several blocks of eateries and galleries set inside appealing redbrick buildings—Bank Square Coffeehouse serves artisan coffee and craft beer, and Meyer's Old Dutch serves tasty burgers and crispy-chicken sandwiches.

Continue to **Poughkeepsie** (pop 32,730), the Mid-Hudson region's largest city and home of the tree-shaded campus of **Vassar College** and its acclaimed **Frances Lehman Loeb Art Center** museum. My favorite activity: buy picnic supplies from Lola's Cafe, then ascend the staircase and stroll across the **Walkway Over the Hudson**, a 1.3-mile 1889 railroad bridge that was converted into a linear park in 2009—the views are incredible, especially at sunset. Continue a few miles north to **Hyde Park**, an attractive river town that's famous for its **Home of Franklin D. Roosevelt National Historic Site**. Take a fascinating tour of his Federal-style mansion and explore the **Franklin D. Roosevelt Presidential Library and Museum**, which was established in 1941 and was the first of its kind. Its archives and exhibits explore the lives of both FDR and First Lady Eleanor Roosevelt, whose own estate, Val-Kill, is just a few miles away at the **Eleanor Roosevelt National Historic Site**. Hyde Park is also home to the **Vanderbilt Mansion National Historic Site**, which is anchored by a grandiose 54-room Beaux-Arts mansion completed in 1899 by McKim, Mead & White, and the main 70-acre campus of the vaunted **Culinary Institute of America**, which has enchanting grounds and gracious buildings. The colorful behind-the-scenes campus tours are a must for foodies, as is dining in one of the excellent restaurants—elegant Bocuse, with its refined French cuisine, is the favorite for a special occasion dinner, but I'm partial to having breakfast or lunch at the airy and inviting Apple Pie Bakery Cafe.

Backtrack to Poughkeepsie and cross the river for a foray into the foothills of the famed **Catskills Mountains**, a rugged range of lofty peaks and steep valleys that extends about 50 miles west to the Delaware River and northeastern Pennsylvania. Stop in the college town of **New Paltz** (home to SUNY New Paltz) and take a walk along **Historic Huguenot Street**, a 10-acre village and living history museum of early 1700s stone houses settled by Calvinist Huguenots. Continue northwest of Mountain Rest Rd and Mohonk Rd—stop if you have a few hours to hike, play golf, dine, or enjoy the spa (day passes are required) at the famous **Mohonk Mountain House**, a lavish late-19th-century resort set on an idyllic alpine lake. Then continue north through the Catskills and across Ashokan Reservoir to **Woodstock**, a prominent artists colony since the late Victorian days of the Hudson River School and Arts and Crafts movements—it would later become a beacon of the US counterculture movement. Although this picturesque village on Tannery Brook has been attracting free spirits for generations, the iconic 1969 rock and folk music festival that bears its name actually occurred 60 miles southwest on Max Yasgur's farm in **Bethel**. At any rate, downtown abounds with intriguing art galleries, crafts shops, and cafes and is also home to the renowned **Woodstock Playhouse**.

Head southeast back into the Hudson Valley to visit **Kingston**, a small and historic city of around 23,000 that became New York's first capital in 1777. Head to the quaint waterfront at the confluence of Roundout Creek and the Hudson River, where you can explore the engaging **Hudson River Maritime Museum**, then venture into Uptown's **Stockade District**, a warren of colorfully painted Victorian buildings that house trendy boutiques and eateries. Kingston has in recent years become one of the state's premier culinary destinations, with venues like Lola (wood-fired pizzas), Kingston Bread & Bar bakery, and the Stockade Tavern earning plenty of acclaim.

Take Rte 199 back across the river and curve down through the quaint and artsy village of **Rhinebeck** before turning north past the attractive gardens and buildings of **Bard College** and by the cute Victorian village of **Tivoli**. Continue to **Olana State Historic Site**, the magnificent Middle Eastern–inspired 1872 home and 250 acres of gardens that make up the estate of Hudson River School painter Frederic Edwin Church. After touring this majestic property, you can either drive or hike 6 miles (round-trip) across the **Hudson River Skywalk**, a scenic pedestrian path that runs along the southern side of the cantilevered **Rip Van Winkle Bridge** to the village of **Catskill** and the **Thomas Cole National Historic Site**, which preserves the 1812 home and studio of the founder of the Hudson River School movement. Just north of Olana, **Hudson** (pop 6100) is a tiny but densely developed former industrial village that has morphed into a trendy—some might say twee—borough of cafes, cocktail lounges, art galleries, and vintage stores that would look right at home in Williamsburg, Brooklyn. Say what you will about the relentlessly hip vibe, Hudson offers no shortage of chic and delicious diversions—I like Kitty's Market Cafe for coffee, pastries, and bacon-egg sandwiches, and Lawrence Park for wine and cocktails. Continue up Rte 9H through charming **Kinderhook**, where you can take a surprisingly engrossing tour of **Martin Van Buren National Historic Site**, the home of the eighth (and first truly obscure) US president (and the only one for whom English was a second language— he grew up speaking Dutch). From here it's about a half-hour drive to Albany.

ALBANY TO THE THOUSAND ISLANDS

Settled in 1614 and the state capital since 1797, **Albany** has only around 100,000 residents but enjoys a prominent role among Empire State cities. This striking metropolis on the Hudson River is known for its impressive architecture, from the ornate Richardsonian Romanesque 1899 **New York State Capitol Building** to adjacent **Empire State Plaza**, a 98-acre tract of sleek International-style civic buildings—including the superb **New York State Museum** and **The Egg** theater complex—completed in 1976 under the direction of Wallace K. Harrison (the creative force behind Lincoln Center's Metropolitan Opera House and the UN complex). After walking around downtown, drop by venerated Jack's Oyster House, where power brokers and politicos have hobnobbed since 1913. Then head west a few blocks for a stroll along eclectic **Lark Street**, with its gracious town houses and colorful cafes, ending with a ramble around the flower beds of enchanting **Washington Park**.

It's about a 40-minute drive north to **Saratoga Springs** (pop 28,500), whose name derives from this historic resort community's abundance of curative mineral springs, which

the Mohawk and Iroquois tribes used for centuries. By the mid-1800s, the town boasted some of the largest and most lavish hotels in the Northeast. The famous **Saratoga Race Course**, one of the nation's oldest thoroughbred horse racing venues, opened in 1863, and the esteemed **Saratoga Performing Arts Center** (SPAC) opened a century later. The town continues to draw fans of racing, music and dance, and healing waters; SPAC, the **National Museum of Dance and Hall of Fame**, and **Saratoga Automobile Museum** are on the grounds of 2379-acre **Saratoga Spa State Park**, which preserves a number of natural springs as well as **Roosevelt Baths & Spa** inside the 1935 Gideon Putnam Hotel. As of this writing, the historic Lincoln Baths building is slated to reopen later in 2022 as the home of the new **Children's Museum at Saratoga**. For all of its formal attractions, much of the fun of Saratoga lies simply in walking around its bustling downtown, which is rife with notable eateries (Hamlet & Ghost, Henry Street Taproom) and interesting boutiques.

Continue up I-87, aka the Adirondack Northway, to **Lake George**, a touristy, family-friendly beach town on the south shore of the narrow 33 mile long lake for which it's named— several outfitters offer scenic steamboat cruises. It's also a southern gateway to **Adirondack Park**, a 9375-square-mile preserve—roughly the size of New Hampshire—that contains a mix of public, state-owned wilderness and private land (including more than 100 municipalities). Established in 1892, this hiking, fishing, and boating paradise boasts 46 prominent mountain peaks, more than 10,000 pristine lakes, and thousands of miles of rivers and streams. Follow Rte 9N up the west shore of Lake George to **Ticonderoga** to visit **Fort Ticonderoga**, an imposing star-shaped stone garrison perched over the narrow south arm of Lake Champlain that figured prominently in the French and Indian and Revolutionary wars. From July through early October, a car ferry makes the half-mile Lake Champlain crossing to Shoreham, VT. Continue on Rte 9N up through **Crown Point**, where you can view the remnants of another prominent colonial fort at **Crown Point Historic Site**, and then along the scenic west shore of Lake Champlain to picturesque **Westport** before cutting inland through **Elizabethtown** and **Keene** to the Adirondacks' most famous community, **Lake Placid**. Home to fewer than 2500 year-round residents, this idyllic alpine village hosted the 1932 and 1980 Winter Olympics. You can learn about the town's sports legacy at the **Lake Placid Olympic Museum** and by touring facilities where top athletes from around the world still train, including the **Olympic Ski Jump** and **Bobsled and Luge** complexes and

Herb Brooks Arena. The latter is named is named for the coach who led the US ice hockey team to a highly unexpected gold medal—what became known as the "Miracle on Ice." There's fantastic hiking nearby, including such great bang-for-your-buck treks as the 1.8-mile **Mt Jo Loop** and the 4.2-mile out-and-back jaunt to **Marcy Dam**, and downtown Lake Placid enjoys a lovely setting on **Mirror Lake**. Terrific restaurants overlooking the water include Top of the Park for creative tapas and the Breakfast Club for heavenly cinnamon-nutmeg French toast.

Continue west through this magnificent mountainscape, stopping for a look around the captivating village of **Saranac Lake** and continuing to **Tupper Lake**, where you should set aside at least a couple of hours—more if you have kids with you—to explore the **Wild Center**, a thrilling contemporary indoor-outdoor museum that features boardwalk and elevated treetop trails, nearly 1000 rescued and rehabilitated live native animals, guided canoe trips on a picturesque bend in the Raquette River, and beautifully designed interactive exhibits on Native American culture and natural history—there's also a lovely lakeside cafe. Turn south on Rte 30 through a series of classic Adirondacks hamlets, including **Long Lake** and **Blue Lake**, which is home to the renowned **Adirondack Experience, The Museum on Blue Mountain Lake**. As a kid whose grandparents owned a summer lodge on Long Lake, I spent many hours exploring this 121-acre seasonal living history museum; it comprises nearly two dozen buildings and outdoor exhibits that bring to life every aspect of the region's human and natural history. Along with the Wild Center, it's still one of my favorite attractions in Upstate New York. Have lunch in Blue Mountain Lake at Chef Darrell's, a restored 1940s stainless-steel diner that serves up hearty burgers and fresh-baked pies.

Follow Rte 28 west along the shores of more small lakes to **Old Forge** and then out of the Adirondacks and up to **Alexandria Bay**, one of the most picturesque of several New York villages in **Thousand Islands**. Actually comprising something in the neighborhood of 1870 different islands, this beautiful, laid-back archipelago extends along the St Lawrence River's US-Canada border from the northeastern tip of Lake Ontario for about 50 miles downstream. You can access a number of prominent attractions from the New York side, including the opulent and eccentric **Boldt Castle**—which occupies its own small island and can be reached by tour boat or ferry—and **Thousand Islands Winery**, one of several noted vintners in the region. As you explore the south shore of the St Lawrence River, also check out the **Antique Boat Museum** and **Rock Island Lighthouse State Park** (reached by tour boat) in **Clayton** and **Tibbetts Point Lighthouse** in **Cape Vincent**. Personally, I think it's worth the effort to drive across the border from Alexandria Bay into Ontario, and then head west along the picturesque **Thousand Islands Parkway**. Go at least as far as dapper **Gananoque**, which is home to the highly regarded **Thousand Islands Playhouse** and has a number of charming eateries, shops, and B&Bs. You can return to the US the way you came or continue 20 miles southwest to **Kingston** (*see* Lakes Ontario, Erie, and Huron chapter p. 201), and take a ferry to **Wolfe Island** and then another back across the border into Cape Vincent.

THOUSAND ISLANDS TO COOPERSTOWN

For the most scenic drive to Rochester, take I-81 south to **Pulaski** and then follow the mostly two-lane roads along Lake Ontario's southern shoreline through **Oswego** and **Sodus**. An attractive, upbeat city of 212,000, **Rochester** abounds with gracious old homes and outstanding museums, and it boasts a diverse, accomplished restaurant and bar scene. On the estate of the photography pioneer who founded Eastman Kodak, the stellar **George Eastman Museum** features a striking contemporary visitor center and cafe, several galleries of photo exhibits, and the entrepreneur's gracious Georgian Revival mansion and gardens. A must if you're traveling with young ones is the 282,000 sq ft **Strong National Museum of Play**, which is routinely ranked among the country's best children's museums. I also like visiting the **National Susan B. Anthony Museum and House**, where the suffragist and women's rights activist resided the final 40 years of her life, and **High Falls Terrace** park, where you can walk out on a pedestrian bridge to view the dramatic downtown waterfall that marks the beginning of the Niagara Escarpment. Have a snack afterward at the 1905 **Public Market**, which has more than 300 vendors, or in the hip **Neighborhood of the Arts**, whose acclaimed restaurants include Lento and Nosh.

Drive about a half-hour southeast to **Canandaigua**, an all-American-looking town of about 10,000 with a wide Main Street that leads the northern shore of the 16-mile lake for which it's named. This picturesque body of water is one of the largest of the **Finger Lakes**, a series of 11 narrow, curving north-south lakes carved by glaciers. The region is known for its romantic B&Bs and waterfront lodges, its lively marinas, and—especially since the 1990s—its outstanding wineries. There are about 130 of them, and they specialize in aromatic cool-weather grapes such as Riesling, Gewürztraminer, and Cabernet Franc as well as less common (in the US anyway) varietals like Zweigelt, Lemberger, and Seyval. Head east to **Geneva**, another of the region's larger towns, this one at the northern tip of **Seneca Lake**. To visit some outstanding wineries—including **Anthony Road, Keuka Spring Vineyards**, and one of the region's pioneer operations, **Konstantin Frank**—drive down Seneca Lake's western shore to **Dresden**, turn west through **Penn Yan**, and continue down the west shore of **Keuka Lake**.

Follow I-86 south to the small city of **Corning** (pop 10,600), the headquarters for Corning Inc., the famed glass and ceramics manufacturer and founder of the outstanding **Corning Museum of Glass**—with more than 50,000 glass objects, some dating back nearly 4000 years, this is a bona fide must-see. Across the Chemung River in Corning's colorful **Gaffer District**, you'll find several art and glass-blowing studios as well as some excellent eateries and craft breweries (Market Street Brewing and Iron Flamingo are both superb). Follow Rte 414 north to **Watkins Glen** at the southern tip of Seneca Lake and explore the breathtaking

400 ft deep gorge and staircase-lined waterfalls of **Watkins Glen State Park**. Continue up the lake's eastern shore, stopping for more tastings at **Red Newt, Atwater**, and **Hazlitt 1852** vineyards (as well as first-rate whiskies and grappa at **Finger Lakes Distilling**). When you get to **Ovid**, turn east and then south along the undulating western shore of **Cayuga Lake**, where you might stop at **Sheldrake Point Winery** or **Finger Lakes Cider House** before going for a hike to the awesome 215 ft tall cascades at **Taughannock Falls State Park**.

You'll soon reach hilly and picturesque **Ithaca**, which is home to both **Ithaca College** and **Cornell University**. Verdant parks fringe Cayuga Lake's curving southern shore, which is also where you'll find the beloved **Ithaca Farmers' Market**. Downtown, especially pedestrianized **Ithaca Commons**, bustles with fun shops and eateries, including Moosewood, the legendary vegetarian restaurant that opened in 1973 and spawned a still-popular vegetarian cookbook series. Drive east through central New York's **Leatherstocking Country**—a verdant and fertile swath of the Mohawk and Upper Susquehanna valleys—to **Cooperstown**. Even casual fans will probably recognize this town on Otsego Lake as the home of the **National Baseball Hall of Fame**, and as someone who grew up obsessed with the national pastime, this beautifully designed three-story museum is one of my ultimate happy places. You can view highlights from the collection of some 40,000 pieces of baseball memorabilia and see plaques of its more than 340 inductees. But there's actually much more to this village. At the north end of **Otsego Lake**, you can attend the acclaimed **Glimmerglass Festival**, the nation's second largest summer opera festival (it runs for about six weeks starting in early July). And back closer to town, the superb **Fenimore Art Museum** has been built around the handsome former farmhouse of the great American novelist James Fenimore Cooper (the *Leatherstocking Tales, The Last of the Mohicans*) and has impressive collections of folk, Indigenous, and American landscape art. Just across the street, Cooper's former farm is now the **Farmers' Museum**, a 23-building living history campus with a remarkable collection of agricultural implements and artifacts. End the day with a sunset dinner at Blue Mingo Grill, which has a terrace overlooking the lake, or with a Belgian-style farmhouse saison and a bowl of truffle-parmesan frites at acclaimed Brewery Ommegang.

BEST EATS

- **Brasserie 292** Perfectly prepared French classics—mussels Provençal, duck confit with lentils and bacon—are the specialty of this downtown Poughkeepsie restaurant with pressed-tin ceilings and red-leather booths. 845-473-0292, brasserie292.com.

- **Silvia** Have a seat on the deck or overlooking the kitchen at this farm-to-table bistro in Woodstock. Standout dishes include smoked chicken and cauliflower schnitzel with capers and lemon. 845-679-4242, silviawoodstockny.com.

- **Gaskins** This romantic yet unpretentious restaurant in tiny Germantown—midway between Kingston and Hudson—features regionally sourced comfort fare, plus superb beers from a nearby sibling business, Suarez Family Brewery. 518-537-2107, gaskinsny.com.

- **Lil' Deb's Oasis** This funky, playfully decorated spot in Hudson serves as both a stellar pan-Latin eatery (try the crispy sour-cherry-glazed pork belly with fermented chiles) and a spirited LGBTQ-embracing neighborhood bar. 518-828-4307, lildebsoasis.com.

- **15 Church** Cap off a day of spa-soaking, concert-going, or horse race-watching at this refined Saratoga Springs restaurant. The food itself is visually stunning—think garganelli pasta with rabbit ragout or artichoke velouté with apricot sofrito. 518-587-1515, 15churchrestaurant.com.

- **Salt of the Earth Bistro** Set inside an inviting Lake Placid farmhouse, this casually elegant eatery presents a world tour of delicious dishes, including shrimp with an Ethiopian peanut sauce and pork chops with pineapple fried rice. 518-523-5926, saltoftheearthbistro.com.

- **Kitchen at Captain Visger House** After exploring the Thousand Islands, enjoy a leisurely repast in this Victorian home (it also has four B&B guestrooms) near the riverfront in Alexandria Bay. The contemporary menu changes weekly. 315-681-3422, captainvisgerhouse.com.

- **Owl House** Close to downtown Rochester museums and hotels, this intimate neighborhood bistro offers an eclectic menu of international eats, with plenty of vegan and vegetarian options and inventive cocktails as well. 585-360-2920, owlhouserochester.com.

- **The Stonecat** This homey, unfussy eatery with sweeping views from its covered deck is my go-to for hearty, creative dining after a day of wine-touring on Seneca Lake. Bounteous salads and regionally sourced steaks and grills are offered along with suggested local wine pairings. Hector, 607-546-5000, stonecatcafe.com.

- **Thompson and Bleecker** This convivial brick-walled tavern in Ithaca Commons specializes in blistered-crust Neapolitan pizzas, house-made pastas, and boldly flavored antipasti. Note the impressive organic wine list. 607-319-0851, thompsonandbleeckerpizza.com.

George Eastman Museum, Rochester *Previous* The Thousands Islands, on the New York and Ontario border

BEST SLEEPS

- **Abbey Inn & Spa** An hour north of New York City, this gorgeously transformed 1902 convent sits on a leafy 65-acre bluff with magnificent Hudson Valley views, 42 posh hotel rooms, a soothing spa, and a farm-to-table restaurant. 914-736-1200, theabbeyinn.com.

- **Hasbrouck House** With 29 smartly furnished rooms, lofts, and suites this posh hideaway in the Catskill foothills boasts two dapper restaurants, a cozy bar, and a century-old swimming pool. Stone Ridge, 845-687-0736, hasbrouckhouseny.com.

- **Hotel Kinsley** Steps from the buzzy eateries of Kingston's historic Stockade District, this collection of four stylishly renovated buildings offers 43 rooms decked out with creature comforts. Restaurant Kinsley serves stellar contemporary American fare. 845-768-3620, hotelkinsley.com.

- **Rivertown Lodge** This boho-chic boutique hotel in Hudson is a good value and features custom-designed furnishings and airy common areas with wood-burning fireplaces. The tavern is a local hotspot for weekend brunch. 518-512-0954, rivertownlodge.com.

- **Adelphi Hotel** A landmark hotel in the venerable Broadway Historic District, the Adelphi has been welcoming Saratoga Springs vacationers since 1877, and the 32-room property will add at least another 170 rooms and numerous amenities by mid-2023. 518-678-6000, theadelphihotel.com.

- **Mirror Lake Inn** Downtown Lake Placid's postcard-perfect waterfront retreat opened in 1924 and offers an appealing range of accommodations, from romantic suites with fireplaces and jetted tubs to multi-bedroom family units with spacious living areas. 518-523-2544, mirrorlakeinn.com.

- **1000 Islands Harbor Hotel** Surrounded on two sides by water, this family-friendly Clayton hotel has a patio and firepits with splendid views of the St Lawrence River, along with an indoor pool, and a festive restaurant. 315-686-1100, 1000islandsharborhotel.com.

- **Watkins Glen Harbor Hotel** Overlooking the marina at the southern tip of Seneca Lake, this contemporary four-story lodge is convenient to the best wine-touring in the Fingers Lakes as well as the attractions in Corning and Ithaca. 607-535-6116, watkinsglenharborhotel.com.

- **Otesaga Resort Hotel** This dignified 1909 grande dame on Cooperstown's lakefront offers a full slate of recreational experience, from golf and spa treatments to several restaurants and bars. It's a 10-minute walk from the National Baseball Hall of Fame. 607-547-9931, otesaga.com.

CAMPING

The options for camping increase significantly the farther you get from New York City, but you can find some inviting spots in the Hudson Valley, including So-Hi Campgrounds near Kingston and Camp Catskills near Hudson. Glamping venues, like Treetopia in Catskill and Woodstock Meadows in Woodstock, are also popular in these parts. Farther north, reliable campgrounds include Coldbrook Resort near Saratoga Springs, Lake George Escape, Saranac Lake Islands, and Lake Durant near Blue Mountain Lake. Wellesley Island State Park has 432 sites in the gorgeous Thousand Islands, and Sned-Acres and Watkins Glen/ Corning KOA are good bets in the Finger Lakes.

Shops in downtown Hudson *Opposite* Lower Town, Quebec City

Quebec's Cities, Mountains, and Fjords ✦

Enjoy incredible French-influenced food, fashion, and architecture without leaving North America on this captivating journey through Quebec's storied cities and majestic national parks.

HOW LONG?

7 days; add an extra day each to see more of Ottawa, Mont-Tremblant, Montreal, and Quebec City.

WHEN TO GO

Quebec has plenty of charm in every season, even in the middle of winter when there's snow in the mountains and ice sculptures, arts festivals, and fireplace-warmed bistros in the cities. I tend to avoid March to mid-May, which can be wet and muddy, and my favorite time is September to October for the crisp evenings and brilliant fall color. Summer is beautiful but touristy.

NEED TO KNOW

It really helps to speak even a few simple French phrases in Quebec, as outside largely bilingual Montreal, Mont-Tremblant, and the more touristy areas of Quebec City, English isn't widely spoken, especially in rural areas.

→ Distances
Total distance, one-way: 750 mi (1207 km)
- Ottawa, ON to Montreal, QC: 180 mi (290 km)
- Montreal, QC to Quebec City, QC: 260 mi (418 km)
- Quebec City, QC to Tadoussac, QC: 300 mi (483 km)

⊜ Daytime Temperatures
January: 15-22°F (-9 - -5°C)
July: 75-80°F (24-27°C)

ⓘ More information
- Ottawa tourism, ottawatourism.ca
- Mont-Tremblant tourism, mont-tremblant.ca
- Montreal tourism, mtl.org
- Eastern Townships tourism, easterntownships.org
- Quebec City tourism, quebec-cite.com
- Saguenay tourism, tourisme.saguenay.ca

◉ SNAPSHOT

A trip through southern Quebec offers a rich diversity of wilderness and urbanity. With their striking riverfront settings and decidedly old-world personalities, Montreal and Quebec feel unmistakably European, and just across the border in Ontario, Ottawa has a wealth of attractions. These vibrant metropolises are strung together by a series of fresh-aired forests, stony mountains, and quaint river hamlets.

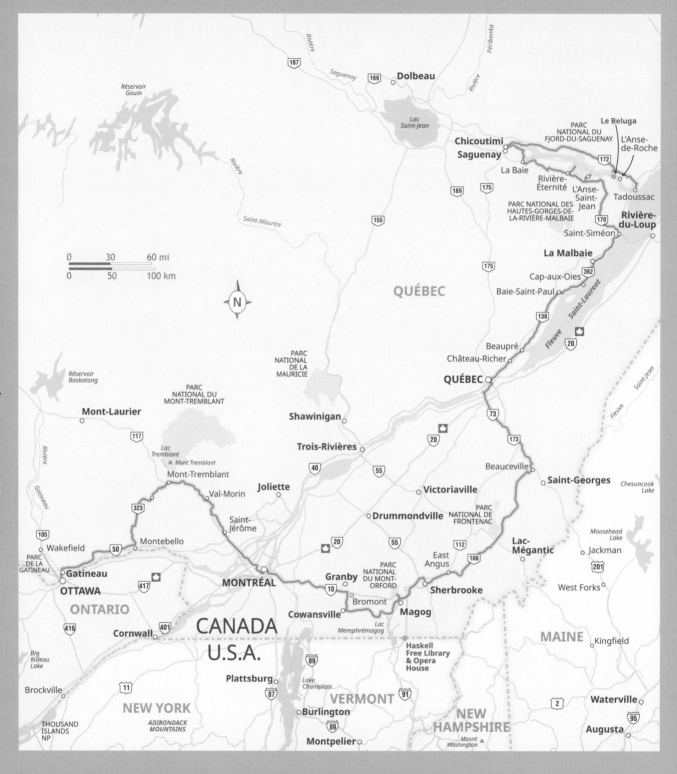

City View

Ottawa

Canada's national capital, Ottawa is the second largest city (pop 935,000) in Ontario but it's just across the river from Gatineau (formerly known as Hull) on the Quebec border and makes a convenient start to this road trip.

Car-friendly rating: Fair-Good. Except for its compact city center, where parking in commercial lots and hotels can get moderately expensive, Ottawa is a fairly diffuse city that quickly feels and looks suburban—complete with ample street parking—within a few miles' drive in any direction.

What to see in a day: My favorite—and I think the prettiest—way to experience the city's key sites is to make a roughly 4-mile walking or biking loop along both sides of the Ottawa River, starting and ending where Wellington St crosses the **Rideau Canal** (Escape Bicycle Tours, a couple of blocks away, has bike rentals); note that both bridge crossings on this route do have dedicated bike/pedestrian lanes. Walk down the steps and stroll along this picturesque canal to **Bytown Museum**, which occupies an 1820s stone warehouse and has great exhibits about the construction and legacy of this waterway. One of the joys of visiting Ottawa in winter is skating along Rideau Canal (sometimes dubbed the world's largest skating rink). Cross the canal and explore hip **ByWard Market**, the name of a bustling 1826 building and also the blocks around it teeming with diverse restaurants and shops—it's the perfect place to pick up local maple syrup, artisan cheeses, and beavertails (Canada's beloved fried-dough pastries). Eateries worth checking out include Fairouz Cafe for modern Middle Eastern cuisine and Sidedoor for creative Asian street food. Continue along the meandering paths through **Major Hill's Park**, with its views of the river and canal locks. Cross the street and tour the superb Moshe Safdie-designed **National Gallery of Canada**, which contains collections of Indigenous and Canadian art, then walk across the 1901 **Alexandra Bridge** into **Gatineau**, QC. Take a tour of the **Canadian Museum of History**, an airy, light-filled modern building designed by renowned Indigenous Canadian architect Douglas Cardinal. The well-designed exhibits are divided chiefly among key spaces, the First Peoples Hall and the Canadian History Hall. Follow the **Voyageurs Pathway** along the riverfront, enjoying the vistas toward Ottawa's imposing Neo-Gothic-style Parliament buildings, then return across the Ottawa River via the **Portage Bridge**. Back on the Ottawa side of the river, I recommend a brief detour just west to the **Canadian War Museum**, another of the city's notable architectural works that also boasts a trove of military artifacts and artworks.

Follow Wellington St east downtown, ending your tour with a walk around **Parliament Hill** and then taking the elevator to the campus's observation deck atop the 322 ft tall **Peace Tower**. Beyond the city center, Ottawa also has several walkable neighborhoods with indie dining and retail scenes, including **Westboro** and—on the south side of downtown—**Bank Street**, which has strong LGBTQ roots and myriad interesting shops and cafes.

Where to stay: I like staying amid the buzzy eateries and bars of ByWard Market, with the sleek **Andaz, Ottawa**—which has a gorgeous 16th-floor rooftop bar—offering stylish accommodations. Nearby, **Le Germain Hotel Ottawa** is another posh and contemporary option. Overlooking Rideau Canal and Parliament, the **Fairmont Chateau Laurier** is a courtly beauty from 1912—high tea here is a longtime tradition. **Alt Hotel Ottawa** and **Arc The Hotel** are good mid-range options.

Canadian Museum of History

OTTAWA, ON TO MONTREAL, QC

Although it's possible to reach Montreal in a couple of hours by following fast and wide Hwy 50 roughly parallel to the Ottawa River on its journey to the St Lawrence Seaway, the far more interesting way is to cut north from **Montebello** and follow Hwy 323 up to the alpine vacation village of **Mont-Tremblant**, where you can explore the national park of the same name. A popular recreational resort since a rail line from Montreal was completed in 1904, this colorful town on the even more colorfully named Devil's River is famous for its championship auto racetrack and for having the largest ski resort in Eastern Canada. **Mont-Tremblant Resort** lies at the lower end of 8 mile long Lac Tremblant and consists of a bustling village with chalet-style condos, hotels, and restaurants. During the warmer months, you can take the gondola to the 2871 ft summit, one of the highest in the Laurentian Range, for a panoramic view from the observation tower and to go hiking and mountain-biking. The highlight for me is attending the 30-minute **Birds of Prey Show**, during which you're treated to an up-close look at trainers interacting with eagles, kestrels, and great horned and snowy owls. It's a winding, picturesque 90-minute drive down through the towns of Val-Morin and Saint-Jerome to reach Montreal.

SIDETRACK

From Ottawa it's a half-hour drive north up Hwy 105 (a more scenic alternative to faster and parallel Hwy 5) through the gently rolling Gatineau River valley to **Wakefield**, QC, a quaint village notable for its fire engine-red, 288 ft long covered bridge (it's a replica of the 1915 original that burned in the 1980s). This quirky arts community with about 2000 residents and a slew of galleries and eateries is a favorite outdoor-recreation destination: canoeing, paddle boating, swimming, snowshoeing, and more. On your return back to Ottawa, stop for a hike around **Gatineau Park**, which features more than 100 miles of trails around lakes and through emerald forests—the slightly steep 2.5-mile **Luskville Falls loop** is a good one. End your adventure with a thermotherapy session in the cool and hot outdoor soaking pools at **Nordik Spa-Nature Chelsea**, which also offers a range of body treatments as well as healthy meals in the intimate Restö eatery and terraced Biërgarden.

Top Fairmont Le Chateau Frontenac Hotel, Quebec City
Opposite top Old Montreal *Opposite bottom* Notre-Dame Basilica

MONTREAL, QC TO QUEBEC CITY, QC

Follow Hwy 10 east from Montreal, which leads into a popular weekend-getaway region known as the **Eastern Townships**. Extending to the Vermont border, it's made up of around 15 key communities and is characterized by glistening lakes, hardwood forests, rolling hills, organic farms, and vineyards. Hop off Hwy 10 south of **Granby** and head into the picturesque town of **Bromont**, stopping for a snack at Cafe Bar Backbone, a fun eatery set inside a climbing gym, and then continuing to **Balnea Spa**, a gorgeous, mostly outdoor retreat with soaking pools and hiking trails surrounding lovely Lac Gale. Follow the country roads to the western shore of **Lake Memphremagog**, a picturesque 32 mile long sliver of water that dips into northern Vermont; the 1901 **Haskell Free Library and Opera House** actually straddles the US-Canada border (residents of either country may enter through the front door, which is in **Derby**, VT, and then continue into the **Stanstead**, QC part of the building to visit the library stacks). There are a few popular beaches at the north end of Lake Memphremagog, where you can explore charming downtown **Magog**. It's a 15-minute drive north to **Mont-Orford National Park**, a 23 sq mile patch of steep mountains that's known for its ski resort in winter and for hiking the rest of the year. Along the route, Aux 2 Tomates is a terrific find for well-prepared thin-crust pizzas and natural wines. Continue east to the Eastern Townships' largest city of **Sherbrooke** (pop 162,000), which is set along the banks of the Magog and Saint-Francois rivers, and then to through the verdant meadows and lakes of **Frontenac National Park** en route to **Beauceville** from which it's an hour's drive to Quebec City.

City View
Montreal

Cosmopolitan, vibrant, and steeped in history, Quebec's largest city (pop 1.8 million) fringes the north shore of the St Lawrence River, its downtown of office towers set against the 745 ft rocky bluff—Mont Royal—for which it's named. With one of North America's most exciting culinary, art, music, and design scenes, Montreal hums with creative energy. And whether you visit in summer when sidewalk terraces swell with diners or in winter when lounges and dance clubs buzz with revelers, this bilingual (French is the predominant language) metropolis feels positively exuberant year-round. Stay for two or three days if your schedule permits.

Car-friendly rating: Fair. In densely settled downtown and Old Montreal, you'll likely need to park in a garage or lot; rates are relatively moderate. Given the excellent subway system and close proximity of central attractions, it's best not to rely much on your car in this part of the city. Up the hill—in the lively Plateau, Mile End, and Mile-Ex areas—street parking is easier to come by, although pay close attention to signage, as residential permits and other restrictions may come into play.

What to see in a day: On a short visit, I recommend focusing on **Old Montreal**. Though undoubtedly touristy, it's also an engaging warren of ancient stone buildings, many of them housing fashionable galleries, boutique hotels, and romantic restaurants—such as Helena for modern Portuguese fare, the French brasserie Holder, and Dispensa Italian Grocery for mouthwatering sandwiches to enjoy from a bench on the promenade overlooking the river. Spend time exploring the **Pointe-a-Calliere Museum**, a trove of archaeological history inside a striking contemporary structure that has been constructed to preserve the excavated remnants of 17th-century buildings. Then make your way along the district's narrow lanes, past the 69 ft towers of neo-Gothic **Notre-Dame Basilica**, with its 6800-pipe organ, and amid the tony boutiques of 19th-century **Bonsecours Market**. Next, venture a bit north and west to explore the neighborhoods where many of Montreal's most talented makers, artists, entrepreneurs, and chefs are earning a name for themselves. Blvd Saint-Laurent and rue Saint-Denis are lined with both classic and cool hangouts in **Plateau Mont Royal**. Saint-Laurent then passes through hip **Mile End**, once the heart of the city's still-vibrant Jewish community and birthplace of the city's iconic smoked meat and bagel incarnations. The creative energy continues beyond into the adjacent **Mile-Ex** and **Little Italy** neighborhoods. You could spend days attempting to eat your way through any of these districts—my favorite is Mile End, and I'm partial to Ta Chido for

Oaxacan-style tortas, Tsukuyomi for ramen, and Fairmount for legendary Montreal bagels. Whether in the morning or around sunset, do make a trek through the city's green heart, 692-acre **Mont-Royal Park**. From the sprawling **Kondiaronk Belvedere** terrace, you'll enjoy views of the city skyline and the green hills beyond.

Where to stay: Old Montreal may just be the most romantic hotel district in North America (it's likely tied with Old Quebec), and there are dozens of options. The **Hotel William Gray**, a pair of venerable 18th-century buildings that have been given a contemporary update, is the ultimate retreat, but I also love the mid-century vibe and pop-art sensibility of 33-room **Hotel Uville**. Among the classics, **Hotel Place d'Armes** is a beautiful hotel with a fabulous rooftop bar. A few blocks south in up-and-coming Griffintown, **Hotel Alt Montreal** is a sleek tower with smartly designed rooms and reasonable rates. And overlooking the Plateau's leafy Saint-Louis Square, **Hotel de l'ITHQ** is situated at and run by the city's most prestigious hospitality college and is also a good deal.

QUEBEC CITY, QC TO TADOUSSAC, QC

The area now know as Quebec City was originally an Iroquois settlement, Stadacona, that was abandoned after increased fighting with the French. In 1608, the explorer Samuel de Champlain established a fort here, making it one of the oldest extant European settlements in North America. Today, visiting the city—especially the Old Quebec quarter—truly does give the sense of having been transported to France. With a population of about 535,000 and only a handful of modern office towers, the provincial capital feels surprisingly small and cozy. I like to approach the city center by way of the **Montcalm** neighborhood, driving along **Grande Allee** until it reaches the lawns and meandering paths of the **Plains of Abraham**, a gracious 240-acre park that was the site of a crucial 1759 battle between the British and French armed forces during the Seven Years' War. It's set on a dramatic promontory that shows off the city's lofty setting high above the St Lawrence River, and it's home to the outstanding **National Museum of Fine Arts of Quebec**. The park is lovely for strolling or jogging. If you really want

to get your heart racing, descend the nearly 400 steps of the wooden **Cap-Blanc Stairs** down a rocky cliff face to **Bassin Brown Park** by the river's edge (bear in mind, you'll have to return up those same stairs). Continue north from the park around the formidable and impressive (and still active as a military installation) **Quebec Citadelle**, which was completed in 1850, and by the imposing Second Empire–style **Parliament Building of Quebec** to **Place D'Youville**, one of the historic hearts of the city center and the boundary of **Old Quebec** (this densely settled part of the city is best explored on foot). **Rue Saint-Jean** passes through the square and is lined for many blocks in either direction with interesting eateries and shops.

Walk east through Old Quebec's **Upper Town**, a perfectly preserved warren of narrow cobblestone streets and mostly stone 18th- and 19th-century buildings with steep metal roofs. Visit the imposing 1647 **Cathedral-Basilica of Notre-Dame de Québec**, the regal **Place d'Armes Park**, and the boardwalk along **Dufferin Terrace**, which offers fantastic views of the river and Lower Town and lies beneath the iconic **Fairmont Le Chateau Frontenac Hotel**, with its castle-like copper roofs and fanciful turrets. Built in 1893, the Chateau Frontenac is the city's most recognizable feature—even if you don't stay here, be sure to peek inside. The 612-room property abounds with amenities, including an indoor pool, a spa, and multiple restaurants, and even offers guided tours if you want to learn more of its storied past. From Dufferin Terrace, you can either take the funicular—which dates to 1879—or walk down the curving narrow lanes that lead into **Lower Town**, with its quaint galleries, romantic restaurants, and direct frontage on the river. The **Museum of Civilization**—with a stunning 1988 design by Moshe Safdie—is an absolute must, with engrossing exhibits on Quebec's 11 First Nations and the province's complicated 415-year European history. Continue up through the **Old Port** district and then along narrow Rue Saint-Paul. You can return to Upper Town, but my preference is to continue west beneath the Hwy 440 overpasses into one of the city's most intriguing neighborhoods, **Saint-Roch**. A formerly industrial and working-class residential area that fell into a steep decline in the late 20th century, the neighborhood has since the early 2000s morphed into a fashionable, hip quarter of international dining, third-wave coffeehouses, and craft breweries. Restaurants like Izakaya Hono and La Korrigane Brasserie earn plenty of buzz, and you'll find some good, mid-priced, modern hotels here, too.

Follow Hwy 138 east along the north shore of the St Lawrence River. Less than a half hour later in **Chateau-Richer**, the small **Cuivres d'Art Albert Gilles Boutique et Musee** is an interesting stop—it showcases the intricate and internationally recognized decorative arts of the Gilles family, which has been creating beautiful copper works for several generations. About an hour farther in **Baie-Saint-Paul**, pick up Hwy 362 and continue 30 miles to **La Malbaie**, for many decades known as Murray Bay. In the mid-19th century the village became a fashionable resort town known for one of the continent's oldest golf courses along with its dozens of grandiose vacation "cottages" (really mansions), many owned by American business tycoons, including US President William H. Taft, who summered here throughout his life. The town is home to the uber-opulent **Fairmont Manoir Richelieu** and celebrated restaurants like Chez Truchon Bistro, Boulangerie Pains d'Exclamation, and La Maison du Bootleggers, which is named for the illicit rum-running activities that occurred in this 1860s building during Prohibition. Notable attractions include **P'tit Bonheur Art Gallery** and—about a half hour north—**Hautes Gorges de la Rivière Malbaie National Park**, a dramatic and deep river gorge famed for its 6.6-mile Acropole des Draveurs hiking trail.

Continue to **Saint-Simeon**, then cut inland on Hwy 170—which becomes part of the **Fjord Route**, a 146-mile scenic road that follows both sides of majestic Saguenay Fjord—to the city of Saguenay for 65 miles to where it empties into the St Lawrence River. Established in 1983, **Saguenay Fjord National Park** preserves one of North America's longest—and southernmost—fjords, a narrow ribbon of river that's 900 ft deep in places and is lined by cliffs that tower as high as 1150 ft. It's a relatively undeveloped park with two main sections—Baie-Éternité on the south shore and Baie-Sainte-Marguerite on the north—and limited facilities, but therein lies part of its charm. It rarely feels crowded, even during the summer high season (which does attract its share of cruise ships). It also offers a slew of activities, including hiking, kayaking, biking, and whale-watching cruises—four kinds of whales inhabit these waters: blue, minke, fin, and beluga.

Turn right from Hwy 170 and follow the road to **L'Anse-Saint-Jean**, one of the best access points for exploring the fjord. At **Voile Mercator** you can book a half-day cruise up and down the fjord on a sailboat, while adjacent **Fjord en Kayak** rents boats and also offers kayak paddles that provide a wonderful perspective on the surrounding cliffs. Have a lunch of savory or sweet buckwheat crepes at Cafe du Quai or a well-crafted beer at La Chasse-Pinte Brasserie Cooperative. Continue back on Hwy 170 to **Riviere Éternité** to visit **Le Fjord du Saguenay Discovery and Visitors Centre**, which has well-designed exhibits that tell the story of the glaciers and geological forces that shaped this remarkable landscape. Then set out on the 4.6-mile round-trip hike to **Cap Trinite** and the 30 ft tall 1881 **Statue of Our Lady of Saguenay**—this somewhat arduous and mostly uphill ramble offers some of the most astonishing vistas in the park.

Continue west to scenic **La Baie**, the oldest and easternmost of three formerly separate municipalities (Chicoutimi and Jonquiere are the others) that are now boroughs of the consolidated city of Saguenay, the region's main economic and population center. La Baie overlooks the narrow and quite funny-sounding **Ha! Ha! Bay**, which is an arm of the fjord, and here you can tour the **Musee du Fjord**, an interactive natural science museum with an impressive aquarium. A 15-minute drive west, **Chicoutimi** is home to Saguenay's main commercial district—you'll find plenty of lively eateries and shops along Rue Racine. Before driving over Hwy 175 to the other shore, I recommend walking at least partly across the 1930s **Pont de Sainte-Anne**, which was closed to car traffic back in the 1970s and today serves only pedestrians and bikes—the views from this 1500 ft long bridge are terrific.

Saguenay Fjord National Park *Opposite* Lower Town funicular, Quebec City

Across the river, turn east on Hwy 172 to drive the Fjord Route's northern side, portions of which hug the shoreline, offering stupendous water views. The 75-mile drive to Tadoussac offers several interesting diversions, including **Parc Aventures Cap Jaseux**, an adrenaline-fueled park and resort that offers kayak trips, a via ferrata climbing experience, and a zip-lining and tree-top canopy tour—this eco-friendly, family-friendly property also has a variety of innovative camping, glamping, and cabin accommodations. About an hour east in **Baie Sainte-Marguerite** you can visit the park's other main visitor center, **Le Beluga**, which has a fantastic permanent exhibit about these graceful 3000-pound mammals that swim far upriver. Next, follow the turnoff from Hwy 172 down to **Anse de Roche** for sweeping fjord vistas, hiking along a portion of the Fjord Trail, and lunch overlooking the beach at charming La Casta Fjord Cafe. The Fjord Route continues to Hwy 138 and the colorful village of **Tadoussac**, at the mouth of Saguenay Fjord, where it enters the St Lawrence Seaway. It has a good selection of restaurants and lodgings, including **Hotel Tadoussac** a stately, red-roofed Victorian property whose rooms could stand some updating but enjoy a beautiful setting on Tadoussac Bay. Stop by the town's **Marine Mammal Interpretation Centre** to learn more about whales, or book a whale-watching cruise from one of several outfitters. Then take a car ferry for a 10-minute ride across the river to **Baie Ste-Catherine**, another small hub of travel services that's also home to the **Pointe-Noire Interpretation and Observation Centre**, which dispenses information about the surrounding **Saguenay–St Lawrence Marine Park**. From here it's a 20-mile drive back to Saint-Simeon and the main route back to Quebec City.

Top Winter Carnival, Quebec City Middle The terrace at the Fairmont Le Manoir Richelieu, La Malbaie *Bottom* Sagueney Fjord, Anse de Roche

BEST EATS

- **Le Petite Cachée** A fireplace and timber-beam ceiling create an inviting ambience at this Mediterranean-inspired spot across the road from Mont-Tremblant's marvelous Devil's Waterfall. Specialties include veal tagine and saffron seafood risotto. 819-425-2654, lapetitecachee.com.

- **Seb L'Artisan Culinaire** This refined farm-to-table restaurant on the bustling main drag in Mont-Tremblant turns out artfully plated dishes like Arctic char with miso beurre blanc and venison loin with an elderberry demi-glace. 819-429-6991, seblartisanculinaire.com.

- **Restaurant Le Hatley** Plan for a leisurely and luxurious repast at this contemporary French-Canadian restaurant inside the posh Manoir Hovey hotel. The lakefront setting in North Hatley, near Magog and Mont-Orford, is enchanting. 819-842-2421, manoirhovey.com.

- **Vin Polisson** Curating a thoughtful selection of mostly old-world natural wines is the mission of this sleekly intimate bar in downtown Sherbrooke that also serves up delicious food. Try the tender short ribs with a mushroom demi-glace. 819-791-2442, vinpolisson.com.

- **Chez Rioux & Pettigrew** Dining in this warmly lighted restaurant in an 1860s former general store on palpably romantic Rue Saint-Paul truly captures the essence of Old-World Quebec City. The food, on the other hand, is original and modern—and delicious. 418-694-4448, chezriouxetpettigrew.com.

- **Buvette Scott** This bright and cheery neighborhood bistro on Quebec City's lively Rue Saint-Jean dispenses shareable plates of delicious French bites: guinea fowl liver pâté, oysters on the half shell, pappardelle with veal cheek ragu. The wine list is top notch. 581-741-4464, buvettescott.com.

- **La Grange aux Hiboux** The intimate "owl barn" serves classic French fare and overlooks a beautiful section of the Saguenay River's Ha! Ha! Bay. The adjoining inn has four overnight rooms. La Baie, 418-544-7716, lagrangeauxhiboux.com.

- **Bistro Cafe Summum** This stylish contemporary eatery in the lively Chicoutimi neighborhood of Saguenay (there's a second outpost in La Baie) serves modern European fare, like beef tataki and scallops with lemon-tarragon cream. 418-544-0000, bistrocafesummum.com.

BEST SLEEPS

- **Hotel Quintessence** This posh 30-room lodge on the shore of Lac Tremblant is an easy walk from the cafes, shops, and myriad activities of Mont-Tremblant Resort village. The property includes a pool and a spa. 819-425-3400, hotelquintessence.com.

- **Espace 4 Saisons** The stylish digs at this contemporary boutique inn on the edge of Mont-Orford National Park are a welcome retreat after a day of hiking, boating, or winter skiing. A bistro and burger pub serve tasty food, and there's a pool, spa, and game room. 819-868-1110, espace4saisons.com.

- **OTL Gouverneur** This snazzy mid-rise on the edge of downtown Sherbrooke is the most urbane hotel between Montreal and Quebec and has cushy rooms with plush bedding and marble bathrooms. 819-780-8800, otlhotelsherbrooke.ca.

- **Hotel Le Germain** The flagship property of Canada's hip and sophisticated Germain Hotels group occupies a stately 1912 building in Quebec City's Old Port. The 143 rooms have bold color schemes and goose-down comforters. 418-692-2224, germainhotels.com.

- **Hotel Pur** amid the hip cafe culture and indie retail of Quebec City's Saint-Roch neighborhood, this moderately priced boutique property rises 18 stories and features sleekly outfitted rooms with tall windows. 418-647-2611, marriott.com

- **Fairmont Le Manoir Richelieu** Perched high on a terraced promontory with commanding views of the St Lawrence River, this chateauesque 1929 resort hotel in La Malbaie makes a fashionable overnight retreat on the journey from Quebec City to Saguenay. It boasts a renowned golf course, spa, and dining room. 418-665-3703, fairmont.com.

- **Gite du Haut des Arbres** With eight cozy and stylish rooms, a deck and small pool with panoramas of the Saguenay River, and an inviting living area warmed by a fireplace, this modern guest house is a charming base for visiting the national park and downtown Chicoutimi. 418-815-4667, giteduhautdesarbres.com.

CAMPING

Even within a short drive of the region's cities, you'll find tranquil lakes, glades, and mountain ranges with scenic campgrounds, many of them offering glamping-style canvas tents or cabins as well as more conventional sites. Wesley Clover Parks has an attractive setting just west of Ottawa, and Camping de la Diable has a beautiful riverside location in Mont-Tremblant. Try Camping Au Plateau 5 Etoiles outside of Montreal, Camping Parc Bromont and Camping Magog Orford in the Eastern Townships, and Camping de la Joie to be near Quebec City. In the Saguenay Fjord region, beautiful locales for sleeping under the stars include Camping de L'Anse, Camping Bleuvet, and Camping Tadoussac.

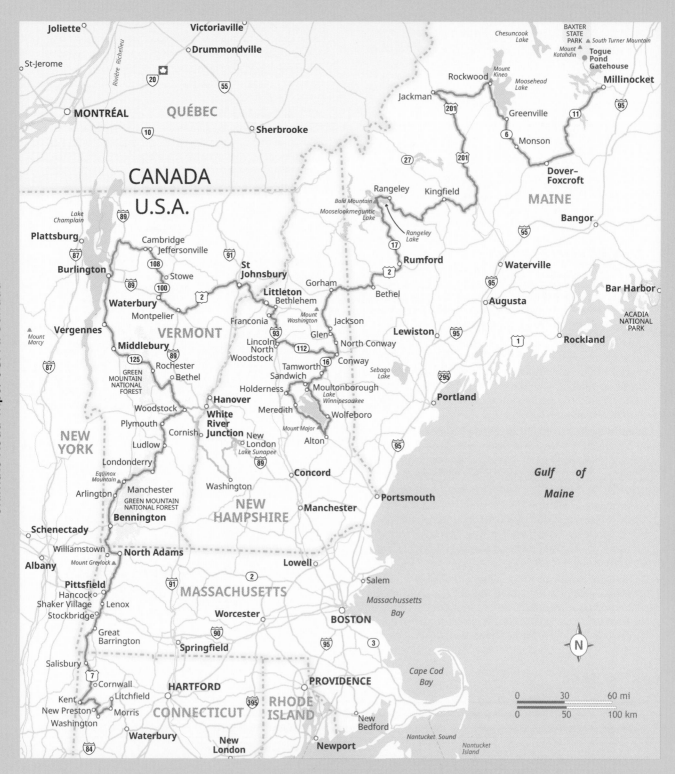

Joliette
St-Jerome
Victoriaville
Drummondville

MONTRÉAL
QUÉBEC
Sherbrooke

CANADA
U.S.A.

Plattsburg
Burlington
Lake Champlain

Cambridge
Jeffersonville
Stowe
Waterbury
Montpelier

St Johnsbury
Littleton
Bethlehem
Franconia

Gorham
Bethel

MAINE
Bangor
Waterville
Augusta

Bar Harbor
ACADIA NATIONAL PARK
Rockland

Chesuncook Lake
BAXTER STATE PARK
South Turner Mountain
Mount Katahdin
Togue Pond Gatehouse
Millinocket

Rockwood
Mount Kineo
Moosehead Lake
Greenville
Monson
Dover-Foxcroft

Jackman

Rangeley
Kingfield
Bald Mountain
Mooselookmeguntic Lake
Rangeley Lake
Rumford

VERMONT
Vergennes
Mount Marcy
Middlebury
Rochester
Bethel
GREEN MOUNTAIN NATIONAL FOREST
Woodstock
Plymouth
Cornish
Ludlow
Londonderry
Equinox Mountain
Manchester
GREEN MOUNTAIN NATIONAL FOREST
Arlington
Bennington

Mount Washington
Lincoln
North Woodstock
Jackson
Glen
North Conway
Conway
Tamworth
Sandwich
Holderness
Meredith
Moultonborough
Lake Winnipesaukee
Wolfeboro
Mount Major
Alton

Hanover
WHITE RIVER JUNCTION
New London
Lake Sunapee
Washington
Concord

NEW HAMPSHIRE
Manchester

Portsmouth

Portland

Sebago Lake

Lewiston

Gulf of Maine

NEW YORK
Schenectady
Williamstown
Albany
Mount Greylock
Pittsfield
Hancock
Shaker Village
Stockbridge
Lenox
North Adams

MASSACHUSETTS
Lowell
Worcester
Springfield

Salem
Massachussetts Bay

BOSTON

Great Barrington
Salisbury
Cornwall
Kent
Litchfield
New Preston
Morris
Washington
Waterbury

HARTFORD
CONNECTICUT
New London

PROVIDENCE
RHODE ISLAND

Newport
New Bedford

Cape Cod Bay
Nantucket Sound
Nantucket Island

N

0   30   60 mi
0   50   100 km

New England's Mountain Towns ★

Scenic, winding country roads connect interior New England's dozens of charming lake towns and alpine hamlets, which abound with colorful galleries, sophisticated restaurants, and engaging museums.

HOW LONG?

10–12 days.

WHEN TO GO

From mid-September through mid-October, this is one of the world's most captivating destinations for viewing fall foliage. The leaves begin changing color earliest in the north (in central Maine and northern New Hampshire and Vermont), with the Berkshires and Litchfield Hills peaking closer to mid-October. Expect sometimes intense traffic on scenic roads, especially on weekends, and steep hotel rates (and two- or three-night minimum stays). Summer is also the high season in interior New England, while winter appeals with its wealth of snow sports and cozy restaurants and inns warmed by fireplaces. The odd season out? Early spring, which can be wet, muddy, and prone to biting black flies.

NEED TO KNOW

Although parts of this region can be popular for skiing and snowboarding in winter, other areas—especially around the region's many big lakes—shut down for parts of the winter months.

➜ Distances
Total distance, one-way: 1000 mi (1609 km)
- Millinocket, ME to Wolfeboro, NH: 400 mi (643 km)
- Wolfeboro, NH to Burlington, VT: 270 mi (435 km)
- Burlington, VT to Manchester, VT: 150 mi (241 km)
- Manchester, VT to Litchfield, CT: 160 mi (267 km)

ⓘ Daytime Temperatures
January: 22-33°F (-6-1°C)
July: 75-80°F (24-27°C)

ⓘ More information
- Moosehead Lake tourism, destinationmooseheadlake.com
- White Mountains tourism, visitwhitemountains.com
- New Hampshire Lakes Region tourism, lakesregion.org
- Stowe tourism, gostowe.com
- Manchester tourism, manchestervermont.com
- Berkshires tourism, berkshires.org
- Litchfield Hills tourism, discoverlitchfieldhills.com

◉ SNAPSHOT

Come for the spectacular fall color, gorgeous summer hiking, or crisp-aired winter recreation. This vertiginous landscape of pristine lakes, hardwood forests, roaring rivers, and dewy meadows abounds with both rustic and worldly charms. Nature is the foremost draw in upper New England, but you'll find countless opportunities to dine in chef-driven bistros, peruse fine art in acclaimed galleries, and curl up by the fire in stately country inns.

In remote interior Maine, activities like hiking, fishing, and boating on pristine mountain lakes draw visitors from spring through autumn (in winter there's skiing at Sugarloaf and a few other popular resorts). This is a rural, unpretentious part of New England—no-frills lodges and motels and casual pancake houses, diners, and pubs are the norm. As you follow this itinerary west and south through Vermont, the Berkshires in Massachusetts, and the Litchfield Hills in Connecticut, you'll encounter many more posh inns and sophisticated restaurants, along with the higher prices that come with them.

This drive begins in **Millinocket**, the gateway to one of the Northeast's most spectacular wildernesses, **Baxter State Park**—the main visitor center is downtown, and a second one is at the **Togue Pond Gatehouse** at the park's southern entrance, 18 miles north. The horizon is dominated by Maine's highest peak, 5267 ft **Mt Katahdin**, which is also the northern terminus of the 2190-mile **Appalachian Trail**. It's an ambitious undertaking to hike Katahdin, but in just a few hours you can appreciate the grandeurs of this pristine place, which is more than five times the size of Acadia National Park. Go for a stroll around **Daicey Pond**, have a picnic on the west shore of **Abol Pond**, or make the 3.5-mile trek up **South Turner Mountain**—it's steep, but it's also the shortest of any of the park's high-peaks excursions. Or book a rafting or tubing excursion along the frothy Penobscot River from one of the several excellent outfitters in the area, including **Northern Outdoors** and **Penobscot Adventures**.

To get to **Moosehead Lake**, you have the option of making the intriguing but rather taxing 2.5-hour drive via the southern end of Baxter State Park on **Golden Road**, a remote backcountry logging route through **Kokadjo** and **Lily Bay**. Although it offers decent odds of spying a moose, more than half of this 70-mile road is unpaved and sporadically quite rough and rutted, and because much of this land has been logged over the years, the scenery isn't as spectacular as you might hope. The more practical and I think prettier drive is on Rtes 11 and 6, which pass through rolling farmland, unpretentious logging and mill towns, and lush woodlands. About 15 miles before Greenville, you'll arrive in **Monson**, a lively little hamlet on Lake Hebron that's in the midst of a striking transformation. In the mid-2010s investors from the Libra Foundation, a Portland-based social justice–minded organization—began buying up and rehabbing run-down downtown buildings; one now contains the outstanding At The Quarry restaurants and others have notable art galleries and shops.

Whatever route you follow on this first leg, you'll pass through vast backcountry and just a handful of hardscrabble villages. Although it may feel as though you've crossed into the Arctic Circle (at least in comparison with the more populous Maine coast), this is still central Maine. A massive tract—larger than Connecticut and Rhode Island combined—of almost completely undeveloped wilderness extends north from Baxter State Park and Moosehead Lake to the Canadian border.

Greenville is the largest community on the largest body of water entirely within New England, Moosehead Lake, but it's still really just a village, with around 1650 residents and a handful of restaurants and shops, several outdoor outfitters, a few hotels, and lots of cabin rentals. In the village center, perched at the southern tip of this 75,000-acre lake, tour the small but excellent **Moosehead Marine Museum** and book a half-day cruise around the lake on the museum's restored 1914 steamship, the *Katahdin*. A highlight of these sails is passing beneath the majestic 700 ft cliffs of **Mt Kineo**, which is the centerpiece of a 1200-acre peninsular state park that was developed in the 1880s as a posh summer resort. I recommend visiting the park by taking a 15-minute shuttle boat ride (it's not accessible by road) from **Rockwood**, a picturesque hamlet 20 miles up Rte 6 from Greenville. The island's hotel was torn down in the 1930s, but you can play a round of golf on the historic course and have lunch in the clubhouse restaurant and bar. My favorite activity is hiking the steep but enjoyable 3.4-mile loop to the top of Mt Kineo and ascending a 60 ft fire tower for mesmerizing 360-degree vistas.

From Rockwood it's a relaxing three-hour drive through a handful of diminutive villages—including **Jackman**, just 15 miles south of the Canadian border, and **Kingfield**, the gateway to acclaimed **Sugarloaf** ski area and the popular mountain biking terrain of the **Carrabassett Valley**—to **Rangeley**, which anchors a beautiful region of six big lakes (and dozens of smaller ones) and is famous for fishing, hiking, and winter sports. The two most popular are **Rangeley Lake** itself and the engagingly named **Mooselookmeguntic Lake**. For a commanding view, hike 1.1 miles to the fire tower atop **Bald Mountain**. Then learn about the region's ecology and human history at the terrific **Outdoor Heritage Museum** in **Oquossoc** before heading south on Rte 17, the **Rangeley Lakes National Scenic Byway**. Stop at the **Height of Land** overlook to snap a few photos and maybe even hike a short stretch of the Appalachian Trail—this is one of the best vantage points in the state for fall foliage.

The Cog Railway, from atop Mt Washington
Previous Lake Champlain, Burlington

Continue southwest through the mill–turned–ski resort towns of **Rumford** and **Bethel**. The latter, with its gracious town green and several lodgings and eateries (I like Butcher Burger for well-crafted gastropub fare), is home to acclaimed **Sunday River** ski resort as well as the impressive **Maine Mineral and Gem Museum**, which occupies a contemporary building with a garden of geological wonders out front and fascinating interactive exhibits inside showcasing western Maine's rich mining history and a remarkable collection of meteorites. US 2 leads into the eastern side of New Hampshire's **White Mountains**, a vertiginous region that covers about a quarter of the state and contains nearly 50 peaks that rise above 4000 ft. In **Gorham**, head south on Rte 16 to tiny **Glen** to explore **Mt Washington**, which at 6288 ft is the highest peak in the northeastern US. In addition to hiking (the shortest routes to the top are about 8.5 miles round-trip), the two ways to the summit are via the 1858 **Cog Railway**, which is near the grand dame **Mt Washington Hotel** in **Bretton Woods** (and located on the west side of the mountain, an hour's drive away), and—my favorite—by driving the **Mt Washington Auto Road**. This 7-mile journey some 4600 ft up a skinny, tortuous road isn't for the faint of heart, but the views at the top, as well as the **Extreme Mount Washington** meteorology museum, are worth the effort (you can also ride up on a guided bus tour or, in winter, snow coach). Prepare for chilly weather at the top, where temperatures can drop to -50 degrees in winter and snow is possible even in July.

Rte 16 continues through quaint **Jackson**, complete with its Instagram-worthy covered bridge and a bounty of sophisticated country inns (the **Inn at Ellis River** and **Inn at Thorn Hill** are both fantastic) and hearth-warmed taverns. The fall leaf peeping (and winter cross-country skiing) is superb. Continue through **North Conway**, a touristy and often traffic-clogged strip of outlet malls that's unfortunately become a bit of a victim of its own commercial development success.

Follow Rte 16 down through **Tamworth**, where you can take a tour of the critically acclaimed artisan spirits maker **Tamworth Distilling**, visit the quirky but engaging **Remick Country Doctor Museum and Farm**, and watch a summer-stock performance at the nearly century-old **Barnstormers Theatre**. Then loop through New Hampshire's **Lakes Region**, which offers up some of the loveliest scenery in the state. Take Rte 109 along the eastern side of New England's second largest lake, **Winnipesaukee**, stopping in **Moultonborough** at the **Loon Center** to learn about these elegant birds—hearing the eerie howls of these animals is one of my favorite things about passing my summers on a lake in New Hampshire. Then visit the **Castle in the Clouds**, a grand 1910s hilltop estate that's now open for tours—and in summer for lakeview lunches and jazz dinners on the lofty patio of the museum's Carriage House restaurant. You'll soon reach upscale **Wolfeboro**, which bills itself as America's oldest summer resort (vacationers have been coming since shortly before American Independence). It boasts Lake Winnipesaukee's prettiest downtown, with a quirky mix of shops, galleries, and eateries from the Yum Yum Shop bakery to the Country Bookseller.

Lake Winnipesaukee view from Mt Major

WOLFEBORO, NH TO BURLINGTON, VT

As you circle around the southern tip of the lake, watch sea planes depart and land on narrow **Alton Bay**, then pull off to make the 3-mile round-trip scramble up several granite ledges and chasms for a grand lake view from atop 1786 ft tall **Mt Major**. Continue along Winnipesaukee's western shore, past the old-fashioned, kid-approved amusement parks, game arcades, ice cream and hot dog stands, and scenic cruises and train rides of **Weirs Beach** and **Meredith**—the latter has several popular hotels on the lake's edge. Then follow US 3 to **Holderness** on enchanting **Squam Lake**, which has several inviting country inns and was the setting of the sentimental Henry Fonda–Katharine Hepburn film classic *On Golden Pond*. Hike the nature trails and see the gardens and animal enclosures of 230-acre **Squam Lakes Natural Science Center**, stopping for a lobster roll or fish and chips on the dock at Walter's Basin, before cutting east northeast through quaint **Sandwich** and returning through Tamworth to **Conway**.

Head west on the iconic 35-mile section of Rte 112 officially called the **Kancamagus Highway** but more commonly referred to by locals as "The Kanc." The designated National Scenic Byway climbs through a dazzling stretch of the White Mountains and is completely free of commercial development. During peak foliage (the first two weeks of October), you don't want to miss this road. But I strongly recommend driving it early on a weekday to avoid the inevitable traffic backups.

Of the route's several picturesque pull-offs, my favorite is the easy half-mile ramble to **Sabbaday Falls**. The road continues into the touristy but spirited ski towns of **Lincoln** and **North Woodstock**, where several attractions compete for the attention of kids and adults—the **Lost River Gorge and Boulder Caves** is my top pick. Head north on I-93, but after just a few miles something unexpected happens: the interstate narrows to just a single lane in either direction for 8 miles as it threads a deep valley within **Franconia Notch State Park**, which offers easy hikes through dramatic **Flume Gorge** and views of the granite cliff that before it collapsed under its own force in 2003 held the famous human-face-like profile known as the **Old Man of the Mountain**.

Up the road in tiny **Franconia**, stroll the flower gardens and peek inside the **Frost Place Museum**, which preserves the beloved American poet's 1915–20 place of residence, then order a pile of gingerbread flapjacks at Polly's Pancakes Parlor, a local tradition since the 1930s. Head northeast to **Bethlehem** with its appealing galleries and eateries, including the sunny beer garden Rek-Lis Brewing, then cut west into the once workaday mill town of **Littleton**, whose Main Street now blooms with appealing indie businesses, including the League of New Hampshire Craftsmen gallery, Crumb Bum bakery, and Just L mid-century antiques. End your tour with a wood-fired pizza and a stein of Indikator Doppelbock at handsome Schilling Beer Taproom, with its inviting terrace on the picturesque Ammonoosuc River.

Crossing the Connecticut River, with New Hampshire's White Mountains in your rearview mirror, Vermont's similarly spectacular **Green Mountains** appear before you. This 250-mile north-south range forms the state's central spine. Although only five of its peaks exceed 4000 ft, this is a strikingly beautiful mountainscape dotted with charming villages. Head west through what's known as the **Northeast Kingdom** to St Johnsbury (pop 7370), stopping—especially if you have a four-legged friend with you—at the unusual **Dog Mountain Home of Stephen Huneck Gallery**, a pet-friendly 150-acre oasis of leash-optional walking trails and peaceful ponds anchored by the farmhouse of the late author, wood carver, and furniture maker Stephen Huneck. The town's **Fairbanks Museum and Planetarium** is also excellent. Continue southwest on US 2 into **Montpelier** (pop 7250, the least populous state capital in the US) before turning northwest and paralleling the Winooski River (and I-89, a quicker option if time is short) to **Waterbury**, which is home to the headquarters of world-famous, tie-dye-embracing **Ben & Jerry's**. Yup, it's on the hokey side, but it's a lot of fun, too. You can tour the factory, pay homage to past favorites (remember Wavy Gravy and Dublin Mudslide?) in the Flavor Graveyard, and—naturally—order a few scoops to enjoy on the patio.

Follow Rte 100 north to one of Vermont's most scenic villages, **Stowe**, which abounds with both down-home and stylish lodgings, eateries, and boutiques, and is famous for skiing and mountain-biking on its namesake mountain. You can learn the history of the town's favorite pastime at the **Vermont Ski and Snowboard Museum** before driving north up one of the prettiest roads in the Green Mountains, Rte 108, which becomes an extremely tight (it's a single lane for a stretch) ribbon of blacktop through several miles of boulders and rocky outcroppings as it passes through **Smugglers Notch**. The road is closed in winter, at which time you can explore it on a snowmobile tour through nearby Smugglers' Notch Resort. In **Jeffersonville**, head west to I-89, and follow it south to Vermont's largest city, **Burlington** (pop 45,000), which hugs the eastern shore of the Northeast's largest freshwater body of water, Lake Champlain. The views from downtown's pretty **Waterfront Park** of New York's dramatic Adirondack Mountains are dazzling. This youthful, progressive college town (home to the **University of Vermont**) is a hot spot for farm-to-table dining, from the casual (American Flatbread) to the refined (Hen of the Woods). You'll find a number of popular shops, bars, and eateries on pedestrianized **Church Street.**

BURLINGTON, VT TO MANCHESTER, VT

South of Burlington, US 7 leads through a fertile valley that's long been known for dairy farming. Appropriately, the **Vermont Cheesemakers Festival** takes place here each August. Having more than once nibbled my way through this showcase of more than 40 artisanal cheese producers, I recommend attending on an empty stomach. It takes place at the redbrick coach barn of **Shelburne Farms**, a 1400-acre Victorian estate with lakeview grounds and gardens designed by Frederick Law Olmsted, an acclaimed dairy, a children's farmyard, a farm store, and lovely seasonal inn and restaurant. The town is also home to the excellent **Shelburne Museum**, a living-history campus with nearly 40 buildings moved here from around the state, plus an extensive collection of pre-automobile-age carriages. Farther south, explore the historic buildings, art galleries, storytelling programs, and agricultural operations of 148-acre **Clemmons Family Farm**, a highlight among the 22 sites on the state's African American Heritage Trail and one of New England's largest black-owned family farms.

SIDETRACK

If you have a few hours, or ideally a full day, make the 110-mile loop back into New Hampshire to explore stunning **Lake Sunapee** and the surrounding countryside. From Woodstock, drive east through **Quechee**, stopping to see the beautifully crafted contemporary glass of the **Simon Pearce** factory, which occupies a water-powered mill. The road soon crosses a bridge over oft-photographed **Quechee Gorge**—there's a state park and trails that lead down to the water's edge. Continue into **White River Junction**, a formerly industrial mill village that's become a hip food-and-art hub—the Turkish cafe Tuckerbox, brunch spot Piecemeal Pies, and coffeehouse-lifestyle boutique Juel Modern Apothecary are all standouts. Drive north to **Norwich**, which is worth a stop for its outstanding **Montshire Museum of Science** and a snack at **King Arthur Baking Company**, a shop and cafe that attract artisan bread bakers.

Cross the Connecticut River into **Hanover**, home to the Colonial-style campus of **Dartmouth College**. Stop to tour the diverse collections of the **Hood Museum of Art**. Next door, the **Hopkins Center for the Arts** bears a strong resemblance to the opera house at New York City's Lincoln Center—both were designed by Wallace K. Harrison. Zip down I-89 to New London, and then follow Rte 103A around the eastern side of pristine **Lake Sunapee**, a 6 sq mile alpine lake framed by a 3000 ft namesake mountain that's popular for hiking and skiing. Walk around the gardens and the 1890 mansion at **John Hay Estate at the Fells**, the former home of the distinguished statesman who served as President Lincoln's personal secretary. Head west through Newport, detouring down Rte 31 through rugged **Pillsbury State Park** to **Washington**, which—as a resident I'm admittedly biased—has one of the prettiest village greens in New England. Along the eastern banks of the Connecticut River, visit **Cornish**, the quaint hamlet where reclusive novelist J.D. Salinger resided. Here you can explore the gorgeous gardens, lawns, and historic buildings of **Saint-Gaudens National Historic Site**—the celebrated sculptor created many of his most memorable works here. The town is also known for its covered bridges, the longest of which—the 445 ft **Cornish-Windsor Bridge**, built in 1866—you can drive through back to Vermont. In **Windsor**, the **American Precision Museum**, occupies an 1846 factory and contains an exhaustive collection of early industrial machinery, tools, and inventions. It's about a 20-minute drive northwest back to Woodstock.

On your way into **Middlebury**, a classic New England village anchored by the verdant campus of prestigious **Middlebury College**, stop for a view of **Belden Falls** and a walk alongside Otter Creek via the easy **Trail Around Middlebury** loop, before enjoying a hoppy ale on the deck of Otter Creek Brewing or a crisp Pearsecco at renowned Woodchuck Cider House. You'll find several excellent art galleries downtown—the **Vermont Folklife Center** is especially interesting. Rte 125 zigzags east over the Green Mountains, offering several appealing places to hop out and stretch your legs, including **Texas Falls** and **Riley Bostwick Wildlife Management Center**. Head south through **Rochester** and **Bethel**, dropping by **La Garagista Farm and Winery** to sample expressive wines and ciders that have earned a cult following in this part of the world. A few miles south, **Woodstock** is one of Vermont's most bewitching small towns; gracious Colonial, Federal, and Victorian houses and upscale shops line the main thoroughfare and flank the elliptical town green, across from which the **Middle Covered Bridge** spans the curving Ottauquechee River. The late business magnate and conservationist Laurence Rockefeller and his family have played a significant role in preserving the town's appearance. He and his wife founded the venerable **Woodstock Inn** and also established the **Marsh-Billings-Rockefeller National Historical Park**, where you can tour the period-furnished mansion and surrounding 555 acres of gardens, grounds, and carriage paths where the Rockefellers resided. Across the street, explore the farmhouse, barns, and fields of one of the state's longest-operating farms at **Billings Farm and Museum**.

Head west on US 4 and Rte 100A to **Plymouth**, stopping to see the **Calvin Coolidge Historic Site**, the relatively modest home in which the 30th US president was raised and also took the oath of office (he was there visiting his family when his predecessor, Warren Harding, died). Follow Rte 100 on a scenic journey past **Okemo** ski area, through the picturesque villages of **Ludlow** and **Londonderry**, and then west past **Bromley** ski area into **Manchester**, which is made up of two main villages: **Manchester Center** has a more modern feel, in part because its downtown abounds with factory outlet stores, but there are some independent gems here, including Northshire Bookstore. A few miles down Rte 7A, past the headquarters of the respected outdoor gear company Orvis, **Manchester Village** contains an impressive historic district of beautifully restored, mostly Colonial buildings, including the famously posh **Equinox** resort. The **American Museum of Fly Fishing** is filled with memorabilia and exhibits that relate to the sport that's so central to rural New England life, and just south of town, the region's must-see is **Hildene**, the imposing early-20th-century summer retreat of Robert Todd Lincoln, son of Abe Lincoln and a future statesman and railroad executive in his own right. The grounds, which include both formal gardens and a boardwalk through peaceful wetlands flanking the Battenkill River, are a highlight. On your way south, it's worth paying the $20 toll to make the 5.2-mile drive up beautiful Skyline Drive atop 3855 ft **Mt Equinox**—the views are astounding.

MANCHESTER, VT TO LITCHFIELD, CT

As you continue south, take slower and more scenic Rte 7A rather than US 7. You'll enter **Arlington**, an easygoing village that looks as though it belongs on the cover of a magazine. In fact, on more than one occasion, it appeared on one. The legendary illustrator Norman Rockwell lived in Arlington from 1939 to 1953 and created dozens of his famously wholesome, all-American paintings and *Saturday Evening Post* magazine covers here, often enlisting locals as models. At the rustic **Sugar Shack** which sells maple syrup and candies, you can view dozens of reproductions of his works and other memorabilia about his life. Continue down toward **Bennington**, where in the distance you'll spy an obelisk rising high above the treetops. This is the **Bennington Battle Monument**, a 306-ft tower built in 1891 to honor the town's favorable role in the Revolutionary War. You ascend an elevator to the top for sweeping views of the countryside, including the stately campus of **Bennington College**, which is worth a walk-through to admire its striking buildings and contemporary art installations. This quaint Colonial village is also home to the engaging **Bennington Museum**.

Crossing into Massachusetts, you enter the Berkshires, which are geographically an extension of the Green Mountains but culturally—and artistically—feel more like an extension of New York City and Boston. **Williamstown**, yet another dapper New England college town, offers a good introduction to the region's impressive arts scene, with its exceptional **Williams College Museum of Art** and **Clark Art Institute**—the latter stands out for its stunning modern addition designed by acclaimed architect Tadao Ando, and its enormous windows overlooking the surrounding greenery. From June through August you can attend the prestigious **Williamstown Theatre Festival**. A few miles east, **North Adams** had been a somewhat prosaic mill town that fell on hard times with the closure in 1985 of the massive Sprague Electric plant. Fast-forward to 1999, and this industrial compound's beautiful redbrick buildings were transformed into the Massachusetts Museum of Contemporary Art, or **Mass MoCA**. I've visited this incredible 280,000 sq ft venue on several occasions and I'm pretty sure I still haven't seen every gallery—it's truly one of the Northeast's greatest architectural and arts marvels. Adjoining the campus are several excellent eateries, including A-OK Berkshire Barbecue, Tunnel City Coffee, and Bright Ideas Brewing. As you venture south on Rte 8, you can drive or hike to the 3491 ft summit of the state's highest peak, **Mt Greylock**, which is crowned with the striking Massachusetts Veterans War Memorial Tower.

Continue down through **Pittsfield** (pop 43,000), the region's largest community, which is notable for its **Pittsfield Museum** and **Arrowhead**, the home of *Moby Dick* author Herman Melville, but if you had to choose one thing to see in the area, I suggest **Hancock Shaker Village**, which is one of the most interesting of a handful of Northeastern US communities from this nearly obsolete religious sect that's open to the public. Now a living history museum, this compound of late-18th- and 19th-century buildings, including a striking round stone barn, presents arts and crafts demonstrations and is surrounded by lush gardens. Farther south, the affluent resort community of **Lenox** has drawn generations of well-heeled families, who built lavish summer estates throughout town and in the surrounding countryside, especially during the Gilded Age. Some of these are open for tours, including **The Mount**, where American novelist Edith Wharton resided from 1902 to 1911, and **Ventfort Hall Mansion and Gilded Age Museum**. Lenox is best known for two seminal performing arts venues, **Shakespeare and Company**—which presents plays year-round by the Bard in a mix of indoor and outdoor theaters—and **Tanglewood**, an acclaimed 200-acre summer performance space that's been the summer home of the Boston Symphony Orchestra since 1937 but also hosts top pop, jazz, and folk acts. The cultural riches have imbued the town with a wealth of romantic, if spendy, restaurants, country inns, and spa and health retreats—the most famous being **Canyon Ranch**, **Kripalu Center**, and **Miraval**.

Continue south through **Stockbridge** to visit **Chesterwood**—the turn-of-the-20th-century estate of sculptor Daniel Chester French—and the **Norman Rockwell Museum** (the artist lived in this town the final 25 years of his life), where you can visit his relocated former studio. The village is anchored by the **Red Lion Inn**, a rambling if idiosyncratic hotel that dates back to 1773, and it's the inspiration for Arlo Guthrie's beloved, nearly 19-minute folk song "Alice's Restaurant,"

Mass MoCA, North Adams

which was based on an actual (now defunct) local eatery. Pop inside the homey Lost Lamb cafe for a latte and an almond croissant, then follow US 7 down through the mountains to **Great Barrington**, a fashionable weekend getaway of urbane eateries and fine shops that's equidistant from both Boston and Manhattan. While in town, duck into SoCo Creamery for a scoop of banana brownie ice cream.

Follow Rte 41 south to Salisbury, in the northwestern corner of Connecticut's **Litchfield Hills**, a warren of quaint villages, dense forests, and small family farms that—like the neighboring Hudson River Valley—is highly popular with New Yorkers; celebrities with homes here include Meryl Streep, Seth Meyer, Patti Lupone, and Dustin Hoffman. Continue through charming **Salisbury** and rejoin US 7, following it down through **Cornwall**, stopping for a photo of the scenic, single-lane **West Cornwall Covered Bridge**, which was built in 1841 and crosses the serene Housatonic River. Continue through **Kent**, then along the rippling shores of **Lake Waramaug**—whose pastoral scenery reminds some of Switzerland—and into **New Preston** and **Washington**, villages that abound with fine antiques shops, stylish boutiques, and renowned art galleries. Turn northeast up through the region's cultural and spiritual heart, **Litchfield**, stopping for a hike amid the lush wetlands, boardwalks, and bird-watching platforms of the 4000-acre **White Memorial Conservation Center**, with its excellent natural history exhibits.

BEST EATS

- **Furbish Brew House** With a laid-back dining room and ample seating on a brick terrace with lake views, this casual Rangeley eatery specializes in well-crafted beers, wood-fired pizzas, and slow-smoked baby back ribs. 207-864-5847.

- **Thompson House Eatery** This farmhouse restaurant in Jackson is one of the few White Mountains restaurants I'll plan an entire weekend around. The locally sourced menu might feature braised chicken ragout with black truffles or miso-glazed salmon with stir-fry soba noodles. 603-383-9341, thethompsonhouseeatery.com.

- **Tim-Bir Alley** Savor superb farm-to-table fare at this cozy brick-walled bistro in Littleton. Espresso-rubbed steaks and seared scallops are standouts. 603-444-6142, travelers-gourmet.com.

- **Cork** Offering a sleek and airy contrast to Stowe Village's traditional taverns and pubs, this modern wine shop and restaurant is a fun place to try new vinos alongside an array of creative foods. 802-760-6143, corkvt.com.

- **Honey Road** James Beard semifinalist Cara Chigazola-Tobin presents boldly flavored Middle Eastern dishes—Vermont quail with date labne, lamb kofta with figs and hazelnuts—at this smart-casual Burlington bistro. 802-497-2145, honeyroadrestaurant.com.

- **Worthy Kitchen** Snag a comfy wooden booth or patio table at this farm-to-table roadhouse in Woodstock. There's an extensive beer selection to pair with hearty portions of Vermont cheddar mac-and-cheese and buttermilk-fried chicken. 802-457-7281, worthyvermont.com.

- **Silver Fork** Set in a late-1890s building that formerly housed Manchester Village's public library, this art-filled restaurant features deftly crafted New England cuisine with a few Caribbean twists, like Creole shrimp mofongo. 802-768-8444, thesilverforkvt.com.

- **Mezze Bistro** Following a visit to the Williamstown Theatre Festival, tuck into plates of refined contemporary American fare. Butternut squash schnitzel, and duck ragout over orecchiette pasta are among the highlights. 413-458-0123, mezzerestaurant.com.

- **Nudel** This intimate Lenox storefront serves international small plates that rely heavily on local produce and meats. Start with kimchi noodles with peanut sauce, followed by pan-seared Arctic char with cucumber-seaweed salad and sriracha aioli. 413-551-7183, nudelrestaurant.com

- **Arethusa al Tavolo** On the main road between New Preston and Litchfield, this flagship restaurant centered around a thriving dairy farm serves sensational seasonal fare. Check out neighbors Arethusa Farm Dairy for farm-to-cone ice cream and Arethusa A Mano bakery for heavenly pastries. 860-567-0043, arethusaaltavolo.com.

BEST SLEEPS

- **Blair Hill Inn** The fanciest lodging in interior Maine, this 10-room Relais & Chateaux boutique hotel in Greenville sits high on a grassy lawn with panoramic views of Moosehead Lake. There's a spa and a fantastic farm-to-table restaurant. 207-695-0224, blairhill.com.

- **Rangeley Inn** More than half of the 27 rooms in this sky-blue Victorian inn have private decks with views of Rangeley's Haley Pond, and there's a convivial tavern. 207-864-3341, therangeleyinn.com.

- **Glen House** From many rooms and the terraces of this eco-friendly boutique hotel at the start of the Mt Washington Auto Road, you can behold New England's highest summit. Start the day with a lobster Benedict in Notch Grille. 603-466-3420, theglenhouse.com.

- **Inn at Thorn Hill & Spa** A standout among several inviting—and cushy—country inns in Jackson, this 18-unit 1890s property offers luxurious spa treatments and rarefied cuisine. 603-383-4242, innatthornhill.com.

- **Pickering House** This restored 1813 yellow farmhouse in Wolfeboro offers Lake Winnipesaukee's most urbane accommodations. The adjacent Pavilion bistro serves artfully prepared seasonal cuisine. 603-569-6948, pickeringhousewolfeboro.com.

- **Sunset Hill House** Soak up sweeping views of the White Mountains from the terrace and pool of this stately 1880 hotel. A popular nine-hole golf course adjoins this inviting inn up the road from Franconia Notch State Park. 603-823-7244, thesunsethillhouse.com.

- **Trapp Family Lodge** Established in the 1950 by the Austrian family that inspired *The Sound of Music,* this festive chalet-style resort rests on more than 2000 verdant acres between Stowe village and ski resort. Myriad family-friendly activities are offered. 802-253-8511, trappfamily.com.

- **Hotel Vermont** Burlington's most sophisticated lodging overlooks two leafy parks and offers commanding views of Lake Champlain. A fireplace warms the high-ceilinged lobby, and James Beard-recognized Hen of the Wood restaurant is next door. 802-651-0080, hotelvt.com.

- **Woodstock Inn** With an enviable setting on Woodstock's classic village green and a spectacular LEED-certified 10,000 sq ft spa, this grand 142-room resort offers downright plush accommodations, four restaurants, and a slew of activities. 888-338-2745, woodstockinn.com.

- **Kimpton Taconic Hotel** Although it has a beautiful Colonial design, this three-story boutique hotel with a dramatic wraparound veranda abounds with contemporary comforts a heated plunge pool and tech-savvy rooms. Enjoy dinner in the inviting Copper Grouse tavern. 802-362-0147, taconichotel.com.

- **Porches Inn** Imaginatively fashioned out of a row of restored Victorian mill workers' homes across the river from Mass MoCA, the 47 rooms have a playfully modern aesthetic, with vintage furniture and contemporary art. 413-664-0400, porches.com.

- **Blantyre** This fabulously Gatsby-esque redbrick castle was built on a Lenox hilltop in 1901 and is now an opulent inn with 23 rooms, plus a restaurant helmed by Michelin-starred chef Daniel Boulod. 844-881-0104, blantyre.com.

- **White Hart Inn** Built in 1806 on Salisbury's town green, this warmly appointed 16-room property features an impressive collection of modern artwork and a fine restaurant and casual cafe. 860-435-0030, whitehartinn.com.

- **Winvian** To end your journey with a truly memorable splurge, book one of the 18 cottages on this Litchfield Hills estate with a stellar restaurant and spa. Each accommodation has its own theme and design, from log cabin to treehouse—there's even a suite fashioned out of a 1968 Sikorsky helicopter. 860-567-9600, winvian.com.

CAMPING

Interior New England is a camping and hiking paradise, especially in northern Vermont, New Hampshire, and Maine. Some beautiful locales in the latter include Katahdin Stream in Baxter State Park, Moosehead Family Campground in Greenville, and Rangeley Lake State Park. Across the border in the White Mountains, consider Crawford Notch near Mt Washington and Lafayette Place in Franconia Notch State Park, while Long Island Bridge has a gorgeous setting on Lake Winnipesaukee. Smugglers Notch near Stowe and North Beach in Burlington are top choices in northern Vermont, and Quechee/Pine Valley KOA is a favorite near Woodstock. Farther south, consider Mt Greylock and October Mountain State Forest in the Berkshires, and Housatonic Meadows or Lake Waramaug State Park in the Litchfield Hills.

Top Saint-Gaudens National Historic Site, Cornish
Middle Fall foliage in Washington
Bottom Pickering House Inn, Wolfeboro

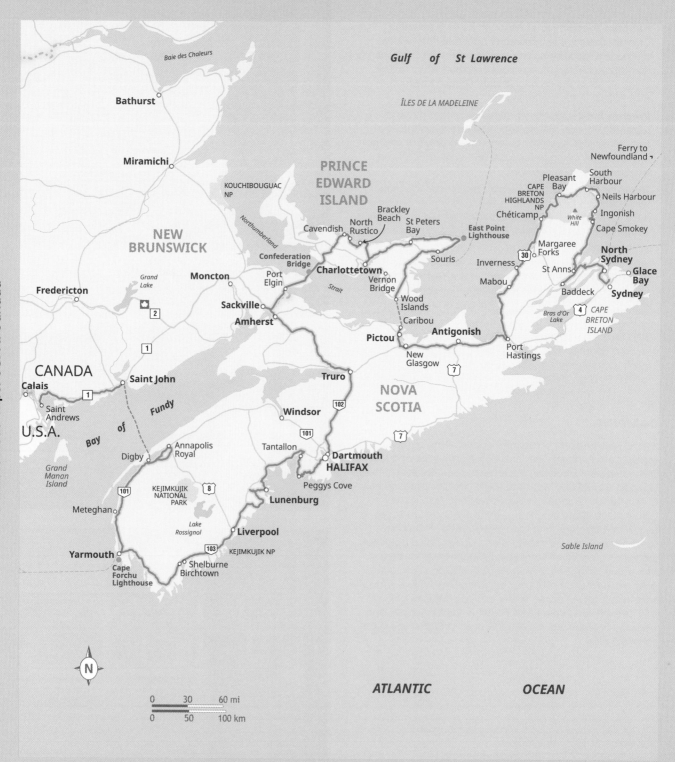

Baie des Chaleurs

Gulf of St Lawrence

ÎLES DE LA MADELEINE

Bathurst

Miramichi

Ferry to
Newfoundland

KOUCHIBOUGUAC
NP

PRINCE
EDWARD
ISLAND

Pleasant
Bay

South
Harbour

CAPE
BRETON
HIGHLANDS
NP

Neils Harbour

NEW
BRUNSWICK

Chéticamp

Ingonish

White
Hill

Cape Smokey

Cavendish

North
Rustico

Brackley
Beach

St Peters
Bay

East Point
Lighthouse

Confederation
Bridge

Charlottetown

Souris

Margaree
Forks

Inverness

St Anns

NORTH
SYDNEY

Fredericton

Grand
Lake

Moncton

Port
Elgin

Vernon
Bridge

Mabou

Baddeck

Glace
Bay

Sydney

Northumberland

Strait

Wood
Islands

2

Sackville

Caribou

Bras d'Or
Lake

CAPE
BRETON
ISLAND

4

Amherst

Pictou

New
Glasgow

Antigonish

1

Port
Hastings

CANADA

Saint John

Truro

7

Calais

Fundy

NOVA
SCOTIA

Saint
Andrews

Bay

Windsor

102

U.S.A.

of

101

7

Grand
Manan
Island

Digby

Annapolis
Royal

Tantallon

Dartmouth
HALIFAX

8

KEJIMKUJIK
NATIONAL
PARK

Peggys Cove

Lunenburg

Sable Island

Meteghan

Lake
Rossignol

Liverpool

KEJIMKUJIK NP

103

Yarmouth

Shelburne
Birchtown

Cape
Forchu
Lighthouse

ATLANTIC   OCEAN

N

0   30   60 mi

0   50   100 km

The Canadian Maritimes 🍁

On this coastal journey through Canada's three Maritime Provinces—New Brunswick, Nova Scotia, and Prince Edward Island—the blend of pristine natural scenery and colorful art, music, food, and nautical history is intoxicating.

HOW LONG?

9–10 days; add an extra day or two to explore more of Halifax, Prince Edward Island, and Cape Breton Island.

WHEN TO GO

Like Quebec and New England, the Maritimes are a classic summer and early autumn destination. Come earlier for the sunny beaches and verdant parks and gardens, and then enjoy the colorful foliage from late September through October. Chilly winter has its charms, plus lower prices and fewer crowds, but the PEI–Nova Scotia ferry shuts down, as do a number of beachside inns and restaurants. Spring is a mixed bag, with wind, rain, and fluctuating temperatures, but by mid-May the region's gardens begin to burst with color.

NEED TO KNOW

The two ferry crossings on this itinerary can be bypassed by longer road routes. Services are more limited in remote areas like Cape Breton Island during the off-season; keep your gas tank topped and check hours or make reservations at restaurants.

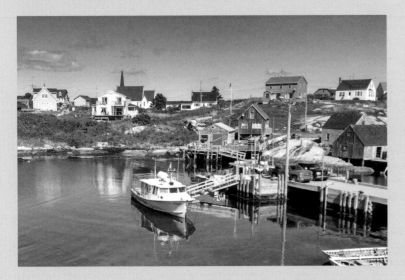

→ Distances
Total distance, one-way: 1150 mi (1851 km)
- St Andrews, NB to Annapolis Royal, NS: 135 mi (217 km)
- Annapolis Royal, NS to Halifax, NS: 325 mi (523 km)
- Halifax, NS to Wood Islands, PEI: 350 mi (563 km)
- Wood Islands, PEI to Sydney, NS: 335 mi (539 km)

ⓘ Daytime Temperatures
January: 25-30°F (-4 - -1°C)
July: 72-75°F (22-24°C)

ⓘ More information
- St Andrews tourism, standrewsbythesea.ca
- St John tourism, discoversaintjohn.com
- Yarmouth and Acadian Shores tourism, yarmouthandacadianshores.com
- Halifax tourism, discoverhalifaxns.com
- Prince Edward Island tourism, tourismpei.com
- Cape Breton Island tourism, cbisland.com

👁 SNAPSHOT

You're never more than 30 miles from the sea on this relaxing journey, mostly on rural two-lane roads, through Canada's friendly and fascinating Atlantic provinces. The landscape is full of surprises: the world's highest tides in the Bay of Fundy, dramatic red rock cliffs on the north coast of Prince Edward Island, and spectacular rocky promontories and lush forests in Cape Breton Highlands. In even the smallest villages, you can find delicious fresh seafood—lobsters are more abundant, and cheaper, here than in Maine. And opportunities to visit ancient lighthouses, colorful maritime museums, and eclectic art galleries abound.

ST ANDREWS, NB TO ANNAPOLIS ROYAL, NS

St Andrews has been a popular getaway for sailors, golfers, and fishing enthusiasts since the early 1880s. The town lies just over a mile across the St Croix River from Robbinston, ME, and it's less than a 30-minute drive from the nearest official border crossing between Calais, ME and St Stephen, NB. Activity in town revolves around the harborfront—colorful shops, seafood restaurants, and pubs line Water Street, and fishing charters and whale-watching cruises depart from **Market Wharf**. At the west end of Water Street, have a stroll through **Centennial Park** before visiting the adjacent **St Andrews Blockhouse National Historic Site**, where you can tour a wooden barracks and storehouse that dates back to the War of 1812.

Drive about an hour east to **St John** (pop 71,000), a colorful Colonial port city that bustles with cargo ships year-round and cruise ships from May through October. With a compact, peninsular downtown and narrow streets lined with Colonial and Victorian buildings, it's a great city for a stroll. Visit the vendors in spirited **St John City Market**, the country's long-running farmers market—pick up a breakfast sandwich or a bagel at historic Slocum & Ferris or a latte at Java Moose and enjoy it on a bench overlooking the gardens in **King's Square** or down the hill on the **Boardwalk** facing the St John River. Then stop by the **New Brunswick Museum**, which has well-curated collections of art and history, but the highlight is the display of whale skeletons and models. The city sits on the north bank of the **Bay of Fundy**, a huge estuary that separates New Brunswick from Nova Scotia; its greatest claim is its high tides—the range is more than 50 ft in places, which is about 15 times the globe's average range. One of the best places to see this phenomenon is the **Reversing Falls Rapids**, where the St John River meets the bay. When the tide rises, the sheer force causes the river to roil and swirl backward and up a series of cascades; at low tide, the river flows back down into the sea. You can see it well from the gravel trail at **Fallsview Park** and from the **Skywalk** observation deck on the west side of **Reversing Falls Bridge**. A little beyond the bridge, hilly **Wolastoq Park** offers great views of the waterfront and the city skyline and is dotted with carved wooden statues of prominent local figures (and one very large beaver). A few blocks away go inside the **Carleton Martello Tower**, one of nine stone fortresses still standing in Canada—this one dates to 1813.

To reach the scenic southwestern coast of Nova Scotia, you have two options: drive 6.5 hours around the Bay of Fundy via Moncton and Truro, or take a 2.5-hour ferry trip across the bay to Digby, NS. If you can afford it (the fare is around C$225 one-way in summer for a vehicle and two passengers), I recommend the ferry crossing—it's a relaxing, beautiful journey. Once you're across the bay, drive a half hour northeast to **Annapolis Royal**. You might never guess from visiting this quiet riverfront settlement of around 500 that it served as Nova Scotia's capital until 1749 (when Halifax took on the honor) and that it's been the site of more military altercations than any place in North America. You can learn about the area's topsy-turvy history at **Port-Royal National Historic Site**, which features a replica of France's first permanent settlement in the New World, and at **Fort Anne National Historic Site**, which the British established in 1629 to defend against the French. Other draws include the lush **Annapolis Royal Historic Gardens**, a 17-acre spread that's set around a re-created 17th-century Acadian cottage, and the hugely popular **Annapolis Royal Farmers & Traders Market**, where more than 100 vendors exhibit on and Wednesday mornings during the warmer months.

ANNAPOLIS ROYAL, NS TO HALIFAX, NS

Backtrack for a look around historic **Digby**, with its compact and walkable village center and several good waterfront lunch spots. From here it's a six-hour drive around the southwest end of the Nova Scotia peninsula to Halifax, but these scenic coastal towns contain enough distractions to add several more hours to your adventure, especially if you detour down around the many craggy necks and peninsulas. Shipbuilding and fishing were central to the early prosperity of many communities, and these industries remain important in many places. The Mi'kmaq Nation inhabited the region for centuries before they were dispossessed by groups of French Acadians, New England Planters, and American Loyalists who had sided with the British Crown. Among the latter were former slaves who fled and served alongside British forces in exchange for their emancipation. To learn more about this important chapter in Canadian history, visit the **Black Loyalist Heritage Society** in **Birchtown**, near Shelburne.

This coastal road, most of it along Hwy 3, is also known as the **Nova Scotia Lighthouse Route**—quite a few of these historic structures still operate. Popular ones include **Cape Saint Mary Lighthouse Park** near Meteghan and the photogenic **Cape Forchu Lighthouse** near Yarmouth. Try creamy seafood chowder in the park's Keeper's Kitchen, which has splendid ocean views. **Yarmouth** (pop 6600) is one of the most prominent and picturesque towns along the drive. During its late-19th-century heyday, it was one of North America's leading centers of shipbuilding, and today it's the terminus of ferries to Bar Harbor, ME. You'll find several small history museums in the compact downtown, which overlooks pretty Yarmouth Harbor, including a branch of Halifax's **Art Gallery of Nova Scotia**. As you continue east, stop by Tusket Falls Brewing for a refreshing Pina Colada Gose and a fried chicken sandwich or thin-crust pizza. As you continue up the coast check out the 17-acre **Historic Acadian Village of Nova Scotia** in Lower West Pubnico, the **Dory Shop Museum** in the quaint Colonial harbor town of **Shelburne**, and the Seaside unit of **Kejimkujik National Park** in Port Joli.

About an hour before you get to Halifax, you'll come to **Lunenburg**. With its steep hills, colorfully painted 18th- and 19th-century houses, and vibrant gallery and dining scene, this spirited village flanks a pair of sheltered harbors and has been designated a UNESCO World Heritage site. Spend a couple of hours touring the outstanding **Fisheries Museum of the Atlantic**, which occupies a historic seafood-processing building on the harbor—you can hop aboard venerable old ships, visit a small aquarium, and learn the stories of the generations of Mi'kmaq people and Europeans who have relied on the bounty of these waters. Eclectic galleries and smart boutiques line the narrow lanes of **Old Town**. Fans of fine spirits should check out **Ironworks Distillery**, which produces first-rate rums and an enticing rhubarb liqueur inside an ancient blacksmith shop.

When you get to **Tantallon**, turn right and follow the eastern shore of **St Margarets Bay** down to famous **Peggy's Cove**, whose tranquil harbor, stately red-and-white lighthouse, colorful lobster boats, and massive coastal boulders have attracted painters, photographers, and sightseers for nearly 200 years. You'll find a handful of art galleries in town (my favorite is the amusingly named co-op, **Hags on the Hill**) and a few casual seafood eateries. A terrific way to gain a different perspective on the landscape is to take a sightseeing excursion or a longer and more in-depth puffin- and seal-watching cruise with **Peggy's Cove Boat Tours**.

The largest city and cultural polestar of Canada's Maritime Provinces, **Halifax** (pop 350,000) is a hilly mixture of old and new. The city sits along the west side of a picturesque harbor, across from the smaller city of **Dartmouth**. An excellent place to start a tour of the city is the superb **Maritime Museum of the Atlantic**, which anchors downtown's bustling Waterfront. Here you can learn more about two major catastrophic events that shaped the city—the

Peggy's Point Lighthouse *Previous* Peggy's Cove

devastating Halifax Explosion of 1917 and sinking of the *Titanic*. The ship sank in 1912 about 700 miles southeast of Halifax, and the city became the final port of call of those passengers who died—121 victims are buried in a special section of **Fairview Lawn Cemetery** in the city's **West End**. Outside the museum, a broad wooden boardwalk extends for about 2.5 miles along the harbor, passing hotels, beer gardens, seafood restaurants, ferry terminals, sculptures and murals, the **Halifax Seaport Farmers' Market**, and the superb **Canadian Museum of Immigration at Pier 21**. It's inside a building that processed nearly 1 million immigrants from 1928 through 1971, and thoughtful exhibits share their artifacts and first-person accounts.

There's a good cache of dining options near where Bishop St meets the waterfront, including Sea Smoke for Asian fusion, the Bicycle Thief for modern Italian, and Alexander Keith's for craft beer and pub fare. From the harbor, walk through downtown—stopping to admire the extensive and eclectic collection at the **Art Gallery of Nova Scotia**—and continue up the hill to tour the **Halifax Citadel National Historic Site**, a star-shaped rampart built in the early 19th century. Then stroll through the 16-acre Victorian-era **Halifax Public Gardens**.

HALIFAX, NS TO WOOD ISLANDS, PEI

The 3 hour drive from Halifax to Prince Edward Island (PEI) is straightforward and pleasant if not particularly exciting. You can break things up a bit with a brief stop at the **Fundy Discovery Site** in **Truro**, which sits near the end of Cobequid Bay, one of the easternmost arms of the Bay of Fundy. Next to this small visitor center, the path along the Salmon River is one of the better places in the province to view the Bay of Fundy's dramatic tidal bore. A little beyond **Amherst**, I suggest detouring slightly into New Brunswick for a walk around peaceful **Sackville Wildfowl Park**, a 55-acre preserve laced with trails and boardwalks that's ideal for viewing migratory birds. Just off the main park trail in the cute village of **Sackville**, quirky Black Duck Cafe serves locally sourced fare.

Roughly 45 minutes north, cross the **Confederation Bridge** to **Prince Edward Island**. Prior to the 1997 construction of this 8 mile long structure (it's Canada's longest), you could reach PEI only by ferry. This 2190 sq mile island—it's about one-sixth the size of Vancouver Island—was home to the Mi'kmaq People before being colonized by the French from 1605 until the Treaty of Paris in 1763, at which time it transferred to the British. In 1873, six years after Canadian Federation, PEI officially joined the country as its seventh—and by far smallest—province. Known for its beautiful, windswept beaches and dramatic red cliffs as well as abundant seafood (PEI mussels and Malpeque oysters are famous worldwide), the island also has deep associations with author Lucy Maud Montgomery's beloved *Anne of Green Gables* novels. From the bridge it's a 40-minute drive to **Cavendish**,

Lunch at the Chowder House, Neils Harbour, Cape Breton Island

the epicenter of *Anne of Green Gables* tourism. Here you'll find many family-friendly attractions—a Ripley's Believe It Or Not museum, the Avonlea shopping village (lots of gift stores and candy shops), a water park, and various amusements—that delight young and old fans of the books. The top draw is **Green Gables Heritage Place**, an 1830s farmhouse that belonged to relatives and neighbors of Montgomery and that served as the fictional home of the young protagonist, Anne Shirley; it's been expanded and restored so its rooms look as the book depicts them. The property also includes a new interpretive center and the stone foundation of the author's childhood home.

But Cavendish has other charms as well, including a significant section of shoreline that's part of **Prince Edward Island National Park**. You can access **Cavendish Beach** and enjoy sweeping water views from the sea cliffs by following the **Gulf Shore Parkway** east to the pretty **North Rustico**, which has its own pretty beach and a bustling harbor and marina. To explore more of PEI National Park, follow Hwy 6 east to **Brackley Beach**, which has a handful of noteworthy diversions, including the **Great Canadian Soap Co.**, a family-run goat farm and natural-soap producer that also sells goat's milk cheeses and ice cream, and the **Dunes Studio Gallery & Cafe**, a beautifully designed timber-and-glass arts and crafts gallery. Head north back into the park to walk along the sweeping sands of Brackley Beach, drive another segment of picturesque Gulf Shore Parkway, and explore the dunes beneath **Covehead Harbour Lighthouse**.

Less than a half-hour south you'll enter PEI's capital, **Charlottetown**, a friendly and walkable city of around 40,000 that overlooks a protected harbor. It's a fairly easy place to explore in a half day, starting downtown at the **Confederation Centre of the Arts**, which contains a well-respected art gallery, the main city library, and a performance venue that hosts concerts and shows, including a musical adaptation in the summer of—you guessed it—*Anne of Green Gables*. Along **Great George Street** and pedestrianized **Victoria Row** you'll find several inviting eateries, galleries, and shops. Save room for dessert at the beloved local ice cream shop, Cows. Continue down to the waterfront for a ramble through **Victoria Park**, the city's largest green space, then continue east along the boardwalk, stopping to admire the period furnishings and gardens of **Beaconsfield Historic House**, an imposing painted lady Victorian built for an affluent shipbuilder in 1877. End up again by the water at breezy **Confederation Landing** and **Peakes Quay Marina**, enjoying lunch or an early dinner at adjacent **Founders' Food Hall**, whose vendors include Datcha for French Caribbean dishes, Famous Peppers Fiamma for pizza, and Receiver Coffee (in the historic Brass Shop building) for espresso drinks and Monte Cristo sandwiches. Charlottetown also has a lively pub scene that's particularly popular with students from the University of PEI; Upstreet Craft Brewing and Gahan House Pub turn out well-crafted ales and good food.

If you're short on time, head south from Charlottetown to Wood Islands to continue by ferry back to Nova Scotia, but my recommendation is to make a loop around the rural and photogenic eastern side of the island. This trip adds three to six hours to your journey, depending on how much you stop and linger. Follow Hwy 2 northeast up to **St Peters Bay**, a tiny village at the end of a calm harbor—casual Rick's Fish & Chips is a great lunch stop along the way. Take Hwy 313 around the other side of the bay to **Greenwich Interpretation Centre**, the main museum and visitor center of PEI National Park. It's filled with engaging exhibits on the island's natural history, including the high dunes you can explore in this easternmost section of the park. Continue around to the tip of the island to oft-photographed **East Point Lighthouse**, a 64 ft with artifacts, photos, and other items about its past on each of the building's five floors. As you return along the south shore, pull off to stroll the sugary-white sands of **Basin Head Provincial Park**, which has an interpretive center and a small fisheries museum overlooking the channel that bisects the beach. Other fun stops include the 1880 lighthouse in **Souris**, the famed FireWorks Feast farm tour (reserve this well in advance) and dinner at the romantic **Inn at Bay Fortune**, and **Roma at Three Rivers National Historic Sit**. Here you can enjoy a traditional meal, prepared using an ancient stone oven, at a 1730s trading post that's now a park and living history museum.

WOOD ISLANDS, PEI TO SYDNEY, NS

At the southeast end of PEI, from May through December, you can continue your journey by ferry in **Wood Islands**—if you have some extra time, walk around enchanting **Wood Islands Provincial Park**, with its stately 1876 lighthouse and museum. The ferry ride to **Caribou**, on central Nova Scotia's north shore, takes about 75 minutes. In winter, when the ferry can't run because of ice in the Northumberland Strait, you can drive here—allow a little over three hours from Charlottetown. As you head south on Hwy 106, stop briefly for a look around the charming harborfront of **Pictou**, a historic town with a scenic wharf, a handful of small

museums, and one fantastic cookie bakery, Mrs. MacGregor's Shortbreads. It's a 90-minute drive east to reach the apex of spectacular natural scenery in the Maritimes: **Cape Breton Island**. At nearly 4000 sq miles, it makes up about one-fifth of the province's total land area. Separated from the rest of Nova Scotia by a not-quite-mile-wide causeway, it doesn't exactly feel like an island—it takes only a minute to drive here via the Canso Causeway Bridge (the **Nova Scotia Visitor Information Centre** in **Port Hastings** is a useful resource). But with its spectacular sea cliffs, friendly villages, and well-preserved Mi'kmaq, Scottish Gaelic, Irish, and Acadian heritage, Cape Breton feels special. You should allow at least a couple of days to see the main sights, but a week on this enchanted isle wouldn't be too much, especially if you're fond of hiking.

Indeed, this is a nature lover's milieu. The most beautiful (northern) section of the island is encircled by one of Canada's most spectacular scenic routes, the **Cabot Trail** (Hwy 30), a 185-mile loop that mostly follows the coast and passes through the heart of majestic Cape Breton Highlands National Park. From Port Hastings, drive up Hwy 19, known as the **Ceilidh Trail** in honor of this area's vibrant Scottish roots, as it curves along the island's west coast for 70 miles through the quaint towns of **Mabou** and **Inverness**. The latter is known for its stunning windswept beachfront—order a crab-cake sandwich at the Inverness Beach Hut Eatery—and the **Cabot Cape Breton** and **Cabot Cliffs** golf courses, a pair of dazzling Scottish links–style tracks that regularly rank among the best in the world. The Ceilidh Trail ends in tiny **Margaree Forks**, where it joins with the Cabot Trail. Before you continue up the coast, I recommend a brief detour east through the lush Margaree River Valley along a gorgeous inland section of the Cabot Trail. After about 6 miles, stop by delightful **Margaree Salmon Museum**, with its informative exhibits devoted to the delicious fish that's a staple in both Scottish and Atlantic Canadian kitchens.

Backtrack to Margaree Forks and follow the Cabot Trail up the coast to **Cheticamp**, the largest of Cape Breton's francophone communities, with about 3000 residents; it's a good place to stock up on groceries, gas, and other supplies before entering the national park. Serving as both a cultural center and a unique museum dedicated to the town's Acadian heritage, **Les Trois Pignons** also showcases a craft for which this town has earned international acclaim: hooked rugs. The galleries display hundreds of both historic and contemporary examples of these detailed tapestries that often depict famous people, places, and stories. Nearby you can feast on

traditional local dishes—Fricot Acadien (a hearty chicken-potato stew), salt cod gratin—in the waterfront dining room of L'abri Restaurant and Bar. The Cabot Trail soon enters the western side of **Cape Breton Highlands National Park**, a 366 sq mile marvel of emerald woodlands, plunging canyons, and sheer cliffs overlooking the south entrance to the Gulf of St Lawrence—it's also where you'll find Nova Scotia's highest point, 1750 ft White Hill. Stop to pick up trail maps at the park's **Chéticamp Visitor Center** and to set out on a hike. The 5.6-mile **Acadian Trail** is a rigorous loop past a dramatic waterfall and offers outstanding scenery, but if you have time for only one hike on this side of the park, make it the 6-mile **Skyline Trail Loop**. On my last ramble along this windy promontory, we saw moose and coyotes, and the views were my favorite of any place in Nova Scotia. The boardwalk staircase leads down to an ocean overlook that's an amazing place to watch the sunset. Nearby, the .3-mile **Bog Trail** is an easy, family-friendly boardwalk trek through a highland bog— it's a favorite for birdwatching.

The adventure continues to the village of **Pleasant Bay**, where the Rusty Anchor serves good burgers and seafood on a deck overlooking the water and the **Whale Interpretive Center** provides an interesting overview of the 16 species of these magnificent mammals that inhabit the waters off Cape Breton. The Cabot Trail then turns inland and crosses a mountainous section of park. When you see water again at **South Harbour**, turn left and drive to the **White Point Trailhead** for a mostly level 1.5-mile out-and-back hike to a promontory overlooking the island's eastern shore. Follow the road down to **Neils Harbour**, another good place to break for a bite to eat overlooking the sea—either for a savory bite at the Chowder House or something sweet at Neils Harbour Lighthouse ice cream shop. The road continues south, hugging the coast, to the park's last major parcel, a thin, tapering peninsula in **Ingonish**, which is also notable for the rambling old seaside hotel, the red-roofed **Keltic Lodge at the Highlands** and its highly acclaimed golf course, **Cape Breton Highlands Links**. Drive out to make the 2.8-mile **Middle Head** loop hike out to the tip of this dramatic peninsula. Continue south, stopping for a stroll on pristine **Ingonish Beach**, and then follow the road as it climbs up around the harbor and crosses dramatic **Cape Smokey**—the overlook and picnic area are worth a stop for a photo. Continue south to **St Anns** to visit the **Gaelic College**, a nonprofit educational organization that since 1938 has worked to preserve Highland Scottish Gaelic culture in Cape Breton. The beautiful hilltop campus presents traditional music and dance concerts, storytelling, and kilt-making and weaving demonstrations, and features a great museum on Highland Scottish culture as well as a fantastic gift shop.

Drive another 15 minutes down the Cabot Trail to **Baddeck**, the last major town along the route and a good regional base with several charming restaurants and inns. It sits on the north shore of **Bras d'Or Lake**, a huge estuarial lake on whose shore the Scottish-born inventor Alexander Graham Bell built a lavish summer estate, Beinn Bhreagh, in 1885—it became his primary home, and he died there in 1922. His descendants continue to live in this private home, but you can explore Bell's legacy at the **Alexander Graham Bell National Historic Site**, a 25-acre park and museum. The town has a few culinary highlights, including Baddeck Lobster Suppers, a seasonal restaurant that offers tantalizing all-you-can-eat lobster, salmon, crab, and steak dinners and the island's most celebrated craft-beer producer, Big Spruce Brewing. Backtrack to St Anns, and then follow Hwy 105 to the island's only true city, **Sydney** (pop 30,000), a former steel-mill town that's also the terminus of ferries to Newfoundland. Beside the ferry terminal in **North Sydney**, you'll find the Lobster Pound and Moore, which might just be the most revered place on the island to eat these prized crustaceans. Sydney is a good base for visiting a couple of other notable Cape Breton attractions, the 18th-century **Fortress of Louisbourg National Historic Site** on Louisbourg Harbour, and **Glace Bay**, where you can visit the **Miners Museum**—it sits atop a once-prolific coal mine—and **Marconi National Historic Site**, from which Guglielmo Marconi sent the first successful transatlantic radio transmission in 1902. Sydney's attractive downtown overlooks the Sydney River and has a nice array of eateries as well as a couple of interesting local history museums and the excellent **Cape Breton Centre for Craft and Design**, which sells work by the island's leading artisans.

Fisheries Museum of the Atlantic, Lunenburg
Opposite Meat Cove, Cape Breton Highlands National Park

SIDETRACK

When I learned that Sydney lies just over 100 miles from the southwestern tip of Newfoundland, an island I've always wanted to visit, I nearly booked a ferry ticket right on the spot. But tacking on a side trip to **Newfoundland** can be an ambitious, time-consuming undertaking, especially if your main goal is to visit the island's largest city and provincial capital of Newfoundland and Labrador, **St John's**. That innocent-sounding 110-mile ferry crossing to **Port Aux Basques** takes 7 or 8 hours and costs about C$210 for a car and two passengers (and another C$55-C$175 for a private room). It's also worth remembering that Newfoundland is big—about the size of Tennessee, but with slower and more circuitous roads. It takes about 10 hours to drive across the island to St John's. There's interesting scenery along the way—the scenic harbor town of **Corner Brook**, a two-hour side trip to the spectacular alpine scenery and lakes of **Gros Morne National Park**, the lakefront aviation hub of **Gander** (with its compelling **North Atlantic Aviation Museum**). But it's still a long haul.

St John's (pop 109,000) is highly regarded for its colorful houses, enchanted harbor setting, hip and urbane food and art scene, and proximity to myriad parks and natural attractions, so give yourself at least three days to explore this lovely city. For your return, you can make the long drive back to Port Aux Basques (where the ferry runs year-round), or during the summer months drive 90 minutes to **Argentia** and make the 16-hour trip by ferry back to Sydney (this one costs about C$500 for a car and two passengers and another C$180-C$250 for a private room). None of this is to say that this wouldn't be a fantastic excursion—I can't wait to do it myself. But give yourself plenty of time to fully enjoy the experience.

BEST EATS

- **Rossmount Inn** Your dinner at this casually refined restaurant in one of the most romantic guest houses in St Andrews is sure to delight and sure to vary each evening according to what's fresh—maybe a chanterelle puree soup with truffle foam one night or brown butter-poached halibut the next. 506-529-3351, rossmountinn.com.

- **Thandie** The exposed brick walls and timber ceilings of this inviting Indian restaurant in downtown St John will warm your spirits every bit as much as the deftly prepared saag, korma, and vindaloo curries. The steaks and cedar-planked salmon are delicious, too. 506-648-2377, singhdining.com.

- **Founders House** Stop by this neatly preserved 1870s New England-style home while exploring quaint Annapolis Royal—it's a favorite for weekend brunch or a relaxing dinner. The upmarket Canadian fare leans toward seafood and farm-raised meats, and there's an impressive wine list. 902-532-0333, foundershousedining.com.

- **Beach Pea Kitchen & Bar** The clean lines of this white-walled dining room provide a soothing contrast to Lunenburg's colorful downtown. Flavorful house-made pastas and a risotto of scallop and rabbit are among the menu standouts. 902-640-3474, beachpeakitchen.com.

- **Edna** In a city with plenty of high-profile restaurants, it was in this intimate neighborhood bar-bistro in the North End that I enjoyed my favorite meal in Halifax. The inventive modern coastal fare—tuna poke, halibut cheeks with smoked potatoes—consistently delivers. 902-429-2550, ednarestaurant.com.

- **The Press Gang** Set inside a wonderfully atmospheric timber-and-stone 1759 building, this beloved downtown Halifax seafooder features live piano on Friday and Saturday nights, one of the province's best single-malt scotch selections, and stellar oysters. 902-423-8816, thepressgang.ca.

- **Blue Mussel Cafe** We went to this casual, open-air restaurant overlooking the glorious harbor in North Rustico expressly to devour a giant bowl of PEI mussels (steamed in white wine and garlic). They were delicious, but what blew us away was the "bubbly bake" of lobster, halibut, and scallops in a decadent cheddar-cream sauce. 902-963-2152, bluemusselcafe.com.

- **Claddagh Oyster House** This softly lighted, casually swanky restaurant on Charlottetown's restaurant row is renowned for thick, 50-day-aged, local-pasture-raised steaks, but there's great seafood, too. And save room for the classic sticky date pudding. 902-892-9661, claddaghoysterhouse.com.

- **Red Shoe Pub** It's the festive toe-tapping nightly live music, and watching locals of all ages dance to it, that's made this unassuming Mabou restaurant on Cape Breton's Ceilidh Trail famous, but the food is fantastic, too. 902-945-2996, redshoepub.com.

- **Black Spoon Bistro** This dapper modern Canadian restaurant near the ferry terminal in North Sydney is worth a special trip. Consider the maple curry spring rolls to start, followed by tender pork ribs with a bourbon-bacon barbecue sauce. 902-241-3300, blackspoon.ca.

BEST SLEEPS

- **Algonquin Resort** This shingle-style, red-roofed Victorian grande dame occupies a commanding hilltop in the bewitching seaside town of St Andrew, its upper-floor rooms (some with patios) offering views of Passamaquoddy Bay. The golf course is one of the best in Canada. 506-529-8823, algonquinresort.com.

- **Chipman Hill Suites** Offering nightly as well as extended-stay accommodations in several smartly restored, mostly mid- to late-19th-century houses throughout downtown St John, this unique property offers options for just about every budget and style. 506-693-1171, chipmanhill.com.

- **Smugglers Cove Inn** You're but a stone's throw from the picturesque harborfront and dozens of fine galleries and restaurants in lovely Lunenburg at this upmarket 20-room inn with well-appointed, unfussy rooms, many of them with balconies. 902-634-7500, smugglerscoveinn.ca.

- **Prince George Hotel** Downtown Halifax's most refined lodging, this modern redbrick midrise is two blocks from Halifax Citadel and a 10-minute stroll down the hill to the Waterfront Boardwalk. Perks include a well-equipped fitness center and indoor pool as well as a first-rate restaurant and bar. 902-425-1986, princegeorgehotel.com.

- **Around the Sea** Each of the four spacious condo-style suites inside this distinctive vacation home overlooking Prince Edward Island National Park and the sea in North Rustico has a full kitchen, living area, and a 50-foot deck. But what makes this place truly special is that this round building rotates slowly, ensuring a water view at various points in the day. 866-557-8383, aroundthesea.ca.

- **The Great George** The 54 traditionally furnished rooms and suites in this centrally located Charlottetown hotel occupy 17 adjacent, carefully restored buildings that date as far back as 1846. There are several excellent restaurants just steps away. 902-892-0606, thegreatgeorge.com.

- **Inn at Bay Fortune** Set on a glistening bay on the eastern end of Prince Edward Island and famed for its FireWorks Feast dining experiences, this posh country inn

on 48 acres is the ultimate gourmet getaway. The sister property, the Inn at Fortune Bridge, is just down the road. 902-687-3745, innatbayfortune.com.

- **Glenora Inn** Part of the fun of staying at this rural property in Mabou, especially for aficionados of fine scotch, is that the accommodations—which range from classic inn and lodge rooms to lavish chalets—are next to an acclaimed distillery. There's also a restaurant and pub where you can sample the whiskies. 902-258-2662, glenoradistillery.com.

- **Cabot Cape Breton** The warmly appointed rooms and villas are among the most luxurious in Nova Scotia, and they're especially popular with guests planning to play on the two world-class links-style golf courses. But even nongolfers will appreciate this spectacular location in Inverness and dining in the exceptional Panorama Restaurant. 902-258-4653, cabotcapebreton.com.

- **Castle Rock Country Inn** This inviting, reasonably priced boutique hotel sits high on a bluff with unobstructed views of Cape Breton Highlands National Park's eastern shoreline, including beautiful Middle Head Peninsula. Restaurant Avalon serves superb seafood. 902-285-2700, castlerockcountryinn.com.

———

CAMPING

This is an extremely popular activity in the Maritimes, and especially on Prince Edward Island and in Cape Breton. In coastal New Brunswick, top options include Kiwanis Oceanfront in St Andrews and Parc New River Beach near St Andrew. In lower Nova Scotia, consider Ellenwood Lake near Yarmouth and King Neptune in Peggy's Cove near Halifax. PEI favorites include Cavendish KOA Holiday and Prince Edward Island National Park near North Rustico, Cornwall/Charlottetown KOA, and Campbell's Cove near East Point. And on Cape Breton Island, best bets are Cheticamp Campground, MacIntosh Brook inside Cape Breton Highlands National Park, Broad Cove in Ingonish, and North Sydney/Cabot Trail KOA.

Top Summerside waterfront on Prince Edward Island
Bottom Colorful crab pots

Coastal New England and Long Island ★

The Northeast's rugged coastline offers a beguiling mix of quirky frozen-in-time fishing villages, family-friendly beaches and resort towns, and fabulous mansions and hotels built during America's Gilded Age.

HOW LONG?

10–12 days; add an extra day each for side trips to the islands or to see more of Newport, Boston, and Portland.

WHEN TO GO

Make this trip in May to mid-June or mid-September to mid-November for fewer crowds and traffic and friendlier shoulder-season prices but still generally mild weather. Winter can be a bargain if you're okay with bundling up, and you'll have beaches all to yourself.

NEED TO KNOW

Even during the shoulder seasons, weekend traffic can be extreme, and hotels book up fast. Many hotels enforce two- to seven-night minimums in summer and on spring and fall weekends.

→ Distances
Total distance, one-way: 800 mi (1287 km)
- Oyster Bay, NY to Newport, RI (with ferry): 165 mi (266 km)
- Newport, RI to Provincetown, MA: 140 mi (225 km)
- Provincetown, MA to Rockport, MA: 160 mi (257 km)
- Rockport, MA to Portland, ME: 120 mi (193 km)
- Portland, ME to Bar Harbor, ME: 165 mi (266 km)

ⓘ Daytime Temperatures
January: 30-40°F (-1-4°C)
July: 75-85°F (24-29°C)

ⓘ More information
- Long Island tourism, discoverlongisland.com
- Mystic and Southeastern CT tourism, ctvisit.com/mystic
- Newport tourism, discovernewport.org
- Cape Cod tourism, capecodchamber.org
- Boston tourism, bostonusa.com
- Portsmouth tourism: goportsmouthnh.com
- Portland tourism, visitportland.com
- Acadia National Park, nps.gov/acad

◎ SNAPSHOT

The jagged Atlantic shoreline that twists and turns in a northeasterly direction from Long Island around Cape Cod and up through coastal Maine is considered one of America's premier vacation playgrounds, with many compelling things to see and do. Tour hands-on living history museums and gloriously restored mansions, browse galleries and shops in quirky Colonial villages, feast on lobster and chowder at "in the rough" seafood shacks, and amble along breezy beaches and rocky shorelines.

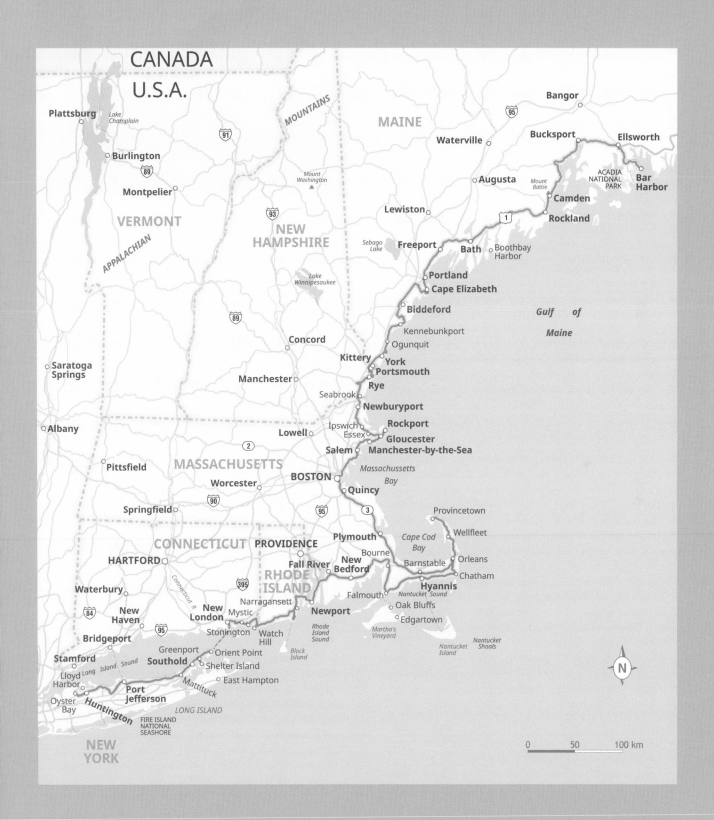

CANADA
U.S.A.

Plattsburg

Lake Champlain

Burlington

Montpelier

VERMONT

APPALACHIAN

Saratoga Springs

Albany

Pittsfield

Springfield

CONNECTICUT

HARTFORD

Waterbury

New Haven

Bridgeport

Stamford

Lloyd Harbor

Oyster Bay

Huntington

Port Jefferson

NEW YORK

MOUNTAINS

Mount Washington

NEW HAMPSHIRE

Lake Winnipesaukee

Concord

Manchester

Lowell

MASSACHUSETTS

Worcester

PROVIDENCE

RHODE ISLAND

Fall River

New London

Mystic

Stonington

Watch Hill

Narragansett

Newport

Rhode Island Sound

Block Island

Greenport

Orient Point

Southold

Shelter Island

Mattituck

East Hampton

LONG ISLAND

FIRE ISLAND NATIONAL SEASHORE

Long Island Sound

Connecticut R.

MAINE

Bangor

Waterville

Augusta

Lewiston

Sebago Lake

Freeport

Bath

Boothbay Harbor

Portland

Cape Elizabeth

Biddeford

Kennebunkport

Ogunquit

Kittery

York

Portsmouth

Rye

Seabrook

Newburyport

Ipswich

Essex

Rockport

Gloucester

Manchester-by-the-Sea

Salem

BOSTON

Quincy

Plymouth

Bourne

New Bedford

Barnstable

Falmouth

Oak Bluffs

Edgartown

Martha's Vineyard

Hyannis

Nantucket Sound

Nantucket Island

Nantucket Shoals

Provincetown

Wellfleet

Orleans

Chatham

Cape Cod Bay

Massachussetts Bay

Bucksport

Ellsworth

ACADIA NATIONAL PARK

Bar Harbor

Mount Battie

Camden

Rockland

Gulf of Maine

N

0   50   100 km

Vineyards on the North Fork of eastern Long Island
Previous Perkins Cove, Ogunquit

OYSTER BAY, NY TO NEW LONDON, CT

Start your journey amid the rolling estates and glacially sculpted coves of central **Long Island's North Shore**, in the small town of **Oyster Bay**. It's just 35 miles from Midtown Manhattan, an even shorter drive from JFK or La Guardia airports, and just 25 miles from the East Coast's major highway, I-95. Attractive little towns are strung along the North Shore's scenic country roads (Rtes 25A, 25, 48), which traverse one of the most acclaimed wine regions in the eastern US. The area has a similar feel—with its Colonial hamlets, bustling marinas, and white clapboard buildings—to coastal New England. And you'll be treated to great views of Long Island Sound, Great Peconic Bay, and Gardiners Bay throughout your drive.

Oyster Bay is the centerpiece of central Long Island's so-called Gold Coast, a region of the North Shore where New York industrialists built often absurdly ostentatious homes and that was both immortalized and critiqued in F. Scott Fitzgerald's *Great Gatsby*. It's home to **Sagamore Hill National Historic Site**, an 83-acre hilltop estate where President Theodore Roosevelt resided most of his adult life. You can tour his ornately furnished Victorian home, explore a museum with exhibits about his life, and stroll the grounds, which include a short nature trail down to a pebbly beach overlooking **Cold Spring Harbor**.

Several much larger nearby estates have been converted into lovely parks, including **Planting Fields Arboretum**, with its 67-room Tudor Revival mansion as well as greenhouses, an herbarium, and fragrant gardens, and **Caumsett State Historic Park Preserve**, whose dramatic setting on **Lloyd Neck Peninsula** offers cooling breezes on hot summer days—you can laze on the beach and swim in Long Island Sound, too. The estate is anchored by the fabulous former home of banking and business magnate Marshall Field and is laced with nature and horseback trails and formal gardens. In the larger neighboring town of **Huntington**, another fabulous estate, **Oheka**, stood in for Xanadu in the movie classic *Citizen Kane* and is now a country inn and restaurant. Just down the road, Kerber's Farm is a great place to snag picnic supplies to enjoy on the grounds of these grand estates—try the delectable potato chip–crusted fried-chicken sandwich.

Head east along the shoreline, past farms and vineyards, to **Mattituck**, the heart of eastern Long Island's exceptional wine country. More than 40 vintners have tasting rooms, and while a range of grapes are grown here, the most prolific varietals hail from France's Bordeaux region (Merlot, Cabernet Franc, Cabernet Sauvignon), which has a similar terroir. A few properties that offer tasting experiences include **Lenz**, a regional pioneer with tastings inside a handsome old barn; **Macari Vineyards**, whose crisp Sauvignon Blanc is best enjoyed from a spacious deck; and **Osprey's Dominion**, which offers a short menu of snacks but also (this is a rarity around here) encourages guests to bring food to picnic on the pastoral grounds.

You'll find a smattering of B&Bs and restaurants throughout the North Fork, many in the main commercial hub, **Greenport**, a tiny former whaling village with a pretty waterfront and an unpretentious feel (especially compared with the conspicuously showy Hamptons on the island's South Fork). From casual takeout spots like Goldberg's Famous Bagels and 1943 Pizza Bar to a handful of legit culinary destinations, such as the Frisky Oyster and Fortino's, the town has evolved into a bona fide culinary destination. From downtown, make the short ferry ride to the north end of **Shelter Island**, a beautiful 29 sq mile patch of undulating forests and tranquil beaches that's accessible only by boat. It's one of my favorite spots for a country drive or a bike ride (there are rental shops near the ferry terminal). I recommend savoring a relaxing meal at the Flying Goat or 18 Bay and ideally overnighting at one of the island's romantic inns.

From Greenport, drive 9 miles to **Orient Point** and then take an 80-minute ferry across Long Island Sound to New London, Connecticut. Ferries cross several times daily, more frequently in summer, and the ride is utterly relaxing. Book ahead during busy times, and note that fares are around $60 to $65 for a car and one driver, plus about $20 for additional adult passengers. The nonferry alternative requires driving busy highways back across Long Island and then along the Connecticut Coast—a mostly mundane four-hour drive that can take much longer with traffic.

NEW LONDON, CT TO NEWPORT, RI

Once off the ferry in **New London,** head east along the coast to **Mystic,** where you can easily spend a full day exploring the nation's largest maritime museum, **Mystic Seaport,** as well as the excellent **Mystic Aquarium,** famous for its beluga whales, seals and sea lions, dozens of African penguins, and countless other sea creatures. More than 60 restored buildings are arranged on a 20-acre tract along the river to resemble a typical New England port village, and you can watch craftspeople at work, view an astounding collection of maritime art, and tour several historic ships (including world's last surviving wooden whaler).

Follow US 1 toward Rhode Island's **Narragansett Bay,** where you'll pick up Rte 138 (right near the underrated **Gilbert Stuart Museum,** birthplace of the portraitist who painted the image of George Washington that now appears on the US dollar bill), and cross two soaring bridges to get to Newport. Without stops, the drive takes a little over an hour, but I like to break things up with stops in the colonial Connecticut shipbuilding village of **Stonington** or upscale **Watch Hill,** RI, which has a handsome lighthouse and one of the nation's oldest operating carousels. Another fun shore town is **Narragansett,** with its excellent beaches and famous, family-friendly seafood eateries, including Aunt Carrie's, a rambling 1920s counter-service eatery acclaimed for clam cakes, broiled sea scallops, and Rhode Island–style (with a clear broth as opposed to cream) clam chowder.

SIDETRACK

There are three famous resort islands just off the coast of southern New England, all of them well worth a day trip: **Martha's Vineyard** and **Nantucket** are accessible by ferry from Cape Cod, and less touristy and smaller **Block Island**—a romantic patch of beaches, formidable sea cliffs, and romantic Victorian inns—is reached by ferry from Narragansett's Point Judith. Bringing your car onto these ferry boats is expensive. I prefer parking on the mainland and renting a bike, walking, or taking buses to explore these islands. Martha's Vineyard is the largest of the three and is home to some beautiful little villages, including **Menemsha** with its superb fishing markets, and **Edgartown,** which has several upscale restaurants and inns. Getting to Nantucket involves the longest ferry ride, but its a walkable village center boasts chic shops and eateries and the outstanding **Whaling Museum.**

NEWPORT, RI TO PROVINCETOWN, MA

One of the country's five largest cities at the time of the American Revolution, **Newport** has just 25,000 residents today, but this monied yachting enclave at the southern tip of Aquidneck Island has developed into one of coastal New England's most beloved vacation destinations. It has more museums, hotels, and restaurants than many cities 10 times its size, so you may wish to spend an extra day or two here, especially if you enjoy touring opulent mansions.

Throughout the 19th century, this town cooled by ocean breezes became a desirable summer retreat among wealthy barons of industry and agriculture. Vanderbilts, Astors, and other affluent families built spectacular mansions—which they quaintly dubbed "summer cottages"—along **Bellevue Ave.** Many of these palaces now operate as museums. The most gawked at is Cornelius Vanderbilt II's 70-room Renaissance Revival white elephant, **The Breakers,** but it's the commission of a different Vanderbilt (Cornelius's brother Frederick), **Rough Point,** that I consider the most interesting of the bunch. Tobacco heiress Doris Duke resided in this oceanfront manor until her death in 1993, and it's furnished largely as she left it—the idiosyncratic mix of museum-quality and prosaic furnishings gives it a more lived-in feel than most of its neighbors. You can view the exteriors of several mansions by walking along the 3.5-mile **Cliff Walk.** Also on Bellevue Ave, don't miss the **International Tennis Hall of Fame,** an extensive Victorian Shingle-style museum and tennis facility designed by Charles McKim and Stanford White in 1881.

Newport also boasts a number of meticulously preserved Colonial homes and buildings, such as **Touro Synagogue,** the nation's oldest place of Jewish worship, and the **Redwood Library and Athenaeum,** a gorgeous neoclassical building that has operated continuously as a lending library since 1750. Newport's harbor-facing downtown, where you'll find the majority of its historic buildings, is best explored on foot or by local trolley, as parking can be a challenge. There's one notable Newport feature best explored by car: **Ocean Drive,** a winding 10-mile route that begins amid Bellevue Ave's mansions and weaves around the rocky coves of the city's southern shore. You can park and walk by the sea at **Brenton Point State Park** and at 200-acre **Fort Adams State Park,** which overlooks both Narragansett Bay and Newport Harbor and is home to a sprawling Colonial fort— each summer the park hosts the internationally renowned Newport Jazz and Newport Folk festivals.

The Beehive Loop, Acadia National Park

Continue up the coast, crossing into southeastern Massachusetts to **Cape Cod**, the picturesque hook-shaped 340 sq mile peninsula that's been synonymous with summertime family vacations for generations. Made up of 15 towns, each with its own distinct charms and personalities, the Cape lends itself to leisurely vacations; many visitors come for a week or more, rent cottages, and spend their days relaxing on the beach, cycling the Cape's extensive network of bike paths, and feasting on fresh seafood. It's a highlight of any coastal trip, but heavy traffic and exorbitant hotel rates can prove challenging during the peak late May to early September vacation season. From the bridges that lead onto Cape Cod to Wellfleet and Provincetown—two charming towns on the outer reaches of the Cape—it's about a 90-minute drive without heavy traffic.

PROVINCETOWN, MA TO SALEM, MA

Following US 6 along the Cape's narrow outer hook, you'll reach the bustling seaside community **Provincetown**, which has been one of the world's leading LGBTQ resort destinations for decades. The town's main strip, **Commercial Street**, offers blocks of prestigious art galleries, hip boutiques, colorful drag bars and dance clubs, and both casual and sophisticated restaurants, and the **Provincetown Art Association and Museum** hosts outstanding exhibits. **Wellfleet** is much smaller than Provincetown but also has a number of cool little shops and eateries, and outside of town, the **Wellfleet Cinemas** drive-in has been screening movies under the stars since 1957—the flea market held here three days a week in summer is a blast.

Much of the Outer Cape comprises the protected dunes, beaches, marshes, and woods that make up **Cape Cod National Seashore**. Stop at **Salt Pond Visitor Center** in **Eastham** for exhibits, maps, and information about this wonderful place for gentle nature walks, breezy beach strolls, and visits to historic maritime facilities, including **Nauset** and **Highland** lighthouses and **Old Harbor Life-Saving Station Museum**. The national seashore also boasts the most stunning of the Cape's beaches, including **Herring Cove** and **Race Point** in Provincetown, **Marconi Beach** in Wellfleet, and **Coast Guard Beach** in Eastham.

Leaving Provincetown, you can follow US 6 all the way back to the Sagamore Bridge en route to Boston. But my preference, once I get to Orleans, is instead to take parallel Rte 6A through the picturesque Colonial hamlets of **Brewster**, **Dennis**, **Barnstable**, and **Sandwich**. Creaky old antiques shops, atmospheric seafood shacks, and handsome

SIDETRACK

It's just a half-hour drive from the Mt Hope Bridge at the northern tip of Aquidneck Island to the capital of Rhode Island, **Providence**, a city of about 180,000 set at the head of Narragansett Bay. A youthful and creative city that's home to several acclaimed colleges, Providence has one of the Northeast's most exciting culinary and arts scenes. On your way from Newport, take your time driving through the attractive bay town of **Bristol**. Note the red, white, and blue stripe down Hope St, the town's main thoroughfare—it's a nod to Bristol's having hosted the country's earliest Fourth of July celebration (it's still enormously popular).

In Providence, head for historic and picturesque **College Hill**, where the stately campuses of both Brown University and Rhode Island School of Design (RISD) blend almost imperceptibly. Tour the world-class collections of art and furniture at the **RISD Museum**, and walk south along **Benefit St**, with its several blocks of neatly preserved Colonial homes and buildings, including the gorgeous **Providence Athenaeum**, where both Edgar Allan Poe and H.P. Lovecraft spent many hours. Walk down the hill to the riverfront and cross the sleek pedestrian- and bike-only **Michael S. Van Leesten Memorial Bridge**, which spans the Providence River and offers great views toward the downtown skyline. End your day with dinner in the adjoining **Broadway** and **Federal Hill** neighborhoods. The latter is Providence's long-standing Italian enclave, with dozens of old-school trattorias, bakeries, and cafes—standouts include Enoteca Umberto for home-style pastas and Pastiche Fine Desserts for cannoli, cookies, fruit tarts, and tiramisu. Broadway is the city's hip haunt of craft cocktail bars and farm-to-table bistros, with hallowed spots including Nicks on Broadway and the Slow Rhode leading the way. If you're going directly to Cape Cod from Providence, head east on I-195.

Boston

Established in 1630, New England's largest city is a favorite destination of history and art lovers. You can visit dozens of pivotal American Revolutionary War sites as well as superb galleries and museums both in the city proper and—just across the Charles River—in **Cambridge**, which is home to both Harvard University and Massachusetts Institute of Technology (MIT). Beyond its formal museums, it's also a great city for strolling, its narrow streets lined with redbrick and brownstone homes, tony boutiques, and both classic and contemporary restaurants.

Car-friendly rating: Poor. As easy and enjoyable as it is to explore Boston on foot or by using the extensive rapid-transit system (which includes underground and above-ground rail network, known as the "T," as well as buses), driving here pretty much sucks. One-way, crooked, and narrow streets are commonplace; local drivers have a reputation for being—how shall I put this?—hurried; and street parking is extremely limited. Public garages and hotels have some of the country's priciest parking, too. If you're staying for more than a day, consider parking outside the city at a long-term commuter lot (such as Riverside, Alewife, or Wonderland) and taking the T into the city.

What to see in a day: Start with a stroll through **Boston Common** and adjacent **Public Garden**, admiring the gold-domed **Massachusetts State House**. Then walk a portion of the 2.5-mile **Freedom Trail**, a red-painted path that connects 16 of the city's seminal Colonial sites, including the **Old State House**, **Faneuil Hall** (which adjoins **Quincy Public Market**), and the **Paul Revere House**. Next explore the narrow, cobblestone streets of Colonial **Beacon Hill**, the trendy shopping and dining of the **Back Bay**, and, a little beyond, the LGBTQ-popular **South End**. Other key areas worth seeking out include **Fenway-Kenmore**, home to baseball's iconic **Fenway Park**, the renowned **Museum of Fine Arts, Boston,** and the more idiosyncratic and even more compelling **Isabella Stewart Gardner Museum.** Not far east of Faneuil Hall, along the city's waterfront facing **Boston Harbor**, you can visit the excellent **New England Aquarium** and the **Institute of Contemporary Art** (maybe my favorite building in the city). A cross the river in **Cambridge**, the museums of **Harvard University**—including the **Harvard Art Museums** and the **Arthur M. Sackler Museum**—are superb, and the surrounding neighborhood and venerable Harvard Yard are fun to explore. Some noteworthy attractions in the city's outskirts can be visited with relative ease by car, including the **John F. Kennedy Presidential Library and Museum** at Columbia Point, **Bunker Hill Monument** in Charlestown, **Arnold Arboretum** in Jamaica Plain, and **Adams National Historical Park** (the home of John, Abigail, and John Quincy Adams) in the nearby town of Quincy.

Where to stay: You'll find plenty of mostly upscale hotels within a 10-minute walk of Boston Common, including posh retreats like the **Four Seasons** and **The Langham** and more moderately priced boutique gems, including the **Revolution Hotel** and **The Godfrey**. To avoid driving and parking downtown, you might consider an outlying hotel that offers free parking and is within walking distance of a T station, such as **Hilton Garden Inn** by Logan Airport and **Holiday Inn Express Boston–Quincy**.

Top **Boston view from Cambridge** *Bottom* **Fenway Park**

captains' homes line this route, which takes about 45 minutes longer than US 6, more with stops. Once off the Cape, you'll come to **Plymouth**, the town famously founded by the Pilgrims, who sailed here aboard the *Mayflower* in 1620. You can learn about the community's complicated history, which has tended to be whitewashed by history books over the centuries, at the **Plimoth and Patuxet Museums**, which does a very good job of interpreting the lives of both the Pilgrims and native Wampanoag tribe that had lived here for at least 10,000 years before their arrival. It's an excellent, immersive museum but one that you need at least three hours to fully appreciate.

Just 20 miles northeast of Boston, the small seafaring city of **Salem**, infamous for the witch trials of 1692, is perfect for a walk along the redbrick sidewalks abundant with stately 18th- and 19th-century homes. Break things up with lunch at Gulu-Gulu Cafe (great coffee, crepes, and panini sandwiches) or Bambolina (delicious wood-fired pizzas). Learn more about the city's dark history at the informative **Salem Witch Museum**, which occupies an ominous-looking Gothic Revival church, but don't miss the impressive **Peabody Essex Museum** or the meticulously preserved 1668 **House of the Seven Gables**, the centerpiece of Salem resident Nathaniel Hawthorne's 1851 novel.

SALEM, MA TO PORTSMOUTH, NH

Salem lies just southwest of **Cape Ann**, the smaller but no less scenic of the state's famous capes. Follow Rte 127 east through Manchester-by-the-Sea and Gloucester. The road snakes through Colonial residential neighborhoods and past some grand old seaside mansions (**Hammond Castle Museum** is one that you can take a very cool tour of), passing by a number of inviting stretches of shore. A bustling fishing port on a protected harbor, **Gloucester** has sizable Italian and Portuguese communities, the descendants of immigrants who arrived in the 19th century to work in the city's prolific shipbuilding and fishing industries. Sebastian Junger's gripping book about an ill-fated commercial fishing boat, *The Perfect Storm*, was based on an actual 1991 event in Gloucester, and the film adaptation starring George Clooney and Mark Wahlberg was filmed here. The town also developed into an artist colony in the early 19th century; much of the current and very impressive art scene is focused on the **Rocky Neck Art Colony**, a collection of galleries and studios on a peninsula that juts into Gloucester's Inner Harbor.

Continue along the shore via Rte 127A to impossibly adorable **Rockport**, a compact waterfront village of narrow lanes

dotted with clapboard Colonial and Victorian houses and cottages, many of them containing fine galleries and eateries, such as Roy Moore Lobster, which opened in 1918. Take Rte 127 up around the tip of the cape, stopping to scamper over the sea boulders at **Halibut Point State Park**, and then looping down to pass through the pleasing villages of Ipswich and **Essex**, home to Woodman's of Essex, which is credited with having invented the fried clam in 1916. Stop by **Castle Hill on Crane Estate**, a 2100-acre hilltop expanse of glorious gardens and sweeping views over Ipswich Bay. You can amble around the property and tour the palatial Great House (which you may recognize as Jack Nicholson's lair of iniquity in *The Witches of Eastwick*). Stop afterward at family-friendly **Russell Orchards** to pick strawberries, blueberries, and apples, mingle with friendly critters in the barnyard, and buy scones or seasonal fruit pies. It's about a 90-minute drive—follow the coast as much as possible for the best scenery—to **Portsmouth**, the largest city along New Hampshire's 18-mile shoreline. About 22,000 people live in this compact seaport known for its well-preserved Colonial buildings, many of them open to the public. A highlight is **Strawbery Banke**, a 10-acre village of more than three dozen restored structures. End your adventures on the sprawling back patio of Earth Eagle Brewings, which serves hefty burgers and jumbo hot dogs with interesting toppings, plus well-crafted ales and refreshing cocktails.

PORTSMOUTH, NH TO PORTLAND, ME

Cross the Piscataqua River into the outlet-shopping mecca of **Kittery**, ME, and follow scenic Rte 1A up the coast through a string of pretty oceanfront communities—**York Beach** and **Cape Neddick**—to diverse and charming **Ogunquit**, where you can tour the small but excellent **Ogunquit Museum of American Art** and check out the shops and seafood eateries (The Trap, Footbridge Lobster, and others) of **Perkins Cove**. From here, walk the stunning 1.3-mile **Marginal Way** footpath along a series of sea cliffs into the cute downtown, with its hip bars and restaurants. Extremely popular with LGBTQ visitors, Ogunquit reminds me of a smaller version of Provincetown.

It's about 40 miles to Portland from Ogunquit, and the trip can take anywhere from 45 minutes via I-95 to two or three hours if you follow the alluring two-lane roads that curve along the coast through the old-money enclave of **Kennebunkport**, the honky-tonk beach vacation town of **Old Orchard Beach**, and the stunningly situated shore community of **Cape Elizabeth**, where you can visit the

famed, oft-photographed **Portland Head** lighthouse, Maine's oldest, dating back to 1791. You can break up the journey in **Biddeford** with breakfast or lunch at the Palace Diner, a diminutive 1920s greasy spoon with a justly deserved reputation for exceptional food, from fluffy buttermilk flapjacks to crispy fried chicken sandwiches.

Before you spoil your appetite, however, keep in mind that **Portland** is one of America's most vaunted foodie cities, despite having only around 65,000 residents. This handsome little metropolis is surrounded by water and overlooks several beautiful islands. Great views can be had from the grassy lawns of the **Western Promenade** and **Eastern Promenade**, two hilltop parks that bracket the city. The **Portland Museum of Art** features extensive holdings of painters who have immortalized the region's natural scenery, such as Winslow Homer, Edward Hopper, and Andrew Wyeth. Next, make the pleasing walk through downtown along **Congress St** and then down to the historic **Old Port** district, with its narrow lanes, bustling wharves, and colorful mix of seafood markets, indie shops, and convivial taverns. Fantastic eateries are everywhere: Tandem Coffee for first-rate espresso drinks, Eventide Oyster Co. for fresh-shucked bivalves, Hot Suppa for down-home Southern fare, Duckfat for Belgian-style frites and luscious milkshakes, the Holy Donut for sweet treats, and Novare Res Bier Cafe for international brews.

SIDETRACK

From Bath, after passing through **Wiscasset** (home of the famous lobster shack Red's Eats), a right turn onto Rte 27 leads south to **Boothbay Harbor**, an idyllic yachting enclave that's ideal for shopping and noshing on seafood—try the rustic Tugboat Inn, or consider spending the night at one of several stunning lodgings, such as the Topside Inn and Linekin Bay Resort. Boothbay Harbor's greatest draw is the expansive **Coastal Maine Botanical Gardens**. Peaceful trails lace the more than 300 acres of formal plantings, art installations, a delightful children's garden, and shady riverside woodlands.

Top Lobster salad at Wentworth by the Sea, New Castle

PORTLAND, ME TO BAR HARBOR, ME

Take I-295 to get from Portland to **Freeport**, where you can visit the enormous flagship of famed outerwear store **L.L. Bean**. Continue along US 1 through the attractive Colonial shipbuilding center of **Bath**, where I recommend exploring the superb **Maine Maritime Museum**, and then continuing through a series of small, historic towns through Maine's mid-coastal region to Rockland.

You'll find some of mid-coastal Maine's most bewitching scenery along the shore of West Penobscot Bay, starting with **Rockland**. Once merely a workaday supply center serving the needs of the region's swankier resort towns, this town of about 7300 has enjoyed a recent renaissance thanks in part to the opening of the renowned **Farnsworth Art Museum**, known for its estimable collection of works by Andrew Wyeth (as well as his father, N.C., and son Jamie), along with many other luminaries of American painting. The museum is the centerpiece of Main St, whose striking redbrick Italianate buildings house one-of-a-kind shops and eateries.

A dramatic stretch of US 1 continues north along Penobscot Bay through quaint **Rockport**, a vaunted artists colony set around a glorious little harbor, and **Camden**, an affluent summer getaway for generations whose harbor is filled with antique wooden-masted sailboats and schooners, including a fleet of historic Windjammers—several outfitters in town offer day and happy hour sunset sails on the bay. Stroll around downtown, relax in Olmsted Brothers–designed **Harbor Park,** or make the short but rather steep 1.1-mile round-trip hike up to the top of Mt Battie in **Camden Hills State Park**. From the historic observation tower at the top, which you can also drive to, the bay views are stupendous.

As you continue up US 1, take the remarkable **Penobscot Narrows Bridge** across the Penobscot River and into **Bucksport**. Built in 2007, this soaring cable-stayed structure is the world's tallest bridge observatory; you can take an elevator to the top of the 420 ft high West Tower to enjoy 360-degree views and check out adjacent **Fort Knox**, a formidable granite fortress constructed in the mid-19th century.

Follow US 1 and then Rte 3 onto **Mount Desert Island**, home to the picturesque resort town of Bar Harbor as well as most of Acadia National Park. **Bar Harbor** was established as a fishing and shipbuilding town in the 1760s, but by the middle of the next century, prestigious American landscape painters, including Thomas Cole and Frederic Church, were drawn here by the alluring harbor, granite cliffs and mountains, and sheltered beaches. The town soon attracted wealthy visitors, many of whom—Rockefellers, Astors, and Vanderbilts among them—built massive summer homes. The downtown is one of the prettiest in the state; Main St is lined with appealing shops and eateries, and both the Village Green and waterfront Agamont Park are great spots to relax with a dish of coriander–lemon curd or blueberry-buttermilk ice cream from Mt Desert Island Ice Cream.

Home to the highest peak on the Eastern Seaboard (1530 ft **Cadillac Mountain**) and a marvelously diverse landscape of rugged and rocky coastal headlands and pristine forests and beaches, **Acadia National Park** is one of the great natural treasures of New England. After stopping by **Hulls Cove Visitor Center**, drive the beautiful Park Loop Rd, taking in the views from the many rocky ledges. The **Nature Center** and **Abbe Museum** are worth a stop, and lunch at the historic Jordan Pond House restaurant is my favorite way to break up the adventure—it's famous for its fluffy fresh-baked popovers with butter and strawberry jam. Although you can drive to the summit of Cadillac Mountain, it can be tough finding a parking spot; I prefer hiking to the top. Other great treks in the park include neighboring and less crowded **Dorr Mountain** and climbing the ladders and rungs of the short but quite vertical **Beehive Loop**, which overlooks one of the park's loveliest stretches of shoreline, **Sand Beach**. If you have an extra day or want to get away from the crowds, set aside a few hours to explore the park's quieter western side, checking out the trails around **Beech Mountain** and **Echo Lake**.

Top Oheka, Huntington *Opposite* Red's Eats, Wiscasset

SIDETRACK

For many who vacation on Maine's coast, Bar Harbor is the end of the road. But the state's rugged coastline stretches for well over 100 more miles to the Canadian border, where you'll find some fascinating diversions. Allow about two hours to get to the tiny Maine border town of **Lubec**, which has an unpretentious little downtown with a handful of casual lodging and dining options—the Home Port Inn & Restaurant is a welcoming place for both. After spending the night, you can rise early and drive to **Quoddy Head State Park** to watch the sunrise from the easternmost point in the United States or, if you're like me, sleep in and visit the park after breakfast. Either way, set aside an hour or two to walk around the 49 ft tall candy-striped **West Quoddy Head Lighthouse** and explore the park's peaceful, windswept nature trails. Another neat activity in this part of the world is driving over the only bridge onto Canada's **Campobello Island** (from the Canadian mainland you can get to this wooded island of about 880 residents by ferry only). I once jogged across this bridge carrying nothing but my passport to the amusement of the border agents on both sides. My goal was to visit **Roosevelt Campobello International Park**, the 2800-acre summer hideaway of Franklin and Eleanor Roosevelt. It's a lot of fun touring the 1897 house and learning more about the couple in the excellent visitor center.

BEST EATS

- **Sandbar** This dapper contemporary bistro in quaint Cold Spring Harbor has one of the region's top wine lists and serves up both the classics (chopped salads, New York strip steak) and more inventive fare. 631-498-6188, sandbarcoldspringharbor.com.

- **Abbott's Lobster in the Rough** At this beloved counter-service seafood spot near Mystic, order a complete lobster feast (with clam chowder, steamers, mussels, and sides) or a la carte lobster rolls and crab cakes while enjoying spectacular views of Long Island Sound. Noank, 860-536-7719, abbottslobster.com.

- **Matunuck Oyster Bar** Near Narragansett, this cheerful restaurant has outdoor seating on several levels, including a roof deck and a barge docked on Salt Pond Harbor—it's great for a leisurely repast of oysters and other local specialties from the sea. 401-783-4202, rhodyoysters.com.

- **White Horse Tavern** America's oldest restaurant dates to 1673 and has wide-plank floors and low-beamed ceilings. It's also one of Newport's better spots for lavish Continental fare. 401-849-3600, whitehorsetavern.com.

- **Stoneacre Garden** The shareable international bites—Korean short rib tacos, udon noodles with lobster—at this lively downtown Newport restaurant are best enjoyed on the deck looking out over Newport Harbor. The boozy brunches on weekends are good fun. 401-619-8400, stoneacregarden.com.

- **Mac's Shack** In this white-clapboard restaurant on Wellfleet's Duck Creek, sup on lobster, sushi and sashimi, Ritz Cracker-crusted bluefish. It's part of a mini empire of eateries, with locations in Chatham, Eastham, and Provincetown, too. 508-349-6333, macsseafood.com.

- **Strangers and Saints** This warmly lighted Provincetown bistro inside an imposing Greek Revival house pleases all tastes with its eclectic menu of Mediterranean-influenced tapas, shareable mains, and inventive pizzas. 508-487-1449, strangersandsaints.com.

- **Settler** Steps from campy Salem sights like the Samantha Stephens *Bewitched* statue and campily creepy Witch Dungeon Museum, this sleek yet cozy neighborhood bistro produces contemporary American food, with a menu that changes daily to reflect what's fresh and local. 978-744-2094, settlersalem.com.

- **Cure** A standout among Portsmouth's acclaimed dining scene, this romantic neighborhood bistro with redbrick walls and pressed-tin ceilings turns out exceptional seasonal New England fare and fine cocktails. 603-427-8258, curerestaurantportsmouth.com.

- **Northern Union** An upscale eatery and wine bar, this is a lovely destination for a romantic dinner after a day of beach relaxation or before catching a show at the renowned Ogunquit Playhouse. 207-216-9639, northern-union.me.

- **Chaval** Consistently sublime Spanish and French fare along with winning service has elevated this West End brasserie to among Portland's most raved-about dining destinations. 207-772-1110, chavalmaine.com.

- **Terlingua** Don't be put off by the unassuming setting in Portland's East End—this buzzy market, quirky eatery and beer garden specializes in mouthwatering barbecue with nods to Texas (smoked brisket) and Mexico (Baja fish tacos and mezcal). 207-956-7573, terlingua.me.

- **The Honey Paw** Close to Portland's Old Port District, this hip pan-Asian restaurant serves boldly seasoned fare like wok-charred eggplant with spicy Szechuan chilies, velvety mapo tofu, and lobster laksa with rice noodles and fish cakes. 207-774-8538, thehoneypaw.com

- **Primo** Foodies drive for miles to dine on the seasonally inspired Italian and Mediterranean fare Victorian farmhouse south of downtown Rockland. Share the charcuterie board before graduating to linguine with local crab and chiles. 207-596-0770, primorestaurant.com.

- **Long Grain** You might not expect sensational Thai food in tiny Camden, but Long Grain is special. The daily rotating curry is always delicious, as are the house-made rice noodles stir-fried with Thai basil, mushrooms, and pork belly. 207-236-9001, longgraincamden.com.

- **Project Social** Everything is terrific at this lively grill and craft-cocktail bar on Bar Harbor's Main St with an enchanting garden patio. The menu is meant for sharing and features Mediterranean dips, grilled veggies, and local shellfish. No phone, socialbarharbor.com.

BEST SLEEPS

- **Oheka** This chateauesque castle on Long Island's highest point is the second largest house in the United States. Sleep in one of the 32 luxurious guest suites and dine in the superb OHK Bar & Restaurant. Huntington, 631-659-1400, oheka.com.

- **Greenporter Hotel** A short walk from Greenport's excellent restaurants and picturesque harbor, this mid-century motor lodge has been updated into a sleek yet casual boutique hotel offering convenience and reasonable rates. 631-477-0066, greenporterhotel.com.

- **Steamboat Inn** The 11 rooms in this inn overlooking the Mystic River have marvelous water and drawbridge views and lots of cushy touches, including whirlpool tubs and fireplaces. A generous full breakfast is included. 860-536-8300, steamboatinnmystic.com.

- **Town and Tide Inn** This small compound of Victorian houses enjoys an ideal location near Newport's Cliff Walk and Bellevue Ave mansions. The 12 rooms have a clean, contemporary look, and in-room spa experiences can be arranged. Newport, 401-845-9400, townandtideinn.com

- **The Wayfinder** A team of local restaurant and design entrepreneurs pooled their talents to convert a prosaic property on the north side of town into a stylish yet affordable 197-room retreat with free parking, a seasonal pool with bar service, and a terrific restaurant, Nomi Park. 401-849-9880, thewayfinderhotel.com

- **Crowne Pointe** Perched on a hill within a quick stroll of Provincetown's top bars and eateries, this tastefully appointed hotel abounds with amenities that you won't often find elsewhere here: a full-service spa, a pool and hot tub, and free on-site parking (which is truly rare in Provincetown). Across the street, the sister property the Brass Key is also lovely. 508-413-6638, crownepointe.com.

- **Nauset Beach Inn** The only lodging that's actually located inside Cape Cod National Seashore, this small compound's cheerfully furnished cottages have big picture windows overlooking the dunes, beach, and ocean. 508-255-2364, nausetbeachinn.com.

- **Hawthorne Hotel** Set on the south edge of Salem's verdant town common, this stately 1925 grande dame has a beautiful lobby and an atmospheric, wood-paneled tavern. With free parking, it's also a great base for exploring Boston (just a half hour away) and Cape Ann. 978-744-4080, hawthornehotel.com

- **Bearskin Neck Motor Lodge** This simple, moderately priced 1960s motel has eight fashionably upgraded rooms and sits right on the ocean at the end of historic Rockport's main thoroughfare. 978-546-6677, bearskinneckmotorlodge.com.

- **Wentworth by the Sea** This spectacular white wedding cake of a hotel just outside Portsmouth dates to 1874 and offers top-notch amenities, including two restaurants, a fabulous spa, and heated indoor and outdoor pools. 603-422-7322, marriott.com.

- **Trellis House** From this utterly enchanting eight-room B&B surrounded by lush gardens and greenery, you're steps from Ogunquit's famed Marginal Way coastal path and within walking or trolleying distance of the beach and local bars and restaurants. 207-646-7909, trellishouse.com.

- **Press Hotel** This seven-story 1920s Old Port building that once housed the city's newspaper has been given new life as a hip 110-room hotel with old-fashioned writing desks, local art, a rooftop deck, and a scene-y farm-to-table restaurant. 207-808-8800, thepresshotel.com.

- **Inn at Diamond Cove** On Great Diamond Island, just a 25-minute ferry ride from Old Port, this distinctive hotel fashioned out of late-19th-century army barracks has spacious, stylish suites—some with kitchens—that feature porches or balconies, and a large pool and acclaimed waterfront restaurant. 207-805-9836, innatdiamondcove.com.

- **Island View Inn** Laze on the sundeck overlooking West Penobscot Bay, go for a swim in the pool, or explore the colorful villages of nearby Rockland and Camden. This dapper yet reasonably priced 21-room inn has everything you need for a day or two of relaxation. Rockport, 207-596-0040, strawberryhillseasideinn.com.

- **Bar Harbor Grand Hotel** A contemporary reconstruction of the grand 19th-century Rodick Inn, which was torn down in 1906, this casually elegant retreat with a rocking chair-lined porch is a short walk from good restaurants and a short drive from Acadia National Park. 207-288-5226, barharborgrand.com.

CAMPING

Along this somewhat densely populated route, it's possible to find RV parks and tent camping venues, but you might find it challenging to find truly remote campgrounds. Excellent locales for pitching a tent include North of Highland Camping Area and Nickerson State Park, both near Cape Cod National Seashore (tent camping is prohibited inside the park itself); Seawall and Blackwoods campgrounds in Acadia National Park; Wildwood State Park on eastern Long Island's North Shore; Melville Ponds north of Newport; Cape Ann Camp Site in Gloucester; Dixon's Campground in Cape Neddick, ME; and Camden Hill State Park in ME.

Opposite Rehoboth Beach

Delaware River and Chesapeake Bay ★

Water plays a starring role in this odyssey through the Mid-Atlantic states, which offers an up-close view into America's Colonial and Industrial eras but also takes in glorious views of pristine beaches and quaint bayside and riverfront villages.

HOW LONG?

8–10 days; add an extra day each to see more of Philadelphia, Baltimore, and Washington, DC.

WHEN TO GO

The region's cherry, azalea, and magnolia trees and flower gardens burst with color from April through June, and September and October offer mild weather and the possibility of having beaches almost to yourself. Summer is high season on the shore, which can be ideal for family fun but can also mean heavy traffic on the roads to the beach and pricey hotel rooms. Winter offers the best value, and although it can be cold and even snowy, daytime highs sometimes climb into the 50s and 60s.

NEED TO KNOW

The ferry from Cape May to Lewes departs several times daily in summer but less often the rest of the year; reservations aren't required but are a good idea. None of the three big cities along this itinerary—Philadelphia, Baltimore, and Washington, DC—are ideal for cars, especially in the downtown areas. Consider using public transit.

→ Distances
Total distance, one-way: 800 mi (1287 km)
- Bethlehem, PA to Cape May, NJ: 180 mi (290 km)
- Cape May, NJ to Norfolk, VA: 200 mi (322 km)
- Norfolk, VA to Richmond, VA: 100 mi (161 km)
- Richmond, VA to Annapolis, MD: 200 mi (322 km)

ⓘ Temperatures
January: 35-50°F (2-10°C)
July: 83-88°F (28-31°C)

ⓘ More information
- Lehigh Valley tourism, discoverlehighvalley.com
- Bucks County tourism, visitbuckscounty.com
- Philadelphia tourism, visitphilly.com
- Cape May tourism, capemay.com
- Norfolk tourism, visitnorfolk.com
- Richmond tourism, visitrichmondva.com
- Washington, DC tourism, washington.org
- Annapolis tourism, visitannapolis.org
- Baltimore tourism, baltimore.org

◉ SNAPSHOT

This hook-shaped route through the Mid-Atlantic coastal plain connects vibrant cities and meticulously preserved Colonial villages with long stretches of both developed and undeveloped shoreline. History lovers appreciate the remarkable museums of the Lehigh Valley, Philadelphia, Colonial Williamsburg, and Washington, DC, but those in search of family-friendly beach resorts and peaceful wildlife preserves will find much to enjoy as well.

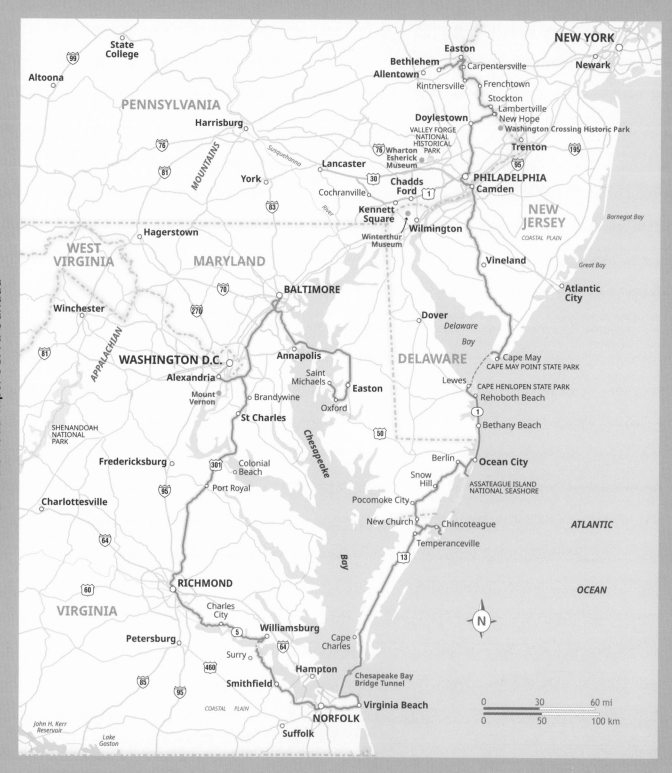

LEHIGH VALLEY, PA TO REHOBOTH, DE

The hilly, green, and culturally rich **Lehigh Valley** comprises a string of small eastern Pennsylvania cities—**Easton**, **Bethlehem**, and **Allentown**—along the Lehigh River near its confluence with the Delaware River. The area was long associated with Bethlehem Steel, once the nation's second largest steel manufacturer. Factories here struggled during the late 20th century, but Lehigh Valley has rebounded and is now the fastest-growing part of the state. Start in Bethlehem, with its trove of well-preserved Colonial and Victorian homes. The **Historic Bethlehem Museums and Sites** is a walkable campus of nearly 20 buildings that showcase the heritage of the town's early Moravian settlers—don't miss the **Kemerer Museum of Decorative Arts**. Across the river, some 10 acres of former steel works have been converted into mixed-use buildings, restaurants, pedestrian paths, and the exceptional **National Museum of Industrial History**. Other worthwhile draws include the impressive **Allentown Art Museum** as well as two family favorites in Easton: the **National Canal Museum** and the **Crayola Experience**, whose kid-friendly exhibits are devoted to the town's most famous product, Crayola crayons.

From Easton follow rural, forested Rte 611 along the curving west bank of the Delaware River south to **Kintnersville** and then Rte 32 on the Pennsylvania side of the river or Rte 29 on the New Jersey side (you can hop back and forth across at a few points). You'll soon reach the bustling twin villages of **New Hope**, PA and **Lambertville**, NJ, which are connected by a handsome 1904 bridge with a cantilevered pedestrian pathway. Both towns have long attracted artists, actors, writers, and other creative spirits. You can learn about the area's critical role in the American Revolution at **Washington's Crossing Historic Park**, which details Gen. George Washington's famous surprise attack on British-aligned Hessian mercenaries on Christmas Day 1776. Since the late 1930s, New Hope's **Bucks County Playhouse** has been one of the country's top summer theaters. Head west on US 202—stopping in quaint **Lahaska** to browse the antiques shops and eateries of **Peddler's Village**—to **Doylestown**, with its lively downtown of elegant eateries as well as several renowned attractions: **Moravian Pottery and Tileworks Museum**, **Fonthill Castle**, the **Michener Art Museum**, and the fascinating **Mercer Museum**, an eccentric six-story 1916 concrete castle packed with Americana, ancient carriages and fire engines, and various tools and furnishings. It's about an hour south to Philadelphia.

SIDETRACK

Rising to about 2200 ft above sea level, the **Poconos** are a gorgeous tract of wooded mountains, placid lakes, and rushing waterfalls immediately north of the Lehigh Valley and rising steeply to the west of the Delaware River and **Delaware Water Gap National Recreation Area**. From Bethlehem drive about 30 miles north to reach **Stroudsburg**, with its tree-lined streets, galleries, and cafes. From here you could spend anywhere from a few hours to a long weekend exploring the region's other bewitching towns—including **Jim Thorpe**, **Tannersville**, **Hawley**, and **Honesdale**—and iconic kid-friendly attractions, such as the **Lehigh Gorge Scenic Railway, Lake Wallenpaupack,** and **Camelbeach Mountain Waterpark**. Especially beautiful drives through the Poconos include US 209, Rte 507, and Rte 402.

From Philadelphia allow about two hours to reach the southern tip of the Jersey Shore, the Victorian resort town of **Cape May**. Popular as a vacation getaway since the mid-1700s, peninsular Cape May has lovely beaches and streets lined with ornately restored, fanciful Victorian houses and inns (the imposing **Congress Hall** hotel is a standout)—the entire 3-square-mile town has been designated a national historic landmark. Three car-free downtown blocks of **Washington St** are lined with gift shops and eateries, but Cape May feels decidedly less commercial than the rest of the Jersey Shore. Be sure to tour the astonishingly grand **Emlen Physick Estate** and experience the untarnished natural scenery, such as the nature trails and bird-watching terrain of **Cape May Wetlands State Natural Area**, which adjoins the commanding 1859 **Cape May Lighthouse**. You can ascend the 199 steps to the top for marvelous view of the shore.

To continue your journey along the eastern shore of Delaware, Maryland, and Virginia—better known as the **Delmarva Peninsula**—you can either take a car ferry 15 miles across the mouth of the Delaware River to charming **Lewes** (I find this to be by far the more relaxing and scenic option) or drive up around the bay, taking I-295 across the Delaware Memorial Bridge. However you get here, do stroll around cute and laid-back Lewes and also the more touristy but colorful downtown of **Rehoboth Beach**, which abounds with both casual and sophisticated restaurants and bars and is the weekend home of President Joe Biden. **Cape Henlopen State Park**, between the two towns, has lovely beaches and nature trails.

CITY VIEW
Philadelphia

One of the nation's oldest and most storied cities, Philadelphia is also the nation's sixth largest, with a population of 1.6 million. Flanking the Delaware River and bisected by the smaller—and quite scenic—Schuylkill River, Philadelphia offers a tantalizing mix of old and new, from some of the most important sites of America's founding to stylish, of-the-moment restaurants, hotels, and arts spaces. I recommend budgeting two days here, but even in a single afternoon you can fit in several memorable attractions.

<u>Car-friendly rating:</u> Poor. Central Philadelphia, where you'll find most key attractions and hotels, is densely populated and historic, with quite a few narrow one-way streets—fortunately, it's laid out on a logical grid. Street parking is tough to come by, and hotel and garage lots are pricey, so it's best to navigate on foot or stay in the close-in suburbs west of the city or by the airport and use the regional SEPTA rail system to get into the city center. In a few interesting but less central neighborhoods, such as Northern Liberties and South Street, it's easier to find street parking.

<u>What to see in a day:</u> The best parts of the city can be divided into three main areas. Closest to the Delaware River, there's **Old City**, home to **Independence National Historical Park**, highlights of which include **Independence Hall**, **Carpenters' Hall**, and the **National Constitution Center**. To the east and south, you'll find some stellar dining options, too, including the celebrated Israeli restaurant Zahav and the trendy Asian-fusion spot Buddakan. A couple of miles away on the northwest side of downtown, **Fairmount Park** is a glorious 2000-acre swath of greenery overlooking the Schuylkill River that's also home to the outstanding **Philadelphia Museum of Art** (whose east entrance stairs you'll recognize from the movie *Rocky*). Two more amazing art museums are near here: the **Barnes Foundation** and the **Rodin Museum**. In between these areas is **Center City**, where I like to relax on a park bench in leafy **Rittenhouse Square** before noshing my way through the colorful food stalls in historic **Reading Terminal Market**. The area has dozens of trendy eateries and bars, including The Love, Vernick Food and Drink, and Tavern on Camac, which is one of the country's oldest and most beloved gay bars.

Where to stay: A reasonably priced, pleasantly furnished boutique hotel in outer Philadelphia's historic Chestnut Hill neighborhood, the **Chestnut Hill Hotel** has free parking and is a short walk from SEPTA trains to the downtown; it's also convenient for visiting Longwood Gardens and Valley Forge battlefield. The upscale **Inn at Penn**, near the University of Pennsylvania, is a stylish option that's also a bit away from downtown crowds. If you're willing to pay the steep parking fees in City Center, consider the beautifully designed **Canopy by Hilton Philadelphia**, which occupies a gorgeous late-19th-century former office building, or the trendy **Kimpton Hotel Monaco**, which is steps from Independence National Historical Park.

City Hall, Philadelphia *Opposite* Mercer Museum, Doylestown

SIDETRACK

The rolling countryside west of Philadelphia yields pleasing country drives to a variety of compelling attractions. As you drive along US 30 through the affluent and leafy **Main Line**, quick detours lead to **Valley Forge National Historical Park**, which served famously as George Washington's 1777-78 Revolutionary War encampment, and the strangely wonderful little woodwork-filled fairy-tale-esque **Wharton Esherick Museum**. US 30 continues another 50 miles west to **Lancaster**, the spirited heart of **Pennsylvania Dutch Country**. Its thriving downtown historic district abounds with eclectic restaurants and galleries but is perhaps best known for the **Central Market Lancaster**, a grand 1889 building that houses the country's oldest continuously operating farmers' market. The 60 vendors carry all manner of goodies, including Amish pickled vegetables, Puerto Rican empanadas, Polish pierogies, and Pennsylvania Dutch horseradish, apple butter, and soft pretzels. I like to overnight at one of the distinctive lodgings, such as the hip **Lancaster Arts Hotel** or stately **Lancaster Marriott at Penn Square**. Return to Philadelphia through **Kennett Square** and the picturesque **Brandywine Valley**—home to the world-class, 1077-acre **Longwood Gardens**—and **Chadds Ford**, where you can tour the exceptional **Brandywine River Museum of Art**, with its extensive collection of works by local son Andrew Wyeth and a striking glass wall that overlooks the river. From here it's just a 10-minute drive south over the Delaware border to the fabulously opulent estate of industrialist and horticulturalist Henry Francis du Pont, **Winterthur Museum, Garden, and Library**, which consists of a 175-room period-furnished mansion and more than 60 acres of exquisite gardens.

REHOBOTH, DE TO NORFOLK, VA

Continue south through a 30-mile stretch of exuberant if rather commercialized Delaware and Maryland shore towns—including **Dewey Beach** and **Ocean City**, with its hulking beach hotels and touristy restaurants with goofy names like Big Pecker's and King Cone ice cream. It amazes me how quickly the excessive development gives way just a few miles south to the quiet pastoral scenes of tree-lined country roads and 300-year-old farmsteads. Continue to the north end of **Assateague Island National Seashore**, which preserves a mile-wide, 37 mile long barrier island of breezy beaches, salt marshes, and prolific animal life, including the famous wild ponies immortalized in Marguerite Henry's celebrated children's book, *Misty of Chincoteague*. Also watch for piping plovers, brown pelicans, great egrets, and myriad winged creatures. At the modern **Assateague Island Visitor Center**, view natural history exhibits before driving across the Verrazano Bridge onto the island. Skip the more crowded state park and drive south through the national seashore, enjoying the undeveloped beaches, dunes, nature trails, and even portions of an abandoned road that had been laid down in 1962 as part of a huge commercial beach development that never came to pass. Keep an eye out for the celebrated brown-and-white ponies, and check out some of the calm bay-facing sections of the island—they offer outstanding birdwatching.

Just inland, stop in the Victorian village of **Berlin** to peruse the distinctive shops or grab a bite at a laid-back cafe. Continue south an hour to the friendly Virginia town of **Chincoteague**, which is on a small barrier island of the same name that adjoins Assateague Island's southern tip. Here you can visit sweeping **Assateague Beach** and **Toms Cove Visitor Center**, stopping to admire the stately 143 ft tall **Assateague Lighthouse**. Back in Chincoteague, grab a scoop of homemade blackberry ice cream at Island Creamery or indulge in fried seafood and gourmet hot dogs from a waterfront table at ChincoTiki Caribbean Bar and Grill. Continue south on US 13, stopping in the tidy Victorian railroad town of **Cape Charles**, with its stately mansions and a great little beach overlooking Chesapeake Bay. It's a captivating place for sunset cocktails or dinner, either at The Shanty, which overlooks the town's harbor and marina, or at the more upmarket Oyster Farm at Kings Creek. From here US 13 continues south both under and over the mouth of Chesapeake Bay via the dramatic 17.6-mile **Chesapeake Bay Bridge Tunnel**. Completed in 1964, it consists mostly of an over-sea bridge and a stretch of causeway but also features two 1 mile long sections of tunnel that burrow 60 ft beneath the water.

NORFOLK, VA TO RICHMOND, VA

The Chesapeake Bay Bridge Tunnel emerges on the northwest side of **Virginia Beach**, which is the most populous of several prominent municipalities that make up southeastern Virginia's **Hampton Roads** region. Drive east on US 60, which curves around the city's meandering and, as you go south, heavily developed beachfront, where you can saunter along the classic boardwalk and out on the pier for some great people-watching. Turn inland on Virginia Beach Ave and stop for a gander around downtown's dynamic **ViBe Creative District**, an art-filled quadrant of indie businesses and a good place to stop for a first-rate cold brew at Three Ships Coffee Roasters or a more substantial bite—and to sample artisan beers and whiskies—at Barrel 17. To learn about the region's marine life, check out the kid-friendly **Virginia Aquarium and Marine Science Center** south of downtown. Continue west about 15 miles to **Norfolk**, which overlooks a deepwater harbor on the southern branch of the Elizabeth River. The creative and cultural hub of Hampton Roads, this attractive city of 245,000 boasts several historic, colorful neighborhoods with notable food and retail scenes, including **Ghent** and **Park Place**. The **Chrysler Museum of Art** contains a world-class collection with works by Rubens, Tintoretto, Matisse, and other masters. Walk along the **Waterside District**'s scenic paths, visiting the **Nauticus** maritime museum and the hulking gray USS *Wisconsin* BB-64 World War II battleship, which together interpret the rich military and commercial history of Virginia's vibrant Tidewater region.

The fastest way around the southern and western sides of Chesapeake Bay are via dull but efficient I-64 and I-95, but I recommend the more engaging scenic route from Norfolk through **Suffolk** and **Smithfield** to the small town of **Surrey**, followed by a picturesque 20-minute ferry ride across the James River. Here you'll reach the **Historic Triangle**, which comprises **Historic Jamestowne** (established by British colonists in 1607 as the site of America's earliest permanent European settlement), **Colonial Williamsburg** (the capital of Virginia throughout most of the 18th century and a critical hub of the American Revolution), and tiny **Yorktown** (where the British surrendered to 1781, thereby sealing America's independence). If you're an ardent history buff, give yourself a couple of days to immerse yourself in the dozens of museums and attractions, which also include upscale **Kingsmill Resort** and its acclaimed riverfront golf courses and the kid-approved **Busch Gardens Virginia** theme park.

Stop first in Historic Jamestowne to walk amid the buildings and nature trails and also make the scenic **Island Drive** loop through this 1500-acre riverfront living history museum. If you have at least two hours, it's worth paying the admission to enter the settlement's buildings—such as the **Jamestown Museum** and the **Powhatan** Indigenous village—and climb aboard its historic tall ships. From here drive the 23-mile **Colonial Parkway**—a scenic road operated by the National Park Service—along the north bank of the James River, through the heart of Colonial Williamsburg, east along the south bank of the York River, and into tiny Yorktown to tour the **American Revolution Museum** and go for a short walk through the historic village. Return on the parkway, stopping for at least an hour to explore 300-acre Colonial Williamsburg—the **Governor's Palace** and **Arboretum** are two highlights, but also try visiting some of the shops where artisans (silversmiths, coopers, shoemakers) practice traditional crafts.

From Williamsburg follow Rte 5 beneath towering trees and beside rolling farmsteads along the north bank of the James River through beautiful, agrarian **Charles City County**. Along the route, much of it lined by a bike path, stop for sandwiches and craft beer on the shaded deck at Spoke + Art Provisions. You'll soon pass several sprawling Virginia estates, including two that were homes of US presidents: John Tyler's **Sherwood Forest** and William Henry Harrison's **Berkeley Plantation**, which is centered around a stunning 1720s Georgian manor house overlooking the James River. Another enjoyable stop is **Shirley Plantation**, where you can sample elegant wines at one of Virginia's best vineyards.

Continue into **Richmond**, the state's handsome and hilly state capital (pop 260,000), with features a string of lovely parks along the James River. Of the several excellent museums, my favorite is the **Virginia Museum of Fine Arts**, with its contemporary McGlothlin wing, sunny sculpture garden, and notable collections of African art, Faberge eggs, and Art Nouveau and Art Deco decorative arts. Admire the gracious, historic homes and bustling cafe culture of the **Fan District** and adjacent **Carytown**, and the hip bars and eateries of the up-and-coming **Scott's Addition Historic District**, where you can savor a cucumber lemon Gose in the beer garden at Ardent Ales or a luscious frozen delight at Gelati Celestia. Especially if you have kids in town, it's worth making the half-hour drive southwest to Moseley to explore the outstanding **Metro Richmond Zoo**, highlights of which include the chance to feed giraffes and penguins, view cheetahs up-close, and hang out with goats, camels, and llamas in the zoo's barnyard.

Ultimate Road Trips: USA & Canada

RICHMOND, VA TO ST MICHAELS, MD

Follow US 301 through the bucolic communities of Virginia's Tidewater region, crossing the Potomac River near quaint **Colonial Beach**. In **Brandywine**, MD turn north onto Rte 5 and follow I-495 west to **Alexandria**, a small, historic city on the west shore of the Potomac. The **Old Town** area, with its cobblestone lanes and 18th-century homes, abounds with sidewalk cafes, ice cream parlors, and fashionable boutiques. From the parks and pedestrian path along the waterfront outside the excellent **Torpedo Factory Arts Center**, you can see the skyline of the nation's capital just upriver. Just 10 miles downriver, visit George Washington's storied 500-acre estate, **Mount Vernon**—fans of small-batch spirits should schedule a tasting in the restored distillery. Continue to the small, energetic city of Annapolis, which is both Maryland's capital and one of the oldest cities in the Mid-Atlantic region.

Annapolis makes a perfect base for daytime trips into Washington, DC and Baltimore, which are each less than an hour away. This historic metropolis (pop 40,000) offers its own intriguing attractions, including the stately 336-acre campus of the **US Naval Academy**, which you can explore after first checking in at the **Armel-Leftwich Visitor Center**. Definitely visit the superb **US Naval Academy Museum**. Afterward, wander in the shadows of the **Maryland State House**, the oldest capitol building in the US in continuous use, and then through the downtown's picturesque historic district. A favorite activity in this nautically inclined city is getting out on the water, which you can accomplish by booking a sailing excursion on Chesapeake Bay or even just taking one of the city's many water taxis around the harbor or to the terrific **Annapolis Maritime Museum**.

From Annapolis drive east across the soaring Chesapeake Bay Bridge back onto the Delmarva Peninsula to **Easton**—with its pretty tree-lined streets, inviting restaurants, and well-regarded **Academy Art Museum**—and the villages of Oxford and St Michaels. Surrounded by water on three sides, **Oxford** is a laid-back jewel from which you can take the nation's oldest privately owned car ferry across the Tred Avon River to **Bellevue**. Continue beautiful **St Michaels**, home to the celebrated **Inn at Perry Cabin** resort as well as a number of great little eateries, such as Corah's Corner, Theo's Steaks, and Talbot 208. From here you can return the way you came to Annapolis or follow US 301 north up the Delmarva Peninsula to Philadelphia, which is about two hours away.

Ocean City

SIDETRACK

Established in 1790, **Washington, DC**, the nation's capital, is not just a center of politics, it's an engaging and diverse city with an incredible collection of 17 free museums and a zoo administered by the Smithsonian Institution, some of the world's most recognizable monuments, and a collection of pleasant, walkable neighborhoods. It's a wonderful city for fans of history, families, foodies, and even nature lovers, but it can also be a little overwhelming for a short visit, given all there is to see and do. Arrive armed with a strategy. Focus your time around the **National Mall**, which is where 11 of the **Smithsonian Museums** are located, including such icons as the **Air and Space Museum**, the **Museum of American History**, and the striking **Museum of African American History and Culture**. Then walk west along the Mall, curving around the **Washington Monument** (look north for a view of the **White House**), and continue by the reflecting pool to see the **Lincoln Memorial** and Maya Lin's moving **Vietnam Veterans Memorial**.

CITY VIEW
Baltimore

More historic than, though overshadowed by, Washington, DC, the thriving port city of Baltimore beckons with first-rate museums, one of the country's best preserved Colonial neighborhoods (Fells Point), and an attractive setting on the beautifully redeveloped Inner Harbor.

Car-friendly rating: Fair. Compared with Washington, DC and Philadelphia, it's a little easier both to drive around and park in this less dense city, and as public transit options aren't as practical for visitors, a car can be useful. Driving is toughest downtown and around the Inner Harbor, but I can usually find street parking in Federal Hill, Fells Point, and Mt Vernon, and overnight hotel parking is typically a bit cheaper than in other large East Coast cities.

What to see in a day: Start in historic **Federal Hill** at the **American Visionary Art Museum**, which occupies a striking building with excellent rotating exhibits and enchanting landscaped sculpture plazas. Climb the steps up into **Federal Hill Park**, a grassy, tree-shaded bluff with sweeping views of downtown and the **Inner Harbor**, whose touristy wharves are mostly the domain of chain restaurants and shops, but the **Maryland Science Center** and **National Aquarium** are excellent, family-friendly attractions. You can either take a short water taxi ride across the harbor to **Little Italy** and walk a few blocks or drive around the harbor to reach **Fells Point**, with its 18th- and 19th-century houses and interesting restaurants, bars, and shops. Don't miss bustling **Broadway Market**, home to Connie's Chicken and Waffles and Taharka Brothers Ice Cream. Continue several blocks to **Mt Vernon**, another district with stately 19th-century buildings. It's anchored by the 178 ft tall **Washington Monument** and is home to the superb **Walters Art Museum**, and it's another hub of fun dining and nightlife (it's also the heart of the city's LGBTQ community). Then drive a couple of miles north to explore the leafy campus of **Johns Hopkins University**, visit the stellar **Baltimore Museum of Art**, check out the quirky cafes and offbeat shops in the retro-hip **Hampden** neighborhood (which has appeared in many of the movies made by famously irreverent queer filmmaker John Waters), and perhaps end your day with dinner at one of this area's outstanding restaurants, such Woodberry Kitchen or True Chesapeake Oyster Co., inside historic **Whitehall Mill** marketplace.

Where to stay:. Fells Point is home to several noteworthy lodgings, including the swanky **Sagamore Pendry**, which occupies a handsomely transformed 1914 pier building that juts into the harbor, and the historic, moderately priced, and reputedly haunted **Admiral Fells Inn**. Mt Vernon also has a couple of hip upscale properties, **The Ivy** and **Revival Baltimore**.

The Inner Harbor *Opposite* The Crayola Experience, Easton

BEST EATS

- **Union and Finch** Savor inventive takes on soul-warming comfort fare—poutine with duck jus gravy and goat cheese curds, chicken and waffles with honey aioli—at this relaxing neighborhood bistro on an unassuming street in Allentown. 610-432-1522, unionandfinch.com.

- **Salt House** Thick wooden beams, dim lighting, and stone and stucco walls create a cozy vibe in this romantic 18th-century modern American restaurant steps from New Hope's famous Bucks County Playhouse. Note the superb craft cocktails. 267-740-7908, facebook.com/thesalthousenewhope.

- **Exit Zero Filling Station** At this stylishly converted former service station in Cape May, you'll find flavorful Thai and Indian curries (try the spicy bang bang chicken and shrimp), decadent cake-batter milkshakes, a well-considered kids' menu, and a huge, covered patio. 609-770-8479, exitzero.com.

- **Blue Moon** Not only is this bright blue-and-yellow craftsman bungalow home to the friendliest little gay bar in LGBTQ-popular Rehoboth Beach, it's also a fantastic restaurant serving up seasonal American fare, such as velvety sweet corn-and-lump crab bisque and short rib Stroganoff with spätzle, creme fraiche, and horseradish. 302-227-6515, bluemoonrehoboth.com.

- **Blacksmith** Acclaimed chef-owner Justine Zegna sources poultry, seafood, and produce from the surrounding Maryland shore at this casually hip lunch and dinner spot in quaint Berlin, a quick hop from Ocean City and Assateague National Seashore. Try the shrimp and grits with a bacon-bourbon cream sauce. 410-973-2102, blacksmithberlin.com.

- **Woody's Serious Food** Next to the KOA campground and Maui Jack's Waterpark on Chincoteague Island, this colorful, open-air barbecue joint is a festive stop for both Memphis- and Carolina-style pulled pork, smoked chicken, and ribs. Save room for the banana pudding. 410-430-4429, woodysseriousfood.com

- **Toast** The name of this funky, art-filled space in Norfolk's eclectic Park Place neighborhood hints at its popularity both for leisurely weekend brunches and clinking cocktail glasses over evening dinners. The hearty Southern-influenced food is a good value. 757-226-9655, toastplace.com.

- **Fat Dragon** Have a seat beneath the red lanterns, exposed air ducts, and high ceilings of this late-night industrial-chic space in Richmond's trendy Scott's Addition, and feast on new wave Asian fare, including beef-jalapeno fried rice, Szechuan chicken wings, and shrimp-and-bacon ramen. 804-354-9888, fatdragonrva.com.

- **Ada's on the River** This rather glamorous supper and brunch spot with soaring windows and a scene-y patio overlooking the Potomac River is steps from Old Town Alexandria. Wood-fired steaks, swordfish, and rack of lamb are among the specialties. 703-638-1400, adasontheriver.com.

- **Miss Shirley's Cafe** The downtown Annapolis location of this boozy and beloved Baltimore-based brunch and lunch spot serves up artfully plated Southern fare, such as crab cake-and-fried green tomato Benedicts and gumbo with andouille, chicken, shrimp, and crawfish. 410-268-5171, missshirleys.com.

- **Bridges Restaurant** With a huge waterfront terrace offering dazzling sunset views over Prospect Bay, this popular eatery on Kent Island is midway between Annapolis and Easton. It's a great place to sample soft-shell crabs, grilled rockfish and grits, and other Maryland delicacies from the sea. 410-827-0282, bridgesrestaurant.net.

BEST SLEEPS

- **Historic Hotel Bethlehem** This stately 1922 grande dame with an inviting lobby framed by towering Palladian windows lies within steps of Bethlehem's 18th-century museums and homes as well as several excellent restaurants. 855-264-2598, hotelbethlehem.com.

- **Ghost Light Inn** With unparalleled Delaware River views, an outstanding Jose Garces restaurant (Stella), and an ideal location beside the Bucks County Playhouse, this contemporary boutique hotel is New Hope's swankiest. You'll also find inviting rooms a few doors down at the smaller sister Inn, the Carriage House. 267-740-7131, ghostlightinn.com.

Top Graduate Annapolis hotel *Bottom* Chili pork dumplings, Fat Dragon, Richmond *Opposite* Mabry Mill, Blue Ridge Parkway

- **Boarding House** In contrast with Cape May's frilly Victorian inns, this chicly updated mid-century-modern motor lodge has a cool surfer vibe, airy and unfussy pet-friendly rooms with local art and vintage surfboards, a rooftop sundeck, and complimentary access to Montreal Beach Club. 609-884-4884, boardinghousecapemay.com.

- **Inn at Canal Square** Choose from 22 elegant rooms and suites at this laid-back, Nantucket-inspired hotel on the pretty harbor in Delaware's historic Lewes Beach. It's a short drive from the bustle of Rehoboth but away from the crowds. 302-644-3377, theinnatcanalsquare.com.

- **The Edge** On its own tiny, peaceful island with fabulous views of osprey nests and Isle of Wight Bay, this romantic, aptly named inn is on the periphery of heavily developed Ocean City. A pedestrian bridge connects to the wonderful Fager's Island restaurant. 410-524-5400, fagers.com.

- **Refuge Inn** Families and couples appreciate the large indoor-outdoor pool, inexpensive rentals, and opportunities to feed the friendly resident ponies at this peaceful 70-room property overlooking the pristine salt marshes of Virginia's Chincoteague Island. 757-336-5511, refugeinn.com.

- **Glass Light Hotel** The stylishly sophisticated rooms in this converted 1912 office tower have tall windows with great views of Norfolk's scenic harbor. Amenities include a hip restaurant, a gallery of contemporary art glass, and inviting common areas. 757-222-3033, glasslighthotel.com.

- **Linden Row Inn** Made up of seven artfully restored Greek Revival row houses on the west side of downtown Richmond, this mid-priced 70-room boutique hotel is close to great restaurants and museums. 804-783-7000, lindenrowinn.com.

- **Kimpton Lorien** Within an easy stroll of Alexandria's Old Town and the lively Potomac Riverfront, this snazzy hotel has a superb spa, two see-and-be-seen restaurants, and arty rooms with clawfoot tub and ultra-plush bedding. Kids can borrow Micro Kickboard scooters for free. 703-894-3434, lorienhotelandspa.com.

- **Graduate Annapolis** This downtown Annapolis hotel has playfully decorated rooms with art and memorabilia that pay homage to the US Naval Academy and St John's College campuses. The Trophy Room restaurant offers well-crafted American food and drink. 410-263-7777, graduatehotels.com.

- **The Inn at Perry Cabin** With gracious lawns, Adirondack chairs, and a dock facing a protected harbor on Chesapeake Bay, this Colonial-style resort with a nautical vibe perfect for a romantic getaway. Book a treatment in the elegant spa, an outing on one of the hotel's classic sailboats or yachts, or a round of golf on the exceptional Pete Dye-designed golf course. 410-745-2200, innatperrycabin.com.

CAMPING

Much of this itinerary passes through cities and densely populated areas, where camping is limited, but there are some good options, such as Benjamin Rush State Park outside Philadelphia, Patapsco Valley State Park near Baltimore, and Pohick Bay Regional Park south of Washington, DC (close to Mount Vernon, VA). Other notable camping venues in less urban areas include Colonial Woods Family Camping Resort, which is convenient both to Lehigh Valley and New Hope; Seashore Campsites and RV Resort near Cape May; Cape Henlopen State Park on the Delaware Coast; Assateague Island National Seashore and Chincoteague Island KOA Resort at the opposite ends of Assateague Island; Virginia Beach KOA in the Hampton Roads area; and Williamsburg/Busch Gardens Area KOA, which puts you close to all of that area's key attractions and is just 40 minutes from Richmond.

The Eastern Appalachians ★

Explore the rocky ridges and lush woodlands of the East Coast's highest and longest mountain range as you drive through America's longest linear park—the Blue Ridge Parkway.

HOW LONG?

5 days; add an extra day each to see more of Asheville, Atlanta, and Great Smoky Mountains National Park.

WHEN TO GO

May to early June for blooming flowers and rushing waterfalls, summer for refreshingly cooler weather than the rest of the Southeast, and mid-September to mid-October for colorful foliage. The parkways can be icy in winter, and many facilities along these routes close during this time.

NEED TO KNOW

Be careful driving these rural alpine routes at night, and even around dawn or dusk, when white-tailed deer, elk, and other wildlife are more likely to be present. This route's higher elevations are also prone to fog. Top off your tank frequently, as gas stations can be sparse. Cell service can be spotty on the parkways and in the national parks.

→ Distances

Total distance, one-way: 800 mi (1287 km)
- Atlanta, GA to Cherokee, NC: 190 mi (306 km)
- Cherokee, NC to Asheville, NC: 90 mi (145 km)
- Asheville, NC to Blowing Rock, NC: 95 mi (153 km)
- Blowing Rock, NC to Roanoke, VA: 175 mi (282 km)
- Roanoke, VA to Front Royal, VA: 225 mi (362 km)

Daytime Temperatures

January: 35-55°F (2-13°C)
July: 75-90°F (24-32°C)

More information

- Atlanta tourism, discoveratlanta.com
- Great Smoky Mountains National Park, nps.gov/grsm
- Blue Ridge Parkway, blueridgeparkway.org, nps.gov/blri
- Asheville tourism, exploreasheville.com
- Roanoke tourism, visitroanokeva.com
- Shenandoah National Park, nps.gov/shen

◉ SNAPSHOT

One of the few regions in the eastern United States that looks and feels as ruggedly spectacular and undeveloped as the West, the Appalachians offer a mix of incredible natural scenery and friendly mountain communities—such as Asheville and Roanoke—that are rich in regional art, food, and music. Much of this drive is along the Blue Ridge Parkway and Skyline Drive, two linked roads that span 574 miles and were designed expressly for drivers to enjoy the scenery at an unhurried pace.

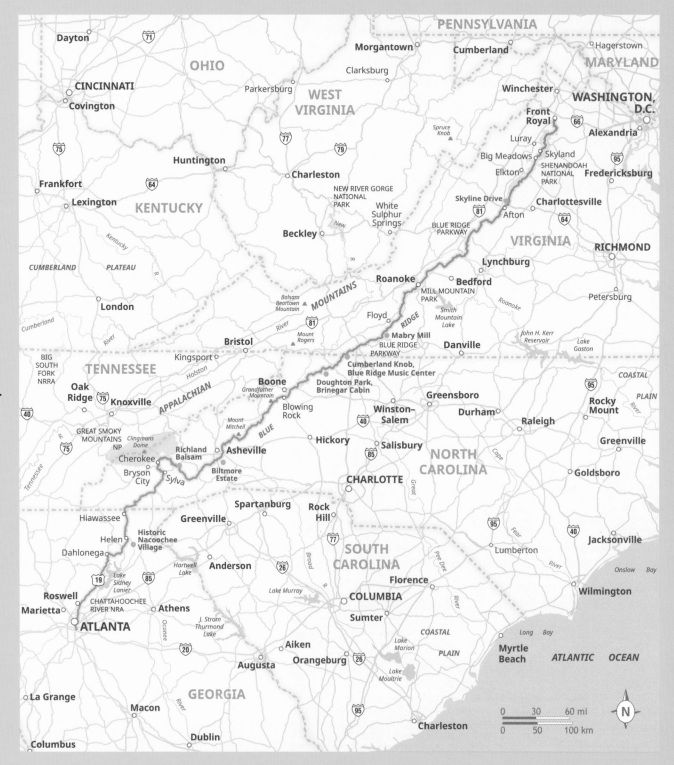

Atlanta

Home to one of North America's biggest international airports (it's the headquarters of Delta Airlines), Atlanta is a handy place to start or finish this trip. A lively, modern, if somewhat sprawling, city with a fantastic food scene and some funky, pedestrian-friendly neighborhoods, it's the largest film and TV production hub outside Hollywood, and it's also packed with exceptional attractions that appeal to kids of all ages, including the Georgia Aquarium, Children's Museum of Atlanta, and the Center for Puppetry Arts, whose Jim Henson Wing displays hundreds of "retired" Muppets.

Car-friendly rating: Fair-good with freeways snaking through and around it, Atlanta feels more like LA than any place east of the Mississippi. Rush-hour traffic snags are a problem, but the city was developed with cars in mind, and it's relatively easy to find free or inexpensive street parking in many neighborhoods. Exceptions are Downtown and Midtown, where you'll likely have to spend money on a garage or valet parking.

What to see in a day: Just southeast of Downtown, visit the historic **Sweet Auburn** district, a focal point of America's Civil Rights Movement and home to **Martin Luther King Jr. National Historical Park**. Appealing neighborhoods nearby include **Grant Park**, with its excellent **Zoo Atlanta** and the **Beacon Atlanta**, a former industrial campus that's been converted into a multicultural center of cool restaurants, art spaces, and retailers. Nearby **East Atlanta Village** and **Little Five Points** are thriving hubs of cafe culture, indie retail, and neatly restored early-20th-century homes and storefronts. Then head to trendy and LGBTQ-popular **Midtown** to check out the latest exhibits at the excellent **High Museum of Art**, and to stroll amid the gorgeous greenery of the **Atlanta Botanical Garden** and adjacent **Piedmont Park**. From either area it's an easy drive to **Ponce City Market**, an impressive mixed-use development fashioned out of a stately 1920s Sears Roebuck warehouse and housing an outstanding international food hall, several upmarket retailers, and a family-friendly rooftop entertainment center with minigolf, old-school amusements, and a fun bar with skyline views.

Where to stay: I recommend staying in one of the less central neighborhoods, which are better for cars and close to lots of good restaurants and shopping. Distinctive properties with plenty of charm and character include the quirky and reasonably priced **Artmore Hotel** in Midtown, the sleek and luxurious **Bellyard** in West Midtown, and the **Wylie** and the **Hotel Clermont**, a pair of hip boutique hotels near Little Five Points. There's also a good selection of chain properties with free parking around the airport and north of the city proper in the Perimeter area, which is convenient for starting your drive toward North Carolina.

Top: Atlanta skyline. *Bottom:* Food trucks in Grant Park.

ATLANTA, GA TO CHEROKEE, NC

This is the only part of this trip that's along conventional roads rather than designated scenic parkways administered by the National Park Service. You can choose from several routes, all of them starting amid the suburbs north of Atlanta but soon entering the lush, rolling foothills of the Appalachians, the East Coast's defining mountain range, which stretches from northeastern Alabama for nearly 2000 miles into Newfoundland, Canada. The **Appalachian Trail**, a legendary hiking route that extends 2193 miles along the spine of this mountain range and was immortalized in Bill Bryson's engrossing memoir *A Walk in the Woods*, begins on Springer Mountain in Fannin County, GA and twists and turns all the way to central Maine. About 600 to 800 intrepid trekkers complete this five- to seven-month journey each year, but more than three million people hike a portion of it.

Follow Rte 400 and then US 19 north to the bucolic college town of **Dahlonega**, which in 1828 experienced one of the nation's earliest gold rush booms (it peaked after about a decade but sporadic mining continued for decades). You can learn of this colorful period at the **Dahlonega Gold Museum**, which occupies downtown's 1836 courthouse building, and—just outside town—take a 40-minute underground tour of **Consolidated Gold Mine**, once the largest gold-mining operation in the East. Home to the pretty campus of the University of North Georgia, Dahlonega has a gracious town square and abounds with good eateries and tasting rooms—this is the heart of Georgia's wine country.

From Dahlonega, follow Rtes 52, 115, and 75 to the exuberantly Bavarian-themed village of **Helen**. If your kitsch detector didn't already light up when you drove past Cleveland's bizarre **Babyland General Hospital**, a massive Greek Revival–style toy store that birthed the Cabbage Patch Kids craze, it will once you see Helen's fanciful Alpine-style gingerbread-trim buildings, many of them housing candle and cuckoo clock emporia, festive beer gardens with dirndl-clad servers, and old-world restaurants (Bodensee is one of the best) dispensing big platters of schweinebraten, schnitzel, apple strudel, and other German delicacies. Have a walk through the town's circa-1870s **Historic Nacoochee Village**, stopping by Nora Mill Granary, which overlooks the Chattahoochee River and has a gift shop proffering cornmeal, pancake mixes, and flour stone-ground on site. Or have a glass of Chardonnay at one of oldest wineries in the state, **Habersham**.

It's about a two-hour drive to Cherokee, and as you venture north, the route climbs over loftier mountain ridges—some as high as 3000 ft—and dips down through increasingly dramatic valleys. Shortly before reaching Sylva, I (an admitted cat lady) like to stop by the quirky **American Museum of the House Cat**, which is festooned with murals and packed with art and collectibles depicting adorable felines. **Cherokee** is at the entrance to Great Smoky Mountains National Park and offers a good range of travel services, a nice tree-shaded park along the Oconaluftee River, and the excellent **Museum of the Cherokee**. Nearby **Bryson City** is another appealing gateway to the Smokies, with a bustling downtown and some fun diversions, from scenic train rides on the **Great Smoky Mountains Railroad** to guided whitewater rafting excursions on the Nantahala River.

SIDETRACK

Although Dahlonega lies just 20 miles from the southern terminus of the Appalachian Trail, actually reaching this spot by car is challenging as it requires navigating windy, unpaved forest roads. The better option is driving a half hour west to **Amicalola Falls State Park**, where from several overlooks you can behold the imposing 729 ft tall cascades for which the park is named and hike as much or as little as you'd like of the 7.5-mile "Appalachian Approach" Trail to Springer Mountain. There's also a historic lodge, a visitor center, and a stone arch under which those who attempt hiking the entire famously arduous trail usually begin their journey.

Thomas Jefferson's Monticello, Charlottesville
Opposite The terrace at the Omni Grove Park Inn, Asheville

CHEROKEE, NC TO ASHEVILLE, NC

A 522,419-acre expanse of rugged peaks, dense hardwood and spruce-fir forests, and roaring rivers, **Great Smoky Mountains National Park** straddles the North Carolina–Tennessee border and is the largest national park in the eastern United States. Much of the wilderness isn't easily accessed by car, but in a day you can easily traverse the park south to north. Start at the well-designed **Oconaluftee Visitor Center** and walk around the adjacent, open-air **Mountain Farm Museum**, an excellent place to learn about the region's Indigenous Cherokee heritage. Then drive north along Newfound Gap Road, detouring for an hour to 6643 ft **Clingmans Dome**, where a moderately steep half-mile trail leads to an observation tower that crowns this highest peak along the Appalachian Trail. Back on Newfound Gap Road, continue north and go for a drive on the lovely though sometimes busy 6-mile **Roaring Fork Motor Nature Trail**, where you can take a short, pleasant hike to **Grotto Falls**.

With a bit more time, you can drive west through the historic settlements of **Elkmont** and **Cades Cove**, driving scenic **Cades Cove Loop Road**. You can either return the way you came (about a two-hour drive) or make the longer (by an hour or so) but highly enjoyable loop around the park's west side via Foothills Parkway, then continue south alongside Chilhowee Lake and meander along a spectacular section of US 129 known as the **Tail of the Dragon** (and much beloved by motorcyclists).

There's something intoxicatingly pure about driving the **Blue Ridge Parkway**, a billboard-free 469-mile two-lane ribbon of blacktop that's maintained by the National Park Service and accesses some of the South's most breathtaking natural scenery. Exploring this artfully laid-out road is easy, and there's no fee; you just hop on, observe the leisurely 45 mph speed limit, and stop where you wish. The road follows the upper ridge line of the Blue Ridge Mountains, one of the major subranges of the Appalachians, stubbornly thumbing its nose at the faster and more direct highways that parallel parts of it.

The parkway starts near Oconaluftee Visitor Center in Great Smoky Mountains National Park. Right after you pull onto the road, at milepost 469.1, the attractive painted wooden "welcome" sign makes a popular photo op. Allow two to three hours to get to Asheville via the parkway, but you can exit at numerous points and take faster conventional roads if you're low on time or it gets dark. I avoid driving the windy parkway at night when it's hard to see what dangers lie ahead, much less the scenery.

There's an especially high number of designated turnouts on this southern 170-mile section of the road, which passes through some of the Southeast's loftiest terrain, including 6053 ft **Richland Balsam** pass, the road's highest point. Keep an eye out for grazing elk along the side of the road. At milepost 451, stop at **Waterrock Knob**, a high meadow with spectacular panoramic views as well as a small visitor center and bookstore with interpretive displays. It's an idyllic picnic spot. About 20 miles later you'll reach 5721 ft **Mt Pisgah**, which has several rewarding hiking trails as well as a historic lodge, restaurant, and campground. Just before the parkway crosses the French Broad River near Asheville, go for a stroll through the **North Carolina Arboretum**, admiring its 434 acres of demonstration gardens, azalea groves, and landscaped streams and ponds.

Asheville (pop 92,000) is the urban jewel of the Blue Ridge Parkway—a center of maker culture, outdoor recreation, and craft-beer and food. Devote a half day to exploring the 8000-acre **Biltmore Estate**, which is anchored by a resplendent—if rather somber—250-room castle built by Richard Morris Hunt in 1895 for one of Victorian America's most storied tycoons, George Vanderbilt. I find the adjacent formal gardens more interesting, along with the estate's many other offerings, which include the excellent Biltmore Winery, a working dairy farm, and the Outdoor Adventure Center, where you can book guided bike tours, kayak trips, and horseback rides. With its eclectic Art Deco, Victorian, and Arts and Crafts architecture, downtown Asheville buzzes with cool restaurants and bars. It's heaven for beer lovers—I like Wedge Brewing and Wicked Weed. Malaprops is an inviting indie bookstore with a cute cafe, and you can treat yourself to exquisite truffles, gelato, and drinking chocolates at French Broad Chocolate Lounge. Just down the hill, the up-and-coming **River Arts District** is a pedestrian-friendly warren of studios and galleries specializing in ceramics, furniture-making, and fine art.

Just north of the park, **Gatlinburg** and **Pigeon Forge** are hugely popular tourist magnets but are also heavily developed and often teeming with crowds. You'll find dozens of rollicking, if sometimes gaudy, family-friendly attractions—amusement parks, dinner theaters and comedy shows, a museum devoted to the *Titanic*, and Dolly Parton's famously campy but beloved **Dollywood** theme resort. If you're delighted by these sorts of diversions, go for it: Gatlinburg—just 3 miles from the park entrance—is the far prettier town. It's another 30 miles to **Knoxville**, which overlooks the Tennessee River and is an appealing midsize city that's a good overnight base if you want to stay longer in the area.

ASHEVILLE, NC TO ROANOKE, VA

You'll encounter some of the most dramatic scenery along the Blue Ridge Parkway between Asheville and Blowing Rock. On the east side of Asheville, stop by the airy and contemporary **Blue Ridge Parkway Visitor Center**, which contains excellent displays on the road's history and topography. A few miles north, don't miss the **Folk Art Center**, which is operated by the renowned Southern Highland Craft Guild. Galleries display regional crafts, both contemporary Southern Appalachian styles and design traditions that date back thousands of years to the region's Indigenous communities. You can watch artisans demonstrate weaving, silk painting, raku pottery, and quilting, and browse the wares in Allanstand, the nation's oldest craft shop.

Numerous opportunities for communing with nature lie just ahead. **Craggy Gardens Picnic Area** (milepost 364) is a rangy plot of outdoor tables set on a gentle wooded slope enveloped by wildflowers, rhododendrons, azaleas, and mountain laurels. Around milepost 355, a side road (Rte 128) climbs 5 miles to the summit of **Mt Mitchell**, which at 6684 ft is the highest US point east of the Mississippi River. It features an observation deck (reached by a short scamper from the parking area), a small history museum, and a casual restaurant serving up no-frills American fare but with eye-popping views.

Around milepost 305, you'll come to a cluster of notable sites, including **Grandfather Mountain**, whose rocky peaks you can visit via a dramatic mile-high swinging bridge, and the greatest engineering marvel along the parkway, the **Linn**

Cove Viaduct, a curving 1243 ft long concrete bridge that hugs the southeastern face of Grandfather Mountain—you can learn about its ingenious design at the Linn Cove Visitor Center. A little beyond, rent a canoe or kayak for a paddle around the rippling shores of Price Lake at **Julian Price Memorial Park**, and then exit the parkway to visit to the charming town of **Blowing Rock**, whose Main St is lined with cute shops as well as the excellent **Blowing Rock Art and History Museum**. It's a 15-minute drive via US 321 to **Boone**, a small city that's home to Appalachian State University and has a good range of lodging options.

As you continue northeast from Blowing Rock, the parkway's charms become a little more subtle and the elevations a bit lower. Sweeping pastures with grazing cows, dewy glades, and wildflower-strewn meadows dominate the landscape. At **Doughton Park** (milepost 238), you can stop for a bite to eat at the Bluffs, an old-time coffeeshop that became the first restaurant on the Blue Ridge Parkway in 1949. The handsome mid-century-style stone-and-timber building reopened in 2021 following an ambitious restoration after a 10-year closure—specialties include fried chicken with hot honey and red-velvet waffles. Nearby, walk around the **Brinegar Cabin**, which is typical of the unfussy late-19th-century homesteads that dotted the Blue Ridge landscape generations ago.

Soon after crossing into Virginia, at milepost 217.5, **Cumberland Knob** is a picturesque spot to stretch your legs on a 2-mile loop trail through a creek and over a waterfall. Nearby at the **Blue Ridge Music Center**, an open-air performing arts venue set against a backdrop of lush mountain greenery, folk and American roots music concerts take place throughout the warmer months, and a visitor center and museum shed light on the rich music heritage of Appalachia. At milepost 176, historic **Mabry Mill** offers blacksmithing and sawmilling demonstrations as well as weekend musical performances, and a modern restaurant serves hearty regional fare—try the pot roast with mashed potatoes, followed by warm blackberry cobbler. A little farther north, you'll encounter one of the prettiest parkway settings in Virginia, the **Smart View Recreation Area**.

Only slightly larger than Asheville, mountainous and leafy **Roanoke** is an excellent base with plenty of good restaurants and (mostly chain) hotels. At milepost 120, follow Mill Mountain Parkway, which twists and turns down a mountainside, accessing great hiking terrain at Chestnut Ridge as well as the family-friendly attractions of **Mill Mountain Park**, which include a zoo, wildflower garden,

Mountain Farm Museum, Great Smoky Mountains National Park
Opposite A pint of local beer at the Everett Hotel, Bryson City

and the 88.5 ft tall Mill Mountain Star, which is illuminated at night—you'll get a nice view of the city skyline from the observation platform at the star's base. In the city's historic downtown, check out strikingly contemporary **Taubman Museum of Art** and—just across the train tracks—the **O. Winston Link Museum**, which occupies the restored Norfolk and Western Railway train station and shows the work of the talented photographer of railroad scenes and Americana. It's a short walk to **Historic Roanoke City Market**, a bustling plaza that hosts a daily farmers market. A cool place to hunt for regional antiques and architectural elements, **Black Dog Salvage** is an amazing 40,000 sq ft showroom beside the **Roanoke River Greenway** path. The company also runs the adjacent, beautifully restored 1911 Stone House as an overnight vacation rental and presents outdoor concerts at the funky Dog Bowl amphitheater.

In **Afton**, just east of where the Blue Ridge Parkway and Skyline Drive meet, you can visit **Veritas Vineyards and Winery** and Blue Mountain Brewery, both of which have expansive shaded patios. Then via I-64 head east 25 miles to the hip and historic college town of **Charlottesville**, home to the stately 1820s campus of the University of Virginia, a vibrant downtown with several excellent restaurants, and **Monticello**, the plantation home of America's third US president, Thomas Jefferson. The estates of presidents James Madison (**Montpelier**) and James Monroe (**Ashlawn-Highland**) are also close by, along with some of the best wineries in the eastern United States, including **Blenheim**, **Keswick**, and **Barboursville**. You can also head west on I-64 just 15 miles to the colorful mountain town of **Staunton** (pronounced STAN-ton), home to a faithful re-creation of Shakespeare's Blackfriars Playhouse—it stages the Bard's works year-round.

At Shenandoah's Thornton Gap Entrance Station (milepost 31.5), follow US 11 west about 10 miles to the small town of **Luray**, famous for **Luray Caverns**, the largest cave network in the eastern United States, which you can tour on a brightly illuminated 1.5-mile walk through a 10-story-high chamber of soaring rock formations and eerie mirrored pools. Luray has a handful of hotels and some good dining options, including Gathering Grounds Patisserie and Broad Porch Coffee

ROANOKE, VA TO FRONT ROYAL, VA

The final leg of the trip includes the northern 115 miles of the Blue Ridge Parkway and all 105 miles of Shenandoah National Park's Skyline Drive. About 30 miles north of Roanoke, the small town of **Buchanan**, with its famous swinging bridge across the James River, makes for a fun detour. At the parkway's **Peaks of the Otter** area, with its mellow pastoral setting, there's a lodge and restaurant overlooking a rippling alpine lake. About 20 miles north, at the **James River Visitor Center**, you can view a historic canal system and locks and walk along a pedestrian bridge that runs directly beneath the road bridge.

Before you know it, at milepost 0, the Blueridge Parkway officially ends on an overpass above I-64, but the road transitions almost seamlessly into **Skyline Drive** and continues along the ridgeline through **Shenandoah National Park**. Skyline Drive looks like the parkway—the main difference is that you pay a $30 fee to enter, and the speed limit is 10 mph slower (at 35 mph). Shenandoah is also closer to the populous Mid-Atlantic corridor, so it's often more crowded than the Blue Ridge Parkway.

Skyline Drive is generally a bit twistier than the Blue Ridge Parkway, and it also offers plenty of appealing scenic turnouts and hiking trailheads. An excellent stop is **Blackrock Summit** (milepost 85), which accesses a gorgeous 1-mile stretch of the Appalachian Trail. Less than an hour north you'll come to the park's two main lodging and dining campuses—**Big Meadow Lodge** and **Skyland Hotel**—as well as some of the park's best hikes. At **Big Meadow**, stop by **Harry F. Byrd Visitor Center**, then make the 2.7-mile loop hike to the crest of **Hawksbill Gap**, which affords grand westerly vistas across Page Valley toward the Allegheny Mountains. An enjoyable trek from **Skyland** is the 1.5-mile trail up to the top of Stony Man peak.

On the northern stretch of Skyline Drive, you'll pass by several more dramatic high points that you can hike to with relative ease, including **Hogback Overlook**, **Little Devils Stairs**, and—near the **Dickey Ridge Visitor Center**—**Signal Knob**. Upon exiting the park's North Entrance, you'll enter the convivial little town of **Front Royal**, from which it's just a 70-mile drive east to Washington, DC. Or you can take I-66 west 10 miles to I-81 and make your way back to Atlanta (a drive of about nine or ten hours without stops).

Downtown Roanoke *Opposite* Waterrock Knob, Blue Ridge Parkway

BEST EATS

- **Capers** With tables overlooking Dahlonega's dapper Courthouse Square, this Mediterranean-inspired gastropub serves tasty dips, salads, flatbreads, and sandwiches. 706-867-0070, capersdahlonega.com.

- **Cúrate** Chef-owned by a team who trained with Spanish chef Ferran Adrià (of El Bulli fame), this buzzy Asheville hotspot in a former 1920s bus station turns out authentic tapas with creative twists; note the extensive sherry and Spanish wine selection. 828-239-2946, curatetapasbar.com.

- **Benne on Eagle** In the cool Foundry Hotel and situated in Asheville's historic Black business district, bustling Benne on Eagle has earned recognition from the James Beard Foundation for its sensational soul food, which marries West African, Caribbean, and Southern recipes and ingredients. 828-552-8833, benneoneagle.com.

- **Plant** Just north of downtown Asheville in the trendy Five Points area, this superb, upscale vegan spot is known for creative fare like bok choy ramen with smoked-tamari broth and lasagna cruda with heirloom tomatoes. 828-258-7500, plantisfood.com.

- **Christa's Country Corner** After hiking or admiring the cascades at Linville Falls, drop by this down-home deli and restaurant in Pineola near milepost 312 of the Blue Ridge Parkway for filling barbecue pork and brisket, chicken and dumplings, and meatloaf. The adjacent store sells local honey, molasses, house-made preserves, and arts and crafts. 828-733-3353, christas.com.

- **Blowing Rock Ale House and Inn** This stellar craft brewery in the cute mountain town for which it's named serves tasty pub fare, from locally raised bison burgers to fried-chicken sandwiches. Upstairs there are five cheerfully decorated guest rooms. 828-414-9600, blowingrockbrewing.com.

- **Lucky Restaurant** Order a finely crafted cocktail and sup on superb farm-to-table fare at this casually swank spot in downtown Roanoke. 540-982-1249, eatatlucky.com.

- **Scratch Biscuit Company** Start the day off right in Roanoke's hip and historic Grandin Village neighborhood with a couple of fluffy biscuits topped with any number of delicious goodies—maybe country ham and eggs, fried Cajun catfish, or blueberry jam. 540-855-0882, scratchbiscuit.com.

- **Blue Wing Frog** An excellent lunch and dinner option near the north entrance of Shenandoah National Park, in Front Royal's historic downtown, this easygoing and eclectic cafe is known for its bountiful salads, shrimp po'boy sandwiches, and a nicely curated beer, cider, and wine list. 540-622-6175, bluewingfrog.com.

BEST SLEEPS

- **Everett Hotel** This upscale boutique hotel in a restored 1905 bank building anchors Bryson City's cute downtown and has a rooftop terrace with mountain views; it's also home to one of the best restaurants in the vicinity of Great Smoky Mountains National Park. 828-488-1976, theeveretthotel.com.

- **Pisgah Inn** Rooms in this motel-style two-story property along one of the most magnificent stretches of the Blue Ridge Parkway are simple, airy, and immaculate, but the real draw is that each has a porch or balcony with rocking chairs and knockout views of mountains and Looking Glass Rock. A casual restaurant serves three meals daily. Canton, 828-235-8228, pisgahinn.com

- **Omni Grove Park Inn** Asheville's stunningly designed 1913 homage to Arts and Crafts decor and architecture is one of the most iconic hotels in the Southeast; it's the kind of place you'll probably want to linger and relax for at least two nights, as the amenities are many, from superb restaurants with terraces overlooking the Blue Ridge Mountains to a fabulous full-service spa with soaking pools and an outstanding golf course. 800-438-5800, omnihotels.com

- **Grand Bohemian Hotel Asheville** Just outside the gate to Asheville's Biltmore Estate amid the shops and eateries of Biltmore Village, this posh, art-filled hostelry has some of the cushiest rooms and suites in the region, plus a fantastic restaurant. 828-505-2949, kesslercollection.com.

- **Switzerland Inn** This chalet-style hotel is just a stone's throw from the Blue Ridge Parkway between Asheville and Blowing Rock and offers handsomely updated Alpine-inspired rooms, A-frame cabins, and even a romantic round cottage; there are three restaurants, too. Little Switzerland, 828-765-2153, switzerlandinn.com.

- **Mountainaire Inn and Log Cabins** A nice choice if you're seeking quietly elegant rusticity as well as close proximity to a lively downtown, this lushly landscaped compound near Blowing Rock's leafy Broyhill Park has traditional inn rooms and cabins with full kitchens—all are smartly decorated with plenty of creature comforts. 828-295-7991, mountainaireinn.com.

- **Primland Resort** About a half hour off the Blue Ridge Parkway, this ultra-posh 12,000-acre spread is part of the chichi Auberge Resorts group and offers opulent accommodations in a stately lodge as well as in roomy cottages and distinctive treehouse units. Meadows of the Dan, 276-633-4413, aubergeresorts.com/primland.

- **Hotel Floyd** An excellent budget option, this four-story hotel is in a friendly, attractive little village less than 5 miles from the Blue Ridge Parkway. 540-745-6080, hotelfloyd.com.

- **Black Lantern Inn** With three stylishly decorated, eco-friendly rooms, this 1920s B&B in downtown Roanoke is close to Mill Mountain Parkway and is one of the city's few truly distinctive overnight options; full breakfast is served weekends. 540-206-3441, blacklanterninn.com

- **Peaks of the Otter Lodge** Overlooking a pristine lake, this mid-priced 63-room hotel in Bedford was built in the mid-1960s and is located directly on the Blue Ridge Parkway, about 35 miles north of Roanoke. 540-586-1081, peaksofotter.com.

- **Big Meadows Lodge and Skyland Inn** The two unfancy but charming lodgings within Shenandoah National Park are only a few miles apart, and both offer gorgeous westerly views (the sunsets are dazzling) and are within walking distance of the park's two popular restaurants as well as numerous hiking trails. Skyland Inn was built in the 1950s and has more of a mid-century vibe, while Big Meadows Lodge dates to the late 1930s and feels a bit more rustic. 877-847-1919, goshenandoah.com.

- **Brookside Cabins** Just 5 miles west of Shenandoah National Park's Thornton Gap Entrance on the outskirts of Luray, this sweet collection of vacation cabins sits alongside a gurgling mountain stream and is a convenient base for side trips to Luray Caverns. 540-743-5698, brooksidecabins.com.

Hawksbill Gap hike, Shenandoah National Park
Opposite New River Gorge National Park

CAMPING

The entire region has loads of great tent and RV camping options. The Blue Ridge Parkway and Shenandoah's Skyline Drive do allow RVs and trailers, although it can be slow-going given the hilly terrain. Some of the best campgrounds include Loft Mountain, Big Meadows, and the smaller and more secluded Lewis Mountain in Shenandoah National Park; and Mount Pisgah, Julian Price, and Peaks of the Otter along the Blue Ridge Parkway. Great Smoky Mountains National Park is one of the top camping destinations in the southeastern US—favorite spots include Smokemont, which is closest to the southern entrance; and Cades Cove, which offers the greatest range of activities and services. Near Helen, Unicoi State Park and Lodge has a beautiful campground, as does Deep Creek Tube Center and Campground in Bryson City and Fancy Gap Cabins and Campground in southern Virginia.

The Western Appalachians ★

The western side of the dramatic Appalachian Range stands out for its rugged terrain and peaceful seclusion, but this journey also passes through several vibrant cities.

HOW LONG?

8 or 9 days; add an extra day or two to explore more of Nashville, Louisville, and Pittsburgh.

WHEN TO GO

Spring through fall are ideal for exploring this part of the country. The upper elevations of the Appalachians offer a cool respite during the warmer months, beautiful blooming gardens in spring, and dramatic foliage in autumn. Winter can be chilly and, in the mountains, treacherous during snowy periods.

NEED TO KNOW

As this route enters rural West Virginia and western Virginia and Maryland, you'll encounter some twisting, steep, and narrow roads, so give yourself plenty of time to navigate this region, and avoid driving in these parts after dark, when wildlife is present.

→ **Distances**
Total distance, one-way: 1130 mi (1819 km)
- Nashville, TN to Louisville, KY: 265 mi (426 km)
- Louisville, KY to Beckley, WV: 370 mi (595 km)
- Beckley, WV to Cumberland, MD: 385 mi (620 km)
- Cumberland, MD to Pittsburgh, PA: 135 mi (217 km)

Daytime Temperatures
January: 35-48°F (2-9°C)
July: 83-90°F (28-32°C)

More information
- Nashville tourism, visitmusiccity.com
- Mammoth Cave National Park, nps.gov/maca
- Kentucky Bourbon Country tourism, bourboncountry.com
- Louisville tourism, gotolouisville.com
- Lexington tourism, visitlex.com
- New River Gorge National Park, nps.gov/neri
- Pittsburgh tourism, visitpittsburgh.com

👁 **SNAPSHOT**

Although this trip is bookended by a couple of dynamic cities, Nashville and Pittsburgh, it passes through some of the most pristine and dramatic wilderness in the eastern United States, offering a mix of spectacular natural grandeur—Mammoth Cave, New River Gorge—and engaging history and culture, including Kentucky's celebrated bourbon distilleries, the Chesapeake & Ohio Canal National Historical Park, and Frank Lloyd Wright's iconic Fallingwater.

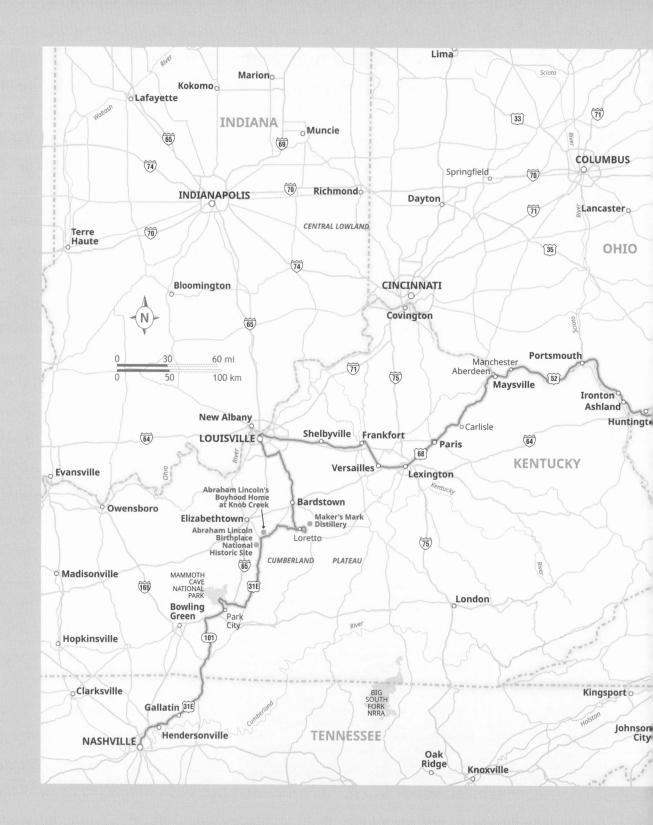

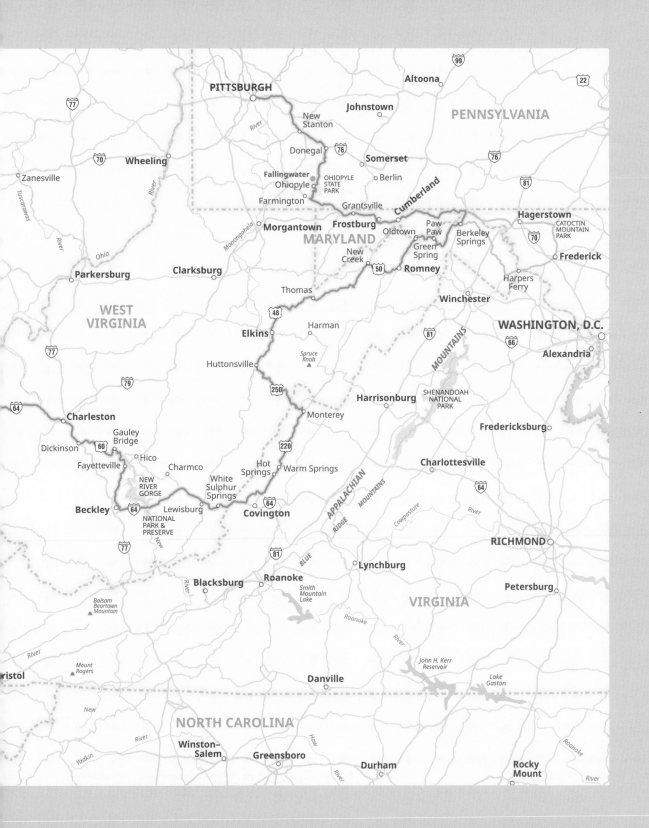

With a wealth of music venues and attractions related to its status as the world's country music capital, **Nashville** also offers an heady mix of historic charm and contemporary vibrancy—especially when it comes to its food, art, and retail. The **Tennessee State Capitol**, a Greek Revival study in marble completed in 1859, dominates a commanding bluff on the north side of downtown—have a walk along the adjacent **Bicentennial Capitol Mall**, stopping to browse and nibble at the **Nashville Farmers' Market**, and then brush up on the region's history at the excellent **Tennessee State Museum**. At the enormous **Assembly Food Hall**, choose from among 30 eateries and bars (Hattie Jane's Creamery for ice cream and Prince's Hot Chicken are two of the stars). Stroll among the neon-lit music clubs and rollicking restaurants that line **Broadway** (aka the Honky Tonk Highway), and then venture across the Cumberland River on the **John Seigenthaler Pedestrian Bridge**. The city's music heritage comes alive at the fantastic **Country Music Hall of Fame**, a strikingly designed contemporary museum that honors the 146 musicians—and counting—who have risen to the top of the ranks of this uniquely American genre. See if there's a show scheduled at the **Ryman Auditorium**, which has been delighting music fans since 1892—it's often a venue for Grand Ole Opry shows. Ardent music fans should drive 15 minutes east to **Music Valley** to attend a performance at the main **Grand Ole Opry** concert hall and tour the extensive indoor gardens of the gigantic (it has nearly 3000 rooms) **Gaylord Opryland Resort**.

Elsewhere in Nashville, fan out into some of the city's hip retail-dining districts, like the **Gulch**, which is home to the outstanding **Frist Art Museum**. Housed in a beautifully converted Art Deco post office building, it presents engaging rotating exhibits and is across the street from the neo-Romanesque **Union Station**, now a swanky hotel. Two other terrific food neighborhoods, both of them also rife with attractive Arts and Crafts and Victorian houses, include **12th Avenue South** (Josephine and Locust are a couple of fantastic restaurants) and **East Nashville**, where I'm partial to Lyra for modern Middle Eastern cuisine and Two Ten Jack for Japanese izakaya fare. West of downtown, explore 132-acre **Centennial Park**, which is anchored by a dramatic full-size replica of the Parthenon (a key site in Robert Altman's iconic film *Nashville*). Continue along West End Avenue into **Belle Meade**, an elegant neighborhood with a pair of top-notch attractions, **Belle Meade Historic Site and Winery** and **Cheekwood**, a 55-acre estate that's home to the **Tennessee Botanical Gardens and Museum**.

As an engaging alternative to I-65, head northeast through the fast-growing Nashville suburbs of **Hendersonville** and **Gallatin** and then north into the hilly Pennyroyal Plateau of central Kentucky to **Park City**, the gateway to **Mammoth Cave National Park**, which contains a portion of what's believed to be the world's longest network of caverns—it's at least 400 miles, and scientists continue to discover new sections. Indigenous communities began mining the caverns as far back as 1200 BCE, and enslaved African Americans were forced to toil long hours in the caves to produce saltpeter (used to make gunpowder). It wasn't until after the Civil War that the cave became a tourist attraction and the 1930s when the Civilian Conservation Corps (CCC) began building infrastructure and blazing trails in anticipation of Mammoth Cave becoming a national park in 1941.

You can reach the park's main attractions, all of which are fun for kids, via the 8.4-mile **Mammoth Cave Parkway**, stopping at the main visitor center to view exhibits and dioramas about the caverns—a footbridge leads to the mid-century **Lodge at Mammoth Cave**, where you'll find two restaurants and a shop selling Kentucky-made crafts and gifts. Whether you book a guided tour or explore the caves on your own (this is a good option if you're short on time), you must buy a ticket; self-guided-tour tickets can be bought only the day of your visit, while guided-tour tickets can be purchased online at recreation.gov (they sometimes sell out weeks ahead, so book early). The two-hour **Historic Tour** is best for first-timers; **Frozen Niagara** (75 minutes) and **Grand Avenue** (four hours) are highly popular, too. The park is also laced with some 85 miles of forested trails and traversed by a 30-mile section of the scenic Green River—several local outfitters offer canoe and kayak tours and rentals.

Drive north on US 31E, stopping for a look around the **Abraham Lincoln Birthplace National Historic Site**, a 344-acre park with a 56-step (in honor of his 56-year life) staircase leading to a grandiose Beaux-Arts–neoclassical museum and memorial building constructed in 1909 that contains a replica of the crude log cabin the president was born in. About 15 minutes northeast you can visit the park's second unit, **Abraham Lincoln's Boyhood Home at Knob Creek**, a 228-acre parcel where the Lincoln family resided during Abe's youth. This area also marks the southern edge of the storied **Kentucky Bourbon Country**, a verdant, undulating patch of bluegrass countryside dotted with both world-famous and smaller bourbon distilleries that stretches between Louisville and Lexington. In 1789 Baptist minister Elijah Craig produced the first batch of this iconic corn

whiskey aged in charred oak barrels. From Knob Creek it's about a half-hour drive on Hwy 52 to tiny **Loretto** to visit the impressive **Maker's Mark Distillery** on Star Hill Farm, which opened in 1953. You can tour the facility and enjoy a tasting, and order delicious lunch—Kentucky-style poutine, bourbon-smoked ribs—and cocktails at Star Hill Provisions cafe.

Head north to **Bardstown** (pop 13,300), the historic heart of bourbon country and Kentucky's second oldest city. Several blocks of neatly preserved brick and clapboard buildings emanate from downtown, which features a number of notable eateries—Bullitt's Winery & Bistro, Scout & Scholar Brewing, and the Old Talbott Tavern among them. There's also great dining and drinking to be had at The Rickhouse, an elegant brick-walled steakhouse on the first floor of **Spalding Hall,** which occupies an 1820s former seminary building that's home to the informative **Oscar Getz Museum of Whiskey History.** The building's grounds are also the site of September's popular **Kentucky Bourbon Festival.** Several other superb distilleries are close by, including **Heaven Hill** and **Four Roses.** It's about a 45-minute drive north to Louisville.

The first week of May, all eyes fall upon Kentucky's largest city, **Louisville** (pop 635,000), when it hosts the world's most illustrious thoroughbred racing event, the **Kentucky Derby.** It's a thrilling time to visit, though plan ahead, as everything books up far in advance. In fact, this attractive riverfront city has much to offer year-round. Graceful Victorian cast-iron buildings line West Main Street, and you can stroll along a landscaped river walk to soak up the impressive panoramas of the downtown skyline at **Louisville Waterfront Park** and by crossing the Ohio River into southern Indiana via the **Big Four Bridge,** which was built for trains in 1895 and converted to pedestrian usage in 2014. Set aside some time to explore the **Louisville Slugger Museum,** which is adjacent to the Hillerich & Bradsby factory, where the ash and maple bats used in Major League baseball games are produced, but also check out the **Frazier International History Museum, Louisville Science Center,** and **Muhammad Ali Center.**

The **East Market District** is a lively warren of eateries and bars—standouts include Butchertown Grocery Bakery,

Top Woodford Reserve Distillery *Middle* Frank Lloyd Wright's Fallingwater *Bottom* Grand Ole Opry, Nashville

La Bodeguita de Mima Cuban Restaurant, and Please & Thank You coffeehouse. The city also has several prominent bourbon distilleries, such as **Evan Williams** and **Old Forester**. Beyond downtown, colorful neighborhoods worth exploring include the **Highlands** and **Cherokee Triangle** districts along Bardstown Road, and **Old Louisville**, home to the gracious campus of the **University of Louisville** and a wealth of stunning Victorian mansions. Visit the **Speed Art Museum**, with its side-by-side 1927 neoclassic main building and dazzling Kulapat Yantrasast–designed 2016 wing—the museum contains the state's foremost collection of Western art, and the grounds are dotted with sculptures. Then check out the legendary 1875 venue of the Kentucky Derby, **Churchill Downs**, where you can explore a museum about its illustrious history.

LOUISVILLE, KY TO BECKLEY, WV

If you're not yet fully sated on bourbon, the two-hour-ish drive to Lexington offers more great opportunities to wet your whistle with whiskey. Head east to **Shelbyville**, where you can stop for a bite of food history at Claudia Sanders Dinner House, a rambling Greek Revival restaurant opened in 1968 by one Claudia Sanders and her colorful, cantankerous husband, Colonel Sanders, by then the retired founder of Kentucky Fried Chicken. Sure enough, fried chicken—prepared with the Sanders's original finger-licking-good recipe—is the top dish here, although the catfish platter is quite tasty, too. Continue east to **Frankfort**, stopping at **Bulleit Distilling** or **Buffalo Trace** along the way. One of the country's smaller state capitals, this leafy city on a curving stretch of the Kentucky River is anchored by the stately 1909 **Capitol**. You can also tour the excellent **Kentucky History Center** as well as the **Old State Capitol Building**, a restored Greek Revival structure that dates to 1850. Follow US 60 southeast, detouring briefly to **Woodford Reserve Distillery**, which produces exceptional bourbon on a beautiful campus of stone buildings.

Continue through historic **Versailles**, where you can book an excursion alongside some of Kentucky's prettiest horse farms on the **Bluegrass Scenic Railroad**, to the state's second largest city and home of the University of Kentucky, **Lexington** (pop 323,000). Start downtown, which has a handful of distinctive hotels, including a branch of the **21c Museum Hotel** and the historic **Gratz Park Inn**. Distilled on Jefferson is a top spot for locally sourced contemporary cuisine and local bourbons, and offbeat Third Street Stuff serves stellar lattes and light cafe fare. Tour

the **Mary Todd Lincoln House**, where the famed first lady resided as a child, and then head south for a stroll through the **University of Kentucky**'s gracious campus and its resplendent **Arboretum, State Botanical Garden of Kentucky**. Also visit **Ashland**, the lavish 1814 mansion of American statesman Henry Clay. On your way north from town, stop by the **Kentucky Horse Park**, where acclaimed thoroughbreds are trained and cared for. You can learn about the state's most famous sport on a behind-the-scenes tour and by visiting the park's **International Museum of the Horse** and **American Saddlebred Museum**.

Take US 68 past some of the region's most picturesque horse farms to **Paris**, which has a quaint downtown of 19th-century buildings and one little gem of a bourbon maker, **Hartfield & Co.** In 2021 the town installed a 20 ft scale steel replica of the Eiffel Tower. A bit south, you can tour one of the most vaunted thoroughbred horse farms in the world, **Claiborne Farm**, whose famous racehorses include the winner of the 2013 Kentucky Derby. The route continues through tiny **Carlisle**, where you can visit the 1795 cabin that was the last Kentucky home of Daniel Boone, and by **Blue Licks Battlefield State Resort Park**, the site of the final military engagement of the Revolutionary War. The road descends down a steep hill into downtown **Maysville**, an inviting river city that was a pivotal stop on the Underground Railroad and is also the birthplace of Rosemary Clooney.

One of my favorite things about road-tripping through the Midwest is driving alongside its picturesque, meandering rivers. After crossing the Ohio River into **Aberdeen**, it's a relaxing 100-mile journey along US 52—the Ohio River Scenic Byway—through a handful of small cities, including **Manchester** and **Portsmouth**, OH and **Ashland**, KY to **Huntington**, WV, a bustling river and railroad town of about 45,000. The downtown historic district makes for a pleasant stroll, which you might end with sausages and hearty German food at Bahnhof WVrsthaus and Biergarten. Continue east on I-64 about an hour to **Charleston**, another river town of 45,000 that's also the state capital—the 292-foot gilt-domed capitol is the tallest building in the state. The city has a handful of attractions that make it worth a stop, including the **West Virginia State Museum** and the **Clay Center**, whose interactive science exhibits are a hit with kids.

Continue down I-64, then cross the Kanawha River to **Dickinson** and take US 60—aka the Midland Trail Scenic Highway—for a beautiful journey along the north bank of this picturesque river to its source—the confluence of the Gauley and New rivers—in **Gauley Bridge**. Stop at the parking area for **Cathedral Falls** and follow the short trail for a view of one of the state's most impressive cataracts, which thunders 60 ft down a series of rocky ledges. You'll then come to **Hawk's Nest State Park**, which offers hiking and picnicking as well as a lodge, restaurant, and nature center—it also has dramatic views into the northern end of **New River Gorge**, which became the country's 63rd national park in 2020.

To delve further into this family-friendly park, turn south on Hwy 5 in Ansted and follow this narrow road through a verdant, pristine forest. You'll soon come to **Adventures on the Gorge**, one of several outfitters that offer activities in this 73,000-acre park, including whitewater rafting, fishing, rock climbing, and hiking. Continue down picturesque **Station Road** to reach the **Canyon Rim Visitor Center**. This light-filled, contemporary building made of local sandstone and oak contains exhibits about the park and has an observation deck with views of the soaring 3030 ft bridge that was constructed in 1977 over the deepest gorge in the Appalachian Mountains. For an even better view, walk down the short trail behind the visitor center for a closer look at the river nearly 900 ft below. Or better yet, book a **Bridge Walk** tour, during which you'll scamper along a narrow catwalk directly beneath the bridge. Across the bridge, the small town of **Fayetteville** is the main services hub for the park, containing a number of motels and cabin rentals as well as several restaurants—Pies and Pints is a good bet for tasty pizza and beer, and the Station Market and Bistro is a great source for picnic supplies.

Other New River Gorge National Park highlights include hiking along the sheer cliffs of the 2.3-mile **Endless Wall Trail**, viewing the dramatic bend in the river at **Grandview State Park**, and visiting the now-abandoned coal-shipping railroad village of **Thurmond**. Continue to the region's largest community, **Beckley** (pop 17,400), to visit the **Beckley Exhibition Coal Mine and Youth Museum**, a remarkable 1880s mine that the city purchased and converted into a historic site for visitors to learn about the industry that's been critical to the region's economy. Tours, led by former miners, take you deep into the underground mine. Nearby **Tamarack Marketplace** is an enormous cultural center where you can browse and purchase arts and crafts produced by nearly 3000 artisans from throughout the state. Before leaving town, stop by the beloved King Tut Drive-In, a 1940s fast-food joint that dispenses wings, burgers, hot dogs, and coconut cream pie.

BECKLEY, WV TO CUMBERLAND, MD

Here in the western Appalachians, a section known as the Alleghany Highlands or—farther north—Allegheny Mountains, this route passes through small villages and along sometimes extremely steep and curvy roads. From Beckley, drive east on I-64 for an hour to quaint **Lewisburg**, where you can take a 45-minute self-guided tour through **Lost World Caverns**, a 1000 ft long underground chamber of stalagmites and stalactites. Colorfully painted Victorian buildings line downtown's main thoroughfare, Washington St. It's a short drive east to **White Sulphur Springs**, a leafy hamlet that's synonymous with one of America's most opulent golf and spa resorts, **The Greenbrier**. With more than 710 elegantly appointed rooms, 20 restaurants and bars, and numerous shops and outdoor activities, this palatial 1913 property occupies a site whose natural mineral springs have drawn visitors since 1778. On a quick visit, stop for lunch and learn about the most fascinating aspect of this property, the 112,544 sq ft bunker built in the early 1960s some 720 ft beneath the hotel and designed to shelter the entire US legislative branch in the event of a crisis (this was, of course, at the height of the Cold War). The existence of the facility was kept from the public until 1992, when it was declassified, and the hotel now gives 90-minute in-depth tours.

Continue into Virginia and follow US 220 on a breathtaking drive through the mountains, stopping to snap a photo of soaring 80 ft **Falling Springs Falls**. At the village of **Hot Springs**, you'll encounter another of the region's venerable resorts, the **Omni Homestead**, a late-Victorian compound with award-winning golf courses and the state's oldest downhill ski area. Countless dignitaries have spent the night here, and at the start of World War II, the property housed nearly 800 detained Japanese diplomats and their families. The tiny village center is also home to the celebrated French restaurant Les Cochons d'Or. Follow US 220 up to **Monterey**, and then turn back into the high mountains of West Virginia via US 250 up to **Elkins**, a picturesque alpine hub of outdoor recreation, and then up US 48 through dramatic hills to **Thomas**, a small hamlet that sits an at elevation of 3035 ft and thrived for many years as a coal-mining center. More recently, artists and entrepreneurs have opened hip cafes, galleries, and lifestyle shops. Continue east to **Romney**, known for its historic **Potomac Eagle Scenic Railroad**, whose excursions provide a chance to view the many eagles that thrive in the verdant South Branch Valley. Turn north up to **Green Spring** and cross the Potomac River into **Oldtown**, MD via the state's only privately owned and operated toll bridge—it'll cost you $1.50 to drive over this single-lane, wooden-plank bridge that dates back to 1937.

Follow windy and scenic Hwy 51 east, partly alongside the historic **Chesapeake and Ohio Canal** (C&O Canal), a narrow 184.5-mile waterway that extends from Cumberland, MD to Washington, DC and is now maintained as a national historic park. You'll soon cross back for a brief foray into the crooked eastern West Virginia panhandle, starting in tiny **Paw Paw**—where you can walk through the **Paw Paw Tunnel**, a 3118 ft long canal passage constructed in 1850 that's still considered an engineering wonder. Continue up the hill to **Berkeley Springs**, an attractive community known since the late 18th century for its curative springs. In the center of town at **Berkeley Springs State Park**, you can book a soak in historic Old Roman and Main bathhouses and view a stone replica of the tub that George Washington relaxed in during his many visits. This enchanting little town also has several galleries and antiques shops and some excellent eateries, including Lot 12 Public House.

SIDETRACK

It's about an hour's drive southeast to **Harpers Ferry**, WV, a tiny hilltop hamlet at the confluence of the Potomac and Shenandoah rivers, directly across from the states of Maryland and Virginia. The town's strategic setting as the northernmost point in the Confederacy figured critically in its outsized role during the Civil War. At **Harpers Ferry National Historical Park**, you can learn about the most critical event of this period, John Brown's unsuccessful abolitionist raid on the town's federal armory. The **Appalachian Trail** passes directly through the park and across the **Winchester and Potomac Bridge**, a railroad-turned-pedestrian crossing, into **Sandy Hook**, MD. Drive 20 miles to **Frederick** (pop 78,200), one of Maryland's most enchanting small cities. With a courtly downtown of carefully restored 18th- and 19th-century buildings, many of them housing distinctive boutiques and restaurants, Frederick has several prominent attractions, including the **National Museum of Civil War Medicine**, **Monocacy National Battlefield**, and picturesque **Carroll Creek Linear Park**. Continue north to **Catoctin Mountain Park**, a stunning swatch of peaks that's maintained by the National Park Service and is also the site of the US presidential retreat, **Camp David**. Head to **Hagerstown**, where you can pick up I-70 and I-68 west through Maryland's panhandle to Cumberland.

Downtown Thomas *Opposite* The Country Music Hall of Fame, Nashville

CUMBERLAND, MD TO PITTSBURGH, PA

Cumberland (pop 19,000), a historic city in far western Maryland's panhandle, once thrived as a pivotal Appalachia transportation hub thanks to its location on a major canal, river, highway, and rail line. Picturesque **Western Maryland Scenic Railroad** excursions on vintage diesel-powered rail cars depart from downtown's 58-acre **Canal Place** park and travel west through a lush, undulating valley to Frostburg. The park also features a stately 1913 train station, interesting history exhibits at the **Allegany Museum**, and **Chesapeake & Ohio Canal National Historical Park**, which is home to the restored canal and towpath—now a bike trail—that mark the western terminus of this once invaluable (during its 1850 to 1875 heyday) transportation passage. A pedestrian bridge leads over Wills Creek to a small park containing the tiny log cabin that served as George Washington's headquarters, first during the French and Indian War and then nearly 40 years later as president and commander in chief during the Whiskey Rebellion. You'll find several good eateries within walking distance, including Ristorante Ottaviani and Baltimore Street Grill. About 10 miles west, **Frostburg** is a quaint old college town (home to **Frostburg State University**) with appealing galleries and one-of-a-kind shops. I-68 continues west to **Grantsville**, home to **Spruce Forest**

Artisan Village, a community of restored cabins that house artists' studios as well as Penn Alps Restaurant and Gift Shop and Cornucopia Cafe. Adjacent **Casselman River Bridge State Park** centers on a small patch of greenery and a single-span 1813 stone-arch bridge.

Take US 40 northwest into southwestern Pennsylvania's **Laurel Highlands** to **Farmington**, best known for its sprawling, family-friendly **Nemacolin** resort, as well as for **Fort Necessity National Battlefield**, the site of a prominent victory for then Colonel George Washington in 1754 during the French and Indian War. Follow Hwy 381 north to **Ohiopyle State Park**, an enchanting setting for hiking and white water rafting on the Youghiogheny (locals call it the "Yough," which rhymes with "hawk") River. Although the population of this tiny village could fit into a school bus, Ohiopyle draws hundreds of visitors on summer and fall weekends. The **Great Allegheny Passage** rails-to-trails path traverses the village on its 150-mile journey between Pittsburgh and Cumberland, and a modern, sun-filled visitor contains exhibits on the area's natural history. The region's tremendous natural beauty has made it a favorite weekend getaway of Pittsburgh industrialists, including the owner of the once-vaunted Kaufmann's Department Store, who in 1936 hired Frank Lloyd Wright to design his weekend house on Bear Run creek. The result, **Fallingwater**, ranks among the world's most visually remarkable residences. This 5330 sq ft home with its unusual cantilevered terraces perched over a rushing waterfall is an incredible work of art and engineering. Tours sometimes sell out, so book well in advance. Nearby you can also tour a less visited Frank Lloyd Wright commission, **Kentuck Knob**, a smaller and less flashy mid-1950s sandstone-and-cypress home that's one of Wright's visionary, decidedly middle-class Usonian designs. It may not have Fallingwater's sheer wow factor, but inch for inch, I find it every bit as interesting. It's about a 90-minute drive northwest through **Donegal** and **New Stanton** to Pittsburgh.

Formerly one of America's leading industrial powerhouses, **Pittsburgh** has largely reinvented itself following a sharp economic decline in the mid-20th century and has emerged as a smaller (pop 303,000) and leaner but undeniably exciting center of art, culture, and education with a diversified, tech- and healthcare-driven economy. It's also a true Appalachian Mountain metropolis surrounded by steep hills that rise above its charmed setting at the confluence of the Ohio, Allegheny, and Monongahela rivers. For an outstanding view, ride the bright-red **Duquesne Incline** funicular to the top of **Mt Washington**. Downtown boasts an impressive

skyline of both historic and contemporary towers, and it's where you'll find a number of stylish hotels, theaters, and performance spaces.

My favorite Pittsburgh neighborhood for exploring, the **North Shore** lies just across the Allegheny River from downtown and contains **PNC Park** (baseball's Pirates) and **Heinz Field** (football's Steelers) as well as the superb **Andy Warhol Museum**, which celebrates the life of the native son and pop art icon. First-rate attractions in the vicinity include the **Carnegie Science Center**, the **National Aviary**, the **Children's Museum of Pittsburgh**, and—set in the historic Mexican War Streets district—the **Mattress Factory** and **Randyland** contemporary art museums. Elsewhere in town, the **John Heinz Pittsburgh Regional History Center** is a highlight of **the Strip** warehouse district, which is also home to old-school eateries like Pamela's Diner and Primanti Bros., known since the 1930s for its sandwiches crowned with mountains of French fries and coleslaw. In **Oakland**, Forbes and 5th avenues anchor the handsome **University of Pittsburgh** and **Carnegie Mellon University** campuses, with their impressive cultural draws—don't miss the **Carnegie Museums of Art and Natural History** and the **Phipps Conservatory and Botanical Gardens**. Farther east you'll discover some of the city's trendy food hubs, such as **Walnut Street** in **Shadyside**, **Bakery Square**—with its sleek Gallery food hall—in **East Liberty**, and **Butler Street** in bustling **Lawrenceville**. For a solid mile, Butler Street is lined with intriguing indie boutiques and eateries—some favorites of mine being Pusadee's Garden for modern Thai fare, Morcilla for Spanish tapas, and Umami for Japanese izakaya cooking.

BEST EATS

- **Peg Leg Porker** A hot spot in Nashville's booming Gulch district, this convivial barbecue joint with a terrace and rooftop bar serves heaping platters of pulled pork nachos, dry-rubbed ribs, and smoked chicken and also makes small-batch bourbons. 615-829-6023, peglegporker.com.

- **Folk** At this rustic-industrial spot in trendy East Nashville, tuck into plates of soul-warming Italian steaks and seafood along with ethereal thin-crust pizzas—try the pie with lamb sausage, preserved hot peppers, and fennel pollen. 615-610-2595, goodasfolk.com.

- **Kurtz** Finish your tour of bourbon distilleries with a satisfying meal at this old-school Southern restaurant across the street from My Old Kentucky Home museum. Try the fried country ham with red-eye gravy and a slice of coconut cream pie. 502-348-8964, kurtzrestaurant.com.

- **610 Magnolia** In this romantic Old Louisville dining room with beamed ceilings and French doors, savor the rarefied contemporary Southern cuisine of James Beard finalist Edward Lee. Consider the duck breast with plum hoisin sauce and charred okra. 502-636-0783, 610magnolia.com.

- **Chik'n & Mi** In a historic house near Louisville's Melrose Arts Center complex, this convivial restaurant specializes in creative takes on Asian comfort fare, including kimchi mac and cheese, miso pork ramen, and crispy fried chicken. 502-890-5731, chiknandmi.com.

- **Tony's of Lexington** This elegant bilevel steakhouse is the perfect locale for a romantic meal and great people-watching. The service is refined, the wine and bourbon selections first-rate, and the food decadently delicious. 859-955-8669, tonysoflexington.com.

- **Livery Tavern** In charming Lewisburg, end a day of adventure in New River Gorge with a meal in this smartly restored 19th-century livery stable that specializes in creative Appalachian fare—think brown sugar-rubbed pork belly, and braised lamb shanks with creamy grits. 304-645-9836, liverytavern.com.

- **Waterwheel Restaurant** In Virginia's crisp-aired Alleghany Highlands, this warmly lighted, high-ceilinged dining room occupies a late-Victorian gristmill that also houses a comfortable country inn. The farm-to-table menu changes seasonally, but you can always add shaved black truffles to any dish. Warm Springs, 540-839-2231, gristmillsquare.com.

- **The Forks** Soak up Appalachian Range views from the deck of this casually sophisticated eatery inside a small Elkins mountain inn. Menu highlights include wild mushroom soup with chive crème fraîche, and coffee-rubbed beef tenderloin with a brandy-peppercorn sauce. 304-637-0932, attheforks.com.

- **Tari's** This art-filled Berkeley Springs cafe enjoys a beloved reputation for regionally sourced Appalachian cuisine, such as Carolina pulled pork with apple butter barbecue sauce and linguine with Chesapeake sea scallops, blue crab, and shrimp. 304-258-1196, tariscafe.com.

- **Poulet Bleu** Run by celebrated Pittsburgh chef Richard DeShantz, this dapper French-American bistro along Lawrenceville's bustling restaurant row serves classics like escargot with garlic butter and steak fries with cognac pepper sauce. Note the extensive list of after-dinner drinks. 412-325-3435, pouletbleupgh.com.

- **Mola** Have a seat in this sleek storefront space in Pittsburgh's trendy East Liberty neighborhood, and enjoy first-rate pan-Asian cuisine, including an extensive sushi selection. 412-365-6688, themolafish.com.

BEST SLEEPS

- **The Russell** Set is a dramatically converted Romanesque-style church in hip East Nashville, this one-of-a-kind 23-room hotel features stained-glass windows and headboards made from old pews. The owners donate part of the revenue from this property and two others (The Gallatin and 506 Lofts) to local homeless shelters. 615-861-9535, russellnashville.com.

- **Hutton Hotel** This sleek, contemporary tower has a great location west of downtown near Music Row, Church Street's LGBTQ scene, Vanderbilt University, and Centennial Park. You can borrow LP players and selections from the vinyl library and even musical instruments to turn your room into a sumptuous music retreat. 615-340-9333, huttonhotel.com.

- **Bourbon Manor** Choose this lovely 10-room early 19th-century B&B in Bardstown as a convenient base for visiting distilleries—Louisville and Lexington aren't far either. You can book a massage in the fireplace-warmed spa room. 502-309-2698, bourbonmanor.com.

- **21c Museum Hotel** Set amid Louisville's West Main Street museum row, this original location of the contemporary art-themed 21c Museum Hotel brand occupies five 19th-century tobacco and bourbon warehouses. You could spend hours exploring the intriguing gallery spaces, and Proof on Main is one of the city's finest restaurants. 502-217-6300, 21cmuseumhotels.com.

- **Resort at Glade Springs** This casually upmarket 200-room property in Daniels is just 12 miles from the southern end of New River Gorge National Park, but it also offers plenty of family-friendly activities on its 4100 wooded acres. 304-763-2000, gladesprings.com.

- **The Greenbrier** There's nothing subtle about this monumental resort in White Sulphur Springs—it's showy and rather enormous, with countless diversions (try to spend at least two nights here to enjoy the amenities). Steeped in history, it's one of the ultimate golf and spa destinations in the Mid-Atlantic region. 855-453-4858, greenbrier.com.

- **Country Inn of Berkeley Springs** Right beside the historic bath houses of Berkeley Springs State Park, this 70-room 1930s hotel in West Virginia's eastern panhandle is an inviting place to relax and restore. A restaurant and two lounges serve very good food and drink. 304-258-1200, thecountryinnwv.com.

- **Savage River Lodge** In a peaceful state forest in western Maryland, on the outskirts of Frostburg, this rustic but comfortable compound offers warmly appointed cabins and spacious yurts with premium bedding, full baths, and gas-log fireplaces. Delicious meals are served in the log cabin-style lodge. 301-689-3200, savageriverlodge.com.

- **Tryp by Wyndham** This hip but affordable 108-room design hotel is filled with local artwork and has two very good restaurants, but it's also steps from several other culinary hot spots in Pittsburgh's lively Lawrenceville neighborhood. 412-567-0555, tryppittsburgh.com.

- **Industrialist Hotel** Close to downtown Pittsburgh's bustling Market Square as well as the theaters and concert venues of Liberty Avenue, this tony boutique hotel occupies the 18-story Arrott Building, which dates to 1902. Rooms have a streamlined and sexy Art Deco vibe, and the Rebel Room serves sophisticated modern American fare and craft cocktails. 412-430-4444, theindustrialisthotel.com.

CAMPING

You'll find plenty of opportunities for sleeping under the stars in this region, especially in the mountains. But even from Nashville to Louisville, you'll find some pleasing campgrounds, such as Cages Bend near Gallatin, Mammoth Cave at the national park, and Louisville South KOA in Kentucky Bourbon Country. Wolford's Landing is a pretty spot in Portsmouth on the Ohio River, and American Alpine Club is a favorite in New River Gorge National Park. As you venture deeper into the Appalachians, consider Bolar Mountain near Hot Springs, Pegasus Farm in Elkins, Blackwater Falls in Thomas, and Little Orleans near Cumberland and Berkeley Springs. Farther north, good bets include Ohiopyle State Park and McConnells Mills State Park north of Pittsburgh.

21c Museum Hotel, Louisville *Opposite* Pittsburgh and the Duquesne Incline from Mt Washington

Coastal Carolinas and Georgia ★

Flanked by pristine barrier islands and dotted with venerable old-world cities, the coast from the Outer Banks to northeastern Florida delights beachcombers, birdwatchers, and bons vivants of all stripes.

HOW LONG?

7 days; add an extra day each to see more of Wilmington, Charleston, and Savannah.

WHEN TO GO

Anytime from March through December can be great for this drive, but each season has its pros and cons, with early spring and late fall a bit cool for some in the Carolinas, but midsummer potentially too hot and humid in Georgia and Florida. April to May and mid-September to mid-November are the sweet spots, although book ahead and prepare for steep rates on weekends. If swimming and beachcombing aren't top priorities, consider visiting in winter, which is still relatively mild and yields fewer crowds and better prices.

NEED TO KNOW

Many of the destinations along this route host major annual festivals, such as Spoleto in Charleston in late spring and St Patrick's Day in Savannah. These can be fun, but they also draw huge crowds and result in sky-high hotel rates.

→ Distances
Total distance, one-way: 850 mi (1368 km)
- Duck, NC to Wilmington, NC: 265 mi (426 km)
- Wilmington, NC to Charleston, SC: 185 mi (298 km)
- Charleston, SC to Savannah, GA: 115 mi (185 km)
- Savannah, GA to St Augustine, FL: 215 mi (346 km)

⊜ Daytime Temperatures
January: 50-68°F (10-20°C)
July: 85-93°F (29-34°C)

ⓘ More information
- Outer Banks tourism, outerbanks.org
- Wilmington tourism, wilmingtonandbeaches.com
- Charleston tourism, charlestoncvb.com
- Savannah tourism, visitsavannah.com
- Golden Isles tourism, goldenisles.com
- Jacksonville tourism, visitjacksonville.com
- St Augustine tourism, visitstaugustine.com

◎ SNAPSHOT

The aesthetic of the curving southeastern US coastline can't be summed up in one exact style: there's the Spanish Colonial influence of America's oldest city, St Augustine; the dignified redbrick Victorians and landscaped squares of Savannah; and the Caribbean-inspired pastels of colonial Charleston, interspersed with modern family-friendly beach and golf resort towns. There's plenty along this route to satisfy every taste and budget, but the region's greatest asset is nature; breezy salt marshes, dune-backed shorelines, and estuarial bays and rivers support a wildly diverse array of wading birds, waterfowl, sea turtles, shellfish, and other creatures.

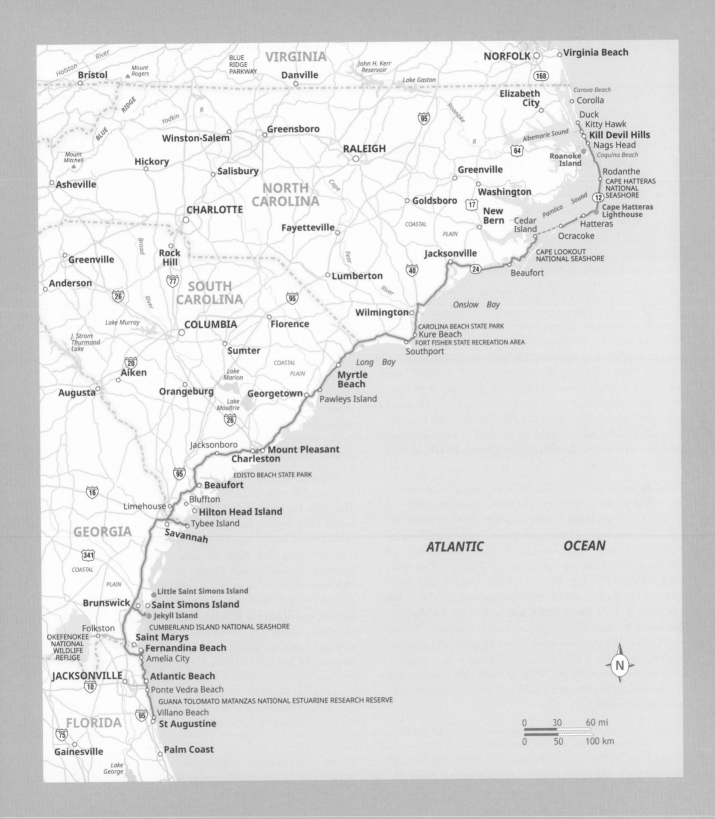

OUTER BANKS, NC TO WILMINGTON, NC

A roughly 200-mile string of narrow barrier islands and peninsulas make up North Carolina's beautiful **Outer Banks**. You can drive nearly the entire length, although the southernmost point, Ocracoke Island, is reached by ferry. A hugely popular vacation destination today, the region was the site of one of America's earliest European settlements—the failed Roanoke Colony in 1587—and has been associated with pirates, shipwrecks, early aviation, and hurricanes ever since. Unfortunately, these low-elevation islands, some of them narrower than 1000 ft, are tremendously vulnerable to the effects of rising sea levels and beach erosion, both of which have been exacerbated severely by climate change, and countless structures as well as roadways along the shoreline have been damaged or destroyed by recent storms.

That said, road-tripping through the salt-aired, dune-flanked Outer Banks is a magical experience, especially the less developed southern section, which is protected within Cape Hatteras National Seashore. From the mainland, US 158 crosses Currituck Sound into the upper span of islands at the town of **Kitty Hawk**. A left turn leads north about 20 miles up Rte 12 through **Duck** and **Corolla**; there are generally fewer homes and businesses the farther north you travel until the paved road dead-ends at **Corolla Beach** (from here, by four-wheel-drive vehicle only, it's possible to continue another 12 miles on unpaved beach roads to **Carova Beach**, at the Virginia border).

Heading south onto Rte 12 leads down through the most densely developed stretch of the Outer Banks for about 15 miles to **Nags Head**. Vacation homes, many of them on stilts for protection during storms, and family-friendly mid-rise hotels line the route, and you'll find some excellent spots for lunch, including the beachy-casual Rundown Cafe and Mama Kwan's Tiki Bar and Grill, both of which offer up fusion-y Pacific Rim and Caribbean fare and colorful tropical cocktails. In **Kill Devil Hills**, stop at **Wright Brothers National Memorial** to see where aviation pioneers Wilbur and Orville Wright conducted their first successful airplane flights; the 430-acre site contains a striking visitor center with an excellent museum, walking paths that trace the path of the original flights, and a 60 ft tall granite monument to their achievement.

At the southern end of Nags Head, take the US 64 bridge across Roanoke Sound to visit **Roanoke Island**, the home of Algonquian Native Americans and then Sir Walter Raleigh's ill-fated 1587 settlement, which you can learn more about at **Fort Raleigh National Historic Site** by attending an outdoor, waterfront performance of the historical musical *The Lost Colony* (shown mid-May to mid-August) and checking out the exhibits in **Lindsay Warren Visitor Center**. Next door, stroll through the 10-acre **Elizabethan Gardens**, and in quaint **Historic Old Manteo** you can tour the excellent **Roanoke Maritime Museum** and book a candlelight walking tour through the village each evening.

Returning to Rte 12, head south into **Cape Hatteras National Seashore**. Within minutes you'll come to pristine dunes at **Coquina Beach** and the short turnoff to **Bodie Island Lighthouse**. If you're up for a workout, climb the 214 steps to the observation deck. At the base, pick up information about the seashore's trails, boating areas, and habitats at the **Bodie Island Visitor Center** and go for a boardwalk stroll through a salt marsh that teems with migratory birds. For the next 40 miles, the road continues south through a mix of undeveloped shoreline and small, laid-back beach towns—**Rodanthe**, **Waves**, **Salvo**, **Avon**—which have a slower, folksier vibe than the Nags Head area. The 13-mile long island that's home to **Pea Island National Wildlife Refuge** preserves critical habitats and nesting grounds for sea turtles as well as dozens of migratory shore and wading birds, including widgeons, American oystercatchers, least terns, and snowy egrets. From the small visitor center, two boardwalk nature trails offer great opportunities for viewing wildlife.

At the southern tip of Hatteras Island, visit the most recognizable structure on the Outer Banks, the **Cape Hatteras Lighthouse**, which at just under 200 ft is the tallest brick lighthouse in the country. You can climb the 257 steps (equal to a 12-story building) to the top for a breathtaking view. Near the base, check out both the **Hatteras Island Visitor Center** and—in the historic lighthouse keepers' quarters—the **Museum of the Sea**. It's about a half-hour drive through the villages of **Buxton**, **Frisco**, and **Hatteras** to reach the free one-hour ferry to Ocracoke Island. The ferry runs about every half hour in summer, but there can be long waits on busy weekends; fortunately, you can kill time if you're delayed at one of the fun waterfront restaurants (Wreck Tiki Bar and Grill is a good option), touristy but colorful souvenir shops, and the intriguing **Graveyard of the Atlantic Museum**, all within walking distance of the terminal.

Assuming you've made reservations for one of the less frequent ferries from Ocracoke Island south to Cedar Island, you'll be taking the most relaxing and scenic route down the

The beachfront, Wilmington *Previous* Forsyth Park, Savannah

coast, eventually to Wilmington. The trip, including both ferry rides, the 20-minute drive across Ocracoke Island, and the final 3 hour drive from Cedar Island ferry terminal takes about 7.5 hours without stops, but Ocracoke Island is a nice place to spend a few hours, or even overnight, so factor that in as well. Alternatively, you could make the 5.5- to 6-hour drive inland to Wilmington by backtracking up Rte 12 to Roanoke Island and continuing west and then south through the historic river towns of **Washington** and **New Bern**, each offering a nice variety of attractions and museums, but I prefer the enchanting scenery of North Carolina's southern shoreline, aka the Crystal Coast.

At 10 sq miles and accessible only by ferry, **Ocracoke Island** feels far more secluded than any other town along this drive— it's peaceful, low-key, and has fewer than 1000 residents. The notorious pirate Blackbeard was killed here in a violent battle in 1718, but these days the most excitement you're likely to encounter is a rush to the bar during last call at 1718 Brewing pub (I'm partial to their tasty sour ales and mango IPAs). Other adventures include lazing on the sand at glorious **Ocracoke Beach**, scampering beneath (you can't climb it) the nation's second oldest operating lighthouse, and viewing old memorabilia and furnishings at the quaint **Ocracoke Preservation Museum**. If you're not spending the night, try to go over on an early ferry and give yourself a few hours for exploring and lunch before continuing on the ferry to Cedar Island, which costs $15 for a car and does accept reservations,

which are a good idea in summer; note that the last ferry is 4:30pm or 5:30pm, depending on the time of year.

Upon landing at **Cedar Island**, it's a 140-mile drive to Wilmington. The first part of this drive is the prettiest, as Hwy 12 and then US 70 pass through the salt marshes of **Cedar Island National Wildlife Refuge** and then along Core Sound, across which you can see another set of barrier islands that are part of **Cape Lookout National Seashore**, a far more remote and wild section of coastline than Cape Hatteras. If you're curious about exploring Cape Lookout, make the 9-mile detour south from US 70 a little west of **Smyrna** to **Harkers Island**, a laid-back fishing village that's home to Cape Lookout's headquarters and its main **Harkers Island Visitor Center**; here you can book a ferry out to the islands, including to **Cape Lookout Lighthouse** and beach.

Follow US 70 to **Beaufort**, a charming little port community that was founded in 1713 and is a nice stop for a bite to eat or a sunset cocktail in the bustling downtown overlooking Taylor Creek. There's also an excellent branch of the **North Carolina Maritime Museum** and several blocks of neatly preserved Colonial and Victorian homes. For the best scenery on the rest of the drive, after crossing into **Morehead City**, head south to **Atlantic Beach** and follow coastal Rte 58 west along this pretty barrier island, then pick up Rte 24 to **Jacksonville**—home to the largest US marine base, Camp Lejeune—and US 17 to Wilmington.

WILMINGTON, NC TO CHARLESTON, SC

An artsy, historic port city on a deep, protected river inland from a glorious beachfront, **Wilmington** (pop 125,000) feels a bit like two other famous coastal cities farther south—Charleston and Savannah. But it has lower profile than the other two, despite having become an increasingly popular place to live and vacation—it's both less expensive and usually less crowded, too. The lively downtown flanks a beautiful stretch of the Cape Fear River, which you can appreciate during a stroll—I like doing this around sunset—along the nearly 2 mile long **Wilmington Riverwalk**, which has cafes, markets, and a scenic marina. Across the river you'll see the imposing World War II–era *Battleship North Carolina*, which you can visit by water taxi. A couple of blocks inland, Front Street is lined with both hip and homey bars and restaurants—stop for a pick-me-up at Bespoke Coffee and Dry Goods or wind down with a Sauvignon Blanc at Fortunate Glass wine bar.

South of downtown, check out small **Cameron Art Museum**, which has excellent rotating shows and a terrific cafe; in fall 2021 it unveiled the remarkable Colored Troops Public Sculpture Project, a life-size bronze featuring 11 Black soldiers who were among the 1600 who fought valiantly on this site during the Civil War's Battle of Forks Road. A few miles east, wander amid the 67 acres of manicured gardens, moss-draped live oaks, and flowering magnolia and camellia trees at **Airlie Gardens** before continuing across Bradley Creek to upscale **Wrightsville Beach**, where you can admire the ocean from historic **Johnnie Mercer Fishing Pier**, shop for souvenirs and beach-picnic supplies at 1919 Robert's Grocery, or linger for a leisurely repast at one of several good eateries. I recommend the Workshop, which serves excellent coffee drinks and smoothies, and East Oceanfront Dining at the Blockade Runner Beach Resort, with a patio overlooking the water (the Sunday jazz brunch is especially enjoyable) and lovely ocean-view accommodations, too.

Follow US 421 south along the **Cape Fear Peninsula**. A hidden gem is **Carolina Beach State Park**, where you can rent a kayak from **Paddle NC** and navigate among the seabirds along a wide stretch of the Cape Fear River or walk the easy but fascinating Venus Flytrap Trail, one of the only places in the world where these small carnivorous plants exist in the wild. For sustenance, head to the Southerly for a made-from-scratch country ham and cheddar biscuit sandwich or to the Fork 'N' Cork for a pint of local beer and the signature Duck Goose Burger: ground duck patty with goose pâté, fried duck egg, and port wine–cherry sauce. A few miles south in **Kure Beach**, walk around the Civil War ramparts and

museum at **Fort Fisher State Historic Site**, the gorgeous beach across the road at **Fort Fisher State Recreation Area**, and the superb **North Carolina Aquarium at Fort Fisher**, which has both fascinating indoor exhibits (the playful sea otters are a crowd favorite) and walking paths through gardens teeming with birdlife.

Head south via the **Fort Fisher Ferry** for a scenic 35-minute ride across the Cape Fear River to picturesque **Southport**, which has appeared in many of the films and TV shows produced in the Wilmington area, from *Dawson's Creek* to *Crimes of the Heart*. Continue into South Carolina and down its coastline for nearly 150 miles to Charleston. En route you'll pass through or around (your choice) **Myrtle Beach**, a favorite destination of college spring breakers that can also be fun for kids or anyone who loves amusement parks, wax museums, and outlet shops; but it's also often overrun with tourists and marred by excessive—and not especially attractive—commercialism. Farther south you'll pass through some quaint and less frenetic coastal towns, such as **Pawleys Island** and the pretty colonial port community of **Georgetown**, before eventually crossing the dramatic Arthur Ravenal Jr. Bridge into historic Charleston.

CHARLESTON, SC TO SAVANNAH, GA

Few places suggest romance more palpably than **Charleston**, a meticulously preserved peninsular city at the confluence of the Ashley and Cooper rivers that's an exemplar of Southern civility, amazing food, venerable art galleries, and historic preservation. Its palm-shaded lanes and pastel-hued 18th- and 19th-century residences, churches, and converted shipping warehouses feel right out of a fairy tale. I suggest spending two or three days here, which allows time to explore some of the interesting sites farther afield, like the massive plantation homes north of the city along **Ashley River Road** (Rte 61), and perhaps one or two nearby beach-resort communities, such as **Sullivan's Island** or **Folly Beach**.

Start your explorations by visiting the **Historic Charleston Foundation**, which sponsors many of the city's top festivals and operates two fine homes open to the public, **Aiken-Rhett House** and **Nathaniel Russell House**. Then head to **Waterfront Park**, a gorgeous slice of tree-shaded greenery with a graceful riverfront promenade. **Meeting St** runs north-south through the heart of downtown and is lined with prominent attractions, including the superb **Charleston Museum**, which was established in 1773 and contains an exhaustive collection of early furnishings, textiles, artwork, and extensive natural history exhibits. Then book a ferry out to **Fort Sumter National Monument**, the site of the fateful fortress at the mouth of Charleston Harbor, where an attack by South Carolina militia on April 12, 1861, set off the Civil War. Half-hour ferry rides depart three or four times per day from downtown's **Liberty Square Visitor Educational Center**. One neighborhood that's changed dramatically of late is **Upper King St**. Once a workaday warren of nondescript businesses, it's blossomed into one of the country's trendiest culinary neighborhoods, a veritable restaurant row of buzzworthy establishments, both casual—Pink Bellies Vietnamese, Rodney Scott's BBQ, Leon's Oyster Shop—and glamorous, such as Maison and The Ordinary.

It's a straightforward two-hour drive to Savannah, but there are a handful of potential detours to tempt you, including the hour-long side trip to **Edisto Island**, which is home to a number of close-knit Gullah (low-country African American) hamlets and the unspoiled sands of **Edisto Beach State Park**. You could also stop in **Hilton Head**, a chichi golf and beach resort developed in the 1950s and primarily of interest if you wish to relax at a cushy spa hotel. On a short daytrip, though, you can stroll the 68 acres of nature trails at the **Coastal Discovery Museum** and have lunch at one of the excellent restaurants clustered around **Harbour Town** and **Sea Pines** villages. Farther south, stop in the picturesque colonial port town of **Beaufort** (pronounced "BYEW-fert," in contrast with the like-named North Carolina town, "BOH-fert"). In this enchanting town on Port Royal Island, overlooking the curving Beaufort River, you'll find a wealth of stately old homes, along with appealing independent shops and restaurants, many along **Bay St**.

SAVANNAH, GA TO ST AUGUSTINE, FL

A dignified city that Gen. James Oglethorpe put on the map in 1733, **Savannah** has survived devastating fires and was spared destruction by Gen. William T. Sherman during the Civil War. It's bounced back from the neglect of its historic district during the mid-20th century, enjoyed a remarkable comeback partly spurred by John Berendt's endearing account of eccentric locals, *Midnight in the Garden of Good and Evil*, and entered into a contemporary arts–driven renaissance heralded by the rapid growth of the **Savannah College of Art and Design (SCAD)**. It opened in 1978 and now enrolls more than 14,000 students and owns dozens of downtown buildings, including the stunning **SCAD Museum of Art**, which resides inside the 1856 former headquarters of the Central of Georgia Railway and presents provocative rotating installations and well as works from an impressive permanent collection.

Downtown Georgetown

SIDETRACK

Two more very interesting detours await you as you approach the Florida border. At exit 3 of I-95, drive west for 35 miles through **Folkston** to reach the **Suwannee Canal** section of **Okefenokee National Wildlife Refuge**, which protects most of the eponymous 685-square-mile swamp, the largest in the contiguous United States. This dense landscape of peat bogs, bald cypress and tupelo stands, and pine forests supports alligators, black bears, and myriad birds, amphibians, and reptiles. At the Suwannee Canal section, you can see exhibits and a film in the visitor center, walk along the **Chesser Island Boardwalk** to a wildlife observation tower, and drive 7.2-mile **Swamp Island Dr**; you can also rent bikes and boats or book guided tours through the refuge's concessionaire, **Okefenokee Adventures**.

Back at exit 3 head east 10 miles through picturesque **St Marys** to **Cumberland Island National Seashore Museum and Visitor Center**, which overlooks the St Marys River. Here you can learn about and book a ferry to explore 36,347-acre **Cumberland Island**, a breathtaking and almost entirely undeveloped barrier isle just off southeastern Georgia's coast. Rangers lead nature walks, and you can view the ruins of the Queen Anne-style estate, **Dungeness**, or take a tour of the still well-preserved **Plum Orchard** mansion. There are no shops or restaurants, so bring your own food. Ferries depart from St Marys in the morning, returning in the late afternoon, so this is a full-day experience or ideal for an overnight if you choose to camp or stay in the island's historic **Greyfield Inn**, whose rates include all meals.

Carefully preserved though it is, Savannah is a vibrant, free-spirited city that embraces both its rich history—numerous buildings are open for tours, the must-see being the **Owens-Thomas House**—and its edgy modern side, which manifests itself in the many outstanding restaurants and fine shops. The downtown historic district is anchored by 22 lushly landscaped squares, each with park benches, statuary, and distinctive architectural features. You could spend an afternoon strolling among them, stopping at one of the classic restaurants, such as casual Clary's Cafe for greasy-spoon breakfast fare and Crystal Beer Parlour for fried chicken and hefty burgers. Or for a fancier experience, the Olde Pink House serves rarefied Southern fare in an elegant 1771 mansion. An engaging way to get acquainted with the city's distinctive design is with a guided walk, led by author Jonathan Stalcup, with **Architectural Savannah**. Also visit the **Telfair Museums**, which comprise the original 1818 Telfair Academy, with 19th- and 20th-century paintings and period furnishings, and the strikingly contemporary Jepson Center, which was designed by Moshe Safdie and contains a superb contemporary art collection. Make the 15-mile drive to **Tybee Island**, a laid-back community with sweeping beaches, a long fishing pier, and several lively bars and restaurants. Along the drive out, visit the Civil War–era buildings at **Fort Pulaski National Monument** and explore **Tybee Island Station and Museum**.

From Savannah you *could* make it to St Augustine, FL in less than three hours via the interstate. But I recommend detouring from I-95 to visit the historic and lovely **Golden Isles**, which comprise four barrier islands centered around the colonial port city of **Brunswick**. Take Hwy 99 to US 17 south into the bustling **Old Town**, stopping for a meal at one of the stellar restaurants, such as Reid's Apothecary or Indigo Coastal Shanty. Head east to reach **St Simons Island**, a tastefully but heavily developed vacation destination with upscale resorts and eateries, but my preference is to take the Sidney Lanier Bridge to **Jekyll Island**, which served as a winter retreat for affluent barons of industry from 1888 until 1942. Having declined in popularity during the Depression and then being evacuated for security purposes during World War II, the state of Georgia bought the 5700-acre island, and the island's stunning beaches, miles of bike trails, and 240-acre historic district (containing a number of Gilded Age mansions) are now open to the public and are great fun to explore. There's also an interesting mix of dining and lodging options. A must-see is the **Georgia Sea Turtle Center**, a nonprofit that educates the public about Georgia's famous loggerhead sea turtles and rehabilitates those in need of medical care.

Soon after crossing into Florida, head east on Rte 200 to **Amelia Island**, the southernmost of the barrier islands that stretch from north of Charleston down the Georgia coast. This 13-mile long island has three communities, with historic **Fernandina Beach** at the top. Continue east to the beach and then follow Rte A1A south down the coast. From Amelia Island, Rte A1A crosses the Nassau River and continues through the pristine dunes of **Little Talbot Island State Park** and then to **Fort George Landing**, where you catch a short ferry ride across the St Johns River to **Mayport** and continue through a string of coastal communities east of Jacksonville, including **Atlantic Beach**, **Jacksonville Beach**, and tony **Ponte Vedra Beach**. The road continues for about 15 miles along a narrow barrier island through **Guana Tolomato Matanzas National Estuarine Research Reserve** before crossing the Tolomato River into St Augustine.

Established by Spanish explorers in 1565 and thus the nation's oldest city, **St Augustine** has a compact downtown of both opulent Spanish Colonial and Victorian architecture (the campus of **Flagler College** stands out in particular), picturesque streets lined with cheerful galleries and eateries, and a wealth of inviting B&Bs and inns. Pedestrian-only **St George Street**, which leads north from central **Cathedral Square** to majestic **Castillo de San Marcos National Monument** is especially charming. For a sweet treat, have a dish of ice cream at Mayday—I like the flavor with dark chocolate and spicy local datil chiles. Later, stop by **San Sebastian Winery**, which produces not only fine vino but respected ports and cream sherries. You can have a drink in the winery's rooftop bar, which has live jazz and serves tapas.

SIDETRACK

This itinerary sticks close to the ocean and bypasses Florida's most populous city, **Jacksonville**, but it's an easy 20- to 30-minute detour west to this sprawling metropolis with more than 930,000 residents. Leveled by a massive fire in 1901, most of the city lacks the Spanish Colonial look that's typical of northeastern Florida, but you'll find some beautiful homes and engaging neighborhoods, especially **Riverside** and **San Marco**, which lie across the St Johns River from each other. Stop for a bite to eat in hip and historic **Five Points**—try Hawkers Asian Street Food or Alewife Craft Beer. And explore the **Cummer Museum of Art and Gardens**, with its impressive European and American masterworks and Meissen porcelain. Another major draw is **Jacksonville Zoo and Gardens**.

BEST EATS

- **Blue Water Grill and Raw Bar** Relax at an outdoor table overlooking Pirate's Cove Marina at this lively Manteo restaurant that offers bountiful salads, tuna sashimi, broiled oysters and hearty pastas and steaks. There's an excellent sister restaurant in Nags Head, Blue Moon Beach Grill. 252-473-1955, bluewatergrillobx.com.

- **Ketch 55 Seafood Grill** Midway down Hatteras Island, in the chill beach village of Avon, this casual tavern is a great choice for Caribbean jerk chicken, soft-shell-crab sandwiches, and steamed Carolina shrimp with cocktail sauce and drawn butter. 252-995-5060, ketch55.com.

- **City Kitchen** You're treated to gorgeous views of Beaufort's Town Creek Marina at this unfussy gathering spot known for creatively prepared crab cakes, Korean-style pork belly tacos, and rich sticky toffee pudding for dessert. 252-648-8141, facebook.com/citykitchenfoods

- **Manna** Sup on refined farm-to-table fare at this romantic, high-ceilinged restaurant in historic downtown Wilmington. Hickory-smoked pork chops and local speckled trout are regulars on the changing menu, and the bar and wine program is superb. 910-763-5252, mannaavenue.com

- **Seabird** Helmed by a James Beard chef, this Wilmington bistro occupies a beautiful vintage-chic space. Share a seafood tower before moving on to enticing mains like swordfish schnitzel glazed in preserved lemon jam. 910-769-5996, seabirdnc.com.

- **Xiao Bao Biscuit** Near Charleston's white-hot Upper King St restaurant row, this sweet spot in a historic storefront doles out heavenly pan-Asian dishes "inspired by kick-ass grandmothers everywhere," from spicy Sichuan pork-and-tofu mapo doufu to tapioca shrimp dumplings with fermented sausage. 843-743-3880, xiaobaobiscuit.com

- **Bertha's Kitchen** Don't be deterred by the line for this no-frills counter-service dining room north of downtown Charleston. You'll be glad you persevered after devouring the mouthwatering soul food—turkey wings, barbecued pig's feet, and smothered pork chops with generous sides of yams and hoppin' john. 843-554-6519.

- **Fig** This warmly lighted bistro earns kudos for its artfully plated contemporary cuisine. The menu changes daily, but you might start with lamb tartare before graduating to a low-country bourride of white shrimp, mussels, and butterbeans. 843-805-5900, eatatfig.com

- **Lost Local** A convivial stop on Beaufort's trendy Bay St, this friendly eatery turns out elevated street tacos (braised barbecue pork in slow-simmered collard greens, blackened shrimp with chipotle crema), plus Creole-style eat-and-peel shrimp. The craft beer list is phenomenal. 843-379-3838, lostlocal.com.

Top Arthur Ravenel Jr. Bridge, Charleston *Middle* The Grey, Savannah *Bottom* Historic houses, Charleston

- **Cotton and Rye** This refined Savannah staple makes many of its signature dishes, from pâtés to artisan breads, from scratch. The daily changing plate of local seafoods is perfect for sharing, but you'll want the fried-chicken thighs with hot honey all to yourself. 912-777-6286, cottonandrye.com.

- **The Grey** In a converted Art Deco 1930s Greyhound bus station, this scene-y restaurant helmed by acclaimed chef Mashama Bailey is the kind of place you want to linger over your meal, savoring the extensive chef's tasting menu. Up front, the Diner Bar is fun for drinks and tasty appetizers. 912-662-5999, thegreyrestaurant.com.

- **Eighty Ocean** Enjoy a romantic dinner in this casually elegant dining room at the historic Jekyll Island Club Resort, which is also one of the most inviting lodgings on the island. The menu leans traditional Italian, but emphasizes local seafood. 912-635-5238, jekyllclub.com.

- **Timoti's Seafood Shack** A standout even among several swankier restaurants in historic Fernandina Beach, on Amelia Island, this easygoing counter-service spot with outdoor seating on a garden patio serves wild-caught seafood. 904-310-6550, timotis.com.

- **Ice Plant** Duck into this 1927 factory building with soaring ceilings for an expertly mixed cocktail. Dine on delicious gastropub fare, from shrimp ceviche to house-made pimento cheese with guava-datil pepper jelly. St Augustine, 904-829-6553, iceplantbar.com.

- **Mojo Old City BBQ** In an airy, conversation-filled outpost of a beloved Florida chainlet, sample outstanding regional barbecue, from Texas-style beef brisket to Carolina-inspired pork, along with a fine selection of whiskies. 904-342-5264, mojobbq.com.

BEST SLEEPS

- **Sanderling Resort** With 120 rooms, two big pools, a first-class spa, and two great restaurants, this elegant but unpretentious beachfront resort in Duck is one of the most desirable retreats in the Outer Banks. Luxury suites overlook the ocean. 855-412-7866, sanderling-resort.com.

- **Inn on Pamlico Sound** It's a short drive to Cape Hatteras Lighthouse from this yellow boutique hotel with a beach and a long boardwalk on the sound. Most rooms have decks with waterfront views, and the romantic cafe serves sophisticated coastal fare. 866-726-5426, innonpamlicosound.com.

- **Captain's Landing Waterfront Inn** In case you needed an incentive to spend a night on tranquil Ocracoke Island, this 10-unit lodging on Silver Lake Harbor offers spacious suites with private decks on the water, full kitchens, and views of the lighthouse. 252-928-1999, thecaptainslanding.com.

- **Hotel Ballast** You can't beat the views of the riverfront or the proximity to historic downtown Wilmington at this Hilton-managed mid-rise hotel with a large pool and three restaurants. 910-763-5900, hotelballast.com

- **Restoration Hotel** Historic Charleston has seen a spate of new, uber-trendy design hotels in recent years—my favorite is this opulent boutique property made up of suites and spacious condo-style residences with full kitchens and multiple bedrooms. 843-518-5100, therestorationhotel.com.

- **Shem Creek Inn** Across the Cooper River from downtown Charleston in historic Mount Pleasant, this attractive but easy-on-the-wallet hotel overlooking a pristine creek has 51 simply but sleekly decorated rooms with decks, fridges, and microwaves. 843-881-1000, shemcreekinn.com

- **City Loft Hotel** A chic mid-century-modern motor lodge in Beaufort's historic downtown, this 22-room property has a decidedly contemporary flair: rooms have bold color schemes, and the perks include loaner bikes and a hip cafe. 843-379-5638, citylofthotel.com.

- **Perry Lane Hotel** This swanky hotel filled with striking local art is a rare slice of modernity in Savannah's historic downtown. With 360-degree views, the rooftop pool, which adjoins the trendy Peregrin bar, is a perfect place to unwind. 912-415-9000, perrylanehotel.com.

- **Kehoe House** An elegant redbrick 1890s mansion overlooking one of downtown Savannah's prettiest squares, this 13-room gem exudes romance. Rates include a lavish full breakfast and afternoon wine and hors d'oeuvres. 912-232-1020, kehoehouse.com.

- **Beachview Club** Close to the famous Jekyll Island Golf Club, this intimate 38-room hotel enjoys sweeping views of verdant lawns, moss-draped live oak trees, rolling dunes, and the ocean. 912-635-2256, beachviewclubjekyll.com.

- **Amelia Schoolhouse Inn** East of the Amelia River in Fernandina Beach, this upscale 17-room inn occupies a stately redbrick 1886 school building that underwent a gorgeous makeover and transformation in 2019. In the back there's a pretty pool and courtyard. 904-310-6264, ameliaschoolhouseinn.com.

- **Elizabeth Pointe Lodge** This clapboard, gambrel-roof inn on a beautiful stretch of Amelia Island beachfront looks as though it could have been airlifted here from Martha's Vineyard. Curling up with a book in a rocking chair on the lodge's elegant verandah is a perfect way to greet the day. 904-277-4851, elizabethpointeameliaisland.com.

- **Collector Inn** This 1-acre compound has been created out of nine historic homes fringed by aromatic gardens and tranquil courtyards. The 30 rooms have fireplaces and walls made of St Augustine's local coquina limestone, and there's a gorgeous bar serving up cocktails and tapas. 904-209-5800, thecollectorinn.com.

- **Casa Monica Resort and Spa** This ornate, Moorish Revival-inspired compound in St Augustine is an elegant place to stay that also has inviting venues for cocktails and dinner, Costa Brava and the hip Cobalt Lounge. 904-827-1888, marriott.com.

CAMPING

Both primitive and developed campgrounds line the route from the Outer Banks to Florida, most of them set behind the dunes (to protect both people and wildlife, camping isn't usually permitted directly on the beach). OBX and Oregon Inlet campgrounds are popular in the upper Outer Banks, while Cape Hatteras KOA and Cape Point are good bets in Cape Hatteras Seashore, and Carolina Beach State Park and Fort Fisher State Recreation Area have lovely settings near Wilmington. In South Carolina beautiful James Island County Park campground is midway between Charleston and the beaches, while Skidaway Island State Park is one of the loveliest options near Savannah. In Northeastern Florida, top options include Fort Clinch State Park on Amelia Island, Little Talbot Island State Park east of Jacksonville, and North Beach Camp Resort near St Augustine.

Top Seafood and beer at Timoti's, Fernandina Beach
Bottom Castillo de San Marcos National Monument, St Augustine *Opposite* Hotel Ballast, Wilmington

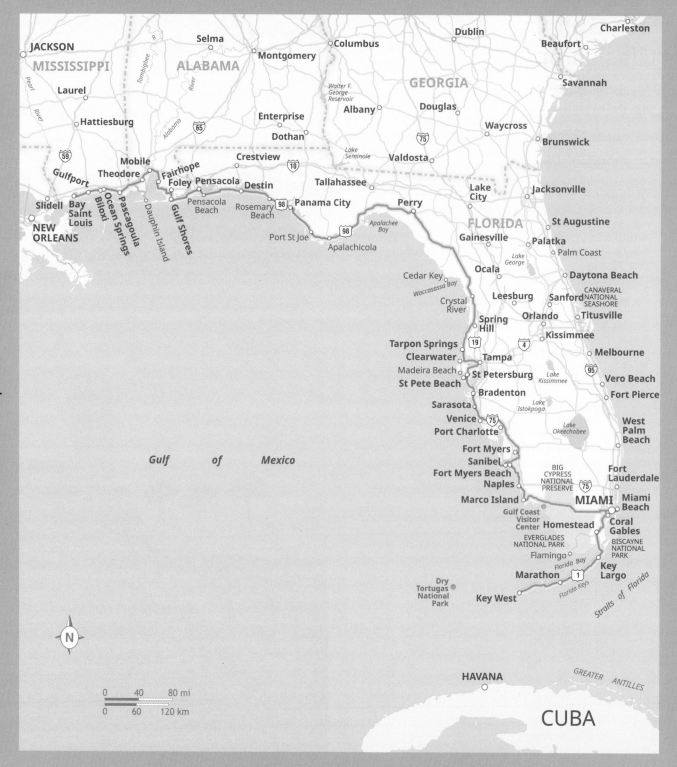

The Gulf Coast:
Mississippi to Florida ★

This curve of the southeastern US coastline abounds with Spanish- and French-colonial architecture, laid-back beach bars and resorts, sugary white-sand beaches, lush mangrove and cypress swamps, and coral keys.

HOW LONG?

8–9 days; add an extra day or two to explore more of St Petersburg and Tampa, the Everglades, or Key West.

WHEN TO GO

Although you may face intense heat and humidity in summer, the Gulf Coast has much to offer year-round. The tradeoff for those hot summer months is that off-season hotel rates can be lower. The dead of winter can get a little cool on the northern Gulf Coast, but it's still warmer than most of the country. Spring offers pleasant temperatures and colorful gardens but also sometimes immense spring break crowds, while fall is a good balance of pleasant weather and manageable crowds.

NEED TO KNOW

Pack lots of sunscreen and mosquito repellent, especially mid-spring to mid-autumn. Book attractions, Everglades activities, and lodgings well in advance during spring break and over the Christmas and New Year's holiday period.

→ Distances
Total distance, one-way: 1125 mi (1811 km)
- Bay St Louis, MS to Pensacola, FL: 170 mi (274 km)
- Pensacola, FL to Tampa, FL: 465 mi (748 km)
- Tampa, FL to Marco Island, FL: 240 mi (386 km)
- Marco Island, FL to Key West, FL: 235 mi (378 km)

⦿ Daytime Temperatures
January: 57-75°F (14-24°C)
July: 90-92°F (32-33°C)

ⓘ More information
- Mississippi Gulf Coast tourism, gulfcoast.org
- Mobile tourism, mobile.org
- Pensacola tourism, visitpensacola.com
- Tampa tourism, visittampabay.com
- St Petersburg tourism, visitstpeteclearwater.com
- Everglades National Park, nps.gov/ever
- Florida Keys tourism, fla-keys.com

⊙ SNAPSHOT

Maybe it's the calm surf or the blissful white coral-shell beaches or the deep cultural ties with the Caribbean, but the Gulf Coast feels completely distinct from the Atlantic and Pacific coasts. It's decidedly slower-paced and noticeably friendlier. Come to savor fresh-caught oysters and Gulf snapper and explore acclaimed art scenes in Ocean Springs, St Petersburg, and Key West. And set aside time to experience the remarkable wildlife and lush wilderness, which you'll discover in parks and preserves up and down the coast, but especially in the Florida Everglades.

BAY ST LOUIS, MS TO PENSACOLA, FL

Begin your adventure about 60 miles east of New Orleans in the twin coastal Mississippi villages of **Bay St Louis** and **Pass Christian**, which are connected by a 2-mile bay bridge and boast long fishing piers and picturesque, historic downtowns abundant with casual seafood restaurants, quirky galleries, and one-of-a-kind shops. After enjoying a relaxed lunch on the palm-shaded patio at Mockingbird Cafe or on the waterfront deck at Shaggy's Pass Harbor, continue east through the cities of **Gulfport** (pop 72,000) and **Biloxi** (46,000). This stretch of US 90 is lined with big casino resorts and family-popular beaches and attractions, like the aquarium at the **Institute for Marine Mammal Studies** and the **Big Play Entertainment Center** amusement park. Continue across Biloxi Bay into **Ocean Springs**, an endearingly charming and historic community with a strong arts presence; it's also where you'll find the **Davis Bayou** section of **Gulf Islands National Seashore**, a mostly off-shore park with islands both in Mississippi and off the Pensacola coast in Florida. Downtown has the most interesting food-and-drink scene on the Mississippi coast—the Greenhouse on Porter and Blue Dog Bistro are lovely options. And it's home to the superb, beautifully designed **Walter Anderson Museum of Art**, which is devoted to the life and works of the famed mid-20th-century wildlife and landscape painter. A short drive southeast at the national seashore, stop by the **William M. Colmer Visitor Center** to view engaging, interactive exhibits on the Gulf's flora and fauna and for a short hike along one of the easy and engaging nature trails. Then continue east through **Pascagoula** and into southwestern Alabama.

Perched over Mobile Bay, southern Alabama's largest city is also one of the South's busiest cargo ports. **Mobile** (pop 187,000) looks and feels a bit like New Orleans, a city with which it shares deep Spanish and French colonial ties—in fact, Mobile boasts the oldest Mardi Gras celebration in the United States, dating back to 1703 (you can learn all about this legacy at the colorful **Mobile Mardi Gras Museum**). A walk around Mobile's colorful downtown, starting in live-oak-shaded **Bienville Square**, reveals dozens of colorful, beautifully preserved buildings from the 1800s (many containing noteworthy restaurants and shops). Downtown also abounds with engaging attractions—the World War II–era **Battleship USS *Alabama*** and the **Gulfquest National Maritime Museum of the Gulf of Mexico**, with its kid-friendly exhibits on the region's seafaring history.

SIDETRACK

I'm very much drawn to the quieter, less developed areas of the Gulf Coast, one of my favorites being **Dauphin Island**. On the way from coastal Mississippi to Mobile, it's just a 25-mile detour from US 90 down Hwys 188 and 193 to this skinny 14 mile long barrier island that's connected to the mainland via the **Dauphin Island Bridge**. With wild dunes, birding preserves, a handful of compelling attractions, and a smattering of friendly, affordable eateries and beach condos, it's a lovely little getaway for a few hours or a whole weekend. On the east side of the island, look for piping plovers and long-legged egrets and herons on the peaceful trails of the **Audubon Bird Sanctuary**, walk along the boardwalk and view more than 100 kinds of native animals at the **Alabama Aquarium at the Dauphin Island Sea Lab**, and explore the original ramparts and cannons of **Fort Gaines**, an 1821 garrison that played a prominent role in the Civil War's Battle of Mobile Bay—during which Admiral David Farragut uttered the immortal order, "Damn the torpedoes!" This is also the western side of the mouth of Mobile Bay. If you wished to continue this drive without visiting Mobile, you could catch a 40-minute ferry ride across to **Fort Morgan** and follow Hwy 180 to rejoin the route in Gulf Shores. Assuming you're headed to Mobile, however, as you drive up Hwy 193 along the bay, be sure to stop in **Theodore** for a walk through **Bellingrath Gardens**, with its 65 acres of camellias, azaleas, and hydrangeas centered around a lavish 1930s country house.

Destin Harbor Boardwalk *Previous* Mexico Beach

Drive east across the northern reaches of Mobile Bay, and then follow US 98 south along the bay's eastern shore through the charming towns of **Fairhope**, with its picturesque fishing pier and courtly tree-lined streets, and then cut southeast through **Foley** and down to **Gulf Shores**, a beachfront resort community filled with hotels and seafood restaurants, as well as outfitters offering dolphin-watching and dinner cruises. Follow Hwy 182 east along the shore, stopping to beachcomb at gorgeous **Gulf State Park**, and then cross the state border onto **Perdido Key** at the very tip of Florida's northwestern panhandle. Celebrate with a plate of raw oysters and a daiquiri at Flora-Bama, an animated party bar and roadhouse on the beach. Head east on Hwy 292, curving up around **Big Lagoon State Park**, where you can amble over the windswept sand dunes on a boardwalk trail to an observation tower and rent kayaks or canoes for a paddle around Wild Grande Lagoon. Then head to **Fort Barrancas**, a 1780s battery with a strategic—and scenic—setting on Pensacola Bay. The property lies within the **Naval Air Station Pensacola**, where you'll also find the 1859 **Pensacola Lighthouse and Maritime Museum** and the outstanding **National Naval Aviation Museum**, which showcases an impressive collection of more than 150 aircraft and spacecraft and offers visitors the chance to test their skills in a flight simulator.

PENSACOLA, FL TO TAMPA, FL

Continue into picturesque downtown **Pensacola**, a city of 54,000 that was established by the Spanish in 1559 and then abandoned for about 150 years following a devastating hurricane. Like Mobile, it retains many aspects of its rich Spanish and French heritage; this is especially apparent in the historic architecture around **Seville Square**, which is shaded by moss-draped live oaks. Just a few blocks west you can visit several small history museums as well as the **Pensacola Museum of Art**, which occupies a stately former jailhouse. Drive south across two bridges to Pensacola Beach—where you can explore the Florida unit of Gulf Islands National Seashore. Draws include several miles of trails though **Naval Live Oaks Nature Preserve** and the 1830s ramparts and batteries of **Fort Pickens**.

Cross back to the mainland near **Navarre Beach Fishing Pier**, and continue east on US 98 for a long, meandering 200-mile journey along the panhandle shore through a series of popular vacation getaways. Starting with the beach town of **Fort Walton Beach**, with its kid-approved **Gulfarium Marine Adventure Park**. In **Destin**, stop for a walk around Destin Harbor Boardwalk, a colorful promenade of lively seafood eateries and quirky gift shops along with tour operators offering kayak paddles, snorkeling trips, and dolphin-watching excursions out around pretty Norriego Point. Tuck into a bowl of Gulf seafood chowder at laid-back Boshamps, and then continue east through the monied enclave of **Rosemary Beach** and the bustling (especially when college spring breakers descend upon it) vacation town of **Panama City Beach**—ZooWorld Zoological Park is a favorite with kids.

Southeast of Panama City, the drive takes on a more relaxed and rural character, as US 98 curves alongside some of the most stunning shoreline scenery in Florida. Try to pass through laid-back **Mexico Beach** when the sun is setting majestically over the Gulf, and stop for a bite to eat or to browse the funky shops along historic Reid Avenue in **Port St Joe**. I recommend detouring south from US 98 and taking the slightly longer but more beautiful route along Hwy 30A, which hugs St Joseph Bay and St Vincent Sound as it meanders toward Apalachicola. If you have time, drive up the narrow **Cape San Blas** peninsula, with its peaceful, breathtaking beaches. My favorite town along this route, **Apalachicola**, reminds me of a smaller and quieter Key West, with its cute downtown of well-maintained 19th-century houses and storefronts. The Station Raw Bar, in a converted auto repair shop, is a cheap and cheerful place to sample shrimp and raw oysters, for which Apalachicola has long been famous. Farther east, stop at **Bald Point State Park** for a beach stroll or swim. Follow US 98 to **Perry**, and then continue south another 170 miles through a sparsely populated region just inland from the Gulf to **Tarpon Springs**. Shortly after it was settled in 1876, Tarpon Springs became popular with Greek immigrants (it still claims the highest percentage of Greek Americans of any city), who settled here to work as divers in the town's prolific natural-sponge industry. You can buy these soft, absorbent sponges and see the fleet of boats at the **Tarpon Springs Sponge Docks** on Dodecanese Blvd, which is also home to several acclaimed Greek restaurants, Mykonos and The Limani among them.

Continue down Alt US19 to **Clearwater**, and then cut east across the bay into the largest city on Florida's west coast, **Tampa** (pop 405,000). On the attractive campus of the **University of Tampa**, check out the **Henry B. Plant Museum**, which is set inside an ornate 1890s railroad hotel and contains fine and decorative art, elegant furniture, and other artifacts that document the region's rise of aristocratic tourism during the Gilded Age. Along downtown's pleasant **Riverwalk**, the **Tampa Museum of Art** occupies a stately contemporary building designed by Rafael Vinoly. I always make a point of visiting **Ybor City**, a historic neighborhood established in the late 19th century as a cigar-manufacturing "company town" that employed and housed thousands of Cuban and southern European workers. This quadrant of handsome brick buildings had become a virtual ghost town by the 1980s, when artists, musicians, and bar owners launched a steady wave of gentrification; it's now a vibrant nightlife and dining district with a mix of LGBTQ and mainstream establishments and **Ybor City Museum State Park**, whose gardens and exhibits document its rich heritage. North of downtown, the city also has a couple of extremely famous family attractions, **ZooTampa at Lowry Park** and **Busch Gardens**, a 335-acre animal theme park founded in the late 1950s. Florida's theme park capital, **Orlando**—the home of **Disney World**, **Universal**, **SeaWorld**, and others—is just a 90-minute drive northeast.

TAMPA, FL TO MARCO ISLAND, FL

Drive over the 6-mile Howard Frankland Bridge, or the shorter and less dramatic Gandy Bridge, heading southwest to **Madeira Beach** and then following the coast south through laid-back **Treasure Island** and **St Pete Beach**. Stop to admire the **Don CeSar**, aka the Pink Palace, a turreted 1920s grand resort. My favorite stretch of this sunny shoreline is **Pass-A-Grille**, a diminutive, low-key beach town that's slightly south from the main road—it's an absolutely stunning place to watch the sunset. A little farther south, 1136-acre **Fort De Soto Park** is ideal for kayaking, snorkeling, and lazing on the beach. From here, cut north around **Boca Ciega Bay Aquatic Preserve** to the engaging little village of **Gulfport**, which has a handful of quirky and inviting eateries, including Pia's Trattoria and Gulfport Brewery and Eatery.

Continue east into **St Petersburg**, a city that in the past 30 years has morphed from a slightly downcast retirement community into one of the Southeast's most vibrant and exciting art and culinary hubs. Start in **Historic Kenwood**, which abounds with hip eateries and shops, and then follow trendy **Central Avenue** east into downtown to visit some of its world-class museums. The most famous, set inside an appropriately Surrealist-inspired 2011 building overlooking Tampa Bay, is the **Salvador Dali Museum**, which contains nearly 2500 of the iconic Spanish artist's works. Other highlights include the **Imagine Museum** and the **Chihuly Collection**, which are both devoted to contemporary glass

art, and the **Museum of Fine Arts**, which I'm a big fan of partly for its superb rotating exhibits but also for its location in **Straub Park** along the enchanting downtown waterfront. Other highlights of this inviting city include the poignant and beautifully designed **Florida Holocaust Museum** and the **Warehouse Arts District**, where you'll find several notable galleries, including **Duncan McClellan**, which occupies a stunningly transformed fish and tomato packing plant and features gorgeous modern glassworks.

Several attractive coastal cities lie ahead, including **Brandenton** and **Sarasota**, which is famous for the **Ringling Estate**, a stately campus established in 1926 by circus magnate and art collector John Ringling and his wife, Mabel. It comprises the grandiose Venetian Gothic mansion **Ca' d'Zan** (the couple's winter home), several exquisite gardens, and the impressive **Ringling Museum of Art**, which contains some 10,000 objects, including works by European masters. Like so many kids who grew up in the northeastern US during the second half of the 20th century, I spent my spring school breaks visiting grandparents in Florida—mine on tiny and residential **Bird Key**, which is one of a handful of barrier islands just off the coast of Sarasota. I still love coming back to wander around **St Armands Key**, with its tony sidewalk cafes set around a landscaped traffic circle (this historic planned village is another legacy of John Ringling), and explore the beaches just south on 8 mile long **Siesta Key**, which boasts some of the most blissful stretches of white sand in the country—**Siesta Beach** is my favorite spot to chill out for an hour or two.

Continue south through **Venice** and around the top of Gasparilla Sound and then cross the Caloosahatchee River into fast-growing **Fort Myers** (pop 87,000), which has an attractive riverfront downtown and is known for its outstanding, family-friendly **IMAG History & Science Center** as well as the **Edison and Ford Winter Estates**, the neighboring winter homes of the famed inventor and automaker—you can take a fascinating tour of this compound that includes their homes, a museum, Edison's laboratory, and botanic gardens. Follow the river southwest and across a curving causeway to **Sanibel Island**, an attractive vacation community with stunning beaches and the engaging **Bailey-Matthews National Shell Museum**. Return to the mainland and drive down Hwy 865 through scenic **Fort Myers Beach** and **Estero Island**, then across pristine **Lovers Island State Park** and down to the southernmost city on Florida's Gulf Coast, **Naples**, which has about 20,000 residents and is known for its lush **Naples Botanical Garden** and a handsome downtown filled with smart shops, respected galleries, posh boutique inns, and elegant restaurants. A little farther south you'll come to **Marco Island**, the only inhabited one of the Ten Thousand Island archipelago and a refuge of fancy vacation homes and upscale hotels.

MARCO ISLAND, FL TO KEY WEST, FL

From where the road from San Marco Island rejoins US 41, aka the Tamiami Trail in this part of the state, it's less than a half-hour drive to the **Gulf Coast Visitor Center**, which is the northwesternmost of the four main visitor centers in **Everglades National Park**. Here you can get information and learn about the many ranger programs and guided tours offered in this 2356 sq mile park (it's the third largest national park in the contiguous US). Although the Everglades has a number of areas and attractions that you can drive to, both its vastness and its amazing wealth of wildlife are best appreciated if you book at least one narrated tour. In the Gulf Coast area, this could be a catamaran boat excursion or a canoe or kayak paddle around **Chokoloskee Bay** and the Ten Thousand Islands, which are a fantastic place to observe sea turtles, dolphins, manatees, and native birdlife. In **Everglades City**, the gateway to this part of the park, you can also learn about the area's ecology and its 2000-year human history at the small but excellent **Museum of the Everglades**, and have lunch at Triad Seafood or Nely's Corner bakery. Back on US 41, you'll drive through the southern end of another vast national park service unit, 720,000-acre **Big Cypress National Preserve**, which borders the Everglades and has its own distinct features. That said, given how much there still is to see in the Everglades, I'd recommend making only a quick stop in Big Cypress—at the **Nathaniel P. Reed Visitor Center**, you can watch an excellent film and check out engaging exhibits about the park, and a short boardwalk trail offers the chance to spot local wildlife. Farther east, the **Oasis Visitor Center** also features a boardwalk and exhibits, and here you can walk part of the **Florida Trail**. About 15 miles farther east, US 41 reenters Everglades National Park. Visit the **Shark Valley Visitor Center**. The main highlight here is **Tram Road**, a paved 15-mile round-trip path that extends deep into the park, accessing hammocks—thick stands of hardwood trees— and an observation deck that offers sweeping views. You can rent a bike and pedal along Tram Road or book a naturalist-narrated tram ride. From here, continue east on US 41 and then south on Hwy 997 toward Homestead to explore more of the Everglades.

Top Downtown Pensacola *Middle* Hippopotamus at Busch Gardens, Tampa *Bottom* Airboat tours in Everglades National Park

In **Homestead** you'll find Everglades National Park's main headquarters at the **Ernest F. Coe Visitor Center**, which has great natural history exhibits and is close to several short walking trails—my favorite is the .8-mile round-trip **Anhinga Trail**. It winds through a sawgrass marsh and is one of the most likely places in the park to see alligators and, as you might expect, anhingas, which are striking long-necked aquatic birds that are well-regarded for their fishing abilities. Continue southwest on Hwy 9336, the main park road, which meanders for nearly 40 miles through the heart of the park to **Flamingo**, where you'll find a variety of activities, from boat tours out around **Whitewater Bay** to kayak and bike rentals. Hurricane Irma badly damaged the main visitor center in Flamingo, and previous hurricanes over the years had destroyed the area's lodgings, but the newly renovated, state-of-the-art **Guy Bradley Visitor Center** along with a new restaurant and hotel are expected to open in Flamingo later in 2022.

Return to Homestead, and take US 1 between Barnes and Blackwater sounds to access the **Florida Keys**, a 180-mile string of more than 800 coral keys that extends from the southern tip of the state's mainland southwest to Key West and divides the Gulf of Mexico from the Atlantic Ocean. US 1 joins this narrow and stunningly beautiful archipelago at **Key Largo**, the uppermost of the inhabited keys. It's home to a number of waterfront resorts (**Playa Largo, Baker's Cay, Dove Creek**) as well as **John Pennekamp Coral Reef State Park**, a mostly offshore refuge that's world-renowned for diving and glass-bottom boat tours. Follow US 1, known here as the Overseas Highway, for 113 miles along a series of narrow keys and more than 40 bridges—including the famous **Seven Mile Bridge**. There are plenty of inviting small towns and attractions along the way, such as the funky **Rain Barrel Village** garden and gallery complex in **Islamorada** and the

SIDETRACK

At the point where US 41 meets with Hwy 997 at the northeastern edge of the Everglades, you're just 20 miles from **Miami**, a dynamic multicultural city on the Atlantic Ocean. There's much to see and do in this region known for incredible food, cutting-edge art and fashion, and luxury spa and beach resorts. Set aside at least a couple of days, or consider ending your trip here, if you want to fully get to know Miami, its beach communities, and its inviting historic neighborhoods, such as **Coral Gables** and **Coconut Grove**. It's relatively easy to explore by car, however, and it's possible to enjoy a satisfying taste of the area in just a half day. I have two strategies for quick visits. The first is to focus on the buzzy **South Beach** neighborhood of **Miami Beach**, a separate city of about 83,000 that's just across the bay from Miami proper. Stroll along the beachfront on **Ocean Drive**, admire the colorfully restored buildings that make up one of the world's iconic collections of Art Deco architecture, and check out the chic retail and dining along **Washington Avenue** and the pedestrianized **Lincoln Mall**. Have lunch on the terrace of a scene-y restaurant—I love historic Joe's Stone Crab, but trendy newer hotspots like Stubborn Seed and the Japanese-Peruvian eatery Chotto Matte are also terrific. The second—and quicker—strategy is to explore the amazing murals and contemporary art of the **Wynwood Art District**, a formerly industrial district of galleries, outdoor installations (don't miss the **Wynwood Walls** murals), and hip eateries northwest of downtown Miami. It's an exciting neighborhood and just maybe the most Instagrammable part of this photogenic city.

As you make your way southwest toward Homestead, it's only about a 10-mile detour to **Biscayne National Park**, a mostly underwater 173,000-acre preserve that also encompasses the northernmost of the Florida Keys, **Elliott Key**. For a quick look, you can simply visit the park's small mainland section, viewing the exhibits, walking out on the dock at **Dante Fascell Visitor Center**, and relaxing on the beach at **Homestead Bayfront Park**. If you have a half day, you can book a three-hour boat tour through the Biscayne National Park Institute out to the most popular of the park's islands, **Boca Chita Key**; there's great birdwatching and even sometimes dolphin viewing on the ride out, and once there you can swim, beachcomb, and take in views of the Miami skyline from the observation deck of a 65 ft tall lighthouse.

birdwatching trails and shallow kayak-friendly waters of **Long Key State Park**. The drive takes two to three hours, so I usually break it up with a leisurely lunch along the way—Lazy Days in Islamorada is a good bet for conch fritters, while Keys Fisheries Market and Marina overlooks the water in **Marathon**.

The drive ends in **Key West** (pop 26,400), the fabled 4.2 sq mile island at the very tip of the Keys. It's home to the **Southernmost Point in the US** (a painted concrete buoy at the corner of South and Whitehead streets marks the spot and makes a fun photo op) and is the southern terminus of US 1, the 2370-mile highway that extends up the Eastern Seaboard to Fort Kent, ME at the Canadian border. As the crow flies, it's just over 100 miles from here to Havana, Cuba. It's hardly surprising that this creative and unconventional town feels so much like its own little Caribbean nation (it's even nicknamed the Conch Republic). I started visiting Key West in the early '90s when it was still considered one of the world's top two or three LGBTQ resort communities (it still draws plenty of queer folks, but much of the gay scene has migrated up to Fort Lauderdale and elsewhere). It felt decidedly more eccentric and less fancy—and touristy—than it does now, especially since its development into a top port of call for major cruise ships. But it's still a special and incredibly charming place, with its own eccentric personality. I never miss a chance to tour the **Ernest Hemingway House**, a gracious mansion that served as the author's residence in the 1930s (partly I like coming here to mingle with the property's large brood of friendly, six-toed cats, many of them descendants of those who belonged to the late author). I also recommend stopping by the **Harry S. Truman Little White House**, where the president regularly vacationed during his term, and **Mel Fisher Maritime Heritage Museum**, with its collection of artifacts salvaged from several 17th-century shipwrecks. But much of the fun is simply sauntering around town, up and down colorful **Duval Street** and along the quieter streets of **Old Town**, and stopping for a bite to eat at the several outstanding eateries. The best Cuban sandwich I've ever eaten came from 5 Brothers Grocery, and I also love offbeat B.O.'s Fish Wagon for soft-shell crab sandwiches and El Siboney for hearty Cuban fare. You never know what you'll discover in this curious community at the literal end of the road.

The waterfront, Destin
Opposite Salvador Dali Museum, St. Petersburg

Set in a remote expanse of the Gulf of Mexico about 70 miles west of Key West, **Dry Tortugas** is one of the most unusual of America's national parks, and it only receives about 80,000 visitors per year (Everglades NP sees that many in a typical month). This small archipelago comprises seven islands, and from Key West you get here either by ferry (the trip takes a little over two hours) or seaplane to the main attraction, **Garden Key**, which is dominated by the country's third largest historic garrison, five-sided **Fort Jefferson**—it was constructed in 1847. You can tour this imposing structure, and the beaches and waters surrounding it are renowned for birdwatching, swimming, and snorkeling. The park's largest island, **Loggerhead Key**, is 3 miles away but isn't served by public transportation; however, you can paddle over by kayak or canoe to walk its sandy paths and admire the 157 ft tall mid-19th-century lighthouse. Although Garden Key has a few campsites, there are no food or lodging concessions in the park, so pack a picnic lunch.

BEST EATS

- **White Pillars** At this gracious mansion near the shore in Biloxi, the vibe is traditional, but the sensational Gulf Coast cuisine reflects the inventive approach of the restaurant's young chef. You might start with a Thai wedge salad with red miso dressing and country ham, followed by cornmeal-fried mahi mahi simmered in a spicy crawfish curry. 228-207-0885, biloxiwhitepillars.com.

- **Vestige** In this intimate gray house in quaint downtown Ocean Springs, savor some of the delicious Southern regional cuisine of James Beard-honored chef Alex Perry—innovative dishes like poached salmon with turnip-currant jam, and wagyu bavette steak with truffle venison jus. 228-818-9699, vestigerestaurant.com.

- **Southern National** A short stroll from historic downtown Mobile's Bienville Square, this airy and sleek restaurant is at the forefront of the city's increasingly incisive culinary edge. Flavorful highlights include loaded sweet potato with berber-spiced lamb and curry yogurt sauce and seafood stew with blackened redfish, crawfish, clams, and green curry coconut broth. 251-308-2387, southernnational.com.

- **Restaurant Iron** This inviting Pensacola storefront space has earned a loyal following for its creative take on Southern cuisine. Consider the tempura fried green tomatoes and goat cheese, and crispy fried gulf oysters and bone-in pork schnitzel with brown-butter spaetzle and muscadine jelly. 850-476-7776, restaurantiron.com.

- **Ulele** With tall windows overlooking beautiful Water Works Park on a bend in the Hillsborough River, this sleek downtown Tampa restaurant celebrates Florida ingredients and both indigenous and European culinary traditions. Flash-fried alligator remoulade, charbroiled Gulf oysters, fire-seared local shrimp with Creole seasoning are among the specialties—save room for the pineapple upside-down bread pudding. 813-999-4952, ulele.com.

- **The Mill** Saunter into this industrial-chic space after a day of exploring St Petersburg's art museums and waterfront, and prepare to be wowed. The cheese-and-charcuterie plates here are among the best I've ever tried (options include octopus bacon and pork belly croutons), and the crispy soft-shell crab with honey-seared watermelon is a revelation. 727-317-3930, themillrestaurants.com.

- **1200 ChopHouse Steak** is the name of the game at this casually upscale restaurant in St Pete Beach that also features an impressive wine list and plenty of terrific local craft beers. Bring your appetite for the 2.5-pound bone-in "tomahawk" ribeye, and upgrade your feast by adding on a Caribbean lobster tail. 727-367-1300, 1200chophouse.com.

- **Selva** Outside of Peru, there may not be a region with better Peruvian food than Florida, and this contemporary space in downtown Sarasota is one of the best, offering up nine different ceviches and a wealth of creative salads and grills, including traditional lomo saltado. 941-362-4427, selvagrill.com.

- **Mad Hatter** Glorious sunsets are part of the charm of dining in this colorful bungalow on Sanibel Island. The contemporary American cooking is superb, too, from rack of lamb with a walnut cherry-pesto crust to saffron bouillabaisse with local shellfish and grouper. 239-472-0033, madhatterrestaurant.com.

- **Tulia Osteria** Set amid the snazzy boutiques and buzzy bistros of Naples's see-and-be-seen 5th Avenue South district, this convivial restaurant with beam ceilings and a romantic patio serves deftly crafted modern Italian dishes, like braised-fennel saltimbocca and chitarra pasta with jumbo lump crab and sea urchin butter. 239-213-2073, osteriatulia.com.

- **Matt's Stock Island Kitchen** With tables overlooking a marina at the Perry Hotel, this dapper, easygoing bistro is outside the touristy fray of Key West proper on a neighboring island that bustles with fishing boats and shipyards. The Florida-Caribbean-inspired food is artfully prepared and boldly flavored. 305-294-3939, perrykeywest.com.

- **Little Pearl** This intimate neighborhood bistro on a quiet lane in Key West's colorful Old Town features an exceptional wine list and presents four-course tasting menus that show off the region's bounty of fresh seafood and produce. You might start with clams steamed in a black-garlic broth, followed by 72-hour braised short ribs with heirloom carrots. 305-204-4762, littlepearlkeywest.com.

BEST SLEEPS

- **The Roost** A short stroll from the restaurant and galleries of quaint Ocean Springs, this live oak-shaded, design-driven boutique inn has custom contemporary furnishings and Walter Anderson artworks. 228-285-7989, roostoceansprings.com.

- **Malaga Inn** Balconies with wrought-iron railings and graceful fountains and courtyards underscore the Creole aesthetic of this refined 39-room inn set in a pair of restored 1862 Mobile town houses. 251-438-4701, malagainn.com.

- **Oyster Bay Boutique Hotel** Steps from the waterfront and Pensacola's picturesque Seville Square, this eco-conscious property has two broad verandas and an updated Victorian design. 850-912-8770, stayoysterbay.com.

- **Hotel Haya** The stylish jewel-toned rooms of this upmarket retreat in Tampa's historic Ybor City entertainment district are set around a large pool and bar. Flor Fina restaurant serves refined pan-Latin fare. 813-568-1200, hotelhaya.com.

- **The Vinoy Renaissance** You'll find plenty of appealing diversions at this 1925 Mediterranean-style grande dame overlooking Tampa Bay in downtown St Petersburg, including 10 tennis courts, two pools, a celebrated golf course, and several acclaimed restaurants. 727-894-1000, marriott.com.

- **The Saint Hotel** Roomy, stylish suites (many with fully stocked kitchenettes) and an attractive pool and lanai make this cozy and reasonably priced compound in St Pete Beach a perfect seaside base for exploring the Tampa Bay region. 727-360-0120, thesainthotel.com.

- **Luminary Hotel** This shiny and chichi 12-story tower opened in 2020 on the Caloosahatchee River in downtown Fort Myers and offers a pleasing balance between urbane sophistication and a laid-back coastal vibe. Amenities include four dining and drinking options and a large fourth-floor pool and deck overlooking the water. 239-314-3800, luminaryhotel.com.

- **Inn on 5th** Check into this classy three-story boutique hotel with 119 luxuriously appointed rooms to be within a short stroll of the tony shops and eateries of Naples' most exclusive street. A full-service spa offers an array of soothing services. 239-403-8777, innonfifth.com.

- **Coconut Palm Inn** With a glorious 450 ft beach on Florida Bay and complimentary kayaks, SUPs, and fishing gear, this Key Largo retreat is ideal for recreation and relaxation. And it's only about an hour from Everglades National Park. Tavernier, 305-852-3017, coconutpalminn.com.

- **La Te Da** This festive, beautifully decorated and maintained 1890s inn is in the heart Key West's colorful Duval St, and it offers its own outstanding restaurant and LGBTQ-popular cabaret and piano bar. 305-296-6706, lateda.com.

- **Pier House Resort** Enjoy a peaceful respite from the hubbub of nearby Mallory Square at this cloistered luxury inn on Key West's scenic waterfront. With one of the finest spas in the Keys, the Pier House also features a private beach, pool, and three breezy restaurants and bars. 305-296-4600, pierhouse.com.

CAMPING

RVing and—to a slightly lesser extent—tent camping are quite popular up and down the Gulf Coast. Davis Bayou is a favorite at Gulf Islands National Seashore in Ocean Springs, Shady Acres has a lovely setting on the Dog River near Mobile, and Fort Pickens is a top choice near Pensacola. Farther down the coast, look to Fort De Soto Park near St Petersburg, Periwinkle Park and Campground Aviary on Sanibel Island, and Naples/Marco Island KOA. Everglades National Park has a pair of popular grounds: Long Pine Key, near the Homestead entrance, and Flamingo, at the end of the park road. And in the Keys, you'll find beautiful sites at Calusa Campground in Key Largo, Jolly Roger RV Resort on Marathon Key, and Boyd's in Key West.

Sea Level seafood shack, Pass Christian
Opposite Southernmost Point, Key West

Index

Andrew Collins (left) with his partner, co-pilot, and always-up-for-an-adventure best friend, Fernando Nocedal.

About the Author

Andrew Collins has written and edited dozens of travel guidebooks on different parts of the United, Canada, and Mexico, including *Destination Pride: A Little Book for the Best LGBTQ Vacations*, for Hardie Grant. An inveterate globetrotter and road-tripper, Andrew lives with his partner, Fernando Nocedal, in Mexico City, while spending much of his time in the Pacific Northwest and New England regions of the United States. Andrew has driven across the United States and Canada more times than he can count, and one of his more ambitious goals is to visit every county in the US. Currently, he's been to 2511 out of 3065 counties (including parishes in Louisiana and boroughs in Alaska). He also teaches travel writing and food writing for New York City's renowned Gotham Writers Workshop. See AndrewsTraveling.com.

PHOTO CREDITS

Published in 2022 by Hardie Grant Explore,
an imprint of Hardie Grant Publishing

Hardie Grant Explore (Melbourne)
Wurundjeri Country
Building 1, 658 Church Street
Richmond, Victoria 3121

Hardie Grant Explore (Sydney)
Gadigal Country
Level 7, 45 Jones Street
Ultimo, NSW 2007

www.hardiegrant.com/au/explore

Maps in this publication contain data sourced from
the following organisations: Made with Natural Earth.
Free vector and raster map data @naturalearthdata.com.

© OpenStreetMap contributors - OpenStreetMap is made
available under the Open Data Commons Open Database
License (ODbL) by the OpenStreetMap Foundation
(OSMF): http://opendatacommons.org/licenses/odbl/1.0/.
Any rights in individual contents of the database are
licensed under the Database Contents License: http://
opendatacommons.org/licenses/dbcl/1.0/

Parks and reserves data - © 2017 Hawaii Statewide GIS,
© Department of Natural Resources Canada 2.0 Open
Government Licence – Canada, © Queen's Printer for
Ontario, 2012-22 Open Government Licence – Ontario,
© 2021 Government of Prince Edward Island, ©
Gouvernement du Québec, 2022 (CC-BY 4.0), Crown
copyright © Province of Nova Scotia Open Government
Licence – Nova Scotia, U.S. Geological Survey (USGS) Gap
Analysis Project (GAP), 2020, Protected Areas Database
of the United States (PAD-US) 2.1: U.S. Geological Survey
data release https://doi.org/10.5066/P92QM3NT,

© Copyright 2019 Tennessee Department of Environment
& Conservation Tennessee State Parks – Smart Parks
Open Data, TIGER/Line® Shapefiles Source: US Census
Bureau, Geography Division

While every care is taken to ensure the accuracy of the data within
this product, the owners of the data do not make any representations
or warranties about its accuracy, reliability, completeness or suitability
for any particular purpose and, to the extent permitted by law,
the owners of the data disclaim all responsibility and all liability
(including without limitation, liability in negligence) for all expenses,
losses, damages (including indirect or consequential damages) and
costs which might be incurred as a result of the data being inaccurate
or incomplete in any way and for any reason.

A catalogue record for this
book is available from the
National Library of Australia

Hardie Grant acknowledges the Traditional Owners of the Country
on which we work, the Wurundjeri people of the Kulin Nation and
the Gadigal people of the Eora Nation, and recognises their continuing
connection to the land, waters and culture. We pay our respects to
their Elders past and present.

Ultimate Road Trips: USA & Canada
ISBN 9781741177862

10 9 8 7 6 5 4 3 2 1

Publisher
Melissa Kayser

Project editor
Megan Cuthbert

Editor
Holly Bridges

Proofreader
Lyric Dodson

Cartographer
Emily Maffei

Design
Andy Warren

Typesetting
Megan Ellis and
Hannah Schubert

Index
Max McMaster

Colour reproduction by Hannah Schubert and Splitting Image
Colour Studio

Printed in China by 1010 Printing International Limited

Publisher's Disclaimers: The publisher cannot accept responsibility
for any errors or omissions. The representation on the maps of
any road or track is not necessarily evidence of public right of way.
The publisher cannot be held responsible for any injury, loss or
damage incurred during travel. It is vital to research any proposed
trip thoroughly and seek the advice of relevant state and travel
organisations before you leave.

Publisher's Note: Every effort has been made to ensure that the
information in this book is accurate at the time of going to press.
The publisher welcomes information and suggestions for correction
or improvement.